Windows 10
Inside Out

Ed Bott
Carl Siechert
Craig Stinson

PHI Learning Private Limited

Delhi-110092
2016

This Indian Reprint—₹ 995.00
(Original U.S. Edition—₹ 10153.00)

WINDOWS 10 INSIDE OUT
by Ed Bott, Carl Siechert and Craig Stinson

Authorized reprint from the English language edition, entitled WINDOWS 10 INSIDE OUT, 1st Edition, 9780735697966 by BOTT, ED; SIECHERT, CARL; STINSON, CRAIG, published by Pearson Education, Inc, publishing as Microsoft Press, Copyright © 2015 by Ed Bott, Carl Siechert, Craig Stinson.

ISBN-978-81-203-5207-0

Published by Asoke K. Ghosh, PHI Learning Private Limited, Rimjhim House, 111, Patparganj Industrial Estate, Delhi-110092 and Printed by Syndicate Binders, A-20, Hosiery Complex, Noida, Phase-II Extension, Noida-201305 (N.C.R. Delhi).

To our families, for their patience and understanding

Contents at a glance

Appendixes

Table of contents

What do you think of this book? We want to hear from you!

Microsoft is interested in hearing your feedback so we can improve our books and learning resources for you. To participate in a brief survey, please visit:

http://aka.ms/tellpress

Introduction

We're back!

The three authors responsible for this edition began working together in 2001. Like many of you, we took a break a few years ago, watching from the sidelines as Microsoft released Windows 8 and Windows 8.1. We've returned for Windows 10 because, quite frankly, we're excited by the possibilities of "Windows as a Service." Unlike with previous versions, which remained largely static until the next big release, you can expect Windows 10 to evolve rapidly.

Much of what we found in Windows 10 is familiar, especially as we dug deep into its core features. The fundamentals of NTFS security and the registry, for example, have remained reassuringly consistent throughout many generations of Windows. But there is also plenty that's new in Windows 10, some of it obvious (the new Start menu) and some not so obvious (Windows Hello).

The challenge of writing a book like this one is that Microsoft plans to keep changing Windows 10, releasing new features every few months instead of every few years. Over time, that means step-by-step procedures for getting tasks accomplished will change (making those routines simpler, we hope). That's why, in this edition, we've tried to focus on the *why* and not just the *how*.

Who this book is for

This book offers a well-rounded look at the features most people use in Windows. It serves as an excellent starting point for anyone who wants a better understanding of how the central features in Windows 10 work. If you're a Windows expert-in-training, or if your day job involves IT responsibilities, or if you're the designated computer specialist managing computers and networks in a home or small business, you'll discover many sections we wrote just for you. And if you consider yourself a Windows enthusiast—well, we hope you'll find enough fun and interesting tidbits to keep you interested because, after all, we're unabashed enthusiasts ourselves.

Assumptions about you

This book was written for people who have some experience with Windows and are comfortable with and even curious about the technical details of what makes Windows work. It touches only briefly on some of the basic topics that you'll find covered in more detail elsewhere (for those, we recommend other Microsoft Press titles, such as *Windows 10 Step by Step* or *Windows 10 Plain & Simple*).

Whether your experience comes from using Windows 8.1 or Windows 7, we expect that you are comfortable finding your way around the desktop, launching programs, using copy and paste operations, and finding information in a web browser. We don't assume that you're a hardware tinkerer, a hacker, a hardcore gamer, or a developer.

How this book is organized

Part 1, "Getting started with Windows 10," offers an overview of what's new in this version, with details on installing and configuring Windows 10, personalizing the Windows experience, connecting to the Internet and local networks, and keeping your user accounts and devices secure.

Part 2, "Working and playing with Windows 10," covers the essentials of using and managing apps and desktop programs, with details on built-in productivity tools (including Mail) and the entertainment apps that help you enjoy your collection of digital photos and music. This section covers the two browsers in Windows 10, the all-new Microsoft Edge and the more familiar Internet Explorer. Finally, it explains how to organize your folders and files and how to find those files when you need them.

Part 3, "System maintenance and troubleshooting," starts with a detailed guide to the different types of hardware you can use with Windows 10, with storage devices getting their own chapter. Additional chapters cover routine maintenance tasks and explore tools and techniques for measuring and improving your computer's performance. The section closes with advice on how to back up your important files, how to recover quickly from problems, and how to troubleshoot issues when they arise.

Part 4, "Windows 10 for experts and IT pros," goes into detail about advanced system-management tools and explains how to set up an advanced network so that you can safely share files, printers, Internet connections, and other resources. Other topics include Windows PowerShell scripting and the powerful Hyper-V virtualization technology built in to the Pro, Enterprise, and Education editions of Windows 10.

Finally, we provide three appendixes of reference information, including a concise look at the differences between Windows 10 editions, an overview of help and support resources, and some details about how the OneDrive cloud storage service works with Windows 10.

Acknowledgments

For this edition of the book, like many before it, we're fortunate to have an expert production team led by Curtis Philips of Publishing.com. Along with technical editor Randall Galloway, copyeditor John Pierce, and proofreader Andrea Fox, our favorite team asked the right questions and made excellent suggestions to cover our lapses. And, as usual, they made it all happen quickly and efficiently, despite all the curveballs that we would throw them.

Although the publishing world has changed tremendously over the past two decades, one constant remains: the folks at Microsoft Press are a delight to work with. Product manager Rosemary Caperton and director of publishing Anne Hamilton carry on this tradition magnificently.

Our sincere thanks go to all these folks.

Errata, updates, & book support

We've made every effort to ensure the accuracy of this book. You can access updates to this book—in the form of a list of submitted errata and their related corrections—at

http://aka.ms/Win10InsideOut/errata

If you discover an error that is not already listed, please submit it to us at the same page.

If you need additional support, email Microsoft Press Book Support at

mspinput@microsoft.com

Please note that product support for Microsoft software and hardware is not offered through the previous addresses. For help with Microsoft software or hardware, go to

http://support.microsoft.com

Free ebooks from Microsoft Press

From technical overviews to in-depth information on special topics, the free ebooks from Microsoft Press cover a wide range of topics. These ebooks are available in PDF, EPUB, and Mobi for Kindle formats, ready for you to download at

http://aka.ms/mspressfree

Check back often to see what is new!

We want to hear from you

At Microsoft Press, your satisfaction is our top priority, and your feedback our most valuable asset. Please tell us what you think of this book at

http://aka.ms/tellpress

We know you're busy, so we've kept it short with just a few questions. Your answers go directly to the editors at Microsoft Press. (No personal information will be requested.) Thanks in advance for your input!

Stay in touch

Let's keep the conversation going! We're on Twitter: *http://twitter.com/MicrosoftPress*

PART 1

Getting started with Windows 10

What's new in Windows 10

Windows 10 is not just another incremental upgrade to the world's most popular PC operating system.

The first clue is the version number. No, you didn't miss Windows 9—Microsoft jumped straight from 8.1 to 10 to underscore the magnitude of change in this release. And make no mistake about it, Windows 10 is dramatically different from the version you're probably using today.

How you react to Windows 10 will be determined in no small part by how you feel about its predecessor.

With the launch of Windows 8 in October 2012, Microsoft removed the familiar touchstones of the Windows user experience—the Start button and Start menu—and replaced them with a radically redesigned Start screen created for use with touch-enabled devices. It also introduced a new class of touch-friendly apps, delivered through a new Windows Store.

The innovations in Windows 8 ushered in a new class of computing devices that a time traveler from 1995 would barely recognize as members of the PC family. But that new design also inspired some passionate and often blunt feedback from Windows users who weren't pleased with the radical changes to an operating system they had spent years mastering.

NOTE

The core code that makes up Windows 10 runs on a broad assortment of hardware, ranging from mobile phones and pocket-size tablets to oversize, touch-enabled smart displays mounted on the walls of corporate conference rooms. In this book, we focus primarily on devices designed to perform the functions associated with traditional PCs. For a discussion of what makes Windows 10 different on small devices, see "Windows 10 on phones and small tablets" in Chapter 13, "Hardware."

Microsoft has reacted to that feedback by reworking the user experience in Windows 10, bringing back the Start menu from Windows 7, combining it with live tiles and other features that were introduced in Windows 8, and tossing in some impressive all-new capabilities. The result should feel significantly more natural for anyone upgrading from Windows 7.

If you skipped Windows 8 and stuck with Windows 7, as we suspect many of our readers did, you have some catching up to do. If you're coming to Windows 10 after spending quality time with Windows 8 and Windows 8.1, you have a different kind of adjusting to do.

In this chapter, we offer a high-level overview of what's new in Windows 10. We start, naturally enough, with the hardware that unlocks many of the signature features in Windows 10.

Next-generation hardware

Every year, Microsoft's hardware partners sell hundreds of millions of PCs running the latest version of Windows. The majority of those PCs still follow traditional form factors: towers designed to fit under a desk, all-in-one PCs that pack the electronics behind a desktop display, and clamshell-shaped laptops with full keyboards and trackpads.

But an increasing percentage—roughly one in every four Windows devices, according to recent research—have diverged from those familiar designs.

The defining characteristic of these next-generation Windows 10 devices is a touchscreen. On touchscreen-equipped laptops, you can choose to perform a task by tapping the screen or by using the keyboard and trackpad. In the case of a tablet running Windows 10, the touchscreen offers the only way to navigate between and within apps.

Then there's the most intriguing category of all: so-called hybrid devices, with a keyboard that can be detached or folded out of the way. The models in Lenovo's perfectly named Yoga series, for example, include touchscreens that can rotate 360 degrees, turning a laptop into a tablet with the keyboard behind the display.

On Microsoft's popular Surface line, shown in Figure 1-1, the Type Cover clicks into place magnetically, allowing the keyboard to flip open for typing and then flip closed to cover the screen. With the Type Cover attached and the adjustable kickstand extended, the Surface Pro looks and acts like a laptop. When you remove the Type Cover and close the kickstand, the Surface Pro becomes a tablet that you can control with a finger or a pen.

On a touchscreen, you swipe and tap to interact with objects on the screen and use an on-screen keyboard to enter and edit text. For devices with detachable keyboards, Windows 10 includes features designed to ease the transition between the traditional PC way of working and the new Tablet Mode.

Figure 1-1 The Surface Pro 3 is the quintessential hybrid device. With the Type Cover attached (left) it works like a laptop. Remove the Type Cover, and it's a tablet.

We offer details on how to master the new user experience, on traditional PCs and touch-screen-equipped devices, in Chapter 3, "Using Windows 10." Our coverage of customization options is in Chapter 4, "Personalizing Windows 10."

The new generation of hardware isn't just defined by peripherals. Modern devices designed for Windows 10 incorporate new features that enhance the security of the startup process. If you've mastered the ins and out of BIOS setup on a legacy PC, you'll need to learn how to configure its replacement, the Unified Extensible Firmware Interface (UEFI). That hardware design in turn enables an additional security feature called Secure Boot, which protects your Windows 10 PC from an insidious form of malware called rootkits. We discuss these features in much greater detail in Chapter 7, "Securing Windows 10 devices."

The Windows 10 user experience

Ironically, if you skipped Windows 8 you missed several major iterations of the Windows user experience that some users found difficult to use on conventional PCs with a keyboard and mouse. By contrast, the Windows 10 user experience feels very much like a smooth evolution of Windows 7.

On a conventional PC, equipped with a keyboard and a mouse or trackpad, Windows 10 starts at the Windows desktop. If you're making the move from Windows 7, this environment, shown in Figure 1-2, should be familiar.

Figure 1-2 After you sign in to Windows 10, you're greeted with the familiar desktop and taskbar.

In the lower left corner is a stylized Windows logo. Clicking that button opens a menu like the one shown in Figure 1-3.

That configuration addresses one of the biggest complaints about Windows 8, which organized programs on a Start screen that occupied the entire display. The new Start menu can be resized to occupy nearly the entire display. If you prefer the Windows 8–style full-screen option, it's available by switching to Tablet Mode, which works even on traditional PCs.

Windows 10 introduces a new visual design, with flat icons and a monochromatic color scheme, as typified by the Settings app shown in Figure 1-4.

Figure 1-3 The Windows 10 Start menu combines the two-column layout from Windows 7 with live tiles from Windows 8.

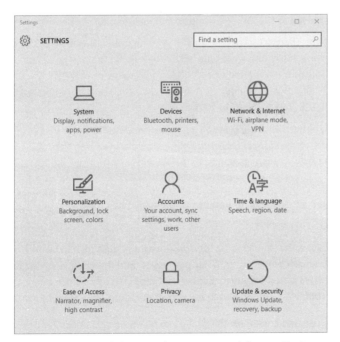

Figure 1-4 The visual design and arrangement of the new Settings app are characteristic of the overall design of Windows 10.

The pieces of Windows 8 that didn't survive

The Windows 8 user interface was radically different from any previous version of Windows. Maybe too radical, based on the clear feedback Microsoft received from customers.

That feedback inspired a thorough rethinking of the Windows user experience, which in turn led to the design you see in Windows 10. In the process, these signature Windows 8 elements were retired:

- **Charms menu.** This vertical row of five buttons, with the Windows logo key at the center, appeared on the right side of Windows 8 PCs in response to a swipe from the right edge or the mouse moving to the upper right corner of the display. Its five functions have been broken up and moved to the new Start menu and to Action Center, which now appears where the Charms once did with a swipe from the right or a click of the Notifications button.

- **Hot corners.** For PCs without a touchscreen, a key navigation principle in Windows 8 involved moving the mouse to a corner and pausing until something happened. Moving the mouse pointer to the upper left corner and then sliding down, for example, exposed a column of thumbnails for switching between running apps. In Windows 10, moving the mouse to a corner does nothing special, and app switching has been moved to the Task View button and its keyboard shortcuts.

- **Start screen.** The Start screen, filled with colorful live tiles, was the first thing a new Windows 8 user saw. Over time, with Windows 8.1 and a subsequent update, the Start screen was modified to make it less jarring. In Windows 10, the desktop is the default first step. If you miss the Start screen, you can restore the experience by expanding the Start menu to full screen or switching to Tablet Mode.

Our experience suggests that the learning curve for Windows 10 is not that steep. But it's ironic that one of the biggest challenges in making the transition from Windows 8 is unlearning these now-missing elements.

Windows 10 isn't just an evolution of features you already knew, however; you'll also find plenty of new capabilities to explore.

Cortana, for example, is the Windows 10 "personal assistant," first seen in Windows Phone 8.1, who takes over the search box if you give her permission and then delivers news headlines, reminders, and answers based on your schedule and your interests. Which interests exactly? That's under your control, using the Notebook shown in Figure 1-5 to tailor your preferences.

We explain how to use and customize this feature in "Cortana and search" in Chapter 3.

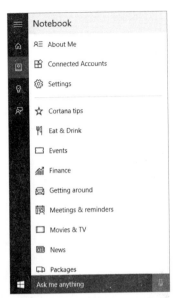

Figure 1-5 With Cortana enabled, clicking in the search box displays personalized reminders and alerts based on settings you specify in the Cortana Notebook.

Another major addition, all new in Windows 10, is the pane that appears on the right side when you swipe in from the right on a touchscreen or click the Notifications button, just to the left of the clock. (In a bit of naming confusion, this new feature is called Action Center, although it's unrelated to the identically named feature from earlier Windows versions.) The top of the pane contains notifications from apps (new messages, weather alerts, alarms, reminders), while the bottom contains handy buttons for performing common tasks, as shown in Figure 1-6.

Figure 1-6 These buttons, which appear beneath notifications in Action Center, allow quick access to system settings.

The new universal apps for Windows 10 are delivered through the Windows Store, just as their predecessors in Windows 8 were, but that's where the resemblance ends. In Windows 10, these so-called modern apps can work in resizable windows alongside conventional Windows desktop applications.

On a tablet, for example, the editing capabilities in the new Photos app work best in full screen. On a large desktop display (or two), the full-screen view is overkill and the app is perfectly usable in a window, as shown in Figure 1-7.

Figure 1-7 The editing controls in the new Photos app are designed so that they work well in a resizable window on desktop PCs with a large display, a keyboard, and a mouse.

For a more thorough look at how modern apps work, see Chapter 8, "Using and managing modern apps and desktop programs."

Fundamental changes in core features

If you're among the substantial population that has stuck with Windows 7 for the past few years, you've missed some interesting and deep-seated changes to some of the core features in Windows. We go into detail about three of those features in this book.

- **File Explorer.** It's no longer called Windows Explorer; beginning with Windows 8, the name officially changed to File Explorer. The addition of a Microsoft Office–style ribbon, shown in Figure 1-8, makes a number of formerly obscure operations more discoverable and dramatically improves search capabilities by adding a Search Tools tab when you click in the search box. Windows 10 adds a Quick Access region in the navigation pane. We cover File Explorer in exhaustive detail in Chapter 12, "Organizing and searching for files."

Figure 1-8 For anyone upgrading from Windows 7, the File Explorer ribbon is all new.

- **Backup and recovery.** If you've ever had to reinstall an older version of Windows, you know how tedious and time-consuming the process can be. Windows 8 introduced "push-button reset" options that automate the process of a clean install, with the option to keep your data or wipe it clean. Windows 10 refines those options impressively, as we explain in Chapter 16, "Backup, restore, and recovery." It also adds the ability to undo a Windows 10 upgrade and restore your previous Windows version, as shown in Figure 1-9.

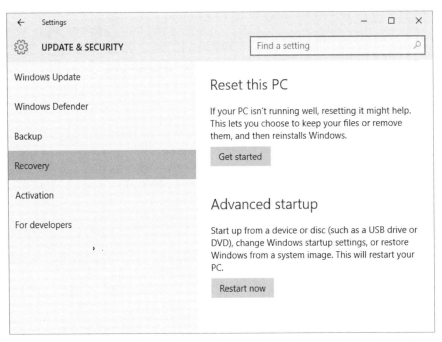

Figure 1-9 The Recovery options in Windows 8 are significantly enhanced in Windows 10, using less disk space and requiring fewer post-restore updates.

- **Task Manager.** This is another familiar Windows 7 utility that received a major make-over in Windows 8. The same improvements are visible in Windows 10: more information about running processes, a new tab for managing processes, and detailed performance information, as shown in Figure 1-10. For an in-depth look at the new Task Manager, see Chapter 15, "System maintenance and performance."

Figure 1-10 The Task Manager Performance tab in Windows 10 offers more information, more clearly organized, than its Windows 7 predecessor.

Windows 10, the web, and cloud services

Internet Explorer has been a part of every version of Windows released in the past 20 years. In Windows 10, for the first time, Internet Explorer isn't the default web browser. Instead, that honor goes to a new browser, Microsoft Edge.

Edge is touch friendly, with a minimal list of controls. Among its unique features is a Reading View button that reformats and rearranges the text of a cluttered webpage to make a less distracting reading experience. You can see this feature in action in Figure 1-11.

Figure 1-11 The Microsoft Edge web browser has simple controls and a Reading View option that reformats text and removes clutter from webpages.

Edge uses a new rendering engine designed with interoperability as a much higher priority than backward compatibility. Internet Explorer is still available for situations where its unique features are essential. We explain the differences between Internet Explorer and Edge, as well as how to configure each one to match your preferences, in Chapter 11, "Browsing the Internet."

Of course, a web browser isn't the only way to connect to shared resources online. When you sign in using a Microsoft account, Windows 10 automatically connects to shared files in the OneDrive service. You can also connect to business-class services using Office 365 and Azure Active Directory.

Working and playing with Windows 10

If you're looking for familiar names in the list of apps included with Windows 10, you'll find plenty—Windows Media Player, Notepad, and Paint, for example.

But much more interesting are the new universal apps that are designed to work on any device running Windows 10. Because these apps are updated automatically via the Windows Store, they can incorporate new features and fix bugs without requiring a separate installation. These apps also allow you to sync settings and data between Windows 10 devices without having to reconfigure accounts or import data.

Windows 10 includes several productivity apps as part of a default installation. Chief among them are the new Mail and Calendar apps, which work with a variety of Internet services, including Microsoft's Outlook.com and Office 365 services as well as Google's Gmail and Apple's iCloud. Figure 1-12 shows a week of appointments in the Calendar app.

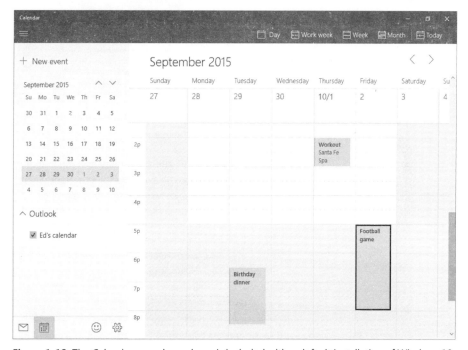

Figure 1-12 The Calendar app, shown here, is included with a default installation of Windows 10. You can switch to the companion Mail app with a click of the icon in the lower left corner.

There are other productivity apps available in the Windows Store, including touch-friendly versions of Word, Excel, and PowerPoint that are included as part of a standard installation in some editions of Windows 10.

For more on work-oriented apps and utilities in Windows 10, see Chapter 9, "Productivity and communication tools."

Windows 10 is also a solid platform for entertainment apps, including digital music and video services that also work on Xbox consoles and Windows 10 phones. The Music app developed exclusively for Windows 10, shown in Figure 1-13, also allows you to access your own personal collection, stored in OneDrive.

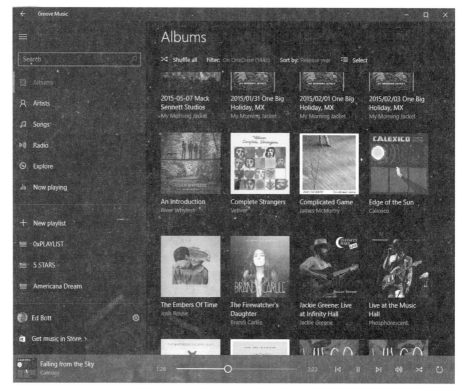

Figure 1-13 The Windows 10 Music app lets you connect via the cloud to a music collection stored in OneDrive's Music folder.

Another hidden gem among the new entertainment features in Windows 10 is built-in support for Miracast adapters, which plug in to an HDMI input on a high-definition TV. Using Miracast, you can tune in to an online video clip and project it to the big screen, with full support for surround sound.

You'll find more details about apps made for fun and games in Chapter 10, "Music, photos, movies, and games."

More updates, more often

Historically, the cadence of Windows has gone something like this: Roughly every three years, a new version of Windows comes out. When you buy a new PC, it includes the latest Windows version; for existing PCs, you can upgrade your current Windows version to the new one (or choose not to upgrade). You then live with that version of Windows until the next one is released and the cycle begins anew.

That's all history now.

Beginning with Windows 10, Microsoft has declared its intention to treat Windows as a service. In the first year after the release of Windows 10, upgrades are free to anyone running Windows 7 Service Pack 1 or Windows 8.1 (except for Windows Enterprise editions, which are available only through Volume License purchases and play by a different set of rules).

Whether you buy a new device with Windows 10 or upgrade an existing one, it is eligible for feature updates, which will be delivered through Windows Update. That's a major change for Windows users, who normally receive only security and reliability updates through these Microsoft-managed channels. Instead of waiting two or three years to be included in a new Windows version or a service pack, new features will be delivered automatically, when they're ready.

The new update process also allows Windows users to choose how soon they want to receive those updates.

Previously, Microsoft developed and tested new Windows features privately, occasionally offering the public an advance look in the form of preview versions before releasing them publicly.

Beginning with Windows 10, those preview releases are built into the development cycle. As new features make their way into Windows, they are delivered to different "flights," starting with internal testers in Microsoft's engineering group, then working out to customers who have opted in to receive preview releases. Each new flight reaches a larger number of people, with fixes for bugs discovered in previous flights incorporated into later ones. Figure 1-14 shows, conceptually, how the flight process works.

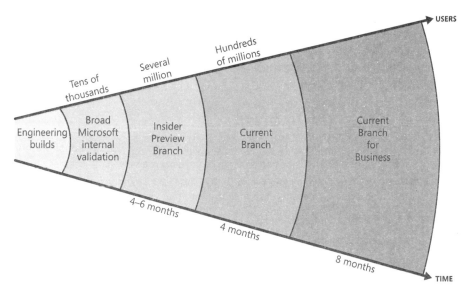

Figure 1-14 For Windows 10, Microsoft is delivering new features in "flights" that eventually reach consumers in the Current Branch.

The official release, installed by PC manufacturers and available to the general public, is officially called the Current Branch. It represents program code that has been thoroughly tested as part of the preview cycle and corresponds to what have traditionally been General Availability releases of new Windows versions or service packs.

This process also allows Microsoft to continue the Windows 10 Preview program, which it started in October 2014. Members of this program, called Windows Insiders, have full access to early test releases of Windows 10 along with frequent updates. In exchange, Microsoft's developers receive unprecedented levels of feedback that shape the development effort in real time. That feedback comes from automated data collection (known as telemetry) and a Feedback app, shown in Figure 1-15, which is installed with every preview release.

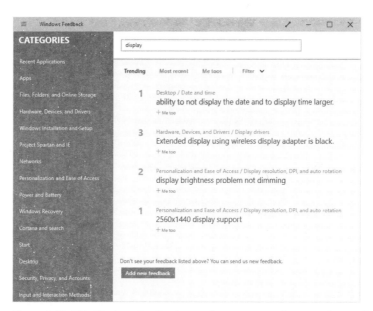

Figure 1-15 This Windows Feedback app allows anyone using a preview version of Windows 10 to report bugs and offer suggestions directly to Microsoft.

Windows 10 for IT pros and experts

The intended scope of this book covers consumers and small businesses using Windows 10. We would need hundreds of additional pages to cover the concerns of IT pros and network administrators responsible for integrating Windows 10 devices into Windows domains using Active Directory.

But if you fall into the IT pro classification, we haven't completely forgotten about you. In particular, we suggest you look at Part 4, where we've assembled information of special interest to power users and administrators.

In those chapters, you'll find information on arcane but incredibly useful topics like editing the Windows registry, troubleshooting performance-related issues, and automating routine tasks.

For those who really want to polish their expert skills, we especially recommend Chapter 21, "Working with Command Prompt and Windows PowerShell," and Chapter 22, "Running virtual machines with Hyper-V," which goes into depth with the powerful, built-in virtualization platform included with Pro and Enterprise editions of Windows 10.

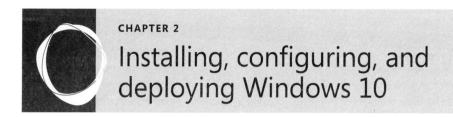

CHAPTER 2

Installing, configuring, and deploying Windows 10

Microsoft's ambitious goal for Windows 10 is to have it running on 1 billion devices within two or three years after its launch.

A few hundred million of those devices will be new PCs, laptops, tablets, and phones that come with Windows 10. But a potentially much larger number will be PCs currently running Windows 7 or Windows 8.1, thanks to Microsoft's unprecedented offer of a free upgrade for those devices. (That offer ends on July 29, 2016, one year after the official launch of Windows 10.)

Among some PC traditionalists, it is a badge of honor to wipe a newly purchased PC clean and then set up Windows from scratch. Even if you're not so fastidious, a clean install is sometimes unavoidable: it's the only option for PCs you build yourself and for virtual machines, and it's sometimes the fastest way to get back up and running after a disk failure.

The same Windows 10 setup program is used for both upgrades and clean installs. For upgrades, the installer is streamlined, offering a minimum of options. Booting from Windows 10 installation media offers a much more complete set of options: choosing a specific physical disk for use in dual-boot (or multiboot) scenarios, creating and formatting partitions, and setting up unattended installations, for example.

In this chapter, we cover both options. We don't include step-by-step instructions to document every possible upgrade or clean installation scenario. Given the nearly infinite number of combinations of PC hardware, comprehensive instructions would be impossible, and besides, we're confident that our readers can make their way through a setup wizard without handholding.

Instead, this chapter concentrates on the big picture, breaking each type of Windows setup into its major steps and explaining what happens (and what can go wrong) in each one. We finish with a checklist to run through after completing an upgrade or clean install.

But first, some suggestions on how to make the setup process as smooth as possible.

Before you start

If you're lucky, your Windows 10 upgrade will be uneventful and the results will be flawless. You can increase the odds of this ideal outcome by taking some common-sense precautions first.

At the top of this list is checking the hardware on which you plan to install Windows 10 to confirm that it meets the minimum requirements (note that this list is unchanged from the system requirements for Windows 7):

- Processor: 1 gigahertz (GHz) or faster

- RAM: 1 gigabyte (GB) (32-bit) or 2 GB (64-bit)

- Free disk space (system drive): 16 GB

- Graphics card: Microsoft DirectX 9 graphics device with WDDM driver

NOTE

The free disk space requirement varies, and Microsoft is continuing to work on improving upgrade scenarios for low disk space. On devices with very small amounts of built-in storage, you might be able to upgrade with as little as 10 free gigabytes. As you approach that threshold, however, you might find that setup fails in unpredictable ways. If you're stuck, check the Microsoft Community forums (*http://answers.microsoft.com*) to see whether there's a workaround for your situation.

Those are fairly modest requirements, and virtually every PC sold in the past six years with Windows 7 or a later version preinstalled should qualify.

For online upgrades to Windows 10, you also need a Microsoft account and Internet access. In fact, regular Internet access is a prerequisite for most of the tasks we describe in this book.

Inside OUT

RIP, Windows Media Center

One of the signature features of Windows for many years has been Windows Media Center. This feature, which debuted as a special edition of Windows XP in 2002, enabled a so-called 10-foot interface for using Windows PCs as an entertainment hub in a living room. Media Center grew steadily from its original design, adding support for high-definition TV and digital cable tuners, to become the centerpiece of the Windows 7 Home Premium, Professional, and Ultimate editions.

After Windows 7 launched, the Windows Media Center team was disbanded and development of the feature ceased. In Windows 8 and 8.1, the Media Center functionality was available as an extra-cost add-on, but it was a simple port of the Windows 7 version, with no new features.

With Windows 10, Windows Media Center is officially retired. When you run Windows 10 Setup to upgrade a PC that has the Windows Media Center feature enabled, it will be uninstalled, and the feature will be completely unavailable after the upgrade is complete. There's no registry magic or secret to enable the feature on Windows 10, either. If Media Center is a make-or-break feature for you, avoid the Windows 10 upgrade on that PC.

Check for potential compatibility problems

In broad terms, any device that is already running Windows 8.1 should be compatible with Windows 10, as should any apps or device drivers installed on that device. There are, however, exceptions to this rule—some of them minor, others more serious. Your likelihood of encountering (usually minor) compatibility issues goes up when upgrading Windows 7 (with Service Pack 1).

The Windows 10 setup program includes a compatibility checker that alerts you to any potential compatibility issues before performing the actual installation. We describe its workings in the section, "Upgrading to Windows 10."

Before you run the setup program, though, it's worth taking inventory of your critical apps and devices and checking with the developer or manufacturer to confirm that those products will be supported under Windows 10. Pay special attention to any app or device that's more than a decade old.

Inside OUT

Use dynamic updates

When you upgrade an existing Windows version using Windows Update, the setup program automatically checks for and downloads dynamic updates. When you start the upgrade process from installation media, you're asked whether you want to get the latest updates. If you have an active Internet connection, be sure to take advantage of this option.

Dynamic updates can include any or all of the following: critical updates to the setup program itself; improved or new versions of boot-critical drivers for storage, display, and network hardware detected on your system; and compatibility updates (also known as shims) for programs you're currently running. Rolling these updates in at the beginning of the process increases the likelihood that your Windows 10 upgrade will be successful. After completing installation, you'll still need to connect to Windows Update to check for critical updates for Windows and the most recent drivers for detected hardware.

Back up your data and settings

Having an up-to-date backup of important files is, of course, good advice for any time. But it's especially important when you're upgrading an operating system.

The simplest way to back up files is to sync them to the cloud. OneDrive sync capabilities are built in to Windows 8.1; a sync utility for Windows 7 is available for download from *http://onedrive.com/download*. Move or copy your files into the OneDrive folder and wait for them to be fully synchronized before proceeding.

With large file collections or slow Internet connections, a sufficiently large USB flash drive or an external hard drive makes a perfectly good target for a local backup. If you're upgrading from Windows 7, you can use its built-in backup program; individual files and folders from those backups can be restored in Windows 10 by using the helpfully labeled Backup And Restore (Windows 7) option. For a complete look at your options, see Chapter 16, "Backup, restore, and recovery."

If you're upgrading from Windows 8.1 and you've signed in with a Microsoft account, your personalized settings are already being synced to OneDrive. From Windows 7, there's no easy way to back up those settings. Although you can find third-party utilities that promise to accomplish this task, it's probably faster (and less risky) to re-create that handful of settings than it is to mess with transfer utilities.

Choose the right package

Those who are able to upgrade online can skip this section. The Windows 10 installer delivered through Windows Update chooses the correct successor to your current edition, downloads it for you in the background, and then walks you through setup.

But for every other Windows 10 installation scenario, you have some decisions to make. To do a clean install or to upgrade using Windows media, you typically download an ISO file, which you can then mount directly or use to create installation media. (Physical copies of Windows 10 are also available in packages in which the installer is on a bootable USB flash drive or a DVD.)

> ## NOTE
> The ISO name is ancient, by modern computing standards, dating back to the mid-1980s. And, strictly speaking, it's also meaningless. The name is shorthand for the file system originally used with CD-ROM media, which was designated ISO 9660 by the standards-setting body that published it. These days, an ISO image file is just as likely to use the UDF file system (ISO/IEC 13346), which is commonly found on larger-capacity optical media such as DVDs and Blu-ray Discs.

Choosing the correct installer involves finding the specific combination of three factors that match your needs:

- **Windows 10 edition.** For installing or upgrading a desktop PC, laptop, or hybrid device, there are two and only two choices: Windows 10 Home or Windows 10 Pro. (Large organizations with volume license contracts can install Windows 10 Enterprise as an upgrade.) We describe the differences between the editions in Appendix A, "Windows 10 editions at a glance."

- **Language.** Windows 10 is available in a large number of languages—111 languages, covering 190 countries and regions, at the time of its initial release. Choose the base language that is appropriate for your installation. You can add language interface packs to translate text that's displayed in commonly used wizards, dialog boxes, menus, and other items in the user interface; however, you can't change the parent language except by reinstalling Windows using an edition built for that language.

- **Architecture.** Windows 10 is available in 32-bit and 64-bit distributions. Most modern CPUs will support either version, and your preference should be for the 64-bit version. In general, 32-bit versions of Windows are appropriate for systems with 2 GB (or less) of RAM, with no option to add memory. Choose a 64-bit version if your system includes 4 GB or more of memory or if you rely on one or more programs that are available only in 64-bit editions. (And note that all of your 32-bit programs, including new and old versions of Microsoft Office, will work fine on a 64-bit copy of Windows, so you needn't fear in that regard.)

If your goal is to purchase a physical or electronic copy of Windows for installation on a new PC or in a virtual machine, the intricacies of Windows licensing require several additional decisions beyond those we just described.

You can choose from the following license types:

- **Full.** A full license is sold directly to consumers as an electronic distribution or a packaged product. With a full license, Windows can be installed on a computer that was not sold with Windows originally, or it can be used as an upgrade. A full license can be transferred to a different computer as long as the underlying copy of Windows is no longer being used on the original location.

- **OEM.** An OEM (original equipment manufacturer) license is one that's included with a new computer. This license is locked to the computer on which it's installed and cannot be transferred to a new computer. OEM System Builder packages are intended for use by small PC makers but are often used by consumers and hobbyists in place of a full license. The system builder is required to provide support for OEM Windows along with the device on which it is installed.

- **Upgrade.** An upgrade license is a discounted copy of Windows that can be installed only on a system that already has an OEM or full license.

- **Volume.** Volume licenses are sold in bulk to corporate, government, nonprofit, and educational customers and are typically deployed by using enterprise management tools. A volume license is available as an upgrade only.

Any PC that was purchased with Windows 7, Windows 8, or Windows 8.1 preinstalled (look for the sticker on the PC itself or on the power supply) is qualified for a free Windows 10 upgrade (the free upgrade offer is good until July 29, 2016). This is true whether the PC came from a large OEM or from a system builder.

You need a full license to install Windows in a virtual machine, on a Mac or other computer that does not come with Windows preinstalled, or in a dual-boot or multiboot setup. That condition can be satisfied with a full (retail or OEM) license of Windows 10 or a full license for an earlier Windows version that supports a Windows 10 upgrade.

NOTE

It's important to understand that the legal and contractual restrictions imposed by license agreements are completely independent of technical restrictions on installation. If you upgrade a system to Windows 10 from Windows 7 and then the system's hard disk fails, you can perform a clean install of Windows 10 and still be properly licensed. Conversely, it is technically possible to install and activate an upgrade version on a computer that doesn't have an underlying license, but doing so violates the license agreement.

Choose your upgrade method

Microsoft strongly encourages online upgrades for anyone running Windows 7 (with Service Pack 1) or Windows 8.1. But you also have the option to perform a custom installation. A custom installation of Windows 10 allows you to start from scratch, with or without your personal data files; you need to reinstall your programs and re-create or transfer settings from another system. An upgrade retains installed programs and settings, but at the risk of creating some compatibility issues.

You'll need to boot from the Windows 10 media and choose a custom installation if either of the following conditions is true:

- **You need to adjust the layout of the system disk.** The Windows 10 installation program includes disk-management tools that you can use to create, delete, format, and extend (but not shrink) partitions on hard disks installed in your computer. Knowing how these tools work can save you a significant amount of time when setting up Windows.

- **You want to install Windows 10 alongside another operating system.** If you want to set up a multiboot system, you'll need to understand how different startup files work so that you can manage your startup options effectively. We discuss this option later in this chapter, in the section "Configuring a multiboot system."

If the system on which you plan to install Windows 10 is already running Windows 7, Windows 8.1, or Windows 10, you can start the setup program from within Windows.

Running setup from within Windows allows you to upgrade from Windows 7 or Windows 8.1, transferring settings and desktop programs to the new installation—provided that the Windows 10 edition is equivalent to or higher than the currently installed Windows edition. If you attempt an unsupported upgrade path, you have the option to transfer personal files only. Table 2-1 shows the supported upgrade paths.

Table 2-1 Supported upgrade paths by edition

Current version	Supported upgrade
Windows 7 Starter, Home Basic, Home Premium	Windows 10 Home
Windows 7 Professional, Ultimate	Windows 10 Pro
Windows 8.1	Windows 10 Home
Windows 8.1 Pro, Windows 8.1 Pro for Students	Windows 10 Pro
Windows Phone 8.1	Windows 10 Mobile

Starting Setup from within Windows does not offer the option to perform a custom install. However, performing an upgrade and choosing Nothing from the list of what you want to keep has the same effect as performing a clean install. After Windows 10 is installed, the Reset option is the preferred way to accomplish the task of repairing a Windows installation that isn't working properly.

Note that the installation media must match the architecture of the installed Windows version. You cannot run the 64-bit setup program on a PC running a 32-bit version of Windows, or vice versa. In addition, you cannot make any changes to the layout of a disk when running Setup from within Windows; you must use existing partitions, and Setup will not recognize or use unallocated space on an attached hard drive.

If you boot from the Windows 10 installation media, you can delete existing partitions, create new partitions, extend an existing disk partition to unallocated space, or designate a block of unallocated space as the setup location. (We describe these actions later in this chapter.) After booting from the Windows installation media, you cannot upgrade an existing Windows installation. Your only option is a custom install.

Using either setup option, you can install Windows 10 on the same volume as an existing Windows version. (You'll find step-by-step instructions in "Performing a clean install" later in this chapter.)

In the next section, we explain what happens behind the scenes when you perform a Windows 10 upgrade or a clean install.

How Windows 10 Setup works

The Windows 10 setup program does its magic using two folders.

- **C:\$Windows.~BT** is a hidden folder that contains the files used during both the online and offline phases of setup. These files are downloaded directly if you upgrade using Windows Update. When you launch Setup from installation media, such as an ISO file or a bootable DVD or USB flash drive, the initial phase of setup creates this folder and copies the setup files to it for temporary use, eliminating the possibility of a setup failure caused by prematurely removing or unmounting the installation media.

- **C:\Windows.old** is created only when you perform an upgrade or do a clean install on a volume that already contains a Windows installation. This folder does double duty. During upgrades, it's used as a transfer location to hold files and settings that are moving from the old installation to the new one. After setup is complete, this folder holds system files from the previous Windows installation as well as any user files that were not migrated during setup.

NOTE

These temporary installation files are deleted automatically after four weeks. Your previous Windows installation is saved indefinitely in Windows.old, allowing you to roll back to the previous version if necessary. On systems with limited storage, you can use the Disk Cleanup utility to remove these files manually. We describe this process in more detail in "Managing disk space" in Chapter 15, "System maintenance and performance."

Upgrading to Windows 10

The streamlined wizard that walks you through a Windows 10 upgrade should be familiar if you've used Windows 8 or 8.1. If most of your experience is with Windows 7, we predict you'll be pleasantly surprised by the improvements in speed (especially on systems with a large number of files) and the reduction in complexity of the entire setup process.

In Windows 10, the upgrade process is optimized for software distribution over the Internet. In those scenarios, the installer file is downloaded using Windows Update and the well-tested Background Intelligent Transfer Service.

No major upgrade is ever risk free, of course, but the Windows 10 installer is designed to be robust enough to roll back gracefully in case of a failure.

When you kick off a Windows 10 upgrade, the setup program performs a series of tasks. First, it runs a compatibility check, which determines whether your PC, peripheral devices, and installed Windows apps will work with Windows 10. (See "Checking compatibility" later in this section for details about warnings that might appear.)

Using Windows Update

Assuming you have a reasonably fast Internet connection, the simplest and fastest way to upgrade to Windows 10 is by using Windows Update. To start that process, click the Get Windows 10 icon in the notification area at the right side of the taskbar, or use the Get Windows 10 link in Windows Update, and then follow the instructions.

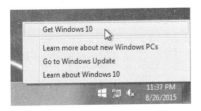

Inside OUT

What if the Get Windows 10 icon isn't visible?

The Get Windows 10 app is a tiny helper app that is automatically installed (via Windows Update) on all PCs running up-to-date versions of Windows 8.1 or Windows 7. If you don't see the icon, here are some possible reasons:

- The KB3035583 update, which delivers the Get Windows 10 app, is not installed. Solution: Check Windows Update and, if necessary, confirm that the update hasn't been hidden. See *https://support.microsoft.com/kb/3035583*.

- Windows is out of date. Solution: For Windows 7, you must have Service Pack 1 installed. Windows 8 PCs must be updated via the Windows Store to Windows 8.1, and Windows 8.1 PCs must have the Windows 8.1 Update (KB2919355) installed. More details are at *http://windows.microsoft.com/en-us/windows-8/install-latest-update-windows-8-1*.

- Your PC is running an Enterprise edition of Windows or is joined to a domain. Solution: Talk with your network administrator about how your organization plans to deploy Windows 10.

That program checks your system configuration for compatibility issues. Assuming your system passes the compatibility test, the app then determines which Windows 10 edition (Home or Pro, 32-bit or 64-bit) is appropriate for the existing installation and configures Windows Update to receive upgrades.

After a restart, Windows Update runs automatically. You should see a dialog box like the one shown in Figure 2-1.

Click Get Started to begin.

Windows Update downloads the necessary installer files in the background, including one large Windows Image file in compressed ESD format, to the C:\Windows\SoftwareDistribution\Download folder. When the download is complete, Windows Update moves Install.esd to the hidden folder C:\$Windows.~BT (along with the other setup files). You can monitor the download progress from Windows Update.

Figure 2-1 Assuming your Internet connection is fast enough, Windows Update is the easiest way to upgrade to Windows 10.

At the end, you see the prompt shown in Figure 2-2. After you restart, the offline portion of the setup process begins.

Figure 2-2 Click Restart Now to switch Setup into offline mode, where the actual installation and migration of settings takes place.

Inside OUT

Upgrade directly from an ISO file

The ISO disc image format was originally devised to make it possible to share DVDs as files, without having to put shiny discs in the mail and wait a few days or weeks. Over time, they've evolved into a virtual alternative that doesn't require discs at all. Beginning with Windows 8, File Explorer supports the capability to mount ISO files directly. (For Windows 7, you need a utility program like the free Virtual CloneDrive from SlySoft, *http://slysoft.com*.)

Obviously, this option won't work for a clean install on a freshly formatted drive, but it's ideal for upgrades. Double-click a saved ISO file in File Explorer to map its contents to a virtual disk, which appears as a DVD drive in the Devices And Drives area of File Explorer, as in Figure 2-3.

Figure 2-3 In this File Explorer window, drive D is a physical drive, but drive E is a virtual drive created by double-clicking and mounting an ISO disc image file.

Double-click to open the mounted disk, and then run Setup to kick off an upgrade. When you no longer need the virtual drive, right-click its File Explorer icon and click Eject.

Using Windows installation media

When you start an online upgrade from within Windows 8.1, the upgrade keeps all your data files and migrates settings, Windows apps, and desktop programs. Upgrades from Windows 7 preserve data files and desktop programs but do not migrate personalized settings such as your desktop background.

If you have Windows 10 installation media, you can also start the upgrade process from within Windows. Open the DVD or USB flash drive in File Explorer and double-click Setup. The resulting wizard walks you through several steps that aren't part of the streamlined online upgrade. The most important of these is the option to transfer files, apps, and settings, a topic we cover shortly.

Checking compatibility

A comprehensive compatibility checker is built into the Windows 10 setup program (it replaces the Upgrade Advisor from Windows 7), and runs as one of the first steps when you kick off an upgrade. A more limited version runs on a clean install, checking for issues such as a BIOS that needs updating or a disk controller or network adapter that has no supported driver.

In most cases, this appraisal turns up nothing, and setup continues without interruption. If this routine finds any issues, however, it notifies you with a warning dialog box. When the compatibility checker turns up any "hard blocks," setup ends immediately, with a message like the one shown in Figure 2-4.

Setup will refuse to continue if your device doesn't have enough RAM or free disk space. Other causes of hard blocks include a CPU or a BIOS that is not supported, as well as the presence of a hard-disk controller or networking device that lacks a driver.

For less severe issues, Setup might warn you that specific apps or devices may not work correctly or will have reduced functionality in Windows 10. You may be given the option to fix the issue and try the upgrade again. In these cases, the compatibility checker offers instructions to deal with specific issues:

- You might need to install updates to your current version of Windows before continuing. If you are upgrading from Windows Update, this task is handled automatically.

- You might need to suspend disk encryption before upgrading.

- Some apps must be uninstalled before the upgrade can continue (in some cases, they can be reinstalled after the upgrade is complete).

- Some apps must be updated to a newer version before the upgrade can be completed.

- After the upgrade, you might need to reinstall language packs.

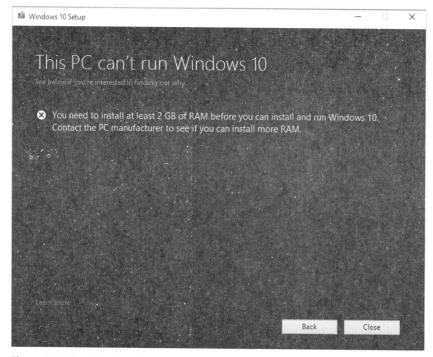

Figure 2-4 A hard block, such as too little memory or an unsupported CPU or network device, will prevent you from installing Windows 10 on a PC.

If the upgrade process ends prematurely for any of these reasons, Setup generally cleans up after itself, although you might have to manually remove some leftovers.

Transferring files, apps, and settings

When you install Windows 10 on a disk volume that already contains a copy of Windows, you must choose what you want to do with user files, settings, and apps. As we noted earlier, online upgrades using Windows Update make this choice for you.

To choose an alternative option, run Setup from installation media or an ISO file. Figure 2-5 shows your options when upgrading from Windows 8.1 to Windows 10.

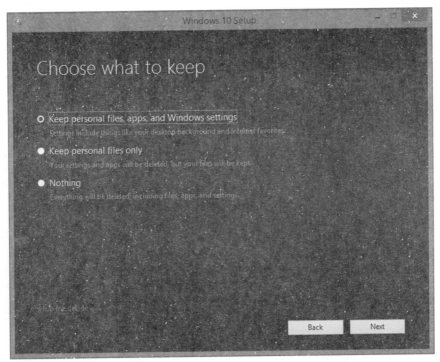

Figure 2-5 When you start a Windows 10 upgrade from installation media, you see the full range of options shown here.

Here's what happens with each option:

- **Keep Personal Files, Apps, And Windows Settings.** All Windows desktop programs and user accounts are migrated. After the upgrade is complete, you need to sign in with your Microsoft account to reinstall apps from the Windows Store and sync saved settings.

  NOTE
  This option is unavailable if you are installing a Windows edition that is not a supported upgrade path from the current edition.

- **Keep Personal Files Only.** This option is the equivalent of a repair installation. Each user's personal files are available in a user profile that otherwise contains only default apps and settings.

- **Nothing.** Choose this option if you want to perform a clean install, with your existing installation moved to Windows.old. Note that the descriptive text, "Everything will be deleted," is misleading. Your personal files, as well as those belonging to other user accounts in the current installation, are not deleted. Instead, they are moved to the Windows.old folder, where you can recover them by using File Explorer.

After the initial prep work, Setup restarts in offline mode, displaying a progress screen like the one shown in Figure 2-6.

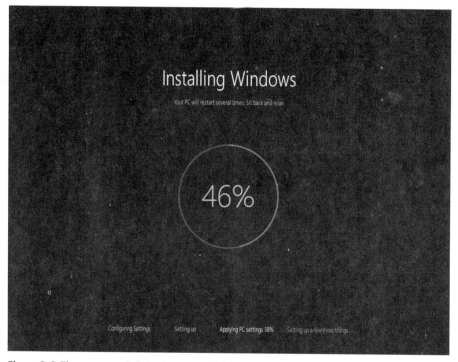

Figure 2-6 The progress circle in the center of this status screen makes one full revolution for each of the phases listed along the bottom of the screen.

In this mode, you can't interact with the PC at all. Your PC is effectively offline as the following actions occur.

Windows Setup first moves the following folders from the existing Windows installation on the root of the system drive into Windows.old:

- Windows

- Program files

- Program files (x86)

- Users

- Program data

During this offline phase, Setup extracts registry values and program data from the Windows.old folder, based on the type of upgrade, and then adds this data to the corresponding locations in the new Windows 10 installation.

Next, Setup lays down a new set of system folders for Windows 10 using the folder structure and files from the compressed Windows image. After that task is complete, Setup moves program files, registry values, and other settings it gathered earlier.

Moving folders minimizes the number of file operations that have to take place, making upgrade times consistent even when individual user accounts contain large numbers of files. (By contrast, the Windows 7 setup program moved files individually, which could lead to some painfully long upgrades.)

To further speed things up, Windows 10 Setup uses hard link operations to move files and folders from the transport location to the new Windows 10 hierarchy. Not having to physically move the file improves performance and also allows for easy rollback if something goes wrong during setup.

Folders associated with individual user accounts are moved when they meet the following criteria:

- Every file in the folder and all of its subfolders is preserved, with no rules defined to exclude some files or subfolders.

- The entire folder is placed within the fresh Windows 10 installation unchanged.

- The target Windows 10 destination doesn't already exist and thus there's no need to merge an existing folder in the target destination with one from the source operating system.

This activity is accompanied by several restarts and can take as long as a few hours, depending on your hardware. At the conclusion of this process, you're confronted with a sign-in screen like the one shown in Figure 2-7.

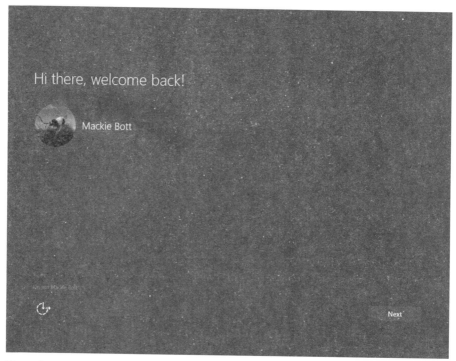

Figure 2-7 In the final stage of setup, signing in with a Microsoft account restores synced settings and apps from OneDrive.

By signing in with a Microsoft account, you can continue setting up Windows 10 by using synced settings. The most current version of each installed app is downloaded and installed from the Windows Store, a process that may continue for several minutes after you sign in.

If you're upgrading from Windows 7 or from a Windows 8.1 PC that was configured to use a local user account, you'll need to sign in using the credentials for that account. After that, you'll have the option to link your account to a Microsoft account or to continue using a local account.

For more on your options when setting up a user account, see Chapter 6, "Managing user accounts, passwords, and credentials."

Performing a clean install

For some veteran Windows users, a clean install is the only option worth considering. Historically, that option means starting up from a bootable USB flash drive containing the Windows 10 installation files and removing all traces of the currently installed Windows version before proceeding with setup.

This is still a perfectly valid installation method, one we'll describe in more detail shortly. But it's no longer the only option, nor is it always the best. For a system that's already running any modern version of Windows, you'll find it much easier to start Setup from within Windows, choose an upgrade install, and choose the option to keep Nothing. After you use Disk Cleanup Manager to remove the old Windows installation, the result is identical to an old-fashioned clean install.

> NOTE
> **For a thorough discussion of how the Push Button Reset option works, see Chapter 16.**

That neat option isn't possible if you are starting with a brand-new hard disk or you want to install a 64-bit Windows 10 edition on a device that's currently running 32-bit Windows, or you want to clean up a messy OEM's partition layout on the system disk, or . . . you get the idea.

For those scenarios, you need to boot into the Windows 10 setup program from a USB flash drive (or a DVD drive, if your PC is equipped with one of those increasingly rare peripherals). You might need to read the manual for your device to learn the magic combination of keystrokes and firmware settings that make it possible to start up using a bootable Windows 10 disc or drive.

After the setup process begins, you can follow the instructions as outlined in this section.

Making bootable media

You can't simply copy installation files to a flash drive and use it to perform a clean install. First, you have to make the disk bootable. When creating a bootable drive, you need to consider two factors:

- **Partitioning scheme: MBR or GPT?** You can use either scheme with a UEFI system; older BIOS-based systems might only be able to recognize MBR partitions.

- **Disk format: NTFS or FAT32?** If you plan to install Windows on a UEFI-based system (such as Microsoft's Surface Pro line), the boot files *must* reside on a FAT32 partition. If the drive is formatted using another file system, the PC will not recognize the device as bootable.

One of the simplest ways to create a bootable install drive from an ISO file is to use the built-in Recovery Media Creator utility. In previous Windows versions, this tool was able to create a bootable drive that included the recovery partition provided by the OEM. If you performed a clean install or removed that recovery partition for space purposes, the recovery drive could be used only for simple repair operations.

In Windows 10, if the Recovery Media Creator can't find an OEM-supplied recovery image, it reconstructs one from currently installed system files. You can use that image to replace the underlying Windows 10 version, and you can use it to perform a clean install. Figure 2-8 shows this utility in operation.

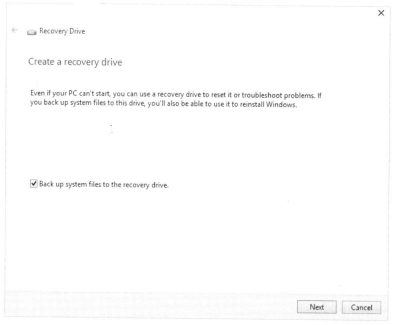

Figure 2-8 Choose the option to add system files if you want to create a recovery drive that you can use to reset the current system.

If you have downloaded an ISO file containing the Windows installation files, you can burn that file to a DVD (assuming the target system has an optical drive from which it can start). Or you can create a blank recovery drive using Windows 8.1 or Windows 10, skipping the option to copy system files to the drive; then mount the ISO file and use File Explorer to copy all of its files and folders to the USB recovery drive.

NOTE

For maximum flexibility in creating installable media, we recommend the free, open source utility Rufus, available at *http://rufus.akeo.ie/*. It allows precise control over partitioning, formatting, and copying installation files to a USB flash drive.

When you boot from that media, you pass through a few introductory screens—choosing a language, accepting a license agreement—and eventually reach the Windows Setup dialog box shown in Figure 2-9. Although you're prompted to choose an installation type—Upgrade or Custom—that's actually a trick question.

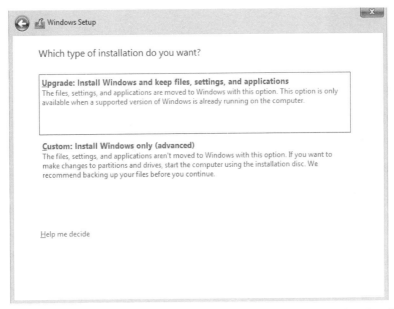

Figure 2-9 When you boot from a USB flash drive or DVD to perform a clean install of Windows, the only option that works from this screen is Custom.

Choosing the Upgrade option raises an error message; you can upgrade Windows only if you start Setup from within Windows.

The Custom option allows you to continue, and you're presented with a list of available disks and volumes. Figure 2-10 shows what you'll see on a system with a single, newly installed hard drive.

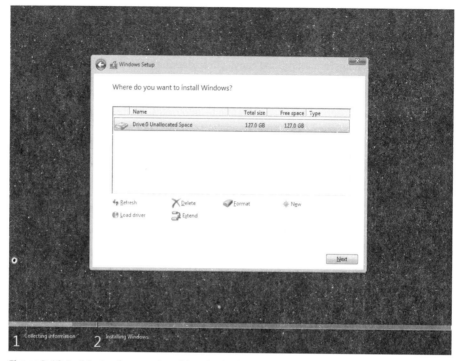

Figure 2-10 In this simple scenario, with a single physical disk that does not contain any partitions, you can click Next to create a partition and install Windows using the entire physical drive.

You can use the tools beneath the list of available drives to manage partitions on the selected drive. These tools allow you to delete an existing partition (for a truly fresh start on a drive that already contains files), create a new partition, format a partition, or extend a partition to include adjacent unallocated space.

For more on managing disks using the full array of Windows tools, see Chapter 14, "Managing disks and drives."

When you click Next, the setup process switches into a lengthy unattended phase in which it lays down the clean Windows 10 image. When that's complete, you get to choose default settings for all new accounts. The default settings are explained in detail in the Use Express Settings screen, shown in Figure 2-11. Click the small Customize Settings link in the lower left corner to open additional pages where you can adjust any of these settings.

If you do a clean install using bootable media for Windows 10 Pro, you're faced with one additional choice immediately after this phase of setup. The dialog box shown in Figure 2-12 asks you who owns your PC. (For an installation of Windows 10 Enterprise, the dialog box asks whether you want to join Azure AD or join a domain.)

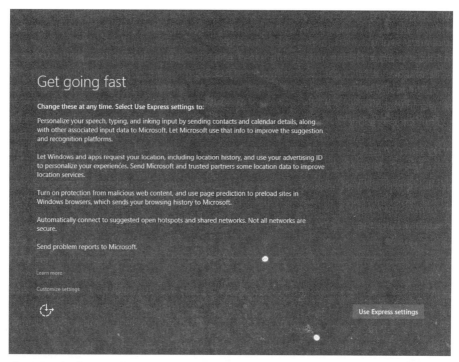

Figure 2-11 When you do a clean install, these default options allow you to configure a user account quickly, without fussing over individual options.

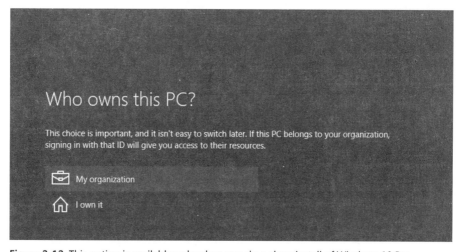

Figure 2-12 This option is available only when you do a clean install of Windows 10 Pro.

Choosing the first option (My Organization) and clicking Next leads you through a slightly confusing series of dialog boxes that allows you to set up a device for access to online services (from Microsoft and others). The credentials are managed in Azure Active Directory and can be linked to services such as an Office 365 account at a workplace or university.

If you own the device, or if it is a company PC that will be joined to a local Windows domain, choose the I Do option.

➤ **For more on setting up user accounts, during or after setup, see Chapter 6.**

Setup and your hard disk

In the previous section, we described the steps for a clean installation on the simplest of all PC configurations: a single hard disk containing unallocated space ready to be automatically partitioned for use as the system drive. Out in the real world, especially among Windows enthusiasts, we know that disk configurations can be much more complex.

On most desktop PCs and on some notebooks, you can connect multiple physical disk drives. You can choose to install Windows 10 to a volume on any IDE or SATA drive (including eSATA drives, which attach to the system via an external cable but appear to Windows as an ordinary internal drive). You cannot, however, install Windows to an external drive connected via USB or IEEE 1394 (FireWire), or to any form of removable media. (The sole exception is the Windows To Go feature, which requires specially built USB drives and an installed copy of Windows 10 Enterprise edition.)

With a new hard disk or an existing one, you might have any of several good reasons to tinker with disk partitions. You might prefer to segregate your operating system files from your data files by placing them on separate volumes, for example, or you might be planning to set up a dual-boot or multiboot system. In any event, it's always easier to make partitioning decisions before setup than it is to resize and rearrange volumes after they're in use.

➤ **For a full inventory of all disk-management tools and techniques available in Windows 10, see Chapter 14.**

Inside OUT

How Windows 10 divides a disk

If you install Windows 10 on a UEFI-based system with a single unformatted disk, Setup creates a default disk layout. Three of its partitions are visible in the Disk Management console, as shown here.

The small (300 MB) recovery partition at the start of the disk contains the Windows Recovery Environment, which allows the system to boot for repair and recovery operations. (For more information, see "Making repairs with the Windows Recovery Environment" in Chapter 17, "Troubleshooting.")

The EFI system partition is even smaller, at 100 MB. It contains the files required for the system to start up, including the Windows Hardware Abstraction Layer and the boot loader (NTLDR).

The largest partition is the primary partition, formatted using NTFS, which contains Windows system files, the paging file, and all user profiles.

A fourth partition, required for every GPT disk, is hidden and not visible in Disk Management. This partition, labeled MSR (Reserved), resides between the EFI system partition and the primary partition and is used for postinstallation tasks, such as converting a basic disk to a dynamic disk. It is visible when you use DiskPart or the partitioning tools available with a custom installation.

PC makers have the option to add custom OEM partitions to this layout, with those volumes containing files that are part of a custom installation. In addition, some PCs contain a second recovery partition, at the end of the drive, that contains files required to restore the original system configuration.

To make adjustments to existing disk partitions, boot from Windows 10 installation media (DVD or bootable USB flash drive) and run through Windows Setup until you reach the Where Do You Want To Install Windows page of the Windows Setup dialog box, shown earlier in Figure 2-10. The collection of tools below the list of disks and partitions is shown in Figure 2-13.

Figure 2-13 Use the disk-management tools in this phase of the Windows 10 setup process to manage disk partitions for more efficient data storage and multiboot configurations.

The system shown in Figure 2-13 includes two physical disks. The first, Drive 0, has been divided roughly in half, with a Windows installation on Partition 4, leaving a block of unallocated space. The second physical disk, Drive 1, has been partitioned but still has most of its space unallocated.

You can accomplish any of the following tasks here:

- **Select an existing partition or unallocated space on which to install Windows 10.** Setup is simple if you already created and formatted an empty partition in preparation for setting up Windows, or if you plan to install Windows 10 on an existing partition that currently contains data or programs but no operating system, or if you want to use unallocated space on an existing disk without disturbing the existing partition scheme. Select the partition or unallocated space, and click Next.

- **Delete an existing partition.** Select a partition, and then click Delete. This option is useful if you want to perform a clean installation on a drive that currently contains an earlier version of Windows. Because this operation deletes data irretrievably, you must respond to an "Are you sure?" confirmation request. After deleting the partition, you can select the unallocated space as the destination for your Windows 10 installation or create a new partition. Be sure to back up any data files before choosing this option.

- **Create a new partition from unallocated space.** Select a block of unallocated space on a new drive or on an existing drive after deleting partitions, and click New to set up a partition in that space.

By default, Windows Setup offers to use all unallocated space on the current disk. You can specify a smaller partition size if you want to subdivide the disk into multiple drives. If you have a 1,500-GB drive, for example, you might choose to create a relatively small partition on which to install Windows and use the remaining space to create a second volume with its own drive letter on which to store data files such as music, pictures, documents, and videos or TV shows.

- **Extend an existing partition by using unallocated space.** If you're not happy with your existing partition scheme, you can use the Extend option to add unallocated space to any partition, provided that space is immediately to the right of the existing partition in Disk Management, with no intervening partitions. If you originally divided a 120-GB notebook hard disk into two equal volumes, you might decide to rejoin the two partitions to give your system drive more breathing room. After backing up your data files to an external drive or to cloud storage, delete the data partition, select the partition you want to make larger, and click Extend. Choose the total size of the extended partition in the Size box (the default is to use all available unallocated space), and click Apply. You can now continue with your installation, restoring your data files after setup is complete.

CAUTION

In both the Disk Management console and the disk-management tools available via Windows Setup, it can be confusing to tell which partition is which. Confusion, in this case, can have drastic consequences if you inadvertently wipe out a drive full of data instead of writing over an unwanted installation of Windows. One good way to reduce the risk of this sort of accident is to label drives well. In Figure 2-13, for instance, you can see at a glance that the first partition on Drive 0 contains a current installation of Windows 10 Pro, the second partition is formatted for data storage, and Drive 1 is empty.

Alert observers will no doubt notice that one option is missing from that list. Unfortunately, Setup does not allow you to shrink an existing disk partition to create unallocated space on which to install a fresh copy of Windows 10. The option to shrink a volume is available from the Disk Management console after Windows 10 is installed, but if you want to accomplish this task before or during setup, you'll need to use third-party disk-management tools.

Configuring a multiboot system

If your computer already has any version of Windows installed and you have a second disk partition available (or enough unallocated space to create a second partition), you can install a clean copy of Windows 10 without disturbing your existing Windows installation. At boot time, you choose your Windows version from a startup menu, like the one shown in Figure 2-14. Although this is typically called a dual-boot system, it's more accurate to call it a multiboot configuration, because you can install multiple copies of Windows or other PC-compatible operating systems.

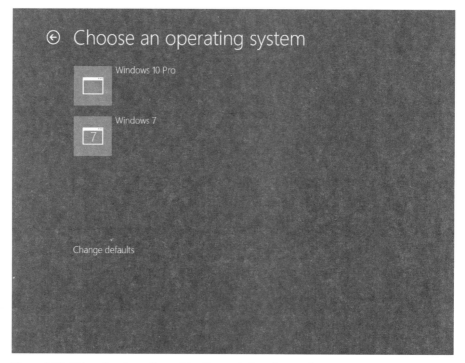

Figure 2-14 This system is configured to allow a choice of operating systems at startup.

Having the capability to choose your operating system at startup is handy if you have a program or device that simply won't work under Windows 10. When you need to use the legacy program or device, you can boot into your earlier Windows version without too much fuss.

This capability is also useful for software developers and IT professionals who need to be able to test how programs work under different operating systems using physical (not virtual) hardware.

For experienced Windows users, installing a second copy of Windows 10 in its own partition can also be helpful as a way to experiment with a potentially problematic program or device driver without compromising a working system. After you finish setting up the second, clean version of Windows 10, you'll see an additional entry on the startup menu that corresponds to your new installation. (The newly installed version is the default menu choice; it runs automatically if 30 seconds pass and you haven't made a choice.) Experiment with the program or driver and see how well it works. If, after testing thoroughly, you're satisfied that the program is safe to use, you can add it to the Windows 10 installation you use every day.

Inside OUT

Use virtual machines instead of hassling with multiboot menus

You can create truly elaborate multiboot configurations using more than a decade's worth of Windows versions. But unless you're running a hardware testing lab, there's no good reason to do that. The much simpler, smoother alternative is to use virtual hardware that faithfully re-creates the operating environment. During the course of researching and writing this book, we installed Windows 10 in virtual machines to capture details of several crucial tasks and processes that can't easily be documented on physical hardware, and we saved many hours compared to how long those tasks would have taken had we set up and restored physical hardware.

We strongly recommend Microsoft's Hyper-V virtualization software, which is a standard feature in the Pro editions of Windows 8.1 and Windows 10 and on recent Windows Server releases. (For more information about Client Hyper-V in Windows 10, see Chapter 22, "Running virtual machines with Hyper-V.")

To run Windows 10 on a Mac, try Parallels, available at *http://parallels.com*. For other operating systems, check out VMware (*http://vmware.com*), which offers excellent virtualization software for use on desktop Windows machines and servers, and the free VirtualBox package from Oracle (*http://virtualbox.org*).

Using any of these solutions, you can install even the most ancient Windows version. Backing up a machine's configuration and restoring it is as simple as copying a file. Legally, you'll need a license for every operating system you install in a virtual machine. If you have a license to use Windows for evaluation purposes, the option to run Windows in a virtual machine can be a lifesaver.

To add Windows 10 to a system on which an existing version of Windows is already installed, first make sure that you have an available partition (or unformatted disk space) separate from the partition that contains the system files for your current Windows version.

The target partition can be a separate partition on the same physical disk, or it can be on a different hard disk. If your system contains a single disk with a single partition used as drive C, you cannot create a multiboot system unless you add a new disk or use software tools to shrink the existing partition and create a new partition from the free space. (The Disk Management console, Diskmgmt.msc, includes this capability; to shrink partitions on a system running an older Windows version, you'll need third-party software. For details, see "Shrinking a volume" in Chapter 14.) The new partition does not need to be empty; if it contains system files for another Windows installation, they will be moved to Windows.old. Run Setup, choose the Custom (Advanced) option, and select the disk and partition you want to use for the new installation.

The setup program automatically handles details of adding the newly installed operating system to the Boot Configuration Data store.

And how do you edit and configure the Boot Configuration Data store? Surprisingly, the only official tool is a command-line utility called Bcdedit. Bcdedit isn't an interactive program; instead, you perform tasks by appending switches and parameters to the Bcdedit command line. To display the complete syntax for this tool, open an elevated Command Prompt window (using the Run As Administrator option) and type the command **bcdedit /?**.

For everyday use, most Bcdedit options are esoteric, unnecessary—and risky. In fact, the only option that we remember using more than once in the past four years is the command to change the text for each entry in the boot menu. By default, the setup program adds the generic entry "Windows 10" for each installation. If you set up a dual-boot system using two copies of Windows 10 (one for everyday use, one for testing), you'll be unable to tell which is which because the menu text will be the same for each. To make the menu more informative, follow these steps:

1. Start your computer, and choose either entry from the boot menu. After startup is complete, make a note of which installation is running.

2. Right-click Start, or press Windows key+X, and choose Command Prompt (Admin) from the Quick Link menu. Click Yes in the User Account Control box to open an elevated Command Prompt window.

3. Type the following command: **bcdedit /set description "*Menu description goes here*"** (substitute your own description for the placeholder text, and be sure to include the quotation marks). Press Enter.

4. Restart your computer, and note that the menu description you just entered now appears on the menu. Select the other menu option.

5. Repeat steps 2 and 3, again adding a menu description to replace the generic text and distinguish this installation from the other one.

A few startup options are available when you click or tap Change Defaults at the bottom of the boot menu, as shown here.

You can choose which installation is the default operating system (this is where descriptive menu choices come in handy) and change the timer that determines how long you want to display the list of operating systems. The default is 30 seconds; you can choose 5 seconds (allowing the default operating system to start virtually automatically) or 5 minutes, if you want to ensure that you have a choice even if you're distracted while the system is restarting. These options write data directly to the Boot Configuration Data store.

For slightly more control over the boot menu timer, use the System Configuration utility, Msconfig.exe. The Boot tab allows you to change the default operating system and set the Timeout interval in any amount between 3 and 999 seconds.

Inside OUT

Installing Windows 10 and Linux in a multiboot configuration

It's possible to install Windows 10 and Linux in a multiboot configuration that works much like the Windows multiboot setup described on the preceding pages. You can set it up to use the Windows 10 boot menu, or you can use a Linux boot loader (most commonly, GRUB) if you prefer. The procedure is a bit more complex than the procedure for installing another version of Windows, and it varies somewhat depending on which Linux distribution you use and which Linux tools (such as partition editors, boot loaders, and the like) you prefer. It's generally easier to set up such a system if the Windows partition is set up first, but it can be done either way: Windows and then Linux, or Linux and then Windows.

An Internet search for "dual boot Linux Windows" turns up plenty of detailed instructions, and if you add the name of your Linux distribution to the search input, you're likely to find the specific steps needed to make it work with Windows 8.1 or Windows 10.

Activating Windows

For more than a dozen years, desktop versions of Windows have included a set of antipiracy and antitampering features. In the past, Microsoft has used different names for these capabilities: Windows Activation Technologies and Windows Genuine Advantage, for example. In Windows 10, these features are collectively referred to as the Software Protection Platform.

The various checks and challenges in Windows 10 are, in essence, enforcement mechanisms for the Windows 10 license agreement, which is displayed during the process of installing or deploying the operating system (you must provide your consent to complete setup). We're not lawyers, so we won't attempt to interpret this license agreement. We do recommend that you read the license agreement, which is fairly straightforward. In this section, we explain how the activation and validation mechanisms in Windows 10 affect your use of the operating system.

Product activation happens shortly after you set up a new PC with Windows 10. Typically, this involves a brief communication between your PC and Microsoft's licensing servers. If everything checks out, your copy of Windows is activated silently, and you never have to deal with product keys or activation prompts.

In the past, activating Windows required entering a 25-character alphanumeric product key. On OEM PCs, this product key is stored in the computer's firmware so it can be automatically retrieved and activated. For retail installations and upgrades, though, entering that product key was mandatory. That's no longer true.

With Windows 10, Microsoft has made a fundamental change to the way it performs product activation on upgrades. The biggest change of all is that the Windows 10 activation status for a device is stored online. After you successfully activate Windows 10 for the first time, that device will activate automatically in the future, with no product key required.

When you upgrade from Windows 7 or Windows 8.1, the Windows 10 setup program checks your current activation status and reports the result to the activation servers. If your current installation of Windows is "genuine" (that is, properly activated), the Windows activation server generates a Windows 10 license certificate (Microsoft calls it a "digital entitlement") for the version to which you just upgraded (Home or Pro). That proof of digital activation is stored in conjunction with your unique installation ID on Microsoft's activation servers.

That unique installation ID is essentially a fingerprint of your PC, based on a cryptographic hash derived from your hardware. That hash is reportedly not reversible and not tied to any other Microsoft services. So although it defines your device, it doesn't identify you. But it does make it possible to store activation status for that device online.

Once that online activation status is recorded, you can wipe your drive clean, boot from Windows 10 installation media, install a clean copy skipping right past the prompts for a product key, and at the end of the process you'll have a properly activated copy of Windows 10.

If you're building your own PC or installing Windows 10 in a virtual machine that doesn't currently have an activated copy of Windows 7 or Windows 8.1, you'll still need a product key for use with a retail Windows 10 package or an OEM System Builder license.

After you successfully activate your copy of Windows 10, you're still subject to periodic antipiracy checks from Microsoft. This process, called *validation*, verifies that your copy of Windows has not been tampered with to bypass activation. It also allows Microsoft to undo the activation process for a computer when it determines after the fact that the product key was stolen or used in violation of a volume licensing agreement.

Validation takes two forms: an internal tool that regularly checks licensing and activation files to determine that they haven't been tampered with, and an online tool that restricts access to some downloads and updates.

If your system fails validation, your computer continues to work, but you'll see some differences: the desktop background changes to black (and if you change it to something else, Windows changes it back to black after one hour), an "activate now" reminder that also tells you your copy of Windows is "Not Genuine" appears on the desktop, and an Activate Now dialog box appears periodically. In addition, your access to Windows Update is somewhat restricted; you won't be able to download optional updates, new drivers, or certain other programs from the Microsoft Download Center until your system passes the validation check.

NOTE

A device that has failed Windows validation can still be used. All Windows functions work normally, all your data files are accessible, and all your programs work as expected. The nagging reminders are intended to strongly encourage you to resolve the underlying issue. Some forms of malware can result in damage to system files that has the same effect as tampering with activation files. Another common cause of activation problems is a lazy or dishonest repair technician who installs a stolen or "cracked" copy of Windows instead of using your original licensed copy. Links in the Windows Activation messages lead to online support tools, where you might be able to identify and repair the issue that's affecting your system. Microsoft offers free support for activation issues via online forums and by telephone.

The activation mechanism is designed to enforce license restrictions by preventing the most common form of software piracy: casual copying. Typically, a Windows 10 license entitles you to install the operating system software on a single computer. If a system builder uses the same product key on a second (or third or fourth) device, you might be unable to activate the software automatically.

As we write this chapter, Microsoft has just begun rolling out the new product activation system in Windows 10. It is possible that some of the details we describe here will change over time.

Entering a product key

When you upgrade a PC that contains a properly activated copy of Windows 7 or Windows 8.1, the freshly upgraded copy is automatically activated as well, with no manual intervention required on your part. At any time, you can check the activation status of your device from the Activation page in Settings, Update & Security, as shown in Figure 2-15.

In some installation scenarios, you might be prompted to enter a 25-character alphanumeric product key that uniquely identifies your licensed copy of Windows. If you experience activation hassles caused by an incorrect product key, you can use the Change Product Key button to set things right, using the dialog box shown in Figure 2-16.

Figure 2-15 Most Windows 10 PCs will be automatically activated, with the successful activation status shown in this dialog box.

Figure 2-16 When you enter the 25-character alphanumeric product key, Windows automatically checks it and prompts you to complete activation.

Here are some key facts you should know about this procedure:

- **The product key is entered automatically on any copy of Windows that is pre-installed on a new PC by a large computer maker.** This configuration is called System Locked Preinstallation (SLP) and allows you to reinstall Windows from recovery media without entering a product key.

- **Your product key matches your edition of Windows.** If you purchase a boxed copy of Windows 10 from a retail outlet, the installation media (typically a DVD) contains a configuration file that automatically installs the edition you purchased: Home or Pro. The product key works only with that edition.

- **Most Windows 10 upgrades don't require a product key.** If you upgrade a properly activated copy of Windows 7 or Windows 8.1 during the free upgrade offer, you don't need to enter a product key. A record of the edition you're licensed to use, Home or Pro, is stored with your hardware ID on Microsoft's activation servers.

- **The architecture does not need to match your product key.** You can use the same key to replace a 32-bit Windows 10 edition with a 64-bit edition, or vice versa.

- **You are not required to enter a product key when performing a clean install of Windows 10.** You're prompted to enter a valid product key to install Windows 10 on a system that does not currently contain a properly activated ("genuine") Windows installation corresponding to the one you're trying to install. If you leave the Product Key box blank and click Next when attempting a clean install of an upgrade edition of Windows, Setup will not continue. You must click the tiny Skip link, just to the left of the Next button.

Activating a retail copy of Windows

When you install Windows 10 on a new PC, it will attempt to contact Microsoft's licensing servers and activate automatically within three days. If the activation process fails, you can activate Windows by connecting to a Microsoft activation server over the Internet or by making a toll-free call to an interactive telephone activation system.

Under most circumstances, activation over the Internet takes no more than a few seconds. If you need to use the telephone, the process takes longer because you have to enter a 50-digit identification key (either by using the phone's dial pad or by speaking to a customer service representative) and then input the 42-digit confirmation ID supplied in response.

The activation process is completely anonymous and does not require that you divulge any personal information. If you choose to register your copy of Windows 10, this is a completely separate (and optional) task.

You're allowed to reinstall Windows 10 an unlimited number of times on the same hardware. During the activation process, Windows transmits a hashed file that serves as a "fingerprint" of key components in your system. When you attempt to activate the same edition of Windows 10 you activated previously, the activation server calculates a fingerprint on the fly, using your current hardware setup, and compares the value against the one stored in its database. If you're reinstalling Windows 10 on hardware that is essentially the same, the fingerprints will match and activation will be automatic.

Just as with earlier Windows versions, the activation process is designed to prevent attempts to tamper with the activation files or to "clone" an activated copy of Windows and install it on another computer. What happens if you upgrade the hardware in your computer? When you activate your copy of Windows 10, a copy of the hardware fingerprint is stored on your hard disk and checked each time you start your computer. If you make substantial changes to your system hardware, you might be required to reactivate your copy of Windows.

Because the activation mechanism assumes (mistakenly) that you've tried to install your copy of Windows on a second computer, Internet activation might not work. In this case, you're required to manually enter a new activation code, which can be obtained from the telephone-based activation support center. You can upgrade almost all components in a system without requiring a new license. You can also replace a defective motherboard and retain the right to reactivate your copy of Windows. (If you upgrade your PC with a new motherboard, that is considered a new PC and might require a new license.)

Activation requirements for OEM installations

If you purchase a new computer with Windows 10 already installed on it, the licensing procedures are different, as are the rules for activation. In the arcane parlance of Windows, system

makers are known as original equipment manufacturers, or OEMs. To make matters more confusing, not all OEMs are created equal; instead, they're divided into two classes:

- Large system builders (Microsoft refers to these firms as named or multinational OEMs
  or, informally, as royalty OEMs) are allowed to install and preactivate Windows using
  System Locked Preinstallation (SLP), mentioned earlier. The preinstalled copy of Windows
  (including the recovery disc) contains configuration files that look for specific information in the system BIOS or firmware. As long as this information matches, no activation is
  required. A new computer from one of these large companies may contain a sticker that
  certifies your installation, but unlike in earlier versions of Windows, that sticker contains
  no product key. The OEM uses a single master key to activate large numbers of computers. If you need to reinstall Windows, you must do so by using the recovery media from
  the same computer (or one with the same motherboard/BIOS combination).

- Smaller firms that build PCs can also preinstall Windows. These OEM copies are called
  System Builder copies, and they do require activation. The rules of the System Builder
  program require the PC manufacturer to use specific tools to preinstall Windows so that
  you accept a license agreement and activate the software when you first turn on the PC.
  In addition, the manufacturer is required to supply the purchaser with the Windows 10
  media (typically a DVD) and affix a product key sticker to the PC's case. If you need to
  reinstall Windows on this computer, you must enter the product key and go through
  activation again.

The license agreement for a retail copy of Windows 10 allows you to transfer it to another
computer provided that you completely remove it from the computer on which it was previously installed. An OEM copy, by contrast, is tied to the computer on which it was originally
installed. You can reinstall an OEM copy of Windows an unlimited number of times on the
same computer. However, you are prohibited by the license agreement from transferring that
copy of Windows to another computer.

Product activation and corporate licensing

Businesses that purchase licenses through a Microsoft Volume Licensing (VL) program receive
VL media and product keys that require activation under a different set of rules from those
that apply to retail or OEM copies. Under the terms of a volume license agreement, each computer with a copy of Windows 10 must have a valid license and must be activated.

Enterprise editions of Windows 10 can be installed using Multiple Activation Keys, which
allow activations on a specific number of devices within an organization, or they can use Key
Management servers to activate computers within their organization. If you encounter activation issues with Windows 10 Pro or Enterprise in a VL deployment, contact the person in your
organization who manages your VL agreement—the "Benefits Administrator" as this person is
called.

Managing Windows activation from the command prompt

Windows 10 includes a command-line tool that you can use to examine the licensing status of a PC, change its product key, and perform other activation-related tasks. Although this feature is primarily intended for automating license administration activities, you can also run the Windows Software Licensing Management Tool interactively. Open a Command Prompt window with administrative privileges and then run the command `Slmgr.vbs`. Run without parameters, this command shows its full syntax in a series of dialog boxes.

One common use of this tool is to display the current licensing status for a device, using the syntax `slmgr.vbs /dli`. Figure 2-17, for example, shows the status of a device that has failed validation and is in Notification mode.

For a much more detailed display of information, use the same command with a switch that produces verbose output: `slmgr.vbs /dlv`.

Figure 2-17 This output from the Windows Software Licensing Management Tool shows a system that is in Notification mode. The Notification Reason code, in the last line, can be useful for troubleshooting.

Tweaking and tuning your Windows 10 installation

When Windows Setup completes, you're signed in and ready to begin using Windows 10. For upgrades and clean installs alike, we suggest following this simple checklist to confirm that basic functionality is enabled properly.

- **Look for missing device drivers.** Open Device Management and look for any devices that have a yellow exclamation mark over the icon or any devices that are listed under the Other category. This is also a good time to install any custom drivers supplied by the device maker and not available through Windows Update. For more on working with device drivers, see "How device drivers and hardware work together" in Chapter 13, "Hardware."

- **Adjust display settings.** You'll want to confirm that the display is set for its native resolution and that any additional tasks such as color calibration have been completed.

- **Check your network connection.** If you skipped network setup during a clean install, you can complete the task now. Open the Network folder in File Explorer to switch from a public network to a private network and allow local file sharing.

- **Verify security settings.** If you use third-party security software, install it now and get the latest updates.

- **Check Windows Update.** You'll get the latest updates automatically within the next 24 hours. Doing the update manually lets you avoid a scheduled overnight restart.

- **Change default programs.** Use this opportunity to set your preferred browser, email client, music playback software, and so on.

- **Adjust power and sleep settings.** The default settings are usually good enough, but they're rarely a perfect match for your preferences. Now is a good time to adjust when your device sleeps and whether it requires a password when it wakes.

Using Windows 10

Regardless of your upgrade path—from Windows 7 or from Windows 8.1—your day-to-day experience changes significantly with Windows 10.

The things you expect Windows to do on your behalf—launching programs, arranging windows on the screen, switching between tasks, finding files, setting notifications, interacting with cloud services, communicating with other people—are basically the same. But the steps you take to accomplish those tasks are different.

The change is more striking if you're moving from a conventional PC or laptop to a touchscreen device. Even if you still have access to a keyboard and mouse or trackpad, the addition of touch fundamentally changes how you interact with Windows and with apps. With a phone or small tablet added to the mix, you have still more options to explore.

In this chapter, we look at the things you tap, click, drag, and drop to make Windows do your bidding. Some, like the taskbar and notification icons, are similar enough to their predecessors that you might miss subtle but significant changes.

Our coverage also includes a section on the unique ways to interact with a tablet running Windows 10. And, of course, we introduce Cortana, the first Windows feature that can literally speak for itself.

A disclaimer, right up front: in this chapter, we are writing about a user experience that is evolving from month to month and that will continue to do so even after the initial release of Windows 10 on July 29, 2015. The screen shots and step-by-step instructions you see here are based on that initial release. It's not only possible, but practically certain, that some of the features we describe here will change in the months after we send this book to the printer as Microsoft delivers on its promise of "Windows as a service."

If you see subtle differences between what's on these pages and what's on your screen, that's the likely reason. We hope our descriptions make it possible to incorporate those changes into your learning.

An overview of the Windows 10 user experience

Before we dive into detailed descriptions of individual features, please join us for a brief tour of Windows 10. Our goal is to introduce the different parts of Windows, new and old, so that we can be sure you're on the same page . . . or at least looking at the same arrangement of pixels.

Figure 3-1 shows the basic building blocks of Windows 10 and offers a hint of its signature visual style.

Figure 3-1 The Start menu and Action Center are at the core of the Windows 10 experience, with the familiar desktop front and center for conventional PCs.

When you first start up a conventional PC running Windows 10, you see the familiar Windows 7–style desktop and taskbar. Clicking the Start button—the Windows logo in the lower left corner—opens the Start menu, which is conceptually similar to its predecessor but differs dramatically in the details.

How the cloud changes your experience

One noteworthy difference between the initial Windows 10 experience and the traditional Windows experience that reached its zenith with Windows 7 is the amount of personalization you see when you sign in on a new PC or device. If you use a Microsoft account you've already used on a different device, the customized settings saved with your account appear automatically on the new device, making it feel familiar right away.

On a clean install or a refresh, you can create a local account, which gives you the standard default layout and themes, as defined by Microsoft. If you sign in to a corporate network, your personalized settings roam according to policies defined by your network administrator. (If your organization allows you to, you can attach a Microsoft account to your domain account, and both your personal and work settings roam together as you switch between devices.)

When you allow your Microsoft account to sync settings between devices, you don't have to go through a tedious process of tweaking the default settings to match those preferences; instead, your visual themes, browser settings, and saved Wi-Fi passwords appear exactly as you expect. If your Microsoft account is connected to OneDrive, your online files, photos, and music collection will be available too. We discuss these features in more detail in Chapter 5, "Networking essentials."

A click on the right side of the taskbar opens Action Center, which is also shown in Figure 3-1. This pane, which uses the full height of your display, contains notifications from apps and services as well as action buttons that allow quick access to settings.

As with previous versions, Windows 10 offers multiple ways to switch between tasks. The Task View button, a new addition to the Windows 10 taskbar, produces the view shown in Figure 3-2, which also illustrates another new feature: virtual desktops. We discuss both features in more detail later in this chapter.

Figure 3-2 Task View allows you to switch quickly between available windows; the new virtual desktop feature allows you to group windows.

> ➤ For more details on how to set up notifications and configure Action Center, see Chapter 4, "Personalizing Windows 10."

Navigating Windows 10

Touchscreens might represent the future of computing, but the present is still ruled by more-or-less conventional desktop and laptop PCs, each equipped with a keyboard and a mouse or touchpad.

For that type of device, the desktop is where you'll likely spend most of your time, and it's what we concentrate on in this section. Tablet Mode has its own set of rules and gets its own section, immediately after this one.

Using and customizing the Start menu

The Windows 10 Start menu, like its Windows 7 counterpart, is divided into two vertical segments. On the left side is a comparatively thin column, with the current user's name and picture at the top. Below that identifying iconography is a list of installed programs, with dedicated shortcuts for File Explorer, Settings, and Power below that.

At the very bottom of the list, you can click or tap All Apps to change the contents of the Start menu's left side so that it looks like Figure 3-3.

Figure 3-3 Clicking All Apps changes the left column in the Start menu to an alphabetical list of available programs.

The scrolling All Apps list is arranged in alphabetical order, in a fashion that's similar to its Windows 7 predecessor. One noteworthy difference: program groups, such as the Windows

Accessories folder, slide downward to open instead of flying out to the right in cascading menus.

On a lightly used system, you can probably find what you're looking for by scrolling through the list of shortcuts on the All Apps menu. Swipe directly on a touchscreen, use two-finger scrolling gestures on a touchpad, or use the scroll wheel with a mouse.

For larger lists of programs, using the search box is the fastest way to find a specific program. For an alternative to scrolling, try this time-saving shortcut: Click or tap any of the letter headings in the list to see the entire alphabet, as shown in Figure 3-4. Then click or tap a letter to jump to the section of the list beginning with that letter.

Figure 3-4 Clicking or tapping any heading in the alphabetical list takes you to this index, where tapping a letter takes you to the programs whose names begin with that letter.

You can change the size and shape of the Start menu by dragging it up (to a maximum height that is 100 pixels below the top of the display), to the right, or both ways. Resizing the Start menu doesn't change the width of the left column, and making the menu wider can be done only in increments corresponding to the width of two Wide tiles. (More on that shortly.)

Customizing the contents of the Start menu

If you're accustomed to the extensive array of customization options for items on the Start menu in earlier Windows versions, you'll need to make some adjustments.

You can remove programs from the Most Used section, but you can't pin program shortcuts to the left side of the Start menu.

You can add or remove shortcuts from the group of options just above the All Apps shortcut and the Power button. Besides the default File Explorer and Settings menu items, locations available for this section include your personal folder, the default folders from your user profile (Documents, Downloads, Music, Pictures, and Videos), and the Network folder. You can also add a HomeGroup shortcut. To see the entire list, open Settings, open Personalization, click or tap Start, and then click or tap Choose Which Folders Appear On Start.

Inside OUT

Which programs are included in the Most Used list?

The list of most used programs—the items that appear below the pinned programs on the left side of the Start menu—is controlled by Windows. In previous Windows versions, this list included only shortcuts to executable files you open, such as .exe files and .msc files. Windows 10 continues this behavior.

Several types of items are excluded by default, so you won't see things like setup programs, installer and uninstaller packages, Control Panel modules, and MMC consoles. You can find a list of what's excluded in the AddRemoveApps value of the registry key HKLM\Software\Microsoft\Windows\CurrentVersion\Explorer\FileAssociation. We do not recommend trying to edit these values manually.

Pin any Windows app to the Start menu, the taskbar, or both, either by right-clicking the program's entry in the All Apps list or by dragging it from that list and dropping it on the right side of the Start menu.

Inside OUT
Master the powerful "other" Start menu

Here's some good news for anyone who misses the system shortcuts from earlier iterations of the Start menu. Most of those tools are available as part of a hidden menu that
appears when you right-click the Start button or press Windows key+X, as shown here:

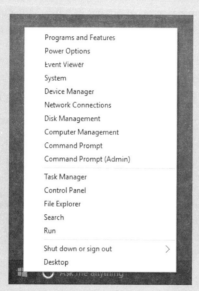

Most of the major system management and troubleshooting tools are on that list,
including Disk Management, Event Viewer, and the Computer Management console.

Windows traditionalists will appreciate the fact that the Shut Down Or Sign Out menu
item is here, along with links to Control Panel and Task Manager. Our personal favorite
is the Command Prompt (Admin) shortcut, which eliminates one minor hassle when it's
time to get work done the old-fashioned way, by typing commands directly. If you're a
PowerShell aficionado, an option on the Navigation tab of the Taskbar And Start Menu
Properties dialog box lets you replace the two Command Prompt options with Power-
Shell equivalents.

Adding and arranging tiles

Anything that appears on the All Apps menu can be dragged to the right side of the Start
menu and placed as a tile. Tiles, which were found on a separate Start screen in Windows 8.1,
behave much the same way in Windows 10, but they are constrained to the Start menu.

Clicking a tile has the same effect as clicking a Start menu program shortcut or a pinned task-bar button. What makes tiles different is the variety of sizes and their ability to display information or notifications from the app, making a tile *live*.

To pin a program as a tile to the right side of the Start menu, drag it into position. As an alternative, right-click its entry in All Apps or the Most Used list on the left side of the Start menu, and then click or tap Pin To Start. The item will take up residence as a medium size tile in the first available empty space on the right side of the menu, from where you can move and resize it as needed.

To remove a program from the right side of the Start menu, right-click it and then click Unpin From Start.

You can adjust the size of any tile by right-clicking the tile to see the menu shown in Figure 3-5.

Figure 3-5 These options are available for most programs acquired from the Windows Store. Not all apps support this full list of sizes.

Note that not all tiles support the full range of sizes shown in this figure. Windows desktop programs, for example, offer only the Small and Medium options.

On a touchscreen, you can accomplish the same tile customization tasks with a long press on the tile. That produces the two options shown in white circles on the right side of the tile in Figure 3-6. Tapping the top option unpins the tile, while tapping the ellipsis in the bottom right reveals a menu with Resize and Live Tile items.

Figure 3-6 On a touchscreen, a long press on any tile produces these controls, which lead to options identical to those on the right-click menu.

NOTE

Options for a specific app might allow additional customization of the live tile. The
Photos app, for example, allows you to choose a specific image for its tile.

Right-clicking the tile for a Windows desktop program produces a menu with an extra set of
options: Run As Administrator, for example.

Tiles can be arranged into groups, with or without custom group names. Drag tiles, one at a
time, into the position you prefer. If the position you choose is sufficiently far from the edge
of an existing group, your tile ends up in a new group of its own. You can move it back to an
existing group or add other tiles to the new group.

A slim bar sits above every group of tiles. By default, this bar is blank. Click (as we have in Figure 3-7) to display a text box where you can type a group name of your choosing. (We created
a group named Microsoft Office here.) Click the horizontal line to the right of the name box to
drag the entire group to a new location.

Figure 3-7 Click above any group of tiles to give that group a descriptive label.

Using and customizing the taskbar

The taskbar is that strip of real estate along one screen edge (bottom by default) that contains, from left to right, the Start button, the search box, program buttons, notification icons, and a clock. The taskbar made its first appearance in Windows 95. In the years since, it has slowly evolved without changing its basic shape

The Windows 10 taskbar continues to serve the same basic functions as its progenitors—launching programs, switching between programs, and providing notifications—with only subtle changes in functionality.

Every running program with a user interface has a corresponding taskbar button. When you close that program, the button vanishes as well, unless it's been pinned to the taskbar. A faint line appears underneath the icon for a running program, and the program with the current focus has a subtle but noticeable transparent shadow to identify it.

The Windows 10 taskbar offers a limited selection of customization options, most of which are available through the Taskbar And Start Menu Properties dialog box (see Figure 3-8). Open it by right-clicking an unoccupied area of the taskbar (if the taskbar is full, right-click the Task View button) and then clicking Properties.

Figure 3-8 For most people, the default options here will be acceptable, especially Lock The Taskbar, which prevents you from accidentally dragging the taskbar to the side of the monitor.

Two items on the Taskbar tab of the Taskbar And Start Menu Properties dialog box control the size and appearance of taskbar buttons:

- **Use Small Taskbar Buttons.** Select this option if you want to reduce the height of taskbar buttons, making them similar in size to buttons in earlier Windows versions. In our experience, buttons of this size are too small for practical use. If you have the eyesight of a hawk, you might beg to differ.

- **Taskbar Buttons.** The default setting for Taskbar Buttons is Always Combine, Hide Labels. This setting instructs Windows to always group multiple windows from a single application (such as Microsoft Word documents) into a single taskbar button. The Hide Labels setting for this option is left over from an old Windows version; Windows 10 does not display labels (window titles) for taskbar buttons.

  With either of the other settings (Combine When Taskbar Is Full or Never Combine), Windows gives each window its own separate taskbar button. It groups windows only when the taskbar becomes too crowded or continues to shrink the size of taskbar buttons as you open more windows. We recommend the default setting here.

➤ **If you have more than one display attached to a Windows 10 PC, some extra customization options are available for the taskbar. See "Configuring the taskbar with multiple displays" in Chapter 4 for details.**

Pinning programs to the taskbar

Pinning a taskbar button makes it easy to find and run favorite programs without the need to open the Start menu or use the search box to find the program's shortcut. To pin a program to the taskbar, simply drag its icon or a shortcut (from the Start menu, from the desktop, or from any other folder) to the taskbar. Alternatively, right-click a program icon wherever you find it and then click Pin To Taskbar.

To remove a pinned program from the taskbar, right-click the pinned icon and then click Unpin This Program From Taskbar. This command also appears on other shortcuts to the program, including those on the desktop and on the Start menu.

You can use task buttons to launch a program that's not currently running or to switch from one running program to another. You can also click a task button to minimize an open window or to restore a minimized window. If those features sound too obvious, here's a trick you might not know: you can open a new instance of a program that's already running—a new Microsoft Word document, for example, or a fresh File Explorer window—by right-clicking the taskbar button and then clicking the program name.

Using Jump Lists for quick access to documents and folders

A Jump List is the official name of the menu that appears when you right-click a taskbar button. Each taskbar Jump List includes commands to open the program, to pin the program to the taskbar (or unpin it), and to close all open windows represented by the button.

In addition, for programs that have been developed to take advantage of this feature, Jump Lists can include shortcuts to common tasks that can be performed with that program, such as Open New Tab on a browser window. For Microsoft Office programs, Adobe Acrobat, and other, similarly document-centric programs, Jump Lists also typically include links to recently opened files.

Figure 3-9 shows the default Jump List for File Explorer.

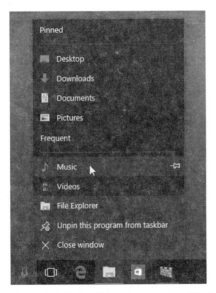

Figure 3-9 Right-click an icon, such as File Explorer, to see a Jump List showing recently opened files and folders with the option to pin items for quick access.

Individual files and folders can't be pinned directly to the taskbar, but you can add them to Jump Lists by using the following techniques.

- To pin a document to the taskbar, drag its icon or a shortcut to any empty space on the taskbar. If the taskbar already has a button for the program associated with the document, Windows adds the document to the Pinned section of the program's Jump List. If the document's program is not on the taskbar, Windows pins the program to the taskbar and adds the document to the program's Jump List.

- To pin a folder to the taskbar, drag its icon or a shortcut to the taskbar. Windows adds the folder to the Pinned section of the Jump List for File Explorer.

- To open a pinned document or folder, right-click the taskbar button and then click the name of the document or folder.

- To remove a pinned document or folder from the Jump List, right-click the taskbar button and point to the name of the document or folder to be removed. Click the pushpin icon that appears.

Changing the order of taskbar buttons

To change the order of buttons on the taskbar, simply drag them into position. Pinned program icons retain their order between sessions, allowing you to quickly find your most-used programs in their familiar (to you) location.

Inside OUT

Use shortcut keys for taskbar buttons

The first 10 taskbar buttons are accessible by keyboard as well as by mouse. Press Windows key+1 for the first, Windows key+2 for the second, and so on (using 0 for the tenth). Using one of these shortcuts is equivalent to clicking the corresponding taskbar button: if the button's program isn't running, it starts; if it has a single open window, you switch to that window; if it has multiple open windows, Windows displays previews of all windows and a "peek" view of the first window.

Note that when you change the order of a taskbar button, you also change the Windows key+number combination that starts that particular program.

Another useful shortcut key is Windows key+T, which brings focus to the first item on the taskbar. At that point, you can repeatedly press Windows key+T, Shift+Windows key+T, or the arrow keys to select other taskbar buttons. When a taskbar button is selected, you can press Spacebar to "click" the button, press the Menu key to display its Jump List, or press Shift+F10 to display its shortcut menu.

Changing the taskbar's size and appearance

The default height of the taskbar is enough to display one button. (If you switch to small buttons, the taskbar automatically shrinks its height to fit.) You can enlarge it—and given the typical size and resolution of computer displays these days, enlarging it is often a great idea. Before you can change the taskbar's dimensions, you need to unlock it. Right-click an unoccupied area of the taskbar; if a check mark appears next to the Lock The Taskbar command, click the command to clear the check mark. Then position the mouse along the border of the taskbar farthest from the edge of the screen. When the mouse pointer becomes a two-headed arrow, drag toward the center of the screen to expand the taskbar. Drag the same border in the opposite direction to restore the original size.

Getting the taskbar out of your way

By default, the taskbar remains visible at all times. If that's inconvenient for any reason, you can tell it to get out of the way. In the Taskbar And Start Menu Properties dialog box, shown earlier in Figure 3-8, select Auto-Hide The Taskbar. With this option selected, the taskbar retreats into the edge of the desktop whenever any window has the focus. To display the task-bar, move the mouse pointer to the edge of the desktop where the taskbar is "hidden."

> ## NOTE
> Regardless of how you set the auto-hide option in the Taskbar And Start Menu Proper-ties dialog box, you can make the taskbar visible at any time by tapping the Windows key or pressing Ctrl+Esc.

Moving the taskbar

The taskbar docks by default at the bottom of the screen, but you can move it to any other edge, including any edge of a secondary screen. To move the taskbar, select a Taskbar Location On Screen option in the Taskbar And Start Menu Properties dialog box.

As an alternative, you can manipulate the taskbar directly: unlock it (right-click an unoccupied spot and then click Lock The Taskbar—unless no check mark appears beside that command, which means that the taskbar is already unlocked). Then drag any unoccupied part of the task-bar in the direction you want to go. (Don't drag the edge of the taskbar closest to the center of the screen; doing that changes the taskbar's size, not its position.)

Adding toolbars to the taskbar

A seldom-used feature of the taskbar is its ability to host other toolbars. Optional toolbars date back to much older versions of Windows, offering shortcuts to folders, documents, and applications. Third parties can also write add-ons that operate entirely within the confines of the taskbar. Built-in toolbars you can choose to install include the following:

- **Address.** The Address toolbar provides a place where you can type an Internet address or the name and path of a program, document, or folder. When you press Enter or click the Go button, Windows takes you to the Internet address, starts the program, opens the document, or displays the folder in a File Explorer window. The Address toolbar is functionally equivalent to the Start menu's Run command or the address bar in File Explorer or the Microsoft Edge browser.

- **Links.** The Links toolbar provides shortcuts to Internet sites; it is equivalent to the Links toolbar in Internet Explorer.

- **Desktop.** The Desktop toolbar provides copies of all the icons currently displayed on your desktop. In addition, it includes links to your Libraries, Homegroup, This PC, Network, Control Panel, and other user profile folders. When you click the toolbar's double arrow, a cascading menu of all the folders and files on your system appears.

To install a new toolbar or remove one you're currently using, right-click any unoccupied part of the taskbar or any existing toolbar. Click Toolbars on the menu that appears, and then choose from the ensuing submenu. A check mark beside a toolbar's name means that it is already displayed on the taskbar. Clicking a selected toolbar name removes that toolbar.

NOTE
You can also display any of the predefined toolbars (listed earlier) or remove any currently displayed toolbar by using the Toolbars tab of the Taskbar And Start Menu Properties dialog box.

In addition, any folder on your system can become a toolbar. To create a new toolbar, right-click an existing toolbar or a spot on the taskbar, click Toolbars, and then click New Toolbar. In the next dialog box, navigate to a folder and click Select Folder.

The folder's name becomes the name of the new toolbar, and each item within the folder becomes a tool.

Controlling how notifications appear

Windows apps are continually notifying you that things have happened: you've received a new message, someone has mentioned you on Twitter or Facebook, or a news app has a breaking news headline to share. Windows gets in the act occasionally as well.

This type of notification appears in Action Center, where each such alert can be dismissed individually or you can clear the entire list with a single click or tap.

Confusingly, these new Action Center notifications, found only in Windows 10, share a name with a classic Windows feature: the notification area, also sometimes called the system tray or the status area, which appears at the right side of the taskbar, just to the left of the clock.

In previous versions of Windows, the taskbar often became crowded with tiny icons. Some of them supply notifications in the form of pop-up messages, but many don't "notify" you of anything and simply offer shortcuts to the parent program.

To deal with notification-area congestion, Windows 10 keeps a few essential icons visible at all times but hides those you aren't actually using. As a result, the notification area doesn't consume an increasingly large chunk of the taskbar; new icons are corralled in a box that appears only when you click the arrow at the left end of the notification area to display the hidden items.

To make an icon visible on the taskbar, drag it from the pop-up box containing hidden icons onto the taskbar. To hide an icon, drag it into the corral.

You can also see a list of notification area icons and specify exactly which ones will appear on the taskbar. To see how many taskbar icons you have and manually switch each one on or off, use your search skills to locate the Select Which Icons Appear On The Taskbar option. (If you want to open this Settings page manually, you'll find it in Settings under the System heading, on the Notifications & Actions tab.) That opens the Settings page shown in Figure 3-10.

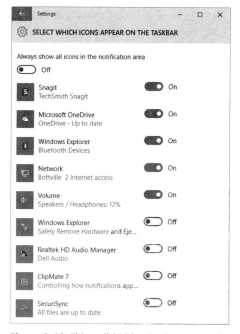

Figure 3-10 This well-hidden Settings page allows you to see a full list of tray icons and decide which ones should appear on the taskbar.

For each notification area icon, you can choose whether to show it on the taskbar at all times or to keep it hidden.

The system icons (Clock, Volume, Network, and so on) can be remanded to the box of hidden icons as well. But if you'd rather banish one or more of them altogether, search for the Turn System Icons On Or Off option, which produces this Settings page. Note that the Power icon is available only on portable PCs.

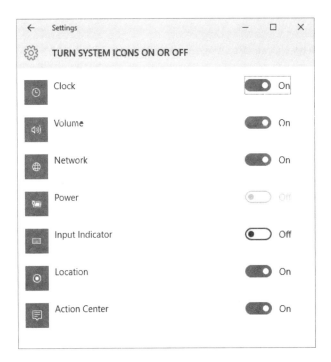

Inside OUT

Use a keyboard shortcut for notification area tasks

If you're one of those users whose fingers never leave the keyboard, you can press Windows key+B to move the focus to the Show Hidden Icons arrow in the notification area. Press Spacebar or Enter to open the box of hidden tray icons. Use the arrow keys to select an icon, and Shift+F10 to display the icon's menu.

Switching tasks

As in previous Windows versions, you can switch to a different program by clicking its taskbar button. And if you're not sure which icon your document is hidden under, hover the mouse pointer over a taskbar button to display a thumbnail image of the window above the button. If a taskbar button combines more than one window (representing multiple Microsoft Excel spreadsheets, for example), hovering the mouse pointer over the taskbar button displays a preview of each window.

If the live thumbnail isn't enough to help you select the correct window, hover the mouse pointer over one of the preview images. Windows brings that window to the fore, temporarily masking out the contents of all other open windows.

The alternative to this manual hunt-and-click technique is a new feature in Windows 10 called Task View, which displays large, live thumbnails of running programs on the screen so that you can switch with confidence.

To begin, click the Task View button or use the Windows key+Tab shortcut. On a touchscreen-equipped device, you can swipe in from the left edge. Figure 3-11 shows the results on a system with seven running programs on a PC operating in Tablet Mode.

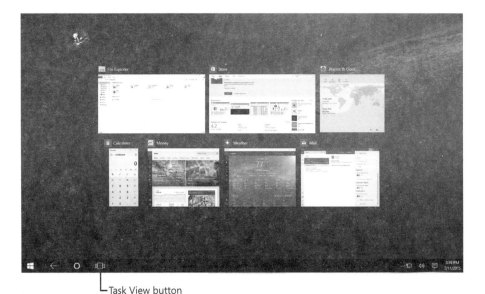

└─Task View button

Figure 3-11 After you switch into Tablet Mode, opening Task View shows running programs using their windowed dimensions, but tapping any thumbnail opens it using the full screen.

Those thumbnails remain open until you do something, usually by clicking or tapping a thumbnail to switch to that window, or by pressing Esc to return to the current window.

If there are too many open windows to fit as thumbnails on the display, use the up and down arrows at the bottom of the screen to scroll through the full list.

The old-fashioned Alt+Tab task switcher, familiar to every Windows user of a certain age, is still available as well. The concept is similar, but the thumbnails are smaller and appear only as long as you continue to hold down the Alt key. Hold down Alt and tap the Tab key to cycle (left to right, top to bottom) through all open windows, with a display that looks like the one in Figure 3-12. When you've highlighted the window you want to bring to the fore, release the Alt and Tab keys.

Figure 3-12 Longtime Windows experts who have the Alt+Tab task-switching shortcut firmly ingrained will be relieved to know it still works in Windows 10.

When using Task View, you also have the option of closing a window by clicking the red X in the upper right corner of the preview or, if your mouse scroll wheel supports clicking, by middle-clicking anywhere in the preview image. Other basic window tasks are available on the shortcut menu that appears when you right-click the preview image.

Switching between virtual desktops

Virtual desktops have been reserved exclusively for power users in previous Windows versions, with the feature requiring the use of third-party utilities.

The idea is straightforward: instead of just a single desktop, you create a second, third, fourth, and so on. On each desktop, you arrange individual programs or combinations of apps you want to use for a specific task. Then, when it's time to tackle one of those tasks, you switch to the virtual desktop and get right to work.

Virtual desktops show up along the bottom of the Task View window. Figure 3-13, for example, shows a Windows 10 system with three virtual desktops configured.

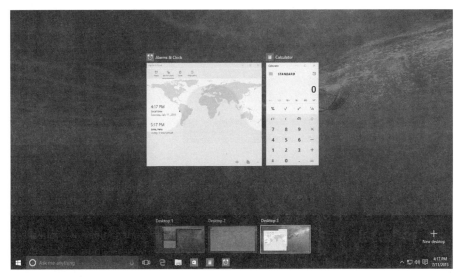

Figure 3-13 In Task View, choose any desktop from the list above the taskbar to see its contents and close programs or drag them to a different desktop.

To create a desktop, click New Desktop in the lower right corner of the Task View window.

And no, there's no option to save virtual desktop configurations so that you can resume with your carefully constructed desktop layout after a restart. You have to start from scratch. We predict (perhaps from wishful thinking) that this feature will make it into a Windows 10 update in the near future.

Using Windows 10 on a touchscreen device

Tablet Mode was specifically designed for sustained use with a touchscreen-equipped device such as a tablet or hybrid PC. We've already discussed the Windows user experience with a conventional PC. Tablet Mode introduces a series of significant changes, automatically if it detects that you're using a touchscreen device without a keyboard attached, or manually if you want to treat a touchscreen-equipped laptop as if it were a tablet. (In fact, you can enable Tablet Mode on a desktop PC without a touchscreen or even a touchpad; the resulting experience might be helpful for someone who occasionally wants that immersive, full-screen environment.)

Turning on Tablet Mode makes the following changes in the Windows 10 user experience:

- Reconfigures the taskbar, bumping up button sizes, adding a back button, replacing the search box with a search button, and hiding all taskbar buttons. The following comparison shows the normal taskbar on top and the same area in Tablet Mode below it.

- All apps run in full screen. It's possible to snap two apps side by side, but they have a thick sizing bar between them, similar to the one introduced in Windows 8.

- The Start menu opens in full screen, with the left column hidden by default and accessible only by tapping a so-called hamburger menu (a stack of three lines that resembles a beef patty between two buns) in the upper left corner of the display.

- Swiping from the left and right enables Task View and Action Center, respectively.

Windows 10 makes some assumptions about your preferences based on your hardware. On conventional PCs with a keyboard and mouse, Tablet Mode is off. On dedicated tablets, this mode is on by default. You can adjust these preferences by using the Settings page shown in Figure 3-14. On a hybrid device with a relatively small touchscreen, you might prefer to have Tablet Mode on full time, for example.

The other essential feature of a touchscreen-equipped device, especially one without a keyboard, is the presence of the extremely versatile Windows 10 Touch Keyboard. It allows text entry into dialog boxes, web forms, your browser's address bar, documents, the search box—anywhere you would normally need a physical keyboard to provide input.

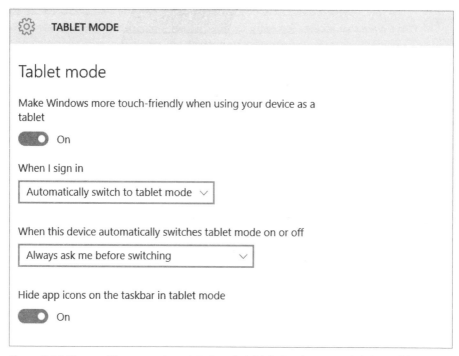

Figure 3-14 These settings are appropriate for a hybrid device that you switch into Tablet Mode occasionally.

Figure 3-15 shows the standard Touch Keyboard layout.

Figure 3-15 This is the standard Touch Keyboard; use the controls in the upper right to move, dock, or close the keyboard.

The Touch Keyboard should appear automatically when you tap to position the insertion point in a place that accepts text entry. On touchscreen-equipped devices, you can make the Touch Keyboard appear by tapping its button, which appears in the notification area on the right of the taskbar. (If this button is hidden, right-click or do a long press on the taskbar and then select the Show Touch Keyboard Button option.)

The limited screen space available for the Touch Keyboard means you have to switch layouts to enter symbols and numbers. Tap the &123 key in the lower left corner to switch between the standard QWERTY layout and the first of two symbol layouts, as shown in Figure 3-16. Note that the layout includes a dedicated number pad, which is extremely handy for working with spreadsheets and performing other data-entry tasks.

Click to see additional symbol layouts

Figure 3-16 Tap the &123 key in the lower left corner to switch between the standard QWERTY keys and this alternate view of symbols and numbers.

In some respects, the Touch Keyboard is more versatile than its physical counterparts. Entering typographic symbols like the interrobang or emoji—the whimsical characters available on all mobile platforms and on Windows 10—doesn't require the use of ANSI codes. Instead, you can enter characters directly. To show the first of more than 30 emoji keyboard layouts, each containing 30 symbols, click the "happy face" button on the bottom row.

With the emoji keyboard layout visible, the bottom row displays keys that you can use to switch between different categories, several of which have multiple layouts, accessible via the left and right arrows below the Tab key. Figure 3-17 shows a useful layout from the Objects & Symbols category.

Figure 3-17 Windows 10 supports hundreds of emoji characters. Pick a category from the bottom row and use the arrow keys to scroll through different character sets, 30 at a time.

NOTE

For a full list of officially supported Windows-compatible emoji characters, see *http://emojipedia.org/microsoft-emoji-list/*.

In addition to the conventional QWERTY layout, the Touch Keyboard comes in some variations, which are accessible by tapping the Switch key in the lower right corner, as shown in Figure 3-18.

Figure 3-18 Tap the Switch key in the lower right corner of any keyboard layout to change to a different arrangement or adjust language preferences.

The Handwriting panel, shown in Figure 3-19, is most useful with devices that support pen input, such as Microsoft's line of x86-based Surface and Surface Pro devices. (The ARM-based

Surface RT and Surface 2 devices do not support Windows 10.) Text you enter in the input box is automatically translated into characters for entry at the current insertion point.

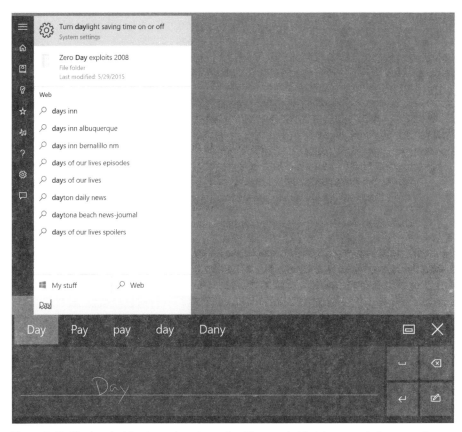

Figure 3-19 The handwriting input box does a frankly remarkable job at translating even sloppy penmanship into readable results.

Handwriting recognition is excellent, even for casual entry. As Figure 3-19 shows, you also have autocorrect options if the recognition engine guesses wrong.

Inside OUT

Using ink and handwriting

When you use a pen to scribble a handwritten note or sketch a figure within a pen-aware application, you create a type of data called ink. Although it superficially resembles a simple bitmap, ink-based data contains a wealth of information in addition to the simple shape. Windows records the direction, pressure, speed, and location of the tablet pen as it moves and stores the resulting marks as a compressed graphic. If you enlarge a piece of data that was stored as ink, Windows uses this stored data to ensure that it keeps its proper shape.

By recognizing the combinations of strokes that represent handwritten letters, the operating system can convert even bad handwriting into text, and with surprising accuracy. You don't have to convert ink into text to get the benefits of handwriting recognition, either. The handwriting recognizer automatically converts handwriting to text in the background, storing the resulting text along with the ink and adding the recognized words and phrases to the search index.

Applications that fully support ink as a data type are relatively rare, but you can perform some remarkable feats with those that do exist. Using Microsoft Word, for instance, you can insert handwritten comments and annotations into a document. Another member of the Office family, OneNote, goes even further, indexing your handwritten notes and allowing you to search through an entire notebook for a word or phrase.

Although you need a pen and a touchscreen that supports digitizing capabilities to add ink to a document using Windows 10, the resulting ink-based data is visible on any Windows-based system, with or without a touchscreen.

The Split Keyboard layout, shown in Figure 3-20 on a Surface 3 in portrait orientation and in Tablet Mode, is extremely odd looking until you imagine trying to tap text with one finger as you hold a tablet in your other hand. With the split layout, you can grip a tablet in portrait or landscape mode and use your thumbs for typing. It takes some practice, but anyone who ever used an old-school BlackBerry phone can confirm that with practice you can achieve startling typing speed.

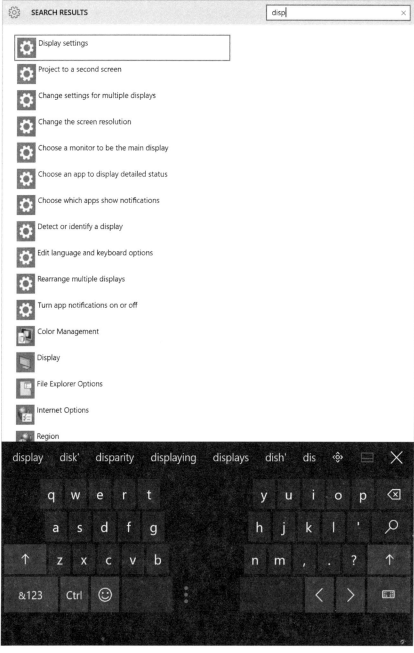

Figure 3-20 This split keyboard layout works best on a smaller tablet, where you can comfortably type with two thumbs.

By default, the Touch Keyboard appears at the bottom of the screen, pushing the contents of the page above it for unobstructed text entry. An X in the upper right corner lets you close any keyboard layout, a second button allows you to lock the keyboard into position, and the four-headed button lets you move a floating keyboard to a more comfortable position on a larger display.

Managing and arranging windows

Windows 10 includes a host of keyboard shortcuts and mouse gestures that greatly simplify the everyday tasks of resizing, moving, minimizing, arranging, and otherwise managing windows. The most useful trick is a collection of "snap" techniques. These have been around for several Windows versions, but Windows 10 adds some extremely useful new tricks to the old familiar methods.

The simplest window-snapping scenario is a PC with a single display, where you want to arrange two windows side by side. You might want to compare two Word documents, move files between the Documents folder and an archive, or do financial research in a web browser and plug the numbers into an Excel spreadsheet.

Drag a window title bar to the left or right edge of the screen, and it snaps to fill that half of the display. As soon as you let go of the title bar, the window snaps into its position and Windows helpfully offers thumbnails for all other open windows to help you choose what to run alongside your first snapped window.

In Figure 3-21, for example, we've just snapped a File Explorer window to the right side of the screen and now have a choice of four other running windows to snap opposite it. (If you don't feel like snapping a second window, just press Esc or click anywhere except on one of those thumbnails. They vanish immediately.)

Here are a few ways you can snap windows in Windows 10 by using a mouse or by dragging directly on a touchscreen:

- Drag the title bar to the top of the screen to maximize the window, or drag the title bar away from the top edge to restore it to its previous window size.

- Drag a window title bar to any corner of the screen, and it snaps to fill that quadrant of the display. This capability is new in Windows 10 and is most useful on large, high-resolution desktop displays.

- Drag the top window border (not the title bar) to the top edge of the screen, or drag the bottom border to the bottom edge of the screen. With either action, when you reach the edge, the window snaps to full height without changing its width. When you drag the border away from the window edge, the opposite border snaps to its previous position.

Figure 3-21 When you snap a window to one edge of the display, Windows shows other windows in thumbnails alongside the snapped window for easy side-by-side arrangement.

Note that the window resizes when the mouse pointer hits the edge of the screen. To use this feature with minimal mouse movement, start your drag action by pointing at the title bar near the edge you're going to snap to.

As soon as you begin dragging a snapped window away from the edge of the screen, it returns to its previous size and position.

Inside OUT

Snap side-by-side windows at different widths

Although Windows automatically arranges side-by-side windows at equal widths, you don't have to settle for symmetry. On a large desktop monitor, for example, you might want to arrange a news feed or Twitter stream along the right side of your display, using a third or less of the total display width and leaving room for Word or Excel to have a much larger share of the screen real estate.

The secret is to snap the first window and immediately drag its inside edge to adjust the window to your preferred width. Now grab the title bar of the window you want to see alongside it, and snap it to the opposite edge of the display. The newly snapped window expands to fill the space remaining after you adjusted the width of the first window.

The rules work the same with multimonitor setups. With two side-by-side monitors, for example, you can drag the mouse to the inside edge of a display and snap a window there, allowing for four equal-size windows lined up from left to right. Dragging the title bar also allows you to move a maximized window from one screen to another on a multimonitor system.

Inside OUT

Shake to minimize distractions

An ancient Windows feature called Aero Shake, first introduced with Windows Vista, survives into Windows 10. Grab the window's title bar with the mouse or a finger and quickly move it back and forth a few times. Suddenly, all windows retreat to the taskbar except the one whose title bar you just shook. This move takes a bit of practice, but it's worth mastering. It requires only three smooth "shakes"—a left, right, left motion is best—not maniacal shaking.

Windows 10 includes keyboard shortcuts that correspond with the preceding mouse gestures. These (and a few extras) are shown in Table 3-1.

Table 3-1 Keyboard shortcuts and gestures for resizing and moving windows

Task	Keyboard shortcut	Gesture
Maximize window	Windows key+ Up Arrow	Drag title bar to top of screen
Resize window to full screen height without changing its width	Shift+Windows key+ Up Arrow	Drag top or bottom border to edge of screen
Restore a maximized or full-height window	Windows key+ Down Arrow	Drag title bar or border away from screen edge
Minimize a restored window	Windows key+ Down Arrow	Click the Minimize button
Snap to the left half of the screen	Windows key+ Left Arrow*	Drag title bar to left edge
Snap to the right half of the screen	Windows key+ Right Arrow*	Drag title bar to right edge
Move to the next virtual desktop	Ctrl+Windows key+ Left/Right Arrow	Three-finger swipe on precision touchpad; none for mouse
Move to the next monitor	Shift+Windows key+ Left/Right Arrow	Drag title bar

Task	Keyboard shortcut	Gesture
Minimize all windows except the active window (press again to restore windows previously minimized with this shortcut)	Windows key+ Home	"Shake" the title bar
Minimize all windows	Windows key+M	
Restore windows after minimizing	Shift+Windows key+M	

* Pressing this key repeatedly cycles through the left, right, and restored positions. If you have more than one monitor, it cycles these positions on each monitor in turn.

The Windows 10 taskbar also exposes some traditional window-management menus. The secret? Hold the Shift key as you right-click a taskbar button. For a button that represents a single window, the menu includes commands to Restore, Move, Size, Minimize, Maximize, and Close the window. For a grouped taskbar button, Shift+right-click displays commands to arrange, restore, minimize, or close all windows in the group.

If you find it disconcerting to have windows snap to a certain size and position when you drag their title bars, you can disable Snap. These options are well hidden on the Multitasking page in System Settings; it's easier to find them by typing **Snap** in the search box.

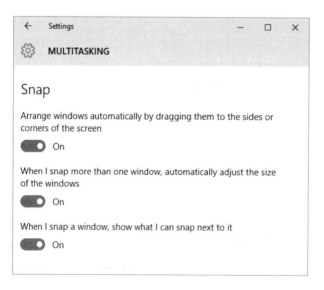

Cortana and search

We start this section with a disclaimer: Search, as a Windows 10 feature and as an online service, is evolving at breathtaking speed. The results that show up in the search box are delivered
by online services that are constantly improving, as are the Windows features you use to make
those requests. Our goal in this section is not to show you how to accomplish specific search
tasks but to help you discover what search is capable of accomplishing for you.

Search is built into Windows 10 as an integral feature that gets prime real estate, just to the
right of the Start button.

By default, on desktop and laptop PCs, this space is occupied by a search box. In Tablet Mode
(or if you change the default setting), a search button appears, which expands into a box when
you tap or click it.

By default, Windows Search is businesslike and efficient, with no personality. You type something in the search box and see results like those shown in Figure 3-22. Windows Search is very
good at finding settings and apps, as you can see.

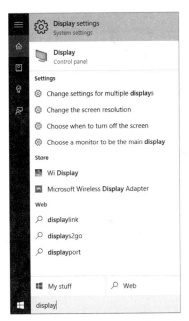

Figure 3-22 Type a word or phrase in the search box, and you get a list of settings and apps that
match the search term, with options at the bottom to search personal files or the web.

If you're more interested in finding a photo or a PowerPoint presentation, enter your search term and then click or tap My Stuff to change the search scope. That immediately expands the size of the search results window, as shown in Figure 3-23, and displays results that match your search terms.

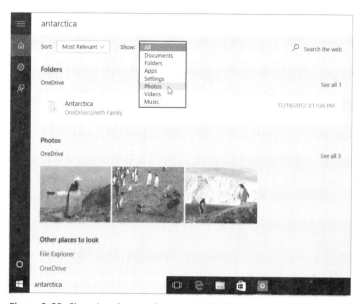

Figure 3-23 Changing the search scope to My Stuff expands the results list and turns up photos, documents, and more, with sort and filter options up top.

➤ For more detailed instructions on how to use Windows Search from File Explorer, see "Using Windows Search" in Chapter 12, "Organizing and searching for files."

Inside OUT

Don't want search? Hide it.

As with most things Windows, you can remove the search button or box completely if you're really convinced you won't use it. You can also specify that you want a button or a box, regardless of whether you're on a PC or tablet. All of these options are in the Taskbar And Start Menu Properties dialog box, on the Toolbars tab.

Cortana, the intelligent search assistant built into Windows 10, adds an adult's voice and a (programmed) sense of humor to the core search experience. It also adds the ability to perform additional tasks, such as adding items to a to-do list, and to deliver regular updates that match your interests, as defined in a notebook full of settings.

In many ways, Cortana today is like a two-year-old prodigy. Despite the pleasant female voice and the mostly natural intonations, "she" is really a web service, which is constantly learning and adding capabilities.

For a partial list of things Cortana can do for you, just ask. Click the microphone button in the search box and say, "What can you do?" That should produce a list like the one in Figure 3-24.

Figure 3-24 If you're not sure what Cortana can do, just ask, "What can you do?"

Because Cortana requires that you grant access to personal information, you need to go through a brief but important setup first. Pay special attention when the setup wizard asks for permission to use your microphone to accept spoken input. (Note: You're perfectly free to say no, but that changes the experience significantly.)

The icon bar along Cortana's left edge is cryptic at first. For a more thorough explanation of what each icon means, click the hamburger menu in the top left corner, next to Cortana's name, to see the list with descriptive labels attached, as in Figure 3-25.

Figure 3-25 Click or tap the hamburger menu in the top left of the Cortana window to display labels identifying what each of the options along the left side does.

The tasks Cortana can complete on your behalf include adding appointments and reminders, creating notes, setting alarms, retrieving a weather forecast, and checking your calendar for upcoming events. Figure 3-26, for example, shows the response when you ask Cortana to set a reminder.

Cortana is most valuable on mobile devices, of course, where the ability to ask a question (literally) and get a useful answer is paramount. But she is a handy assistant in an office as well.

In addition to taking over search duties for files, folders, settings, music, and so on, Cortana can return results based on information you've allowed her to search. Just clicking in the search box allows Cortana to display a scrolling list of useful information: news headlines, stock prices from your watch list, results from your favorite team's latest game, weather forecasts, and reminders on when you need to leave to arrive on time for an appointment.

You establish those interests in an initial, brief interview, but you can expand or change those interests later by visiting the Cortana notebook. To start, click the Notebook icon, just below Home on Cortana's left side. That opens a dialog box like the one shown in Figure 3-27.

Figure 3-26 If you ask Cortana to set a reminder or create an appointment, she responds with this crisply efficient form.

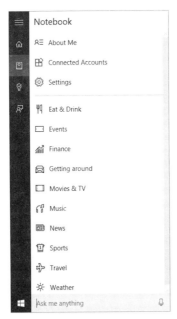

Figure 3-27 Use Cortana's notebook to customize your interests and help make the "Here's what's happening now" summaries more useful.

You have every right to be concerned about privacy when using a service that knows so much about your daily routine. You can read the Cortana privacy policy by following a link at the bottom of the Cortana Settings pane, shown in Figure 3-28.

Figure 3-28 The Cortana Settings pane allows you to read the privacy policy, disable the service and clear local information, or go online and delete all saved information.

The top option on this window turns Cortana off and deletes any locally saved information. To delete personal information saved on Microsoft's servers, click or tap Manage What Cortana Knows About Me In The Cloud and follow the instructions.

Personalizing Windows 10

Every new version of Windows brings some changes to its visual appearance, and Windows 10 is no exception. Another constant is the ability to tweak and refine that appearance to better suit your tastes.

It's your operating system; make it reflect your preferences, your needs, your style. Make it work for you. Windows 10 provides myriad tools for doing just that—tools that we survey in this chapter.

Settings vs. Control Panel

Personalizing Windows to your liking is generally done by applying settings. So it makes sense that many personalization settings are made in a modern app called Settings, which is shown in Figure 4-1. The Settings app made its first appearance in Windows 8, beginning the transition of personalization and other settings from Control Panel, the desktop app that has served this function since the beginning of Windows back in 1985. That transition is not complete, however. In Windows 10 you'll find that some settings are made only in Settings, some can be made only in Control Panel, and some have equivalent functions in both places.

You'll find a shortcut to Settings in the lower left corner of the Start menu. Alternatively, you can launch it with a keyboard shortcut: Windows key+I. To open Control Panel, right-click or long-tap the Start button (or press Windows key+X), and then click or tap Control Panel. Of course, using the search box, you can find and launch either one, as well as find and launch the page or app for individual settings.

In this chapter we guide you to the most effective way to make a specific setting, be it via Settings or Control Panel. But there's no need to memorize a particular pathway. Use the search box in Settings; the results include matches from Settings *and* Control Panel. (The corresponding search box in Control Panel searches only within Control Panel.)

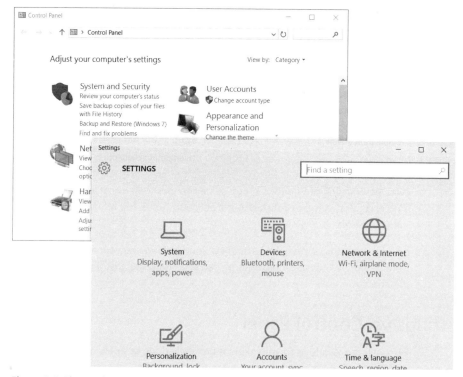

Figure 4-1 The modern Settings app will eventually supplant the old school Control Panel.

Customizing the visual appearance

The most obvious way to personalize your Windows experience is to customize its visual appearance—the desktop background, the window colors, and so on. These settings are made in the aptly named Personalization, a Settings tool that appears when you right-click the desktop and choose Personalize. See Figure 4-2.

NOTE

Confusingly, Control Panel also has a Personalization option—and you can't use it to set backgrounds and colors. Instead, it's the place for working with themes, a topic we take up in "Syncing your settings between computers" later in this chapter.

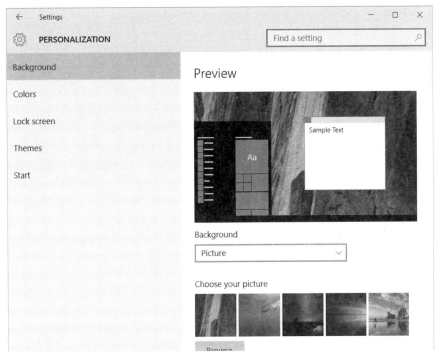

Figure 4-2 Personalization, your home base for setting backgrounds and colors, shows the effect of your settings in a Preview area.

Selecting the desktop background

You can perk up any desktop with a background image. Your background can be supplied by a graphics file in any of several common formats (including .bmp, .gif, .jpg, .png, and .tif). And you're not stuck with a static image, either. You can set up a slide show of images.

To select a background, in Settings choose Personalization, and then click Background. The Background box (see Figure 4-2) offers three types of backgrounds:

- **Picture** displays a photo or other image. Choose one of the pictures provided with Windows or click Browse to choose one of your own pictures.

- **Solid Color** covers the background with a color you select from a palette of two dozen shades.

- **Slideshow** is like the Picture option, but with a twist: At an interval you select (ranging from 1 minute to 1 day), Windows changes to a new picture from your selected picture albums. By default, Windows uses your local Pictures library and your Pictures folder on OneDrive as sources for the slide show. Click Browse to replace these choices.

Inside OUT

Restore the photographs furnished with Windows

When you click Browse to select a new picture, your selection replaces one of the five existing picture choices. But what if you decide you'd rather go back to one of those terrific photos provided with Windows? Getting any one of them back is simple, but not obvious.

Click Browse and navigate to %Windir%\Web\Wallpaper. (On most systems, %Windir% is C:\Windows.) You'll find a handful of nice pictures in subfolders of that folder—including the ones you've displaced.

After you choose an image or set up a slide show, select one of the six Choose A Fit options to let Windows know how you want to handle images that are not exactly the same size as your screen resolution.

- **Fill** reduces or enlarges the image so that it fits the shortest dimension and crops the other edges.

- **Fit** reduces or enlarges the image so that it fits the longest dimension and adds black bars on the other edges.

- **Stretch** reduces or enlarges the image so that it fits both dimensions, distorting the image as necessary.

- **Tile** repeats the image at its original size to fill the screen.

- **Center** displays the image at its original size in the center of the screen.

- **Span** works like Fill to display a single image across multiple monitors.

Here are some other ways to change the desktop background:

- Right-click an image file in File Explorer and choose Set As Desktop Background.

- Right-click an image in Internet Explorer and choose Set As Background.

- Open any image file in Paint, open the File menu, and choose Set As Desktop Background. A submenu lets you choose the Fill, Tile, or Center picture position.

- Use the Photos app to open an image file, click or tap the ellipsis at the right side of the menu bar, and then click or tap Set As Background.

Selecting colors

With a beautiful desktop background in place, your next personalization step might be to select a complementary color for the window borders, Start menu, and taskbar. To do that, right-click the desktop, choose Personalize, and then click Colors to see a screen like the one shown in Figure 4-3.

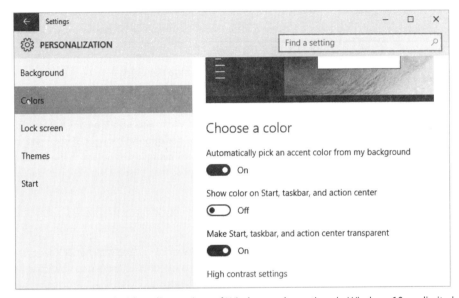

Figure 4-3 Compared with earlier versions of Windows, color options in Windows 10 are limited.

Unlike the dizzying array of options for setting colors for every individual screen element in earlier versions of Windows, Windows 10 offers only the following choices:

- **Automatically Pick An Accent Color From My Background.** The accent color, in varying intensities, is used to highlight selections (such as the word *Colors* in the left pane shown in Figure 4-3), as a background color for taskbar and Start menu icons, and for some text elements in modern apps. When this option is on, Windows selects a color that complements your current background, be it a solid color or a picture. (And if you use a slide show as your background, the accent color changes each time the background picture changes.) Turning this option off displays a selection of colors from which you can choose.

- **Show Color On Start, Taskbar, And Action Center.** Turning this option on applies the accent color as a background to the Start menu, the taskbar, and Action Center. When it's off, those areas have a dark background.

- **Make Start, Taskbar, And Action Center Transparent.** Not "transparent" as in clear glass; more like darkly tinted glass, which allows you to see "through" each of these elements to the underlying desktop. To some, transparency is a cool effect, whereas others find it distracting.

One more option appears on the Colors tab: High Contrast Settings. That option is intended to help users with visual impairments. For more information, see "Overcoming challenges" later in this chapter.

TROUBLESHOOTING

The automatic color option doesn't change the color

Suppose you turn off the first option and select a color, and then later decide you'd rather go back to the automatic color. So you turn on the option to automatically select an accent color and . . . nothing happens. When you turn it on, the automatic option doesn't take effect until the *next time* the background changes. If you want to use the automatic color associated with the current background, return to the background page and select the same background again; that triggers Windows to "automatically" select an accent color.

Customizing mouse pointers

Sometimes it's the little things that make a difference . . . and make your computer uniquely yours. If you think an hourglass depicts the passage of time more unambiguously than a rolling doughnut, you can easily bring back the Windows XP–era shape. You can customize the entire array of pointer shapes your system uses by choosing Mouse in Control Panel, which opens a dialog box like the one shown in Figure 4-4. (If you find yourself on the Mouse & Touchpad page in Settings, scroll down to the bottom. Under Related Settings, click Additional Mouse Options to open the Mouse Properties dialog box.)

On the Pointers tab of the Mouse Properties dialog box, you can select a pointer type in the Customize box and then click Browse to select an alternative pointer shape. (The Browse button takes you to %Windir%\Cursors and displays files with the extensions .cur and .ani. The latter are animated cursors.)

Windows wraps up a gamut of pointer shapes as a mouse-pointer scheme. The system comes with an assortment of predefined schemes, making it easy for you to switch from one set of pointers to another as needs or whims suggest. Figure 4-4 shows the list.

Figure 4-4 Some of the predefined mouse-pointer schemes are better suited than the default scheme for working in challenging lighting conditions.

The pointers included with Windows won't win any cutting-edge design awards; some of them date back to an era when an hourglass actually *was* used for keeping time. However, there are situations where a switch is worthwhile. If you sometimes use your portable computer in lighting conditions that make it hard for you to find the pointer, consider switching to one of the large or extra large schemes. If nothing else, those will give your eyeballs a larger target to pursue.

If you're inclined to roll your own mouse scheme (by using the Browse button to assign cursor files to pointer types), be sure to use the Save As command and give your work a name. That way you'll be able to switch away from it and back to it again at will.

Configuring desktop icons

A fresh, cleanly installed Windows 10 desktop (as opposed to one generated by an upgrade installation) includes a single lonely icon—Recycle Bin. If you want to display other system icons, in the search box (any search box: on the taskbar, in Settings, or in Control Panel) type **desktop**, and then click Show Or Hide Common Icons On The Desktop. The Desktop Icon Settings dialog box, shown next, provides check boxes for five system folders—Computer, User's Files (the root folder of your own profile), Network, Recycle Bin, and Control Panel.

If you're really into customization, you can change any of the five icons that appear in the large box in the center. Note that the Control Panel icon does not appear in this center box even if you select its check box; Windows doesn't provide a way to change it.

To change an icon, select it in the center box and click Change Icon. You'll find an interesting assortment of alternative icons in the file %Windir%\System32\Imageres.dll. (Be sure to use the horizontal scroll bar to see them all.) If none of these suit you, try browsing to %Windir%\System32\Shell32.dll.

After you've populated your desktop with icons, you might want to control their arrangement. If you right-click the desktop, you'll find two commands at the top of the shortcut menu that can help in this endeavor. To make your icons rearrange themselves when you delete one of their brethren, click View and then click Auto Arrange Icons. To ensure that each icon keeps a respectable distance from each of its neighbors (and that the whole gang stays together at the left side of your screen), click View, Align Icons To Grid. And if your icons occasionally get in the way (for example, if you want to take an unimpeded look at the current desktop background image), click View, and then click Show Desktop Icons. (Return to this command when you want the icons back.)

To change the sort order of desktop icons, right-click the desktop and click Sort By. You can sort on any of four attributes: Name, Size, Item Type, or Date Modified. Sorting a second time on any attribute changes the sort order from ascending to descending (or vice versa).

Controlling the appearance of other icons

Windows displays icons around the perimeter of the desktop too: in the notification area (the right or bottom end of the taskbar), in Action Center, and on the Start menu.

The notification area ordinarily shows the date and time, icons that indicate network and battery status, a shortcut for setting speaker volume, and the like. In addition, many programs add icons that serve as shortcuts to various program functions as well as status indicators. And some programs display pop-up messages via the notification area.

Fortunately, you can manage the clutter and the distractions to include only the information you want. You'll find the tools to do so in Settings, System, Notifications & Actions. On that page, click Select Which Icons Appear On The Taskbar and Turn System Icons On Or Off to specify which icons appear. Scroll down a bit to the Show Notifications From These Apps section to specify which ones are allowed to display pop-up messages or play sounds. For more information, see "Controlling how notifications appear" in Chapter 3, Using Windows 10."

Action Center, which appears when you swipe from the right side of the screen or click the Action Center icon in the notification area, includes a collection of action buttons at the bottom of the pane, as shown here.

Other action buttons appear if you click Expand—but the top four buttons are designated as *quick actions*, because all it takes is a swipe and a tap to execute one of these actions. To select your four quick actions, make your choices at the top of the Notifications & Actions page in Settings, System.

The available action buttons depend on the capabilities of your computer, but they may include items such as Wi-Fi, Bluetooth, and Airplane Mode (which let you turn wireless communications on or off with a tap or click); Brightness, Battery Saver, Rotation Lock, and Tablet Mode (which control features normally used only on mobile PCs); and All Settings and Notes (shortcuts to Settings and OneNote, respectively). Quiet Hours turns off notifications temporarily.

Inside OUT

Add or remove icons from the Start menu

By default, in the lower left corner of the Start menu you'll find icons for File Explorer, Settings, Power, and All Apps. If you like, you can add shortcuts to many other commonly used folders. In Settings, choose Personalization, Start, and then tap or click Choose Which Folders Appear On Start. For information about making other changes to the Start menu, see "Using and customizing the Start menu" in Chapter 3.

Configuring the taskbar with multiple displays

If your computer has more than one monitor attached, you have additional options for configuring the taskbar: you can show it on just the main display or on all displays, and you can vary its appearance on each display. To review these options, right-click the taskbar and choose Properties. You'll find them under Multiple Displays at the bottom of the Taskbar tab in the Taskbar And Start Menu Properties dialog box, shown next.

Selecting the first option shows a taskbar on each monitor; if you clear it, the taskbar appears only on the main display. (You specify the "main display" in Settings, System, Display. For details, see "Displays" in Chapter 13, "Hardware.")

The Show Taskbar Buttons On setting determines where the taskbar button for a particular app appears—on all taskbars or only the one where that app's window resides.

The last setting specifies how taskbar buttons are combined on displays other than the main display.

➤ For information about other taskbar settings, see "Using and customizing the taskbar" in Chapter 3.

Customizing the lock screen

The lock screen—the screen that's displayed while your computer is turned on but nobody is signed in—can be changed to your liking too. In Settings, click Personalization, Lock Screen to see your options, as shown in Figure 4-5.

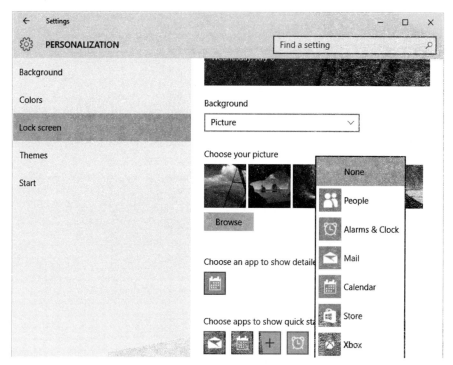

Figure 4-5 Tapping a status icon lets you select which apps you want to appear on the lock screen.

Here you can select a background, using options similar to those available for a desktop background. You can also select one or more apps to display their current status—such as the number of new email messages, upcoming appointments, alarms, and so on—on the lock screen. Tap one of the app icons to see a list of apps that support this feature. You can have only one app display detailed status and only seven apps show quick status. To add another you must first stop showing one of the existing apps.

Additional options for determining what appears on the lock screen can be found in Settings, System, Notifications & Actions. Under Notifications, two options control the ability of app notifications, alarms, reminders, and incoming calls to appear on the lock screen.

Working with fonts

The days when your choice of fonts ended just beyond Arial and Times New Roman are long gone; if you include all the language variants and style variants (bold, italic, and so on), Windows 10 comes with hundreds of fonts.

The headquarters for font management is Fonts in Control Panel, which is shown in Figure 4-6. From this list of fonts, you can select a font (or a font family, which appears as a stack) and then click Preview to open a window that shows the font's characters in sizes ranging from 12 point to 72 point. (A point is a printer's measurement that is still used in modern digital typography. There are 72 points to an inch.)

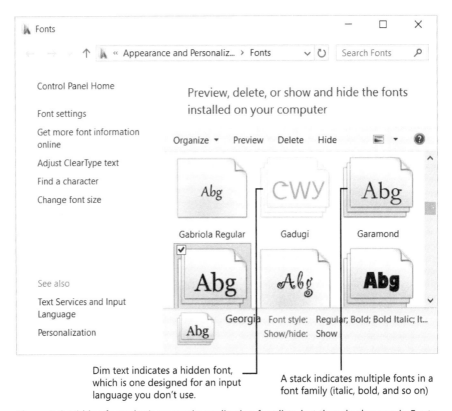

Dim text indicates a hidden font, which is one designed for an input language you don't use.

A stack indicates multiple fonts in a font family (italic, bold, and so on)

Figure 4-6 Hidden fonts don't appear in application font lists, but they do show up in Fonts.

The primary font format used by Windows is TrueType. Windows also supports OpenType and PostScript Type 1 fonts. To install a new font, you can drag its file from a folder or compressed .zip archive to Fonts in Control Panel. But it's not necessary to open Fonts; the simplest way to install a font is to right-click its file in File Explorer and choose Install. Because font file names are often somewhat cryptic, you might want to double-click the file, which opens the font preview window, to see what you're getting. If it's a font you want, click the Install button.

NOTE

PostScript Type 1 fonts normally consist of two or three files. The one you use to install the font—regardless of which method you use—is the .pfm file, whose file type is shown in File Explorer as Type 1 Font File.

Making text easier to read

If you like to work at high screen resolutions but find yourself straining to read the text, you can try the following:

- Look for scaling ("zoom") commands in the text-centric programs you use. Many programs, including most modern word processors, include these scaling features. Scaling text up to a readable size is a good solution for particular programs, but it doesn't change the size of icon text, system menus (such as the Start menu), or system dialog boxes.

- To enlarge part of the screen, use the Magnifier tool. (For more information, see "Overcoming challenges" later in this chapter.)

- Use the scaling options in Display settings. Adjusting the scaling to a higher level enables you to have readable text at higher screen resolutions.

To adjust display scaling, in Settings tap System, Display. Adjust the slider below Change The Size Of Text, Apps, And Other Items, as shown in Figure 4-7. The slider for adjusting display sizes has only three or four (depending on your display hardware) predefined settings; it's not continuously adjustable as a slider control might imply.

Your changes take effect only after you click Apply, which is below the Brightness Level slider (not visible in the figure), and sign out. After you sign in again, test some text-centric applications to see whether you like the result. If you don't, return to the Display settings and try another setting.

> ➤ For information about screen resolution and other display configuration tasks, see "Displays" in Chapter 13.

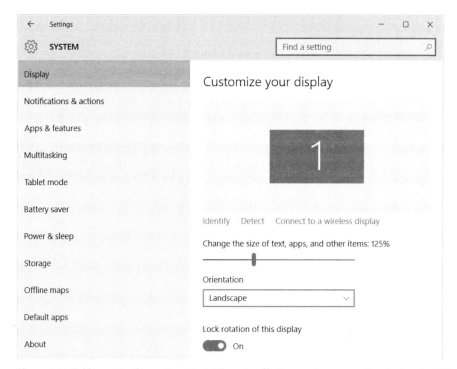

Figure 4-7 Unlike most other options in Settings, to effect your changes on the display size slider, you must scroll down and click Apply.

Using font smoothing to make text easier on the eyes

ClearType is a font-smoothing technology that reduces jagged edges of characters, thus easing eye strain.

To check or change your font-smoothing settings, type **cleartype** in the search box, and then click Adjust ClearType Text. Doing so opens the ClearType Text Tuner, which, in its first screen, has a check box that turns ClearType on when it is selected. The ensuing screens that appear each time you click Next offer optometrist-style choices ("Which is better, number 1 or number 2?") to help you reach ClearType perfection. If you have more than one monitor attached, the ClearType Text Tuner goes through this exercise for each one.

Windows includes seven fonts that are optimized for ClearType. The names of six of these—Constantia, Cambria, Corbel, Calibri, Candara, and Consolas—begin with the letter c—just to help cement the connection with ClearType. If you're particularly prone to eye fatigue, you might want to consider favoring these fonts in documents you create. (Constantia and Cambria are serif fonts, considered particularly suitable for longer documents and reports. The other four are sans serif fonts, good for headlines and advertising.) The seventh ClearType-optimized font, Segoe UI, is the typeface used for text elements throughout the Windows user interface. (Windows also includes a ClearType-optimized font called Meiryo that's designed to improve the readability of horizontally arrayed Asian languages.)

> ➤ **For information about how ClearType works, visit Microsoft's ClearType site at** *w7io.com/0404.*

Calibrating your display's colors

To get the most accurate rendition of images and colors on your screen, you should calibrate it. You've probably noticed, but perhaps not fiddled with, the buttons on your monitor that control various display settings. A tool included with Windows, Display Color Calibration, helps you to calibrate your screen by using your monitor's display controls as well as various Windows settings. With Display Color Calibration, you set gamma, brightness, contrast, color balance, and other settings, all of which are explained in the on-screen descriptions.

To run Display Color Calibration, in the search box, type **calibrate** and then click Calibrate Display Color. If you'd rather click or tap your way to it, open Settings, click System, Display, Advanced Display Settings, Color Calibration. Display Color Calibration opens a full-screen application that leads you through the steps of adjusting your display by making settings and adjusting monitor controls until the images displayed at each step look their best.

NOTE

If you work with color and you need more precise control over the way colors appear on your screen and on your printer, you should explore Color Management, a tool that lets you work with stored color profiles. In the search box, type color management to find this tool.

Making other small visual tweaks

Windows is alive with little animations, such as when you open or close a window. Along with other effects, these can help to direct your focus to the current window or activity. But some folks find them annoying, and an argument can be made that they do take a small bite out of your computer's performance. So if you don't like them, turn them off!

In the search box of Settings or Control Panel, type **performance** and then choose Adjust The Appearance And Performance Of Windows. Alternatively, you can tap your way through this lengthy path: Settings, System, About, System Info, Advanced System Settings, Settings (under Performance). A dialog box like the one shown next opens, allowing you to control animations and other effects on a granular level.

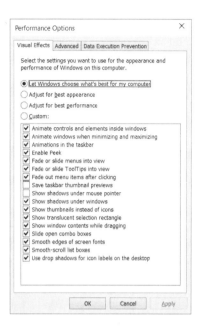

Working the way you like

It's important to look good, and that's what the previous sections of this chapter cover. But even more important is personalizing your computer to work in a way that's comfortable for you, and that's what we address here: specifying your mouse and keyboard preferences, selecting sounds for alerts, and even choosing a screen saver.

> ➤ Customizers often like to change a few other functionality-related features. For information about moving system folders and libraries, see "Relocating personal data folders" in Chapter 12, "Organizing and searching for files." For information about power-management settings, see "Power management and battery life" in Chapter 15, "System maintenance and performance."

Taming your mouse or other pointing device

To teach your mouse new tricks, in Settings visit Devices, Mouse & Touchpad. Settings here under Mouse let you swap the functions of your left and right mouse buttons (great for left-handed folks) and control how much to scroll each time you roll the mouse wheel. You'll find other mouse settings by scrolling to the bottom of the Mouse & Touchpad page and clicking Additional Mouse Options. Doing so opens the Mouse Properties dialog box, shown earlier in Figure 4-4.

Mouse Properties has settings that define a double-click (that is, how quickly you must twice press the mouse button for it to be detected as a double-click instead of two clicks), add visual highlights to the mouse as you move it, and more.

Depending on the mouse you have, you might find additional options in Mouse Properties or in a separate app. For example, if you have a Microsoft mouse, you might see the Mouse And Keyboard Center tab (as shown in Figure 4-4). That tab contains a link that launches an app where you can adjust many more settings, such as assigning useful functions to each mouse button.

If your computer has a precision touchpad, the Mouse & Touchpad page in Settings, Devices has a lot to explore, as shown in Figure 4-8.

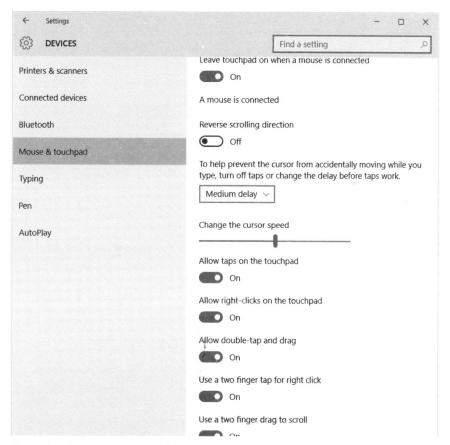

Figure 4-8 Touchpad users are richly rewarded by visiting Mouse & Touchpad and scrolling down to the settings under Touchpad.

Options here let you turn off the touchpad when you have a mouse attached or disable it alto-gether. Those who've been annoyed when the pointer suddenly hops to a new location while they type (usually because a thumb lightly grazed the touchpad) will appreciate—nay, shout hosannas about—the setting that delays cursor moves. Other settings determine what various gestures (tapping, double-tapping, tapping with two or three fingers, dragging with two or three fingers, and so on) will do.

If you use a pen with your computer, visit the Pen page in Settings, Devices. The modest num-ber of settings here control the appearance of the pen cursor and offer another place for left-ies to assert their rights.

Handwriting recognition in Windows is amazing; it has often correctly interpreted our own writing, which we could barely read ourselves. Nonetheless, pen users whose handwriting verges on indecipherable would do well to take a few minutes to train the handwriting rec-ognition system to better read their scrawl. To do that, in Control Panel open Language. Next to your language, click Options, and in the Language Options window click or tap Personalize Handwriting Recognition. This opens a Handwriting Personalization window, which leads to a series of windows in which you can submit handwriting samples, as shown next.

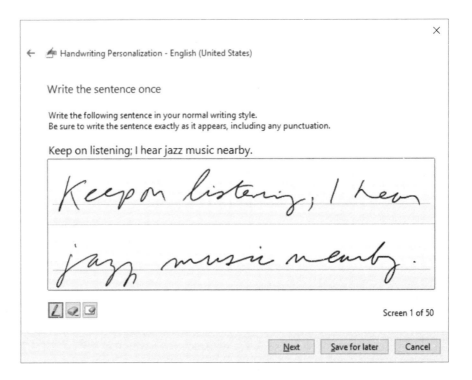

Managing keyboard settings

Keyboard users—yes, there are still a few—will find settings under Keyboard in Control Panel that control how quickly a key repeats when it's held down. And as with a mouse, you might find additional settings in a manufacturer-provided tab or app.

But wait; there's more! In Settings, open Devices, Typing to see options like those shown in Figure 4-9. The options under Spelling and the Add A Period option under Typing work only with modern apps. The other options under Typing work only with the Touch Keyboard. Adding to the confusion, some (but not all) options under Touch Keyboard also work with a physical keyboard. If you often use modern apps or the Touch Keyboard, you'll want to experiment with these settings.

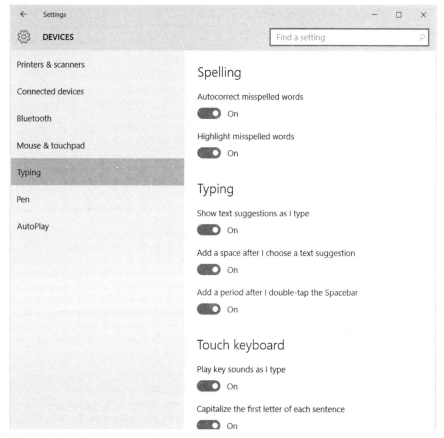

Figure 4-9 For the most part, the options on the Typing page work only with modern apps and with the Touch Keyboard.

Inside OUT

Reconfigure the Caps Lock key to avoid shouting

If you occasionally find yourself accidentally stuck in Caps Lock mode, so that your emails are shouting or your text documents look like a demand letter from a creditor, consider the following tweak.

You can disable the Caps Lock key so that it does nothing whatsoever: Open Registry Editor and navigate to HKLM\System\CurrentControlSet\Control\Keyboard Layout. Add a Binary value called Scancode Map. Set the data for this key to

00000000 00000000 02000000 00003A00 00000000

Close Registry Editor, restart, and you'll never be stuck in Caps Lock again.

Selecting sounds for events

To specify the sounds that Windows plays as it goes through its paces, in the search box type **sounds**, and then click Change System Sounds. In the Sound dialog box (shown here), you can select a predefined collection of beeps, gurgles, and chirps that Windows and various apps play in response to various system and application events.

You can select a sound scheme from the list (a new installation of Windows comes with only a single scheme, called Windows Default), or you can customize the sound schemes. To see which sounds are currently mapped to events, scroll through the Program Events list. If an event has a sound associated with it, its name is preceded by a speaker icon, and you can click Test to hear it. To switch to a different sound, scroll through the Sounds list or click Browse. The list displays .wav files in %Windir%\Media, but any .wav file is eligible. To silence an event, select None, the item at the top of the Sounds list.

If you rearrange the mapping of sounds to events, consider saving the new arrangement as a sound scheme. (Click Save As and supply a name.) That way, you can experiment further and still return to the saved configuration.

Inside OUT

Mute your computer

If you like event sounds in general but occasionally need complete silence from your computer, choose No Sounds in the Sound Scheme list when you want the machine to shut up. (Be sure to clear the Play Windows Startup Sound check box as well.) When sound is welcome again, you can return to the Windows Default scheme—or to any other scheme you have set up. Switching to the No Sounds scheme won't render your system mute (you'll still be able to play music when you want to hear it), but it will turn off the announcement of incoming mail and other events.

If you want to control sound levels on a more granular level—perhaps muting some applications altogether and adjusting volume levels on others—right-click the volume icon in the notification area and choose Open Volume Mixer. Volume Mixer provides a volume slider (and a mute button) for each output device and each running program that emits sounds.

Choosing a screen saver

Screen savers don't save screens. (In long-gone days when screens were invariably CRTs and many offices displayed the same application at all hours of the working day, having an image move about during idle times probably did extend the service life of some displays.) And they certainly don't save energy. But they're fun to watch. To see the current offerings, in the search box type **screen saver**, and then click Change Screen Saver.

In the Screen Saver Settings dialog box (shown next), select an option under Screen Saver. Some screen savers have additional configuration options; click Settings to review your choices.

Tuning Windows to know about you

A personalized experience requires Windows to know some things about you. Not just how to read your handwriting, or your dining preferences, but some basic information: where are you?

Your location affects several settings, such as the current time (more specifically, the time zone), your language and keyboard, and the way dates, times, and numbers are displayed. To set your location, in Settings open Time & Language to display the Date & Time page, as shown in Figure 4-10.

First, be sure to select the proper time zone for your current location. If you're connected to the Internet, the time should be set automatically; Windows periodically synchronizes your computer's clock to an Internet-based time server. (Without an Internet connection, turn off automatic time setting and click Change to set the time manually.)

Then you'll want to review the samples under Formats; many apps use the formats you set here as their default format for displaying dates and times. Initially, these are set based on the country/region you specify during Windows setup, but you can easily change any or all of them by clicking Change Date And Time Formats.

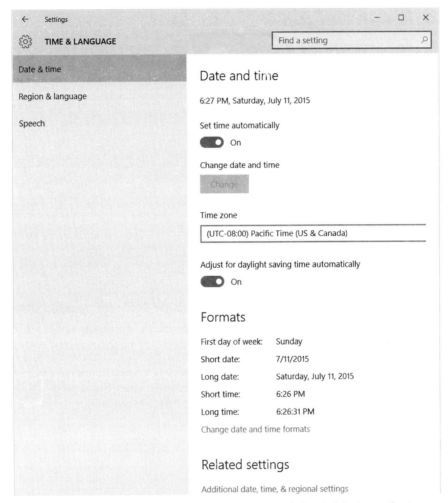

Figure 4-10 A quick way to display this page is to tap or click the clock in the notification area and then tap or click Date And Time Settings.

Inside OUT

Set formats for currency and numbers

Some apps also look to Windows for a default format for displaying monetary amounts (the currency symbol and number format) and numbers (items such as the thousands separator and the decimal symbol)—but you won't find those settings here. Instead, on the Date & Time page in Settings, tap or click Additional Date, Time, & Regional Settings. In the Control Panel window that opens, click Change Date, Time, Or Number Formats, and then click Additional Settings.

If you frequently communicate with people in other time zones, you might want to scroll down to the bottom of the Date & Time page in Settings and click Add Clocks For Different Time Zones. This opens a dialog box in which you can add one or two clocks to the top of the calendar that appears when you click or tap the clock in the notification area, as shown next.

Optionally add clocks for other time zones

Current time at your location

To quickly display a calendar for a month in another year (or another decade), tap here and then use the up and down buttons

Syncing your settings between computers

Windows 10 offers two types of synchronization among computers:

- A *theme* is an über configuration that combines and names the various personalization settings that you can make. Themes can incorporate the desktop background, window color, sound scheme, screen saver, desktop icons, and mouse pointers.

- A more comprehensive collection of synchronization settings encompasses not only themes but various other personalization options:

    - **Web Browser Settings.** Settings you make using the Settings command in Microsoft Edge and the Internet Options command in Internet Explorer

    - **Passwords.** Passwords you've saved in your web browser

    - **Language Preferences.** Settings you make in Settings, Time & Language

    - **Ease Of Access.** Settings you make in Settings, Ease Of Access (for details, see the next section, "Overcoming challenges")

    - **Other Windows Settings.** Various other settings, ranging from window positions to Start menu arrangements to calendar settings—and many more

Note that these are all settings that pertain to your own Microsoft account or domain account (either a work domain or an Azure Active Directory domain). Settings that apply to all users at your computer, such as screen resolution, are not included in the current theme or other synchronized settings. Also, settings associated with a local user account don't get synchronized with other computers.

Working with themes

To select a theme, go to Settings, Personalization, Themes, and then click Theme Settings. A dialog box appears showing predefined themes included with Windows as well as themes you've saved. Simply click one to select it; the theme is applied right away, so if you don't like what you see and hear, you can select another before you close the window.

If you've got all the visual and aural aspects of your profile set up just the way you want them, and you want to be able to experiment further but still return to the current settings, it's time to revisit Theme Settings. At the top of the themes list, in the My Themes category, you'll see Unsaved Theme if you made changes to whatever theme was previously in effect. To make those changes reusable, click Save Theme and supply a name.

If you make additional changes, you'll once again generate an Unsaved Theme entry. There's no limit to the number of themes you can create. Windows saves each group of settings as a .theme file in your %LocalAppData%\Microsoft\Windows\Themes folder. (A .theme file is a standard text file that describes all the theme settings. For complete details about theme files, see "Theme File Format" at *w7io.com/0402*.) You can delete unwanted items from the My Themes list; simply right-click the item you no longer want and choose Delete Theme. Note that you can't delete the theme that's currently in use.

Inside OUT

Share themes with friends or from a local user account

Syncing themes among your devices is effortless when you sign in with a Microsoft account. But even if you use a local account, you still might want to use a theme on your other computers or share it with other users. Because a .theme file is just a text file, it doesn't contain the graphic images of your desktop, the sound files you use for various events, or other necessary files that make up the entire theme experience. For the purpose of sharing themes, Windows uses a .themepack file, which includes the .theme file as well as all other nonstandard theme elements. A .themepack file uses the standard compressed folder (.zip archive) format to envelop its component files. To create a .themepack file of an item in My Themes, right-click it and choose Save Theme For Sharing. Unless you specify otherwise, Windows saves the .themepack file in the default save location of your Documents library.

To use a theme that was saved in .theme or .themepack format, simply double-click it. (Of course, a .theme file won't offer the full experience if the theme's components aren't available on your computer in folders to which you have access. To create a .themepack file—which includes all the necessary files—see the preceding tip.)

Because themes are so easily portable, you can find many compelling Windows themes online. Start your quest by clicking Get More Themes Online (under My Themes in Personalization), where Microsoft offers a nice selection.

Synchronizing other settings

To manage synchronization of various other components, in Settings click Accounts, Sync Your Settings. Figure 4-11 shows the window that appears.

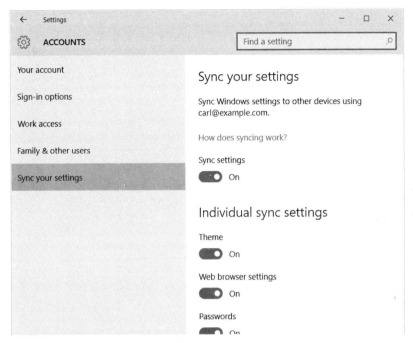

Figure 4-11 You can enable or disable all sync settings with a single setting, or you can control settings individually.

Overcoming challenges

Microsoft has a longstanding commitment to making computing accessible and easier to use for persons with vision, hearing, or mobility impairments. Windows 10 groups these options into the Ease Of Access section of Settings. (Alternatively, you can press Windows key+U to open Ease Of Access Center, the Control Panel equivalent.)

Ease Of Access in Settings provides a prominent link to each of the following settings, which can be used alone or in combination:

- **Narrator.** This tool converts on-screen text to speech and sends it to your computer's speakers. This option allows people who are blind or have severe vision impairments to use Windows.

- **Magnifier.** This tool enlarges part of the screen, making it easier for persons with vision impairments to see objects and read text. (You can also launch Magnifier with a keyboard shortcut: Press Windows key+plus sign to launch it and zoom in. Press again to zoom in more, or press Windows key+minus sign to zoom out.)

- **High Contrast.** This tool uses a high-contrast color scheme (by default, white text on a black background) that makes it easier for visually impaired users to read the screen.

- **Closed Captions.** This tool lets you set the appearance of closed captioning in videos for apps that support closed captioning.

- **Keyboard.** This collection of tools includes an alternate means for Windows users with impaired mobility to enter text using a pointing device. Options that appear when you click Options in On-Screen Keyboard let you control how it works—you can choose whether to select a letter by clicking, for example, or by allowing the pointer to pause over a key for a specific amount of time. Other tools on the Keyboard page allow uses with impaired mobility to more easily deal with key combinations and repeated keystrokes.

- **Mouse.** This page includes tools that make the mouse pointer easier to see for visually impaired users. Another tool enables the numeric keypad to move the mouse pointer instead of by using a mouse.

- **Other Options.** This page includes a smattering of appearance-related options to assist those with visual or hearing impairments.

The easiest way to configure your computer for adaptive needs in one fell swoop is to open Ease Of Access Center in Control Panel and then click Get Recommendations To Make Your Computer Easier To Use, a link near the center of the page. The link launches a wizard, shown here, that walks you through the process of configuring accessibility options.

If you want accessibility options to be available at all times, even before signing in to the computer, click the Change Sign-In Settings link in the left pane of Ease Of Access Center in Control Panel. This option (shown next) applies any changes you make to the sign-in desktop. If you choose not to enable this option, you can still turn accessibility features on or off at the sign-in screen; click the small Ease Of Access icon in the lower right corner of the sign-in screen to display a list of available settings, and then press the Spacebar to enable each one.

Networking essentials

Modern computing is defined by our ability to communicate and share with one another by using devices of all shapes and sizes. These days, most of that activity happens over the world's largest global network, the Internet, using a variety of widely accepted hardware and software standards. The Internet is also the driving force behind cloud-based services, which are transforming the way we work and play.

The same network standards that allow connections to the Internet can also be used to create a local area network (LAN), which makes it possible to share files, printers, and other resources in a home or an office.

In the not-so-distant past, setting up a network connection was a painful process, one that often required professional help. Today, network hardware is ubiquitous, and setting up a network connection in Windows 10 requires little or no technical knowledge. That doesn't mean the process is entirely pain free; troubleshooting network problems can be maddeningly frustrating, and understanding the basics of networking is tremendously helpful in isolating and fixing problems.

In this chapter, we cover the essentials of connecting a Windows 10 device to wired and wireless networks in a home or small office. We also explain how to share resources securely and how to check the status of your network connection to confirm that it's working properly.

At the time we wrote this chapter, we wanted to include a discussion of OneDrive. Unfortunately, Microsoft's release schedule for the new OneDrive synchronization client didn't quite mesh up with the initial release of Windows 10. You'll find a summary of OneDrive and other cloud services in Appendix C, "OneDrive and other cloud services."

> ➤ In larger businesses, networks typically have a Windows server at their heart. We cover the ins and outs of managing and using these larger, more complex networks in Chapter 20, "Advanced networking."

Getting started with Windows 10 networking

Before you can connect to the Internet or to a local area network, your Windows 10 device needs a network adapter, properly installed with working drivers.

Since the release of Windows 7, Microsoft's hardware certification requirements have mandated that every desktop PC, laptop, all-in-one, and portable device include a certified Ethernet or Wi-Fi adapter.

You'll typically find wired Ethernet adapters in desktop PCs and all-in-ones, where a permanent wired network connection is appropriate. These adapters can be integrated into the motherboard or installed in an expansion slot and accept RJ45 plugs at either end of shielded network cables.

Most modern wired adapters support either the Fast Ethernet standard (also known as 100Base-T), which transfers data at 100 megabits per second, or the more modern Gigabit Ethernet standard, which allows data transfers at 1 gigabit (1,000 megabits) per second. In an office or a home that is wired for Ethernet, you can plug your network adapter into a wall jack that connects to a router, hub, or switch at a central location called a patch panel. In a home or an office without structured wiring, you need to plug directly into a network device.

Inside OUT

Connect to a wired network using a USB port

If you crave the consistent connection speed and reliability of a wired network but have a portable PC or mobile device that lacks a built-in Ethernet connection, consider investing in a USB network adapter. A USB 2.0 port will support Fast Ethernet speeds, whereas a modern device with a USB 3.0 or USB Type-C port should be capable of Gigabit Ethernet speeds. Some network docking stations and USB hubs include an Ethernet adapter; this option allows you to use a single USB connection for instant access to a wired network and other expansion devices while you're at your desk, using Wi-Fi when you're on the go.

In recent years, wireless networking technology has enjoyed an explosion in popularity. Wireless access points are a standard feature in most home routers and cable modems, and Wi-Fi connections are practically ubiquitous. You can connect to Wi-Fi, often for free, in hotels, trains, buses, ferries, and airplanes in addition to the more traditional hotspot locations such as cafés and libraries.

All laptops and mobile devices designed for Windows 10 include a Wi-Fi adapter, which consists of a transceiver and an antenna capable of communicating with a wireless access point.

Wireless adapters are also increasingly common in desktop and all-in-one computer designs, allowing them to be used in homes and offices where it is impractical or physically impossible to run network cables.

Ethernet and Wi-Fi are the dominant networking technologies in homes and offices. Alternatives include phone-line networks, which plug into telephone jacks in older homes, and power-line technology, which communicates using adapters that plug into the same AC jacks you use for power. The availability of inexpensive wireless network gear has relegated phone-line and power-line technologies to niche status; they are most attractive in older homes and offices, where adding network cable is impractical and wireless networks are unreliable because of distance, building materials, or interference. (A hybrid approach, useful in some environments, allows you to plug a Wi-Fi extender into an existing power line to increase signal strength in a remote location.)

You don't need to rely exclusively on one type of network. If your cable modem includes a router and a wireless access point, you can plug network cables into it and use its wireless signal for mobile devices or for computers located in areas where a network jack isn't available.

When you upgrade to Windows 10, the setup program preserves your existing network connection. If you perform a clean setup of Windows 10, your wired Internet connection should be detected automatically; you're prompted to enter the access key for a wireless connection during the setup process.

NOTE

In this chapter, we assume you have an always-on broadband connection in your home or office or that you are connecting to the Internet through a public or private Wi-Fi connection with Internet access. Although Windows 10 supports dial-up connections, we do not cover this option.

Checking your network's status

As we noted earlier, most network connections in Windows 10 should configure themselves automatically during setup. Three tools included with Windows 10 allow you to inspect the status of the current connection and either make changes or troubleshoot problems.

Using the network icon and flyout

The most easily accessible network tool is the status icon that appears by default in the notification area at the right side of the taskbar. Its icon indicates the current network type (wired or wireless) and the status of the network. Click that icon to display the network flyout, which displays options relevant to your type of network connection.

Figure 5-1 shows the network flyout for a Surface Pro 3 with a USB Ethernet adapter connected to a wired network and a Wi-Fi connection to the Bottville access point. Both networks
appear to be operating properly. (As we explain later, a status of Limited would indicate problems with the network's ability to connect to the Internet.)

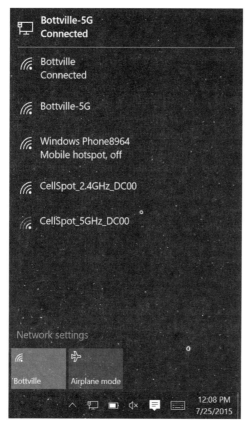

Figure 5-1 On a mobile device, the two buttons at the bottom of this network flyout allow you to
enable or disable Wi-Fi (left) or turn on Airplane Mode (right) to shut down all radios temporarily.

Every available network is shown on this list, including wired connections and wireless access
points that are broadcasting their names. In Figure 5-1, the PC is connected to both a wired
network and a wireless access point. Because the wired connection is faster, it gets priority, sitting at the top of the list with a line separating it from the wireless networks.

The icon for each access point indicates its signal strength. In Figure 5-1, for example, the
router named CellSpot is transmitting and receiving on two different frequencies, with each
one getting its own name. The 2.4 GHz connection appears to be considerably stronger than
the 5 GHz connection.

Two buttons at the bottom of the network flyout are available on laptops and mobile devices. The button on the left shows the name of the currently connected wireless network. Click or tap to temporarily disable Wi-Fi connections; tap again to reconnect to a wireless network. (We cover the details of wireless connections more fully later in this chapter.)

A red X or yellow triangle over the network icon means your Wi-Fi adapter is enabled but not working properly. In Figure 5-2, for example, the yellow triangle with an exclamation point is Windows 10's way of warning that something's wrong with that connection. The network fly-out shows that the wireless adapter is connected to an access point but isn't able to reach the Internet.

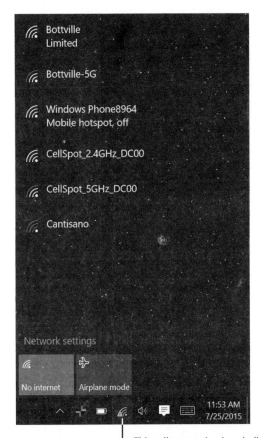

└ This yellow warning icon indicates a wireless problem

Figure 5-2 The familiar warning icon over the wireless icon means there's a problem with the connection. The flyout provides more details: The connection is limited, with no Internet access via Wi-Fi.

➤ For help with troubleshooting network problems (wired and wireless), see Chapter 20.

The Network Settings link at the bottom of the network flyout leads to the Network & Internet page in Settings, with details for the current network shown by default. On a desktop or all-in-one PC with only a wired connection, that page looks something like the one shown in Figure 5-3.

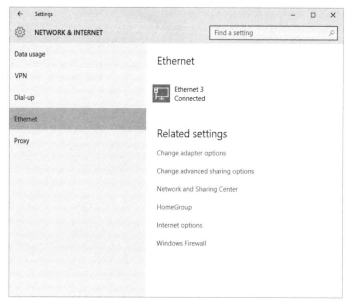

Figure 5-3 The Ethernet heading and the icon shown here confirm that the current connection is wired. All of the options under Related Settings lead to the classic desktop Control Panel.

Inside OUT

Mobile hotspots and other metered connections

Some devices with data connections on a cellular network allow you to turn the device into a mobile Wi-Fi hotspot, sometimes referred to as a "Mi-Fi" device. This capability is invaluable when you need to get some work done on a portable PC and an affordable, reliable Wi-Fi connection isn't available. The list of available network connections in Figure 5-1, for example, includes a phone running Windows 10 Mobile, which is capable of acting as a hotspot once the option is turned on. Most modern smartphones, including iPhones and Android devices, are capable of acting as a hotspot as well, although the cellular data provider must allow this capability.

A mobile hotspot looks like a Wi-Fi network, so you can connect your Windows 10 laptop by using its Wi-Fi adapter. A modern mobile network can be significantly faster than a public Wi-Fi connection. It also has the advantage of being more secure because you're connecting through your trusted mobile device to the carrier's (presumably secure) network rather than to a public Wi-Fi network that could be compromised.

The downside of using a mobile hotspot where you pay by the megabyte or gigabyte is potentially higher costs (especially if you're roaming outside your home network) or the risk that you'll hit your data limit and have your connection throttled or stopped completely. To avoid that possibility, Windows 10 identifies mobile hotspots as metered connections and automatically limits certain types of background activity. By default, the list of restricted activities includes downloads from Windows Update and always-on connections to an Exchange Server in Microsoft Outlook. The Data Usage option in Settings, Network & Internet allows you to see how much data a specific network connection has used in the past 30 days.

If Windows 10 doesn't realize that a specific network is on a pay-as-you-go connection, open the Wi-Fi page under the Network & Internet heading in Settings, and click or tap Advanced Options. Slide the Set As Metered Connection switch to the On position, as shown here:

Clicking the icon for a connected wired network (the one labeled Ethernet 3 in Figure 5-3, for example) displays details about that connection: its IP addresses, Domain Name System (DNS) settings, and network adapter (including manufacturer name and current driver version). Figure 5-4 shows these properties for the virtual network adapter in a Hyper-V virtual machine we used for testing as we worked on this book.

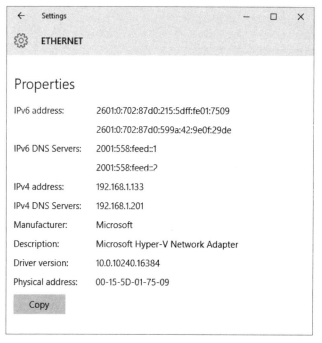

Figure 5-4 These details for a wired network connection are essential for troubleshooting network-ing problems. Click Copy to save the settings to the Clipboard to paste into a help desk ticket or an email message.

You can get to the equivalent information for a wireless connection by selecting the Wi-Fi option on the Network & Internet Settings page and then clicking or tapping Advanced Options.

On the Network & Internet Settings page (shown earlier in Figure 5-3), each item in the list under the Related Settings heading leads to an option in the classic desktop Control Panel. It's possible that some of these functions will have migrated to the modern Settings app by the time you read this.

> ➤ We cover Change Adapter Options and Change Advanced Sharing Options more fully in Chapter 20.

Network And Sharing Center

If you've managed a network in Windows 7, you're probably already familiar with the Network And Sharing Center, which was the hub of almost all networking activities. You can get to the Windows 10 version of the Network And Sharing Center in any of the following ways:

- In the notification area, click the Network icon and then click Open Network And Sharing Center.

- In the search box, begin typing **network** until the Network And Sharing Center item appears at the top of the menu; click it.

- In Settings, click or tap Network & Internet and then click or tap Network And Sharing Center under the Related Settings heading.

- In Control Panel, click Network And Internet, and then click Network And Sharing Center.

- In File Explorer, select the Network folder, open the Network tab on the ribbon, and then click the Network And Sharing Center button.

As you can see in Figure 5-5, this iteration of the Network And Sharing Center is a bit tidier than its predecessors but still firmly entrenched in the desktop Control Panel, offering access to most of the same information and functions.

Figure 5-5 The Network And Sharing Center provides a snapshot of the active network and includes links to nearly every relevant related task or setting.

The block of options along the left side is essentially the same as the choices under the Related Settings heading in the newer Network & Internet page in Settings. The most useful information in the Network And Sharing Center appears in the center, under the heading View

Your Active Networks. In Figure 5-5, you can see that this network is using a wired connection and is configured to be private, allowing other PCs and devices on the same network to view shared resources. (We explain how and why to choose between public and private networks later in this chapter in "Setting network locations.")

Clicking the name of the active connection—in this example, Ethernet—leads to a status dialog box, where a Details button leads to additional information. The list of network details is a bit longer than its counterpart in the Settings app, as Figure 5-6 illustrates.

Figure 5-6 Click the Details button in the status dialog box for a connection (left) to open an information-dense listing of IP addresses and other details (right).

NOTE

Many tasks related to configuring networks require elevation to administrator privileges, as indicated by the shield icon next to commands and on command buttons.

Although there's no obvious way to copy information from the Network Connections Details box (to share with a support engineer, for example, or to paste into a post on a community support forum), it is possible to do so. Use your mouse to select a single row, or hold down Ctrl or Shift and click to select multiple rows, then press Ctrl+C to copy the selection to the Clipboard.

Monitoring network performance in Task Manager

Sometimes it's useful to know not just whether a network connection is working but how well it's handling its primary job of transmitting and receiving packets of data. For a real-time graph of network throughput, open Task Manager, click the Performance tab, and then select a connection name from the list on the left. Figure 5-7 shows a file upload in progress on a wired Ethernet connection.

Figure 5-7 The real-time performance graph in Task Manager lets you see not just whether your network connection is working but also how well.

The scale of the real-time performance graph adjusts dynamically to allow you to see relative differences easily. In Figure 5-7, for example, the Gigabit Ethernet adapter is theoretically capable of sending and receiving data at roughly 1,000 megabits per second. Using that scale, the spikes in this upload, averaging an otherwise impressive 3.3 megabits per second, would be a tiny flat squiggle nearly indistinguishable from the bottom border. With a scale of 11 megabits per second, both the send and receive graphs are capable of telling the story of whether the connection is working as expected.

➤ For more information on basic techniques for identifying problems on Windows networks, see "Troubleshooting networking problems" in Chapter 17, "Troubleshooting." For more advanced troubleshooting help, see Chapter 20.

Inside OUT

IPv6 and Windows 10

The longer you've worked with Windows, the more likely you are to be familiar with the granddaddy of Windows networking, Internet Protocol version 4, also known as IPv4. A default network connection in Windows 10, wired or wireless, uses IPv4 but also enables the newer IP version 6. IPv6 is on by default and has been the preferred protocol in all desktop and server versions of Windows for nearly a decade, since the release of Windows Vista.

Without getting into the minutiae of network addressing, suffice it to say that IPv4, with its addresses based on four groups of numbers from 0 to 255, has a big problem. When the Internet was young, that address space, consisting of 4.3 billion unique combinations of dotted addresses, like 192.168.1.108 or 10.0.0.242, seemed huge. Unfortunately, nobody anticipated just how big the Internet would become, and the authorities who assign IP addresses on the Internet have literally run out of IPv4 addresses.

The solution is IPv6, which uses 128-bit addresses and therefore has a maximum address space of 3.4×10^{38} addresses, which we are confident is enough to last for the next few generations of Internet users. IPv6 is slowly but surely taking over large swaths of the Internet. The giant American Internet and cable provider Comcast has fully enabled its network for IPv6, with most of its competition not far behind. Major mobile carriers are also providing the majority of traffic on native IPv6 connections.

Major content providers are enabled for IPv6 as well. You can read about Microsoft's IPv6 efforts at *bit.ly/ms-ipv6*. Almost all of Google's services now work over IPv4 and IPv6, as does Yahoo. Facebook's giant data centers now run IPv6 exclusively, and Netflix has supported IPv6 for years.

Windows veterans might be tempted to shy away from IPv6, preferring the more familiar IPv4. In our experience, that's a mistake. IPv6 is here to stay. Learn about it and embrace it.

Setting network locations

A desktop PC connected to a wired home or small office network remains in a single location, by definition. In contrast, mobile devices running Windows 10 can connect to different types of networks—a corporate domain, a wireless hotspot at a coffee shop, or a private home network. Each type of network has its own security requirements. Windows uses network locations to categorize each network and then applies appropriate security settings. When you connect to a new network, Windows applies one of three security settings:

- **Public.** This is the default setting for any new, untrusted network connection. Network discovery is turned off for public networks, making it impossible for other people on the same access point to connect to your computer. This option is appropriate for networks in public places, such as wireless hotspots in coffee shops, hotels, airports, and libraries. It's also the correct choice if your desktop or laptop PC is directly connected to a cable modem or other broadband connection without the protection of a router and hardware firewall.

- **Private.** This option is appropriate when you're connecting to a trusted network, such as your own network at home—if and only if that network is protected by a router or residential gateway (a consumer device that combines a cable modem, router, and wireless access point in a single box) or comparable Internet defense. When you make this choice, Windows enables network discovery and allows you to enable the HomeGroup feature for sharing with other users on the network.

- **Domain.** This option is applied automatically when you sign in to Windows using a computer that is joined to a Windows domain, such as your company network. In this scenario, network discovery is enabled, allowing you to see other computers and servers on the network by using accounts and permissions controlled by a network administrator.

  ➤ If you have a mobile computer that connects to multiple networks, keep in mind that the Windows Firewall keeps separate network security profiles for private (home or work), public, and domain-based networks, For more information about Windows Firewall, see "Blocking intruders with Windows Firewall" in Chapter 7, "Securing Windows 10 devices."

The location of the current network is shown in the Network And Sharing Center, below the name of the network.

To change a public network to a private one, or vice-versa, open Settings, click or tap Network & Internet, and then select the Wi-Fi or Ethernet heading in the list on the left. Click or tap the icon for a wired connection or, for a wireless connection, click or tap Advanced Options. That opens the properties dialog box for the active connection, with the Find Devices And Content

option, shown in Figure 5-8, at the top. When this setting is Off, the network is public. Slide the
switch to On to make the network private.

Figure 5-8 Flip this switch to the On position to notify Windows that this is a private network and
it's safe to connect to other network devices. In the Off position, the network location is set to Public
and outside access is blocked.

Inside OUT

Workgroups versus domains

Computers on a network can be part of a workgroup or a domain.

In a workgroup, the security database (including, most significantly, the list of user
accounts and the privileges granted to each one) for each computer resides on that
computer. When you sign in to a computer in a workgroup, Windows checks its local
security database to see whether you've provided a user name and password that
matches one in the database. Similarly, when network users attempt to connect to your
computer, Windows again consults the local security database. All computers in a workgroup must be on the same subnet. A workgroup is sometimes called a peer-to-peer
network.

By contrast, a domain consists of computers that share a security infrastructure, Active
Directory, which in turn is managed on one or more domain controllers running
Windows Server. Microsoft's cloud-based alternative, Azure Active Directory, provides
the same infrastructure without requiring IT departments to manage local servers.
Active Directory and Azure Active Directory can be combined to create effective hybrid
environments. When you sign in using a domain account, Windows authenticates your
credentials against the security database defined by your network administrator.

In this chapter (and throughout this book), we focus primarily on workgroup networks.

Connecting to a wireless network

In this section, we assume that you have already configured a wireless access point (often included as a feature in cable modems and DSL adapters supplied by your broadband provider) and confirmed that it is working correctly.

Whenever your computer's wireless network adapter is installed and turned on, Windows scans for available wireless access points. If it finds at least one (and you're not already connected to a wireless network), it alerts you via the wireless network icon, which looks a bit like an antenna. If you see a bright dot at the end of an otherwise gray antenna, that means connections are available.

Unless you're out in the country, far from civilization, you're likely to see lots of access points available for connection, most of them owned by your neighbors or nearby visitors. Assuming those networks are adequately secured with a password you don't know and can't guess, you'd have no luck connecting to them anyway.

Clicking or tapping the entry for a secured access point reveals a box in which you are expected to enter a passphrase, as in Figure 5-9. If what you enter matches what's stored in the access point's configuration, you're in. Getting in is easy on a network you control, where you set the password. For a secured access point controlled by someone else—a doctor's waiting room, a coffee shop, a friend's office—you'll need to ask the network owner for the passphrase or key.

Figure 5-9 Connecting to a secure network for the first time requires that you correctly enter a passphrase or security key.

Before you reach that security prompt, you're asked whether you want to connect automatically to that network in the future. If this is a place you expect to visit again (or in the case of a coffee shop, again and again and again . . .), say yes to save the credentials. Note that saved Wi-Fi passwords are synced between devices when you sign in with a Microsoft account, so you might find that a brand-new device, one you've never used before, automatically connects to your home or office Wi-Fi without having to ask you.

To disconnect from a Wi-Fi access point, click or tap its entry in the network flyout and then tap Disconnect. Doing so automatically turns off the option to connect automatically to that network in the future.

Windows 10 saves credentials for every Wi-Fi access point you connect to, giving you the option to connect with a tap when you revisit. If that thought makes you uncomfortable, you can see and manage the full list of networks by opening Network Settings and clicking Manage Wi-Fi Settings on the Wi-Fi page. That list can be startling, especially if you're a frequent traveler. Tap any name in the list, and you'll see either one or two buttons, as in Figure 5-10.

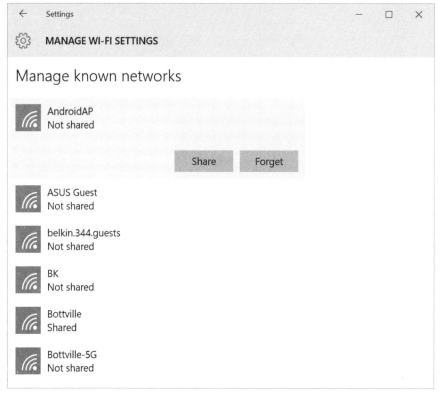

Figure 5-10 Wireless networks you connect to are saved in this list. Tap Forget to delete the saved passphrase and remove the network from the list.

Tapping the Forget button deletes any saved security information and removes the network name from the list. The Share button is available only if you've turned on the option to share network settings with your contacts, a feature that's part of Wi-Fi Sense, which we describe later in this chapter.

Inside OUT

Decoding Wi-Fi standards

The most popular wireless networks use one of several variants of the IEEE (Institute of Electrical and Electronics Engineers) 802.11 standard, also known as Wi-Fi. On modern Wi-Fi networks, you are likely to encounter one of the following three standards (going from oldest to newest):

- **802.11g.** This standard was current up until 2009, just before the release of Windows 7. It's still in wide use on older PCs and wireless access points. It can transfer data at a maximum rate of 54 megabits per second using radio frequencies in the 2.4 GHz range. (Some manufacturers of wireless networking equipment have pushed the standard with proprietary variations that approximately double the speed.) 802.11g-based networks have largely supplanted those based on an earlier standard, 802.11b, which offers a maximum speed of 11 megabits per second.

- **802.11n.** Using this standard, adopted in 2009, you can expect to see dramatic improvements in speed (600 megabits per second) as well as significantly greater range. Unlike the earlier standards, the 802.11n standard allows use of the 5 GHz frequency range as well as 2.4 GHz. However, not all 802.11n hardware supports both bands.

- **802.11ac.** This standard, finalized in 2014, builds on the 802.11n specification and allows multiple links at both ends of the wireless connection, advertising throughput rates of 500 megabits per second per link, with a theoretical maximum speed of up to 2,600 megabits per second.

Although the newer Wi-Fi standards are backward compatible with hardware that uses the older, slower standards, be aware that all traffic on your network runs at the speed of the slowest wireless standard in use; if you've just bought an 802.11ac router, you will see the faster speed only if you replace your old network adapters.

For the maximum throughput, use 5 GHz 802.11ac devices throughout your network. The 5 GHz band is subject to less radio interference than 2.4 GHz and is capable of a higher maximum theoretical data rate. If you must maintain compatibility with older 2.4 GHz devices, the ideal solution is to use a dual-band wireless access point.

Connecting to a hidden network

Every wireless network has a name, formally known as a *service set identifier* but typically referred to as an SSID. Some wireless networks are set up so that they don't broadcast their SSID. Connecting to such a hidden network is a bit more challenging because its name doesn't appear in the list of available networks on the network flyout or in Network & Internet Settings. Making such a connection is possible, however, as long as you know the network name and its security settings.

> ### NOTE
>
> Configuring a router so that it doesn't advertise its name has been incorrectly pro-
> moted by some as a security measure. Although it does make the network less acces-
> sible to casual snoops, lack of a broadcast SSID is no deterrent to a knowledgeable
> attacker. Furthermore, attackers can learn the SSID even when they're not near your
> wireless access point because it's periodically broadcast from your computer, wherever
> it happens to be. We provide these steps to help you connect to a hidden network
> managed by someone else; we don't recommend that you configure your home or
> office network in this fashion.

If one or more nearby networks aren't broadcasting their SSID, you'll see Hidden Network in the list of available networks. Click or tap that entry, and then you'll need to enter the correct SSID before you're allowed to the real security test, your passphrase or security key.

After you jump through that one extra hoop, the process is no different from connecting to a network that broadcasts its name.

To set up your computer so that it connects to a particular nonbroadcasting wireless network whenever you're in range, follow these steps:

1. Open Network And Sharing Center, and click Set Up A New Connection Or Network.

2. In the Set Up A Connection Or Network Wizard, select Manually Connect To A Wireless Network and click Next.

3. Specify the network name (SSID), the type of security used by the network, the encryption type if the network uses WPA or WPA2 security, and the security key or passphrase, as shown in Figure 5-11. Select Connect Even If The Network Is Not Broadcasting. (What is the privacy risk mentioned in the dialog box? When this option is turned on, your computer sends out probe requests to locate the wireless network; an attacker can detect these probe requests and use them to determine the network's SSID. Your computer continues to send these requests even when you're away from your network's access point.) Click Next.

Figure 5-11 Use this well-hidden dialog box to configure a hidden network so that it's always available to connect to automatically.

4. Click Next, and then click Close.

Wireless security

On a conventional wired network, especially in a private home or office, physical security is reasonably easy to secure: if someone plugs a computer into a network jack or a switch, you can trace the physical wire back to the intruder's computer. On wireless networks, however, anyone who comes into range of your wireless access point can tap into your network and intercept signals from it.

If you run a small business, you might want to allow Internet access to your customers by using an open Internet connection. Some Internet service providers create secure guest accounts on their customers' cable modems that allow other customers of that service to connect using their network credentials.

Other than those scenarios, however, you probably want to secure your network so that the only people who can connect to it are those you specifically authorize. Doing that means configuring security settings on your wireless access point or router. When you connect to a network, known or unknown, the level of security is determined by the encryption standard chosen by the network owner and supported by network hardware on both sides of the connection.

Depending on the age of your hardware, you should have a choice of one or more of the following options, listed in order of preference:

- **Wi-Fi Protected Access 2 (WPA2).** Based on the 802.11i standard, WPA2 provides the strongest protection for consumer-grade wireless networks. It uses 802.1x-based authentication and Advanced Encryption Standard (AES) encryption; combined, these technologies ensure that only authorized users can access the network and that any intercepted data cannot be deciphered. WPA2 comes in two flavors: WPA2-Personal and WPA2-Enterprise. WPA2-Personal uses a passphrase to create its encryption keys and is currently the best available security for wireless networks in homes and small offices. WPA2-Enterprise requires a server to verify network users. All wireless products sold since early 2006 must support WPA2 to bear the Wi-Fi CERTIFIED label.

- **Wi-Fi Protected Access (WPA).** WPA is an earlier version of the encryption scheme that has since been replaced by WPA2. It was specifically designed to overcome weaknesses of WEP. On a small network that uses WPA, clients and access points use a shared network password (called a preshared key, or PSK) that consists of a 256-bit number or a passphrase that is from 8 to 63 bytes long. (A longer passphrase produces a stronger key.) With a sufficiently strong key based on a truly random sequence, the likelihood of a successful outside attack is slim. Most modern network hardware supports WPA only for backward compatibility.

- **Wired Equivalent Privacy (WEP).** WEP is a first-generation scheme that dates back before the turn of the century. It suffers from serious security flaws that make it inappropriate for use on any network that contains sensitive data. Most modern Wi-Fi equipment supports WEP for backward compatibility with older hardware, but we strongly advise against using it unless no other options are available.

You might see other encryption options, but those are typically designed for use on enterprise networks and are beyond the scope of this book.

Inside OUT

Beef up security at the access point

If your data is sensitive and your network is in an apartment building or an office complex where you can reasonably expect other people to wander into range with wireless adapters, you should take extra security precautions in addition to enabling WPA. Consider any or all of the following measures to protect your wireless access point from intruders:

- Change the network name (SSID) of your access point to one that doesn't match the hardware defaults and doesn't give away any information about you or your business.

- Disable remote administration of the access point; if you need to change settings, you can do so directly, using a wired connection.

- Whether you decide to allow remote administration of the access point or not, set a strong password so that a visitor can't tamper with your network settings.

- Check the firmware and drivers for wireless hardware (access points and adapters) at regular intervals and install the most recent versions, which might incorporate security fixes.

- Consider using a virtual private network (VPN) for wireless connections. A VPN sends all wireless traffic over an encrypted connection, making it impossible for others to snoop on your wireless traffic. Corporate network administrators can help set up a VPN using your company's security infrastructure. For unmanaged Windows 10 devices, VPN software and services are available.

When setting up a wireless access point for a home or small office, choose a strong passphrase. A passphrase for WPA or WPA2 can be up to 63 characters long and can contain letters (case-sensitive), numbers, and spaces (no spaces at the beginning or end, however). Many devices generate a random alphanumeric key, but you might prefer to use a memorable phrase instead of random characters. If you do, choose a phrase that's not easily guessed, make it long, and consider incorporating letter substitution or misspellings to thwart attackers. Because it can be saved and synced between devices, you shouldn't need to enter it often.

You must use the same encryption option on all wireless devices on your network—access points, routers, network adapters, print servers, cameras, and so on—so choose the best option that is supported by all your devices. If you have an older device that supports only WEP (and it can't be upgraded with a firmware update), consider retiring or replacing that device.

TROUBLESHOOTING

You can't connect to other computers

If you're connecting to a network in your home or office (as opposed to a public hotspot, such as at an Internet café), be sure that the network is defined as a private network (either home or work). By default, Windows errs on the side of security, setting the location of all new networks as Public, and thus not open to connections from other devices on the same network. That's safe, but it also means you won't be able to see other local computers you trust. To see whether this is the problem, open the Network And Sharing Center. If Public Network appears beneath the name of your network, there's an easy fix.

Open File Explorer and click or tap Network in the list on the left. That should display a yellow banner at the top of the list noting that network discovery and file sharing are turned off. Click that banner, and then click Turn On Network Discovery And File Sharing in the resulting menu, as shown in Figure 5-12.

Figure 5-12 If your network location is set to Public, you'll see this banner in the Network folder; click it to make the network private and see other devices on the local network.

That click toggles the network location from Public to Private and should allow you to see the rest of the network (and vice versa). Do this only if you are certain that the other devices connected to this network can be trusted.

Sharing wireless connections with Wi-Fi Sense

Windows 10 includes a pair of new features under the collective heading of Wi-Fi Sense. What they share in common is a desire to make it easier to connect to and share trusted, secure Wi-Fi connections without you and your friends having to ask for passwords.

To manage Wi-Fi Sense, click the taskbar icon for your Wi-Fi network, click Network Settings, and then, on the Wi-Fi page, click Manage Wi-Fi Settings. Figure 5-13 shows the Wi-Fi Sense Settings page.

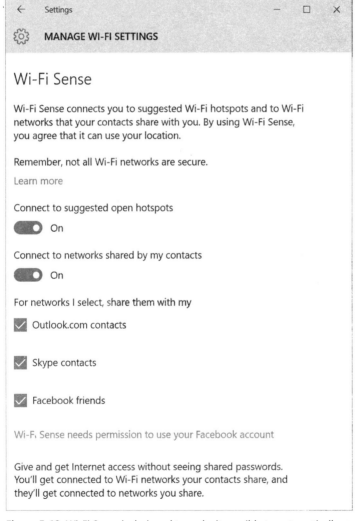

Figure 5-13 Wi-Fi Sense is designed to make it possible to automatically connect to an unfamiliar network that has been suggested by Microsoft or shared by a friend.

The top setting, Connect To Suggested Open Hotspots, allows you to connect automatically to hotspots that are in a database managed by Microsoft. The second group of settings, Connect To Networks Shared By My Contacts, allows you to share a network with friends and family members who are in your Outlook.com, Skype, or Facebook contact lists and are also using Windows 10. Your friends never see the password; instead, they're authenticated securely by Wi-Fi Sense, using encrypted credentials.

Although the option to share networks is on by default, none of your saved Wi-Fi networks are actually shared until you choose to do so. To control sharing for a network, find its entry in the Known Networks list (shown earlier in Figure 5-10) and then use the Share (or Stop Sharing) button for that network name to enable (or disable) sharing.

Sharing files, digital media, and printers in a homegroup

The HomeGroup feature, originally introduced as part of Windows 7 and maintained through Windows 10, allows Windows devices to share resources on a home network. The list of share-able things includes USB-connected printers as well as files from the default libraries: Documents, Music, Pictures, and Videos. You can print a boarding pass, concert tickets delivered via email, or a Word document from your PC, with the documents emerging from a printer attached to a different PC on the same network. The HomeGroup feature also allows you to search across all computers in a homegroup to find pictures from a recent event. Files on other devices are almost as easily accessible as if they were on your own computer.

(Oh, and if you're confused by the capitalization of the term, you're not alone. Microsoft hasn't budged from the conventions it adopted when this feature appeared in Windows 7. The correct spelling is HomeGroup when the term refers to the feature and the associated Control Panel option where you configure it. The collection of Windows computers joined together this way is called a homegroup, with no capitalization. In File Explorer, in dialog boxes and menus, and in this book, the term might be capitalized to indicate that it is part of the name of an option. We apologize profusely for the confusion.)

> ## NOTE
> The HomeGroup feature works only with computers running Windows 7 or later. To share files with computers running other operating systems (including earlier versions of Windows), or to enable users of those computers to access files on your Windows 10 computer, you must use network sharing methods compatible with those older versions. For details, see "Sharing resources with other users" in Chapter 20.

The HomeGroup feature is specifically designed for environments where the connected computers are in a physically secure location (a private home or an office) with users who are fully trusted. Traditional network sharing requires matching account credentials on every device and will not work with devices for which the user has a blank password. HomeGroup is designed to work well regardless of whether computers and user accounts have passwords. Sharing is accomplished through the use of a special password-protected user account. If you're interested in the technical workings, see the "How HomeGroup works" sidebar.

How HomeGroup works

The simplicity of setting up and using HomeGroup belies its complexity. The basic sharing mechanism uses standard sharing protocols that have been part of Windows for many years. Here's the short version: HomeGroup grants share permissions and applies an access control entry (ACE) to each shared object, allowing access to a group called HomeUsers. A hidden, password-protected account (which is required for accessing shared objects over a network connection) named HomeGroupUser$ is a member of HomeUsers and acts as your proxy in accessing shared network resources. (In fact, even if your user account is password protected, HomeGroup still uses the HomeGroupUser$ account instead of your account to connect to a remote computer.) You can work around this setting by selecting the Use User Accounts And Passwords To Connect To Other Computers option in Advanced Sharing Settings. For more information about this setting, see "Configuring your network for sharing" in Chapter 20.

CAUTION

Do not change the password for the HomeGroupUser$ account; doing so is a recipe for disaster. (Note that the account password is *not* the same as the homegroup password.)

But there's much more going on with HomeGroup. Creating or joining a workgroup creates the HomeGroupUser$ account and the HomeUsers group and adds all local accounts to the group. HomeGroup setup also configures Windows Firewall. (Specifically, it enables certain rules in the Core Networking, Network Discovery, and HomeGroup groups. And for computers that are not joined to a domain, it enables rules in the File And Printer Sharing, Windows Media Player, and Windows Media Player Network Sharing Service groups.) In addition, it configures the HomeGroup Provider and HomeGroup Listener services. (HomeGroup also relies on Function Discovery and several other networking services.)

The requirements to implement and use HomeGroup are few:

- At least one computer running Windows 7 Home Premium or above or any edition of Windows 8, Windows 8.1, or Windows 10 to create the homegroup

- All computers in the homegroup running Windows 7 or later

- The network location for all computers must be set to Private. Although domain-joined PCs were able to access homegroup resources in earlier versions, that capability is not available in Windows 10.

For users, setting up HomeGroup is a straightforward process. On one computer—it doesn't matter which one because HomeGroup is a true peer-to-peer networking system without a designated server/controller—you create a homegroup. Then, on other computers, you join the homegroup.

Creating a homegroup

The current HomeGroup status is visible with the details of any active network in Network And Sharing Center. If no homegroup exists, click Ready To Create to begin the setup process. You can also set up the HomeGroup feature at a later time; type **homegroup** in the taskbar or Control Panel search box, and then click HomeGroup in the list of search results.

If no homegroup currently exists on your network, the HomeGroup page in Control Panel informs you of that fact, as in Figure 5-14. Click Create A Homegroup to open a wizard that walks you through the process.

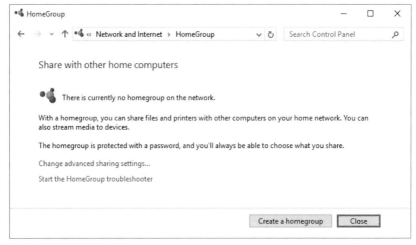

Figure 5-14 You'll see this Control Panel page only once. After your homegroup is created, this page offers options for you to change, join, or leave the homegroup.

Inside Out

Go ahead, change the homegroup password

The homegroup password isn't intended to be highly secure. The only machines that can connect to your homegroup are those that are connected to your wired or wireless network, so even a simple password is sufficient to keep out uninvited guests. To change the randomly generated alphanumeric password to one that's easier to remember, visit the HomeGroup Control Panel from any computer that's already joined the homegroup. Using an administrator's credentials, click the Change The Password option (shown here) and follow the prompts.

In the dialog box that follows, you can enter any password you like (we suggest a memorable passphrase), or click the refresh button until you're satisfied with one of the automatically generated options. As the instructions in this process make clear, you'll need to visit every other computer in the homegroup and manually replace the old password with the new one you just created.

The first step allows you to select which default libraries should be shared with other home-group members and which should remain out of bounds. As the example in Figure 5-15 shows, the Documents folder is excluded from sharing by default, whereas pictures, videos, music, and printers and other shareable devices are included. You can change any of these settings now or later.

Figure 5-15 The first step in setting up a homegroup is to specify which of your default libraries you want to share as well as whether to share printers.

Click Next, and the wizard generates a password for your homegroup, as shown in Figure 5-16. (Behind the scenes, the wizard also sets up the requisite user accounts and security groups, services, firewall rules, and shares.) Click Finish, and you're done.

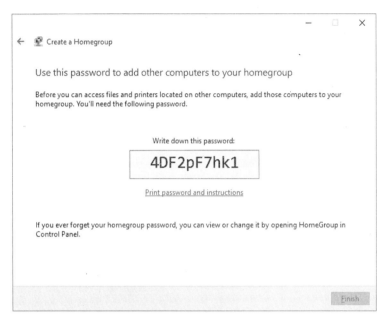

Figure 5-16 You'll use this same (shared) password to join other computers to the homegroup.

Joining a homegroup

After a homegroup has been created, other computers on the network can join it by using a similarly brief process. Open HomeGroup in Control Panel and click Join Now to reach a wizard that informs you that a homegroup already exists and gives you the opportunity to join it.

Click Next, and the wizard asks you to choose the resources you want to share with other devices that are part of the same homegroup. Click Next again to enter the homegroup password. Enter the password and click Next, and you're ready to view resources from other computers in the homegroup. To do that, open File Explorer. In the left pane, expand Homegroup to see a subfolder for each user account on each computer in the homegroup, as shown in Figure 5-17.

By default, every homegroup user has View (read-only) access to the shared personal libraries and folders on other computers in the homegroup.

Fortunately, you're not limited to sharing only the content of the Documents, Music, Pictures, or Videos libraries. If you would like to share other folders or files with users of other computers in your homegroup, you can add the folder (or folders) to an existing library or create a new custom library. (For instructions on working with libraries, see "Working with libraries" in Chapter 12, "Organizing and searching for files.")

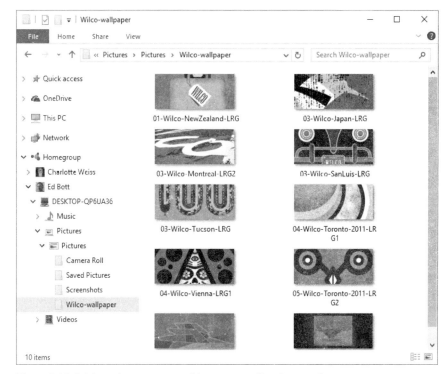

Figure 5-17 Joining a homegroup enables access to libraries on other computers.

To share a folder that's not in a library, locate that folder in File Explorer, right-click and click Share With, and then choose Homegroup (View) or Homegroup (View And Edit), as shown in Figure 5-18. (The same commands are also available on the Share tab of the File Explorer ribbon.)

CAUTION

Don't share the root folder of a drive (for example, D:\). Although sharing the root folder has long been common practice, we recommend against doing so. Because of the way permissions are inherited, changing permissions on the root folder can cause a variety of access problems. A better solution is to create a subfolder within that root folder to hold the files and subfolders you want to share, and then share the subfolder.

Which command you select, of course, determines whether a homegroup user on another computer can create, modify, and delete folders and files within the shared folder. Both options share the selected item with your entire homegroup.

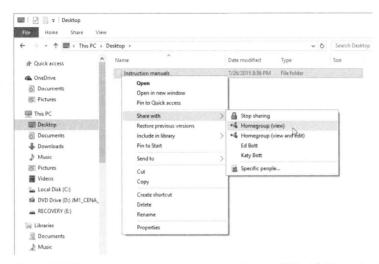

Figure 5-18 In a homegroup, you can choose to share individual folders using this well-hidden option.

To share with only certain individuals, choose Share With, Specific People. Doing so opens the File Sharing dialog box shown in Figure 5-19.

Figure 5-19 Clicking the arrow in the top box displays a list of local user accounts as well as home-group users who have signed in using a Microsoft account.

Using this feature with homegroups allows you to set per-user permissions that override homegroup permissions. So if you allow homegroup users View access, you can allow specific individuals Read/Write access. The time-honored Windows technique to implement this level of sharing is to set up user accounts with matching names and passwords on different PCs. That can lead to management hassles and messy sign-in screens.

NOTE

The File Sharing dialog box describes its two permission levels as Read and Read/Write. In File Explorer's Share With menu, the Homegroup options are View and View And Edit. They are, for all practical purposes, the same set of permissions described differently.

You also use the Share With command on the ribbon or the shortcut menu to prevent sharing of a particular folder or file within a shared library or folder. Select the items, click Share With, and then click Stop Sharing.

Similarly, you can override the default sharing settings for private folder profiles within a library—normally these are shared with View access—by selecting a folder or file within the shared library or folder and clicking Share With.

NOTE

A computer joins a homegroup and, therefore, all users on that computer have access to the homegroup's shared resources. However, sharing options are maintained on a per-user basis; on a computer with more than one user account, each user decides which of his or her libraries to share.

Browsing shared folders and files

If your network location is set as Private, you've probably noticed the Homegroup node in File Explorer's navigation pane. After adding a device to a homegroup, you can work with folders and files from other computers in the Homegroup node just as you use folders and files in your own libraries. Tasks you can perform include:

- Preview and open files

- Play music or view pictures or video (in a folder filled with music files, look for the Play All button on the toolbar)

- Search through all files within a folder, a library, a user node, or the entire homegroup

- Add a shared folder to one of your local libraries

- Add, modify, and delete files (only in libraries or folders shared with Read/Write access)

The Homegroup node also responds politely to right-clicks, displaying a convenient menu that lets you change settings for the homegroup, view the homegroup password, or start a trouble-shooter to figure out why sharing isn't working properly.

Sharing a printer

Printer sharing isn't as big a deal today as it was when the HomeGroup feature debuted many years ago.

Today, we carry boarding passes and concert tickets on our smartphones. And for the rare pages we do need to commit to paper, it's often easiest to save a file to the cloud and then retrieve that file using the PC that has a printer attached.

Still, there's nothing quite like the convenience of sitting on the couch with a Windows 10 tab-let and printing out a document to a printer in your home office.

If a homegroup member computer has a printer connected to one of its USB ports, and if the computer's user has chosen to share its printers (by selecting the Printers And Devices check box in HomeGroup), all homegroup users have access to that printer.

If the printer has been certified by the Windows Logo Program, it shows up automatically in Control Panel's Devices And Printers folder for all homegroup users. HomeGroup obtains the driver files from the host computer whenever possible or downloads them from the Internet if necessary (for example, if the host computer runs 32-bit Windows and your computer has 64-bit Windows installed), and then installs the driver without requiring any user interven-tion. (Note that it might take a few minutes after joining or connecting to a homegroup for HomeGroup to discover the shared printer and install the driver.)

If the shared printer is connected to a desktop computer (but not a laptop) that is in sleep mode, sending a print request to the printer uses Wake On LAN to awaken the computer so that it can perform the print job. After completing the print job, the computer returns to sleep.

Leaving a homegroup

If you decide that HomeGroup isn't for you (or, perhaps, you want to join a different home-group), you can leave a homegroup. Open HomeGroup in Control Panel and click Leave The Homegroup. Because HomeGroup is a true peer-to-peer network, when any computer leaves the homegroup, the homegroup remains intact and all other members are unaffected (except they'll no longer be able to see your computer's resources, of course).

Note, however, that the Homegroup icon remains in File Explorer even after you leave the homegroup. Selecting the icon displays a message that includes an option to join a home-group (if one is detected) or create one.

CHAPTER 6

Managing user accounts, passwords, and credentials

The user account, which uniquely identifies each person who uses the computer, is an essential component in security and in providing a personalized user experience in Windows. Windows allows you to restrict access to your computer so that only people you authorize can use the computer or view its files. User accounts in Windows provide the means by which you can

- Require each user to identify himself or herself when signing in.

- Control access to files and other resources that you own.

- Audit system events, such as sign-ins and the use of files and other resources.

- Sync files and settings between different computers that you use.

If your computer is in a secure location where only people you trust have physical access to it, you might not have such concerns. But you should still create a user account for each person who uses the computer because associated with each account is a user profile that stores all manner of information unique to that user: favorite websites, desktop background, document folders, and so on. With fast user switching, a feature described in this chapter, you can switch between user accounts with only a few clicks.

Working with user accounts

When you install Windows 10 on a new computer, the setup program creates a profile for one user account, which is an administrator account. (An *administrator account* is one that has full control over the computer. For details, see "User accounts and security groups" later in this chapter.) Depending on what type of account you select during setup, that initial account can be either a Microsoft account or a local user account. (For information about these account types, see the next section, "Microsoft account vs. local account.") If you upgrade to Windows 10 from Windows 7 or Windows 8 and you had local accounts set up in your previous operating system, Windows migrates those accounts to your Windows 10 installation.

Local user accounts that you migrate from Windows 7 or 8 maintain their group memberships and passwords.

Through Accounts in Settings, Windows provides a simple post-setup method for creating new accounts and making routine changes to existing accounts. When you launch Accounts in Settings, you'll see a window similar to the one shown in Figure 6-1.

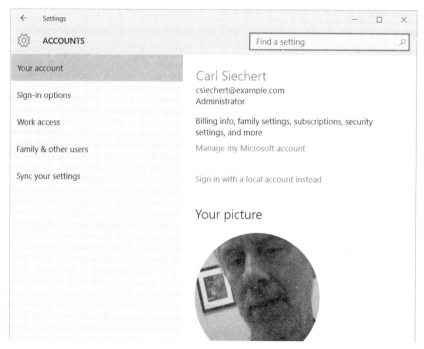

Figure 6-1 Accounts in Settings lets you manage your own account and, if you have an administrator account, manage other accounts.

You'll find different options and settings in Accounts depending on the type of account you use (Microsoft account or local account), whether your account is a member of the Administrators group, and—if your computer is joined to a domain—group policies in effect. In a domain environment, all management of user accounts beyond basic tasks such as selecting a picture is normally handled at the domain level.

And, because the transition from the old-school Control Panel to the modern Settings app is not complete, you'll find that some account-related settings can be made only with User Accounts in Control Panel, which is shown in Figure 6-2.

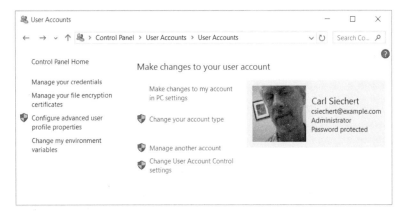

Figure 6-2 The link near the center of the page—Make Changes To My Account In PC Settings— opens Accounts in Settings. Most of the other links here lead to settings that aren't available in Settings, Accounts.

Microsoft account vs. local account

A *Microsoft account* is an online account system that can enhance security of your computer and its data, foster easy synchronization between computers, and enable many online services (such as OneDrive, Cortana, and Skype) as well as access to the Windows Store. Under various names (most recently, Windows Live ID), Microsoft accounts have been around for years. If you've registered for Microsoft services such as Hotmail, Xbox Live, or Zune, you already have a Microsoft account. If you have an email address that ends with msn.com, hotmail.com, live.com, or outlook.com, you have a Microsoft account. However, you do not need a Microsoft address to create a Microsoft account; you can set up a Microsoft account using an existing email address from any domain and any email provider.

A *local account* is one that stores its sign-in credentials and other account data on your PC. This type of account has been the standard in Windows for decades. A local account works only on a single computer.

NOTE
A third type of account, a work account using Azure Active Directory or Windows Server Active Directory, stores account information on a network server. It offers many of the advantages of a Microsoft account, subject to restrictions imposed by the network administrator. These accounts are more common in large businesses and schools. In this book we do not cover their use in depth.

Beginning with Windows 8 and continuing in Windows 10, Microsoft recommends the use of a Microsoft account rather than a local user account. It's not a requirement, however; local accounts are still fully supported. So why use a Microsoft account?

- You can synchronize PC settings between multiple computers. If you use more than one PC—say, a desktop PC at work, a different desktop at home, a laptop for travel, and a tablet around the house—the ability to sync allows your settings to apply to all your computers. Settings include things like your desktop colors and background, your stored passwords, browser favorites and history, your account picture, your accessibility configuration, and so on. The synchronization happens automatically and nearly instantly.

  To view or modify your synchronization settings, open Settings and click or tap Accounts, Sync Your Settings. You can disable synchronization altogether (turn Sync Settings off) or you can turn individual settings on or off.

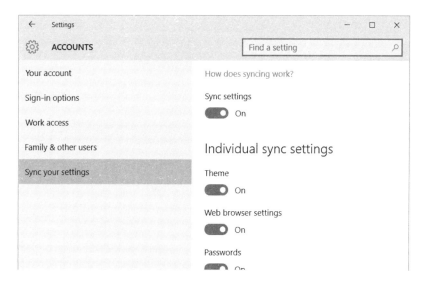

- You can use OneDrive cloud storage and gain access to your data from any computer. (For more information about OneDrive, see Appendix C, "OneDrive and other cloud services.")

- You can download modern apps using the Store app. Without a Microsoft account, you can browse in the Store, but you cannot download apps, music, or videos.

- Some features in preinstalled modern apps require the use of a Microsoft account.

- Cortana, the personal assistant that's part of Windows 10, is available only when you sign in with a Microsoft account.

- With built-in two-factor authentication, a Microsoft account provides security for your PC and its data.

NOTE

It is possible to use OneDrive, make Store purchases, and use some other apps that depend on a Microsoft account even if you sign in with a local account. However, you must sign in to each app individually, and some features might be unavailable or, at a minimum, less convenient to use.

Are there any reasons *not* to use a Microsoft account?

- If you sign in using your Microsoft account password (rather than using a PIN or Windows Hello, as described later in this chapter in "Managing the sign-in process"), your password might be stolen. This could happen if someone is watching over your shoulder as you sign in, for example. Armed with your Microsoft account ID and password, a thief has access to much of your online life. (The moral here, of course, is not to eschew Microsoft accounts; rather, use a sign-in method that uses two-factor authentication and doesn't expose your password.)

- If your home network includes computers running Windows 7 or earlier (that is, versions that do not support the use of Microsoft accounts), connecting to shared resources can be more complicated. For information about working around this problem, see "Sharing resources with other users" in Chapter 20, "Advanced networking."

- Some folks have privacy and data security concerns about storing personal information on the servers of a large corporation, whether it be Microsoft, Google, Apple, Amazon, or others. Microsoft has implemented a single privacy statement that covers most of its consumer products and services. For information about the privacy policy and to make choices about how Microsoft uses your data, visit *account.microsoft.com/privacy*. For more information, see the sidebar "Configuring privacy options."

You can switch between using a Microsoft account and a local account by going to Settings, Accounts. On the Your Account page (shown earlier in Figure 6-1), click Sign In With A Local Account Instead. Windows then leads you through a few simple steps to create a local account, which you'll then use for signing in. If you're already using a local account, the link reads Sign In With A Microsoft Account Instead. A few screens later, you're connected to an existing Microsoft account or a new one you create.

Configuring privacy options

These days, you don't need to be a conspiracy theorist to be concerned about privacy. Some companies abuse your trust by taking your information—often without your knowledge or consent—and sharing it with others who hope to profit from that information. Because Windows 10 is tightly integrated with cloud services (meaning some of your information gets stored on Microsoft-owned servers), and because Microsoft acknowledges using some of your information to provide better service (for example, Windows collects information from your calendar so that Cortana can make better suggestions), some people have privacy concerns about Windows.

But Microsoft is forthcoming about the types of information it collects and, more importantly, what it does with that information. Here, for example, is part of the privacy statement regarding advertising:

> The ads we select may be based on your current location, search query, or the content you are viewing. Other ads are targeted based on your likely interests or other information that we learn about you over time using demographic data, search queries, interests and favorites, usage data, and location data—which we refer to as "interest-based advertising" in this statement. Microsoft does not use what you say in email, chat, video calls or voice mail, or your documents, photos or other personal files to target ads to you.

More important still, Windows includes a raft of options for controlling your privacy. You'll find them in Settings, Privacy, shown next. Here you can specify which apps are allowed to use each of your computer's many devices, whether to disclose your location, whether to let Cortana better know your voice and word pronunciations, and so on. You should examine each of these options carefully and decide for yourself where the proper balance is between your personal privacy and convenience.

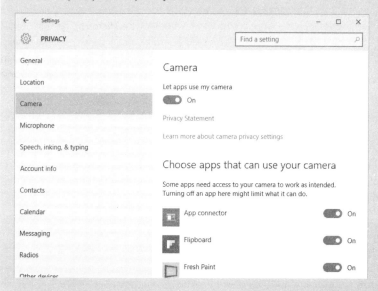

On each page in Settings, Privacy, you'll find a link to the Microsoft privacy statement and links to additional information as well as the controls for making settings. The privacy statement is detailed yet clearly written, and it is an important aid for deciding which options to enable.

Changing account settings

With options in Settings and Control Panel, you can make changes to your own account or another user's account.

To change your own account, open Settings, Accounts to open the Your Account page, shown earlier in Figure 6-1. If you start at User Accounts in Control Panel, click Make Changes To My Account In PC Settings to reach the same destination.

INSIDE OUT

Access the Your Account page quickly

You can jump straight to the Your Account page in Accounts without going through Control Panel or Settings. Simply open the Start menu, click or tap the account picture in the upper left corner of the Start menu, and choose Change Account Settings.

On the Your Account page, you can change your account picture, either by browsing for a picture file or by using your computer's built-in camera to take a picture. If you sign in with a Microsoft account, the Manage My Microsoft Account link opens your default web browser and loads your account page at *account.microsoft.com*. On that page, you can change your password or the name associated with your Microsoft account. Click other tabs along the top of the page to review your subscriptions and Store purchases, change your payment options, get information about all PCs and other devices associated with your Microsoft account, set privacy options, and more.

If you have added one or more users to your computer, you (as a computer administrator) can make changes to the account of each of those users. (For information about adding users, see "Adding a user to your computer" later in this chapter.)

To change a user's account type, in Settings, click Accounts, Family & Other Users. Then click the name of the account you want to change and click Change Account Type. (Your choices are Standard User or Administrator. For details, see "User accounts and security groups" later in this chapter.)

If the person signs in with a Microsoft account, there are no other changes you can make. (You can't make changes to someone else's Microsoft account at *account.microsoft.com*.) For users who sign in with a local user account, you can make a few additional changes, but you must start from User Accounts in Control Panel (shown earlier in Figure 6-2). Click Manage Another Account, and then click the name of the account you want to change. You can make the following changes:

- **Account Name.** The name you're changing here is the full name, which is the one that appears on the sign-in screen, on the Start menu, and in User Accounts.

- **Password.** You can create a password and store a hint that provides a reminder for a forgotten password. If the account is already password protected, User Accounts allows you to change the password or remove the password. For more information about passwords, see "Setting a password" later in this chapter.

- **Account Type.** Your choices here are the same as in Settings, Accounts: Administrator (which adds the account to the Administrators group) or Standard User (which adds the account to the Users group).

If you use a local user account, you can make the following additional changes to your own account (that is, the one with which you're currently signed in) by clicking links in the left pane:

- **Manage Your Credentials.** This link opens Credential Manager, which lets you manage stored credentials that you use to access network resources and websites. For more information, see "Managing and securing your credentials" later in this chapter.

- **Create A Password Reset Disk.** This link launches the Forgotten Password Wizard, from which you can create a password reset tool on removable media.

- **Manage Your File Encryption Certificates.** This link opens a wizard that you can use to create and manage certificates that enable the use of Encrypting File System (EFS). EFS, which is available only in Pro and Enterprise editions of Windows 10, is a method of encrypting folders and files so that they can be used only by someone who has the appropriate credentials. For more information, see "Encrypting information" in Chapter 7, "Securing Windows 10 devices."

- **Configure Advanced User Profile Properties.** This link is used to switch your profile between a local profile (one that is stored on the local computer) and a roaming profile (one that is stored on a network server in a domain environment). With a local profile, you end up with a different profile on each computer you use, whereas a roaming profile is the same regardless of which computer you use to sign in to the network. Roaming profiles require a domain network based on Windows Server. To work with user profiles other than your own, in Control Panel open System and click Advanced System Settings; on the Advanced tab, click Settings under User Profiles.

- **Change My Environment Variables.** Of interest primarily to programmers, this link opens a dialog box in which you can create and edit environment variables that are available only to your user account; in addition, you can view system environment variables, which are available to all accounts.

Deleting an account

You can delete any account except one that is currently signed in. To delete an account, in Settings, Accounts, click Family & Other Users, and click the name of the account you want to delete. Then click Remove. Windows then warns about the consequences of deleting an account, as shown in Figure 6-3.

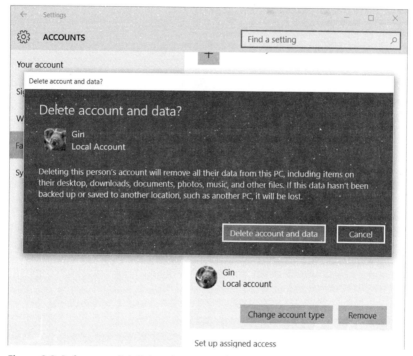

Figure 6-3 Before you click Delete Account And Data, be sure you have saved any data you don't want to lose.

NOTE

User Accounts won't let you delete the last local account on the computer, even if you're signed in using the account named Administrator. This limitation helps to enforce the sound security practice of using an account other than Administrator for your everyday computing.

After you delete an account, of course, that user can no longer sign in. Deleting an account also has another effect you should be aware of: you cannot restore access to resources that are currently shared with the user simply by re-creating the account. This includes files shared with the user and the user's encrypted files, personal certificates, and stored passwords for websites and network resources. That's because those permissions are linked to the user's original security identifier (SID)—not the user name. Even if you create a new account with the same name, password, and so on, it will have a new SID, which will not gain access to anything that was restricted to the original user account. (For more information about security identifiers, see "Introducing access control in Windows" later in this chapter.)

Inside OUT

Delete an account without deleting its data

Earlier versions of Windows included an option for preserving an account's data files—documents, photos, music, downloads, and so on stored in the user's profile—when you delete the user account. Windows 10 offers that option too, but you won't find it in Settings. Instead, open User Accounts in Control Panel. Click Manage Another Account, click the account you want to remove, and then click Delete The Account.

User Accounts gives you a choice about what to do with the account's files:

- **Delete Files.** After you select Delete Files and confirm your intention in the next window, Windows deletes the account, its user profile, and all files associated with the account, including those in its Contacts, Desktop, Documents, Downloads, Favorites, Links, Music, Pictures, Saved Games, Searches, and Videos folders.

- **Keep Files.** Windows copies certain parts of the user's profile—specifically, files and folders stored on the desktop and in the Documents, Favorites, Music, Pictures, and Videos folders—to a folder on your desktop, where they become part of your profile and remain under your control. The rest of the user profile, such as email messages and other data stored in the AppData folder; files stored in the Contacts, Downloads, Saved Games, and Searches folders; and settings stored in the registry are deleted after you confirm your intention in the next window that appears.

Managing the sign-in process

Users of Windows (as well as most other operating systems) are familiar with the time-honored sign-in method: at the sign-in screen, select your name (if it's not already selected) and then enter a password. This continues to be a valid technique in Windows 10.

> NOTE
>
> When you first turn on your computer or return to it after signing out, the *lock screen* is displayed. The lock screen normally shows a snazzy picture, the current time and date, and alerts from selected apps. (You can select your own lock screen picture and specify what information you want displayed on the lock screen. For details, see "Customizing the lock screen" in Chapter 4, "Personalizing Windows 10.") To get from the lock screen to the sign-in screen, click anywhere, press any key, or (if you have a touch screen) swipe up.

Inside OUT

Press Ctrl+Alt+Delete without a keyboard

Some network administrators enable a policy that requires you to press Ctrl+Alt+Delete to switch from the lock screen to the sign-in screen. That's tough to do on a tablet with no keyboard—until you know the trick: press the Windows button (usually on the bezel along the right or bottom edge of the screen) and the power button.

Windows 10 has other sign-in options that add security as well as convenience:

- You can enter a numeric PIN.

- You can trace a pattern of gestures on a picture.

- With appropriate hardware, you can use Windows Hello—a biometric sign-in method that scans your fingerprint, your face, or your iris.

These three methods each provide a form of *two-factor authentication*, a means of identifying yourself with multiple components. In the case of Windows sign-ins, the components include two of the following: something you know (such as a PIN or the gesture pattern), something you have (the device itself), and something that's inseparable from you (your fingerprint, face, or iris).

The device you sign in on acts as an authentication component because your information (the PIN or your biometric data) is stored, in encrypted form, on the device—not on a remote server. So, for example, if someone learns your PIN, they can use it only on that device; they can't use it to sign in to your account on any other device. Or if someone steals your computer, they can't sign in unless they know your PIN.

By comparison, passwords are not as secure. Even if you're vigilant about using a strong password, not writing it down, and ensuring that it's not stolen from you, your user name and password combination could be part of one of those huge data breaches that make the news on almost a weekly basis. Through no fault of your own, your data is in the hands of criminals, who can then use that data to sign in to your account using any computer. Using a PIN with Windows 10, a thief would need to know your PIN and steal your device. And it's even less likely that a thief could nab your device and spoof your biometric data.

In the following sections, we explain how to set up each of these sign-in methods: password, PIN, picture password, and biometric. You configure each of these options on the Sign-In Options page in Settings, Accounts, as shown in Figure 6-4.

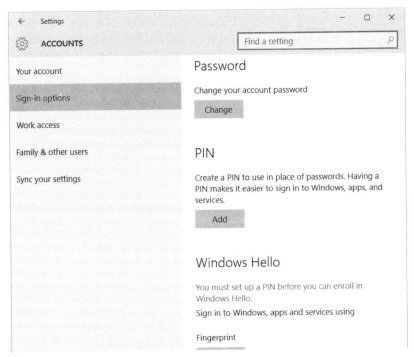

Figure 6-4 Options shown on the Sign-In Options page depend on your computer's hardware. For example, Windows Hello appears only if you have a compatible fingerprint reader or camera.

If you set up more than one option for signing in, you can choose a method other than the default by clicking Sign-In Options on the sign-in screen. This ability might come in handy, for example, if the fingerprint reader fails to recognize your grubby mitt. Icons for each of the options you've set up then appear as shown next; click or tap one to switch methods.

Setting a password

When you create a Microsoft account, you're required to create a password. Similarly, if you add a local user account to your computer, Windows 10 requires you to specify a password. Earlier versions of Windows did not have this requirement, however, so if you upgrade from an earlier version, you might have local accounts that are not password protected.

Now would be a good time to remedy that. After all, associating a password with your user account is your first line of defense against those who would like to snoop around in your files. Because the sign-in screen shows every user account, if you don't set passwords, anyone who has physical access to your computer can sign in simply by clicking a name on the sign-in screen. If the chosen name belongs to an administrator account, the person who clicks it has full, unfettered access to every file and setting on the computer. Requiring a password for each account (particularly administrator accounts) goes a long way toward securing your computer.

> ### NOTE
> If you sign in with a local account, you must add a password before you can use a PIN, picture password, or Windows Hello.

To set or change your own password, open Settings, Accounts. On the Sign-In Options page (Figure 6-4), click or tap Change under Password. You'll first need to enter your old password to confirm your identity. Windows then asks you to enter your new password twice. For a local account, you must specify a password hint. The password hint appears after you click your name on the sign-in screen and type your password incorrectly. Be sure your hint is only a subtle reminder, because any user can click your name and then view the hint. (Windows will not allow you to create a password hint that contains your password.)

NOTE

If you sign in with a local account, you can use a quicker alternative: Press Ctrl+Alt+Delete and click Change A Password. This method has one shortcoming, however: it does not let you enter a password hint.

You can also set or change the password for the local account of another user on your computer. To do so, open User Accounts in Control Panel, click Manage Another Account, and click the name of the user whose password you want to change. Then click Change The Password or (if the account doesn't currently have a password) Create A Password.

CAUTION

If another user has files encrypted with EFS, do not create a password for that user; instead, show the user how to create a password for his or her own account. Similarly, do not remove or change another user's password unless the user has forgotten the password and has absolutely no other way to access the account. (For more information, see the sidebar "Recovering from a lost password.") If you create, change, or remove another user's password, that user loses all personal certificates and stored passwords for websites and network resources. Without the personal certificates, the user loses access to all of his or her encrypted files and all email messages encrypted with the user's private key. Windows deletes the certificates and passwords to prevent the administrator who makes a password change from gaining access to them—but this security comes at a cost!

Recovering from a lost password

It's bound to happen: someday when you try to sign in to your computer and are faced with the password prompt, you will draw a blank.

For a Microsoft account, go to *account.live.com/password/reset*. (Presumably, you'll need to do this from another computer or a mobile device.) A series of questions there allows you to prove your identity and reset your password.

For a local account, Windows offers two tools that help you to deal with this dilemma:

- **Password hint.** Your hint (if you created one) appears below the password entry box after you make an incorrect entry and press Enter. You can create a hint when you set a password.

- **Password reset disk.** A password reset disk allows you (or anyone with your password reset disk) to change your password—without needing to know your old password. As standard practice, each user should create a password reset disk and keep it in a secure location. Then, if a user forgets the password, he or she can reset it using the password reset disk.

Both solutions require a little forethought on your part. You must create the hint when you set your password, and you must create the password reset disk before you actually need it.

To create a password reset disk, you need to know your current password and have removable media available. (You can use a floppy disk, USB flash drive, external hard drive, or memory card.) Follow these steps:

1. Sign in using the account for which you want to create a password reset disk.
2. Insert the removable media you plan to use as a password reset disk.
3. In Control Panel, open User Accounts.
4. In the left pane, click Create A Password Reset Disk to launch the Forgotten Password Wizard.
5. Follow the wizard's instructions.

You can have only one password reset disk for each user account. If you make a new one, the old one is no longer usable.

To use the password reset disk when password amnesia sets in:

1. On the sign-in screen, make an entry in the password box. If you guess right, you're in! If you're wrong, Windows informs you that the password is incorrect.
2. Click OK. The sign-in screen reappears, but with additional text below the password box.
3. If the first bit of additional text, your password hint, jogs your memory, enter your password. If not, click Reset Password to open the Password Reset Wizard.

   The Password Reset Wizard asks for the location of the password reset disk, reads the encrypted key, and then asks you to set a new password, which it then uses to sign you in. Your password reset disk remains usable for the next attack of forgetfulness; you don't need to make a new one.

If you can't remember the password, the hint doesn't refresh your memory, and you don't have a password reset disk, you're out of luck. An administrator can sign in and change or remove your password for you, but you'll lose access to your encrypted files and email messages and your stored credentials.

Using a PIN

To set up a PIN for signing in to your computer, go to the Sign-In Options page (Figure 6-4) and click Add under PIN. After entering your password to confirm your identity, you enter numbers in a dialog box like the one shown here. The minimum length is four digits (0–9 only; no letters or special characters allowed), but your PIN can be as long as you want.

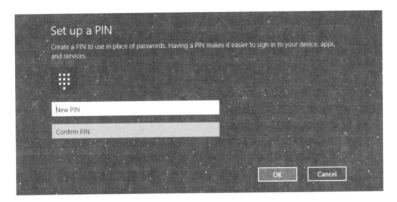

To sign in using a PIN, you can type the numbers on your keyboard. If your computer doesn't have a keyboard, a numeric pad appears on the screen so you can tap your PIN. (If the numeric pad does not appear, tap in the PIN-entry box.)

Using a picture password

A picture password allows you to sign in on a touchscreen using a combination of gestures (specifically, circles, straight lines, and taps) that you make on a picture displayed on the sign-in screen. The easiest way to get the hang of it is to go ahead and create one.

To get started, go to the Sign-In Options page in Settings, Accounts. Under Picture Password, click Add. Verify your identity by entering your password to display the introductory screen shown in Figure 6-5.

After reviewing the description, click Choose Picture. You then get to select one of your own pictures to appear on the sign-in screen. When you're satisfied with your selection, click Use This Picture.

On the next screen that appears, you specify the gestures you'll use to sign in. Your "password" must consist of three gestures. Upon successful entry of your gestures, click Finish.

To sign in with a picture password, on the sign-in screen you must perform the same three gestures: same order, same location, and same direction. You don't need to be *that* precise; Windows allows minor variations in location.

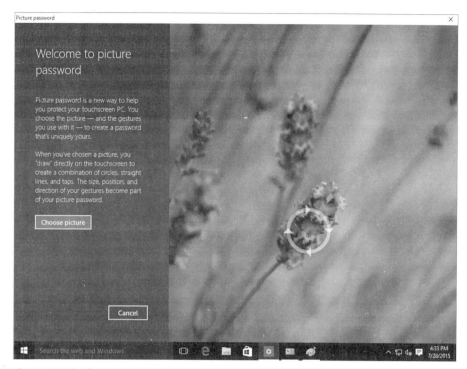

Figure 6-5 The first screen that appears when you set up a picture password explains how it works.

Using Windows Hello for biometric sign-ins

With the proper hardware, you can sign in simply by swiping your fingerprint or, even easier, showing your face in front of your computer's camera. When Windows Hello recognizes a fingerprint, face, or iris, it greets you by briefly displaying your name and a smiley face on the sign-in screen (as shown in Figure 6-6) before going to your desktop.

To use Windows Hello for biometric sign-ins, you need one of the following:

- A fingerprint reader that supports the Window Biometric Framework

- An illuminated 3-D infrared camera such as the Intel RealSense camera that is installed on some computers delivered in 2015 or later; a standard webcam will not work because it could easily be spoofed

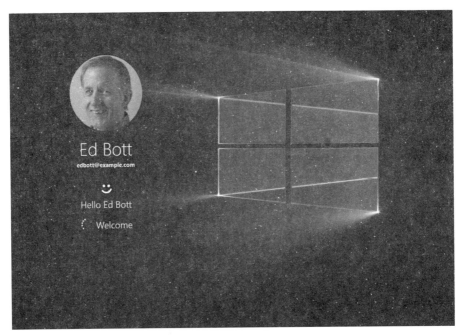

Figure 6-6 Windows Hello greets you, of course, by saying "Hello."

NOTE
You must add a PIN as described earlier in this chapter before you can use Windows Hello.

To set up Windows Hello, go to the Sign-In Options page in Settings, Accounts. Under Windows Hello, click Set Up for the biometric device you want to use. Windows asks you to enter your PIN to verify your identity. After that, you need to enter your biometric data. To be sure it's getting a good read, Windows asks you to scan several times, as shown in Figure 6-7.

If you are setting up fingerprint scanning, you can enroll additional fingers (so that you don't have to be particular about using the same finger all the time) by clicking Add Another after you complete registration for a fingerprint. (To add another fingerprint later, return to Settings, Accounts, Sign-In Options and click Add Another.) You can also associate an additional fingerprint with a different user account on the same device. Sign in to the alternate account and set up the second fingerprint there. When you restart, you can choose your account by choosing the fingerprint associated with that account.

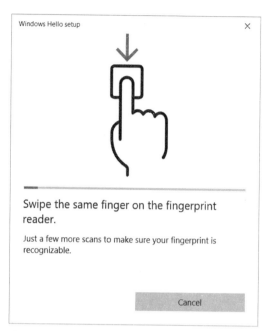

Windows Hello setup   ×

Swipe the same finger on the fingerprint
reader.

Just a few more scans to make sure your fingerprint is
recognizable.

Cancel

Figure 6-7 Setup for Windows Hello guides you through the brief process of scanning and storing your biometric data.

Signing out, switching accounts, or locking your computer

When you're finished using your computer, you want to be sure that you don't leave it in a condition in which others can use your credentials to access your files. To do that, you need to sign out, switch accounts, or lock your computer:

- **Sign Out.** With this option, all your programs close and the lock screen appears.

- **Switch Account.** With this option, your programs continue to run. The sign-in screen appears, ready for the sign-in credentials of the person you select. Your account is still signed in, but only you can return to your own session, which you can do when the user you switch to chooses to sign out, switch accounts, or lock the computer.

- **Lock.** With this option, your programs continue to run, but the lock screen appears so that no one can see your desktop or use the computer. Only you can unlock the computer to return to your session; however, other users can sign in to their own sessions without disturbing yours.

To sign out, switch accounts, or lock your computer, open the Start menu and click or tap your name at the top of the menu to display a menu like the one shown in Figure 6-8.

Figure 6-8 On a computer that's joined to a domain, Switch Account appears instead of individual account names. You can then enter an account name on the sign-in screen.

INSIDE OUT

Use keyboard shortcuts

To lock your computer, you can press Windows key+L. (You might also find it more convenient to use this shortcut for switching accounts; the only difference is that it takes you to the lock screen instead of to the sign-in screen.)

For any of these actions—sign out, switch accounts, or lock—you can start by pressing Ctrl+Alt+Delete, which displays a menu that includes all three options.

Sharing your PC with other users

Whether you're setting up a computer for your family to use at home or to be used in a business, it's prudent to set it up securely. Doing so helps to protect each user's data from inadvertent deletions and changes as well as malicious damage and theft. When you set up your computer, consider these suggestions:

- **Control who can sign in.** Create accounts only for users who need to use your computer's resources, either by signing in locally or over a network. Delete or disable other accounts (except the built-in accounts created by Windows).

- **Change all user accounts except one to standard accounts.** You'll need one administrative account for installing programs, creating and managing accounts, and so on. All other accounts can run with standard privileges.

- **Be sure that all accounts are password protected.** This is especially important for administrator accounts and for other accounts whose profiles contain important or sensitive documents. You might not want to set a password on your toddler's local account, but all other accounts should be protected from the possibility that the tyke (or your cat) will accidentally tap the wrong name on the sign-in screen.

- **Restrict sign-in times.** You might want to limit the computing hours for some users. The easiest way for home users to do this is with Microsoft Family; for details, see "Controlling your children's computer access" later in this chapter.

- **Restrict access to certain files.** You'll want to be sure that some files are available to all users, whereas other files are available only to the person who created them. The Public folder and a user's personal folders provide a general framework for this protection. You can further refine your file-protection scheme by selectively applying permissions to varying combinations of files, folders, and users.

Adding a user to your computer

To allow another user to sign in on your computer, you must add them through Settings, Accounts. Go to the Family & Other Users page, shown in Figure 6-9, which has separate controls for adding members of your family and adding "other users." The difference is that family members are subject to restrictions that an adult member of the family can specify (for details, see "Controlling your children's computer access" later in this chapter), whereas other users have full use of the computer (subject, of course, to limitations imposed by their account type).

NOTE
The Family & Other Users page is available only when you sign in with an administrator account.

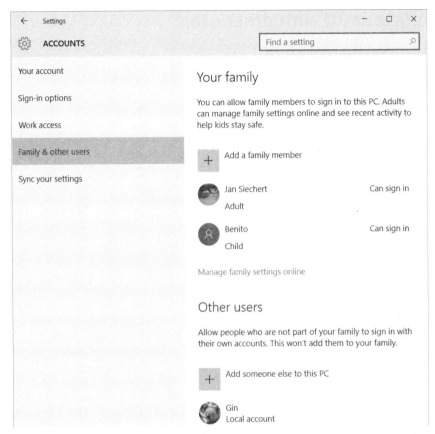

Figure 6-9 Under Other Users, you can add a local account or a Microsoft account. Family members must have a Microsoft account.

To add a user who's not a family member, under Other Users click Add Someone Else To This PC. Windows then asks for the email address of the new user. If the email address is already associated with a Microsoft account, all you need to do is click Next and the new user is ready to go. (The first time the new user signs in, the computer must be connected to the Internet.) If the email address you provide is not associated with a Microsoft account, Windows provides a link to sign up for a new Microsoft account. (Clearly, Windows tries to steer you toward using a Microsoft account at every opportunity.)

What if you want to add a local account? At the first screen—when Windows asks for an email address—instead click the link near the bottom: The Person I Want To Add Doesn't Have An Email Address. In the next dialog box that appears, shown next, Windows offers to set up a new Microsoft account.

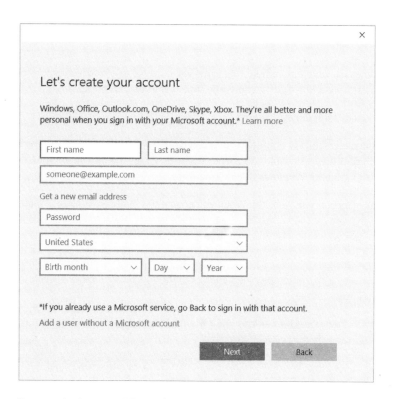

But you don't want a Microsoft account! Look to the bottom of the window, and click Add A User Without A Microsoft Account. Windows then asks you to specify a user name and password for the new user. (If your computer has only local accounts set up, you go directly to this final dialog box, skipping the two that guide you toward a Microsoft account.) Click Next, and your work is done.

Controlling your children's computer access

Previous versions of Windows had a feature called Parental Controls (Windows Vista and Windows 7) or Family Safety (Windows 8), which allowed parents to restrict and monitor their children's computer use. Windows 10 offers similar capabilities, but the implementation is completely different. Those earlier versions stored their settings on your PC, but in Windows 10 family settings are now stored and managed as part of your Microsoft account.

This architectural change has some obvious benefits:

- You don't need to make settings for each child on each computer. After you add a family member on one PC, you manage the settings for each child in the cloud, and those settings apply to all the family PCs where they sign in.

- You can manage your children's computer use from any computer that's connected to the Internet.

Family settings has one requirement that some will perceive as a disadvantage: each family member must have a Microsoft account and sign in with that account.

What can you do with family settings?

- Monitor each child's computer use. You can see what they search for on the web and which sites they visit, which apps and games they use, and how much time they are signed in to each Windows 10 computer they use.

- Block inappropriate websites. When you enable this feature, Microsoft-curated lists of sites that are blocked or explicitly allowed are used by default, but you can supplement these lists with sites that you want to always block or always allow.

- Control each child's use of apps and games. Based on age ratings, you can limit the apps and games a child can download and purchase. You can also block specific apps and games from running.

- Restrict when your children can use the computer, and for how long. Figure 6-10 shows how you specify the hours of use.

At the time of the initial Windows 10 release in mid-2015, family settings features were still in development. By the time you read this, family settings might include changes to the preceding features as well as some additional features. Visit *account.microsoft.com/family* to see the newest adaptation.

To get started with family settings, open Settings, Accounts and click Family & Other Users. (See Figure 6-9.)

> ### NOTE
> **To see the Your Family section of the Family & Other Users page, you must sign in with a Microsoft account, and your account type must be administrator.**

Then click Add A Family Member. Windows asks whether you want to add an account for an adult or a child; the difference is that an adult can manage family settings, whereas a child is controlled by family settings.

You then enter the family member's email address, and if a Microsoft account is not associated with that address, Windows gathers the needed information to set one up. Unlike when you add an "other user," there is no option to use a local account.

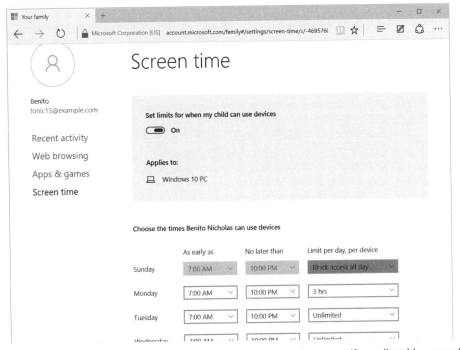

Figure 6-10 With Screen Time settings, for each day of the week you specify an allowable range of times for a child's computer use, plus an overall limit on the amount of computer time.

After you select a Microsoft account for the new family member, Microsoft Family sends an email invitation to that person. The new family member can sign in to your computer right away, but family settings take effect only after he or she opens the email message and clicks the Accept Invitation button. (Until that happens, the word *Pending* appears next to the family member's name on the Family & Other Users page.)

TROUBLESHOOTING

The email invitation never arrives

Despite repeated attempts on your part to use the Family & Other Users page, some-times the invitation isn't sent. To get around this, click **Manage Family Settings Online** (alternatively, browse to *account.microsoft.com/family*). On the webpage that appears, click the **Add** button for a child or an adult.

To view or change settings for child accounts, and to add or remove members from your family (adult or child), on the Family & Other Users page click Manage Family Settings Online. If you (as an adult) use a standard account rather than an administrator account, you won't see the Family & Other Users page. You can, however, still manage family settings. On the Your Account page in Settings, Accounts, click Manage My Microsoft Account. On the webpage that appears, click the Family tab. (If no tabs appear at the top of the page, click the hamburger menu—the icon with three horizontal lines—and choose Family.)

Note that when you sign in to one of your other computers, your family's accounts are already in place; you don't need to add family members on each device. However, by default the other family members cannot sign in to these other devices. To enable access, click the name of the family member and then click Allow.

Restricting use with assigned access

Assigned access is a rather odd feature that allows you to configure your computer so that a certain user (one you've already added to your computer) can run only a single modern app. When that user signs in, the specified app starts automatically and runs full-screen. The user can't close the app or start any others. In fact, the only way out is to press Ctrl+Alt+Delete (or press the Windows button and power button simultaneously), which signs out the user and returns to the sign-in screen.

The use cases for this feature are limited, but here are a few examples:

- A kiosk app for public use

- A point-of-sale app for your business

- A game for a very young child

If you can think of a use for this feature, click Set Up Assigned Access, at the bottom of the Family & Other Users page.

Introducing access control in Windows

The Windows approach to security is discretionary: each securable system resource—each file or printer, for example—has an owner who has discretion over who can and cannot access the resource. Usually, a resource is owned by the user who creates it. If you create a file, for example, you are the file's owner under ordinary circumstances. (Computer administrators, however, can take ownership of resources they didn't create.)

NOTE

To exercise full discretionary control over individual files, you must store those files on an NTFS volume. For the sake of compatibility, Windows 10 supports the FAT and FAT32 file systems used by early Windows versions and many USB flash drives, as well as the exFAT file system used on some removable drives. However, none of the FAT-based file systems support file permissions. To enjoy the full benefits of Windows security, you must use NTFS. For more information about file systems, see "Choosing a file system" in Chapter 14, "Managing disks and drives."

What are security identifiers?

Windows security relies on the use of a security identifier (SID) to identify a user. When you create a user account on your computer (local account or Microsoft account), Windows assigns a unique SID to that account. The SID remains uniquely associated with that user account until the account is deleted, whereupon the SID is never used again—for that user or any other user. Even if you re-create an account with identical information, a new SID is created.

A SID is a variable-length value that contains a revision level, a 48-bit identifier authority value, and a number of 32-bit subauthority values. The SID takes the form S-1-x-y1-y2- .... S-1 identifies it as a revision 1 SID; x is the value for the identifier authority; and y1, y2, and so on are values for subauthorities.

You'll sometimes see a SID in a security dialog box (for example, on the Security tab of a file's properties dialog box) before Windows has had time to look up the user account name. You'll also spot SIDs in the hidden and protected $RECYCLE.BIN folder (each SID you see in this folder represents the Recycle Bin for a particular user) and in the registry (the HKEY_USERS hive contains a key, identified by SID, for each user account on the computer), among other places. The easiest way to determine your own SID is with the Whoami command-line utility. For details, see the following tip.

Not all SIDs are unique (although the SID assigned to your user account is always unique). A number of commonly used SIDs are constant among all Windows installations. For example, S-1-5-18 is the SID for the built-in Local System account, a hidden member of the Administrators group that is used by the operating system and by services that sign in using the Local System account. You can find a complete list of such SIDs, called well-known SIDs, in Microsoft Knowledge Base article 243330 (*w7io.com/1601*).

To determine which users have access to a resource, Windows assigns a security identifier (SID) to each user account. Your SID (a gigantic number guaranteed to be unique) follows you around wherever you go in Windows. When you sign in, the operating system first validates your user name and password. Then it creates a security access token. You can think of this as the electronic equivalent of an ID badge. It includes your user name and SID, plus information about any security groups to which your account belongs. (Security groups are described later in this chapter.) Any program you start gets a copy of your security access token.

Inside OUT
Learn about your own account with Whoami

Windows includes a command-line utility called Whoami (Who Am I?). You can use Whoami to find out the name of the account that's currently signed in, its SID, the names of the security groups of which it's a member, and its privileges. To use Whoami, open a Command Prompt window. (You don't need elevated privileges.)

Then, to learn the name of the signed-in user, type **whoami**. (This is particularly useful if you're signed in as a standard user but running an elevated Command Prompt window—when it might not be obvious which account is currently "you.") If you're curious about your SID, type **whoami /user**. For a complete list of Whoami parameters, type **whoami /?**.

With User Account Control (UAC) turned on, administrators who sign in get two security access tokens—one that has the privileges of a standard user and one that has the full privileges of an administrator.

Whenever you attempt to walk through a controlled "door" in Windows (for example, when you connect to a shared printer), or any time a program attempts to do so on your behalf, the operating system examines your security access token and decides whether to let you pass. If access is permitted, you notice nothing. If access is denied, you get to hear a beep and read a refusal message.

In determining whom to let pass and whom to block, Windows consults the resource's access control list (ACL). This is simply a list of SIDs and the access privileges associated with each one. Every resource subject to access control has an ACL. This manner of allowing and blocking access to resources such as files and printers is essentially unchanged since Windows NT.

What are ACLs?

Each folder and each file on an NTFS-formatted volume has an ACL (also known as DACL, for discretionary access control list, and commonly called NTFS permissions). An ACL comprises an access control entry (ACE) for each user who is allowed access to the folder or file. With NTFS permissions, you can control access to any file or folder, allowing different types of access for different users or groups of users.

To view and edit NTFS permissions for a file or folder, right-click its icon and choose Properties. The Security tab lists all the groups and users with permissions set for the selected object, as shown here. Different permissions can be set for each user, as you can see by selecting each one.

To make changes to the settings for any user or group in the list, or to add or remove a user or group in the list, click Edit. (Use caution. Setting NTFS permissions without understanding the full consequences can lead to unexpected and unwelcome results, including a complete loss of access to files and folders. Before you delve into the inner workings of NTFS permissions on the Security tab, be sure to try the safer and less complicated homegroup sharing or the Share With command. For details, see "Sharing files, digital media, and printers in a homegroup" in Chapter 5 and "Sharing files and folders from any folder" in Chapter 20.)

The access granted by each permission type is as follows:

- **Full Control.** Users with Full Control can list contents of a folder, read and open files, create new files, delete files and subfolders, change permissions on files and subfolders, and take ownership of files.

- **Modify.** Allows the user to read, change, create, and delete files but not to change permissions or take ownership of files.

- **Read & Execute.** Allows the user to view files and execute programs.

- **List Folder Contents.** Provides the same permissions as Read & Execute but can be applied only to folders.

- **Read.** Allows the user to list the contents of a folder, read file attributes, read permissions, and synchronize files.

- **Write.** Allows the user to create files, write data, read attributes and permissions, and synchronize files.

- **Special Permissions.** The assigned permissions don't match any of the preceding permission descriptions. To see precisely which permissions are granted, click Advanced.

UAC, which was introduced in Windows Vista, adds another layer of restrictions based on user accounts. With UAC turned on, applications are normally launched using an administrator's standard user token. (Standard users, of course, have only a standard user token.) If an application requires administrator privileges, UAC asks for your consent (if you're signed in as an administrator) or the credentials of an administrator (if you're signed in as a standard user) before letting the application run. With UAC turned off, Windows works in the same (rather dangerous) manner as pre–Windows Vista versions: administrator accounts can do just about anything (sometimes getting those users in trouble), and standard accounts don't have the privileges needed to run many older programs.

➤ For more information about UAC, see "Preventing unsafe actions with User Account Control" in Chapter 7.

Permissions and rights

Windows distinguishes two types of access privileges: permissions and rights. A permission is the ability to access a particular object in some defined manner—for example, to write to an NTFS file or to modify a printer queue. A right is the ability to perform a particular system-wide action, such as signing in or resetting the clock.

The owner of a resource (or an administrator) assigns permissions to the resource via its properties dialog box. For example, if you are the printer owner or have administrative privileges, you can restrict someone from using a particular printer by visiting the properties dialog box for that printer. Administrators set rights via the Local Security Policy console. For example, an administrator could grant someone the right to install a device driver. (The Local Security Policy console is available only in the Pro and Enterprise editions of Windows 10. In the Home edition, rights for various security groups are predefined and unchangeable.)

> ## NOTE
> In this book, as in many of the Windows messages and dialog boxes, *privileges* serves as an informal term encompassing both permissions and rights.

User accounts and security groups

The backbone of Windows security is the ability to uniquely identify each user. While setting up a computer—or at any later time—an administrator creates a user account for each user. The user account is identified by a user name and is normally secured by a password, which the user provides when signing in to the system. Windows then controls, monitors, and restricts access to system resources on the basis of the permissions and rights associated with each user account by the resource owners and the system administrator.

Account type is a simplified way of describing membership in a security group, a collection of user accounts. Windows classifies each user account as one of two account types:

- **Administrator.** Members of the Administrators group are classified as administrator accounts. By default, the Administrators group includes the first account you create when you set up the computer and an account named Administrator that is disabled and hidden by default. Unlike other account types, administrators have full control over the system. Among the tasks that only administrators can perform are the following:

    - Create, change, and delete user accounts and groups
    - Install and uninstall desktop programs

- Configure automatic updating with Windows Update
- Install an ActiveX control
- Install or remove hardware device drivers
- Share folders
- Set permissions
- Access all files, including those in another user's folder
- Take ownership of files
- Copy or move files into the %ProgramFiles% or %SystemRoot% folders
- Restore backed-up system files
- Grant rights to other user accounts and to themselves
- Configure Windows Firewall

- **Standard user.** Members of the Users group are classified as standard user accounts. A partial list of tasks available to standard user accounts includes

  - Change the password and picture for their own user account
  - Use desktop programs that have been installed on the computer
  - Install system and driver updates using Windows Update
  - Install and run modern apps from the Windows Store
  - Install approved ActiveX controls
  - Configure a secure Wi-Fi connection
  - Refresh a network adapter and the system's IP address
  - View permissions
  - Create, change, and delete files in their document folders and in shared document folders
  - Restore their own backed-up files
  - View the system clock and calendar, and change the time zone
  - Set personalization options, such as themes, desktop background, and so on
  - Select a display dots-per-inch (DPI) setting to adjust text size
  - Configure power options
  - Sign in in Safe Mode
  - View Windows Firewall settings

Assigning an appropriate account type to the people who use your computer is straightforward. At least one user must be an administrator; naturally, that should be the person who administers the computer. All other regular users should each have a standard user account.

What happened to the Administrator account?

Every computer running Windows has a special account named Administrator. In versions of Windows before Windows 7, Administrator was the primary account for managing the computer. Like other administrator accounts, the Administrator account has full rights over the entire computer. But in Windows 10, the Administrator account is disabled by default.

In Windows 10, there's seldom a need to use the Administrator account instead of another administrator account. With default settings in Windows, the Administrator account does have one unique capability: it's not subject to UAC, even when UAC is turned on for all other users. All other administrator accounts (which are sometimes called Protected Administrator accounts) run with standard-user privileges unless the user consents to elevation. The Administrator account runs with full administrative privileges at all times and never needs your consent for elevation. (For this reason, of course, it's rather risky. Any application that runs as Administrator has full control of the computer—which means applications written by malicious or incompetent programmers can do significant damage to your system.)

Inside OUT

And the Guest account?

Historically, the built-in Guest account has provided a way to offer limited access to occasional users. Not so in Windows 10. Although this account still exists, it is disabled by default, and the supported tools for enabling it (the Local Users And Groups console, for example) do not work as expected. In our experience, trying to trick Windows 10 into enabling this capability is almost certain to end in frustration. In the cloud-centric world of Windows 10, the Guest account no longer works as it used to and enabling it can cause a variety of problems. A better solution (if your guests don't have their own device that can connect to your wireless network) is to set up a standard account for guest use.

Security groups allow a system administrator to create classes of users who share common privileges. For example, if everyone in the accounting department needs access to the Payables folder, the administrator can create a group called Accounting and grant the entire group access to that folder. If the administrator then adds all user accounts belonging to employees in the accounting department to the Accounting group, these users will automatically have access to the Payables folder. A user account can belong to one group, more than one group, or no group at all.

In large networks based on Active Directory domains, groups can be a valuable administrative tool. They simplify the job of ensuring that all members with common access needs have an identical set of privileges. We don't recommend creating or using groups other than the built-in Administrators and Users groups on standalone and workgroup-based computers, however.

Permissions and rights for group members are cumulative. That means that if a user account belongs to more than one group, the user enjoys all of the privileges accorded to all groups of which the user account is a member.

Managing and securing your credentials

When you sign in to a password-protected website using Microsoft Edge, the browser asks if you want it to save your user name and password. You might've wondered where Edge stores those credentials. You'll find the answer in Credential Manager, a Control Panel app that is shown in Figure 6-11.

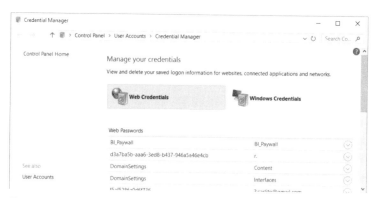

Figure 6-11 To see the details for a credential, click it to expand the entry.

To use Credential Manager, in the search box begin typing **credential** until Credential Manager appears; click it to open the app. Here you can see which credentials have been saved, view the details of each one (including the password for web credentials), and remove credentials you no longer need. Click Windows Credentials to display a list of network-related credentials. On this page, you can also add, back up, and restore credentials.

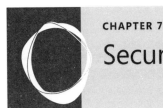

Securing Windows 10 devices

We don't mean to be scaremongers, but they *are* out to get you. Computer attacks continue to increase in number and severity each year. And while the big data breaches—the loss of millions of credit card numbers from a major retailer or the loss of millions of personnel records from the U.S. government—command the most media attention, don't think that the bad guys wouldn't like to get into your computer too. Whether it's to steal your valuable personal data, appropriate your computing resources and bandwidth, or use your PC as a pathway into a bigger target with whom you do business, there are plenty of actors with bad intent.

According to the 2015 Internet Security Threat Report, published by Symantec, 60 percent of all targeted attacks struck small and medium-sized organizations. Like individuals, these organizations often don't have the resources to invest in security—making them juicy targets.

In this chapter, we examine the types of threats you're likely to face at home and at work. More importantly, we describe some of the more significant security improvements made in Windows 10—many of which are in layers you can't see, such as hardware-based protection that operates before Windows loads. Then we explain how to use the more visible security features, including Windows Firewall, User Account Control, BitLocker, and Windows Defender.

Understanding security threats

A decade ago, the threat landscape for Windows users was dominated by viruses and worms. Ah, for the good old days! The modern threat landscape is much more complex and, unfortunately, more insidious. Today, an attacker is likely to be part of an organized crime ring, not an attention-seeking vandal, and attacks are typically designed to go unnoticed for as long as possible.

A rogue program, installed without your knowledge and running without your awareness, can perform malicious tasks and transfer data without your consent. This category of software is often referred to as *malware*.

The goal of the bad guys is to get you to run their software. They might, for example, convince you to install a *Trojan*—a program that appears legitimate but actually performs malicious actions when it's installed. This category of malware doesn't spread on its own but instead uses social engineering (often using popular social networking sites such as Facebook and Twitter) to convince its victims to cooperate in the installation process. As part of its payload, a Trojan can include a downloader that installs additional malicious and unwanted programs. Some Trojans install a "backdoor" that allows an outside attacker to remotely control the infected computer.

What's in it for the bad guys? Money, mostly, gathered in a variety of ways, depending on how the attackers got through your defenses.

A *password stealer* runs in the background, gathers user names and passwords, and forwards them to an outside attacker. The stolen credentials can then be used to make purchases, clean out bank accounts, or commit identity theft.

Bad guys prey on fear with rogue security software (also known as *scareware*), which mimics the actions and appearance of legitimate antivirus software. If you install one of these programs, it inevitably reports the presence of a (nonexistent) virus and offers to remove it—for a fee, of course.

In 2015, the fastest rising star in the malware hall of shame is *ransomware*, a form of digital blackmail in which a program encrypts all your data files and offers to unlock them only upon payment of a ransom.

Phishing attacks, which use social engineering to convince visitors to give away their sign-in credentials, are a separate but potentially devastating avenue to identity theft that can strike in any browser using any operating system.

You can review lists of current malware threats, along with links to details about each one, at the Microsoft Malware Protection Center, *w7io.com/1518*. For a more comprehensive view of the changing threat landscape, the Microsoft Malware Protection Center issues a twice-yearly report, using data from hundreds of millions of Windows users and other sources. You'll find the latest Microsoft Security Intelligence Report at *w7io.com/1501*.

Securing your computer: A defense-in-depth strategy

A multidimensional threat landscape requires a multilayered approach to protecting your PC and your network. The big picture goal is to secure your device, secure your data, secure your identity, and block malware. On a home or small business network, those layers of security include the following:

Use a hardware router to protect your broadband connection. This is an essential part of physical security, even if your network consists of a single PC. We provide an overview of the technology in "Getting started with Windows 10 networking" in Chapter 5, "Networking essentials."

Enable a software firewall and keep it turned on. You can use Windows Firewall, which is included with Windows 10, or a firewall that you obtain elsewhere. To learn more, see "Blocking intruders with Windows Firewall" later in this chapter.

Use biometric sign-in. Biometric sign-in using a fingerprint reader or facial recognition with Windows Hello offers much more than convenience. Because biometric sign-in is linked to a specific device, it provides effective two-factor authentication. If you don't have the necessary hardware, use a PIN or picture password for sign-in—both of which can be more secure than a traditional password. For more information, see "Managing the sign-in process" in Chapter 6, "Managing user accounts, passwords, and credentials."

Set up standard user accounts and keep User Account Control enabled. Standard accounts help to prevent (or at least minimize) the damage that an untrained user can do by installing untrusted programs. User Account Control (UAC) helps in this regard by restricting access to administrative tasks and virtualizing registry and file-system changes. For details, see "Introducing access control in Windows" in Chapter 6 and "Preventing unsafe actions with User Account Control" later in this chapter.

Keep Windows and vulnerable programs up to date. Windows Update handles this chore for Windows, Office, and other Microsoft programs. You're on your own for third-party programs. We provide an overview of security updates in "Staying on top of security updates" later in this chapter.

Use an antimalware program and keep it up to date. Windows Defender, which is included with Windows 10, provides antimalware protection, but many third-party solutions are also available. For details, see "Using Windows Defender to block malware" later in this chapter.

Protect yourself from threats in email messages. At a minimum, your email solution should block or quarantine executable files and other potentially dangerous attachments. In addition, effective antispam features can block scripts and prevent phishing attempts.

Use parental controls to keep kids safe. If you have children who use your computer, family safety features in Windows can help you keep them away from security threats. It also includes options you can use to restrict their computer activities in other ways. For details, see "Controlling your children's computer access" in Chapter 6.

Security And Maintenance, a Control Panel app, monitors many of these areas to be sure you're protected, and it displays an alert if something needs attention. For details, see "Monitoring your computer's security" later in this chapter.

The most important protective layer—and the one that is most easily overlooked—is user education and self-control. Everyone who uses a computer must have the discipline to read and evaluate security warnings when they're presented and to allow the installation only of software that is known to be safe. (Although a user with a standard account can't install or run a program that wipes out the entire computer, he can still inflict enough damage on his own user profile to cause considerable inconvenience.) Countless successful malware attacks worldwide have proven that many users do not have adequate awareness of safe computing methods.

What's new in Windows 10

Because the bad guys are always upping their game, a hallmark of each new version of Windows is a number of new and improved security features. Windows 10 is no exception. Here we enumerate changes available in Windows 10 Home and Windows 10 Pro; several additional features are included with Windows 10 Enterprise on a managed network.

Securing devices

Security features in Windows 10 begin with support for modern hardware designs. Although Windows 10 continues to support legacy hardware, some security features require two elements built in to most newer computers:

- **Unified Extensible Firmware Interface (UEFI).** UEFI is a firmware interface that replaces the BIOS, which has been a part of every PC since the beginning of personal computing. Among other improvements, UEFI enables Secure Boot and Device Encryption, features that are described in the following pages. PCs designed for Windows 8 and later must use UEFI.

- **Trusted Platform Module (TPM).** A TPM is a hardware chip that facilitates encryption and prevents altering or exporting encryption keys and certificates. With a TPM, BitLocker Drive Encryption (described later in this chapter) is more convenient to use as well as more secure. Other security features in Windows 10, such as Measured Boot and Device Guard, require the presence of a TPM.

With UEFI and TPM in place, Windows 10 is able to secure the boot process. (Many recent malware attacks take control of the system early in the boot process, before Windows is fully running and before antimalware programs spring into action. This type of malware is called a *rootkit*.) The Windows 10 boot process steps through the following features:

- **Secure Boot.** Secure Boot, a basic feature of UEFI, prevents the use of any alternative operating system (OS) loader. Only an OS loader that is digitally signed using a certificate stored by UEFI is allowed to run. (A conventional BIOS allows interruption of the boot process to use any OS loader, including one that's been corrupted.)

- **Early Launch Antimalware (ELAM).** Antimalware software—including compatible third-party programs as well as Windows Defender—that has been certified and signed by Microsoft loads its drivers before any other third-party drivers or programs. This allows the antimalware software to detect and block attempts to load malicious code.

- **Measured Boot.** Measurements of the UEFI firmware and each Windows component are taken as they load. The measurements are then digitally signed and stored in the TPM, where they can't be changed. During subsequent boots, measurements are compared against the stored measurements.

Securing data

The increased mobility of PCs also increases the risk of theft. Losing a computer is bad enough, but handing over all the data you've stored on the computer is by far the greater loss. Windows 10 includes new features to ensure the thief can't get your data.

- **Device encryption.** On devices that support InstantGo, data on the operating system volume is encrypted by default. (Formerly called Connected Standby, InstantGo is a Microsoft hardware specification that enables advanced power-management capabilities. Among other requirements, InstantGo devices must boot from a solid state drive.) The encryption initially uses a clear key, but when a local administrator first signs in with a Microsoft account, the volume is automatically encrypted. A recovery key is stored at *onedrive.com/recoverykey*; you'll need it if you reinstall the operating system or move the drive to a new PC.

- **BitLocker Drive Encryption.** BitLocker Drive Encryption offers similar (but stronger) whole-volume encryption, and on corporate networks it allows centralized management. In Windows 10, BitLocker encrypts drives more quickly than in previous Windows versions; additional speed comes from the new ability to encrypt only the part of a volume in use. For more information, see "Encrypting with BitLocker and BitLocker To Go" later in this chapter.

Securing identities

It seems like every week we hear about another data breach where millions of user names and passwords have been stolen. There's a thriving market for this type of information because it enables the thieves to sign in anywhere using your credentials. Furthermore, because many people use the same password for different accounts, criminals can often use the stolen information to hack into a theft victim's other accounts. Windows 10 marks the beginning of the end of passwords.

- **Windows Hello.** With Windows 10, enterprise-grade two-factor authentication is built in. After enrolling a device with an authentication service, the device itself becomes one factor; the second factor is a PIN or a biometric, such as a fingerprint, facial recognition, or an iris scan.

- **Microsoft Passport.** After Windows Hello signs you in, Microsoft Passport enables sign-in to networks and web services. Your biometric data remains securely stored in your computer's TPM; it's not sent over the network.

With this combination of authentication methods, an attacker who has a trove of user names and passwords is stymied. To unlock Microsoft Passport (and, by extension, gain the ability to sign in to your web services), he needs the enrolled device. And a thief who steals your computer needs your PIN or biometric data. Active Directory, Azure Active Directory, and Microsoft Accounts support this new form of credentials; other services are sure to follow.

For more information about Windows Hello, see "Managing the sign-in process" in Chapter 6.

Blocking malware

Since the days of Windows 7, several features that block malicious software have been beefed up:

- **Address Space Layout Randomization (ASLR).** ASLR is a feature that randomizes the location of program code and other data in memory, making it difficult to execute attacks that write directly to system memory because the malware can't find the memory location it needs. In Windows 10, memory locations are scrambled even more. And because the randomization is unique to each device, a successful attack on one device won't work on another.

- **Data Execution Prevention (DEP).** DEP is a hardware feature that marks blocks of memory so that they can store data but not execute program instructions. Windows 10 can't be installed on a system that doesn't support DEP.

- **Windows Defender.** In Windows 7, Windows Defender is a lightweight antispyware program. But starting with Windows 8 and continuing in Windows 10, Windows Defender includes the well-regarded antimalware capabilities of Windows Security Essentials, a free add-on for Windows 7. Windows Defender supports ELAM, described earlier in this chapter, which means that it can defend against rootkits that attempt to co-opt the boot process. For more information, see "Using Windows Defender to block malware" later in this chapter.

- **SmartScreen.** The goal of SmartScreen, introduced in Windows 7, is similar to that of Windows Defender: stop malicious code from running, which is much better than trying to clean up the damage after the fact. But SmartScreen takes a completely different approach: instead of looking for signatures of known bad programs, it checks a hash of each executable downloaded from an online source against Microsoft's application-reputation database. Files that have established a positive reputation are deemed safe and are allowed to run, whereas files with a negative reputation are blocked.

  In Windows 7, SmartScreen is a feature of Internet Explorer and checks files as they are downloaded. Beginning with Windows 8, SmartScreen is an integral part of Windows (and continues to be a feature of Internet Explorer and, in Windows 10, Microsoft Edge). Therefore, it blocks execution of unknown programs not just as you download them in a browser but any time you attempt to run a program from an online source—including those downloaded with a non-Microsoft browser.

Monitoring your computer's security

In Windows 10, security-related options have been gathered in Security And Maintenance in Control Panel, shown in Figure 7-1. (Veteran users of Windows 7 and Windows 8 will recognize this as the new name for what was called Action Center in those earlier operating systems. In Windows 10, *Action Center* refers to the list of notifications and buttons that can appear on the right side of the screen.) You can open Security And Maintenance from Control Panel or Settings: In the search box of either app, type **security** and then click Security And Maintenance. (No keyboard? Open Control Panel, tap System And Security, and then tap Security And Maintenance.)

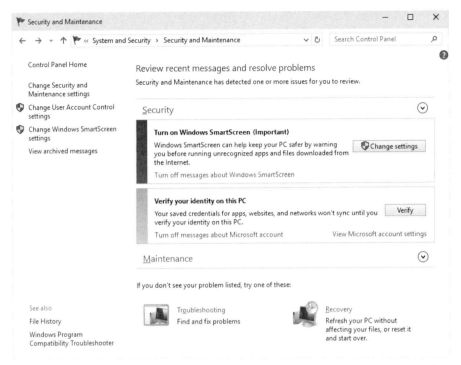

Figure 7-1 Security And Maintenance collects security, maintenance, and troubleshooting information and settings in a single window.

The Security section in Security And Maintenance provides at-a-glance information about your security settings. Items that need your attention have a red or yellow bar, as shown in Figure 7-1. A red bar identifies important items that need immediate attention, such as detection of a virus or spyware or that no firewall is enabled. A yellow bar denotes informational messages about suboptimal, but less critical, settings or status. Next to the bar appear explanatory text and buttons that let you correct the problem (or configure Security And Maintenance so that it won't bother you).

If all is well, the Security category is collapsed and you see nothing in that category when you open Security And Maintenance. Click the arrow to expand the category, and you'll see all the security-related items that Security And Maintenance monitors, as shown in Figure 7-2.

Click to display programs of same type

Figure 7-2 When multiple firewall programs are installed, you can click a link to show a list like this one. Use the Turn On button to enable a program that is currently disabled.

Security And Maintenance is designed to work with third-party firewall, antivirus, and anti-spyware programs, as well as with the programs built in to Windows (Windows Firewall and Windows Defender). Systems with more than one program installed in any of these categories include a link to show a list of such programs. For example, Figure 7-2 shows a system on which Norton Security is installed. The dialog box that appears when you click the link to view installed programs allows you to turn on any installed program that is currently turned off.

If you don't want to be bothered with alerts from Security And Maintenance about one or more security features, click Change Security And Maintenance Settings. After clearing items you don't want monitored in the dialog box shown in Figure 7-3, you won't receive any further alerts, and thereafter Security And Maintenance passively indicates the status as Currently Not Monitored.

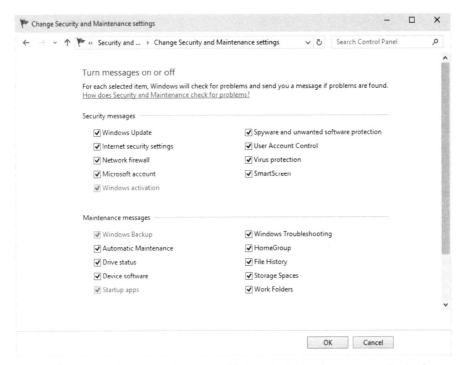

Figure 7-3 You can selectively disable and enable Security And Maintenance monitoring here, or you can manage monitored items individually by clicking links in the main Security And Maintenance window.

Staying on top of security updates

As we noted earlier in this chapter, Microsoft continues to beef up security in Windows. But as new threats emerge, the task is never done, so perhaps the most important step in keeping your system secure is to be sure that you stay current with updates to Windows and other programs. Microsoft issues frequent updates that provide replacements for installed device drivers as well as fixes to code that has been found to be faulty. Some updates provide new features or enhanced performance, while others patch security holes.

To install updates automatically, Windows uses Windows Update. In Windows 10, you'll find Windows Update in Settings under Update & Security. For more information about Windows Update, see "Keeping Windows up to date" in Chapter 15, "System maintenance and performance."

You might be interested in knowing more about current security threats, including those that are addressed by Windows Update: What, exactly, is the threat? How serious is it? What workarounds are available? Microsoft Security Response Center publishes detailed information, in the form of a *security bulletin*, about the threat and the response. To find this information, you can take either of two routes:

- In Windows Update, click Advanced Options, and then click View Your Update History. Click the link below an item for a brief description, and in the box that pops up click the Support Info link for details. Also notice that each item in the list includes a KB (knowledge base) number. You can get detailed information about the update and the problem it addresses by going to *https://support.microsoft.com/kb/nnnnnnn/*, replacing *nnnnnnn* with the seven-digit number following "KB."

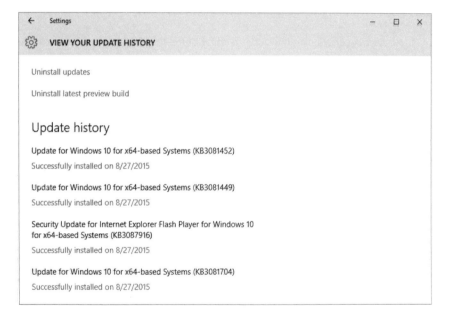

- Visit the Security Advisories and Bulletins page (*w7io.com/0702*). Here you'll find links to chronologically ordered information (most recent first) in the following formats:
  - **Security bulletin summaries.** A single document is published each month containing a complete list of security bulletins published during that month. For each bulletin in the list, you'll find a title and an executive summary, a severity rating (see the following page for more information about these ratings), a list of affected software, and a link to the bulletin.

    You can go directly to a security bulletin summary using this URL: https://technet. microsoft.com/library/security/ms*yy*-*mmm*/, replacing *yy* with the last two digits of the year (for example, use 15 for 2015) and *mmm* with the standard three-letter abbreviation for the month (for example, use "nov" for November).

- **Security bulletins.** Each bulletin contains detailed information about the issue, including a complete list—with version numbers—of software affected by the threat and, for each affected version, an assessment of the severity. Each security bulletin is assigned a name in the following format: MS*yy-nnn*, where *yy* is the last two digits of the year and *nnn* is a consecutive number that starts with 001 each year. For example, the twenty-seventh security bulletin of 2015 is called MS15-027.

  You can go directly to a security bulletin by appending the bulletin number to this URL: *https://technet.microsoft.com/library/security/*.

- **Security advisories.** Advisories describe security issues that might not require a security bulletin (and with it, a security update) but that can still affect your computer's security.

Each security bulletin includes a rating of the threat's severity. These are the four ratings that are used, listed in order of severity (most severe first):

- **Critical.** A critical vulnerability can lead to code execution with no user interaction.

- **Important.** An important vulnerability is one that can be exploited to compromise the confidentiality or integrity of your data or to cause a denial of service attack.

- **Moderate.** A moderate vulnerability is one that is usually mitigated by default settings and authentication requirements. In other words, you'd have to go a bit out of your way for one of these to damage your system or your data.

- **Low.** A vulnerability identified as low usually requires extensive interaction or an unusual configuration to cause damage.

For more information about these ratings, see "Security Bulletin Severity Rating System" at *w7io.com/0703*.

Blocking intruders with Windows Firewall

Typically, the first line of defense in securing your computer is to protect it from attacks by outsiders. Once your computer is connected to the Internet, it becomes just another node on a huge global network. A firewall provides a barrier between your computer and the network to which it's connected by preventing the entry of unwanted traffic while allowing transparent passage to authorized connections.

Using a firewall is simple, essential, and often overlooked. You'll want to be sure that all network connections are protected by a firewall. You might be comforted by the knowledge that your portable computer is protected by a corporate firewall when you're at work and that you use a firewalled broadband connection at home. But what about the public hotspots you use when you travel?

And it makes sense to run a firewall on your computer even when you're behind a residential router or corporate firewall. Other people on your network might not be as vigilant as you are about defending against viruses, so if someone brings in a portable computer infected with a worm and connects it to the network, you're toast—unless your network connection has its own firewall protection.

Windows includes a two-way, stateful-inspection, packet-filtering firewall called, cleverly enough, Windows Firewall. Windows Firewall is enabled by default for all connections, and it begins protecting your computer as it boots. The following actions take place by default:

- The firewall blocks all inbound traffic, with the exception of traffic sent in response to a request sent by your computer and unsolicited traffic that has been explicitly allowed by creating a rule.

- All outgoing traffic is allowed unless it matches a configured rule.

You notice nothing if a packet is dropped, but you can (at your option) create a log of all such events.

Using Windows Firewall with different network types

Windows Firewall maintains a separate profile (that is, a complete collection of settings, including rules for various programs, services, and ports) for each of three network types:

- **Domain.** Used when your computer is joined to an Active Directory domain. In this environment, firewall settings are typically (but not necessarily) controlled by a network administrator.

- **Private.** Used when your computer is connected to a home or work network in a workgroup configuration.

- **Guest or public.** Used when your computer is connected to a network in a public location, such as an airport or a library. It's common—indeed, recommended—to have fewer allowed programs and more restrictions when you use a public network.

If you're simultaneously connected to more than one network (for example, if you have a Wi-Fi connection to your home network while you're connected to your work domain through a virtual private network, or VPN, connection), Windows uses the appropriate profile for each connection with a feature called multiple active firewall profiles (MAFP).

You make settings in Windows Firewall independently for each network profile. The settings in a profile apply to all networks of the particular type to which you connect. (For example, if you allow a program through the firewall while connected to a public network, that program rule is then enabled whenever you connect to any other public network. It is not enabled when you're connected to a domain or private network unless you allow the program in those profiles.)

➤ For more information about network types, see "Setting network locations" in Chapter 5.

Managing Windows Firewall

Windows Firewall is a Control Panel application that provides a simple interface for monitoring firewall status and performing routine tasks, such as allowing a program through the firewall or blocking all incoming connections. To open Windows Firewall, type **firewall** in the search box or in Control Panel. Click Windows Firewall to display a window similar to the one shown in Figure 7-4.

Figure 7-4 Windows Firewall shows status and settings for each currently connected network. The Domain Networks profile appears only on computers that have been joined to a domain.

Enabling or disabling Windows Firewall

The main Windows Firewall application, shown in Figure 7-4, is little more than a status window and launch pad for making various firewall settings. The first setting of interest is to enable or disable Windows Firewall. To do that, click Turn Windows Firewall On Or Off to open the screen shown next. From here you can enable (turn on) or disable (turn off) Windows Firewall for each network type. In general, the only reason to turn off Windows Firewall is if you have installed a third-party firewall that you plan to use instead of Windows Firewall. Most of those, however, perform this task as part of their installation.

As you'll discover throughout Windows Firewall, domain network settings are available only on computers that are joined to a domain. You can make settings for all network types—even those to which you're not currently connected. Settings for the domain profile, however, are often locked down by the network administrator using Group Policy.

The Block All Incoming Connections check box in Customize Settings provides additional safety. When it's selected, Windows Firewall rejects all unsolicited incoming traffic—even traffic from allowed programs or that would ordinarily be permitted by a rule. (For information about firewall rules, see the next section, "Allowing connections through the firewall.") Invoke this mode when extra security against outside attack is needed. For example, you might block all connections when you're using a public wireless hotspot or when you know that your computer is actively under attack by others.

NOTE

Selecting Block All Incoming Connections does not disconnect your computer from the Internet. Even in this mode, you can still use your browser to connect to the Internet. Similarly, other outbound connections—whether they're legitimate services or some sort of spyware—continue unabated. If you really want to sever your ties to the outside world, open Network And Sharing Center and disable each network connection. (Alternatively, use brute force: physically disconnect wired network connections and turn off wireless adapters or access points.)

Allowing connections through the firewall

In some situations, you want to allow other computers to initiate a connection to your computer. For example, you might use Remote Desktop, play multiplayer games, or chat via an instant messaging program; these types of programs typically require inbound connections so that others can contact you.

The simplest way to enable a connection is to click Allow An App Or Feature Through Windows Firewall, a link in the left pane of the main Windows Firewall window. The list of programs and features that initially appears in Allowed Apps, shown in Figure 7-5, depends on which programs and services are installed on your computer; you can add others, as described in the following sections. In addition, program rules are created (but not enabled) when a program tries to set up an incoming connection. To allow connections for a program or service that's already been defined, simply select its check box for each network type on which you want to allow the program. (You'll need to click Change Settings before you can make changes.)

Figure 7-5 Selecting an item and clicking Details displays a description of the program or service.

In each of these cases, you enable a rule in Windows Firewall that pokes a small hole in the firewall and allows a certain type of traffic to pass through it. Each rule of this type increases your security risk to some degree, so you should clear the check box for all programs you don't need. If you're confident you won't ever need a particular program, you can select it and then click Remove. (Many of the list items included with Windows don't allow deletion, but as long as their check boxes are not selected, these apps present no danger.)

The first time you run a program that tries to set up an incoming connection, Windows Firewall asks for your permission by displaying a dialog box. You can add the program to the allowed programs list by clicking Allow Access.

When such a dialog box appears, read it carefully:

- Is the program one that you knowingly installed and ran?

- Is it reasonable for the program to require acceptance of incoming connections?

- Are you currently using a network type where it's okay for this program to accept incoming connections?

If the answer to any of these questions is no—or if you're unsure—click Cancel. If you later find that a needed program isn't working properly, you can open the allowed apps list in Windows Firewall and enable the rule.

Alternatively, you can set up the program from the Allowed Apps window shown in Figure 7-5 without waiting for a Windows Security Alert dialog box to appear. Follow these steps:

1. Click Allow Another App. The Add An App dialog box appears.

2. In Add An App, select the program for which you want to allow incoming connections. Or click Browse and navigate to the program's executable file if it isn't shown in the Apps list.

3. Click Network Types.

4. Select the network types on which you want to allow the program, click OK, and then click Add. (You can also select network types in Allowed Apps after you add the program.)

Restoring default settings

If you've played around a bit with Windows Firewall and perhaps allowed connections that you should not have, you can get back to a known secure state by clicking Restore Defaults in Windows Firewall. Be aware that doing so removes all rules that you've added for all programs. Although this gives you a secure setup, you might find that some of your network-connected programs no longer work properly. As that occurs, you can add again each legitimate program that needs to be allowed, as described on the previous pages.

Advanced tools for managing Windows Firewall

If you have any experience at all configuring firewalls, you'll quickly realize that the Windows Firewall application in Control Panel covers only the most basic tasks. Don't take that as an indication that Windows Firewall is underpowered. To the contrary, you can configure all manner of firewall rules, allowing or blocking traffic based on program, port, protocol, IP address, and so on. In addition, you can enable, disable, and monitor rules; configure logging; and much more. With advanced tools, you can also configure Windows Firewall on remote workstations. Because the interface to these advanced features is rather daunting, Windows Firewall provides the simplified interface described earlier. It's adequate not only for less experienced users, but also for performing the routine firewall tasks needed by information technology (IT) professionals and others.

Nonetheless, our tour of security essentials would not be complete without a visit to Windows Firewall With Advanced Security, a snap-in and predefined console for Microsoft Management Console (MMC) that offers granular control over rules, exceptions, and profiles. To open it, in Windows Firewall click Advanced Settings. Windows Firewall With Advanced Security appears, as shown in Figure 7-6.

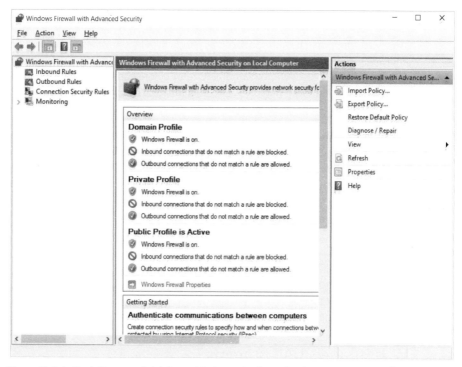

Figure 7-6 In the left pane, click Inbound Rules or Outbound Rules to view, configure, create, and delete firewall rules. The Domain Profile appears even on a computer that is not part of a Windows domain.

The initial view presents information similar to that shown in Windows Firewall. Go just a few steps farther into the cave, however, and you could be lost in no time. The "Windows Firewall with Advanced Security Getting Started Guide" can brighten your path; view it at *w7io.com/1502*. For additional details, see "Using Windows Firewall with Advanced Security" at *w7io.com/0701*.

Inside OUT

Open Windows Firewall With Advanced Security directly

You don't need to open Windows Firewall to get to Windows Firewall With Advanced Security. In the search box, type wf.msc and press Ctrl+Shift+Enter to run it as an administrator.

Preventing unsafe actions with User Account Control

Widely scorned when it was introduced as part of Windows Vista, User Account Control (UAC) intercedes whenever a user or program attempts to perform a system administrative task and asks for the consent of a computer administrator before commencing what could be risky business. Since that rocky start, UAC has been tuned to become an effective security aid—without the annoyance factor that plagued the original implementation.

In Windows 10, user accounts you set up after the first one are standard (nonadministrator) accounts by default; although they can carry out all the usual daily computing tasks, they're prevented from performing potentially harmful operations. These restrictions apply not just to the user; more importantly, they also apply to any programs launched by the user. Even administrator accounts run as "protected administrator" accounts allowed only standard-user privileges except when they need to perform administrative tasks. (This is sometimes called Admin Approval Mode.)

> ➤ **For information about user accounts, see Chapter 6.**

Most programs are written so that they don't require administrator privileges for performing everyday tasks. Programs that truly need administrative access (such as utility programs that change computer settings) request elevation—and that's where UAC comes in.

What triggers UAC prompts

The types of actions that require elevation to administrator status (and therefore display a UAC elevation prompt) include those that make changes to system-wide settings or to files in %SystemRoot% or %ProgramFiles%. (On a default Windows installation, these environment variables represent C:\Windows and C:\Program Files, respectively.) Among the actions that require elevation are the following:

- Installing and uninstalling desktop applications

- Installing device drivers that are not included in Windows or provided through Windows Update

- Installing ActiveX controls

- Changing settings for Windows Firewall

- Changing UAC settings

- Configuring Windows Update

- Adding or removing user accounts

- Changing a user's account type

- Running Task Scheduler

- Restoring backed-up system files

- Viewing or changing another user's folders and files

Within Windows, you can identify in advance many actions that require elevation. A shield icon next to a button or link indicates that a UAC prompt will appear if you're using a standard account.

Shield icons identify links that require UAC elevation

If you sign in with an administrator account (and if you leave the default UAC settings unchanged), you'll see fewer consent prompts than if you use a standard account. That's because the default setting prompts only when a program tries to install software or make other changes to the computer, but not when you make changes to Windows settings—even those that would trigger a prompt for a standard user with default UAC settings. Windows uses autoelevation to elevate without prompting certain programs that are part of Windows. Programs that are elevated automatically are from a predefined list, they must be digitally signed by the Windows publisher, and they must be stored in certain secure folders.

Limitations of User Account Control

User Account Control isn't a security silver bullet. It's one layer of a defense-in-depth strategy.

Some Windows users assume that UAC consent dialog boxes represent a security boundary. They don't. They simply represent a place for an administrator to make a trust decision. If a bad guy uses social engineering to convince you that you need his program, you've already made a trust decision. You'll click at least a half-dozen times to download, save, and launch the bad guy's program. A UAC consent request is perfectly normal in this sequence, so why wouldn't you click one more time?

If this scenario bothers you, the obvious solution is to adjust UAC to its highest level. Among other changes, this setting disables the autoelevation behavior. (For details on how to do this, see "Modifying UAC settings" later in this chapter.) If a program tries to use this subterfuge to sneak system changes past you, you'll see an unexpected consent dialog box from the system. But as soon as you provide those elevated credentials, the code can do anything it wants.

A better alternative is to sign in using a standard account, which provides a real security boundary. A standard user who does not have the administrator password can make changes only in her own user profile, protecting the system from unintended tampering.

Even running as a standard user doesn't provide complete protection. Malware can be installed in your user profile without triggering any system alarms. It can log your keystrokes, steal your passwords, and send out email using your identity. Even if you reset UAC to its highest level, you could fall victim to malware that lies in wait for you to elevate your privileges and then does its own dirty work alongside you.

As we said, enabling UAC is only one part of a multilayered security strategy. It works best when supplemented by a healthy skepticism and up-to-date antimalware software.

Dealing with UAC prompts

At sign-in, Windows creates a token that is used to identify the privilege levels of your account. Standard users get a standard token, but administrators actually get two: a standard token and an administrator token. The standard token is used to open Explorer.exe (the Windows shell), from which all subsequent programs are launched. Child processes inherit the token of the process that launches them, so by default all applications run as a standard user—even when you're signed in with an administrator account. Certain programs request elevation to administrator privileges; that's when the UAC prompt is displayed. If you provide administrator credentials, Windows then uses the administrator token to open the program. Note that any processes that the successfully elevated program opens also run as an administrator.

As an elevation-requesting application attempts to open, UAC evaluates the application and the request and then displays an appropriate prompt. As an administrator, the most common prompt you're likely to see is the consent prompt, which is shown in Figure 7-7. Read it, check the name of the program, click Yes if you're confident that it's safe to proceed, and carry on.

Figure 7-7 Clicking Show Details displays a link to the program's certificate.

If you use a standard account, when a program requires elevation you'll see the credentials prompt, which is shown in Figure 7-8. If the user is able to provide the credentials (that is, user name and password, smart card, or fingerprint, depending on how sign-in authentication is configured on the computer) of an administrator, the application opens using the administrator's access token.

By default, the UAC dialog box sits atop the secure desktop, a darkened representation of your desktop that runs in a separate process that no other application can interfere with. (If the secure desktop wasn't secure, a malicious program could put another dialog box in front of the UAC dialog box, perhaps with a message encouraging you to let the program proceed. Or a malicious program could grab your keystrokes, thereby learning your administrator sign-in password.) When the secure desktop is displayed, you can't switch tasks or click the windows on the desktop. (In fact, they're not really windows. When UAC invokes the secure desktop, it snaps a picture of the desktop, darkens it, and then displays that image behind the dialog box.)

Figure 7-8 To perform an administrative task, a standard user must enter the password for an administrator account.

There's a delay before the secure desktop appears

On some systems, you have to wait a few seconds before the screen darkens and the UAC prompt appears on the secure desktop. There's no easy way to solve the slow-down, but you can easily work around it. In User Account Control Settings (described in the next section, "Modifying UAC settings"), you can take the protection level down a notch. The setting below the default provides the same level of UAC protection (albeit with a slight risk that malware could hijack the desktop), except that it does not dim the desktop.

NOTE

If an application other than the foreground application requests elevation, instead of interrupting your work (the foreground task) with a prompt, UAC signals its request with a flashing taskbar button. Click the taskbar button to see the prompt.

It becomes natural to click through dialog boxes without reading them or giving them a second thought. But it's important to recognize that security risks to your computer are real and that actions that trigger a UAC prompt are potentially dangerous. Clearly, if you know what you're doing and you click a button to, say, change Windows Update settings, you can blow past that security dialog box with no more than a quick glance to be sure it was raised by the expected application. But if a UAC prompt appears when you're not expecting it—stop, read it carefully, and think before you click.

Modifying UAC settings

To review your User Account Control options and make changes to the way it works, in the search box or in Control Panel, type **uac** and then click Change User Account Control Settings. A window similar to the one shown in Figure 7-9 appears.

Figure 7-9 The topmost setting might overwhelm you with UAC prompts; the bottom setting turns off UAC.

Your choices in this window vary slightly depending on whether you use an administrator account or a standard account. For standard accounts, the top setting is the default; for administrator accounts, the second setting from the top is the default. Table 7-1 summarizes the available options.

To make changes, move the slider to the position you want. Be sure to take note of the advisory message in the bottom of the box as you move the slider. Click OK when you're done—and then respond to the UAC prompt that appears! Note that when you're signed in with a standard account, you can't select one of the bottom two options, even if you have the password for an administrator account. To select one of those options, you must sign in as an administrator and then make the change.

Table 7-1 User Account Control settings

Slider position	Prompts when a program tries to install software or make changes to the computer	Prompts when you make changes to Windows settings	Displays prompts on a secure desktop
Standard user account			
Top (default)	✔	✔	✔
Second	✔	✔	
Third	✔		
Bottom (off)			
Administrator account			
Top	✔	✔	✔
Second (default)	✔		✔
Third	✔		
Bottom (off)			

TROUBLESHOOTING

User Account Control settings don't stick

If you find that nothing happens when you make a change to User Account Control settings, be sure that you're the only one signed in to your computer. Simultaneous sign-ins that use Fast User Switching can cause this problem.

Inside OUT

Use Local Security Policy to customize UAC behavior

Users of the Pro and Enterprise editions of Windows 10 can use the Local Security Policy console to modify the behavior of UAC. Start Local Security Policy (Secpol.msc), and open Security Settings\Local Policies\Security Options. In the details pane, scroll down to the policies whose names begin with "User Account Control." For each policy, double-click it and then click the Explain tab for information before you decide on a setting. With these policies, you can make several refinements in the way UAC works—including some that are not possible in the User Account Control Settings window. (Administrators on Windows-based enterprise networks can also configure these options using Group Policy management tools.) For details about each of these policies, see "UAC Group Policy Settings" at *w7io.com/1523*.

Regardless of your UAC setting, the shield icons still appear throughout Control Panel, but you won't see UAC prompts if you've lowered the UAC protection level. Clicking a button or link identified with a shield immediately begins the action. Administrators run with full administrator privileges; standard users, of course, still have only standard privileges.

CAUTION

Don't forget that UAC is more than annoying prompts. Only when UAC is enabled does an administrator run with a standard token. Only when UAC is enabled does Internet Explorer run in a low-privilege Protected Mode. Only when UAC is enabled does it warn you when a rogue application attempts to perform a task with system-wide impact. And, of course, disabling UAC also disables file and registry virtualization, which can cause compatibility problems with applications that use fixes provided by the UAC feature. For these reasons, we urge you not to select the bottom option in User Account Control Settings, which turns off UAC completely.

Encrypting information

Windows provides the following encryption tools for preventing the loss of confidential data:

- Encrypting File System (EFS) encodes your files so that even if someone is able to obtain the files, he or she won't be able to read them. The files are readable only when you sign in to the computer using your user account.

- BitLocker Drive Encryption provides another layer of protection by encrypting entire hard-disk volumes. By linking this encryption to a key stored in a Trusted Platform Module (TPM) or USB flash drive, BitLocker reduces the risk of data being lost when a computer is stolen or when a hard disk is stolen and placed in another computer. A thief's standard approach in these situations is to boot into an alternate operating system and then try to retrieve data from the stolen computer or drive. With BitLocker, that type of offline attack is effectively neutered.

- BitLocker To Go extends BitLocker encryption to removable media, such as USB flash drives.

NOTE

Encrypting File System and BitLocker Drive Encryption are not available in Windows 10 Home. Encrypting a removable drive with BitLocker To Go requires Windows 10 Pro or Windows 10 Enterprise; the resulting encrypted drive can be opened and used on a device running Windows 10 Home.

Using the Encrypting File System

The Encrypting File System (EFS) provides a secure way to store your sensitive data. Windows creates a randomly generated file encryption key (FEK) and then transparently encrypts the data, using this FEK, as the data is being written to disk. Windows then encrypts the FEK using your public key. (Windows creates a personal encryption certificate with a public/private key pair for you the first time you use EFS.) The FEK, and therefore the data it encrypts, can be decrypted only with your certificate and its associated private key, which are available only when you sign in with your user account. (Designated data recovery agents can also decrypt your data.) Other users who attempt to use your encrypted files receive an "access denied" message. Even administrators and others who have permission to take ownership of files are unable to open your encrypted files.

You can encrypt individual files, folders, or entire drives. (You cannot encrypt the boot volume—the one with the Windows operating system files—using EFS, however. For that, you must use BitLocker.) We recommend that you encrypt folders or drives instead of individual files. When you encrypt a folder or drive, the files it contains are encrypted, and new files that you create in that folder or drive are encrypted automatically.

To encrypt a folder, follow these steps:

1. In File Explorer, right-click the folder, choose Properties, click the General tab, and then click Advanced, which displays the dialog box shown next. (If the properties dialog box doesn't have an Advanced button, the folder is not on an NTFS-formatted volume and you can't use EFS.)

2. Select Encrypt Contents To Secure Data. (Note that you can't encrypt compressed files. If the files are already compressed, Windows clears the compressed attribute.)

3. Click OK twice. If the folder contains any files or subfolders, Windows then displays a confirmation message.

NOTE

If you select Apply Changes To This Folder Only, Windows doesn't encrypt any of the files currently in the folder. Any new files that you create in the folder, however, including files that you copy or move to the folder, will be encrypted.

After a file or folder has been encrypted, File Explorer displays its name in green. This minor cosmetic detail is the only change you are likely to notice. Windows decrypts your files on the fly as you use them and reencrypts them when you save.

CAUTION

Before you encrypt anything important, you should back up your file recovery certificate and your personal encryption certificate (with their associated private keys), as well as the data recovery agent certificate, to a USB flash drive or to your OneDrive. Store the flash drive in a secure location. To do this, open User Accounts in Control Panel, and then click Manage Your File Encryption Certificates. If you ever lose the certificate stored on your hard drive (because of a disk failure, for example), you can restore the backup copy and regain access to your files. If you lose all copies of your certificate (and no data recovery agent certificates exist), you won't be able to use your encrypted files. No backdoor exists (none that we know of, at any rate), nor is there any practical way to hack these files. (If there were, it wouldn't be very good encryption.)

To encrypt one or more files, follow the same procedure as for folders. You'll see a different confirmation message to remind you that the file's folder is not encrypted and to give you an opportunity to encrypt it. You generally don't want to encrypt individual files because the information you intend to protect can too easily become decrypted without your knowledge. For example, with some applications, when you open a document for editing, the application creates a copy of the original document. When you save the document after editing, the application saves the copy—which is not encrypted—and deletes the original encrypted document. Static files that you use for reference only—but never for editing—can safely be encrypted without encrypting the parent folder. Even in that situation, however, you'll probably find it simpler to encrypt the whole folder.

Encrypting with BitLocker and BitLocker To Go

BitLocker Drive Encryption can be used to encrypt entire NTFS volumes, which provides excellent protection against data theft. BitLocker can secure a drive against attacks that involve circumventing the operating system or removing the drive and placing it in another computer. BitLocker provides the greatest protection on a computer that has TPM version 1.2 or later; on these systems, the TPM stores the key and ensures that a computer has not been tampered with while offline. If your computer does not have TPM, you can still use BitLocker on your operating system volume, but you must insert a USB startup key or enter a password each time you start the computer or resume from hibernation. Non-TPM systems do not get the system integrity check at startup.

BitLocker To Go, a feature introduced in Windows 7, allows you to encrypt the entire contents of a USB flash drive or other removable device. If it's lost or stolen, the thief will be unable to access the data without the password.

To apply BitLocker Drive Encryption or BitLocker To Go, right-click the drive in File Explorer and then click Turn On BitLocker. BitLocker asks how you want to unlock the encrypted drive—with a password, a smart card, or both. After you have made your selections and confirmed your intentions, the software gives you the opportunity to save and print your recovery key, as shown in Figure 7-10.

Your recovery key is a system-generated, 48-character, numeric backup password. If you lose the password you assign to the encrypted disk, you can recover your data with the recovery key. BitLocker offers to save that key in a plain text file; you should accept the offer and store the file in a secure location.

Figure 7-10 The option of saving the recovery key to your Microsoft account—that is, to your OneDrive—is new with Windows 10.

Inside OUT

Store your recovery keys on OneDrive

Clicking Save To Your Microsoft Account saves the recovery key on your OneDrive, making it accessible anywhere you have an Internet connection. But the trick is finding that key on OneDrive: Go to *onedrive.com/recoverykey*.

With all preliminaries out of the way, BitLocker begins encrypting your media. This process takes a few minutes, even if the disk is freshly formatted. However, if you are in a hurry, you can opt to encrypt only the used space on the drive. This choice can save you a considerable amount of time if your disk contains only a small number of files.

To read a BitLocker-encrypted removable disk, you need to unlock it by using whatever method you have stipulated. If you're prompted for a password that you have lost or forgotten, click More Options and then click Enter Recovery Key. In case you have several recovery-key text files, BitLocker To Go gives you the key's identification code:

Find the entry on OneDrive (*onedrive.com/recoverykey*) or the text file whose name matches the identification code, copy the recovery key from this text file to the BitLocker dialog box, and you'll be granted temporary access to the files, which is good until you remove the disk or restart the computer. At this point, you might want to change the password; open BitLocker Drive Encryption in the System And Security section of Control Panel and click Change Password.

To remove BitLocker encryption from a disk, open BitLocker Drive Encryption in Control Panel and click Turn Off BitLocker. The software will decrypt the disk; allow some time for this process.

➤ **For more information about BitLocker, see *bit.ly/bitlocker-overview*.**

Using Windows Defender to block malware

The best way to fight unwanted and malicious software is to keep it from being installed on any PC that is part of your network. Over the years, malicious hackers have found a variety of ways to install malware: floppy disks, document files, email attachments, instant messaging attachments, AutoPlay on USB flash drives, scripts, browser add-ons . . . and the list goes on. Many of these transmission methods rely on social-engineering techniques designed to lure inattentive or gullible users into opening an infected attachment, visiting an infected website, and so on. Not satisfied with being able to pick off the inattentive and gullible, authors of hostile software are always on the lookout for techniques they can use to spread infections automatically.

Any program that tries to sneak onto your PC without your full knowledge and consent should be blocked. An important layer in a basic PC protection strategy, therefore, is to use up-to-date antimalware software. Into the breach steps Windows Defender, the antimalware program included in Windows 10.

Windows Defender runs as a system service and uses a scanning engine to compare files against a database of virus and spyware definitions. It also uses heuristic analysis of the behavior of programs to flag suspicious activity from a file that isn't included in the list of known threats. It scans each file that you access in any way, including downloads from the Internet and email attachments you receive. (This feature is called *real-time protection*—not to be confused with scheduled *scans*, which periodically inspect all files stored on your computer to root out malware.)

Using Windows Defender

In general, you don't need to "use" Windows Defender at all. As a system service, it works quietly in the background. The only time you'll know it's there is if it finds an infected file; one or more notifications will pop up to alert you to the fact.

Nonetheless, you might want to poke around a bit. To open Windows Defender, type **defender** in the search box, and click the program's shortcut. If a shortcut to Windows Defender doesn't appear or if you don't have a keyboard, open Settings, tap Update & Security, tap Windows Defender, scroll all the way to the bottom, and tap Use Windows Defender.

The Home tab, shown in Figure 7-11, shows the current status and the results of the most recent scan. This tab also tells you whether real-time protection is enabled.

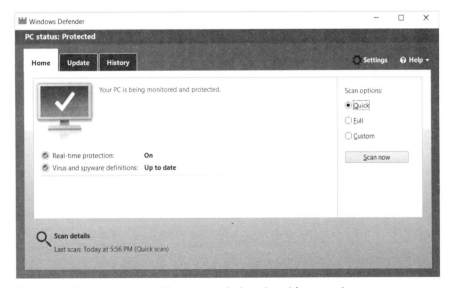

Figure 7-11 The Home tab provides status and a launch pad for manual scans.

To temporarily disable real-time protection (if it is interfering with the installation of a legitimate program, for example), click Settings to open a window in which you can turn off real-time protection. Doing so causes the PC Status banner at the top of the program window to glow red and change from Protected to At Risk; a large Turn On button dominates the Home tab. Windows Defender is so anxious to restore real-time protection, in fact, that it automatically turns it back on when you restart your computer or after some time elapses.

Windows Defender uses Windows Update to retrieve definition files and periodic updates to the detection engine. The Update tab in Windows Defender shows when the definitions were last updated and also features an Update button in case you want to get the latest definitions immediately instead of waiting for Windows Update.

Manually scanning for malware

The combination of real-time protection and periodic scheduled scanning is normally sufficient for identifying and resolving problems with malware and spyware. However, if you suspect that you've been infected, you can initiate a scan on demand. To immediately scan for problems, on the Home tab (see Figure 7-11) under Scan Options, select the type of scan you want to perform and click Scan Now.

The Quick option kicks off a scan that checks only the places on your computer that malware and spyware are most likely to infect, and it is the recommended setting for frequent regular scans. Choose Full if you suspect infection (or you just want reassurance that your system is clean) and want to inspect all running programs and the complete contents of all local volumes. Click Custom if you want to restrict the scan to any combination of drives, folders, and files.

Inside OUT

Run a scan from a script or a scheduled task

Windows Defender includes a command-line utility that you can use to automate scans with a script or a scheduled task. You'll find MpCmdRun.exe in %ProgramFiles%\Windows Defender. For details about using the utility, open an elevated Command Prompt window and run the program with no parameters.

A full scan can be burdensome, especially if you have hundreds of thousands of files scattered around local disks. To minimize the time and system resources, you can specify that Windows Defender skip over locations and file types that you know are safe and haven't been tampered with. To do that, begin by clicking Settings. On the Windows Defender tab in Settings, click Add An Exclusion (under Exclusions) to display a window like the one shown in Figure 7-12.

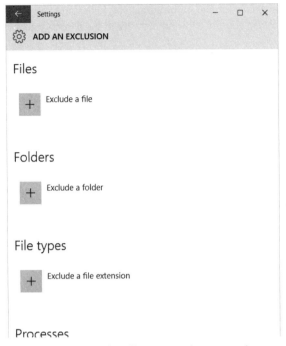

Figure 7-12 Files, folders, file types, and processes that are excluded are ignored during scans. Click the plus icon to add items to the exclusion list.

There you'll find four options that affect scanning:

- **Exclude A File.** Specify files that you know to be safe.

- **Exclude A Folder.** Specify folders that you know to be safe. This is an appropriate option if you have a folder full of previously downloaded system utilities that routinely trigger alerts. Do not use this option with folders where you normally download new files.

- **Exclude A File Extension.** Similarly, you can exclude from scans all files with the file name extensions (such as common scripts) that you specify.

- **Exclude A .Exe, .Com Or .Scr Process.** If you find that a program is routinely detected as a potential threat despite your telling Windows Defender to allow it, consider adding the program to this list. Be sure to specify the process name (Myprogram.exe) and not the program name. This strategy is less risky than excluding the containing folder;

if you grant blanket approval for files in the containing folder, and later some real spyware ends up in the folder, you risk allowing malware to sneak onto your system with no
warning.

To delete an exclusion (so it will no longer be excluded from scans), return to Add An Exclusion, click or tap the name of the exclusion you want to delete, and click Remove.

Dealing with detected threats

If Windows Defender detects the presence of malware or spyware as part of its real-time protection, it displays a warning above the notification area and, in most cases, resolves the problem without you lifting a finger.

To learn more about its findings, in Windows Defender click the History tab. Select Quarantined Items, and then click View Details. As Figure 7-13 shows, Windows Defender shows the
name, alert level, and detection date of the quarantined item or items.

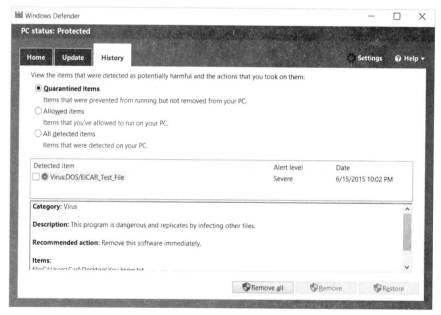

Figure 7-13 The box below the list shows details about the selected item; a link at the bottom of
that box (not shown) leads to online information about the particular infection.

Detected items are moved to a restricted folder (%ProgramData%\Microsoft\Windows
Defender\Quarantine) whose permissions include a Deny access control entry that locks out
the built-in Users and Everyone groups. Executable files in this folder cannot be run, nor can

the folder's contents be accessed from File Explorer. Items moved here can be managed only from the Windows Defender console (preferred) or an elevated Command Prompt window.

Stopping unknown or malicious programs with SmartScreen

SmartScreen, which began as a feature in Internet Explorer in Windows 7, is used to identify programs that other users have run safely. It does so by comparing a hash of a downloaded program with Microsoft's application-reputation database. This occurs when you download a program using Microsoft Edge or Internet Explorer, and when you attempt to run a program that you have downloaded from the Internet—regardless of what browser you use.

Programs with a positive reputation run without any ado. Programs that are known to be bad or that have not yet developed a reputation are blocked. A message similar to the one shown in Figure 7-14 appears.

Figure 7-14 When you attempt to run a downloaded program that doesn't match one in Microsoft's database, a message like this appears.

If you're certain that a program is safe, you can override the block by selecting the check box, which adds a Run Anyway button you can then click. With default settings in place, you'll then need the approval of someone with an administrator account before the program runs. Don't say you weren't warned.

You can adjust the level of SmartScreen protection by going to Security And Maintenance (see Figure 7-1 earlier in this chapter) and clicking Change Windows SmartScreen Settings. Besides the default setting, you can remove the requirement for administrator approval or you can disable SmartScreen altogether.

PART 2

Working and playing with Windows 10

CHAPTER 8

Using and managing modern apps and desktop programs

As the title of this chapter suggests, the programs you can run on Windows 10 fall into two broad categories. One category consists of so-called desktop applications. These are the programs that you may have and could have run under Windows 7 and earlier versions. Windows 10 continues to support such programs. (You may also see these programs described as Win32 applications.) These traditional applications are designed, for the most part, for use with a keyboard and a mouse, and many of them first came into being during the era when desktop machines dominated the computing landscape.

The other category consists of programs delivered through the Windows Store. These programs, optimized for touch and mobile use (although equally usable on desktop systems with traditional input devices) are variously called *modern apps, trusted Windows Store apps,* or *UWP apps*. Windows favors the term *Trusted Windows Store apps*. If you enter the name of one of these programs in the search box on your taskbar, you will see something like the following:

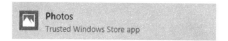

In this book, for the sake of simplicity, we use the designation *modern app*, but Windows opts for the wordier handle for good reason. These apps, available only through the Windows Store, have passed a stringent vetting process and can be trusted to be free of malware. They are also "sandboxed," which means they run in secure isolation, free from potentially hazardous interactions with other running processes.

The current name for the development platform is *Universal Windows Platform*, or *UWP*. The keyword here is *universal*. The platform offers a core application programming interface (API) that allows developers to create a single app package that can be installed on devices with a wide range of sizes and modalities, with adaptive controls that tailor the app to the size and feature set of the target machine. In short, a program you download from the Windows Store to your tablet is likely to work as well on your traditional desktop machine, your all-in-one, your Xbox console, your phone, and your notebook PC.

What's in a modern app

Here are some important characteristics of modern apps:

- **Tiles.** Each app gets a tile, which can be displayed on the Start menu or not, as you choose. To add an app to the Start menu, press the Windows key, click or tap All Apps, right-click the name of the app, and choose Pin To Start Menu. (Similar steps allow you to pin an app to the taskbar or to unpin an app from either location.)

- **Live tiles.** Tiles can be programmed to update dynamically when they're displayed on the Start menu—that is, they can become *live tiles*. Live tiles can, for example, display news headlines, cycle through a set of photos, show calendar information, and so on. If you find a tile to be livelier than you would like, you can render it inanimate by right-clicking it and then clicking Turn Live Tile Off.

- **Notifications and alerts.** Apps can trigger notifications and alerts. To take one example, your calendar app can display appointment information on your lock screen and issue reminders at the appropriate times.

- **Cortana.** Apps can be integrated with Cortana, allowing you to do such things as issue a voice command to send an email.

- **Security and safety.** Modern apps are prevented from accessing system resources. They also don't store their own configuration information in publicly accessible places, such as .ini files.

- **The ability to run without administrative consent.** Because modern apps are certified to be free of potential hazards, you don't need an administrative token to install or run them. You won't find Run As Administrator on the shortcut menus of modern apps; there is no need for it.

- **Power conservation.** By default, an app is suspended within a few seconds if you move away from it. This behavior is particularly valuable on battery-driven systems such as phones and tablets. Apps can be written to run in the background (allowing you, for example, to play music while you work), but this is an exceptional case.

- **Automatic updates.** Modern apps are updated automatically. The Windows Store manages this process for you when an app's publisher makes changes to a program.

- **Per-user installation.** When you install an app, that app is installed only for your user account. Other account holders who want to use the app have to install it as well. Depending on licensing provisions and the number of devices on which you have installed the app in question, other accounts on a system where an app has already been bought and installed might find, on visiting the Windows Store, that the app is identified as "owned." In that case, these users can install the app without going through a payment process. The same is true for other systems that you sign in to with the Microsoft account under which you bought the app.

- **Display adaptability.** If you have a modern app running on systems with disparate form factors, such as a phone and a notebook, you can easily see how the app adjusts its user interface to accommodate the different screen sizes. With many apps, you can see the same adaptability simply by adjusting window size. For example, if you display a month view in Calendar on a large display and then narrow the window from either side, you will note the following adjustment:

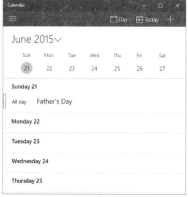

Initially, as you reduce the window's width, Calendar compresses its display but maintains the layout. Eventually, to maintain readability, the program switches to a vertical layout comparable to what you would see on a phone.

Browsing the Windows Store

The Windows Store, much improved and expanded since its debut with Windows 8, is your emporium for games, music, movies, and TV shows, as well as modern Windows apps. The menu across the top of the Windows Store page allows you to switch between these various kinds of offerings. Below the display ad, you'll find some items that the Windows Store thinks you might be interested in, based on what you've downloaded earlier. Farther down is a sort of categorized bestseller list—top free games, games that have received stellar ratings from other users, "new and rising" items, and so on. Figure 8-1 shows how part of the Windows Store appeared on one of our systems around the time of the official launch of Windows 10.

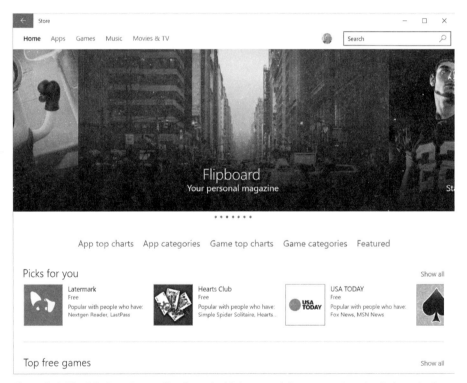

Figure 8-1 The Windows Store offers items it thinks you might want to download given the items you've chosen previously.

If you know more or less what you're looking for, you can use the handy search box to find it. You can search by name or publisher, and the search results will include entertainment offerings (albums and songs, for example), as well as apps.

➤ **For information about using the Windows Store to purchase music, movies, and TV shows, see Chapter 10, "Music, photos, movies, and games."**

If you just want to browse, you can start by clicking App Categories. An alphabetized list of categories appears. When you find something of interest, click it to see details. Figure 8-2 shows a sample of the kind of details you might find. Be sure to scroll down to the rating details and reviews.

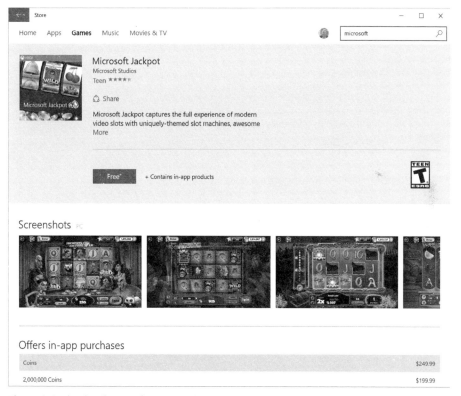

Figure 8-2 The details page for an app shows screen shots, reviews and ratings, and suggestions of what else you might like.

As Figure 8-2 shows, the price for some apps is adorned with an asterisk and the notation that the app comes with "in-app products." This is a delicate way of alerting you that the app, once installed, will be giving you the opportunity to buy extra goodies. Some apps are quite low-key about this; other have been known to be nearly useless without at least some of the extra items. A quick check of the reviews might help you spot an app whose effective price is not what it seems. As Figure 8-3 shows, the details screen should also enumerate the extra offerings:

Offers in-app purchases

Coins	$249.99
2,000,000 Coins	$199.99
900,000 Coins	$99.99
150,000 Coins	$24.99
48,000 Coins	$9.99
20,000 Coins	$4.99
750 Coins	Free

Figure 8-3 The details page for Microsoft Jackpot lists its in-app purchase offerings.

Finding additional information

Scrolling to the bottom of an app's details page reveals some additional useful details:

Features

- Stay up to date with the latest IT Innovations
- Cloud powered modern App provides latest IT Showcase contents leveraging latest Windows features
- Quickly find desired contents using key word search and semantic zoom
- Get Live Notifications, Pin your favorite contents on-to Favorites section for quick access
- Share contents over email, twitter or facebook or save it to OneDrive for any time access
- Read out contents, use app bar to quickly change themes, hide banner and perform more content functions!
- View & access IT Showcase content statistics by media type or by products through Trends Tile
- View localizaed contents specific to regions - click regions under settings to view available regions

Additional information

Published by Microsoft Corporation

Microsoft Corporation

Category
Business

Approximate size 6.9 MB

Age rating For ages 7 and up

Supported processors x86, x64, ARM

Installation Install this app on up to ten Windows 10 devices.

This app has permissions to use
- microphone
- internetClient

Supported languages
English (United States)

Learn more
Microsoft IT Showcase support
Microsoft IT Showcase website

Additional terms
Microsoft IT Showcase privacy policy
Store terms of use

Report this app
Report this app to Microsoft

Items of particular interest here might include the approximate size of the app, the system resources the app is permitted to use (in the example here, the microphone and Internet client), and the number of devices on which the app can be installed.

Buying an app

To begin the process of installing a new app simply click its price. If the app is free (many are), the download and installation process begins at once. If money is required, the payment process is managed through your Microsoft account. (If your Windows 10 user account signs in locally, as opposed to through a Microsoft account, you will be prompted at this point for Microsoft account credentials, and you will be guided to create such an account if you don't already have one.)

While the app is being downloaded and installed, you can follow its progress:

In the progress window, you can also pause or cancel a download. You might want to pause if you have several lengthy downloads going at once and want to prioritize them.

Uninstalling an app

The easiest way to uninstall a modern app is to right-click it on the Start menu or in the All Apps list and then click Uninstall. Because an app is installed per user, uninstalling is as well; if you want to be rid of a program everywhere it has been installed, you need to repeat the procedure to uninstall it.

You can also uninstall both modern and desktop apps by opening Settings, clicking System, and then clicking Apps & Features. The list of installed programs that appears provides useful information about when each app was installed and how much space on disk it is consuming (Figure 8-4). The list includes both modern and desktop apps and can be sorted by size, name, or installation date. Note that the size given for an app includes the data used as well as the application size itself. If you have large music and photo collections, for example, you will see much larger numbers in this column.

To uninstall an app from the Apps & Features list, simply click its name and then click the Uninstall button that appears.

Figure 8-4 The Apps & Features section of Settings provides a way to uninstall both modern and desktop apps.

TROUBLESHOOTING

Modern apps won't uninstall

If the normal uninstall routine for a modern app doesn't seem to work, you can remove the troublesome item by using Windows PowerShell. (See Chapter 21, "Working with Command Prompt and Windows PowerShell," for information about PowerShell.) Use the Get-AppxPackage cmdlet to obtain a list of packages installed on your system. Find the one you want to remove and note its *PackageFullName* property. Then supply this property as a parameter to the Remove-AppxPackage cmdlet. Note that you must be working in a PowerShell session with administrative privileges.

Managing line-of-business apps

Enterprises can develop line-of-business (LOB) apps for use within their organizations. Such apps can be deployed either through a private Business Store—managed and deployed by the Windows Store—or through a process called *sideloading*.

In addition to creating and deploying apps, administrators can also use Group Policy to control the use of all apps, including those that are supplied by Windows itself. For example, an organization might choose to remove the Sports app or prohibit it from running.

The process of distributing a Windows 10 app through a private Business Store requires that an enterprise have Azure Active Directory accounts for each user in the organization. (These accounts are used instead of Microsoft accounts.) Installation files are managed and deployed by the Windows Store, which also tracks license usage. Updates are delivered via normal update channels—Windows Update or Windows Server Update Services (WSUS).

LOB apps distributed within an organization without using the Windows Store don't need to be signed by Microsoft and don't require Azure Active Directory accounts. They do need to be signed with a certificate that is trusted by one of the trusted root authorities on the system.

Apps included with Windows 10

If you click through the Apps & Features list in Settings (see Figure 8-4), you will find that for some items, the Uninstall button is not available. These are apps that are supplied with a default installation of Windows 10, and Windows intends for you to keep them. (You will find a few other apps in the All Apps section of your Start menu that can't be uninstalled.) In the initial release of the operating system, the list of built-in programs included the following, among others:

- Alarms & Clock

- Calculator

- Camera

- Contact Support

- Cortana

- Groove Music

- Mail and Calendar

- Maps

- Movies & TV

- OneNote

- People

- Photos

- Settings

- Store

- Voice Recorder

- Weather

- Xbox

Several of these are relatively lightweight programs with no complexity worth discussing. You can read about some of the others in later chapters of this book. For the productivity and communication programs (including Mail and Calendar, OneNote, and People), see Chapter 9, "Productivity and communication tools." For the more right-brained items (Groove Music, Movies & TV, Photos, and Xbox), see Chapter 10.

Inside OUT

Don't overlook the humble Calculator

It's been around in one incarnation or another since the late 1980s, and it's no match for Excel, but the lowly Calculator app has a few tricks worth knowing about. It includes a programmer mode (specialized for bitwise operations on binary, octal, and hexadecimal values) along with the more common standard and scientific modes. And it can serve as a handy converter for measurements of volume, length, angles, time, and so on. (No, it doesn't do currencies.) Click the hamburger menu (three horizontal lines) in the upper left corner to see its repertoire.

Installing, running, and managing desktop applications

Windows 10 supports virtually all desktop applications that are compatible with Windows 7. If you have upgraded from Windows 7 (or from a Windows 8.1 system that itself was upgraded from Windows 7), all your desktop applications from the earlier environment should be happy and ready to go. Desktop programs can be installed anew in the usual ways, from installation media or by download from the Internet.

Desktop programs appear in the Start menu's All Apps list (or on the Start menu itself if you put them there) alongside modern apps. The only difference you're likely to see there is the absence of a live tile and the shortcut menu that appears if you right-click:

The Run As Administrator and Open File Location commands do not appear on this menu for modern apps. Running modern apps with administrative privileges is never required because such apps don't have the ability to mess with system files. Open File Location is absent from modern app shortcut menus because, as mentioned earlier, modern apps are defined by *package* data structures (in %LocalAppData%\Packages), and Windows assumes you have no need to inspect these structures.

The file locations for desktop apps (usually in a subfolder of %ProgramData%) are useful if you like to create shortcuts to your programs. For example, if you were accustomed to having shortcuts on your desktop to the programs you most frequently use, there's no reason not to populate your Windows 10 desktop the same way. Use the Start menu's shortcut menu to go to a program's file location. Then right-click the item in that folder and click Create Shortcut. The shortcut will appear in the same folder. Copy it, navigate to the desktop, and paste it there.

Running desktop applications as an administrator or another user

As in Windows 7, some desktop applications must be run with an administrative token. If you want to edit the registry, for example, you need to run Registry Editor (regedit.exe) as an administrator. You can run a program as an administrator by right-clicking any shortcut for the program (on the Start menu or elsewhere), choosing Run As Administrator, and satisfying the User Account Control (UAC) prompt with either consent or credentials. Here are two additional ways to do it:

- Start a Command Prompt session as Administrator: press Windows key+X and then choose Command Prompt (Admin). Then, in the Command Prompt window, type the name of the executable file for whichever program you want to run as an administrator. To run Registry Editor, for example, type **regedit**. Because you've already passed UAC inspection for the Command Prompt session, and because whatever you run from Command Prompt is a child process of Command Prompt, you don't have to deal with any further UAC prompts. This method is excellent for situations where you need to run a sequence of programs as an administrator. Keep one administrative-level Command Prompt window open, and run your programs from the command line.

● Type the name of the program you want to run in the taskbar search box, and then press Ctrl+Shift+Enter.

To run a program under a different user account, you can use the Runas command. You can do this from Command Prompt. The syntax is

```
Runas /user:username programname
```

After you issue the command, you'll be prompted to enter the password for the specified user account. Note that the Runas command does not work with File Explorer or with Microsoft Management Console (MMC) snap-ins.

Inside OUT

Use Steps Recorder to troubleshoot misbehaving software

When you need to report details about a software problem to a tech support person, the Steps Recorder tool can prove valuable. Run this program by typing **steps** in the taskbar search box and then clicking the Steps Recorder item that appears. Click Start Record, retrace your steps through the problematic program, and then click Stop Record. Steps Recorder takes a screen shot and time stamp at each crucial juncture (each mouse click or command), and then appends a verbal description of each step. You can add your own comments along the way. After you stop and save your recording, you can share it with tech support. (Steps Recorder is also an excellent tool for creating documentation to be used by others in your organization.)

Dealing with compatibility issues

As mentioned, programs that run without problems on Windows 7 will run equally well on Windows 10. Certain older desktop applications might create problems, however. Windows will attempt to flag potential compatibility problems when you first run such a program. The Program Compatibility Assistant that appears will offer you the alternatives of checking online for solutions (such as downloading a more recent version) or going ahead and running the program.

If you install a program and subsequently run into compatibility issues, a program compatibility troubleshooter may appear. Alternatively, you can run the troubleshooter yourself from Control Panel. You can find it by typing **compatibility** in the Control Panel search box. Under the heading Programs And Features, you will find the link Run Programs Made For Previous

Versions Of Windows. Click this link to launch the troubleshooter, and then click past the opening screen.

The troubleshooter begins by scanning for problems that it can detect automatically. If it finds none, it will present a list of applications installed on your system and let you select the one that's giving you difficulty. Select the offending program and follow the prompts to try to resolve your problem.

Managing programs and processes with Task Manager

Task Manager is a tool that serves two essential purposes. You can use it to track aspects of your system's performance and to see what programs and processes are running and termi-nate items when the normal shutdown methods aren't working.

> ➤ For information about using Task Manager to monitor system performance, see Chapter 15, "System maintenance and performance."

The easiest way to run Task Manager is by means of its keyboard shortcut, Ctrl+Shift+Esc. Fig-ure 8-5 shows the Processes tab of Task Manager. If you don't see a tabular layout similar to that shown in Figure 8-5, click More Details at the bottom of the window.

Figure 8-5 Task Manager is useful for terminating recalcitrant applications and processes, as well as for monitoring system performance.

By default, the items listed on the Processes tab are grouped by type—apps at the top, followed by background processes, Windows processes, and so on. Grouping is optional; clear Group By Type on the View menu if you want a single list.

Note that some of the items in the Apps list have outline controls. You can expand these to see what files or documents are open. In Figure 8-5, for example, the Microsoft Word entry has been expanded to reveal the name of the document that's currently open. The lists are initially sorted in ascending alphabetical order. Click a heading to reverse the sort. You can also click one of the performance headings to see which processes are using resources on your system. Clicking CPU, for example, will give you a constantly updating readout of how your apps and background processes are taxing the CPU.

Terminating a program with Task Manager

The Processes tab also includes a Status column. Most of the time, the entries in this column will be blank, indicating that everything is humming along. If an app hangs for any reason, you will see the words *Not Responding* in this column. In that case, you can attempt to shut down the miscreant by right-clicking its name and clicking End Task. Don't be too quick on the trigger, however; Not Responding doesn't necessarily mean permanently out to lunch. If the program is using every bit of resources to handle a different task, it might simply be too busy to communicate with Task Manager. Before you decide to end the program, give it a chance to finish whatever it's doing. How long should you wait? That depends on the task. If the operation involves a large data set (performing a global search and replace in a large Microsoft Access database, for instance), it's appropriate to wait several minutes, especially if you can hear the hard disk chattering or see the disk activity light flickering. But if the task in question normally completes in a few seconds, you needn't wait that long.

Inside OUT
Be smart about shutdowns

When you shut down an app by clicking End Task, Task Manager zaps the item immediately and irrevocably, closing any open files without giving you a chance to save them. (This is equivalent to choosing End Process on the Processes tab of the Windows 7 Task Manager.) Whenever possible, you should try to close the program by the normal methods before resorting to End Task.

Finding detailed information about a program

To see detailed information about the process that's running an app, right-click the app
and choose Go To Details. This takes you to a related item on the Details tab. Right-clicking
Microsoft Word, for example, takes you to Winword.exe, the name of Word's executable file.
(See Figure 8-6.)

Figure 8-6 Right-clicking an item on the Processes tab takes you straight to the related item
on the Details tab.

For each process, Task Manager includes the following information by default: image name
(the name of the process), process ID (PID), status (running or suspended, for example), user
name (the name of the person or account that initiated the process), CPU (the percentage of
the CPU's capacity that the process is currently using), memory (the amount of memory the
process requires to perform its regular functions, also known as the private working set), and
description (a text field identifying the process). To display additional information for each
process, right-click one of the headings and choose Select Columns.

Inside OUT

Go online to read about programs and processes

Task Manager makes it easy to learn more about items on the Processes or Details tab. Simply right-click an item and choose Search Online. Task Manager opens a browser window and funnels the name of the app and the name of its process to your default search engine. There you'll typically find numerous links to official and unofficial information. If you're suspicious about the legitimacy of anything that shows up in Task Manager, by all means use this tool to find out what others are saying.

Assigning a program to a specific processor

If you have a multi-core or multiprocessor system, you can assign a process to a specific processor—but only after the process is already running. To do this, right-click the process on the Details tab and choose Set Affinity. The following dialog box appears:

To assign a process to a particular CPU, clear the check boxes for the other entries in this dialog box.

Reviewing history

The App History tab, like the Processes tab, provides information about how programs are using system resources. But App History, shown in Figure 8-7, knows only about modern apps; you won't find your desktop applications listed here. App History accumulates its information over some range of time, giving you an approximate idea of how you have been using your computer. If you never clear and restart the history, it will record everything going back to your installation of Windows 10. You can start fresh by clicking Delete Usage History.

Figure 8-7 The App History tab tells you how much CPU time and other resources each modern app has used over a period of time.

As on other Task Manager tabs, you can sort information on the App History tab by clicking column headings. Clicking CPU Time, for example, brings the heavy hitters to the top of the list. Note, however, that Task Manager already calls your attention to the biggest consumers by means of color mapping, with the darkest colors assigned to the largest numbers.

History is interesting, but you might also find the App History tab useful as a program launcher. Right-click any item in any column, and you'll find a Switch To command. If the program is running, this command brings it front and center. If it's not running, Task Manager launches it.

Managing startup programs

Setting up a desktop application to run automatically when you start Windows is easy. If the program's installer doesn't offer to do this for you (many do) and you want the program to run every time you begin a Windows session, create a shortcut for the program in the Startup folder of your Start menu. Here's one way to do it:

1. On your Start menu, right-click the program you want to run at startup and choose Open File Location. You will find a shortcut for the program in the File Explorer window that appears.

2. Open a second File Explorer window and navigate to %AppData%\Microsoft\Windows\ Start Menu\Programs\Startup.

3. Copy the program's shortcut from the first File Explorer window to the second.

Inside OUT

Run a modern app at startup

You will find it challenging to launch a modern app from your Startup folder. You can find the app's executable by starting the program, running Task Manager, right-clicking the program on the Processes tab, clicking Go To Details, right-clicking the process name on the Details tab, and then clicking Open File Location. From there you can create a shortcut and copy it to your Startup folder. At the beginning of your next Windows session, you may find a warning from Windows SmartScreen:

Windows protected your PC

Windows SmartScreen prevented an unrecognized app from starting. Running this app might put your PC at risk.

App: Microsoft.Photos.exe
Publisher: Unknown Publisher

☐ I understand the risk and want to run this app.

Don't run

Windows SmartScreen is a security feature that helps protect you from potential malware. (See Chapter 7, "Securing Windows 10 devices.") Although the app in this example is clearly not a threat, SmartScreen may become wary on seeing it run from an unaccustomed location.

You can bypass SmartScreen by selecting the check box and clicking Run Anyway. But the next obstacle is more problematic:

C:\Program Files\WindowsApps\Microsoft.Windows.Photos_15.710.18110.0_x64__8wekyb3d8bb...   X

❌ C:\Program Files\WindowsApps\Microsoft.Windows.Photos_15.710.18110.0_x64__...\Microsoft.Photos.exe

This application can only run in the context of an app container.

OK

The problem is that modern apps, unlike desktop programs, must be run within the context of elaborate data structures called *packages*. (You can see a list of the packages installed on your system and drill down to their component folders by visiting %LocalAppData%\Packages in File Explorer.) A workaround is to create your Startup folder shortcut not to the app but to a data file associated with the app. If .jpg files are associated with the modern Photos app, for example, create a startup shortcut to one of your .jpg files. At startup, Windows will execute the shortcut, which will launch the app.

Suspending or removing startup items

The problem that many users have with startup programs is not with creating them (that's easy, and in many cases it happens more or less automatically) but getting rid of them. Having too many startup programs not only makes your system take longer to start, it also has the potential to waste memory. If you don't require a program at startup, it's a good idea to get it out of your startup path.

If you've created the startup item in the first place by the method just described, you can remove it by revisiting the Startup folder and exercising the Delete key. Often, the situation is not so simple, however, because—as you'll see next—there are many other ways by which a program can be made to run at startup.

You can see a list of startup processes on the Startup tab of Task Manager. As Figure 8-8 shows, the Startup tab identifies each item by its estimated impact on the time required to start your Windows environment. In the figure, we've sorted on the Startup Impact column, bringing the high-impact items to the top.

You can't remove a startup item from this list, but you can disable it so that the item will not run automatically at your next startup. To do this, right-click the item and then click Disable.

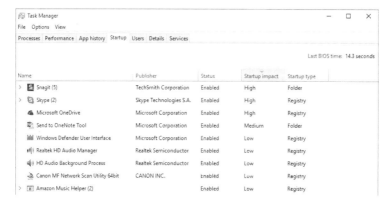

Figure 8-8 The Startup tab in Task Manager shows you which startup programs are enabled and how much impact each is estimated to have on your startup time.

If you're not sure whether an item on the Startup tab is justifying its existence there, try disabling it and restarting. Alternatively, or additionally, you can right-click the item and use the handy Search Online command to learn more about it.

Other ways a program can be made to run at startup

As mentioned, a shortcut in the Startup folder is only one of many ways in which a program can be made to run at startup. Programs that set themselves up to run automatically and administrators who configure systems for others to use have a great many other methods at their disposal, including the following:

- **Run key (machine).** Programs listed in the registry's HKLM\Software\Microsoft\Windows\CurrentVersion\Run key are available at startup to all users.

- **Run key (user).** Programs listed in the HKCU\Software\Microsoft\Windows\CurrentVersion\Run key run when the current user signs in. A similar subkey, HKCU\Software\Microsoft\Windows NT\CurrentVersion\Windows\Run, can also be used.

- **Load value.** Programs listed in the Load value of the registry key HKCU\Software\Microsoft\Windows NT\CurrentVersion\Windows run when any user signs in.

- **Scheduled tasks.** The Windows Task Scheduler (see Chapter 19, "Automating tasks and activities") can specify tasks that run at startup. In addition, an administrator can set up tasks for your computer to run at startup that are not available for you to change or delete.

- **Win.ini.** Programs written for 16-bit Windows versions can add commands to the Load= and Run= lines in the [Windows] section of this startup file, which is located in %SystemRoot%. The Win.ini file is a legacy of the Windows 3.1 era.

- **RunOnce and RunOnceEx keys.** This group of registry keys identifies programs that run only once, at startup. These keys can be assigned to a specific user account or to the machine:

    - HKLM\Software\Microsoft\Windows\CurrentVersion\RunOnce

    - HKLM\Software\Microsoft\Windows\CurrentVersion\RunOnceEx

    - HKCU\Software\Microsoft\Windows\CurrentVersion\RunOnce

    - HKCU\Software\Microsoft\Windows\CurrentVersion\RunOnceEx

- **RunServices and RunServicesOnce keys.** As their names suggest, these rarely used keys can control automatic startup of services. They can be assigned to a specific user account or to a computer.

- **Winlogon key.** The Winlogon key controls actions that occur when you sign in to a computer running Windows. Most of these actions are under the control of the operating system, but you can also add custom actions here. The HKLM\Software\Microsoft\ Windows NT\CurrentVersion\Winlogon\Userinit and HKLM\Software\Microsoft\Windows NT\CurrentVersion\Winlogon\Shell subkeys can automatically launch programs.

- **Group Policy.** The Group Policy console includes two policies (one in Computer Configuration\Administrative Templates\System\Logon, and one in the comparable User Configuration folder) called Run These Programs At User Logon that specify a list of programs to be run whenever any user signs in.

- **Policies\Explorer\Run keys.** Using policy settings to specify startup programs, as described in the previous paragraph, creates corresponding values in either of two registry keys: HKLM\Software\Microsoft\Windows\CurrentVersion\Policies\Explorer\Run or HKCU\Software\Microsoft\Windows\CurrentVersion\Policies\Explorer\Run.

- **Logon scripts.** Logon scripts, which run automatically at startup, can open other programs. Logon scripts are specified in Group Policy in Computer Configuration\Windows Settings\Scripts (Startup/Shutdown) and User Configuration\Windows Settings\Scripts (Logon/Logoff).

The Startup tab in Task Manager is a fine way to disable startup behavior established by registry keys. Note, however, that Task Manager may not list every startup item; in particular, the list does not include items established by Group Policy or Task Scheduler. For a somewhat more complete list, run System Information (type **system information** in the taskbar search box; the utility should appear at or near the top of the search results). Unlike Task Manager, System Information includes items in the All Users startup folder (%ProgramData%\Microsoft\ Windows\Start Menu\Programs\Startup) as well as those in the startup folder for your own account. It also tells you *which* registry keys are responsible for a program's startup status, instead of simply indicating "Registry." Unfortunately, System Information, like Task Manager, also omits Group Policy and Scheduled Tasks items.

For the most comprehensive listing of items that run at startup, as well as a handy tool to prevent certain programs from starting, we recommend Autoruns, a free utility from Windows Sysinternals. Autoruns, which you can download from *w7io.com/2001*, shows all the registry keys and startup locations listed earlier, and it also shows Explorer shell extensions, services, browser helper objects, and more. Autoruns is particularly useful for finding processes that don't belong (such as a Trojan horse or other malware) or that you suspect of causing problems. You can then disable these items without removing them while you test your theory, or you can delete their autorun command altogether.

Select an item, and its details appear at the bottom of the screen, as shown here. Disable an item by clearing the check box next to its name; you can later reenable it by selecting the check box. To clear an item from the autorun list, select it and click Entry, Delete. (Note that deleting removes only the entry in the registry or other location that causes the item to run; it does not delete the program.)

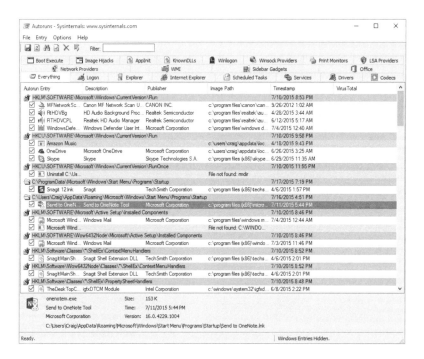

Although the tabs at the top of the Autoruns window filter the list of autorun items into various categories, the number of items can still be daunting. One nice feature of Autoruns is its ability to filter out components that are part of Windows or are digitally signed by Microsoft, as these are presumably safe to run. Commands on the Options menu control the appearance of these items.

You can also use the Compare feature in Autoruns to compare before and after snapshots of the data the program finds. Run Autoruns before you install a new program, save the data, run Autoruns again after you install the program, and compare the results to see what changes to autorun behavior were made by the program's installation.

Setting default programs and file-type associations

Most of the programs you use in Windows are associated with particular file types and protocols. These associations are what enable you, for example, to open an MP3 file in File Explorer and have your favorite audio program play the file, or click an Internet hyperlink in a document or an email message and have your choice of browser take you to the appropriate website. Some of these associations were probably established by the operating system when you performed a clean install or an upgrade from an earlier version of Windows. (The Windows setup program gives you choices in this matter during the installation process, allowing you, for example, to accept the associations that Windows proposes or keep the ones you had established before upgrading.) Regardless of how the associations between programs and file types and protocols are currently set, Windows allows you to see and modify the settings.

Some parts of the user interface used for managing file-type associations and default programs have been migrated to the Windows 10 Settings app, while other parts remain in the old-style Control Panel. Microsoft has indicated that, over time, all of these configuration settings will be available in the Settings app. But as of the July 2015 rollout of Windows 10, this work was still incomplete. You may find yourself using both Settings and Control Panel to get everything set up the way you want it.

For a quick and easy way to set the default app for certain kinds of documents, open Settings, System, and click Default Apps. Figure 8-9 shows an example of what you're likely to see.

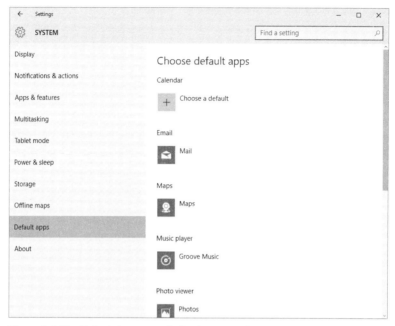

Figure 8-9 The Default Apps page in Settings provides a quick way to change the program associated with certain types of documents.

In the figure, you can see that, for example, the modern Mail app is the default handler for email documents or *mailto* links. To change that, click the Mail icon:

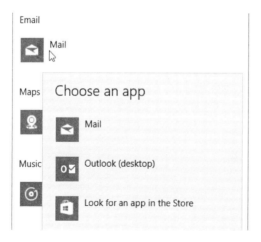

Here, two programs capable of handling email are installed on the system: the modern Mail app and the desktop version of Microsoft Outlook. Mail is currently assigned to this file type. You could change to Outlook or visit the Store to look for something else.

But just because a program is identified in Settings as the default for a file type does not mean that that program is assigned to open *every* file type that it can open. For example, Figure 8-9 shows Groove Music as the default music player. If you scroll to the bottom of the Default Apps list in Settings and click Set Default Apps By Type, however, you arrive in the Set Default Programs section of Control Panel, where you'll discover that Groove Music is the designated player for only 13 of 15 possible file types:

To see which file types Groove Music is assigned to handle and which ones it is not, click Choose Defaults For This Program. A quick glance at the file-type list that appears shows that Windows Media Player is the default for .wav and .wma files, while the rest of the file types are assigned to Groove Music, as shown next.

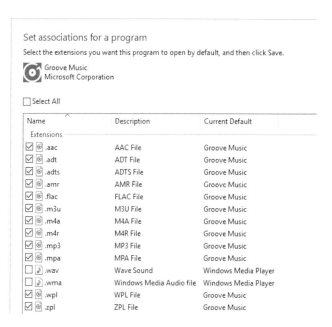

Clicking Select All (or selecting the individual check boxes for .wav and .wma) puts everything in the Groove Music camp.

What if, for some reason, you want to assign a file type in this list—say .mp3—to an altogether different program, perhaps an app that you intend to download from the Windows Store? To do this, return to the Default Apps page in Settings and click Choose Default Apps By File Type. As Figure 8-10 shows, Windows responds with a long alphabetized list of all the file types known to your system.

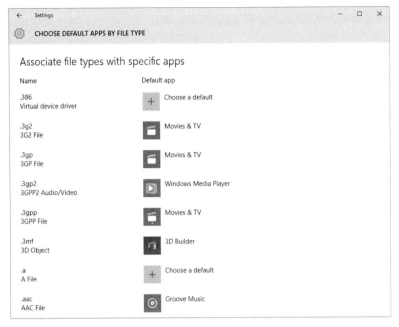

Figure 8-10 By clicking Choose Default Apps By File Type in Settings, you can control the associations for every file type recognized by your system.

Scrolling through the list to the .mp3 entry and clicking the name of the program currently associated with this type allows you to choose a different installed program or visit the Store:

Using a nondefault program ad hoc

If you just want to open a file now and then in an application that's not the default for that file type, there's no need to go through all the business of changing the default application. Simply right-click the file in File Explorer and choose Open With. Windows displays a menu offering the various applications that can open the selected file type. If you don't find the one you want, click Choose Another App. This time a menu similar to the following appears:

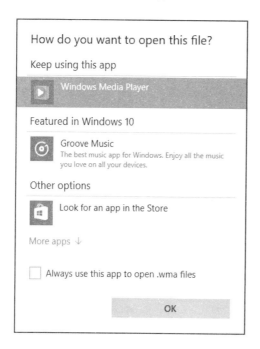

You can do two things in this menu. You can change the default for the selected file type (select one of the listed apps and then click Always Use This App), or you can go for something altogether different by clicking More Apps. Doing this brings up a list of programs, many if not most of which will be completely unsuitable for the selected file type. Select one of these if you're curious to see what will happen. But don't click Always Use This App unless you are quite sure. If the program isn't what you want, it will simply make a nuisance of itself, and you'll have to go to the trouble of making something else the default.

Turning Windows features on or off

If you want to disable or enable certain default Windows features, open Settings and type **turn windows features on or off** in the search box. The dialog box shown in Figure 8-11 appears.

Figure 8-11 The Windows Features dialog box provides a simple way to disable or enable selected programs.

Here you can enable Hyper-V Management Tools (if they're not already enabled), disable Internet Explorer 11 if you have no further need of it, and so on. Note that some of the items in the list have subentries. Those marked by a filled check box have some components enabled and some not.

Setting AutoPlay options

AutoPlay is the feature that enables Windows to take appropriate action when you insert a removable device such as a CD, DVD, or memory card into a drive. The operating system detects the kind of disc or media you have inserted and takes the action that you have requested for that type of media. If you have not already made a decision about what the operating system should do, a window similar to this one appears:

If you don't want Windows to take any action, you can simply click the Close button. Otherwise, clicking or tapping brings you to the screen shown next.

Notice that your choices here are limited to the current default program for the media type (Windows Media Player in this example) and Take No Action. If you don't want to commit to either of these, press Esc.

In any case, if you set a default action for a particular media type and subsequently change your mind and want a different default, you can open Settings and search for **AutoPlay**. Shown in Figure 8-12, AutoPlay in Settings lets you configure some types of media but not (as of July 2015) others. You might need to search for AutoPlay in Control Panel to see the rest.

Figure 8-12 The AutoPlay page in Settings lets you configure AutoPlay behavior for some types of media. You might need to visit Control Panel to configure other types.

In the Control Panel counterpart for this corner of Settings, you will see a dialog box comparable to the one shown in Figure 8-13.

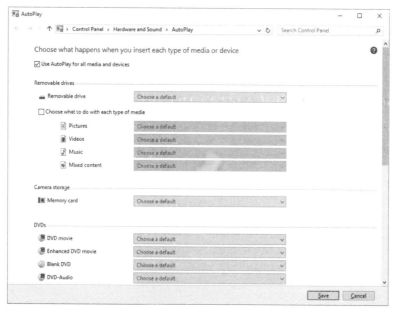

Figure 8-13 For each media type, Windows lets you choose from a list of appropriate possibilities.

Inside OUT

You don't want a default action?

To have no default action for a given media type, choose Ask Me Every Time. To suppress the AutoPlay dialog box completely, choose Take No Action.

Productivity and communication tools

In this chapter and Chapter 10, "Music, photos, movies, and games," we discuss specific programs that are included with a default installation of Windows 10 or available as free downloads from the Windows Store. We break these programs into two large categories, covering those that serve productive purposes in this chapter and those that entertain in the next. (Although we are well aware that the distinction is fuzzy—one person's amusement may certainly be another's business, and some of us find occasional entertainment in the exploration of mundane workaday programs.)

> ➤ For information about Microsoft Edge and Internet Explorer, see Chapter 11, "Browsing the Internet."

The list of tools that come with Windows grows longer with each iteration, largely because every new version, in addition to introducing new items, must continue to support the work habits developed by users of its predecessors. If you have routinely covered your Windows 7 desktop with color-coded sticky notes, for example, you will be pleased to know that the Sticky Notes desktop application is alive and well in Windows 10. (But you might want to explore the Store to see whether a comparable but more richly featured program is available.)

In addition to the obligatory legacy applications, Windows 10 offers a whole set of modern productivity and communication apps, all designed for touch and stylus as well as more traditional input methods. In addition, not installed by default but available without charge from the Store are mobile versions of three Microsoft Office applications—Word, Excel, and PowerPoint. A fourth member of the Office suite, OneNote, is installed by default; you don't have to go to the Store to get it.

We begin our survey with a look at the modern communication and productivity apps.

Mail, Calendar, and People

Although they have separate entries on the Start menu, Mail, Calendar, and People are three faces of a common application. You can switch between Mail and Calendar by tapping or clicking icons in the lower left corner of the window. And the People app, populated by the accounts you set up in Mail or Calendar, provides a directory of potential addressees when you create Mail messages or invite associates to a meeting. Type the beginning of a contact's name or email address on the To line of a message, and if that name or address is among your contacts in People, the To line will be completed for you.

Setting up and using Mail

The first time you open the Mail app, you'll be asked to set up accounts:

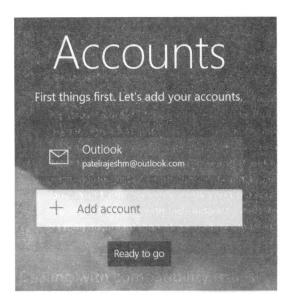

At the top of the list is the Microsoft account you use to sign in to Windows or to Microsoft services such as Outlook.com. Below, you can add more email accounts as needed. Mail supports Exchange, Outlook.com, Gmail, iCloud, POP, and IMAP accounts. The setup process is straightforward, prompting you for your email address and password. You might see additional requests for information and permissions. For a Gmail account, for example, you are presented with the following:

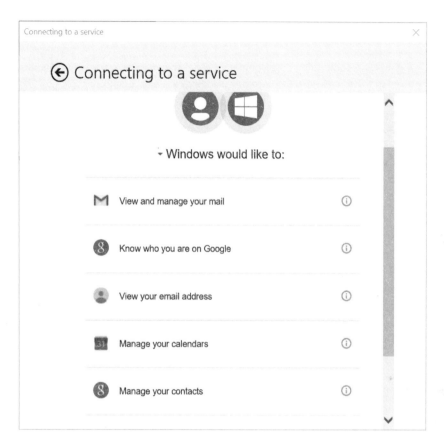

Adding and configuring accounts

To add email accounts subsequently, click the Gear icon in or near the lower left corner of your screen:

The gear is your gateway to settings options for Mail (as for many other modern Windows apps). Click Accounts, then Add Account. To delete or reconfigure an existing account, select it in Settings. Note that you cannot delete (but you can reconfigure) the address associated with your Microsoft account.

Options for reconfiguring an account in Mail are shown in Figure 9-1. The default settings, shown in the figure, reflect the program's intended use as a mail client for users on the go. To save battery and disk space, Mail bases its sync frequency on your usage patterns. If you use Mail now and then only on this computer, the program dials back the sync frequency and reports its decision next to the Currently Syncing heading. In the figure, Mail is fetching your mail only once a day, but if you use the app with any significant frequency, it will fetch messages at shorter time intervals. In any case, you can override the program's decision making and configure a predetermined sync interval by opening the drop-down list at the top of the dialog box.

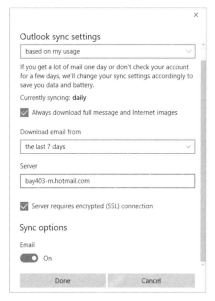

Figure 9-1 By default, the frequency with which Mail syncs messages from your mail server is based on your usage patterns. You can opt to sync more frequently.

Reading and responding to mail

Mail devotes the majority of its screen space to a list of message headers on the left and a reading area on the right. To read a message, tap or click it in the headers pane. To delete a message click or tap the trash can icon near the upper right corner of the header entry:

The icons to the left and right of the trash can let you archive a message or flag it as important. All three of these functions are also available via a shortcut menu if you right-click a message heading.

Creating a new message

To create a new message, click the New Mail icon. Note that the new message window provides an elaborate set of editing tools, derived from Microsoft Word. For example, a wealth of styling options is available via the Format tab on the ribbon. Use the arrows on the ribbon to see the full set of options at your disposal.

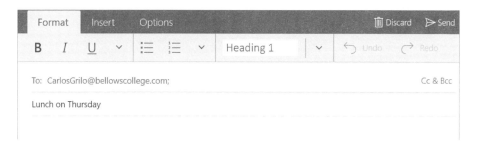

To attach a file to your message, click the Insert tab. You can use that part of the ribbon to insert tables, pictures, and hyperlinks as well. Mail also provides a proofreader; click Options and then click Spelling to check the spelling of your messages.

Using folders

The pane to the left of the message headers provides access to the Drafts and Sent Items system folders. Other folders that you may have created on your mail server appear in an additional pane that appears if you click More, below the system folders. You can move a message from the headers pane to one of your own subfolders by right-clicking the header and then clicking Move.

Setting Quick Actions and other options

On a touchscreen or tablet, you can make quick work of mail-handling tasks by means of Mail's Quick Actions feature (Figure 9-2). Click or tap the gear icon and choose Settings, Options to configure Quick Actions.

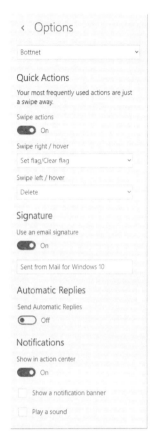

Figure 9-2 The Quick Actions section of the Options pane lets you configure the way Mail responds to swipes with your finger or a stylus and provides easy ways to manage incoming messages.

You can assign one action to a right swipe and another for swiping left. By default, as shown in the figure, putting your finger or stylus on a message and whisking it off to the right flags the message as important (or clears the flag if it has already been set). Dragging in the other direction deletes the message. Alternatives for either direction include marking the message as read or unread and moving a message to a folder.

As Figure 9-2 shows, other parts of the Options pane let you configure a signature that is appended to outgoing messages, turn on automatic replies, and specify how and whether you want to be notified of incoming mail. If you turn on automatic replies, the pane expands so that you can enter your preferred message—for example, "I'm out of the office until the end of the month." You can specify one message for senders within your organization and another for those outside, and you can limit the automatic response sent to people on the outside to those who are on your contacts list.

Once you have flagged a set of messages, you might want to change the message list to show only those you have flagged. To do this, click the arrow to the right of Inbox and then choose Flagged. You can apply a similar filter if you want to see only those messages not marked as read.

One more command worth mentioning is Zoom. If your mobile device is just too small for comfortable reading, click the three dots at the upper right corner of the window, and then choose Zoom from the menu that descends. Magnification options range from 50 percent to 400 percent.

Setting up and using Calendar

In both Mail and Calendar, two icons at the lower left corner let you switch from one app to the other. If you're already running Mail, a quick tap takes you straight to Calendar. Alternatively, you'll find Calendar on your Start menu or the All Apps list.

Accounts set up in Mail are used in Calendar and vice versa. You can add or modify accounts in Calendar as you would in Mail; click the gear icon, and then click Accounts in the Settings pane. If you're using multiple accounts, your Calendar events will be distinguished by color, and if the display gets noisy, you can use the check boxes in the left pane, below the thumbnail calendar, to suppress particular components of your composite calendar, as shown next.

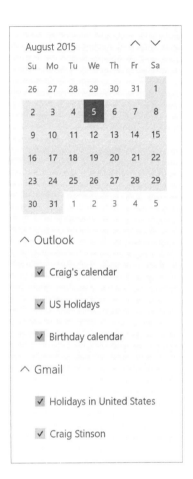

If you don't see this pane at the left of your screen, click or tap the so-called hamburger icon in the upper left corner. Doing this removes or redisplays the left pane (you'll find it useful particularly on a small display).

Adding an event

To add an event to your calendar, either click or tap New Event, or click the calendar itself. If you click New Event, you get the full Details window for the event, shown in Figure 9-3. If you click a day or an hour on the calendar, you get a smaller version of this window, and you can move to the full view by clicking More Details. In either case, if you have Calendar configured to use more than one account, you'll want to specify which account the new event should belong to.

Use the Reminder list to specify your preferences regarding alerts. Calendar defaults to a 15-minute heads-up, but you have lots of alternatives, including None. Note that Calendar's live tile (if you have the app on your Start menu) will also alert you to upcoming events. Cortana can offer reminders as well, of course, depending on how you have configured her.

Figure 9-3 shows the details of a recurring event. To create such an item, simply click Repeat and specify your parameters. Calendar offers daily, weekly, monthly, and yearly options.

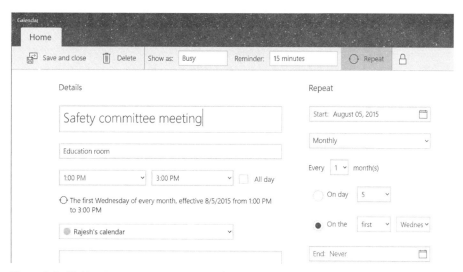

Figure 9-3 Clicking Repeat opens a new set of options, where you can specify yearly, monthly, weekly, or daily parameters for a recurring event.

Inviting others to a meeting

To create a meeting event and invite others to join, add the email addresses of your invitees to the People section of your Details view. Then click Send. Each of the invitees will get a message allowing him or her to send back a yes-no-maybe response:

Recipients can expand the lists next to the Tentative and Decline buttons to add a message of explanation.

Adding or editing contacts with People

People is a simple app that acts as a repository for contacts derived from the accounts you set up in Mail or Calendar. (You can also add or delete accounts in People itself.) As the following illustration shows, People simply lists your contacts:

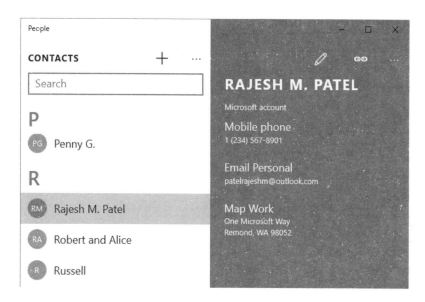

You can edit a contact's information by selecting the contact in the left pane and clicking the Edit icon (shaped like a pencil) on the right. If you have more than one entry for a contact, you can use the Link icon (to the right of the Edit icon) to consolidate them.

Downloading and using Skype

Skype, Microsoft's Internet video telephony and conferencing tool, is not part of a default installation of Windows 10, but you can download the free version by running Get Skype from the Start menu. (If you don't find Get Skype, go to *www.skype.com*.) Microsoft also offers a more richly featured product called Skype for Business (formerly known as Lync), either as a standalone item or as part of the business versions of Office 365. For information about features and pricing of Skype for Business, see *www.skype.com/business*.

After you download the app, Skype will prompt you to create an account or sign in to an existing one. Figure 9-4 shows how your screen might look after you have created your account but before you have added any contacts.

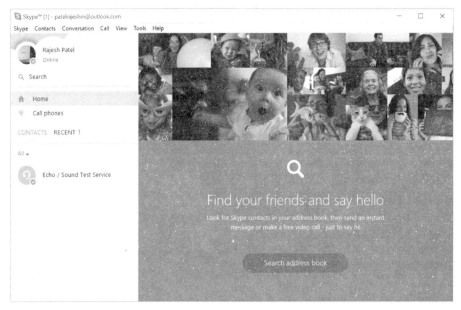

Figure 9-4 After you create a Skype account and sign in, your first actions might be to use the Echo/Sound Test Service link to verify that your camera and microphone are functioning and the Search link to add contacts.

Before you start making calls, you might want to check your video, microphone, and speaker settings. You can do this by clicking Echo/Sound Test Service in the Contacts pane. Alternatively, open the Tools menu, choose Options, and then click either Audio Settings or Video Settings.

To add contacts, click Search (below your name in the upper left corner of the window). Type your contact's Skype account name if you know it or an email address. You can also simply type the contact's name, but this approach might produce a long list of Skype users with identical first and last names. When you find the person you want to add, select the name and click Add To Contacts. Your contact will then receive a request message:

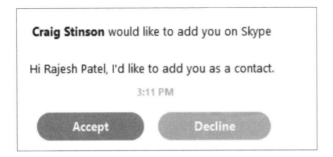

Craig Stinson would like to add you on Skype

Hi Rajesh Patel, I'd like to add you as a contact.

3:11 PM

Accept   Decline

Note that if you receive an unwanted contact solicitation and choose to decline, the Decline button provides additional options to simply block the request or report it as spam.

With your equipment checked out and your contacts list populated, you might then want to flesh out your own profile—the information that your contacts will see about you. The profile screen appears when you click your own name in the upper left corner of the window, and here you can add phone information and many other details. (Click Show Full Profile to see the complete list of fields you can change.) If you shot your profile with the rear-facing camera by mistake or simply want to transmit a different image (there's no requirement that it be you!), click Change Picture.

Placing or answering an audio or video call

To initiate an Internet-to-Internet call, click your contact's name, and then choose one of the options that appear on the right side of the screen:

Click the icon on the right (the one with the plus sign) to add more people to the call. The phone icon in the center makes the call audio only. Choose the camera icon on the left to send video as well. You can also switch in and out of video during the call if the need arises—for example, if the quality of your Internet connection is not strong enough to support video transmission.

Similar buttons appear if someone places a call to you. Before you answer, you'll also get an audio signal to alert you to the call.

Calling people who don't have Skype or aren't online

Skype also lets you place Voice-over-Internet-Protocol (VoIP) calls to people who don't have Skype accounts or are not online. The calls are charged at per-minute rates that vary by country or region. Before placing a call, you can buy credit by opening the Skype menu and choosing Buy Skype Credit. For users in the United States, credit is available in increments of $10 and $25.

When you're ready to call, click Call Phones. On the dialer that appears, open the Choose Country/Region drop-down list, select the country or region you're calling, click the numbers to dial, and then click the phone icon.

Sending text or video messages, pictures, or files

To send a text message, select a contact name, and then type in the text box that appears at the bottom of the window. (You can also send text while you're in an audio or video call.) To send a video message to someone, click the paper-clip icon to the left of the text box, and then click Send Video Message. Your camera will come to life, your shining visage will appear on the screen, and you can click the red Record button when you're ready to start. Click the Send button when you're satisfied and ready to transmit.

To send a photo or a file, click the paper-clip icon and choose Send Photo or Send File.

Using the mobile and desktop versions of OneNote

Windows 10 comes with a modern OneNote app preinstalled. You don't have to grab it from the Store; it should already be there on your system. (If for any reason it's not, you *can* get it from the Store, free of charge.) This is a lightweight mobile version of Microsoft's excellent note-taking application, optimized by the size and spacing of the ribbon's tabs and commands to be used with fingers or a stylus. (It also works fine on systems without touchscreens, of course.)

Also free, but a download away (from *www.onenote.com/download*), is the full-featured desktop version of OneNote, a component of Microsoft Office. (As we write, the downloadable product is OneNote 2013, but OneNote 2016 is standing only a few feet offstage.) If you have a tablet or other touchscreen system, you can use your fingers or stylus with this version of OneNote as well, although the targets on the user interface will be a little smaller.

Because the mobile OneNote is a modern app, it is updated automatically by the Windows Store. The desktop Office applications, including OneNote, may also be updated periodically via Windows Update, but it's possible that Microsoft will be putting more development effort into the modern app.

In any case, there's no compelling reason to choose one or the other. You can use both, and your notebooks will be synced automatically and accessible from either version (as well as from your phone if you have OneNote installed there). OneNote Mobile may be ideal when you're on the go or when you're concerned with reading your notes (and those that others have shared with you) and making simple annotations. For more extensive editing and note taking, and for such things as inserting recorded audio or video notes, you'll probably want the much larger feature set provided by the desktop program.

If you're new to OneNote, the most essential things to know are these:

- Like the other Office mobile apps (Excel, Word, and PowerPoint), OneNote saves every-thing you enter immediately and instantly. If your notebook is stored on OneDrive, you have access to it from anywhere.

- Notes are stored in *notebooks*, which are subdivided into *sections*. Each section consists of one or more *pages*. OneNote gives you a notebook to start with, and that notebook contains a single section (called New Section 1) consisting of a single page (called Unti-tled Page). Sections are identified by tabs arrayed across the top, and pages are listed vertically, on the left (in the mobile version) or the right (in the desktop version). Click the plus signs to add sections or pages.

- OneNote is a free-form editor. You can type or jot anywhere on the page. With drawing tools, you can annotate your annotations.

With the desktop version of OneNote, you can create shared notebooks for collaborative proj-ects. Click File to see a list of your notebooks. To share an existing notebook, click Invite People To This Notebook, below a notebook's name. (The notebook must be stored on OneDrive for this link to be available.) To create a new shared notebook, click File, then New. Choose a loca-tion, supply a name, and then click Create Notebook. In a moment, the following prompt will appear:

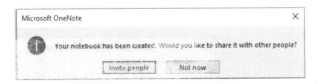

Click Invite People, and then supply email addresses.

Shared notebooks, like all others, are usable in both versions of OneNote, but in the mobile version you're limited to sharing the current page. To do that, click the Share icon at the upper right corner of the window.

Using the mobile versions of Word, Excel, and PowerPoint

Microsoft also provides touch-optimized versions of three major Office programs—Word, Excel, and PowerPoint. Comparable to the mobile edition of OneNote described in the previous section, these mobile Office apps are modern apps that are ideal for quick reads and edits on tablets. Their large and well-spaced user-interface controls make them easy to manage with fingers and styli.

NOTE

The mobile Office apps are free (you can find them in the Windows Store), but their full functionality requires an Office 365 subscription. Without a subscription, you can open and read Office documents, but you cannot edit or save documents. In any case, you should consider these mobile items as on-the-go complements to their desktop suite-mates. For extensive document generation and editing, you'll want the larger feature set that comes with Office 365.

Features common to the mobile Office apps

Here are some important features shared by all three mobile Office apps:

- **Autosave.** Changes are saved instantly and automatically. The name under which the current document is being saved appears in the center of the screen, above the ribbon:

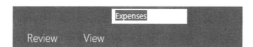

You can change the name by clicking it and typing a new one, but you might find it easier to tap the File menu and then tap Save. As Figure 9-5 shows, the Save command serves the function that is assigned to the Save As command in other programs.

Figure 9-5 The Save command shows you where and under what name your file is being automatically saved. You can rename or copy the file here.

If you are making tentative edits, or if you are concerned that an errant press of your finger or hand might change the file's content awkwardly, consider working with a copy instead of the original. You can make a copy by visiting the Save command.

- **Sharing.** Clicking the Share icon in the upper right corner of the ribbon lets you extend read or read/write privileges to other people. As Figure 9-6 shows, you can attach a message to your invitation. Below the message appear the names of everyone who already has access to the document.

- **Help.** Near the Share icon on all three apps is a lightbulb icon. This provides access to the "Tell me what you want to do" feature (which will also be part of the Office 2016 desktop applications). When you indicate what you want to accomplish here, the program will—if it can—carry out the action you request instead of directing you to an explanation of how to do it. To save you stylus-strokes, a list of commonly requested actions appears, under the heading Try. (See Figure 9-7.) If what you want isn't there, you can type the task. If all else fails—for example, if the program can't understand or carry out your order—you'll be redirected to an Internet help source.

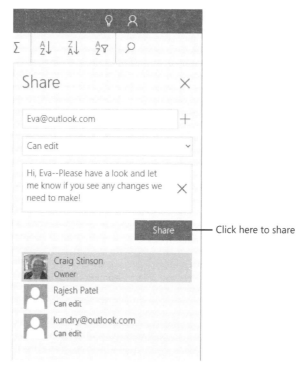

Click here to share

Figure 9-6 Clicking the Share icon lets you send a personalized invitation to a friend or coworker and shows you who is already on the team.

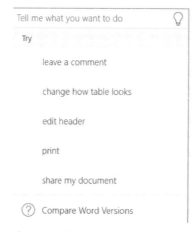

Figure 9-7 "Tell me what you want to do" can provide a quicker alternative to traditional Help commands. If it can, the mobile Office app will carry out your instructions directly, without telling you what to do.

Exploring the mobile Office apps

If you are familiar with the desktop counterparts of the three mobile Office apps, you might want to start exploring the mobile apps by looking at the comparison topics available via the "Tell me what you want to do" feature. These appear below the list of suggested entries. Figure 9-7, for example, shows the topic Compare Word Versions at the bottom of Word Mobile's "Tell me" list. These commands lead you to useful comparisons. Beyond comparing, the best way to learn about these apps is, quite literally, by poking around. Here are a few highlights.

Using Reading view in Word Mobile

Word Mobile has a Reading view that makes perusing a document on a small screen more comfortable. To get there, tap Read on the View tab or click the Read icon, between the "Tell me" icon and the Share icon, near the upper right edge of the screen. As Figure 9-8 shows, the Read tab offers a number of useful options for sizing, coloring, and spacing text. Reading view opens in full-screen mode; to see the Read tab, click the three dots at the upper right side of the window. To get out of Reading view, click Edit on the Read tab.

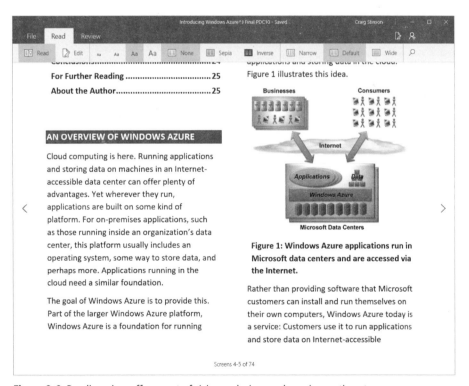

Figure 9-8 Reading view offers a set of sizing, coloring, and spacing options to ease your eyes on a small screen.

Simplifying formula entry in Excel Mobile

Options on the Home tab provide quick access to many of Excel Mobile's commonly used commands. You can create sums here, for example, sort rows in a table, insert rows and columns, and so on. For more complex formula entry, however, click the Formula icon (*fx*) at the left edge, below the ribbon. Using the categorized function list that descends, you can enter the formula you need with a minimum of typing:

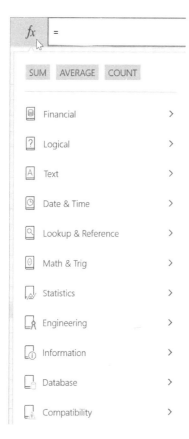

Using your finger as a laser pointer in PowerPoint Mobile

There's no need to use a mouse to highlight important points in a PowerPoint presentation. Start your slide show, and then use your finger to point to the places you want to underscore. After a pause, your finger press will produce a red dot on the presentation, which you can move as you would a highlighter.

Using Maps

Mapping applications have long been one of the indispensable tools of modern life. Microsoft's modern Maps app should serve you well, whether you want to explore a new city, plot a road trip, find a restaurant, print a set of turn-by-turn directions to take with you on the road, or just enjoy aerial views of the world or your neighborhood. (If you search for a restaurant known to Maps, you'll be rewarded with reviews, hours, and website information in addition to a map.)

On first run, Maps asks for permission to track your location information. If you consent, Maps will plant a marker at your current location. When you start Maps, it always opens to whatever map or view you were using last, but pressing Ctrl+Home displays your current location, assuming the program knows what that is.

To find a location, click the Search tool on the left or press Ctrl+F. You can type an address or the name of a place known to Maps—an institution or a restaurant, for example. As in Figure 9-9, Maps shows the location on the map and a couple of street-side pictures below the search string, on the left. A Nearby icon below the pictures provides categorized entries for potential items of interest near the selected location.

Figure 9-9 In addition to displaying your search item on the map, Maps shows pictures and can lead you to nearby attractions.

To get directions, click the Directions icon, directly below the Search icon, and then type your starting and ending points (one of them may already be in place if you just searched for it). Maps responds with a set of turn-by-turn instructions:

Above the turn instructions, you'll find a summary of the route—the distance, traffic conditions, and expected time of travel. Use the printer icon directly below this summary to print the directions as well as the map.

Maps defaults to showing driving directions. To see public transportation information instead, click the bus icon near the upper right corner of the directions pane. For a walking route, click the humanoid icon next to the bus icon. Maps calculates its walking time at a rate of about 2.3 miles per hour. If you usually walk or ride public transit, you can change the default by clicking the gear-shaped Settings icon and opening the Preferred Directions list.

With a set of directions in place, you can click the Go button, at the right side of the summary information, and you can expand the turn information to show maps and route at each point along the way:

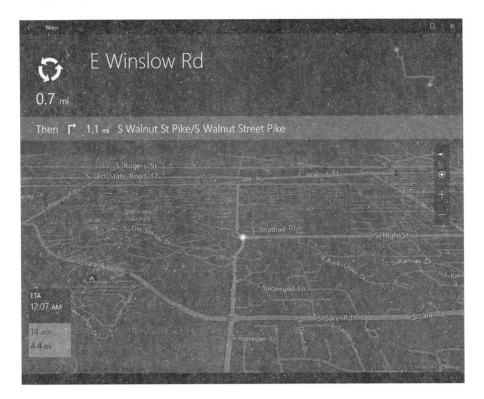

On a GPS-enabled device, such as a phone with Windows 10, Maps will give you spoken directions. If your device does not have GPS capability, silent images such as this will appear. (Please don't attempt to read these images and instructions while you drive; your passenger will be happy to act as navigator.)

On the right side of a map's display, Maps offers a panel of additional options, allowing you to change the compass heading, switch between plane and elevation views, display your current location, switch between aerial and street views, and zoom in and out. Clicking Map Views, the fourth of these icons, yields the flyout options shown next.

Maps also includes a 3D Cities feature (the last icon in the panel on the left side of the screen), which lets you display aerial images of a large selection of cities in various parts of the world. When you need a break from your labors, you can travel vicariously to Aix-en-Provence or drop in for an overhead look at the Dresden Frauenkirche:

Using Alarms & Clock

As the name implies, Alarms & Clock will give you a nudge at a prescribed time. You can configure an alarm to sound once only or to repeat on particular days. For example, if you use an alarm to rouse you from sleep, you can have one alarm for workdays and another for weekends. As this image shows, you can also attach a text message to an alarm—to let you know why you're being roused.

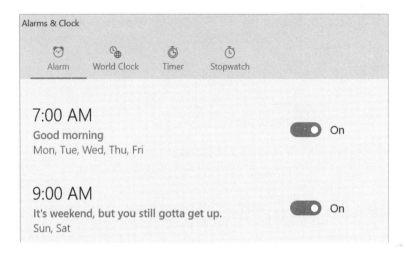

Alarms will also wake your computer from sleep—provided your hardware supports InstantGo. For more information about this feature, previously known as Connected Standby, see *bit.ly/InstantGo*.

To set a new alarm, click the plus sign on the Alarm page. Be sure to click the Save icon on the New Alarm page when you have things set up as you want them. To remove an item from your collection of alarms, right-click it and click Delete.

On the World Clock page, you can check out the time in any part of the world and compare it with your local time. Click the plus sign to add a city. The display uses shading to show where the sun is up and where it's not, as shown next.

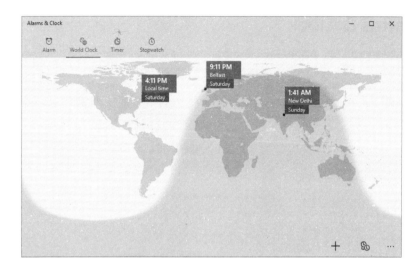

The remaining two pages in Alarms & Clock provide basic timer and stopwatch functionality. Alarms & Clock is a simple app. If you need something more elaborate, visit the Store.

The info apps: News, Weather, Sports, and Money

Windows 10 provides four excellent apps, powered by MSN (*www.msn.com*), that can keep you up to date about things going on around you (or lead you down the path to total self-distraction, depending on your inclinations). You can peruse the current headlines, drill down by category, search for anything you don't immediately find—and either read immediately or save items to your reading list to look at later. (The Reading List app is discussed in the next section.) All the info apps implement live tiles; pin them to your Start menu to get quick headlines.

News

The News app presents large tiles for recent headline stories, smaller tiles for stories of subordinate interest (be sure to scroll to see the whole list), and a menu across the top that lets you filter by category:

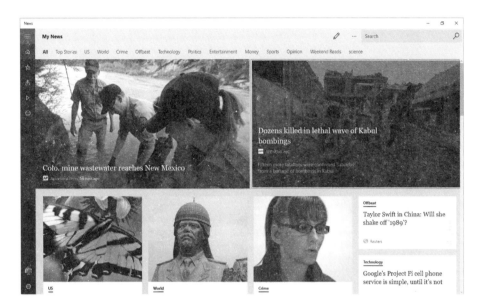

The horizontal menu across the top covers many categories but doesn't include local news. For that, click the fourth icon in the vertical toolbar on the left:

If you're looking for a story about a particular topic that doesn't happen to bubble up to the top of one of the category pages, try the Search field. As Figure 9-10 shows, News will present what MSN has about your search topic, along with other items judged to be related.

The horizontal menu of news categories might not include some you'd like to see and others you never want to bother with. To customize, click the Interests icon:

The My Interests page shows all your current categories. To remove a category, click the green check mark. To add others, select one of the items in the menu on the left, and then click the plus sign for a category you want to add.

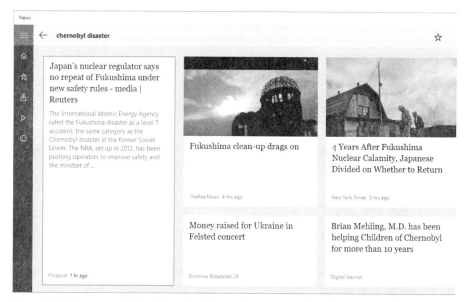

Figure 9-10 Here a search for "Chernobyl disaster" summons a few Chernobyl items plus several others that MSN judges to be related.

Weather

The Weather app offers a wealth of forecasted and historical information about virtually any city in the world, including your own:

Scroll down the Forecast page to see details about the day—sunrise, sunset, wind speed, humidity, and more. Below that you'll find record highs, lows, and rainfall. You might also find such tidbits as the number of times thunderstorms have occurred on this day over the past 30 years. More interesting details await you on the Maps and Historical Weather pages. Click the icons in the panel on the left to display these.

If there are cities you regularly track, visit the Places page, shown next:

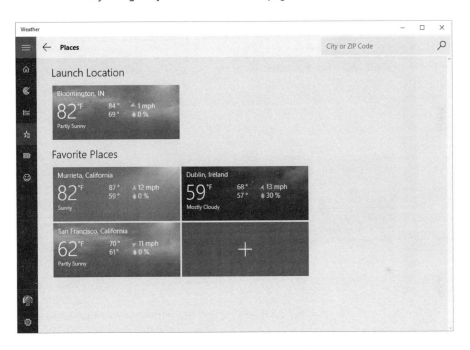

Click the plus sign to add a city. Right-click a city to remove it.

Finally, visit the News page for current weather stories.

Sports

With the Sports app, you can follow news stories about your favorite teams or sports:

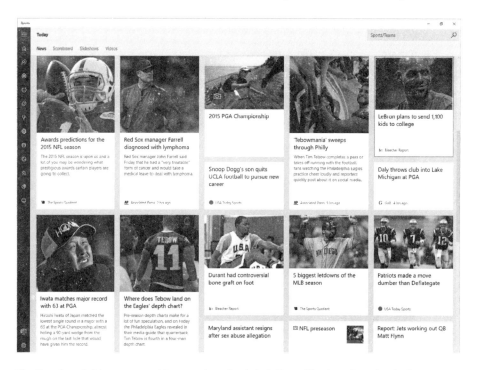

The list of available sports and leagues is truly global. If you like American football, you can follow the NFL, but Europeans who have a different definition of football can choose from no fewer than 42 separate leagues on the continent. You can also track Australian Rules football, cricket, and rugby. Or you can see a scoreboard of all the games currently going on:

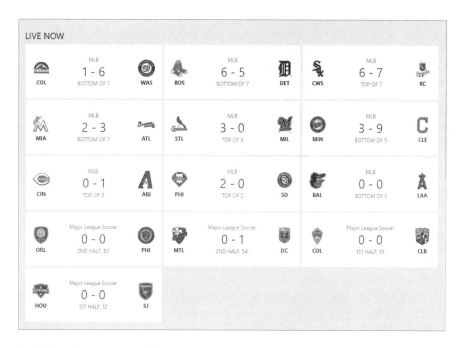

By drilling down on one of the current games, you can view detailed information in something close to real time:

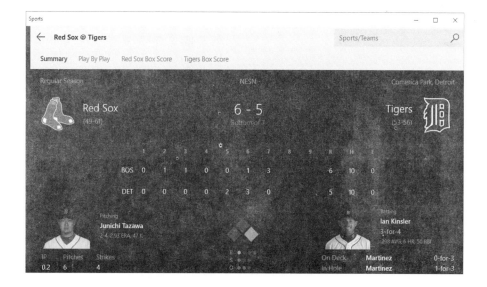

In your exploration of Sports, don't neglect to visit My Favorites (the third icon from the bottom in the panel at the left). There you can add the teams that you are particularly interested in following. Sports will feed updates from these teams to its live tile.

Money

As Sports does for games, Money lets you track market action in an approximation of real time. Below the news stories on the Home page, a dashboard shows the current action in several major markets:

Click a market to see more detail:

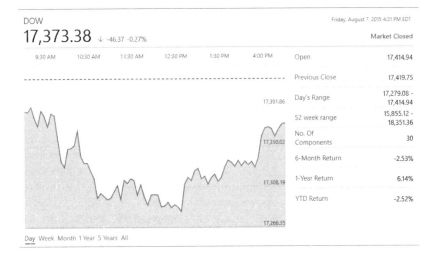

The Money app covers stocks, bonds, commodities, and currencies. Click the World Markets icon (sixth from the top in the panel at the left) to see a map of the world with summaries of many regional markets. Click the Currency Converter icon (fourth in the panel) to check current conversion rates. The Watchlist icon (third from the top) lets you add stock symbols of particular interest. On your Watchlist page, Money supplies news stories as well as price data.

Sharing and saving news stories

When you find a story that you want to keep or send to someone else, open the story and then click the Share icon:

A menu will appear showing sharing options:

Choosing Mail opens your default mail client. If you choose OneNote, you'll see OneNote's proposed destination notebook and section. Use the drop-down list to change the destination.

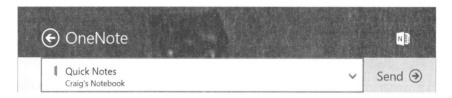

If you choose Reading List App, a confirmation appears providing the name and source of your story. Open the Categorize list to specify which Reading List category will serve as your destination. (See the following section for information about Reading List app categories.)

Preserving items of interest with Windows Reading List

The first thing to know about the Windows Reading List app is that it is completely separate from the reading list *feature* that's part of the Microsoft Edge web browser. (Introduced in Windows 8, the app predates the browser.) Moreover, the reading list the app maintains is also separate from the one you might create in Edge. Windows Reading List is not installed by default; you can install it for free from the Store.

> **For information about using the reading list feature in Microsoft Edge, see "Using Reading List, an alternative to Favorites" in Chapter 11.**

The Reading List app is ideal for those who browse news stories with the expectation of read-ing them thoroughly later. Nearly any story that you open in one of the info apps (described in the previous section) can be saved to the Reading List app. Most webpages that you open in Edge (but not in browsers that are desktop applications) can be saved either to the Reading List app or to the reading list in Edge. Stories that you save to the Reading List app are avail-able on any computer on which you sign in using the Microsoft account under which the item was saved. For example, you can browse at home and then read your selections on your tablet or laptop as you ride the train to work.

The Reading List app organizes saved items in categories. The app gives you six categories to start with—Finance, Food, Health, News, Sports, and Travel. You can create and delete catego-ries at will. Anything not stored in a category goes into an additional bin called Uncategorized:

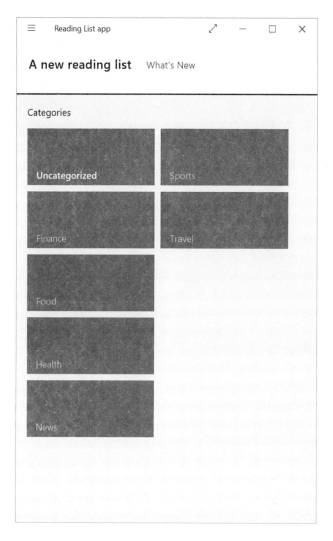

To save a story or webpage to the Reading List app, click the Share icon near the upper right corner of the window, and then select Reading List from the list of sharing options. You'll have an opportunity to choose a category in the confirmation dialog box that the Reading List app presents, as shown next.

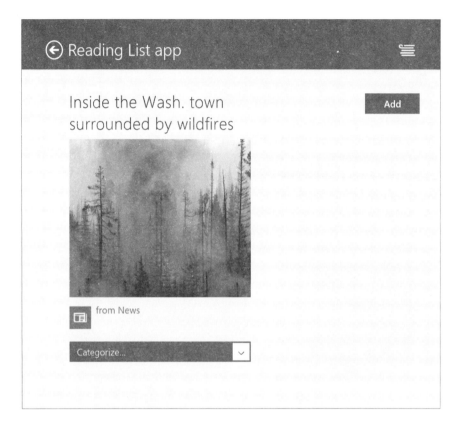

When you open the Reading List app, you see the most recent items you have added (in descending chronological order) regardless of how they're categorized. This time-ordered display gives you another method of finding your material. To get to your categories, right-click anywhere in the window other than on a story tile, and then choose the category you want.

To open a story, simply click its tile. To put an uncategorized item into a category, right-click its tile. A menu that shows your current categories pops up from the bottom of the screen, and you can make a selection. An item at the bottom of this category list lets you create a new category.

You can keep stories in the Reading List app for as long as you like, but as a space-saving measure, the app removes the image from a story's tile after three months.

To delete an item, right-click it and then click Delete. Deleted items are kept in an archived state for, by default, 30 days. If you want another look at something you've deleted, right-click in the app (not on a tile) and click Recently Deleted. You can change the archival time to either

10 days or 60 days. To do this, click the hamburger menu, choose Settings, and then choose
Options.

Voice Recorder

The Sound Recorder application that was included with Windows versions dating back to the
Middle Ages (well, perhaps not *quite* that long) has been replaced by a shiny new modern app
called Voice Recorder. The Voice Recorder app, which creates files in the .m4a format, is great
for recording speeches, lectures, and interviews. There is no maximum time for a recording,
and you can mark the recording at interesting junctures while your speaker speaks. During
subsequent playback, a simple click on the marked timeline will bring you back to a place you
found noteworthy.

To start recording, click the microphone icon in the left pane. While recording is in progress,
Voice Recorder presents a flag icon that you can use to mark points of interest. The three time
indications at the bottom of the following illustration indicate marks that have already been
made.

When you have finished recording, Voice Recorder's left pane adds the new recording to the
list of those you've already made, as shown next.

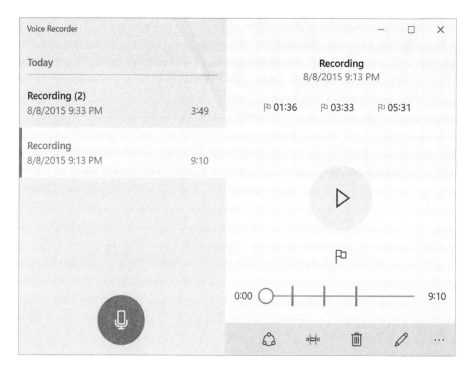

To change a recording's name to something descriptive, click the pencil icon on the toolbar in the right pane.

Voice Recorder includes a Trim command, by means of which you can shorten a recording. When you click the second icon on the toolbar, black handles appear at the beginning and end of the timeline:

Drag the handles forward or backward and click the check mark to trim your recording.

CHAPTER 10

Music, photos, movies, and games

Not that long ago, your PC was the indispensable hub of digital media. Music and movies were delivered on shiny discs, and you needed a desktop or laptop PC to rip CDs, watch DVDs, transfer photos from your digital camera, and share your photos on social media.

Today, the explosion of mobile devices and cloud-based entertainment services means the PC is no longer a hub, and shiny discs are now an endangered species. The PC is still uniquely qualified for tasks that involve editing and managing a media collection and syncing it with cloud services, but for playing those files you're more likely to use a smaller mobile device.

The three core media apps included with Windows 10—Groove Music, Photos, and Movies & TV—are tightly connected to the cloud. Like other apps built on the Universal Windows Platform, they're touch-friendly but also work well in a window on a conventional PC.

If you're worried that the digital media landscape in Windows 10 will be completely alien, we can reassure you that a few of your familiar touchstones remain: Windows Media Player is still available for playing music and movies on a desktop or portable PC. Likewise, the venerable Windows Photo Viewer and, yes, Microsoft Paint are still around, virtually unchanged from their Windows 7 incarnations.

In the living room, it's still possible to connect a PC to a home entertainment system directly, although the experience is less enjoyable than it used to be now that Windows Media Center is no longer available with any edition of Windows 10 (in fact, Media Center is removed from your system when you upgrade from a prior edition). More modern alternatives include streaming content from a Windows tablet or PC to a large display (like your big-screen TV) by using built-in support for the Miracast standard. And if your living room or rec room includes an Xbox One game console, it's easy to connect to a Windows 10 PC.

But before we talk about apps, let's review the basics of how Windows 10 organizes media files.

Managing your digital media libraries

In the Windows world, digital media files are managed just like other files. As with earlier versions, Windows 10 creates default libraries for Music, Pictures, and Videos, and it uses metadata in files stored within folders in those libraries to organize their contents.

> ➤ For a detailed discussion of how to view and manage metadata in files, see "Managing file properties and metadata" in Chapter 12, "Organizing and searching for files."

In Details view, files in these locations are arranged in columns that reflect their content. The default Music folder, for example, displays song titles, contributing artists, and the name of the album containing those songs. After selecting multiple MP3 files, you can use the properties dialog box to change the album or artist title for the entire group, as shown in Figure 10-1. (This editing is supported in all widely used digital media formats, including Windows Media Audio and several lossless formats we discuss later in this chapter.)

Figure 10-1 Use the properties dialog box to edit metadata for music files, such as changing the album title for a selection of tracks.

When you use File Explorer to open folders that contain music, photos, or videos, Windows adds a custom tab to the ribbon, with tasks appropriate for that type of data. Figure 10-2, for example, shows the Music Tools tab, with options to play files from the current folder, add them to a playlist, or "cast" them to a device such as a Miracast-enabled TV or an Xbox One (a topic we discuss in more detail later in this chapter).

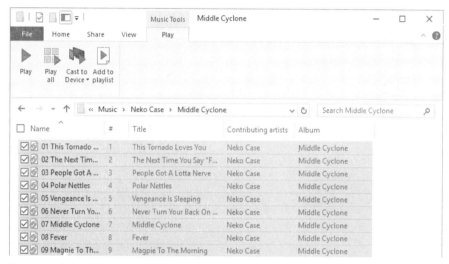

Figure 10-2 For folders containing music files, the File Explorer ribbon adds a custom Music Tools tab with commands for direct playback to the default player app.

Likewise, folders containing digital image files contain a custom Picture Tools tab like the one shown in Figure 10-3, which offers an extremely limited set of customization options as well as the ability to bore your friends and family with a slide show cast to your Xbox One or other compatible device.

Despite the new look, all the new digital media apps use the tried-and-true library capabilities in Windows 10 to determine which files to display when you open the respective app. You can customize the selection of folders included in each library by clicking the gear icon to open Settings in any of the three apps. Figure 10-4, for example, shows the dialog box that appears when you click or tap Choose Where We Look For Music in the Groove Music app.

Figure 10-3 The Picture Tools tab appears automatically on folders containing images, offering simple rotation tools and slide-show capabilities.

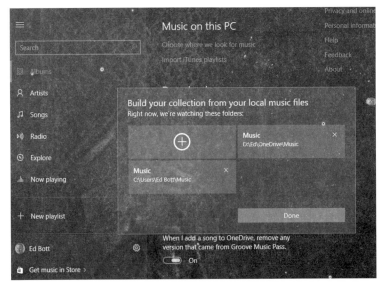

Figure 10-4 Every digital media app in Windows 10 includes a setting to adjust which folders are included in the corresponding library.

Note that any changes you make to the selection of folders in any of the three core digital media apps are automatically reflected in the corresponding Windows 10 library and vice versa.

And, of course, as befits a cloud-centric operating system, all those apps are also integrated with OneDrive. The Photos app, for example, includes the contents of your OneDrive Camera Roll folder, which contains photos you upload from mobile devices (iPhones and Android devices are supported, as are Windows phones). You can upload pictures to OneDrive manually or configure your phone so that new photos are automatically uploaded to OneDrive for safekeeping and sharing.

Similarly, you can store your music collection in OneDrive and stream or download its contents to any Windows 10 device using the Groove Music app.

Music

No, you're not seeing double. Windows 10 includes two programs whose primary purpose is to play digital music files.

- Groove Music is a Universal Windows app and the default app for playing music files in Windows 10. It's the direct successor to the Xbox Music app from Windows 8.1, and it traces its ancestry (at least indirectly) to the late, lamented Zune Music app. Using Groove Music, you can stream or download your music collection from OneDrive, play music files in a variety of formats, and stream customized playlists from the Groove Music service based on a single track, an album, or an artist. With a Groove Music Pass, you can listen to any album in the service's vast collection and download those album tracks for offline listening on up to four devices.

- Windows Media Player in Windows 10 is virtually identical to the version shipped with Windows 7. (The single, very large exception is support for files saved using formats based on lossless compression.) The most distinctive feature of Windows Media Player compared with Groove Music is its ability to play CDs and rip their contents to digital formats. It can also sync content with some older models of portable music players.

Both programs create indexed libraries from the contents of folders in your Music library. The indexes are stored separately.

Groove Music

Every installation of Windows 10 sets Groove Music as the default music player. Figure 10-5 offers an overview of the program's interface.

Figure 10-5 The Groove Music app's contents pane shows your entire collection by default. You can switch to a view by artist or show all songs by using links on the left.

The design of the Groove Music app isn't difficult to figure out. A menu pane on the left allows you to change the way your collection is displayed (Albums, Artists, or Songs). You can start a customized streaming playlist by clicking Radio, browse new albums available for purchase (or for playback with a Groove Music Pass) by using the Explore button, or display the current playlist by clicking Now Playing. Your custom playlists appear at the bottom of the left pane.

Figure 10-6 shows the options when you click to display the contents of an individual album. (The four options to the right of the album cover are visible because we clicked More.)

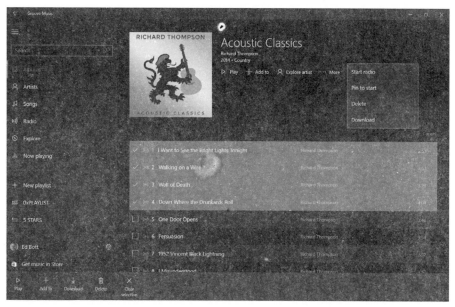

Figure 10-6 The options at the bottom apply only to the current selection. Use the Add To option to send tracks or an entire album to a custom playlist.

As we noted earlier, Groove Music integrates neatly with OneDrive. Any compatible files you save to the Music folder in OneDrive are available for playback when you sign in on any Windows 10 device. The resulting collection can be displayed along with locally stored files or maintained separately. Use the Filter menu, as shown in Figure 10-7, to specify your preferences.

Search terms you enter in the box at the top of the menu show results from your collection by default, as shown in Figure 10-8. You can change the scope to Full Catalog to show additional results, which are available for purchase or, with a Groove Music Pass, for streaming and download.

Figure 10-7 Use the Filter menu to show only a subset: albums saved in the OneDrive Music folder, for example, or those available offline.

Figure 10-8 Searches display results that match artists, albums, and songs from your collection by default. Use the Full Catalog option to see additional results from the Store.

TROUBLESHOOTING

You can't hear any sound from your speakers

Modern PCs often have multiple playback channels, in both digital and analog formats. Audio playback hardware can be found in a variety of locations: on your motherboard; as an optional feature on an add-in video card, with multichannel sound typically delivered over an HDMI cable; on an add-in sound card; or through headphones connected physically or wirelessly using a Bluetooth connection. It's not unusual to find multiple audio playback options in a single PC, especially one that has been upgraded extensively.

If your hardware and drivers appear to be installed correctly but you're unable to hear any sound, right-click the speaker icon in the notification area at the right side of the taskbar and choose Playback Devices. This opens the Sound dialog box from Control Panel, with the Playback tab selected. Look for a green check mark next to the device currently designated as the default playback device. In the following example, the built-in speakers are disabled, and headphones connected via Bluetooth are used for communications programs and for playback. To change the default playback device, click the Speakers/Headphones option (the exact wording varies depending on how the driver developer chose to implement it) and then click Set Default.

➤ For details on how to configure hardware and install drivers to unlock the functionality of those devices, see Chapter 13, "Hardware."

Using Windows Media Player to rip CDs

If you prefer the familiar Windows Media Player interface to the more modern Groove Music app, relief is a search away. We don't recommend Windows Media Player for new Windows 10 users, but if you're already comfortable with its quirks and you don't want to access your music collection from the cloud, it's a thoroughly appropriate choice.

We don't include exhaustive instructions for Windows Media Player in this edition (if you're interested in that, pick up a copy of *Windows 7 Inside Out*). The one task Windows Media Player can perform that Groove Music can't is to convert ("rip") tracks from an audio CD and save them in digital formats on your local hard drive.

Figure 10-9 shows a CD (selected in the left pane in Windows Media Player) with its tracks being ripped to the local hard drive.

Figure 10-9 The best reason to use Windows Media Player is to rip an audio CD to digital format, a task that Groove Music can't perform.

When you're connected to the Internet, Windows Media Player consults its online data sources to determine the name of your disc, as well as the names of the artist(s) and tracks and the genre of music the disc contains. This information is used to automatically tag and name tracks. You can use Windows Media Player or File Explorer to change those tags if necessary.

Windows Media Player copies each CD track to a separate file and stores it, by default, in the Music folder of the currently signed-in user (%UserProfile%\Music). Using the album metadata, Windows Media Player creates a folder for each artist and a subfolder for each album by that artist.

The digital files you create by ripping a CD are completely free of technical restrictions on your ability to play them back or make identical copies: you can listen to the saved tracks on your PC or on a mobile device, burn a collection of tracks to a custom CD, or copy those tracks to another PC or to OneDrive. Before you use Windows Media Player to rip a CD, however, it's wise to check the program's settings.

For practical purposes, files copied from audio CDs to your hard disk must be compressed; if you rip tracks to your hard disk using the uncompressed WAV format, a typical 60-minute CD will consume more than half a gigabyte of disk space. Compressing the files means you can store more music on your hard disk, and it makes the process of backing up and streaming music files easier and more efficient.

When it comes to compression, your first choice is simple: lossy or lossless? Most popular algorithms used to compress audio (and video) files are lossy, which means that they achieve compression by eliminating data. In the case of audio files, the data that's tossed out during the compression process consists mostly of frequencies that are outside the normal range of human hearing. However, the more you compress a file, the more likely you are to degrade its audio quality to the point where you'll notice it.

Windows 10 allows you to rip tracks using three different lossless compressed formats: Windows Media Audio Lossless, Apple Lossless Audio Codec (ALAC), or Free Lossless Audio Codec (FLAC). We recommend FLAC, which is widely supported and stores music files efficiently without sacrificing any information. In theory, at least, a track ripped in a lossless format should be indistinguishable from the original.

NOTE
Although you can play files saved in FLAC format from a local disk, you cannot stream this format from OneDrive.

Deciding on the type and amount of compression involves a tradeoff between disk space and audio quality. The level of compression is determined by the bit rate you select for your copied files. Higher bit rates preserve more of the original sound quality of your audio tracks but result in larger files on your hard disk or portable player. Lower bit rates allow you to pack more music into limited space at a cost in fidelity.

For compatibility with the maximum number of devices, the widely used MP3 format is best.

To set your preferences after inserting a CD, click the Rip Settings button on the Player toolbar. (You can also reach this dialog box by clicking Organize and then Options, and then clicking the Rip Music tab.) Click Format, and then choose one of the six available formats, as shown in Figure 10-10. If you choose a format that allows lossy compression, use the slider at the bottom of the dialog box to choose a quality level.

Figure 10-10 Before ripping a CD, be sure to choose a format and quality level here.

As long as you have that dialog box open, use the options at the top to change the location where your ripped files are saved and to define the default naming convention for individual tracks.

Managing photos and digital images

Windows 10 includes three built-in apps suitable for viewing, managing, and editing photos in digital image formats. In this section, we concentrate on the Photos app, with a nod to two older desktop programs—Windows Photo Viewer and Paint—which exist primarily for compatibility's sake.

As with its music and movie counterparts, the Photos app displays the contents of all files it finds in your Pictures library. It also includes the option to show photos and videos from One-Drive, even if those files are not synchronized with your PC or tablet.

Figure 10-11 shows the relatively simple user interface of the Photos app, with the entire collection available for browsing and editing.

Figure 10-11 By default, the Photos app organizes your collection of digital pictures by date, with the newest photos displayed first.

Several options in the Photos app's Settings page are worth checking before you invest a lot of time and energy learning its inner workings. Figure 10-12 shows these options, with the two most important at the top of the list.

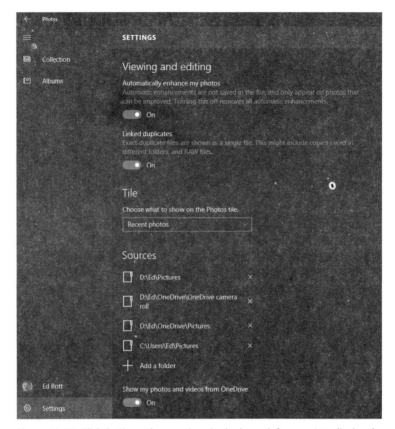

Figure 10-12 Click Settings (the gear icon in the lower left corner) to display these options.

Digital photography purists will probably want to disable both of the options at the top of this list, or at least be aware that they're enabled.

The first option automatically "enhances" photos as they're displayed. The underlying file isn't altered, but the image you (and your audience) see in the app might be changed to make it look better—at least in the eyes of the Photos app's algorithms.

The Linked Duplicates setting is intended to eliminate the frustration of seeing multiple copies of the same image. This can occur if your camera captures images in RAW format but also saves a lower-resolution copy for easier downloading on space-sensitive mobile devices. You can see the full selection of image files by using File Explorer.

Finally, at the bottom of the list is a switch that allows you to include photos and videos from OneDrive. This option includes every photo and every video in every folder. If you prefer to see only files in selected folders that are synced to your local PC or device, turn this option off and add the local synced OneDrive folders to your Pictures library.

Clicking an individual photo opens it for viewing, sharing, and editing, with an array of tools appearing in a bar above the image, as shown in Figure 10-13. Note that we've clicked the ellipsis at the end of the menu bar to show a drop-down menu of additional options.

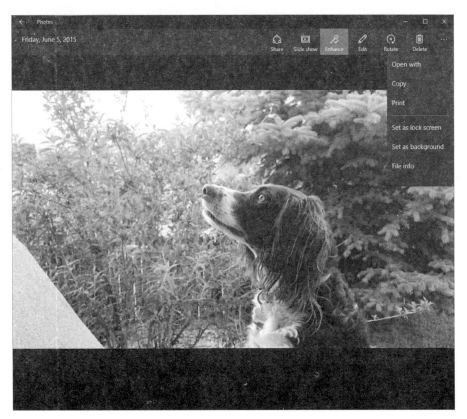

Figure 10-13 By default, the Enhance option is selected in the menu bar. In addition to options for sharing and editing this photo, you can click the ellipsis to the right of the menu bar for more options.

Choose the File Info option to see selected details about the image, as shown here, with a clickable link to open the folder containing the image in File Explorer.

Using the Photos app to crop and edit pictures

The greatest strength of the Photos app is its collection of lightweight editing tools. After opening an image, click or tap the pen icon to see the full set of editing tools, as shown in Figure 10-14.

For quickly turning a casual shot into something worth keeping and sharing, the tools in the Basic Fixes category are extremely useful. Here's what each one does:

- **Enhance.** Use this option to allow the app's algorithms to analyze the image and make basic changes. You're likely to see the image straightened and the color balance or contrast corrected, for example.

- **Rotate.** This control lets you shift the angle of the picture 90 degrees at a time, to fix images that are sideways or upside down.

- **Crop.** Cut out extraneous material, using either a free-form selection or a standard aspect ratio. (See more details following this list.)

- **Straighten.** This option lets you move the horizon of the image in either direction, one degree at a time, for those occasions when you were holding the camera at a slight angle when the picture was snapped.

- **Red Eye.** Removes the red-eye effect caused by using a flash when snapping photos of people. (Note that this has no effect on pictures of dogs and cats and other nonhuman species.)

- **Retouch.** Click this tool to change the mouse pointer to a tool that blurs anything you click with it. Use it to remove distractions and clutter from an image.

Figure 10-14 Select one of the five options on the left to see editing tools in that category on the right.

The Crop tool is probably the one you'll use most often. Figure 10-15 shows it in action.

Figure 10-15 When cropping, use the tool on the menu bar to display this list of preset aspect ratios.

Drag any corner to make the crop area larger or smaller. After setting the correct size, click the photo and drag the portion you want to keep into the crop area. Click the check mark to save your changes.

The photo editing options available on the right side of the image change based on what you select on the left side. The following options are available in addition to the Basic Fixes tools we listed previously:

- **Filters.** Select from six predefined tones that highlight different shades (blue, gold, and so on); the final choice is black and white.

- **Light.** Change the brightness and contrast or emphasize or deemphasize highlights and shadows. The figure following this list shows an example of this feature in use.

- **Color.** Change the temperature, tint, or saturation of the image—for example, to compensate for a blue tint from indoor lighting. The final option in this group allows you to "color boost" a specific area by dragging a pin icon onto the spot to get the boost.

- **Effects.** The two options here allow you to create a vignette, with the center section you select in focus and the surrounding area slightly out of focus (you can see this effect applied to the image in Figure 10-16), or use the Selective Focus option to highlight a key portion of the image while blurring the rest.

Figure 10-16 shows the editing tools available for the Light category.

Figure 10-16 Selecting Light on the left exposes a set of editing tools on the right. Using these tools effectively takes a little practice.

Using these editing controls takes a little practice. When you click Brightness, for example, a circle appears to its left with a large white dot next to it, as shown on the right here. Drag that circle clockwise or counterclockwise to make the image brighter or dimmer (with the number in the center of the circle increasing or decreasing according to your changes). The other con-trols work in a similar fashion.

After making changes to a photo, you can save it (replacing the original) or save a copy. The respective controls are available above the photo itself.

Organizing photos into albums

Previously, we've discussed tools for managing an entire collection. The second option in the menu bar on the left side of the Photos app allows a more focused view of photos.

The Albums feature also illustrates a theme we've discussed repeatedly in this book. Our cov-erage is based on the Photos app as it existed at the time of the initial Windows 10 release, on July 29, 2015. In that release, the Albums feature feels decidedly unfinished, and we're confident that the app you're using as you read this section will be more polished (and will continue to improve over time).

One of the biggest disconnects in the release we discuss here is between the Albums feature at *OneDrive.com* and the feature of the same name in this app. In OneDrive, you create albums manually and can add photos from any folder. In the Photos app, albums are created auto-matically, based on dates and events. You can refine the selection by removing photos, but you can't combine two albums into one.

Switching to Albums view in the Photos app produces a scrolling list of all automatically cre-ated albums, as shown in Figure 10-17.

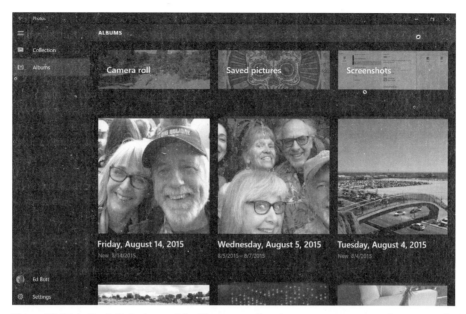

Figure 10-17 In the initial release of the Photos app, there's no way to create an album manually. These albums were automatically generated by the app.

The algorithm that creates albums adds a label to each one, based on the date the photos were taken, and then picks a cover photo and a selection of photos to include in the album. You can customize the name, change the cover photo, and select a different batch of photos. To start, open the album and then click or tap the pen-shaped Edit button. That opens an editing window like the one shown in Figure 10-18.

As with all such changes, be sure to click or tap the check mark (at the top of the page) to save your changes.

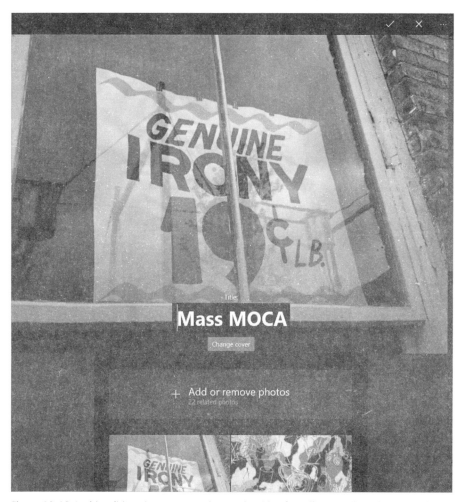

Figure 10-18 In this editing view, you can change the title of an album, replace the cover photo, and add or remove photos from the album itself.

Windows Photo Viewer and Paint

For compatibility purposes, Windows 10 includes the Windows Photo Viewer desktop app. Figure 10-19 shows this app, which is capable of displaying a single photo at a time and has no editing options aside from the capability to rotate a photo 90 degrees. Its user interface clearly dates back to a bygone era.

Figure 10-19 The Windows Photo Viewer app, still included with Windows 10, sports a user interface from the Windows Vista era.

We can't really think of a good reason why someone would use this legacy app in place of the more modern Photos app. Its only distinguishing feature is the capability to burn a slide show to CD or DVD, a task you can also accomplish with any number of third-party apps.

And then there's Microsoft Paint (Mspaint.exe), which has been a part of Windows since version 1.0. Despite its age, Paint still has a few useful tricks up its sleeve. Its most useful feature is the capability to save an image in an alternative format—if you've saved an image in the space-hogging Windows Bitmap format, for example, you can quickly convert it to a much more efficient, compressed format, such as PNG or JPEG, by using the Save As option on the File menu, as shown in Figure 10-20.

The Paint app also allows you to resize an image, a capability that is useful if your original image was captured at a very high resolution (with a correspondingly large file size) and you plan to post it on a webpage or share it via email, where the large file size might be unwelcome.

Figure 10-20 Use Paint's File menu to convert an image to a different format.

To shrink an image using Paint, click Resize on the Home tab. That opens the dialog box shown in Figure 10-21, which allows you to specify a percentage or an actual height or width, measured in pixels. The decrease in file size can be substantial.

Figure 10-21 Use Paint to change the size of an image file; this option is useful when you plan to post an image online and file size is a concern.

Watching movies, recorded TV shows, and video clips

The Movies & TV app is similar in design to Groove Music and Photos. Of the three, it is probably the simplest to use, doing its handful of required tasks very well.

Inside OUT

What about DVDs?

In a significant break from the past, Windows 10 doesn't include the capability to play DVDs (or MPEG-2 files ripped from DVDs). That decision is a reflection of two market realities: Most new PCs don't include optical disc drives at all, and the cost of royalties for DVD playback software is significant. Microsoft offers a DVD Player app that is free for anyone who upgrades a Windows 7, Windows 8, or Windows 8.1 PC that included Windows Media Center; this app should be installed automatically and be available in the All Apps list on any device that was upgraded from a previous version of Windows that contained Windows Media Center.. If you don't qualify for that app, we recommend the free VLC software, which contains the necessary codecs and is available in a desktop version (from *videolan.org*) and also in a modern version from the Windows Store.

The left-side menu bar in the Movies & TV app allows you to see content you've purchased from the Windows Store (previous purchases from the Xbox store are also included and can be played back). Figure 10-22 shows a typical TV library.

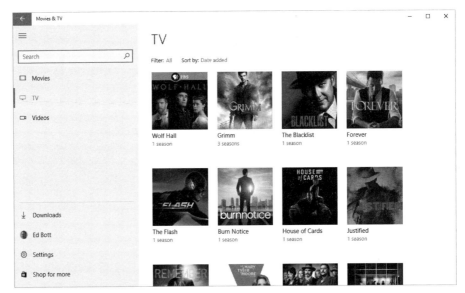

Figure 10-22 Movies and TV programs you've purchased through an Xbox or from the Windows Store are available for playback here.

The Videos page allows you to see your collection of personal video files captured in compatible formats, such as those in MP4 formats recorded on a modern smartphone. The player window, shown in Figure 10-23, includes the typical controls for playback, with a slider bar that allows you to move to a specific point in the file.

Figure 10-23 Click the double-headed diagonal arrow to zoom a video to full screen, hiding elements such as the title bar and playback controls.

Miracast

You have a high-definition video on your Windows 10 laptop or tablet. You have a large high-definition TV connected to a surround-sound system in your living room. If you have a long enough HDMI cable, you can connect your laptop's video output to a spare HDMI input on the big-screen TV. That option works, but it's an awkward solution at best. So how do you bring that video to the big screen without tripping over a 15-foot cord?

One answer, if you have the right hardware, is to stream your laptop display (with 5.1 surround sound) to the larger, louder living-room system. For this task, you can choose from a variety of wireless standards, each one backed by a large hardware or software company. Windows 10 natively supports a standard called Miracast, which is designed for wirelessly mirroring a mobile display and streaming high-quality sound between mobile devices and large displays, with (in theory) perfect fidelity.

In homes, Miracast is mostly an entertainment option, good for projecting YouTube videos and the occasional webcast to a larger screen. This setup is also effective for a conference room or a classroom, where the Miracast adapter can be permanently attached to a large-screen display and available for connection from any Windows 10 device.

To project your laptop or tablet display using Miracast, you need a compatible receiver, such as a TV or Blu-ray player that also supports the standard, or an external adapter that connects to your TV's HDMI port. Although the Miracast standard is relatively new, the technology behind it is well tested, and there are an increasing number of compatible devices on the market. The most versatile option is a thumb drive–sized adapter like the Microsoft Wireless Display adapter shown in Figure 10-24, which plugs into an HDMI input on a TV or monitor and draws power via a USB adapter.

Figure 10-24 The Microsoft Wireless Display adapter plugs into an HDMI port and draws power via a USB connection, turning a TV into a Miracast receiver.

A Miracast receiver uses Wi-Fi Direct to turn itself into a special-purpose wireless hotspot. Connecting a Miracast-compatible device to that invisible hotspot allows the device to mirror or extend its display to the larger screen.

After preparing the Miracast receiver to accept incoming connections (usually a simple matter of turning it on and selecting the matching input on the TV), open Windows 10's Action Center and click or tap the Connect button. That opens up a panel that lists available devices, where you can click or tap the entry for your Miracast receiver, with the goal of making a connection like the one shown in Figure 10-25.

Figure 10-25 Tapping the Connect button at the bottom of the Windows 10 Action Center allows you to connect to a Miracast device and mirror your laptop or tablet display to a larger device such as a TV.

The first time you encounter a Miracast adapter, you're prompted to add it, installing a device driver in the process. (You can see previously paired and available devices in the Connect pane.) On subsequent visits, that device should be available as a target you can tap or click in the Connect pane. After successfully connecting to the Miracast receiver, you can duplicate the display on your laptop or tablet to the larger screen, allowing you to wirelessly project a PowerPoint presentation to a conference room TV, watch a livestream in your living room, or cue up a music playlist for a party.

All three built-in Windows 10 media apps include a Cast option that allows you to send the current video and audio output to a previously configured device.

After you make a Miracast connection, you can change the projection mode just as you would with a second display connected directly to your PC. Options available in the Connect pane allow you to extend the display, so that you can watch a webcast or a video conference call on the large screen while you work on your laptop; use the second screen only; or use the PC screen only, severing the Miracast connection.

Xbox and other forms of online entertainment

Microsoft's Xbox One game console connects with Windows 10 devices in several ways. (In fact, as we write this section, Microsoft has announced plans to run a customized edition of Windows 10 on the Xbox One, an upgrade that should happen in November 2015.)

If you own an Xbox One console, we recommend that you check out two Windows 10 apps.

Xbox One SmartGlass, shown in Figure 10-26, turns a Windows 10 touchscreen device into a very capable remote control for your console. You can tap, slide, and type to control games, navigate the Xbox home screen, and pause or play back media files.

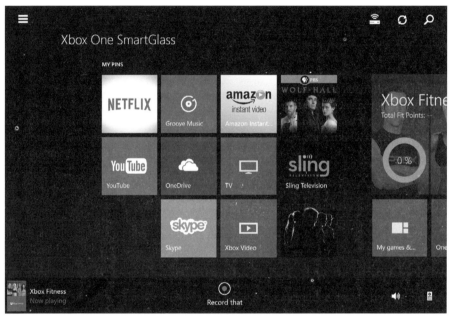

Figure 10-26 The Xbox One SmartGlass app for Windows 10 allows you to use a touchscreen device to control your Xbox One console remotely.

The Xbox app for Windows 10 allows more direct connections to an Xbox One, including the capability to stream games directly from the console to a Windows 10 device for immediate play even if someone else is using the TV that the Xbox One is connected to.

As Figure 10-27 shows, you can see your entire activity feed, connect with friends, and record games by using this versatile app.

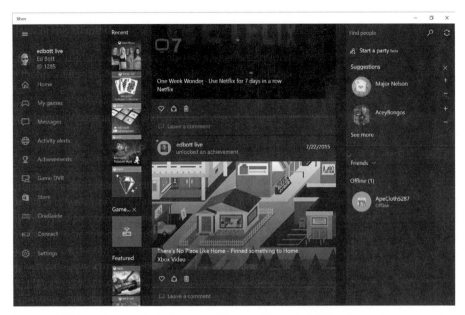

Figure 10-27 The Xbox app includes most of the capabilities that diehard Xbox gamers want to see.

Browsing the Internet

It's a well-known phenomenon in software development: as applications get simpler and easier to use, they get more complex under the covers. Microsoft says that in developing its new web browser, Microsoft Edge, some 220,000 lines of code were deleted from the old browser, Internet Explorer 11. But more than 300,000 lines of code were added. The deletions removed baggage from the past—no longer needed or wanted in a modern browser. The additions brought new and useful features, such as the reading list and web notes, and integration with Cortana, plus support for new web-development standards and better interoperability with other modern browsers.

For the Windows 10 user, the one apparent complexity introduced by Edge is the presence of two Microsoft browsers. Edge is the default, but Internet Explorer remains as an alternative. (You'll find it in the All Apps section of your Start menu, within the subfolder Windows Accessories.) Quite unlike the situation in Windows 8.1, however, which had both a modern and a desktop variant of Internet Explorer, the two browsers in Windows 10 are totally distinct. Edge is a modern browser built to modern standards; Internet Explorer is an aging browser encumbered in many ways over the years by the need to maintain compatibility with old-style web-design practices. In the years ahead, Microsoft will continue to provide technical support and security updates for Internet Explorer 11, but development will be focused entirely on Edge.

Large organizations and other users who rely on older web technologies such as ActiveX for their intranets or line-of-business web applications might have reason to make Internet Explorer the default browser. Most others will prefer Edge for its uncluttered design, touch-friendliness, new features, speed, and, above all, its enhanced security. Like all other modern apps adhering to the Universal Windows Platform, Edge *always* runs in a protected environment. This is not to say you can't damage your system by downloading malicious goods or falling for phishing scams. (SmartScreen Filter will warn you about sites that might be dangerous, but it can't restrain you from choosing unwisely.) But Edge does eliminate many of the security hazards—particularly rogue ActiveX controls and browser helper objects—that have plagued Internet Explorer over the years.

> ➤ **For information about SmartScreen Filter, see "Using SmartScreen Filter to avoid phishing scams and dicey downloads" later in this chapter.**

For most users the choice is straightforward: use and enjoy Edge, but keep Internet Explorer on hand for the occasional website that requires it. (A simple command in Edge lets you open the current page in Internet Explorer.)

In this chapter, we survey Edge—with frequent comparisons with the still present, still-useful Internet Explorer 11.

NOTE

Edge, like Windows 10 itself, is a work in progress and will receive frequent updates. Certain features that are not in place as we write (shortly after the official launch of Windows 10 in July 2015) may in fact be part of the version of Edge that you are using. For example, the ability to sync favorites between computers using the same Microsoft account was only a promise at launch; by the time you read this book, it may be an actuality. An extension model, based on JavaScript and HTML technologies, is also promised for later in 2015. At initial release, the only extensions supported by Edge were Adobe Flash Player and PDF rendering, both built in to the browser.

Why the new browser?

From a high altitude, the history of Internet Explorer, from its inception in 1995 to the present, can be seen as a competition between antagonistic ambitions—to adapt to new web-development standards (and to new competing browsers, such as Mozilla Firefox and Google Chrome) while maintaining compatibility with the past. Each new version of the browser made improvements to its predecessors. But because so many sites had been developed on the assumption that they would be viewed through older versions of browsers, the newer browsers had to include the means to emulate the older. So, for example, the Compatibility View option introduced in Internet Explorer 8 allowed users to correct some display problems that arose with sites that had been written for Internet Explorer 7. Moreover, older releases remained in use as newer releases arrived, presenting developers with the headache-inducing need to support numerous variant browser versions. (As of spring 2014, Internet Explorer 8 was reported to still have 20 percent of the browser market, despite the release of three later versions; developers could not comfortably ignore that large a user population.)

With Edge, Microsoft has set out to create a clean-slate, modern browser, free of compatibility freight and free of the most egregious security hazards. The focus is on support for current and forthcoming web standards and interoperability, so that sites developed for other modern browsers will run with minimal or no modifications on Edge.

After 20 years of service, the Trident rendering engine of Internet Explorer, Mshtml.dll, has been rewritten for the new Edge rendering engine, Edgehtml.dll. (The *rendering engine* is what translates HTML and other web code into an intelligible, navigable website.) Among the technologies not included in the new rendering engine are the following:

- ActiveX

- Browser helper objects

- Document modes

- Vector Markup Language (VML)

- VBScript

> ➤ For more detailed information about the changes in EdgeHTML, see the Microsoft Edge Dev Blog, at *http://blogs.windows.com/msedgedev*, as well as the blog post "Microsoft Edge: Building a safer browser," at *bit.ly/ms-edge-intro*. For more about technologies that are either in development or under consideration for Edge, see *http://dev.modern.ie.*

Browser basics

The following sections outline some of the essentials of browsing in either Edge or Internet Explorer. We discuss, among other things, how to make your choice of default browser and default search engine.

Setting or changing your default browser

Edge is Microsoft's recommended default browser. To make a different browser your default, open Settings and search for **default apps**. Under Choose Default Apps, click Web Browser. The menu that appears will list Edge, Internet Explorer, and any other browsers you happen to have installed on your system. (You'll also see the option to visit the Store.)

> ➤ For information about fine-tuning your default settings—for example, assigning particular browsers to particular web protocols—see "Setting default programs and file-type associations" in Chapter 8, "Using and managing modern apps and desktop programs."

Within Edge, you can open the current page in Internet Explorer by clicking the ellipsis icon at the far right of the toolbar (see Figure 11-1) and then clicking Open With Internet Explorer. If you are working in an environment in which Enterprise Mode has been enabled, sites configured to open in Enterprise Mode will automatically be displayed in Internet Explorer.

User interface basics in Edge

Edge continues the trend toward visual simplicity (the minimization of "chrome") that has been characteristic of recent iterations of Internet Explorer. But whereas the menu bar in Internet Explorer is optional (you can make it appear or disappear by pressing the Alt key), Edge has no menu bar. What you see is what there is—with the exception of two possible customizations:

- You can add the Home button to your toolbar by clicking More Actions (the ellipsis icon), choosing Settings, scrolling to the bottom of the Settings pane, clicking View Advanced Settings, and then turning on the switch below Show The Home Button. There you can also type the address of the home page you want to use. On narrow screens, the Home button might push other controls too close together for finger navigation, but otherwise it's a handy item to have on board.

- You can display the Favorites bar by clicking More Actions, then Settings, then Show The Favorites Bar.

Figure 11-1 shows the landmarks in Edge (with the Home button displayed) and Internet Explorer 11. Note that controls in Edge are spaced to ease use on touchscreens.

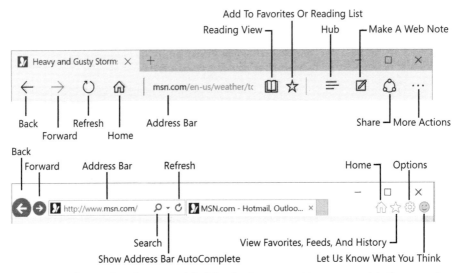

Figure 11-1 The user-interface controls in Edge (top) are spaced to accommodate fingers and a stylus. Internet Explorer (bottom) offers similar controls in a more traditional layout.

Using the Start page in Edge

Unless you have configured it to do otherwise, a new instance of Edge opens on the Start
page. (You can also reach the Start page by entering **about:start** in the address bar.) As
Figure 11-2 shows, the Start page asks for your next destination and presents a large field in
which you can respond. You can enter either a Uniform Resource Locator (URL) or a search
string here.

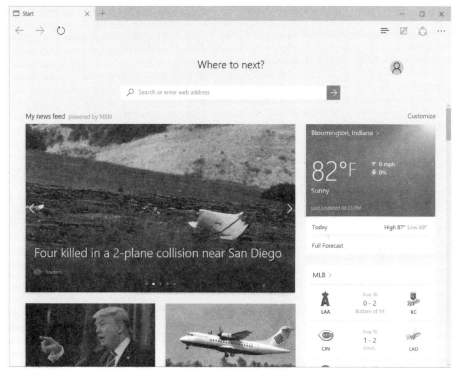

Figure 11-2 In the large input field atop Edge's Start page, you can type either a web address or a
search string.

If Edge can parse your input as a web address, it takes you there directly. Otherwise, it passes
your keystrokes to your default search provider.

If the Start page is not present, simply type in the address bar, which functions the same way as the Start page's input field. In either place, Edge does its best to simplify your typing task. While you type, the browser offers a list of potential sites and search suggestions:

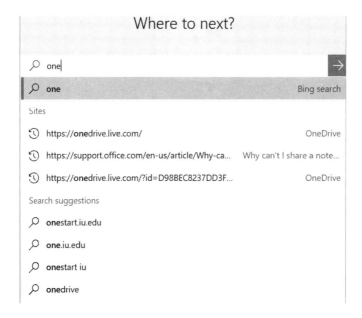

The icon that looks like a clock in retrograde motion marks sites derived from your browsing history. The search suggestions that appear below this group are based on information gathered by Cortana about your interests and location.

As Figure 11-2 shows, the rest of the Edge Start page, below the input field, is not given over to empty white space (the browser is not *that* Spartan); instead, it's filled with news-feed tiles, perhaps also including some tips about how to use Edge effectively. Here again, the browser does its best to track your interests, based on choices you have made in the info apps, your location, your selections in the Cortana Notebook, and so on. You can customize the news feed by clicking Customize in the upper right corner.

Cortana may pop up in your browser immediately if you type something about which she is particularly knowledgeable. Enter a flight number or the name of a currency, for example, and you will get status or rate information:

Cortana already knows a great many useful facts, and as time goes on you can expect the breadth of her expertise to expand.

Using tabs

Like all modern browsers, Internet Explorer and Edge allow you to keep multiple pages open on separate tabs in the same application window and switch between them quickly. This feature is a tremendous timesaver for anyone doing research or trying to juggle multiple tasks.

Tab grouping in Internet Explorer

The tab grouping feature in Internet Explorer allows you to identify groups of related tabs visually. When you open a new tab by clicking a link in the current tab, Internet Explorer displays the original tab and the newcomer in the same color, showing you at a glance that the two tabs hold related content. Any additional tabs you generate from pages also acquire the same color. Right-clicking a tab within a tab group reveals commands to close all tabs in the current group, close all tabs not in the current group, and remove the current tab from the group.

Creating and manipulating tabs

In either browser, you can open a new tab in any of several ways:

- To open a new blank tab, press Ctrl+T, or click the New Tab button, just to the right of the current tabs.

- To open a link in a new tab without shifting focus from the current tab, right-click the link and choose Open In New Tab, or hold down Ctrl while you click the link.

- To open a link in a new tab and shift focus to the newly opened tab, hold down Ctrl+Shift and click.

- To duplicate a tab, press Ctrl+K, or right-click the tab and choose Duplicate Tab.

To close any open tab, click the X at the right side of its tab or press Ctrl+W.

To reposition a tab within an array of tabs, drag the tab you want to move laterally. To peel a tab off from the current browser window and make it appear in a new window, drag the tab upward or downward.

If more tabs are open than will fit in the browser window, a scrolling arrow appears to the left of the first tab or the right of the last (or both). Click the arrow to scroll in the indicated direction. You can also use keyboard shortcuts to cycle between tabs: press Ctrl+Tab to move from left to right or Ctrl+Shift+Tab to go from right to left.

When you have a lot of tabs open, particularly if you are working with more than one browser window, you might prefer to navigate by hovering your mouse pointer over the Edge or Internet Explorer icon on the taskbar. In Internet Explorer, Windows displays either thumbnails or names for all open tabs, and you can point to the one you want. If you point to a tab in a browser window, a ScreenTip shows the page title and web address. In Edge, each separate browser window gets its own thumbnail, but seeing individual tabs requires switching to that window.

Setting tabbed browsing options

If you regularly open large numbers of tabs, you will probably want to tweak the way your browser handles tabs. To see the options available in Edge, click More Actions, then Settings. Toward the bottom of the pane you'll find Open New Tabs With. Click the field below to unfurl this set of choices:

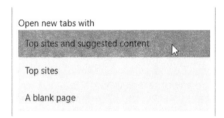

If you choose the first option or second option, new tabs will open with one or two rows (depending on screen width) of "top sites" suggestions:

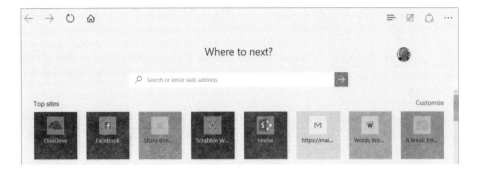

After you've used Edge for a while, the Top Sites section of the new tab page should reflect your actual browsing history and become a useful navigational tool. Initially, however, you might find the selection a bit arbitrary. You can eliminate any sites that you don't want to see by pointing to the thumbnail and clicking the X.

A comparable but slightly different set of options is available in Internet Explorer. To find them, click Tools, then Internet Options. On the General tab of the Internet Options dialog box, click Tabs. In the Tabbed Browsing Settings dialog box, open the drop-down list below When A New Tab Is Opened, Open.

Reopening closed tabs

Did you accidentally close a tab before you were quite finished with it? No problem. In either browser, right-click any tab that's currently open and choose Reopen Closed Tab. Your most recently closed page will reappear in its previous location. You can repeat this procedure for other tabs you may have closed. If you like keyboard shortcuts, Ctrl+Shift+Tab reopens closed tabs without you having to move the mouse.

Internet Explorer, but not Edge, includes a command that lets you reopen a particular closed tab without having to reopen others that were closed later. Right-click a tab and choose Recently Closed Tabs. A menu will appear from which you can choose the page you want to revisit.

Restoring your last session

The new tab page in Internet Explorer includes a Reopen Last Session link that reloads every page that was open the last time you closed Internet Explorer. This can spare you some anguish if you accidentally close the browser when you meant to close only the current tab.

It can really rescue you if you sit down at your machine and find that your system has been restarted in your absence.

Be aware that if you have two or more Internet Explorer sessions open, each in a separate window, Reopen Last Session revives only the tabs that were open in the session that was closed last.

Edge automatically opens all tabs that were previously open if you restart Windows without closing Edge first. A separate setting will open each new session with the tabs that were open in the previous session even if you close Edge first. To avail yourself of this option, click More Actions, then Settings. Under Open With, choose Previous Pages.

Customizing your home and startup pages

Edge distinguishes between a home page and startup pages. Startup pages, of which you may have one or more, appear at the beginning of each new session. The home page, of which you may have but one, arrives only when you click the Home button—which is not displayed by default but can easily be added to your toolbar.

To configure startup pages, click More Actions, then Settings. As Figure 11-3 shows, your options are to open with the default Start page (about:start), the new tab page, the pages you had open when you last closed the browser, or one or more pages of your own choosing.

If you select A Specific Page Or Pages, Edge will propose MSN and Bing. If you want something else, click Custom. Then use the plus sign and address box to express your preferences. (If you're already looking at a page you want at startup, click in the address bar, press Ctrl+C to copy the page's URL, and then click in the Settings pane address box and press Ctrl+V to paste.)

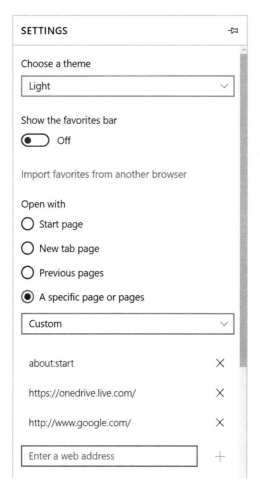

Figure 11-3 You can use the Open With section of the Settings pane to tell Edge how you want to begin a session.

To use a home page, open the Settings pane, click View Advanced Settings, and then turn on the switch below Show The Home Button. Once the button has been enabled, a box will appear in which you can name a home page:

You can think of the Home button as a favorite-favorite shortcut. Link it to a page that you use frequently but not invariably. Assign as startup pages those that you must see every time you go to work in Edge.

Internet Explorer makes no comparable distinction between home and startup pages. But you can set multiple home pages by clicking Tools, then Internet Options. Fill out the Home Page section of the General tab with one or more URLs, each on a separate line:

Note that the Startup section of this dialog box lets you dispense with home pages altogether and stipulate that each new session should begin with the tabs that were open in the last one.

Changing your default search provider

On a clean installation, Microsoft Bing, unsurprisingly, is the default search provider for both of Microsoft's browsers. With a few simple steps, you can change the default in either browser. The one gotcha is that to change the search provider in Edge, you must first have visited the search provider's website. You don't have to do anything there; you just have to have been there at least once for the provider to show up on the list of available search engines.

With that excursion completed, start in Edge by clicking More Actions, Settings, View Advanced Settings. Toward the bottom of the Advanced Settings pane, you'll see the name of your current default search provider:

To make a change, open this drop-down list and choose Add New. On the screen that follows, you will find a list of search candidates (sites that you have visited that support the OpenSearch standard):

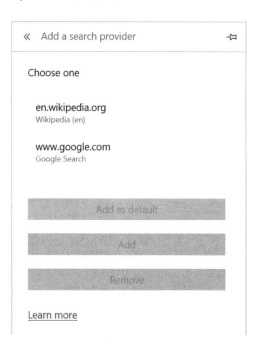

Select one and then click either Add As Default or Add (or Remove, if you want it off the list). If you click Add, Edge will not make it the default but will make it available in the Advanced Settings pane. If you want to use a certain search provider only some of the time, you can go to Advanced Settings and select it, without changing the default that will apply to searches in subsequent sessions.

To change providers in Internet Explorer, start by clicking Tools, Manage Add-Ons. The Search Providers section of the Manage Add-Ons dialog box, shown in Figure 11-4, displays a list of your current providers.

Figure 11-4 The Manage Add-Ons dialog box lists your current providers and offers a link whereby you can add more.

Near the lower left corner of the dialog box, if your eyes are good, you will find the link Find More Search Providers. Clicking this link takes you to the Internet Explorer Gallery, where you can make a selection. Click a provider, then click Add To Internet Explorer. In the confirmation dialog box that arrives next, you will have the opportunity to make your new provider the default:

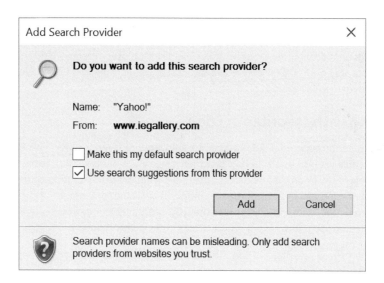

If you choose not to make the added provider the new default, you can still easily use the
new search engine as an occasional alternative to the current default. When you search in the
address bar, below the list of suggested sites, you'll find small icons for all your listed search
providers (Figure 11-5). Click here to perform an ad hoc search with a nondefault provider.

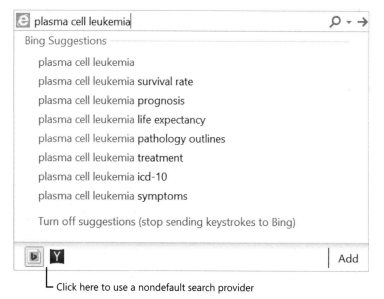

Figure 11-5 When you search in the address bar, Internet Explorer offers icons to let you select a
nondefault search provider.

Using favorites, history, and the reading list

The favorites and history lists, grouped under the new Hub user interface in Edge, will help you find your way back to sites you've already visited. The new reading list feature in Edge is a handy alternative to favorites.

Browsing with favorites in Edge

Like every other browser, Edge lets you build a repository of favorite sites—sites that you know or suspect you'll want to return to now and then. Once a site has been designated a favorite, you can reopen it with only a few clicks, instead of having to search for it again or pull it up from your browsing history. (Your browsing history is available for reuse as well, of course, but it's often better to use history for sites that you need to return to unexpectedly. For more about this feature, see "Browsing through history" later in this chapter.)

To add a site to your favorites in Edge, click Add To Favorites Or Reading List. That's the star icon near the right side of your browser window. As Figure 11-6 shows, the dialog box that appears gives you a choice between adding a site to your favorites and adding to your reading list. Click Favorites if that's not already underscored.

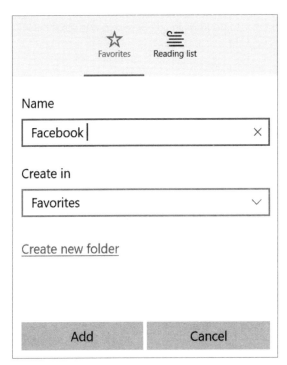

Figure 11-6 As part of its effort to keep the user interface controls well spaced for touch friendliness, Edge combines Add To Favorites and Add To Reading List in a single dialog box, accessed via the star icon on the toolbar.

Edge proposes the title of the current website as the name for your favorite and a folder destination for the new shortcut. Initially you may have only two folders, called Favorites and Favorites Bar. You can use the Create New Folder link to expand this repertory. (The Favorites Bar folder is special because the favorites you store there can be displayed as a toolbar at the top of your screen. To display the Favorites Bar, click More Actions, then Settings, and then click the switch labeled Show The Favorites Bar.)

NOTE
The quickest way to add the current page to your favorites is by pressing Ctrl+D.

Inside OUT
Always rename favorites

Get in the habit of assigning a descriptive name when you save a favorite. Make sure the name you choose contains the words your future self is likely to use as search terms. Steer clear of extra-long file names. Web designers often create outrageously long page titles, packing descriptions and keywords together with the goal of ranking higher on search engines. Shorter, more meaningful names are easier to spot when you're scrolling through a folder full of favorites. And speaking of folders, by all means use them to categorize your favorites. The more favorites you accumulate, the gladder you'll be that you did.

Navigating to a favorite site in Edge

To use your favorites, once you have created them, click the Hub icon. That's the one that looks like this:

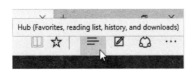

You can also get to the Hub by pressing Ctrl+I.

As Figure 11-7 shows, the Hub is a multipurpose affair. The four icons at the top take you, from left to right, to Favorites, Reading List, History, and Downloads. We'll look at the other three Hub sections at later points in this chapter.

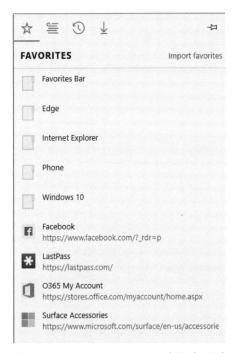

Figure 11-7 Favorites are accessed via the Hub, which also provides entrée to your reading list, history, and downloads.

Click a favorite to launch it in the current tab. To launch it in a new tab, right-click it and then click Open In New Tab. The menu that appears when you right-click also gives you the means to rename or remove a shortcut.

NOTE
If you have enough room on your screen and you expect to be working with several shortcuts, pin the Hub. The pane will remain open until you click the X, which replaces the pin icon in the upper right corner.

Importing favorites from other browsers

To import favorites that you have created in another browser, open the Hub, click the Favorites tab, and then click Import Favorites. (You have to be in the Favorites folder, not a subfolder, when you do this.) Edge will offer a selection consisting of whatever other browsers it finds on your system:

Select the check boxes for the browsers from which you want to import favorites.

TROUBLESHOOTING

You can't find your Edge favorites

Internet Explorer saves its favorites in a subfolder of your user profile, %UserProfile%\
Favorites; Edge does not, at least in its current incarnation. (That feature is scheduled
to be added in a future upgrade, perhaps even by the time you read this.) Like the
executable files for modern apps, favorites that you create in Edge, a modern app, are
tucked away in a folder deeply nested under %LocalAppData%\Packages. To be exact,
the location is %LocalAppData%\Packages\Microsoft.MicrosoftEdge_8wekyb3d8bbwe\
AC\MicrosoftEdge\User\Default\Favorites. If you find that address difficult to remember, don't despair; you can't do anything useful with the File Explorer entries there
anyway. For example, if you try to add a favorite by creating a file alongside the others,
Edge will simply ignore it. And no, you can't sync your favorites with other devices by
syncing that obscure folder.

Using the reading list, an alternative to favorites, in Edge

Favorites are a great way to preserve and categorize website addresses to which you expect to
be returning periodically. When you just need to save something for later perusal, the reading list in Edge might be a better alternative. Any webpage can be saved to the reading list. It
doesn't have to be text-oriented, although the reading list feature is perfect for long articles
that you don't have time to read at the moment.

To save the current page to the reading list, click the Add To Favorites Or Reading List icon. A simple dialog box appears:

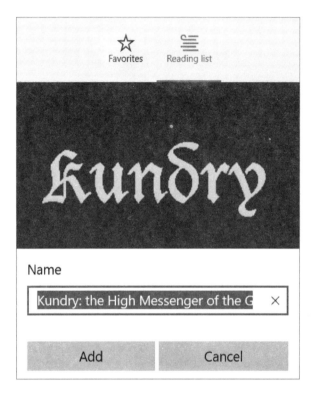

Edge proposes the name of the page as the name of your reading list item, but you can (and often should) replace that with something easier to recognize. Above the name field, Edge displays an image taken from the page you're saving, assuming that it finds one near the beginning of the page.

When you're ready to read your saved item, click the Hub, then the Reading List tab. Your pages are ordered chronologically with the most recent on top (see Figure 11-8). Click and read.

Figure 11-8 Edge sorts your reading list in descending chronological order.

When you've finished with an item, right-click it and choose Remove.

> ➤ The reading list maintained by Edge is separate from the one created by Windows Read-
> ing List. For information about the latter, see "Preserving items of interest with Windows
> Reading List" in Chapter 9, "Productivity and communication tools."

Browsing with favorites in Internet Explorer

To add a site to your favorites in Internet Explorer, do any of the following:

- Press Ctrl+D.

- Click Favorites, or press Alt+C or Ctrl+I to open the Favorites Center, and then click Add
  To Favorites.

- Pin the Favorites Center, and then drag the icon to the left of the webpage address in
  the address bar to the Favorites list. If you want the item to go inside an existing subfolder that isn't open, point to the folder icon and wait. After a pause, the folder opens,
  and you can drop the shortcut in its proper place within the subfolder.

- Right-click anywhere within the current page, and then click Add To Favorites. This
  action adds the current page to the Favorites folder. If you point to a link on the page
  and choose this menu option, the newly created shortcut picks up the title and address
  of the link.

All of these methods, except the drag-and-drop procedure, produce the Add A Favorite dialog
box, shown in Figure 11-9.

Figure 11-9 Internet Explorer proposes to use the page title as the name for the favorite. Replace
the default page title with a shorter, simpler name to make the favorite easier to find.

The Create In drop-down box allows you to save the new favorite within the top level of the
Favorites folder or choose a subfolder. You can also create a new subfolder. Each favorite is
saved as an Internet shortcut (a file with the extension .url) in the Favorites folder in your user
profile.

You can edit these shortcuts the same way you edit any other kind of shortcut. Right-click the
shortcut or folder in the Favorites Center to rename, copy, or delete the shortcut. You can also

use File Explorer to rename your favorites and organize them into folders. A quick way to get to your Favorites folder in File Explorer is to type **favorites** in the search box.

To save all open tabs in the current window as a folder of new favorites, open the Favorites Center, click the down arrow next to Add To Favorites, and choose Add Current Tabs To Favorites. After you specify a folder name and location, Internet Explorer saves all open tabs in that folder. If the folder name you enter already exists, the current tabs are added to that folder.

Syncing favorites in Internet Explorer

Synchronizing your Internet Explorer favorites is simple and automatic if your systems are set up to sync settings via a Microsoft account. In Settings, search for **sync**. Choose Sync Your Settings, and then make sure that Web Browser Settings is turned on:

If Web Browser Settings is on, then any Internet Explorer favorite you create on one system will appear on all other systems you sign in to with the same Microsoft account.

Working with pinned sites in Internet Explorer

The idea behind pinned sites in Internet Explorer is straightforward: you can open a website in a tab and then drag an icon from the address bar (or drag the tab itself) onto the taskbar, where it's pinned just like a program. If the site has a custom icon (also known as a *favicon*), the shortcut for the pinned site uses it instead of the generic Internet Explorer icon.

Here, for example, we've created pinned sites for four news sources and lined them up side by side on the right side of the taskbar:

When you open a pinned site, its appearance is subtly different from a normal website. It maintains its privileged position on the taskbar, complete with personalized icon, which makes it easy for you to quickly get back to a site you use regularly. The personalized icon appears in the upper left corner of the browser window as well, and the Back and Forward buttons take on the same color as the icon.

Browsing through history

Edge and Internet Explorer each maintain their own history of the sites you visit. If you need to return to a site and you neglected to make it a favorite (or save it to your reading list in Edge), you should be able to find it by looking through the history listings. It's not an ideal way to retrace your steps because the history is exhaustive and duplicative. You're likely to find an individual entry for each visit you made to a particular site, for example. More problematic, the sites are listed by their official titles, not by the friendly names you would probably have assigned to favorites. So to get back to a site via history, you might need to comb through a lot of distractions. It helps greatly, of course, if you know when you last opened the site you want to revisit. Both browsers gather their entries into time-interval bins such as Today or Last Week. Edge also adds a time stamp to sites that you opened during the last several days; if you know you discovered a site yesterday evening, this time stamping can help narrow your search.

History in Edge

To inspect your history in Edge, click Hub, and then click History (it's the third icon from the left). Alternatively, press Ctrl+H. As Figure 11-10 shows, Edge presents sites in descending chronological order, beginning with a category called Last Hour if it happens that the current day has barely begun.

Use the outline controls at the left to expand date categories. Don't click the X at the right side of a date heading unless you'd like to expunge that segment of your history. As you move your mouse pointer down through the sites, X icons appear to the right of each in turn. You might want to use those icons to get rid of sites that happen to be in the historical record but that you know you'll never need to reopen; doing so might make it easier to find the sites you do want.

Should it happen that history records that you went to Contoso.com every day in the last three weeks, you might want to avail yourself of another expunging option. Right-click one of the entries for this site and choose Delete All Visits To Contoso.com. (You probably don't need this history to find your way back.)

If you want to erase the entire history, click Clear All History at the top of the list. (You can also clear your browsing history via the Settings pane, as we'll see later in this chapter.)

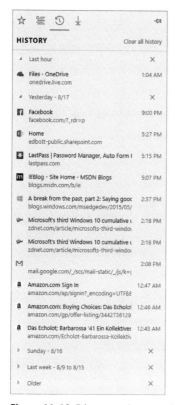

Figure 11-10 Edge organizes your browsing history in descending chronological order.

History in Internet Explorer

Internet Explorer hides your browsing history on the third tab in the Favorites Center. You can get there by clicking Favorites and then clicking the History tab or by pressing Ctrl+H. At the top of the history pane, you'll find a handy drop-down list that lets you arrange entries by date, site, most visited, or the order visited today (see Figure 11-11). Most important, perhaps, the list includes a Search History option. The search tool won't find content buried on a page, but it will find words that appear in page titles. For example, suppose you visited the website of an airport shuttle service and looked at the home page, a page called Rates, and another called Reservations. You don't remember the name of the company or which day you were pondering a limo ride, but you do remember that you went to the Reservations page. Search your history for "reservations," and you'll find what you need.

Figure 11-11 You can sort Internet Explorer's History list in a variety of memory-jogging ways. For best results, try the Search History option.

Managing downloads

Downloading documents and programs is straightforward. Both browsers provide progress reports such as the following while the download is under way:

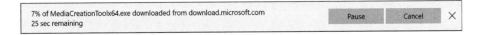

If you change your mind midstream, you can click Cancel. If you need to pause while you do something else, there's a button for that as well. When the download is complete, another message asks you what you want to do with it:

For an executable, you'll have the option to run the new download. For a document, an Open button will appear in place of Run.

Clicking View Downloads in Edge takes you to a list of your downloads.

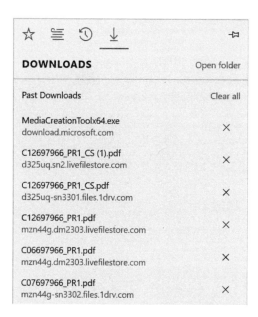

You can also get to this list in Edge by clicking the Hub icon and selecting the fourth icon from the left. Clicking entries in this list lets you open any downloaded document or run any downloaded executable—just as you could do in your Downloads folder (by default, This PC\ Downloads) in File Explorer; you can go to that folder directly by clicking Open Folder. If the Downloads list in Edge becomes cluttered, you can use the X controls to eliminate particular items, or clear the whole list at once with the Clear All link. Note that these actions delete nothing from your store of downloads; they simply tidy up the list in the browser.

To get to the comparable set of features in Internet Explorer, click Tools, View Downloads.

Using SmartScreen Filter to avoid phishing sites and dicey downloads

The term *phishing sites* refers to websites designed by scammers to resemble online commerce and banking sites. The scammer's goal is to fool you into visiting the site (often by enticing you to click a link in an email message) and have you fill in sensitive information such as your sign-in credentials, account numbers, and details about your identity.

SmartScreen Filter, introduced with Internet Explorer 7, detects known and suspected phishing sites and does its best to deter you from falling prey. The feature does its detective work with the help of an allow list, a set of rules, and a server-based block list that is continually updated. The initial check is heuristic, looking at the content of the page itself; if all the images are from a bank's website, for example, but the submit button goes to a URL containing an IP address, red flags go up.

If SmartScreen Filter thinks you're headed to a dodgy page, it displays a bold warning before you ever get there. An icon in the address bar identifies the address as an Unsafe Website, and a banner on the warning page itself provides one-click egress.

SmartScreen Filter also steps up to warn you about downloads it considers to be potentially hazardous. Such a warning does not necessarily mean the download is unsafe (the feature bases its judgment on information that Windows users supply to Microsoft, but it is not infallible). But unless you're sure that the download is from a trusted source, you should heed the warning.

To make sure that SmartScreen Filter is on in Edge, click More Actions, Settings, View Advanced Settings. The switch you're looking for is at the bottom of the Advanced Settings pane:

Help protect me from malicious sites and
downloads with SmartScreen Filter

 On

To enable SmartScreen Filter in Internet Explorer, click Tools, Safety, Turn On SmartScreen Filter. If the link says "Turn Off . . . ," that means the feature is already enabled.

Making text more readable

Edge and Internet Explorer both provide easy ways to make text and graphics on a webpage larger or smaller. If you're working on a touchscreen or on a device with a precision touchpad, you can zoom in and out with the standard touch gestures. Spread two fingers on a page to make the content larger; bring two fingers together to make it smaller.

With a wheel mouse, you can zoom in or out by holding down the Ctrl key while you roll the wheel forward or back. Zooming with the mouse wheel has the advantage of maintaining the position of whatever object you're pointing to when you begin zooming. Suppose, for example, that you're zooming in to get a better look at a graphic element lying near the right edge of the screen. If you use other zooming methods, the element you care about will eventually drift out of the window. But if you zoom in by pointing to it and rolling the wheel, the element retains its position relative to your mouse pointer as it gets larger.

If a mouse is not at hand, hold down Ctrl and press the Plus Sign to increase magnification; do the same with the Minus Sign to zoom back out. To return to normal (100%) magnification, press Ctrl+0.

Should you forget these shortcuts, you can always go to the menu. In Edge, click More Actions. The Zoom command with its Plus and Minus icons is near the top of the pane. In Internet Explorer, click Tools, and then Zoom.

Using Reading View in Edge

Zooming in is an excellent way to make small text easier on the eyes. But for more improvement in reading comfort, try Reading View in Edge. Introduced in Windows 8 with the modern app version of Internet Explorer, Reading View removes distracting elements from a webpage to let you focus on the text you're actually trying to read. You might find Reading View especially valuable on narrow tablets or phones, where text of interest can easily get crowded out by nonessential elements. Figures 11-12 and 11-13 show the same page in normal display and in Reading View.

In converting a page to Reading View, Edge removes such distractions as ads and navigational display elements, while retaining hyperlinks, source information, and graphics that are integral to the article. Generous amounts of white space, a soft sepia background, and a specially designed font further augment readability. (The background and font size can be customized.)

Reading View also makes some intelligent layout decisions. Notice in Figure 11-13, for example, that the byline and date have been moved from above the title, where they appear in Figure 11-12, to below it, where you would expect to see them in a conventional newspaper or magazine article. Similarly, on wide screens in landscape mode, Reading View is likely to create a multicolumnar display. On narrow screens, it sticks with a single column.

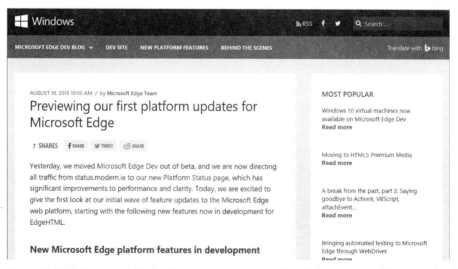

Figure 11-12 In its normal display, the text you want to read might be surrounded by navigational elements and ads.

Previewing our first platform updates for
Microsoft Edge

Microsoft Edge Team
Microsoft Edge Dev Blog | August 18, 2015 10:00 am

Yesterday, we moved Microsoft Edge Dev out of beta, and we are now directing all traffic
from status.modern.ie to our new Platform Status page, which has significant improvements to performance and clarity. Today, we are excited to give the first look at our initial wave of feature updates to the Microsoft Edge web platform, starting with the
following new features now in development for EdgeHTML.

New Microsoft Edge platform features in development

CSS

File APIs

Figure 11-13 In Reading View, the navigational elements have been removed (although hyperlinks
are retained), and a generous amount of white space has been added to enhance readability.

To display a page in Reading View, click the Reading View icon, which resembles an open
book; it's the first in the set of icons at the right side of the toolbar. If Reading View is not
available (because the page is not suitable for that kind of display), the icon will be dim. (The
icon might also be dim for a few seconds while Edge analyzes your page to see whether it
can be displayed in Reading View.) To switch back to normal view, click the Reading View icon
again or click the Back icon.

Reading View is not available in Internet Explorer 11.

Customizations for Reading View appear in two drop-down boxes in the Settings pane (click
More Actions, then Settings):

Reading

Reading view style

Default	∨

Reading view font size

| Medium | ∨ |

The alternatives to Default for Reading View Style are Light, Medium, and Dark. If you choose Dark, Reading View switches to a reversed format, with white text on a black background, with blue retained for hyperlinks. For Reading View Font Size, your choices are Small, Medium, Large, and Extra Large.

Sharing webpages from Edge

Got something to share? Click the Share icon. Edge responds with a list of installed apps that can receive your offering, as shown in Figure 11-14.

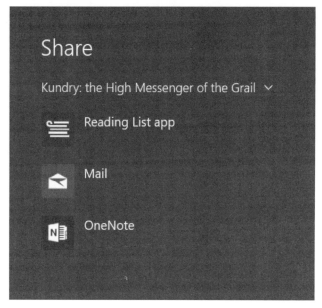

Figure 11-14 Clicking the Share icon reveals a list of programs installed on your system to which you can send a copy of the current page.

The system from which you are sharing may offer a different set of targets—perhaps including Facebook or an RSS reader, for example. If you have previously shared pages to Mail, the addresses of your recent recipients will appear at the top of the list.

At the top of the Share pane you'll find the name of your page, and to the right of that is a small drop-down arrow. Click the arrow if you want to share a screen shot of the page (for example, if you're sending a picture rather than text). Otherwise, Edge will share a link to the current page.

Annotating Edge pages with web notes

The web note feature in Edge lets you draw on, highlight, add text annotations to, and clip sections of webpages that you want to call attention to. Edge turns your webpage into a static graphic image on which you can draw with your fingers or a stylus (on a touchscreen) or use the mouse on a nontouch monitor. After you've marked up a page, you can email it, send it to your OneNote notebooks (or other sharing target), or simply save it to your own favorites or reading list. Figure 11-15 shows an example of a page with a red encirclement and some yellow highlighting.

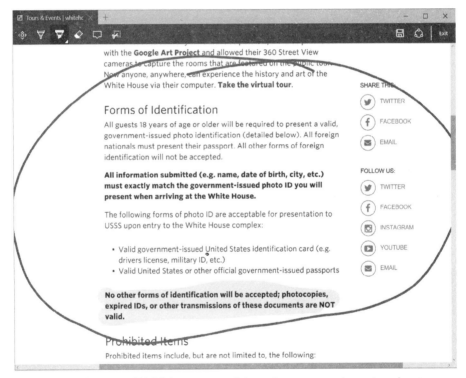

Figure 11-15 The pen and highlighter are two of the tools you can use to create web notes.

To begin creating a web note, click Make A Web Note, the icon to the left of Share near the right edge of the toolbar. Edge opens a set of drawing tools for your use, shown next:

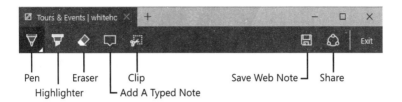

Pen | Eraser | Clip | Save Web Note | Share
Highlighter | Add A Typed Note

Click the drop-down arrows on the Pen and Highlighter tools to reveal size and color options. If your stylus or mouse goes astray, you can use the Eraser tool and try again. To get rid of all the marks you've made, you can click the drop-down arrow on the Eraser tool and choose Clear All Ink. (Alternatively, you can exit drawing mode and then come back for another go.)

To add a text box to the page, click Add A Typed Note, and then click to indicate where you want the text to go. To copy a snippet to the Clipboard, click the Clip tool, then select the area you want to copy.

The Save Web Note tool, on the right side of the toolbar, offers OneNote, Favorites, and Reading List as destinations. If you save to your favorites or the reading list, you'll be able to pull the page back up at any time and review your annotations. The Share icon presents the usual set of sharing choices (see the previous section).

Inside OUT

Use a web note to freeze a webpage

Website content tends to be ephemeral. If you need to capture the current state of a rapidly changing webpage, grab it with a web note and save it to your reading list, favorites, or OneNote. If you don't care to annotate it, you can simply click Make A Web Note and then click Share. There are many other ways to take screen shots, but this one is right at hand as you browse, and it captures the entire page, not just what you see in the confines of your screen. When you reopen your web note from wherever you put it, you can quickly switch back to the "live" version of the site by means of the Go To Original Page link that appears atop the web note.

Managing and troubleshooting add-ons in Internet Explorer

The Toolbars And Extensions section of the Manage Add-Ons dialog box, shown in Figure 11-16, provides information about whatever ActiveX controls, browser helper objects, and other add-ons you have installed in Internet Explorer. You can inspect version numbers, see how many times an add-on has been used or blocked, and view details of the performance impact of any add-on. More important, you can disable an add-on completely, either as a troubleshooting step or as a way to improve the performance and reliability of Internet Explorer.

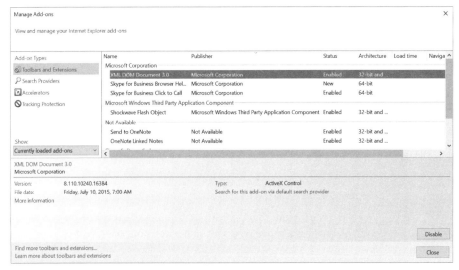

Figure 11-16 Select an item from the list of installed add-ons to enable or disable it. You can view a summary of details about the item in the pane below the list.

When you select an item in the list of add-ons, you can see more details about it in the pane below, including the publisher's name, the version number and file date (if available), and the add-on type. Buttons in the lower right corner let you disable or enable the add-on.

If you're ready to be completely overloaded with information, double-click an add-on's name in the list. If the selected add-on is an ActiveX control, you see an information-rich dialog box like the one shown next:

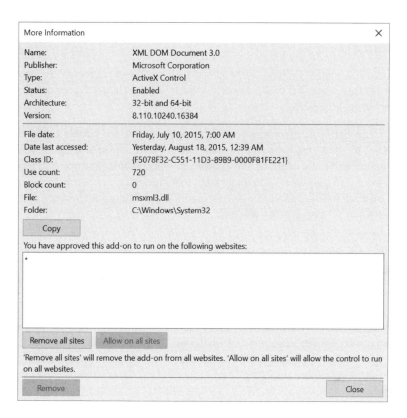

In the large box here, the asterisk—the wildcard character for "all"—indicates that you have approved the add-on to run on all sites. If you're particularly cautious, you might want the option to approve websites on a site-by-site basis. In that case, click the Remove All Sites button. From that point forward, whenever you visit a site that uses that ActiveX control, Internet Explorer will request your permission to run it.

Privacy and security issues

In Windows 10, you can eliminate most security concerns by browsing whenever possible in Edge. Because the new browser runs in a sandboxed environment, what happens in Edge stays in Edge, so to speak. That is to say, nothing that you do in Edge is going to damage your system by exploiting a third-party add-on. Privacy issues, on the other hand, will always accompany our visits to the web, in part because privacy choices are a matter of personal preference, involving tradeoffs between convenience and the desire to be left alone. We discuss those tradeoffs and the settings by which they're implemented in the following sections.

Allowing or not allowing your browser to save sign-in credentials

Both Edge and Internet Explorer will happily store user IDs and passwords in a secure location, simplifying their reuse. The data is saved in a "vault," a folder to which your user account does not have direct access.

Saving credentials is an optional feature. It can save you time and trouble when you're revisiting sites—shopping sites, for example—that require you to sign in to an account. But if you think that someone else might be sitting down at your computer and going to those same sites without your permission, you might want to forego the convenience. To turn credential saving on or off in Edge, click More Actions, Settings, View Advanced Settings, and then put this switch in whichever position you favor:

The Manage My Saved Passwords link below the switch produces a list of all the credentials that Edge has collected, with a handy X next to each in case you want to remove particular items. If you click an entry in this list, Edge provides the URL, user name, and encrypted password in a dialog box similar to this:

You can modify the user name or password in this dialog box, but for your security, Edge will not show you (or anyone else using your computer) the current password. (You can, however, inspect passwords by means of Credential Manager, discussed in a moment.)

To reach the comparable setting in Internet Explorer, click Tools, Internet Options. Go to the Content tab of the Internet Options dialog box and click Settings in the AutoComplete section. The option to save passwords (and be prompted for approval each time Internet Explorer finds new credentials to save) appears in the AutoComplete Settings dialog box, along with numerous similar options:

Viewing and deleting credentials with Credential Manager

The Manage Passwords button in the AutoComplete Settings dialog box takes you to Credential Manager, a destination you can also reach by searching for Credential Manager in Control Panel. The Web Credentials section of Credential Manager displays a list of user names and passwords saved by either Edge or Internet Explorer. Clicking an item reveals details, as shown in Figure 11-17.

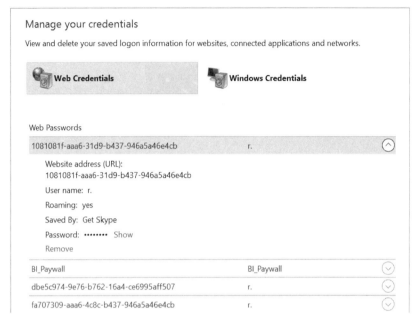

Figure 11-17 Credential Manager, a part of Control Panel, lists all web credentials saved by either browser.

The Remove link here provides a way to clean out credentials you no longer need. The Show link lets you see the password you saved, but for your security it requires you to reenter the password by which you sign in to Windows.

Blocking pop-ups

Windows that pop up unexpectedly while you're browsing aren't usually malicious, but they can be annoying. Both browsers offer the ability to suppress them.

In Edge, visit the Advanced Settings pane and make sure that Block Pop-Ups is set to On. It's only an on-off switch; there are no further options here, but when you encounter a site that requires a blocked pop-up, you will have the option to add it to a safe-sites list.

To shut down pop-ups in Internet Explorer, click Tools, Internet Options, go to the Privacy tab, and select Turn On Pop-up Blocker. For fine-tuning, click Settings to get to the following dialog box:

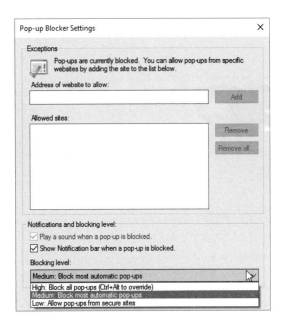

The pop-up blocker defaults to a medium level of scrutiny, which means that it blocks "most" pop-ups. The low and high alternatives let you accept pop-ups only from secure sites (those to which you connect via an HTTPS URL) or accept no pop-ups from any site.

The top of this dialog box is devoted to a safe-sites list. You can build it manually by copying URLs to the Address Of Website To Allow box and clicking Add. Or you can build it as you go; when you come to a site that requires a pop-up, you can choose to have the blocker ignore that site in the future.

Clearing your browser history and other personal information

Your browser keeps a copy of webpages, images, and media you've viewed recently. This cached information—combined with cookies, saved form data, and saved passwords (although these are saved to generally inaccessible locations)—might give another person who has access to your computer more information than you might want him or her to have.

To wipe away most of your online trail in Edge, click More Actions, Settings, and then click Choose What To Clear. These steps take you to the set of check boxes shown in Figure 11-18. To get to the comparable location in Internet Explorer, click Tools, Safety, Delete Browsing History.

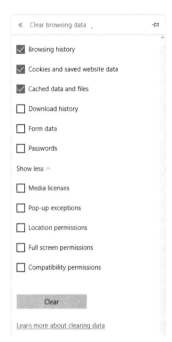

Figure 11-18 The options under Clear Browsing Data in Edge, and the corresponding choices in Internet Explorer, let you specify which elements of your history you want to erase.

The most important of these choices are as follows:

- **Browsing History.** This is simply a list of sites you've been to, whether you went to them directly or followed another site's hyperlinks, since you last cleared your history.

- **Cookies And Saved Website Data.** A *cookie* is a small text file that enables a website to store persistent information on your hard disk. Cookies, particularly first-party cookies, are generally benign and more often than not useful. Note that removing cookies via this option does not block their arrival in the future. (To do that, see "Blocking cookies and sending do-not-track requests" later in this chapter.)

- **Cached Data And Files.** These are local copies of pages and media content from sites that you visit. The browser "caches" this data to speed up its display on subsequent visits.

- **Download History.** This is the list that appears on the History tab of the Hub. Deleting this history here (or clicking Clear All in the Hub—the actions are equivalent) does not remove the downloads themselves, which remain where you put them.

- **Form Data.** Your browser stores some information—for example, your shipping or email address—that you use to fill out forms, simplifying reuse. You can erase its memory here.

- **Passwords.** As mentioned earlier (see "Allowing or not allowing your browser to save sign-in credentials"), there are pros and cons associated with caching passwords. If you change your mind after you've allowed the browser to store these credentials, you can erase the data here.

Squelching history temporarily with InPrivate browsing

If you want to cover your tracks only for a particular browsing session, don't bother fussing with history settings or clearance. Simply open an InPrivate window. In Edge, click More Actions, New InPrivate Window. In Internet Explorer, press Ctrl+Shift+P or click Tools, Safety, InPrivate Browsing. When you subsequently close the InPrivate session, any data the browser has stored (session cookies and other temporary files) is deleted.

Be aware that browsing privately is not the same as browsing anonymously. Sites you visit can record your IP address, and your network administrator or Internet service provider can see which sites you connect to and can capture any unencrypted information that you transmit or receive.

During an Internet Explorer InPrivate session, toolbars and extensions are disabled by default. If you want them enabled, click Tools, open the Internet Options dialog box, and go to the Privacy tab. Then clear the Disable Toolbars And Extensions When InPrivate Browsing Starts check box.

Blocking cookies and sending do-not-track requests

Cookies—small bits of information that websites store on your hard disk—come in two flavors. First-party cookies are used by the site that you are currently visiting, generally for such purposes as personalizing your experience with the site, storing shopping-cart information, and so on. Third-party cookies are used by a site other than the one you're visiting—such as an advertiser on the site you're currently visiting.

Cookies do not carry executable code (they're text files) and can't be used to spread viruses or malware; they can't scurry around your hard disk reading your address book and financial records, for example. A cookie can provide a website only with information that you supply while visiting the site. The information a cookie gathers can be read only by pages in the same domain as the one that created the cookie.

Nevertheless, privacy concerns arise when advertisers and web-analytics companies begin to correlate the information from third-party cookies to build a profile of your activities. Because it's not always obvious who's sending you a cookie and what purposes that cookie serves, some people are understandably wary about allowing cookies on their systems.

Both browsers allow you to block either all cookies or third-party cookies. In Edge, click More Actions, Settings, View Advanced Settings. Then open the drop-down list below the Cookies heading. You'll see the following simple set of choices:

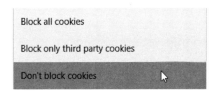

In Internet Explorer, click Tools, Internet Options. On the Privacy tab, click Advanced. In the Advanced Privacy Settings dialog box, shown in Figure 11-19, you can express your prefer-ences separately for first-party and third-party cookies. In addition to accepting or blocking cookies, you can ask to be prompted each time a first or third party wants to deliver or update a cookie. You are likely to find this choice more trouble than it's worth. In addition, you can also choose to allow all session cookies—cookies that are deleted at the end of your browsing session.

Figure 11-19 It's hard to think of a reason for blocking first-party cookies while allowing cookies from third parties, but Internet Explorer will let you do it.

In a separate dialog box (click Sites on the Privacy tab of the Internet Options dialog box), you can block individual domains from serving cookies or allow them to.

Suppressing unwanted data collection by sending do-not-track requests

Manually blocking cookies is a tedious and error-prone process. A better way to request that advertisers refrain from collecting and storing personal data from your browser is by sending do-not-track requests.

The do-not-track (DNT) standard, introduced first with Firefox in 2011, is now included with most modern browsers. If DNT is enabled, when you visit a site, the browser sends a header requesting that the site refrain from passing information about you to third parties. This is not a guarantee that the site will honor your request (and it's possible that you will still receive third-party cookies), but DNT has found widespread acceptance among mainstream advertisers.

In Windows 8, the option to send do-not-track requests was turned on by default (included with Internet Explorer's "express settings"). This provoked controversy and resistance from both competing browsers and the advertising industry because the standard, as codified by the World Wide Web Consortium (W3C), stipulates that DNT requests result from an active decision by end users. Microsoft reversed its position on the matter, and in both Edge and Internet Explorer, DNT is initially turned off. To turn it on in Edge, click More Actions, Settings, View Advanced Settings and set Send Do Not Track Requests to On. In Internet Explorer, click Tools, Safety, Turn On Do Not Track Requests.

Configuring security zones in Internet Explorer

Internet Explorer uses a system of "security zones" to let you configure security settings differently for different categories of websites. The zones are called Internet, Local Intranet, Trusted Sites, and Restricted Sites, and you can configure them by going to the Security tab of the Internet Options dialog box, shown in Figure 11-20.

The four zones are intended to be used as follows. The Restricted Sites zone, designed for sites that you trust the least (or explicitly distrust), has the highest security settings—that is, the maximum in safeguards. The Trusted Sites zone has, by default, a medium level of protection, blocking the download of unsigned ActiveX controls and prompting for permission before downloading other material considered potentially unsafe. The Internet Zone—with medium-high settings—is reserved for all nonintranet sites that you have not assigned to the Trusted Sites or Restricted Sites zone. The Intranet Zone, with low security settings, is populated with intranet sites that you have not explicitly moved to Trusted Sites or Restricted Sites, sites that bypass your proxy server, and all network servers accessed via a UNC path (*server_name*).

Figure 11-20 Use this dialog box to add sites to specific zones in Internet Explorer or to modify the security settings associated with a zone.

To add sites to a zone, select the zone and click Sites. To change the security settings for a zone, adjust the slider or click Custom Level.

CHAPTER 12

Organizing and searching for files

Unless you use your computer exclusively as a game machine, learning to manage your "stuff"—your documents, programs, and communications—is probably the single most critical computing skill you need to acquire. Because the continual growth in storage capacity encourages a corresponding increase in digital retentiveness, keeping track of files, media items, and other documents is more crucial than ever.

The redesigned File Explorer (in Windows 7 it was known as Windows Explorer) is rich with organizational power tools, including live-icon previews of file contents (for applications and document types that support this capability), a preview pane that allows you to peek inside a file's contents without actually opening it, and a details pane that displays file properties and lets you add descriptive tags to files. In this chapter, we dive deeply into this rich feature set and explain how Windows 10 can help you organize your data files.

Organizing is just the first step to a well-ordered documentary life, of course. Finding things again when you need them is every bit as crucial. Windows 10 incorporates a powerful indexing service and search engine that can help you find what you need quickly and with a minimum of effort wherever it may reside.

Exploring File Explorer

You can't become a Windows expert without mastering File Explorer. This general-purpose tool is used throughout Windows for general file-management tasks, for opening and saving files in Windows programs, and even in parts of the Windows shell. The more you understand about how File Explorer works, the more effective you'll be at speeding through tasks without unnecessary delays. Because it's vital to know your way around, we'll begin this chapter with a short tour.

Figure 12-1 shows the major landmarks in a typical File Explorer display.

Figure 12-1   File Explorer includes the navigation and display elements shown here, some of which can be customized.

Inside OUT

Use a keyboard shortcut to open File Explorer

You can find File Explorer in a variety of places in Windows 10, but if you're handy with the keyboard, don't bother hunting for it. Press Windows key+E to get there directly.

If you've used any of the recent versions of Microsoft Office, or if you're coming to Windows 10 by way of Windows 8, then you won't be startled to see the ribbon atop File Explorer. If, by any chance, this aspect of the user interface is new to you, the only thing you need to know is that it replaces the old system of drop-down and cascading menus with a set of top-level tabs—Home, Share, and View in the example shown in Figure 12-1. When you click a tab, an appropriate set of options appears below it:

You'll notice that the various commands under a tab are organized into groups—Clipboard, Organize, New, Open, and Select on the Home tab, for example. More important points to note are the following:

- The command bar from Windows 7 days is gone. The ribbon itself provides the context-specific commands that used to appear on the command bar.

- When certain items are selected in the contents pane, an additional tab appears at the right side of the ribbon, with commands relevant to the context. If you select a picture folder, for example, or one or more picture files in any folder, a Manage tab bearing picture-related commands appears:

- The ribbon can be minimized or not, according to your preference. If the ribbon is mini-mized, as it is in Figure 12-1, the commands appear only when a tab is selected. If it's not minimized, they're always visible. To switch from one view to the other, right-click the ribbon.

- Most of what's on the ribbon is also available on the menus that appear when you right-click files or folders. If you ever become impatient when trying to find a command on the ribbon, simply right-click and look there. Microsoft adopted the ribbon to reduce the number of cascading submenus that we all used to have to traverse. But sometimes the old ways seem simpler; it's your choice.

To the left of the ribbon tabs, displayed in blue, is the File menu. There you will find com-mands for opening a new File Explorer window; for opening Windows PowerShell and the command prompt (Cmd.exe), with and without administrative privileges; a list of recently used folders for quick navigation; and more.

Inside OUT

Use the keyboard instead of the mouse (if you prefer)

Hardcore keyboard users will appreciate that any command on the ribbon can be accessed and applied without the mouse. Press Alt, then notice the letters and numbers that appear under the ribbon tabs and the Quick Access Toolbar. Press one of those letters—H for Home, for example—and the appropriate tab itself appears, adorned with its own set of shortcut letters. Follow the shortcuts to your destination.

The design of the ribbon—its purpose—is to put the commands you use most often front and center, easy to find. A secondary benefit is that it makes less frequently used commands easier to discover. Here are a few gems that merit your attention:

- The Copy Path command, on the Home tab, puts the path of the current folder or file on the Clipboard. This is handy for sending someone a link to a network share via email. (As an alternative, you can click in the address bar and press Ctrl+C, or you can press Shift as you right-click, and then click Copy As Path on the shortcut menu.)

- The Move To and Copy To commands, also on the Home tab, drop down a list of likely targets (recently used folders) for your move and copy operations.

- The Zip command, on the Share tab, instantly creates a Zip (compressed) file from the current selection, thereby providing an alternative to the time-honored approach of right-clicking and choosing Send To, Compressed (Zipped) Folder. (See "Using compressed (zipped) folders" later in this chapter.)

- On the View tab, you'll find handy commands for showing or not showing files and folders with the Hidden attribute. Another command nearby lets you assign the Hidden attribute to the current selection.

Customizing the Quick Access Toolbar

As its name implies, the Quick Access Toolbar—that set of icons in the upper left corner of File Explorer, above the ribbon—puts commonly used functions close at hand (or close to your mouse pointer). If you'd like those items a few centimeters closer, you can move the Quick Access Toolbar below the ribbon by clicking the arrow at the end to display the menu shown here:

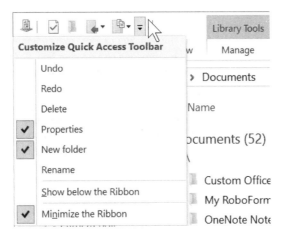

This menu also lets you change the items that appear on the Quick Access Toolbar. Here, for example, we've set up the toolbar to offer Properties and New Folder. Any command on the ribbon in File Explorer can be added to the Quick Access Toolbar—not just the few that are shown in the preceding illustration. To add a command, right-click it and then click Add To Quick Access Toolbar, as we've done here with the Move To and Copy To commands. To remove it, right-click it on the Quick Access Toolbar and then click Remove From Quick Access Toolbar.

Navigating in File Explorer

In its default arrangement, File Explorer displays the navigation pane with a handful of starting points for navigating through files on your computer and on your network:

NOTE

On a Windows 10 device that is joined to a domain, you cannot create a homegroup, but you can join one that has been created by someone else on your home network. In that case, the Homegroup node will be available in File Explorer only if a homegroup is available for you to join.

Displaying the navigation pane is optional (to remove it, click the View tab, open the Navigation Pane drop-down menu, and clear the Navigation Pane check box), but unless you need every bit of available screen space for the contents pane (perhaps with the addition of the preview pane or details pane), you'll probably find it convenient to keep the navigation pane in view. It helps you with navigation, of course, but it also serves as a handy drop target when you're moving or copying files or folders.

The Quick Access node at the top of the navigation pane is new in Windows 10. When it's selected, File Explorer displays a collection of recently used folders and another of recently used files. Windows makes some intelligent choices about what to display under Quick Access, but you can customize this to suit your needs. In the Frequent Folders section, you'll find some folders marked with pins and others without one. The pinned folders always appear under Quick Access (unless you unpin them). The unpinned folders are ones that you have recently worked with, and these folders are replaced by others if you begin to use them less frequently. You can unpin a pinned folder by right-clicking it and then clicking Unpin From Quick Access. And you can make any folder anywhere a permanent resident of Quick Access by right-clicking it and then clicking Pin To Quick Access.

The Recent Files section of Quick Access contains files that you have recently worked with, sorted with the most recently used at the top. By right-clicking a file name and clicking Open File Location, you can go directly to the folder in which the file resides. If you find that you don't need to see a particular file (and want to make room for another), you can right-click that file and then click Remove From Quick Access.

Quick Access is an extremely handy navigational tool because it gathers together the stuff you're most likely to be concerned with, regardless of where that stuff is actually stored. But if you don't need it, or you're not keen on having passersby see what you've been working on, you can suppress either or both the Frequent Folders section or the Recent Files section. To do this, click the View tab and then click Options. On the General tab of the Folder Options dialog box, you'll find the check boxes you need in the Privacy section. (If you just want to cover your immediate tracks without changing the overall behavior of File Explorer, it's probably simpler to click Clear in the Privacy section.)

The OneDrive node is also new in the Windows 10 File Explorer. Note that a click here does not take you to the cloud. Instead it opens the folder %UserProfile%\OneDrive, which stores local copies of documents that you have synced with OneDrive. (For more details about One-Drive, see Appendix C, "OneDrive and other cloud services.")

By clicking the View tab and then opening the Navigation Pane drop-down menu, you can avail yourself of three additional options related to this pane:

- **Expand To Open Folder.** By default, selecting a folder in the contents pane has no effect on the navigation pane. If you select Expand To Open Folder, File Explorer opens the parent folder of the folder you select in the contents pane, making it easier to see the parentage and neighborhood of the selected item.

- **Show Libraries.** If you choose to directly manage files stored in libraries (see "Working with libraries" later in this chapter), you might want to include them in your navigation pane. If you select the Show Libraries option, all of your libraries—those that Windows provides and any that you create yourself—appear in a node in the navigation pane. If you want to see only particular libraries, click the Libraries node heading, and then right-click each library you want to remove and click Don't Show In Navigation Pane. To restore a library to this node, use the Show In Navigation Pane command. Both commands are also in the Manage group on the Libraries tab.

- **Show All Folders.** For the most inclusive navigation pane, select Show All Folders. The resulting tree will include, in addition to your libraries, your profile folders (click your user name in the navigation pane to expand this item), any media folders on your network to which you have access (these will appear directly under This PC), Control Panel, and the Recycle Bin. (For more about your profile folders, see the next section.)

What's what and where in a user profile

A *user profile* contains all the settings and files for a user's desktop environment. In addition to personal documents and media files, this profile includes the user's own registry settings, cookies, browser favorites, and user data and settings for installed programs.

By default, each user who signs in to a computer has a local user profile, which is created when the user signs in for the first time. Local user profiles are stored in %SystemDrive%\Users. Each user's profile is stored in a subfolder where the user account name is the folder name (for example, C:\Users\Katy). The entire path for the current user's profile is accessible via another commonly used environment variable, %UserProfile%. If you have File Explorer's navigation pane set to show all folders, you can see the subfolders of your profile by clicking your user name in the navigation pane.

Here's a rundown of the major profile folders. Because apps can add their own data to the profile, your system might have some additional profile folders.

- **Contacts.** This folder first appeared in Windows Vista and was designed to store contact information used by Windows Mail. It is not used by any programs included in Windows 10 and is maintained for compatibility purposes with third-party personal information management programs.

- **Desktop.** This folder contains items that appear on the user's desktop, including files and shortcuts. (A Public counterpart also contributes items to the desktop.) A link to this location appears in the Quick Access section of the navigation pane.

- **Documents.** Most applications use this folder as the default location for storing user documents.

- **Downloads.** This folder, which was introduced in Windows Vista, is the default location for storing items downloaded from websites. A link to this location appears by default in the Quick Access section of the navigation pane.

- **Favorites.** Internet Explorer favorites are saved in this folder by default. To open it quickly in File Explorer, type the shortcut **shell:favorites** in the address bar.

- **Links.** This folder contains shortcuts that appear under the Quick Access heading in the navigation pane. You can create shortcuts here directly, but it's easier to drag items from a file list or the address bar directly to the navigation pane.

- **Music.** This folder is the default location for ripped CD tracks. Most third-party music programs store downloaded tracks in a subfolder here.

- **Pictures.** If you transfer images from external devices (such as digital cameras) or save images from external locations, they end up here.

- **Saved Games.** This folder is the default storage location for apps that can save a game in progress.

- **Searches.** This folder stores saved search specifications, allowing you to reuse previous searches.

- **Videos.** Video files that you download from external services or from external devices are saved here by default.

Application data

The hidden AppData folder, introduced in Windows Vista, is used extensively by programs as a way to store user data and settings in a place where they'll be protected from accidental change or deletion. This folder contains application-specific data—customized dictionaries and templates for a word processor, junk sender lists for an email client, custom toolbar settings, and so on. It's organized into three subfolders, named Local, LocalLow, and Roaming. The Roaming folder (which is also accessible via the environment variable %AppData%) is for data that is made available to a roaming profile (a profile stored on a network server; the server makes the profile available to any network computer where the user signs in). The Local folder (which is also accessible via the system variable %LocalAppData%) is for data that should not roam. The LocalLow folder is used only for Internet Explorer Protected Mode data.

Subfolders under AppData\Local include the following:

- **Microsoft\Windows\History.** This hidden folder contains the user's Internet Explorer browsing history. You can open it directly by using the shortcut **shell:history**.

- **Temp.** This folder contains temporary files created by applications. The %Temp% variable points to AppData\Local\Temp.

Subfolders under AppData\Roaming\Microsoft\Windows include the following:

- **Libraries.** You'll find files that define the contents of default and custom libraries here.

- **Network Shortcuts.** This folder contains shortcuts to network shares that appear in the This PC folder. The folder is not hidden; you can add your own shortcuts here, although it is easier to right-click in This PC and choose Add A Network Location.

- **SendTo.** This folder contains shortcuts to some of the folders and applications that appear on the Send To submenu. Send To is a command that appears when you right-click a file or folder in File Explorer (or on the desktop). The SendTo folder is not hidden. You can add your own items to the Send To menu by creating shortcuts here. Type **shell:sendto** in the address bar to open this folder and add or delete shortcuts.

Inside OUT

Expand the Send To menu

Normally, the Send To menu displays a limited selection of items, including the Desktop and your Documents library as well as any removable storage devices and mapped network drives. To see an expanded Send To menu that includes all folders in your user profile, hold down Shift and then choose Send To from the shortcut menu. The list expands to include your profile folders:

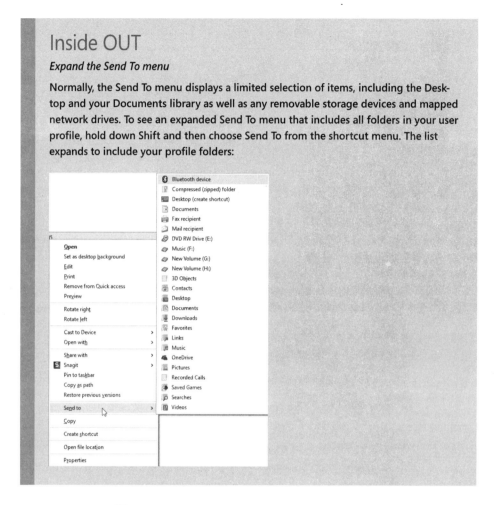

Common profiles

Windows creates a local user profile for each user account, storing the profiles in subfolders of %SystemDrive%\Users with folder names that match the account names. In addition to these user profiles, the operating system creates two others:

- **Public.** The Public profile contains a group of folders that mirror those in your user profile. You can see the Public Documents, Public Music, Public Pictures, and Public Videos folders in their matching libraries. The advantage of these folders is that other users can save files to these locations from different user accounts on the same computer or from across the network.

- **Default.** When a user signs in to a computer for the first time (and her account is not set up to use a roaming profile or mandatory profile), Windows creates a new local profile by copying the contents of the Default profile to a new folder and giving it the user's name. Note that the Default folder is hidden, and you must approve a User Account Control (UAC) consent dialog box to add files to it. You can configure the Default profile the way you want new users' initial view of Windows to appear. Note, however, that some of the customizations that you make to the Default profile might not be copied to profiles for new users. For more information about this topic, see the series of articles by Windows MVP Mitch Tulloch at *w7io.com/21101*.

CAUTION
In the unlikely event that Windows is unable to access your user profile when you sign in, the system might create a temporary user profile in %SystemDrive%\Users\Temp, warning you at sign-in that it has done so. Any changes you make to this temporary profile (including any files you save in its data folders) will be deleted when you sign out.

Working with libraries

A *library* is a virtual folder that aggregates the contents of multiple folders stored on your computer or on your network. You can sort, filter, group, search, arrange, and share the data in a library as if it were in a single location. Windows 10 gives you several by default: Documents, Music, Pictures, Saved Pictures, and Videos. You can create additional libraries to suit your storage needs, and you can customize any library by changing or adding to the physical folders that make up that library.

The important things to understand about libraries are the following:

- A library can encompass multiple folders on multiple disks.

- Libraries are automatically indexed for fast searching, provided their component folders are indexed. Thus, for example, you can open a library, enter a search term in its search box, and quickly pull up all matching documents, even if they're located on far-flung corners of your storage empire.

- Library files are automatically backed up by the Windows 10 File History feature.

Here are some usage scenarios for libraries:

- **Large digital media collections.** You keep your favorite music in the Music folder on your notebook so that you have it available when you leave home. The bulk of your collection, including large high-definition movie files and albums you don't listen to regularly, are stored on an external hard drive. By arranging content on the external drive into Music, Pictures, and Videos folders and then adding those folders to the corresponding libraries, you have full access to your entire collection when you're home and connected to the external drive.

- **Workgroup projects.** You and some coworkers are collaborating on a project. Your drafts are stored in a subfolder of the Documents folder on your local hard disk. You also need access to shared graphics on a network file server, and final drafts from you and your coworkers will be saved in another shared network folder. By adding the local Drafts folder and the two network folders to a custom library, you can search and browse through all those files from one virtual location.

- **Homegroup projects.** At the end of every year, you create a holiday newsletter to send to friends and family. You create a custom library that includes one local folder where you copy photos that will go in the newsletter. You also save the draft of the newsletter there. With two clicks, you can share the custom library with your homegroup so that other family members can add their own files and photos to the project.

- **School-related or work-related projects.** You keep documents, notes, spreadsheets, and other files organized in subfolders, one for each client or project you're working on. Adding those subfolders to a custom library allows you to quickly browse a single subfolder or search through all folders at once. Searching for proposals, contracts, or homework assignments can help you find a document you did for a previous project, adapt it for a new project, and save it quickly in the correct subfolder.

Figure 12-2 illustrates a library search. Here we've created a custom library called School and searched for the term *tulip*. File Explorer returns four items—two Word files, a webpage, and a JPEG image—stored in four different locations. We could, of course, have searched globally, but the search results would likely have included extraneous material not related to schoolwork.

Figure 12-2 The custom library shown here includes four folders on two local drives. Search results cover all four locations.

To create a new library, click the Libraries heading in the navigation pane, and then click New Item, Library on the Home tab. (Alternatively, right-click Libraries in the navigation pane, and then click New, Library.) Give the new library a descriptive name and then press Enter. Your newly created library appears in the navigation pane. Click the Include A Folder button to populate the library.

Using the Include Folder dialog box, select the folder you want to use as the default location for saving files in this library and then click Include Folder. That opens the library and lists the contents of the folder you just selected.

To add more folders to the library, click the Manage tab. Then click Manage Library to get to the Library Locations dialog box:

In this dialog box, you can delete folders as well as add them, of course, and you can also change the library's default save folder. The default save folder is important for applications that expect to save their documents in particular places—a music service, for example, that expects to save downloaded songs in a certain folder within the Music library. It's also the folder that File Explorer will use if you drag a file to the library's heading in the navigation pane.

What locations can you add to a library? The most important consideration is that the folder must be indexed so that it can be included in searches. Folders and network shares in any of the following locations are eligible for inclusion:

- The system drive.

- An additional volume on an internal local drive formatted using NTFS or FAT32.

- An external USB or IEEE 1394 (FireWire) hard drive, formatted using NTFS or FAT32.

- A USB flash drive, if the device appears in the navigation pane, under the This PC heading.

- A shared network folder that is indexed using Windows Search; this includes any shared folder from another computer in your homegroup.

- A shared network folder that has been made available offline and is therefore available in your local index.

  ➤ For more details on how to manage the search index, see "Configuring search and index-ing options" later in this chapter.

To delete a library, simply right-click it in the navigation pane and click Delete. The library is gone, but its component folders and their contents remain.

Inside OUT

Open a file or folder location from a library

Because libraries are virtual folders, it's sometimes difficult to perform operations directly on their contents. If you want to see a file or folder in its actual location in File Explorer, right-click and choose Open File Location or Open Folder Location.

Using compressed (zipped) folders

Depending on the file type, you can dramatically reduce the amount of disk space used by one or more files by compressing those files into a zipped folder. Don't be fooled by the name: a zipped folder (also known as a Zip file or archive) is actually a single file, compressed using the industry-standard Zip format and saved with the .zip file name extension. Any version of Windows can open a file saved in this format, as can other modern operating systems. The format is also accessible with the help of many third-party utilities. Thus, zipped folders are an ideal way to compress large files in order to send them in email or transfer them across a network, including the Internet.

> ### TROUBLESHOOTING
>
> *Your application can't open zipped files*
>
> File Explorer compresses and decompresses files in zipped folders on the fly, displaying the contents of an archive in a window that closely resembles a folder. But most applications do not support this format. Thus, to view a WordPad document stored in a zipped folder, you need to double-click the zipped folder in File Explorer to display its contents and then double-click the file. If you try the same task using WordPad's Open command, you'll open the binary Zip file itself and display its unreadable contents. (If you want to edit a file stored in a Zip file, be sure to extract it to a local or network folder first.)

To create a new archive using zipped folders, follow these steps:

1. In File Explorer, display the folder in which you want the new archive to reside.

2. Right-click any empty space in the folder, and then click New, Compressed (Zipped) Folder.

3. Name the folder.

To add files and folders to your archive, drag and drop them onto the zipped folder icon in File Explorer (or double-click to open the zipped folder in its own window and then drag items into it). You can also use the Clipboard to copy and paste items. To remove an item from the zipped folder, double-click the folder to display its contents, right-click the item, and then click Delete.

You can also create a compressed folder from the current selection by clicking Zip on the Share tab in File Explorer. Windows creates an archive file with the same name as the selected object. Use the Rename command (or press F2) to replace the default name with a more descriptive one.

To extract individual files or folders from a zipped folder, open it in File Explorer and then drag the items you want to extract to a new location, or use the Clipboard to copy and paste. To extract all items from a zipped folder to a specific location, right-click the zipped folder icon and then click Extract All, or open the zipped folder in File Explorer and click Extract All on the Extract tab on the ribbon.

Inside OUT

Add password protection to zipped folders

When creating a new archive, you no longer have the option to add a password to protect the file from casual snoops (that feature disappeared with Windows 7). If you need password protection, you can use a third-party program. You have many choices, including the venerable WinZip (*winzip.com*), which costs $30 per copy. An attractive freeware alternative is 7-Zip (*7-zip.org*), which supports a huge number of compression formats, and also allows you to secure compressed files using 256-bit Advanced Encryption Standard (AES) encryption. It integrates neatly into File Explorer.

Displaying or suppressing check boxes

File Explorer offers two modes of file and folder selection—with and without check boxes. You can switch between them by means of the Item Check Boxes command on the View tab.

With check boxes on, you can select multiple items that are not adjacent to one another simply by selecting each one in turn; no need to hold down the Ctrl key. In any case, though, Ctrl-selecting and Shift-selecting work as they always have, with or without check boxes.

Arranging data in File Explorer

You can adjust the display of any individual folder's contents in File Explorer by means of options in the Layout section of the View tab. As Figure 12-3 shows, your choices are numerous: icons in various sizes, Tiles, List, Details, and Content. Display options are folder-specific and persistent.

Figure 12-3 The View tab provides a large set of options for displaying content in File Explorer.

You can get a look at each display option by hovering the mouse over it on the View tab. File Explorer gives you a preview of each choice, making it easier for you to decide.

The range of options for the various icon views is larger than it looks. Although there are four discrete choices available on the View tab—small, medium, large, and extra large—the actual number of sizes is 76. You can cycle smoothly through all 76 sizes by choosing one of them, holding down the Ctrl key, and turning the wheel on your mouse. With each step, you'll see the icons grow or shrink (although at some of the smaller sizes the change is barely perceptible).

Content view, introduced in Windows 7, is intended primarily for use with search results. In the case of documents, it shows a fairly lengthy snippet of text with the matching search items highlighted.

List view displays file names only. If you have a large number of items in the folder you're working with, the list snakes; that is, you read down the first column, then up to the top of the second, and so on. Details view provides a multicolumn tabulation of your files. The column headings vary by folder type, but you can tailor them in any case. To add or remove a column heading, put your folder in Details view, click the View tab, click anywhere in the row of headings, and then click Add Columns. (Alternatively, right-click anywhere in the row of column headings.) If the list of column headings that appears doesn't include the one you want, click Choose Columns (at the bottom of the list). As Figure 12-4 shows, the Choose Details dialog box that appears next provides you with a wealth of choices. In fact, Figure 12-4 shows only the first 15 choices in a vast array of possibilities.

Figure 12-4 Use this dialog box to select which headings are displayed in Details view.

In the Choose Details dialog box, you can also use the Move Up and Move Down buttons to change the order in which column headings appear. (You can also change the column order in File Explorer by dragging headings with the mouse.)

As you'll discover momentarily (see "Sorting, filtering, and grouping" later in this chapter), headings in Details view are important for sorting data as well as simply displaying it.

Inside OUT
Change display settings in Open and Save dialog boxes

In many programs, you can change display settings in common file-management dialog boxes, although you will not find a View tab there. To switch between an icon view and Details view (or to make any other comparable switch), right-click an open space within the dialog box (you might have to enlarge the dialog box first), then click View.

Initially, all folders intended for the storage of user data (including those you create) are assigned one of five folder templates. These templates define the default headings that File Explorer considers appropriate for the content type. These headings are used atop columns in Details view and are available on the Sort By menu in all other views. The logic is straightforward: you'll probably want to sort a folder full of MP3 tracks by track number, but that column would be superfluous in a folder full of Microsoft Word documents. And the Date Taken column is extremely useful for filtering digital photos, but it isn't much use with any other kinds of data.

Table 12-1 lists the default column headings available in each of these five templates. It also lists additional headings that are not included by default but might be useful for each template.

Table 12-1 Standard folder templates

Template	Default headings	Additional headings
General Items	Name, Date Modified, Type, Size	Date Created, Authors, Tags, Title
Documents	Name, Date Modified, Type, Size	Date Created, Authors, Categories, Tags, Title
Pictures	Name, Date, Tags, Size, Rating (in libraries); Name, Date, Type, Size, Tags (in folders)	Date Created, Date Taken, Dimensions, Rating
Music	Name, [Track] #, Contributing Artists, Album	Type, Size, Date Created, Date Modified, Album Artist, Bit Rate, Genre, Length, Protected, Rating, Year
Videos	Name, Date, Type, Size, Length	Date Created, Date Modified, Media Created, Dimensions

Inside OUT

Customize folder templates

Not sure what folder "type" you're in? Right-click a blank space in the folder and then click Customize This Folder, or tap the Alt key to reveal the menu bar, and then choose View, Customize This Folder. (If this option isn't available, you're viewing a system folder whose template can't be changed.) On the Customize tab of the properties dialog box for the selected folder, look at the selection in the Optimize This Folder For drop-down list, which shows the folder type that's currently in effect.

Sorting, filtering, and grouping

Regardless of the view settings you've chosen for a folder, you can adjust the way its contents are displayed at any time by changing the sort order, filtering the contents by one or more properties to include only selected items, and grouping and arranging the contents by a particular heading. In any view, these options are available by right-clicking anywhere in the contents pane and choosing a Sort By or Group By option. In most cases, however, these actions are easier to accomplish by switching to Details view and using the column headings, which is also the preferred way to filter.

Sorting a folder's contents   To sort a folder in Details view, click the heading that you want to use as a sort key. For example, to sort by Date Modified, click the Date Modified heading. Click again on the same heading to reverse the sort order. The current sort order is indicated by an up arrow or down arrow above the heading to indicate whether the sort is in ascending or descending order.

In all other views, right-click any empty space in the contents pane and select a value from the Sort By menu. A bullet next to Ascending or Descending indicates the current sort order; choose the other option to reverse the sort order.

Filtering folder contents   In Details view only, you can use headings to filter the contents of a folder. If you rest your pointer on a heading, a drop-down arrow appears at the right. Clicking the arrow reveals a set of filter check boxes appropriate for that heading. In some cases (the Tags heading, for example, as shown in Figure 12-5), the filter list is built on the fly from the contents of the current file list.

Select any check box to add that item to the filter list; clear the check box for an item to remove it from the filter. After you filter the list in Details view, you can switch to any other view and the filter will persist. (Look in the address bar to see the specific filter applied, and click the previous breadcrumb to remove all filtering without switching back to Details view.)

Figure 12-5 When you click the drop-down arrow next to a column heading, a set of filtering options appropriate for the heading appears.

If you filter by Size, you get a set of choices based on the file sizes that Windows deems appropriate given the current folder contents, as shown here:

A filter can use multiple check boxes and multiple headings. So, for example, you could filter a picture folder based on ratings as well as a "date taken" value, resulting in a file list like this one:

When a folder is filtered, check marks appear to the right of headings used for filtering (see the Rating and Date headings in the preceding illustration). The values on which you have filtered appear in the address bar.

When you select multiple check boxes in the same heading, File Explorer displays items that match any of the selected check boxes. When you select filtering check boxes from two or more separate headings, however, File Explorer displays only items that satisfy the criteria applied to each heading (in Boolean terms, it uses the conjunction AND between the headings).

Inside OUT

Use the date navigator to zoom through time

If you click a date heading, the filter options display a date navigator like the one shown next, with common date groupings available at the bottom of the list. You can also click Select A Date Or Date Range and use the calendar to filter the file list that way.

The date navigator is much more powerful than it looks at first glance. Use the calendar to zoom in or out and narrow or expand your view of the contents of a folder or a search. Initially, the calendar shows the current month, with today's date highlighted. Click the month heading to zoom out to a display showing the current year as a heading with the current month highlighted. You can then drag or hold down Ctrl and click to select multiple months, as shown here:

Click the year to zoom out again to show the current decade. Click once more to show the current century. In any calendar view, you can use the arrows to the left and right of the column heading to move through the calendar a month, year, decade, or century at a time. To zoom back in, click any month, year, decade, or century on the calendar control. This technique is especially valuable with folders or search results containing hundreds or thousands of files and folders.

Grouping folder contents   If sorting and filtering don't give you enough ways to organize or locate files, try grouping. Grouping generates a display comparable to the one shown in Figure 12-6. Here we have grouped a set of picture files by their tags.

Figure 12-6 You can group items in any view. Here we have grouped some pictures by tag in Details view.

When you group items, File Explorer collects all the items that have some common property, displaying each group under a heading that can be expanded or collapsed in most views. List view offers a particularly interesting perspective, with each group of results appearing under a column heading. The grouped arrangement is saved as part of the custom view settings for that folder; the next time you open the folder, it will still be grouped.

To group items in a File Explorer window, open the View tab, click Group By, and then click the property you want to use. File Explorer displays a dot before the selected property. You can remove the grouping by returning to Group By and choosing None.

Inside OUT

Zip through File Explorer with keyboard shortcuts

Pressing Ctrl+N in File Explorer opens a new window on the same folder. Ctrl+W closes the current window. (These keyboard shortcuts function the same way in Internet Explorer.) The following additional keyboard shortcuts work in File Explorer:

- **Alt+Up Arrow** Go up one level.
- **Alt+Right Arrow** Go forward.
- **Alt+Left Arrow** Go back.
- **Alt+D** Move the focus to the address bar and select the current path.
- **F4** Move the insertion point to the address bar and display the contents of the drop-down list of previous addresses.
- **Alt+Enter** Show properties of the selected file.
- **Tab** Cycle through the following elements: navigation pane, file list, column headings, address bar, search box.
- **F11** Switch in and out of full-screen mode.
- **Ctrl+Shift+N** Create a new subfolder in the current folder.
- **Ctrl+Shift+E** Expand the navigation pane to the current folder.

Managing file properties and metadata

Every file you view in File Explorer has a handful of properties that describe the file itself: the file name and file name extension (which in turn defines the file type), the file's size, the date and time it was created and last modified, and any file system attributes. These properties are stored in the file system itself and are used for basic browsing and searching.

In addition to these basic file properties, many data file formats can store custom metadata. These additional properties can be added by a device or by software; in some cases, they can be modified by the user. When you take a digital picture, your camera or smartphone might add the device make and model, exposure time, ISO speed, and other details to the file when it's saved. When you rip a CD using Windows Media Player, it retrieves details about the artist and album from the Windows Metadata service and adds them to the MP3 or WMA files. Microsoft Word automatically adds your name to the Author field in a document you create; you can fill in additional properties such as keywords and comments and save them with the file.

Inside OUT

Rate your favorite digital media files

For digital photos, music, and other media files, you'll notice that the Rating field is available in the details pane. Instead of providing a box to enter free-form text or a number, this field shows five stars, all of which are shown in gray initially. You can rate any file on a scale of one to five stars by clicking the appropriate star in the details pane. Adding ratings is a great way to filter large media collections so that they show only the entries you've previously rated highly. Ratings are also useful in playlists and screen savers.

The details pane, which you can display by clicking Details Pane on the View tab, displays a thumbnail of the selected file (if a thumbnail is available), plus quite a few properties. In the following illustration from a subfolder in the Pictures library, you can see the date the photo was taken, the make of the camera, the dimensions of the picture, the exposure settings, and quite a bit more.

001
JPG File

Date taken:	3/12/2015 4:39 PM
Tags:	Add a tag
Rating:	☆ ☆ ☆ ☆ ☆
Dimensions:	3456 x 5184
Size:	7.92 MB
Title:	Add a title
Authors:	Add an author
Comments:	Add comments
Availability:	Available offline
Camera maker:	Canon
Camera model:	Canon EOS REBEL T5i
Subject:	Specify the subject
F-stop:	f/10
Exposure time:	1/250 sec.
ISO speed:	ISO-100
Exposure bias:	0 step
Focal length:	33 mm
Metering mode:	Pattern
Flash mode:	No flash, compulsory
Date created:	4/10/2015 12:30 AM
Date modified:	3/12/2015 4:39 PM

The properties displayed in the details pane might not be everything the operating system knows about the selected file, however. For the complete list, right-click the item and click Properties (or select the item and press Alt+Enter). Then click Details in the properties dialog box.

Figure 12-7 shows a side-by-side comparison of the properties dialog box and the details pane for a music track. Note that the properties dialog box includes such exotica as Period, Mood, Beats-Per-Minute, and Initial Key.

Figure 12-7 The details pane is simple to use and invaluable, but the properties dialog box might offer a more exhaustive set of properties.

In either place, the details pane or the properties dialog box, you can edit many (but not all) of the item's properties. Some properties, such as file size, are calculated by the file system or are otherwise fixed and cannot be directly modified. But you can edit custom metadata if the format of the underlying file allows you to do so.

To enter or change a property's value, simply click and type. If you add two or more words or phrases to a field that accepts multiple entries (such as Tags or Authors), use semicolons to separate them. Press Enter or click Save to add the new or changed properties to the file.

You can edit properties for multiple files at one time. This is especially useful when you're correcting an error in an album or artist name; just select all the songs in the album's folder. When more than one file is selected, you'll note that some properties in the details pane (such as track numbers and song titles) change to indicate that the specified field contains multiple values. A change you make to any field will be written to all of the files in your selection.

Metadata is saved within the file itself, using industry-standard data storage formats. Software developers who need to create a custom file format can make its metadata available to Windows by using an add-in called a property handler, which opens the file format to read and write its properties. Because metadata is saved within the file itself, the properties you edit in File Explorer or a Windows program are fully portable. This means

- You can move files to other computers, even those running other operating systems, without losing the files' tags and other metadata.

- You can edit a file in an application other than the one in which it was created without losing any of the file's properties (assuming the other application properly adheres to the file format's standard for reading and writing metadata).

- A file's properties are visible to anyone who has read access to the file.

You can edit custom properties (including tags) only in files saved using a format that accommodates embedded metadata. For digital image files, Windows supports the JPEG, GIF, and TIFF formats, but you cannot save metadata in bitmap images and graphics files saved in PNG format because these formats were not developed with metadata in mind. Among music file formats, MP3, WMA, and FLAC fully support a wide range of properties designed to make it easy to manage a music collection; files saved in the uncompressed WAV (.wav) format do not support any custom tags. Plain text and Rich Text Format (.rtf) files do not support custom metadata; files saved in Word formats expose a rich set of additional properties, as do all other native file formats from Microsoft Office programs.

In some cases, you'll find that you're unable to view or edit metadata in a file even though the underlying format supports metadata. In that case, the culprit is a missing property handler. In some cases, you can lose data in this situation if you're not careful. This might happen, for example, if you create a file using WordPad and save it in the Office Open XML Document format. If you then open that file using Word, you can add properties such as author name, title, and comments. When you save the file, the file name extension (.docx) remains unchanged. However, if you reopen the document in WordPad, you'll see an information bar at the top of the document warning you that the program does not support all the features of the file format.

If you make some changes and attempt to save the document under the same name or a different name, you'll see the following stern warning:

Believe that warning. If you choose the Save option, any custom properties you saved in an earlier version of the file will be stripped out permanently.

Inside OUT
Remove personal metadata for privacy's sake

Metadata within a file can tell a lot about you. Cameras record data about when a picture was taken and what camera or smartphone was used. Microsoft Office automatically adds author and company information to documents and spreadsheets. With user-created tags, you can add personal and business details that might be useful on a local copy but are unwise to disclose to the wider world.

To scrub a file of unwanted metadata, select one or more files in File Explorer, click the Home tab, click Properties, and then click Remove Properties. This opens the Remove Properties dialog box, an example of which is shown here:

At this point, you have two choices. The default option creates a copy of your file (using the original file name with the word Copy appended to it) and removes all properties that can be changed, based on the file type. The second option, Remove The Following Properties From This File, allows you to select the check boxes next to individual properties and permanently remove those properties from the file when you click OK. (If no check box is visible, that property is not editable.)

Of course, common sense should prevail when it comes to issues of privacy. This option zeroes out metadata, but it does nothing with the contents of the file itself. You'll need to be vigilant to ensure that a digital photo doesn't contain potentially revealing information in the image itself or that sensitive personal or business details aren't saved within a document's contents.

Recovering lost, damaged, and deleted files and folders

It takes only a fraction of a second to wipe out a week's worth of work. You might accidentally delete a folder full of files or, worse, overwrite an entire group of files with changes that can't be undone. Whatever the cause of your misfortune, Windows includes tools that offer hope for recovery. If a file is simply lost, try searching for it (see "Using Windows Search" later in this chapter). For accidental deletions, your first stop should be the Recycle Bin, a Windows institution since 1995. If you don't find what you're looking for in the Recycle Bin, your next recourse is a considerably more powerful recovery tool called File History.

> ➤ For information about File History, see "Using File History to protect files and folders" in Chapter 16, "Backup, restore, and recovery."

Recovering files and folders with the Recycle Bin

The Recycle Bin provides protection against accidental erasure of files. In most cases, when you delete one or more files or folders, the deleted items go to the Recycle Bin, not into the ether. If you change your mind, you can go to the bin and recover the thrown-out items. Eventually, when the bin fills up, Windows begins emptying it, permanently deleting the files that have been there the longest.

The following kinds of deletions do not go to the Recycle Bin:

- Files stored on removable disks

- Files stored on network drives, even when that volume is on a computer that has its own Recycle Bin

- Files deleted from a command prompt

- Files deleted from compressed (zipped) folders

You can bypass the Recycle Bin yourself, permanently deleting an item, by holding down the Shift key while you delete the item. You might want to do this if you need to get rid of some very large files and you're sure you'll never want those files back. Skipping the Recycle Bin in this case will reclaim some disk space.

You can also turn off the Recycle Bin's services permanently, as we explain in the following section.

Changing Recycle Bin settings

To see and adjust the amount of space currently used by the Recycle Bin for each drive that it protects, right-click the Recycle Bin icon on your desktop and then click Properties. In the Recycle Bin Properties dialog box (shown in Figure 12-8), you can select a drive and enter a different value in the Custom Size box. Windows ordinarily allocates up to 10 percent of a disk's space for recycling. (When the bin is full, the oldest items give way to the newest.) If you think that amount of space is excessive, enter a lower value.

Figure 12-8 You can use the Recycle Bin Properties dialog box to alter the amount of space devoted to the bin—or to turn the feature off for selected drives.

NOTE

If you don't see a Recycle Bin icon on your desktop, it's probably hidden. To make it visible, type **desktop icons** in the Windows search box. Next, in the search results, click Show Or Hide Common Icons On The Desktop. Then, in the Desktop Icon Settings dialog box, select the Recycle Bin check box and click OK. If you use the Show All Folders option in File Explorer, you'll have access to the Recycle Bin from the bottom of the navigation pane.

If you'd rather do without the Recycle Bin for a particular drive, select the drive in the Recycle Bin Properties dialog box and then select Don't Move Files To The Recycle Bin. Remove Files Immediately When Deleted. This action is equivalent to setting the maximum capacity to 0.

Whether the Recycle Bin is enabled or disabled, Windows normally displays a confirmation prompt when you delete something. If that prompt annoys you, clear the Display Delete Confirmation Dialog check box.

Restoring files and folders

When you open the Recycle Bin, Windows displays the names of recently deleted items in an ordinary File Explorer window. In Details view (see Figure 12-9), you can see when each item was deleted and which folder it was deleted from. You can use the column headings to sort the folder—for example, to display the items that have been deleted most recently at the top, with earlier deletions below. Alternatively, you can organize the bin by disk and folder by clicking the Original Location heading. If these methods don't help you find what you're hoping to restore, use the search box.

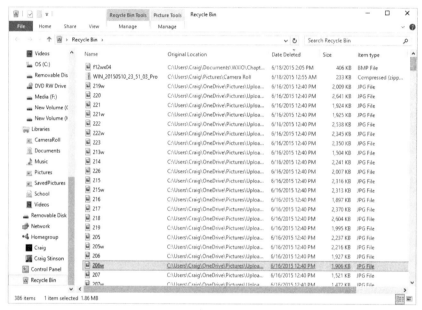

Figure 12-9 Sorting the Recycle Bin in Details view can help you find what you need to restore; so can the search box.

Note that deleted folders are shown only as folders; you don't see the names of items contained within the folders. If you restore a deleted folder, however, Windows re-creates the folder and its contents.

The Restore commands on the Manage tab (Restore All Items and Restore The Selected Items) puts items back in the folders from which they were deleted. If a folder doesn't currently exist, Windows asks your permission to re-create it. Note that if your Recycle Bin contains hundreds or thousands of deleted files dating back weeks or months, Restore All Items can create chaos. That command is most useful if you recently emptied the Recycle Bin and all of its current contents are visible.

If you want, you can restore a file or folder to a different location. Select the item, click the Home tab, click Move To, and then choose a new location. Or, simplest of all, you can drag the item out of the Recycle Bin and put it where you want it.

Purging the Recycle Bin

A deleted file sitting in your Recycle Bin takes up as much space as it did before it was deleted. If you're deleting files to free up space for new programs and documents, transferring them to the Recycle Bin won't help. You need to remove them permanently. The safest way to do this is to move the items to another storage medium—a different hard disk or a removable disk, for example.

If you're sure you'll never need a particular file again, however, you can delete it in the normal way, and then purge it from the Recycle Bin. Display the Recycle Bin, select the item, and then press Delete.

To empty the Recycle Bin entirely, click Empty Recycle Bin on the Manage tab.

Relocating personal data folders

Although the organizational scheme that Windows has adopted for personal data folders—the visible subfolders of %UserProfile%—is suitable for many users, the scheme has one potential defect: it combines data and system files on the same physical volume. For a variety of reasons, some users prefer to separate their documents and other profile data. These reasons might include the following:

- Large collections of data, in particular digital media files, have a way of overwhelming the available space on system volumes, eventually necessitating their removal and relocation to a separate, larger volume.

- Separating data from system files makes restoration easier in the event of system corruption (for example, by malware).

- Separation reduces the size and time devoted to image backups, encouraging their regular use.

- Separation can make it easier, when the time comes, to upgrade the operating system.

On a large system volume, it might not be a problem to keep data files and system files together on the same disk. But if you have installed Windows on a solid state drive—an excellent strategy for performance—the space on your system drive is likely to be at a premium. It's a good idea to keep at least 20 percent of your system drive free. If you find your space shrinking below that threshold, you should probably consider relocating some of your personal data folders.

Inside OUT

Get industrial-strength file management with Robocopy and RichCopy

Dragging files between folders in File Explorer is fine for some tasks, but when it comes to heavy-duty file management you might want a better tool. If you're willing to do a little typing in exchange for power and flexibility that you can't get with File Explorer, get to know Robocopy.

Robocopy (the name is short for Robust File Copy) was introduced with the Windows Server 2003 Resource Kit and is included in Windows 10. Its many strengths include the ability to copy all NTFS file attributes and to mirror the contents of an entire folder hierarchy across local volumes or over a network. If you use the right combination of options, you can recover from interruptions such as network outages by resuming a copy operation from the point of failure after the connection is restored.

The Robocopy syntax takes some getting used to. If you're familiar with the standard Copy and Xcopy commands, you'll have to unlearn their syntax and get used to Robocopy's unconventional ways. The key difference is that Robocopy is designed to work with two directories (folders) at a time, and the file specification is a secondary parameter. For details, type **robocopy /?** at a command prompt.

If you aren't keen on the idea of using a command-line tool, check out RichCopy, a graphical copy utility written by Microsoft engineer Ken Tamaru. You can read about RichCopy and download the bits at *bit.ly/richcopy*.

The easiest, safest way to accomplish this goal is to store personal data in folders on a separate volume, and then include those folders in your libraries. (For information about using libraries, see "Working with libraries" earlier in this chapter.) This approach leaves you with a default set of profile folders, which you can still use when it's convenient to do so, but it keeps the bulk of your personal information in a separate place.

Not everyone loves libraries, however, and there's no requirement to love them. You can still move some or all of your profile subfolders in Windows 10, just as you could in earlier versions. To relocate a user profile folder by editing its properties, follow these steps:

1. In the navigation pane, click your account name (you might need to display all folders first) to open the root folder of your profile.

2. Right-click a folder that you want to relocate, and choose Properties. (Or select the folder, and then click Properties on the Home tab.)

3. On the Location tab of the properties dialog box, enter the address that you want to relocate the folder to. For example, to move the Downloads folder from C:\Users\Craig\ Downloads to F:\Users\Craig\Downloads, you could simply replace the C with an F at the beginning of the path.

4. Click OK. Windows asks permission to create the target folder if it doesn't already exist. Click Yes. A Move Folder dialog box similar to this one appears:

5. Unless you have some good reason not to move the existing files from the original location to the new one, click Yes.

It's really not a good idea *not* to click Yes in this dialog box. First, it's difficult to imagine why you would want some of your personal documents in a given category on one disk and the rest on another. (If you want to keep your existing files separate from those you save in the future, move the old files to a subfolder in the new location instead of leaving them in the old location.) Second, because %UserProfile% is a system-generated folder, not an ordinary data folder that corresponds to a fixed disk location, leaving some files behind will give you two identically named subfolders in %UserProfile%.

Using Save locations

Save locations, a new feature in Windows 10, provides a quick and easy way to see which disks Windows will use to save new documents in various categories. At Settings, System, Storage, you will see a display similar to the following:

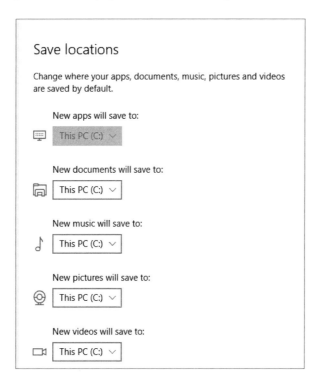

You can open the drop-down menu for a category to change the save location for that category.

Using Windows Search

Perhaps more than any other feature in Windows, the search tools have the potential to change the way you work. If your filing philosophy involves the digital equivalent of throwing everything into a giant shoebox, you'll be startled at how easy it is to find what you're looking for. Even if you consider yourself an extremely well-organized Windows user, we predict that you'll find ways to integrate the new search tools into your everyday routine.

Searching everywhere

If you're accustomed to the way that search worked in Windows 7 or Windows 8.1, the difference you're likely to notice first is that Windows 10 takes a "search everywhere" approach. Internet searching is tightly integrated with file searching, and both are integrated with your personal assistant, Cortana.

When you begin typing into the search box on your taskbar (it's located directly to the right of the Start menu button), Cortana (assuming you have enabled her) pops up and checks to see if you're making a request that she can handle—such as "remind me to call Russell at 8 this evening." If you enter what appears to be a search term, Cortana steps aside, and Windows Search presents a categorized list of possible hits, comparable to the one shown in Figure 12-10.

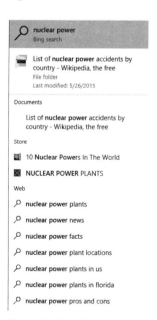

Figure 12-10 Windows Search searches everywhere, both locally and on the web.

In this example, our search term was "nuclear power," and Windows has returned a number of items. The Bing search item at the top of the list represents the search tool's judgment about what we're most likely looking for—in this case, a general web search through our default web search service. Immediately below that, however, is a folder and a document, both found in our local file resources. As it happens, both relate to the same item, a file and supporting documents downloaded from Wikipedia. Below that are a couple of items of possible interest in the Windows Store. And finally, the search tool gives us a set of more specific web searches.

At the bottom of the search results pane, not shown in Figure 12-10, are two handy buttons, labeled My Stuff and Web:

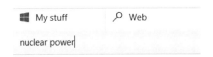

These buttons let you restrict your search to local resources or the Internet. If you click My Stuff, the search tool gives you an expanded results pane, again categorized. (In this example, the results were organized into Documents, OneDrive, Folders, and Photos.)

The results pane is sorted by default according to relevance—the system's judgment about what you're most likely to want. You can use a drop-down list to switch from relevance to most recent. A second drop-down list lets you filter the results pane according to type—Documents, Folders, Apps, Settings, Photos, Videos, Music.

Finally, in case the My Stuff hits don't include what you're looking for, there's a handy Search The Web button that redirects your inquiry to the Internet.

This "search everywhere" approach is ideal when you're not exactly sure whether you want a local item or something from the web. When you know you want a local file, as you'll see momentarily, it's typically quicker to search within File Explorer.

Configuring search and indexing options

At its heart, Windows Search relies on a speedy, powerful, and well-behaved indexing service that does a fine job of keeping track of files and folders by name, by properties, and (in supported formats) by contents. All of those details are kept in the search index, a database that keeps track of indexed file names, properties, and the contents of files. As a rule, when you do most common types of searches, Windows checks the index first and returns whatever results it finds there.

NOTE

The search index is stored by default in %ProgramData%\Microsoft\Search\Data. Default permissions for this folder are set to allow access only to the System account and to members of the Administrators group. This folder contains no user-editable files, and we recommend that you leave its contents undisturbed.

Inside OUT

When do searches skip the index?

Although we focus mostly on indexed searches in this section, Windows 10 actually includes two search engines. The second engine is informally known as *grep* search (the name comes from an old UNIX command derived from the full name *global | regular expression | print*). Windows Search uses the index whenever you use the search box on the taskbar, in libraries, and in locations that are part of a homegroup. In those circumstances, search looks only in the index and ignores any subfolders that are excluded from the index.

Windows uses the grep search engine if you begin your search from the This PC folder, from the root of any local drive (including the system drive), or from a local file folder. Grep searches include the contents of all subfolders within the search scope regardless of whether they're included in the search index. For a more detailed examination of nonindexed searches, see "Advanced search tools and techniques" later in this chapter.

To build the index that makes its magic possible, Windows Search uses several separate processes. The index is constructed dynamically by the Windows Search service, SearchIndexer.exe. The indexer crawls through all locations that are prescribed to be indexed, converting the content of documents (in supported formats) into plain text and then storing the text and metadata for quick retrieval.

The Windows Search service begins running shortly after you start a new Windows session. From that point on, it runs in the background at all times, creating the initial index and updating it as new files are added and existing ones are changed or deleted. Protocol handlers do the work of cracking open different data stores to add items to the index. Property handlers allow Windows Search to extract the values of properties from items and store them properly in the index. Filters extract the contents of supported file types so that you can do full-text searches for those items.

Which files and folders are in the index?

Indexing every 0 and 1 on your hard disk would be an exhausting task—and ultimately point-less. When you search for a snippet of text, you're almost always looking for something you wrote, copied, or saved, and you don't want the results to include random program files that happen to have the same snippet embedded in the midst of a blob of code. So the default set-tings for the indexer make some reasonable inclusions and exclusions.

Certain locations are specifically included. These include your user profile (but not the AppData folder), the contents of the Start menu, and your browser history. Offline files stored in the client-side cache (CSC) are automatically included in your local index. You can explicitly add other folders to the index, but Windows 10 eliminates the need to do that. Instead, just add the folder to a library; when you do so, Windows automatically adds that folder to the list of indexed locations and begins indexing its contents without requiring any additional steps on your part.

CAUTION

Data from Microsoft Outlook 2010 and subsequent versions is not stored in the index. The ability to find messages using Windows Search was removed because these recent versions of Outlook provide their own search tools. For more information, see *support.microsoft.com/en-us/kb/2385524*.

To see which folders are currently being indexed, open the Indexing Options dialog box. You can get there in various ways, including by entering **Indexing Options** in the search box on the taskbar. As Figure 12-11 shows, the Indexing Options dialog box initially shows the top level of folders that are included in the index.

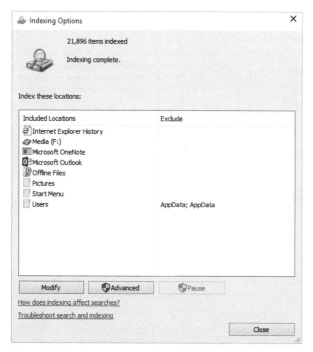

Figure 12-11 The Indexing Options dialog box shows the top level of locations that are included in the index. Subfolders (for example, all the profile subfolders of Users) are not shown here.

To get more information about what's being indexed, click Modify. Figure 12-12 shows the elaborate dialog box that results.

CAUTION

We strongly recommend that you not try to manage locations manually using the Indexed Locations dialog box. If you add a folder to a library and then remove it from the list of indexed locations, the folder will remain in the navigation pane under the associated library, but none of its contents will be visible in the library itself.

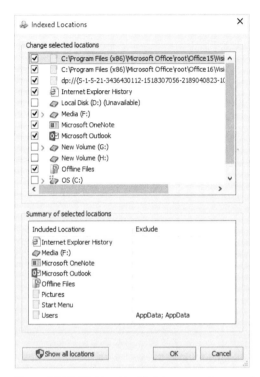

Figure 12-12 Clicking Modify lets you see in more detail which locations are being indexed. Adding a folder to a library automatically selects the corresponding check box here.

In its default view, the Indexed Locations list shows only locations that are accessible to your user account. To see (and manage) locations from other user profiles, click Show All Locations. As the User Account Control (UAC) shield icon makes clear, you'll need to be signed in as an administrator (or provide an administrator's credentials) to continue.

Within that list of indexed locations, the Windows Search service records the file name and properties (size, date modified, and so on) of any file or folder. Files marked as System and Hidden are indexed but are displayed in search results only when you change File Explorer settings to show those file types. Metadata for common music, image, and video file formats is included in the index by default. The indexer also includes the contents of a file and its custom properties if the file format has an associated property handler and filter. Some of the more common file formats supported by filters included with Windows 10 are shown in Table 12-2.

Table 12-2 Some file formats that support content indexing

File format	Extension
HTML	.ascx, .asp, .aspx, .css, .hhc, .hta, .htm, .html, .htt, .htw, .htx, .odc, .shtml, .shtml, .sor, .srf, .stm, .wdp, .vcproj
MIME	.mht, .mhtml
Office	.doc, .dot, .pot, .pps, .ppt, .xlb, .xlc, .xls, .xlt
Plain text	.a, .ans, .asc, .asm, .asx, .bas, .bat, .bcp, .c, .cc, .cls, .cmd, .cpp, .cs, .csa, .csv, .cxx, .dbs, .def, .dic, .dos, .dsp, .dsw, .ext, .faq, .fky, .h, .hpp, .hxx, .i, .ibq, .ics, .idl, .idq, .inc, .inf, .ini, .inl, .inx, .jav, .java, .js, .kci, .lgn, .lst, .m3u, .mak, .mk, .odh, .odl, .pl, .prc, .rc, .rc2, .rct, .reg, .rgs, .rul, .s, .scc, .sol, .sql, .tab, .tdl, .tlh, .tli, .trg, .txt, .udf, .usr, .vbs, .viw, .vspcc, .vsscc, .vssscc, .wri, .wtx
XML (xmlfilt.dll)	.csproj, .user, .vbproj, .vcproj, .xml, .xsd, .xsl, .xslt
Favorites	.url
Journal file	.jnt
Rich Text Format	.rtf
WordPad	.docx, .odt
XML Paper Specification	.dwfx, .easmx, .edrwx, .eprtx, .jtx, .xmlps

Inside OUT

Add text from faxes to the search index

Picture file types are not included in the list of formats in Table 12-2 because images by definition consist of colored pixels rather than words, and they thus contain no content to index. But one image format is a noteworthy exception to that rule. If you use a device or service to receive pages sent from a remote fax machine, the received faxes are saved using Tagged Image File Format (TIFF), but the original document usually consists of at least some text. Windows includes code that can perform optical character recognition on received faxes saved as TIFF files and include the recognized text in the search index. To enable this feature, open Control Panel and click Turn Windows Features On Or Off (under the Programs And Features heading). In the Windows Features dialog box, select Windows TIFF IFilter and then click OK.

To see which file formats support indexing, open the Indexing Options dialog box and click the Advanced button (you'll need to supply an administrator's credentials to do so, although elevation is silent if your sign-in account is a member of the Administrators group). On the File Types tab of the Advanced Options dialog box (see Figure 12-13), you will find a long list of file name extensions. By default, the check box next to every item in this list is selected, meaning that all of the listed file types are included in the index. As we describe later, not all of them support content indexing, however.

Figure 12-13 Installing Microsoft Office adds a slew of new indexing filters, as shown on the right.

The list of formats on the File Types tab on your computer might include more file types if you've installed Windows programs that include custom property handlers and filters, such as those installed with recent versions of Microsoft Office. Figure 12-13, for example, shows a side-by-side view of common Word document formats before and after installing Microsoft Office 365. The original list includes a generic Microsoft Office filter for .doc and .dot files as well as a WordPad filter for .docx files. After installing Office, the Office Open XML Format Word Filter takes over content indexing and also adds support for additional document and template formats. Any file with one of these extensions that is stored in an indexed location has its full contents added to the index, courtesy of the new filters.

Each of the file types in this list can be indexed in one of two manners by using the option buttons below the list—Index Properties Only or Index Properties And File Contents. The latter option is selected by default for any file type that has a registered filter, and the name of the associated filter is listed in the Filter Description column. If you don't need to search content in a file type that has a filter and would normally be indexed, you can save some processing overhead by selecting the file type and choosing Index Properties Only. If you need content indexing where none is currently provided, you can try switching a file from Index Properties

Only to Index Properties And File Contents. In that case, the indexer will use the Plain Text filter—which might or might not yield satisfactory results.

Windows Search does not index the content of files that are saved without a file name extension, nor does it index contents of files that are protected by Information Rights Management (IRM) or digital rights management (DRM).

A handful of locations are specifically excluded from indexing. Even if you manually specify that you want your system drive (normally C) to be included in the index, the following files and folders will be excluded:

- The entire contents of the \Windows folder and all its subfolders (the Windows.old folder that is created by an upgrade installation of Windows 10 is also excluded)

- \$Recycle.Bin (the hidden folder that contains deleted files for all user accounts)

- \Users\Default and all of its subfolders (this is the user profile template used to create a profile for a new user)

- The entire contents of the \Program Files and \Program Files (x86) folders and all of their subfolders

- The \ProgramData folder (except the subfolder that contains shortcuts for the shared Start menu)

Monitoring the index, and tuning indexer performance

The status message at the top of the Indexing Options dialog box offers real-time updates on what the indexer is doing at the moment. "Indexing complete" means there are no pending tasks. The status message lists the number of items (files, folders, and so on) that are currently in the index.

"Indexing paused" means the service has temporarily stopped all indexing tasks; you'll see this message if you check the indexer status shortly after you start the computer because the default setting for the Windows Search service is Automatic (Delayed Start).

If indexing tasks are currently under way, the status message will display an increase or decrease in the number of items indexed as new, changed, and deleted files are processed. The indexer is designed to throttle itself whenever it detects that the system is working on other, presumably more important tasks. As a result, you'll most likely be told that "Indexing speed is reduced due to user activity" when you first check.

That message indicates that the indexing service has backed off in response to your activity and is operating at a fraction of its normal speed. If the number of files to be indexed is big enough (if you copied a folder full of several thousand documents, for instance), you'll see the indexing speed pick up dramatically after you keep your hands off the keyboard and mouse for a minute or so.

The exact speed of indexing depends on a variety of factors, starting with the speed of your CPU and storage subsystem and including as well the number, size, and complexity of documents and whether their full contents are being indexed. Unfortunately, the status message in the Indexing Options dialog box doesn't include a progress bar and doesn't indicate how many files are yet to be indexed, so there's no easy way to tell whether the current task is barely under way or nearly complete. If you haven't recently added any new folders to the index but have simply been changing a few files in the course of normal work, the index should stay close to complete (assuming you've ever had a complete index).

Some websites for performance-obsessed Windows users complain about the performance hit that Windows Search causes; some even recommend disabling the Windows Search service to improve overall system performance. We recommend that you leave it running. In our experience, the Windows Search service uses only a small percentage of available CPU resources even at its busiest. The indexing service is specifically designed to back off when you use your computer for other activities, switching to low-priority input/output (I/O) and allowing foreground I/O tasks, such as opening the Start menu, to execute first. When Windows 10 first builds its index, or if you copy a large number of files to the system at once, indexing can take a long time and cause some spikes in CPU and disk activity, but you shouldn't notice any impact on performance.

File Explorer accesses the index directly, so even if the indexer is busy processing new and changed files it shouldn't affect the speed of a search operation. In normal operation, retrieving search results from even a very large index should take no more than a few seconds.

Other index maintenance tasks

The Indexing Options dialog box is also your gateway to buttons and check boxes that let you rebuild a corrupted index, change the location where the index stores its data, add folders to the index, change how the index deals with particular file types, and so on. To perform any of these maintenance tasks, display the Index Settings tab of the Advanced Options dialog box, shown in Figure 12-14.

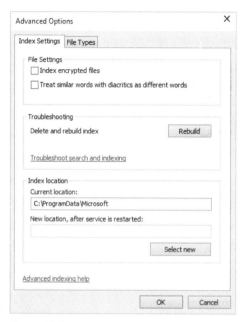

Figure 12-14 You can use this dialog box to rebuild an index that has stopped functioning properly.

It's not supposed to happen, but if your index stops working properly (or if you just performed major file maintenance and you want to give the index a fresh start), click Rebuild in the Troubleshooting area. Then give your system time to re-create the index. Be aware that rebuilding the index might take a considerable amount of time.

For security reasons, the contents of encrypted files are not included in the index by default. (Properties such as the name, date, and size of such files are indexed.) If you use Encrypting File System and you need those files indexed, select Index Encrypted Files in the File Settings area. This limitation does not apply to drives protected with BitLocker Drive Encryption.

By default, the index files live in subfolders of %ProgramData%\Microsoft\Search. If you install a faster hard disk on your computer, you might be able to improve search performance by moving the index files to the new disk. (Note that the index must reside on a fixed disk.) Simply type or paste the full path of the folder you want to use in the Current Location box. (The path must not be greater than 128 characters in length.) Be prepared to restart your computer and wait while the index is rebuilt.

Although this option sounds like an appealing performance tweak, we recommend you think twice before trying it. The actual difference in performance is likely to be minor, and you can expect to encounter problems reestablishing the index if you have to restore your system drive from a backup and you don't also restore the volume containing the index.

Basic search techniques

You can search wherever you see a search box. Specifically, that means the following:

- From the search box on the taskbar

- From the search box in the upper right corner of any File Explorer window

- From Settings or Control Panel

- From a common file dialog box

When you type in the search box on the taskbar, in a library, or in a homegroup location, the list of results is drawn from the search index. The list includes files whose names or properties contain the specified text; for files in formats that include appropriate property handlers and filters, the results will include items whose contents contain the text you entered. The scope of the search depends on your starting point. From the taskbar search box, you'll search the entire index, but you can restrict the scope to a specific location by selecting that location in File Explorer and using its search box.

The following rules govern how searches work:

- Whatever text you type must appear at the beginning of a word, not in the middle. Thus, entering **des** returns items containing the words *des*ire, *des*tination, and *des*troy but not un*des*irable or sad*des*t. (You can override this behavior by using wildcard characters, as we explain in "Advanced search tools and techniques" later in this chapter.)

- Search terms are not case-sensitive. Thus, entering **Bott** returns items with Ed Bott as a tag or property, but the results also include files containing the words *bott*om and *bott*le.

- By default, searches ignore accents, umlauts, and other diacritical marks. If you routinely need to be able to distinguish, say, Händel from Handel, open the Indexing Options dialog box, click Advanced (you'll need administrative credentials), and then select Treat Similar Words With Diacritics As Different Words.

- To search for an exact phrase, enclose the phrase within quotation marks. Otherwise, you search for each word individually.

Searching from the taskbar

The search box on the taskbar has a multiple personality. Its primary role is to help you find shortcuts to applications on the All Apps menu and tasks in Settings or Control Panel. When you type a search term that matches an item in any of those locations, the results appear almost instantaneously. But this box also offers access to everything else in the search index:

websites in your history folder; saved favorites; any shared network folders that are included in any of your libraries; and, of course, files and folders in your file system.

The search box (here and elsewhere) is a "word wheel"—which means that the search begins as soon as you start typing, and each new character you type refines the results. If you type the letters *m* and *e* into the search box on the taskbar, you'll see results for Windows Media Player as well as the Windows Memory Diagnostic. You'll also see various Settings items (Media Streaming Options, Messaging Privacy Settings, and so on), folders and documents that begin with those two characters, and a smattering of websites.

Because the word wheel action is snappy and the taskbar search is optimized to find items on the Start menu, typing a few characters here can be a great alternative to hunting up a program shortcut from the All Apps section of the Start menu. Typing **media** into the search box, for example, produces a list like this:

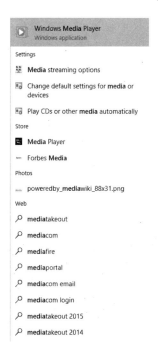

The scope of a search from the taskbar covers the entire index, including document files, folders, Internet shortcuts, objects on a Microsoft OneNote page, and more. Results, as we noted earlier, are ranked by relevance and categorized.

The results pane lists only a few hits for each of the categories. The category headings, how-ever, are links, and clicking a link brings up a more complete list. Here, for example, is what you might see if you click the Settings link in the previous example:

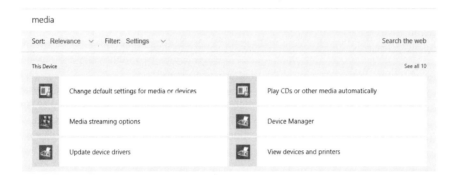

Even this is not complete, however. Clicking the See All link at the right side of this display adds four more items to the result set.

Inside OUT
You can search for programs that aren't on the Start menu

Searching from the taskbar's search box can be a good way to run a program that isn't on the Start menu—such as Registry Editor or an .msc console. (To run an .msc console, type the full name, including the .msc extension.) The taskbar's search looks for exe-cutables in system folders that are not ordinarily indexed. Because the search engine's word-wheel feature works only with indexed locations, however, you need to type the full name before it appears in the search results. You also need to identify the program by the full name of its executable file, rather than its friendly title. Typing **Registry Editor** in the search box gets you nothing (unless you happen to have created a short-cut and saved it under that name). Typing **regedit** summons the program.

Searching from File Explorer

When you know that what you're looking for is stored in a library folder somewhere, it's more efficient to search for it from File Explorer. Select the likely parent folder in the navigation pane (or select Libraries if you're not sure which library folder it's in), then begin typing in the File Explorer search box.

Search results for indexed folders appear so quickly that you may have a substantial number of hits before you type the second or third character in the search string. At this point, Windows may simplify your task by recalling earlier search strings and presenting you with a list of possible completions:

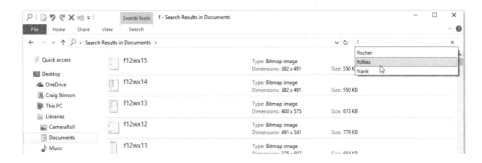

Inside OUT

See all files in a folder and its subfolders

If you have opened File Explorer to a particular folder and you want to avoid the tedium of opening subfolders to view their contents, try using the wildcard character that's been around as long as Microsoft has been making operating systems. Entering an asterisk (*) in the search box immediately returns all files in the current folder and all its subfolders. Assuming the list is of manageable size, you can then group, filter, sort, or otherwise rearrange the items within the folder to find exactly what you're looking for.

Once you have a set of search hits, a contextual Search tab appears on the ribbon, offering you a wealth of options to refine and re-search:

The options in the Refine group let you narrow the search by date range, size range, and kind. The Kind list includes such things as Document, Picture, Music, Folder—and many more. The Other Properties list is context-specific. In a music folder, for example, this list will offer Album,

Artists, Genre, Length, Folder Path, Year, Rating, and Title; in a Pictures folder, you'll see Date Taken, Tags, Type, Name, Folder Path, and Rating.

If you find you've initiated your search from the wrong location, try Search Again In, in the Location group of the Search tab. Or just switch to a different node in the navigation pane and start again.

Inside OUT

Search from a common dialog box

Like the search box in File Explorer, the search box in a common Open or Save As dialog box takes as its default scope the current folder and its subfolders. Searching from a dialog box might not sound all that nifty at first. After all, if you're trying to open a file and you don't know exactly where it is, you can always hunt for it from a File Explorer folder and then double-click it when the Windows Search engine ferrets it out. But searching from a dialog box can be quite useful if you're already in the dialog box and find yourself confronted by too many files.

Advanced search tools and techniques

For search needs that go beyond the options presented on the Search tab, Windows offers the Advanced Query Syntax (AQS). AQS is the official name for the set of rules that Windows Search follows when interpreting what you type in the search box. (You'll find detailed documentation of AQS at *w7io.com/0903*.)

NOTE

You can use any of these search formulations in the File Explorer search box but not in taskbar searches.

In addition to keywords, AQS supports the following types of search parameters, which can be combined using search operators:

- **Kinds of items.** Folders, documents, pictures, music, and so on
- **Data stores.** Specific databases and locations containing indexed items
- **File properties.** Size, date, tags, and so on

The most basic query typically begins with a keyword (or a portion of a word) typed in the search box. Assuming that you begin typing in a location that supports indexed searches (the taskbar search box or your Documents library, for example), the list of search results will include any item in that location containing any indexed word (in its name or properties or content) that begins with the letters you type. You can then narrow the search by using additional parameters. In every case, these consist of a word that AQS recognizes as a property or other index operator, followed by a colon and the value for that operator.

The value that immediately follows the colon can take several forms. If you want a loose (partial) match, just type a word or the beginning of a word. Thus, **type:Word** will turn up files of the type Microsoft Word Document, Microsoft Word 97 – 2003 Document, Microsoft Word 97 – 2003 Template, Microsoft Word Macro-Enabled Document, and so on. To specify a strict (exact) match, use an equal sign and, if necessary, quotation marks, as in this example: **type:="Microsoft Word Document"**.

You can also use Boolean operators (AND, OR, and NOT) and parentheses to combine criteria. If you have fond memories of MS-DOS, you'll welcome using * and ? as wildcards, and you can dramatically change the behavior of a search by means of the innocuous-looking tilde (~) character (which forces Windows to perform a strict character search in indexed locations; see the discussion later in this section).

> ➤ Of course, all of these techniques become much more useful when you're able to reuse your carefully crafted search criteria, as we explain in "Saving searches and clearing search history" at the end of this chapter.

Searching by item type or kind

To search for files with a particular file name extension, you can simply enter the extension in the search box, like this:

```
*.ext
```

(Note that this method of searching does not work for .exe or .msc files.) The results will include files that incorporate the extension in their contents as well as in their file names—which might or might not be what you want. You will get a more focused search by using the ext: operator, including an asterisk wildcard and a period like this:

```
ext:*.txt
```

NOTE

As with many properties, you have more than one way to specify an exact file name extension. In addition to ext:, you can use fileext:, extension:, or fileextension:.

File name extensions are useful for some searches, but you'll get even better results using two different search properties: Type and Kind. The Type property limits your search based on the value found in the Type field for a given object. Thus, to look for files saved in any Microsoft Excel format, type this term in the search box:

```
type:excel
```

To find any music file saved in MP3 format, type this text in the search box:

```
type:mp3
```

To constrain your search to groups of related file types, use the Kind property. Table 12-3 lists many (but not all) of the options available with this search term.

Table 12-3 Limiting items in search results by kind

Kind syntax	Returns as search results
kind:=calendar kind:=appointment kind:=meeting	Appointments and meetings stored in iCalendar and vCalendar files
kind:=communication	Email messages and attachments that you have saved as files
kind:=contact kind:=person	vCard files, Windows Contact files
kind:=doc kind:=document	Text files, Microsoft Office documents, Adobe Acrobat documents, HTML and XML files, and other document formats
kind:=folder	File folders, search folders, compressed (Zip) files, and cabinet files
kind:=link	Shortcuts to programs and files, Internet shortcuts
kind:=music kind:=song	Groove Music or Windows Media Player playlists and audio files in supported formats, including MP3, WMA, FLAC, and WAV
kind:=pic kind:=picture	Picture files in any indexed format, including JPEG, GIF, bitmap, PNG, as well as icons and shortcuts to image files
kind:=program	Windows and MS-DOS applications, batch and VBScript files, saved registration entries, Windows Installer packages, and program shortcuts
kind:=video	Movie files and clips in any indexed format

Changing the scope of a search

You can specify a folder or library location by using folder:, under:, in:, or path:. Thus, **folder:documents** restricts the scope of the search to your Documents library, and **in:videos mackie** finds all files in the Videos library that contain *Mackie* in the file name or any property.

Searching for item properties

You can search on the basis of any property recognized by the file system. (The list of available properties for files is identical to the ones we discuss in "Arranging data in File Explorer" earlier in this chapter.) To see the whole list of available properties, right-click any column heading in File Explorer and then click More. The Choose Details dialog box that appears enumerates the available properties.

When you enter text in the search box, Windows searches file names, all properties, and indexed content, returning items where it finds a match with that value. That often generates more search results than you want. To find all documents of which Jean is the author, omitting documents that include the word Jean in their file names or content, you would type **author:jean** in the search box. (To eliminate documents authored by Jeanne, Jeannette, or Jeanelle, add an equal sign and enclose jean in quotation marks: **author:="jean"**.)

When searching on the basis of dates, you can use long or short forms, as you please. For example, the search values

modified:6/15/15

and

modified:06/15/2015

are equivalent.

To search for dates before or after a particular date, use the less-than (<) and greater-than (>) operators. For example:

modified:>11/16/12

would search for dates later than November 16, 2012. Use the same two operators to specify file sizes below and above some value.

Use two periods to search for items within a range of dates. To find files modified in September or October 2014, type this search term in the Start menu search box:

modified:9/1/2014 .. 10/31/2014

You can also use ranges to search by file size. The search filters suggest some common ranges and even group them into neat little buckets like the ones shown here, so you can type **size:** and then click Medium to find files in the range 100 KB to 1 MB.

Again, don't be fooled into thinking that this list represents the full selection of available sizes. You can specify an exact size range, using operators such as >, >=, <, and <=, or you can use the ".." operator. For example, **size:0 MB..1 MB** is the same as **size:<=1 MB**. You can specify values using bytes, KB, MB, or GB.

Inside OUT

Make your searches flexible

You don't need to enter a precise date as part of a search term. Instead, Windows Search recognizes "fuzzy" date qualifiers like *today, yesterday, this week,* and *last month.* This technique lets you create saved searches that you can use to quickly open a window showing only the files you've worked on this week or last week. A search that uses dates picked from the calendar wouldn't be nearly as useful next month for identifying current projects, but one built using these relative dates will continue to be useful indefinitely.

Using multiple criteria for complex searches

You can use the Boolean operators AND, OR, and NOT to combine or negate criteria in the search box. These operators need to be spelled in capital letters (or they will be treated as ordinary text). In place of the AND operator, you can use a plus sign (+), and in place of the NOT operator, you can use a minus sign (–). You can also use parentheses to group criteria; items in parentheses separated by a space use an implicit AND operator. Table 12-4 provides some examples of combined criteria.

Table 12-4 Some examples of complex search values

This search value	Returns
Siechert AND Bott	Items in which at least one indexed element (property, file name, or an entire word within its contents) begins with or equals Siechert and another element in the same item begins with or equals Bott
title:("report" NOT draft)	Items in which the Title property contains the word report and does not contain a word that begins with draft
tag:tax AND author:Doug	Items authored by Doug that include Tax in the Tags field
tag:tax AND author:(Doug OR Craig) AND modified:<1/1/14	Items authored by Doug or Craig, last modified before January 1, 2014, with Tax in the Tags field

NOTE

When you use multiple criteria based on different properties, an AND conjunction is assumed unless you specify otherwise. The search value **tag:Ed Author:Carl** is equivalent to the search value **tag:Ed AND Author:Carl**.

Using wildcards and character-mode searches

File-search wildcards can be traced back to the dawn of Microsoft operating systems, well before the Windows era. In Windows 10, two of these venerable operators are alive and well:

- *   The asterisk (also known as a star) operator can be placed anywhere in the search string and will match zero, one, or any other number of characters. In indexed searches, which treat your keyword as a prefix, this operator is always implied at the end; thus, a search for **voice** will turn up *voice, voices,* and *voice-over.* Add an asterisk at the beginning of the search term (***voice**), and your search will also turn up any item containing *invoice* or *invoices.* You can put an asterisk in the middle of a search term as well, which is useful for searching through folders full of data files that use a standard naming convention. If your invoices all start with INV, followed by an invoice number, followed by the date (INV-0038-20140227, for example), you can produce a quick list of all 2014 invoices by searching for **INV*2014***.

- ?   The question mark is a more focused wildcard. In index searches, it matches exactly one character in the exact position where it's placed. Using the naming scheme defined in the previous item, you could use the search term **filename:INV-????-2014*** to locate any file in the current location that has a 2014 date stamp and an invoice number (between hyphens) that is exactly four characters long.

To force Windows Search to use strict character matches in an indexed location, type a tilde (~) as the first character in the search box, followed immediately by your term. If you open your Documents library and type **~??v** in the search box, you'll find any document whose file name contains any word that has a *v* in the third position, such as *saved, level,* and, of course, *invoice.* This technique does not match on file contents.

Searching nonindexed locations

In both the previous examples, we described the behavior of searches in indexed locations, such as a library or a folder within a library. In other locations, the grep search engine kicks in. By default, anything you enter in one of these locations is treated as a character search that can match all or any part of a word. Thus, if you open a data folder that is not in a library and enter the search term **voice**, you'll get back *voices* and *voice-over* and *invoice.* The behavior of wildcards varies slightly as well. In a grep search, **??voice** matches *invoice* but not *voice.* In an indexed search, the wildcards at the beginning of the term are ignored in favor of loose matches. (Extra question marks at the end of a search term are ignored completely.)

When Windows does a grep search of the folder's contents, a green progress bar traversing your address bar warns you that the search is likely to be slow. While the search is still under way, you can click the Search tab and refine the search.

By default, when searching nonindexed locations, Windows looks at file names and basic properties (date modified and size) only. You can change this behavior so that Windows searches the contents of files that include a property handler and filter. To do this, click the Search tab, click Advanced Options, and then click File Contents. Be aware that this can add significantly to your search times.

Inside OUT

Search shared remote folders

When you connect to a shared folder on a networked computer, the search engine can detect whether Windows Search is running and whether the location you've accessed is already part of the remote index. If it is, great! Your query gets handed off to the remote search engine, which runs it on the other machine and returns its results to your computer. Note that for an indexed search of a shared folder, that folder must be included in the list of indexed locations on the remote computer, and the remote computer must be running version 4.0 or later of Windows Search. All versions of Windows released since 2008 are supported.

Saving searches and clearing search history

After you have completed a search and displayed its results in File Explorer, you can save the search parameters for later reuse. Click Save Search on the Search tab. The saved search is stored, by default, in %UserProfile%\Searches. You can reexecute the search at any time, against the current state of the index, by clicking it in the navigation pane or Searches folder.

When you save a search, you are saving its specification (technically, a persistedQuery), not its current results. If you're interested in the XML data that defines the search, right-click the saved search in your Searches folder, choose Open With, and choose Notepad or WordPad.

Recent searches are also included in a history list. To see what you have searched for, click in the search box in File Explorer, click the Search tab, and then click Recent Searches. If the list of recent searches gets unwieldy or you want to cover your tracks, click Clear Search History at the bottom of this list.

TROUBLESHOOTING

Your search returns unexpected results

If Windows Search does not perform as expected, try typing **fix search** in the taskbar search box. Then click Find And Fix Problems With Windows Search. The troubleshooter that appears automatically finds and fixes any problems that it can detect. If it finds none, it leads you through a series of steps to identify and resolve your problem.

PART 3

System maintenance and troubleshooting

Hardware

It's probably only a slight exaggeration to say that no two computers are alike. Motherboards, storage devices and controllers, video and network adapters, and peripherals of all shapes and sizes combine to create a nearly infinite number of possible computer configurations.

The good news for anyone using Windows 10 is that most of these devices should just work. For most common hardware upgrades, Windows detects the device automatically and installs a driver so that you can use the device and its full array of features. This chapter covers those installations as well as devices that need to be added manually, those that have optional configuration steps, and of course troubleshooting devices.

In this chapter, we cover the nerve center of hardware, Device Manager, with an explanation of how drivers work. We also explain how to set up specific device configurations, including multiple monitors, Bluetooth adapters, and printers.

Adding, configuring, and removing hardware devices

Since its introduction in Windows 95, Plug and Play technology has evolved tremendously. Early incarnations of this technology were notoriously unreliable, leading some users to dismiss the feature as "plug and pray." As this now-mature technology enters its third decade, however, hardware and software standards have converged to make most device configuration tasks completely automatic.

Any computer that was certified as compatible with Windows 7 or later supports the Plug and Play device standard, which handles virtually all the work of configuring computer hardware and attached devices. A Plug and Play device identifies itself to Windows by using unique identifiers in a well-organized hierarchy, listing its required resources (including drivers), and allowing software to configure it.

Plug and Play devices can interact with the operating system, with both sides of the conversation responding to device notification and power management events. A Plug and Play driver can load automatically when Windows detects that a device has been plugged in, and it can suspend and resume operation properly along with the system.

NOTE

Although it's still possible to find older devices that require non–Plug and Play inputs, such as scanners, plotters, and similar peripherals that connect to serial and parallel ports, these legacy devices are becoming increasingly rare. If you own this type of device, we recommend retiring it if possible and replacing it with a supported modern alternative. If you have no choice but to keep it around, look for a community of fellow owners of that device; they're the most likely to be able to help you with configuration issues.

Installing a new Plug and Play device

When you install a Plug and Play device for the first time, Windows reads the Plug and Play identification tag in the hardware's BIOS or firmware. It then compares that ID tag with a master list of corresponding tags drawn from all the Setup Information files in the %SystemRoot%\Inf folder. If it finds a signed driver with a matching tag, it installs the correct driver file (or files) and makes other necessary system modifications with no intervention required from you. If everything goes as expected, the only subtle indication you might see is a progress dialog box (typically minimized) that displays a green bar over its taskbar icon and then vanishes when its work is complete.

NOTE

Any user can plug in a new device and begin using it if a driver for that device is included with Windows 10 or is available via Windows Update. Installing a new driver that is downloaded from a third-party site and is digitally signed by a third party rather than by Microsoft requires an administrator's credentials.

If Windows detects a Plug and Play device (after you've plugged it into a USB port, for instance) but cannot locate a digitally signed driver that matches the device, it doesn't provide any warning notification. Instead, a stub for the device is installed as it awaits the arrival of a proper driver. These partially installed devices appear in Device Manager, under the Other Devices heading, with a yellow exclamation point over the device name, as in Figure 13-1.

Figure 13-1 If Windows 10 can't find drivers for a new Plug and Play device, it adds a yellow exclamation point to the Device Manager listings and files the devices under the Other Devices heading.

TROUBLESHOOTING

Drivers for built-in devices are missing

Device Manager might show some devices in the Other Devices category, with a yellow exclamation point indicating that the correct drivers are missing, after a clean installation of Windows 10. This usually occurs on a PC where some low-level devices built into the motherboard aren't recognized during Windows 10 setup. The usual cure for this sort of problem is to check with the device manufacturer to see whether drivers are available for download; pay special attention to chipset drivers, which add the necessary entries to the Windows Plug and Play database to allow the correct built-in drivers to be installed.

When Windows Update can't find a signed driver (and, thankfully, those occasions are becoming rarer as the Windows ecosystem matures), you need to manually install a device driver, a topic we cover in more detail later in this chapter.

The built-in Windows drivers are perfectly adequate for many device classes. Some devices, especially complex ones like scanners and all-in-one printers, might require utility software and additional drivers to enable the full range of features for that device.

How device drivers and hardware work together

Before Windows can work with any piece of hardware, it requires a compatible, properly con-figured device driver. Drivers are compact control programs that hook directly into Windows and handle the essential tasks of communicating your instructions to a hardware device and then relaying data back to you. After you set up a hardware device, its driver loads automati-cally and runs as part of the operating system, without requiring any further intervention on your part.

Many of the individual technologies used in Windows 10 devices use minidriver models, where the device driver is made up of two parts. Typically, Microsoft writes a general class driver that handles tasks that are common to devices in that category. The device manufacturer can then write device-specific code to enable custom features.

Windows 10, even more than its recent predecessors, includes a surprisingly comprehensive library of class drivers that allow most devices to function properly without requiring any additional software. There are class drivers for pieces of hardware that are, these days, typically integrated into a larger system: audio devices, network adapters, webcams, and display adapt-ers, for example. Windows 10 also includes drivers for external add-ons (wired and wireless) including printers, monitors, keyboards, scanners, mice and other pointing devices, smart-phones, and removable storage devices.

This core library is copied during Windows setup to a protected system folder, %SystemRoot%\System32\DriverStore. (Driver files and associated elements are stored in the FileRepository subfolder.) Anyone who signs in to the computer can read and execute files from this location, but only an installation program working with authorization from a member of the Adminis-trators group can create or modify files and folders there.

You can add new drivers to the driver store in a variety of ways, including the following:

- Windows Update offers drivers when it detects that you're running a device that is com-patible with that driver but is currently using an older version. (You can also search for the most recent driver via Windows Update when installing a new device.)

- A Windows cumulative update may refresh the driver store with new and updated drivers.

- As an administrator, you can add signed third-party drivers to the driver store by run-ning an installer program. All drivers added to the driver store in this fashion are saved in their own subfolder within the FileRepository folder, along with some supporting files created by Windows 10 that allow the drivers to be reinstalled if necessary.

Any driver that has been added to the store is considered to be trusted and can be installed without prompts or administrator credentials. All drivers, new or updated, that are copied here from Microsoft servers are certified to be fully compatible with Windows 10 and are digitally signed by Microsoft.

Inside OUT

Copy the FileRepository folder before a clean reinstall

If you're planning a clean reinstall of Windows 10 using bootable installation media rather than the Reset function, consider copying the FileRepository folder from %SystemRoot%\System32\DriverStore to removable media, such as a USB flash drive. After your clean install is complete, you can quickly reinstall any custom drivers by using the Update Driver option from Device Manager and specifying that saved folder as the location for the new driver files.

A Windows hardware driver package must include a Setup Information file (with the extension .inf). This is a text file that contains detailed information about the device to be installed, including the names of its driver files, the locations where they are to be installed, any required registry settings, and version information. All devices with drivers in the DriverStore folder include Setup Information files in the %SystemRoot%\Inf folder.

Although the Setup Information file is a crucial part of the driver installation process, you don't work with it directly. Instead, this file supplies instructions that the operating system uses during Plug and Play detection, when you use a setup program to install a device, or when you manually install a driver update.

CAUTION

The syntax of Setup Information files is complex, and the intricacies of .inf files can trip up even experienced software developers. If you find that a driver setup routine isn't working properly, you might be tempted to try editing the Setup Information file to work around the hang-up. Trust us: that approach is almost certain to fail. In fact, by tinkering with .inf files to install a driver that is not certified to be compatible with your hardware, you run the risk of corrupting registry settings and making your system unstable.

When Windows completes the installation of a driver package, it performs all the tasks specified by the Setup Information file and copies the driver files themselves to %SystemRoot%\System32\Drivers.

Inside OUT

For Windows 10, signed drivers only

Beginning with the release of Windows 10, all new kernel-mode drivers must be submitted to Microsoft and digitally signed by the Windows Hardware Developer Center Dashboard portal. (Kernel-mode drivers run at the same level of privilege as Windows itself, as opposed to user-mode drivers, which run in the context of the currently signed-in user and cannot cause the system to crash.) Additionally, beginning 90 days after the release of Windows 10, any new drivers submitted to Microsoft must be signed by a valid Extended Validation Code Signing Certificate—a higher-cost option that provides extra assurance about the identity of a software publisher.

The net effect of these changes is to make it extremely difficult for malware to be delivered as part of a driver update. Drivers that were properly signed under the previous rules and were released before those two Windows 10 milestones will continue to work, but Windows 10 will not load new kernel-mode drivers unless they are signed by that Microsoft-controlled portal.

Driver signing establishes an initial threshold of trust, but by itself it's not necessarily an indicator of quality. For that you need to look at the signature a little more closely.

The highest level of quality is found with drivers that have passed compatibility and reliability tests for that category of device, as defined in Microsoft's Hardware Lab Kit. Those devices earn the right to use the Windows logo and can be included on Microsoft's Certified Products List.

Hardware developers who simply want to deliver a signed driver to their customers can submit the driver to Microsoft and "attest" to its quality rather than submitting actual test results. The Attested Signing Service signature is different from the one for a logo-certified device, but Windows 10 treats them the same, allowing either type of signed driver to be installed with no prompts by any user.

In the distant past, users could change default settings to allow installation of unsigned drivers and even completely eliminate warnings about the accompanying security risks. Those options are available by changing advanced startup settings in Windows 10, but they require disabling Secure Boot and fundamentally undermine the device's security. As a result, we strongly recommend against using them.

Getting useful information from Device Manager

The more you know about individual hardware devices and their associated driver versions, the more likely you are to make short work of troubleshooting problems or configuring advanced features for a device. In every case, your starting point is Device Manager, a graphical utility that provides detailed information about all installed hardware, along with controls that you can use to configure devices, assign resources, and set advanced options.

NOTE

In Windows 10, Device Manager also includes categories that don't represent actual hardware—print queues, for example, or anything under the Software Devices heading. In this section, we focus only on physical hardware devices and their associated drivers.

To open Device Manager (Devmgmt.msc), type **device** in the search box and then click its entry from the top of the results list. Power users can click the Device Manager shortcut on the Quick Access menu that appears when you right-click the Start button or press Windows key+X. (Device Manager is also available as a snap-in under the System Tools heading in the fully stocked Computer Management console.)

As Figure 13-2 shows, Device Manager is organized as a hierarchical list that inventories every piece of hardware within or connected to your computer. The default view shows devices by type.

Figure 13-2 Click the arrow to the left of any category in Device Manager to see individual devices within that category.

To view information about a specific device, double-click its entry in Device Manager's list of installed devices. Each device has its own multitabbed properties dialog box. Most hardware devices include a selection of tabs, including General and Driver. The General tab lists basic facts about the device, including the device name and type, the name of its manufacturer, and its current status, as in the example in Figure 13-3.

Figure 13-3   The General tab supplies basic information about a device and indicates whether it is currently functioning properly.

The Driver tab, shown in Figure 13-4, lists version information about the currently installed driver for the selected device. Although the information shown here is sparse, it covers the essentials. You can tell at a glance who supplied the driver and you can see who digitally signed it; you can also determine the date and version number of the driver, which is important when considering whether you should download and install an available update.

Figure 13-4 The Driver tab, which is available for every installed device, offers valuable information and tools for managing installed drivers.

Clicking the Driver Details button on the Driver tab leads to another dialog box that lists the names and locations of all files associated with that device and its drivers. Selecting any file name from this list displays details for that file in the lower portion of the dialog box. (We'll get to the other buttons in the next section.)

Click the Details tab for a potentially overwhelming amount of additional information, arranged in a dialog box that allows you to see one property and its associated value at a time. You can see the full list of properties by clicking the arrow to the right of the current entry in the Property box; Figure 13-5 shows the typically dense result.

Figure 13-5 Most of the device properties you can select from this list return obscure details, but a few are useful for troubleshooting purposes.

Choosing a property tucks the list away and displays the value associated with that property, as in the example shown here, which lists the Plug and Play IDs associated with the selected device.

TROUBLESHOOTING

Device Manager shows an unknown device

Most modern hardware built for Windows 7 or later just works with Windows 10. But occasionally you might find mysterious entries under the Other Devices heading in Device Manager, with few or no details, no associated drivers, and no clue about what to do next. This problem is most likely to appear after you perform a clean install of Windows 10 on a device originally designed for another operating system, but it's also possible for the issue to occur with older external hardware.

You can often get important clues by opening the properties dialog box for the device and looking on the Details tab. The Hardware IDs property, in particular, can be invaluable. The string VID_ followed by a number is a Vendor ID code; PID_ is a Product ID code. Use your favorite search engine to look on the web for a combination of those two values. For best results, limit the scope of your search to **site:catalog.update. microsoft.com**.

In addition to this basic information, the properties dialog box for a given device can include any number of custom tabs. The USB hub built into the motherboard of the PC shown in Figure 13-6, for example, adds a custom tab (Power) that allows you to view how much power is available for devices connected to ports on a particular USB hub (although it might take some further sleuthing and some trial and error to figure out which of the PC's physical ports are associated with that hub).

Figure 13-6 Yes, the properties dialog box for this USB hub includes separate tabs for Power and Power Management.

By design, the information displayed in Device Manager is dynamic. When you add, remove, or reconfigure a device, the information stored here changes as well.

Enabling and disabling devices

Any device listed in Device Manager can be disabled temporarily. You might choose this option if you're certain you won't need an installed device under normal conditions but you want to keep it available just in case. On a desktop PC with a permanent wired Ethernet connection, for example, you can keep a Wi-Fi adapter installed but disabled. That configuration gives you the option to enable the device and use the wireless adapter to connect to a mobile hotspot when the wired network goes out of service.

Right-click any active entry in Device Manager to see the Disable menu. To identify any device that is currently disabled, look for the black, downward-pointing arrow over its icon in Device Manager, as shown here. To turn a disabled device back on, right-click its entry in Device Manager and then click Enable.

Adjusting advanced device settings

As we mentioned earlier, some devices include specialized tabs in the properties dialog box available from Device Manager. Controls on these additional tabs allow you to change advanced settings and properties for devices. For example:

- Network cards, modems, input devices, and USB hubs often include a Power Management tab that allows you to control whether the device can force the computer to wake up from Sleep mode. This option is useful if you have fax capabilities (yes, some businesses still use faxes) enabled for a modem or if you use the Remote Desktop feature over the Internet on a machine that isn't always running at full power. On both portable and desktop computers, you can also use this option to allow Windows to turn off a device to save power.

- The Volumes tab for a disk drive contains no information when you first display the properties dialog box for that device. Click the Populate button to read the volume information for the selected disk, as shown in Figure 13-7, and click the Properties button to check the disk for errors, run the Defrag utility, or perform other maintenance tasks. Although you can perform these same tasks by right-clicking a drive icon in File Explorer, this option might be useful in situations where you have multiple hard disks installed and you suspect that one of those disks is having mechanical problems. Using this option allows you to quickly see which physical disk a given volume is stored on.

Figure 13-7 After you click the Populate button, the Volumes tab lists volumes on the selected drive and gives you full access to troubleshooting and maintenance tools.

CAUTION

DVD drives offer an option to change the DVD region, which controls which discs can be played on that drive. The DVD Region setting actually increments a counter on the physical drive itself, and that counter can be changed only a limited number of times. Be extremely careful with this setting, or you might end up losing the capability to play any regionally encoded DVDs in your collection.

- When working with network cards, you can often choose from a plethora of settings on an Advanced tab, as shown in the following example. Randomly tinkering with these settings is almost always counterproductive; however, you might be able to solve specific

performance or connectivity problems by adjusting settings as directed by the device
manufacturer or a Microsoft Support article.

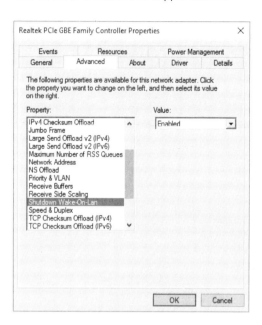

Updating and uninstalling drivers

If you're having a hardware problem that you suspect is caused by a device driver, your first
stop should be Device Manager. Open the properties dialog box for the device, and use the
following buttons on the Driver tab to perform maintenance tasks:

- **Update Driver.** This choice opens the Update Driver Software dialog box, which we
  describe in the next section.

- **Roll Back Driver.** This option uninstalls the most recently updated driver and rolls
  back your system configuration to the previously installed driver. This option is available
  from Safe Mode if you need to remove a driver that is causing blue-screen (Stop) errors.
  Unlike System Restore, this option affects only the selected device. If you have never
  updated the selected driver, this option is unavailable.

- **Uninstall.** This button completely removes driver files and registry settings for the selected device and, if you select the appropriate option, completely removes the associated driver files as well. Use this capability to remove a driver that you suspect was incorrectly installed and then reinstall the original driver or install an updated driver.

Inside OUT
Create a safety net before tinkering with drivers

When you install a new hardware driver, Windows automatically attempts to create a new System Restore checkpoint. That doesn't mean it will be successful, especially if a problem with your System Restore settings has caused this utility to suspend operations temporarily. To make certain that you can roll back your changes if necessary, set a new System Restore checkpoint manually before making any kind of hardware configuration change. (For more details, see "Rolling back to a previous restore point" in Chapter 16, "Backup, restore, and recovery.")

Disabling automatic driver updates

Microsoft uses the Windows Update mechanism to deliver drivers for many devices. This feature allows you to plug in a new device with relative confidence that it will work without extra effort on your part. It also allows you to automatically receive updated drivers, which typically fix reliability, stability, and compatibility problems.

The dark side of driver updates is that they can occasionally cause a previously functional device to act up or even shut down. For that reason, some cautious Windows users prefer to disable automatic driver updates. To find this well-hidden option, type **device installation** in the search box and click the top result, Change Device Installation Settings. That opens the dialog box shown in Figure 13-8, which is set by default to Yes, Do This Automatically. When you change the setting to No, a group of additional options, previously hidden, appears.

Selecting the Never Install Driver Software From Windows Update offers some assurance that an unexpected driver update won't clobber your working setup. It does, of course, impose an additional maintenance burden, as you have to manually monitor devices for driver updates and apply them using the techniques we describe in the remainder of this section.

The final option in the dialog box, which is selected by default, allows Windows Update to retrieve icons and support information for devices, allowing a more accurate depiction of installed devices in the Devices And Printers window, which we describe in the next section.

Figure 13-8 If you're willing to accept the burden of manually checking for driver updates in exchange for the assurance of not being inconvenienced by a defective driver update, use these settings.

Updating a device driver manually

Microsoft and third-party device manufacturers frequently issue upgrades to device drivers. In some cases, the updates enable new features; in other cases, the newer version swats a bug that might or might not affect you. New Microsoft-signed drivers are often (but not always) delivered through Windows Update. Other drivers are available only by downloading them from the device manufacturer's website. Kernel-mode drivers must still be digitally signed before they can be installed.

If the new driver includes a setup program, run it first so that the proper files are copied to your system. Then start the update process from Device Manager by selecting the entry for the device you want to upgrade and clicking the Update Driver button on the toolbar or the Update Driver option on the right-click shortcut menu. (You can also click Update Driver on the Driver tab of the properties dialog box for the device.)

That action opens the dialog box shown in Figure 13-9.

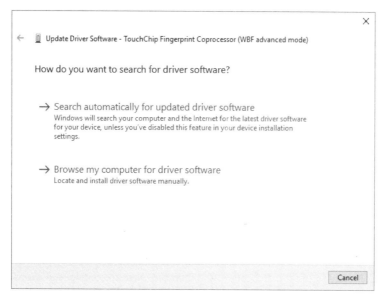

Figure 13-9 When manually updating a driver, try the automatic option first unless you want to select a specific driver you previously downloaded.

Click Search Automatically For Updated Driver Software if you want to look in local removable media and check Windows Update. Click Browse My Computer For Driver Software if you want to enter the location of a downloaded driver package or choose from a list of available drivers in the driver store. Clicking the latter option opens a dialog box like the one shown in Figure 13-10, with two options for manually selecting a driver.

Figure 13-10 If you've downloaded a driver package that doesn't include an installer, select its location here to allow the update to proceed.

If you've downloaded the driver files to a known location or copied them to removable storage, click Browse to select that location, and then click Next to continue. (If you have a copy of the FileRepository folder from a previous Windows installation on the same hardware, you can choose that location.) With the Include Subfolders option selected, as it is by default, the driver update software will do a thorough search of the specified location, looking for a Setup Information file for the selected device; if it finds a match, it installs the specified driver software automatically.

Use the second option, Let Me Pick From A List Of Device Drivers On My Computer, if you know the driver software you need is already in the local driver store. In general, choosing this option presents a single driver for you to choose. If you need to install an alternative driver version that isn't listed, clear the Show Compatible Hardware check box, as we've done in Figure 13-11, and then choose a driver from an expanded list of all matching devices in the device category.

Clear this check box to see all available drivers in this category

Figure 13-11 Clear the check box here only if you are certain that Plug and Play has selected the wrong driver and you want to manually install a different driver.

Inside OUT

Make sure that update is really an update

How do you know whether a downloaded version is newer than the currently installed driver on your system? A good set of release notes should provide this information and is the preferred option for determining version information. In the absence of documentation, file dates offer some clues, but they are not always reliable. A better indicator is to inspect the properties of the driver files themselves. After unzipping the downloaded driver files to a folder on a local or network drive, right-click any file with a .dll or .sys extension and choose Properties. On the Version tab, you should be able to find details about the specific driver version, which you can compare with the driver details shown in Device Manager.

Rolling back to a previous driver version

Unfortunately, updated drivers can sometimes cause new problems that are worse than the woes they were intended to fix. This is especially true if you're experimenting with prerelease versions of new drivers. If your troubleshooting leads you to suspect that a newly installed driver is the cause of recent crashes or system instability, consider removing that driver and rolling your system configuration back to the previously installed driver.

To do this, open Device Manager and double-click the entry for the device you want to roll back. Then go to the Driver tab and click Roll Back Driver. The procedure that follows is straightforward and self-explanatory.

Uninstalling a driver

There are at least three circumstances under which you might want to completely remove a device driver from your system:

- You're no longer using the device, and you want to prevent the previously installed drivers from loading or using any resources.

- You've determined that the drivers available for the device are not stable enough to use on your system.

- The currently installed driver is not working correctly, and you want to reinstall it from scratch.

Inside OUT

Manage Plug and Play drivers

Removing and reinstalling the driver for a Plug and Play device requires a little extra effort. Because these drivers are loaded and unloaded dynamically, you can remove the driver only if the device in question is plugged in. Use the Uninstall button to remove the driver before unplugging the device. To reinstall the device driver without unplugging the device, open Device Manager and choose Action, Scan For Hardware Changes.

To remove a driver permanently, open Device Manager, right-click the entry for the device in question, and click Uninstall. (If the entry for the device in question is already open, click the Driver tab and click Uninstall.) Click OK when prompted to confirm that you want to remove the driver, and Windows removes the files and registry settings completely. You can now unplug the device.

If you installed the driver files from a downloaded file, the Confirm Device Uninstall dialog box includes a check box (shown in Figure 13-12) that allows you to remove the files from the driver store as well. This prevents a troublesome driver from being inadvertently reinstalled when you reinsert the device or restart the computer.

Figure 13-12 Be sure to select this check box if you want to prevent a troublesome driver from being inadvertently reinstalled.

Note that you can't delete driver software that is included with Windows 10.

Troubleshooting sporadic hardware errors

When your computer acts unpredictably, chances are good that defective hardware or a buggy device driver is at fault.

In those circumstances, using a powerful troubleshooting tool called Driver Verifier Manager (Verifier.exe) is a terrific way to identify flawed device drivers. Instead of your computer locking up at a most inopportune time with a misleading Blue Screen of Death (BSOD), Driver Verifier stops your computer predictably at startup with a BSOD that accurately explains the true problem. Although this doesn't sound like a huge improvement (your system still won't work, after all), Driver Verifier Manager performs a critical troubleshooting step: identifying the problem. You can then correct the problem by removing or replacing the offending driver. (If you're satisfied that the driver really is okay despite Driver Verifier Manager's warning, you can turn off Driver Verifier for all drivers or for a specific driver. Any driver that Driver Verifier chokes on should be regarded with suspicion, but some legitimate drivers bend the rules without causing problems.)

Driver Verifier works at startup to thoroughly exercise each driver. It performs many of the same tests that are run as part of the Windows certification and signing process, such as checking for the way the driver accesses memory.

Beware: If Driver Verifier Manager finds a nonconforming driver—even one that doesn't seem to be causing any problems—it will prevent your system from starting. Use Driver Verifier only if you're having problems. In other words, if it ain't broke . . .

To begin working with Driver Verifier Manager, open an elevated Command Prompt window and type **verifier**. In the Driver Verifier Manager dialog box, shown here, select Create Standard Settings. (If you want to assess current conditions before proceeding, select the last option, Display Information About The Currently Verified Drivers.)

When you click Next, you get a list of all currently installed drivers that match the conditions you specified. Note that the list might contain a mix of hardware drivers and some file-system filter drivers, such as those used by antivirus programs, CD-burning software, and other low-level system utilities.

At this point, you have two choices:

- Go through the list and make a note of all drivers identified and then click Cancel. No changes are made to your system configuration; all you've done is gather a list of suspicious drivers, which you can then try to remove or disable manually.

- Click Finish to complete the wizard and restart your computer. Don't choose this option unless you're prepared to deal with the consequences, as explained in the remainder of this sidebar.

If your computer stops with a blue screen when you next sign in, you've identified a problem driver. The error message includes the name of the offending driver and an error code.

Driver Verifier has been included with every version of Windows since Windows 2000 and is included with Windows 10. For information about using Verifier, see the Microsoft Support article 244617, "Using Driver Verifier to identify issues with Windows drivers for advanced users," at *support.microsoft.com/kb/244617*. To resolve the problem, boot into Safe Mode (press F8 during startup) and disable or uninstall the problem driver. You'll then want to check with the device vendor to get a working driver that you can install.

To disable Driver Verifier so that it no longer performs verification checks at startup, run Driver Verifier Manager again and select Delete Existing Settings in the initial dialog box. Alternatively, at a command prompt, type **verifier /reset**. (If you haven't yet solved the driver problem, of course, you'll be stopped at a BSOD, unable to disable Driver Verifier. In that case, boot into Safe Mode and then disable Driver Verifier.)

You can configure Driver Verifier so that it checks only certain drivers. To do that, open Driver Verifier Manager, select Create Standard Settings, click Next, and select the last option, Select Driver Names From A List. This option lets you exempt a particular driver from Driver Verifier's scrutiny—such as one that Driver Verifier flags but you are certain is not the cause of your problem.

Fine-tuning hardware and printer settings

In Windows 7, Microsoft introduced the Devices And Printers folder. It lives on in Windows 10, within the classic Control Panel, under the Hardware And Sound category, where it offers a slightly old-fashioned look at installed devices you're likely to interact with. Figure 13-13 shows Devices And Printers with its two namesake categories expanded. Note the photo icons, which are downloaded automatically as part of the driver installation for some devices and add a touch of realism to the contents of this folder.

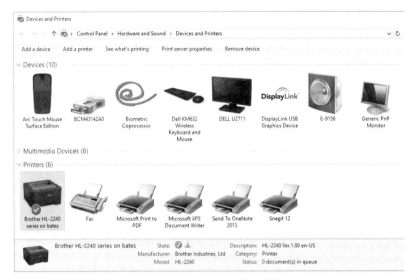

Figure 13-13 The Devices And Printers folder looks spiffier than Device Manager, but it doesn't allow you to do much with devices.

Double-click any item here to see an abbreviated properties dialog box, which contains a shortcut to the more complete properties dialog box from Device Manager. Shortcut menus are available for some devices, such as monitors, keyboards, and mice. The shortcut menu for the Microsoft Arc Touch Mouse shown here includes commands that open settings for it and other input devices.

Three commands are common to all of these context menus: Create Shortcut, Troubleshoot, and Properties. Devices that aren't working properly are flagged with yellow exclamation points, with the same familiar symbol added to that device's Troubleshoot command.

The shortcut menus for storage devices allow you to browse files stored on that drive. Right-click the icon for your computer itself and you'll find a rich assortment of options, including System Properties, Network Settings, Bluetooth Settings, and Power Options.

The Create Shortcut command plants a shortcut on your desktop, which makes the device's context menu accessible outside Devices And Printers. If you create a shortcut to the entry for your computer, for example, you can right-click that shortcut to go straight to such places as Sound Settings or Power Options.

The Properties command provides an alternative route to the dialog boxes that have traditionally been provided by Device Manager.

Printers and print queues

To install a modern printer that plugs into a USB port on the PC where you plan to use it, just connect the device. Plug and Play does the rest of the work. (See "Installing a new Plug and Play device" earlier in this chapter.)

> ### NOTE
> Although it's possible that there are still some non–Plug and Play printers out there, connecting to creaky parallel ports on PCs from the late Cretaceous period, we are happy to bid those devices adieu, and we urge you to do the same. We don't cover manual connection options for legacy devices in this book.

Wireless printers that connect over Wi-Fi or by using Bluetooth also support Plug and Play. Follow the manufacturer's instructions to complete the wireless connection, or skip ahead a few pages to our explanation of the Add A Printer option.

> ➤ You can share a printer for use by other users on the same local network. The simplest way is using the HomeGroup feature, which we describe in "Sharing files, digital media, and printers in a homegroup" in Chapter 5, "Networking essentials." On business networks, the procedure is more formal; see "Sharing a printer" in Chapter 20, "Advanced networking."

To configure a printer or work with documents in a print queue, double-click the printer's icon in the Devices And Printers folder. Depending on the type of printer, you will see either a simple printer-queue dialog box or a more elaborate display, like the one shown in Figure 13-14. Note that it includes printer settings, configuration options, and links to webpages where the maker of the device is eager to sell you accessories and supplies such as ink and toner cartridges.

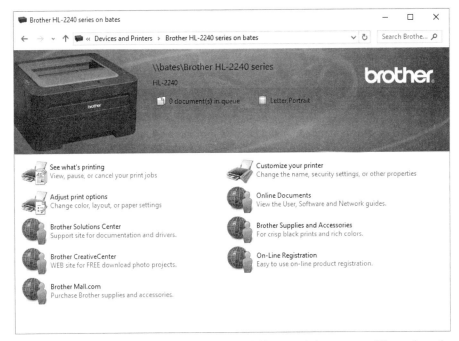

Figure 13-14 Despite the fancy formatting, the available controls here are no different from those you'd see by right-clicking the printer icon and using its shortcut menu.

For a multifunction device, this page might include options to scan documents and photos using the built-in scanner, and to download software and obtain support information from the manufacturer.

The display, with a photo of the actual printer model to reassure you that you're in the right place, might be dramatic, but the available controls for the network-connected printer shown in the Devices And Printers folder are no different from those you would see if you right-click the printer icon and use its shortcut menu.

The top part of the display provides status information. In Figure 13-14, for example, you can see that the Brother HL-2240 series laser printer is set to print in portrait mode on letter-size paper and currently has no print jobs waiting. The options below let you see and manage documents in the print queue or adjust print options (switch from portrait to landscape, for example, or feed an envelope by using a different paper tray). If the Customize Your Printer option is available, click it to open a dialog box where you can manage the general device settings available for this class of device, as shown in Figure 13-15.

Figure 13-15 Change the name of the printer and check its currently available features here. Also consider printing a test page before you tackle a big job, just to be on the safe side.

Printers aren't exactly like snowflakes, but there are far too many variations in hardware and software design for us to offer more than the most general advice: get to know your printer by inspecting these settings, and don't be afraid to read the manual.

To make a wireless or networked printer available locally, click Add A Printer on the Devices And Printers toolbar. If the planets are properly aligned, the autodiscovery software might locate your printer and walk you through setting it up. If you're not so lucky, click The Printer I Want Isn't Listed to open the manual options shown in Figure 13-16.

Among the "other options" available on this page in the Add Printer Wizard, you can connect to a network printer using its Universal Naming Convention (UNC) name. The printer in Figure 13-14 earlier, for example, was connected to a printer on a server named Bates, making its UNC address \\BATES\Brother HL-2240 Series. You can also use an IP address for a device that has a permanently assigned address, and enlist the help of a wizard to connect a wireless or Bluetooth printer.

Figure 13-16 The Add Printer Wizard offers numerous paths to connect to a printer, even one that's "a little older."

Inside OUT

Find a printer's TCP/IP address or host name

Often the easiest way to determine the TCP/IP address or host name for a printer is to use the printer's control panel to print a configuration page, which usually includes this information.

One of the simplest ways to connect to a shared network printer doesn't involve any wizards at all. Just use File Explorer to browse to the network computer, where you should see an entry for any shared printer available to you. Double-click that icon to begin the process of connecting to that printer. Because Windows requires a local copy of the network printer's driver, you'll need an administrator's credentials, and you are likely to see a dialog box similar to the following, with a bright yellow banner that means "Proceed with caution."

If you're confident that the shared network printer is safe and trustworthy, click Install Driver. In a moment, you'll receive a success message and be given the opportunity to make the new printer your default.

Inside OUT

Use a compatible driver

If you can't find a driver that's specifically designed for your printer, you might be able to get away with another driver. Check the hardware documentation to find out whether the printer emulates a more popular model, such as a Hewlett-Packard Laser-Jet. If so, choose that printer driver, and then print some test documents after completing setup. You might lose access to some advanced features available with your model of printer, but this strategy should allow you to perform basic printing tasks.

Keyboards, mice, touchpads, and pens

Windows 10 supports a wide range of input devices. Most wired keyboards and mice configure themselves automatically at startup. Bluetooth devices need to be paired first (a topic we cover a bit later in this chapter). For a wireless device that uses a USB-connected radio transceiver, you might need to go through an initial pairing process.

When an external keyboard and mouse are installed, you'll find some basic customization abilities available for generic keyboard and mouse functions in the classic Control Panel. Enter **keyboard** or **mouse** in the search box to see the corresponding shortcuts for these two groups of options, as shown in Figure 13-17. Both of these dialog boxes include a Hardware tab with details about the device and its installed driver.

Figure 13-17 Windows 10 includes basic support for keyboards and mice; check the Hardware tab in either of these dialog boxes to get more device details.

You'll find some additional mouse configuration options in Settings, under the Devices heading. (See "Taming your mouse or other pointing device" in Chapter 4, "Personalizing Windows 10.") The Mouse & Touchpad Settings page offers only minimal options when a basic mouse or pointing device is attached.

But the Touchpad heading expands tremendously when a *precision touchpad* is included as part of a mobile device. All members of the Surface family that are capable of running Windows 10 support this input standard, as do some portable PCs from other manufacturers (typically premium models intended for a business audience). The precision touchpad driver supports a wide range of gestures and additional settings, including options to disable the touchpad completely or when a mouse is attached. Figure 13-18 shows just a few of these options—the list continues for another full screen.

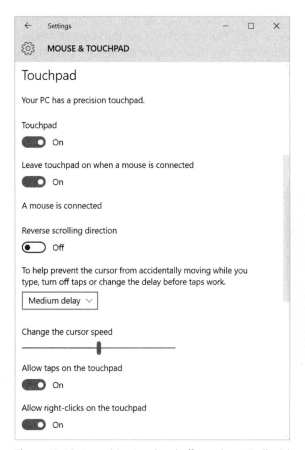

Figure 13-18 A precision touchpad offers a dramatically richer set of options for a pointing device. This dialog box is from the Microsoft Surface 3 running Windows 10.

The most useful options with a precision touchpad expand tapping and dragging options, allowing a two-finger tap to serve as a right-click substitute, for example, or to double-tap and then drag a window. Default gestures include a two-finger scroll and a three-finger swipe that shows Task View when swiping up and minimizes the current window when swiping down.

If your device doesn't include precision touchpad support, you might still have access to a broader range of touchpad behaviors. Devices that include a Synaptics ClickPad, for example, have access to many of the same gestures through a utility that hooks into the Mouse Properties dialog box.

Some third-party mice include separate control modules that allow you to customize the behavior of the pointing device. Many Microsoft devices use the Microsoft Mouse And Keyboard Center utility, with options that vary depending on the device model. Figure 13-19 shows one of the highly customized, device-specific pages available in this app. (Remarkably, this app even gets the color of the Arc Touch Mouse right.)

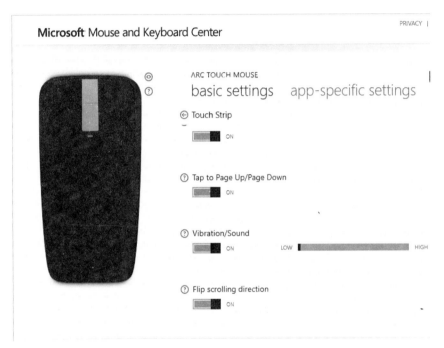

Figure 13-19 This control software, the Microsoft Mouse And Keyboard Center, is capable of identifying a specific device and even noting its color. These options aren't available for generic mice.

For devices that include a pen, you'll find a few configuration options on the Pen page, under the Devices heading in Settings. If you're having trouble getting the pen's input to register properly when you tap, try running the Calibrate utility, which is available via a button on the Tablet PC Settings page in Control Panel. (Search for **calibrate** and you'll find this otherwise well-hidden option.)

Displays

Of all hardware categories in the modern PC world, the display category is the most mature, with any display capable of configuring itself as soon as it's connected.

In general, you'll need to visit the Display pages in Settings only when something goes wrong, which isn't often.

Here are the three display settings you need to pay attention to:

- **Resolution.** Every display has a native resolution, one where the number of physical pixels matches the number of pixels Windows wants to show. Configuring the display at a non-native resolution generally results in a subpar viewing experience, often with a blurry, stretched display. That's probably why you have to take an extra step and go to the Advanced Display Settings page to see and change resolution. Figure 13-20 shows a 27-inch high-resolution monitor running at its native resolution of 2560 x 1440 pixels, as indicated by the word "(Recommended)" in the label.

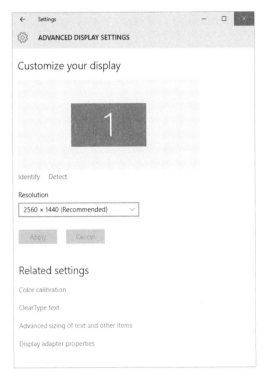

Figure 13-20 The "(Recommended)" after this option indicates that it's the native resolution and most likely the correct choice.

- **Scaling.** On high-resolution monitors, you can increase the apparent size of apps and text. Scaling the display is a necessity when using a high resolution on a relatively small screen. Full HD (1920 x 1080) might look great on a 24-inch desktop monitor, but on an

11-inch display, actually seeing those icons and reading the accompanying text labels would require superhuman vision at 100 percent scaling. On a system with a single display, you can adjust the scaling by using a slider below the thumbnail of the current monitor on the Display page in Settings.

➤ We cover scaling in "Making text easier to read" in Chapter 4.

● **Multiple displays.** When you attach a second (or third or fourth) display to Windows 10, the Display page in Settings changes. Thumbnails in the preview pane (Figure 13-21) show each display at its relative size (in terms of resolution), and you can drag the displays to either side of one another (or even stack one on top of the other). You can also adjust the alignment of the two displays to match their actual physical alignment, with the goal of having your mouse pointer move naturally between displays without a jarring shift when crossing the bezels.

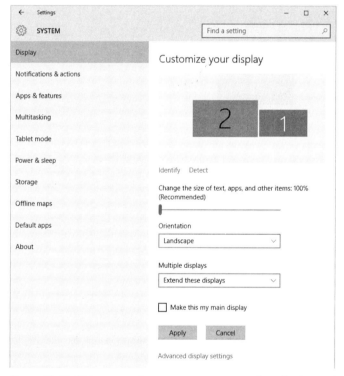

Figure 13-21 With two monitors, you can arrange each so that it matches the physical layout. Pick a display and click Make This My Main Display to control how the taskbar behaves.

Bluetooth devices

Bluetooth is one of those rare standards that passes the "it just works" tests consistently. These days virtually every portable device supports Bluetooth for wirelessly connecting headsets and pairing fitness devices. Many desktop PCs include Bluetooth support as well, for connecting keyboards and mice.

Before you can use one Bluetooth device with another, you have to pair it, a process that generally involves making the external device discoverable, switching to the Bluetooth tab in Settings, and then following some instructions. Figure 13-22 shows a Surface pen, made discoverable by holding down a special button combination for several seconds. Tapping Pair completes the connection and makes the device usable with Windows 10, running in this example on a Surface 3 tablet.

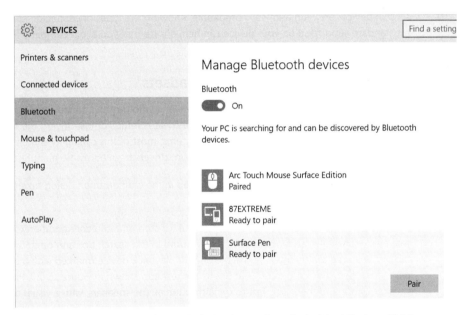

Figure 13-22 Before using a Bluetooth device, it must be paired with a Windows 10 PC.

One sure-fire indication that the Bluetooth Settings page in Figure 13-22 is on a mobile device is the presence of an on-off switch for the Bluetooth adapter. Desktop PCs don't normally allow Bluetooth to be disabled, a wise precaution given that doing so could render the keyboard and mouse—and thus the entire PC—unusable.

USB devices

Universal serial bus, more commonly known as USB, is one of the oldest and most reliable Plug and Play standards in the world. Through the years, the USB standard has progressed from version 1.1 to 2.0 to 3.0, with the latest jump making a monumental difference in the speed of data transfer between USB-connected devices. The new USB 3.1 standard is probably the greatest evolution of all, offering the ability to power full-size laptops, transfer data at blistering speeds, and even drive high-resolution displays.

Confusingly, a new USB Type-C connector is arriving at the same time as USB 3.1 begins to appear in high-end computing machinery. The USB Type-C connector is reversible (no more flipping the USB plug three times until you find the right orientation). These new connectors are compatible with older USB devices, but only with an adapter.

All USB devices are Plug and Play compatible. Knowing the types of connectors and the highest standard supported on your device can help ensure that you avoid compatibility hassles and carry the right cables.

Speakers, microphones, and headsets

Windows 10 supports a broad array of high-quality audio outputs, capable of delivering multi-channel surround sound to sophisticated home theater setups or just driving the tiny speakers on a laptop. As with other hardware subsystems, most of this capability is built into the Windows core drivers and doesn't require custom drivers from hardware manufacturers.

A few useful built-in capabilities are buried deep in the configuration dialog boxes of the Windows 10 audio subsystem.

The first allows you to test your surround-sound (or stereo) audio configuration to confirm that every speaker is working properly. Enter **audio** in the search box and open the Playback tab of the Sound dialog box. Choose the default playback device (marked with a green check mark) and then click Configure. That opens the test app shown in Figure 13-23. Pick your speaker layout and then click Test to cycle through all the speakers, with a visual display showing which one should be playing.

Windows 10 also allows you to designate a playback device, typically a headset, for use as the default communications device, as shown in Figure 13-24. After making that designation, you can change playback behavior so that other sounds automatically reduce their volume when your communication device is in use and the sound of, say, loud music would interfere with your communication.

Figure 13-23 This speaker setup test allows you to confirm that you haven't accidentally wired the right speakers to left and vice versa.

Figure 13-24 This well-hidden option allows you to reduce other sounds (music and notifications, for example) when Windows detects that you're trying to communicate.

CHAPTER 14

Managing disks and drives

When you get right down to it, storage defines what you can and can't do with Windows. A big hard disk (or two or three) makes it possible for you to download and store an enormous amount of digital music, photos, and video; manage large-scale, data-intensive projects; and keep your entire collection of digital resources safely backed up.

Using today's gigantic disks effectively, however, often entails partitioning them intelligently so that separate volumes can be assigned distinct purposes. For a variety of reasons, we recommend, for example, that you keep your operating system and personal data on separate volumes, that (if possible) you make a full image backup of the volume on which the Windows system files are stored, and that you make regular and frequent backups of your valuable data. All of this requires some planning and some familiarity both with disk-management concepts and with management tools that Windows 10 provides.

➤ **For more information, see Chapter 12, "Organizing and searching for files," and Chapter 16, "Backup, restore, and recovery."**

In this chapter, we'll look at the disk-management tools provided by Windows 10 and survey some of the scenarios under which you might find these tools of use.

The Windows 10 disk-management tools

The principal disk-management tool in Windows 10 is the Disk Management console (Diskmgmt.msc). For those who need to incorporate disk-management tasks in scripts (as well as for those who simply prefer carrying out administrative tasks at the command prompt), Windows also provides a powerful command-line program called DiskPart. Everything you can do with Disk Management you can also do by using DiskPart; you just have to work harder and more carefully. Accessing Windows Management Instrumentation (WMI) through Windows PowerShell provides another method for managing disks. This method offers capabilities that are not available with the Disk Management console or DiskPart, and it has the additional advantage of custom programmability, which can be useful when you need to perform disk-management operations repeatedly on different computers.

Knowing when to use which tool is the secret of disk wizardry in Windows 10. Disk Management, for example, is ideal for shrinking and expanding volumes, while the Clean command in DiskPart makes short work of preparing a disk to be formatted for a new role. That command has no counterpart in Disk Management.

Running Disk Management

To run Disk Management, type **diskmgmt.msc** at a command prompt, or press Windows key+X and then click Disk Management. You need administrative credentials to run Disk Management. Figure 14-1 illustrates the Disk Management console.

Figure 14-1 Use the Disk Management console to gather information about and manage hard disks and removable disks.

Disk Management provides a wealth of information about physical disks and the volumes, partitions, and logical drives in place on those disks. You can use this utility to perform the following disk-related tasks:

- Check the size, file system, status, and other properties of disks and volumes

- Create, format, and delete partitions, logical drives, and dynamic volumes

- Assign drive letters to hard disk volumes, removable disk drives, and optical drives

- Create mounted drives

- Convert basic disks to dynamic disks and vice versa

- Create spanned and striped volumes

- Extend or shrink partitions

Disk Management displays information in two panes. In its default arrangement, the upper pane lists each volume on your system and provides information about the volume's type, status, capacity, available free space, and so on. You can carry out commands on a volume by right-clicking in the first column of this pane (the column labeled Volume) and choosing a command.

In the lower pane, each row represents one physical device. In the headings at the left of each row, you see the name by which the device is known to the operating system (Disk 0, Disk 1, and so on), along with its type, size, and status. To the right are areas that display information about the volumes of each device. Note that these areas are not by default drawn to scale. To change the scaling used by Disk Management, click View, then Settings. You'll find various options on the Scaling tab of the Settings dialog box.

Right-clicking a heading at the left in the lower pane displays commands pertinent to an entire storage device. Right-clicking an area representing a volume provides a menu of actions applicable to that volume.

Managing disks from the command prompt

To use DiskPart, start by running Cmd.exe with elevated privileges. You can do that by pressing Windows key+X and then clicking Command Prompt (Admin).

> ➤ **For more information about the command prompt, see Chapter 21, "Working with Command Prompt and Windows PowerShell."**

When you run DiskPart, it opens a console window and dumps you at the DISKPART> prompt. If you type **help** and press Enter, you see a screen that lists all available commands, like the one shown next.

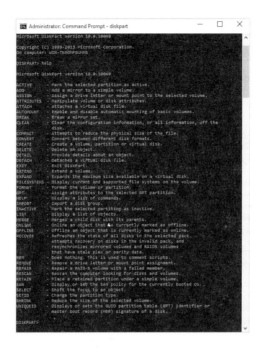

Even if you don't prefer the command line and don't intend to write disk-management scripts, you should know about DiskPart because, if you ever find yourself needing to manage hard disks from the Windows Recovery Environment (Windows RE), you will have access to DiskPart but you won't have access to the Disk Management console. (Windows RE is a special environment that you can use for system-recovery purposes if a major hardware or software problem prevents you from starting Windows.)

Windows also includes a second command-line tool for file-system and disk management, called Fsutil. This utility allows you to find files by security identifier (SID), change the short name of a file, and perform other esoteric tasks.

CAUTION

Fsutil and DiskPart are not for the faint of heart or casual experimentation. Both are intended primarily to be incorporated into scripts rather than for interactive use. DiskPart in particular is dense and cryptic, with a complex structure that requires you to list and select objects before you act on them. For more details about DiskPart, see Microsoft Support article 300415, "A Description of the DiskPart Command-Line Utility" (*w7io.com/2501*). Although this article dates from Windows XP days and some of the comparisons it makes between DiskPart and the Disk Management console are out of date, its tutorial information about the syntax and usage of DiskPart is still accurate.

Understanding disk-management terminology

The current version of Disk Management has simplified somewhat the arcane language of disk administration. Nevertheless, it's still important to have a bit of the vocabulary under your belt. The following terms and concepts are the most important:

- **Volume.** A volume is a disk or subdivision of a disk that is formatted and available for storage. If a volume is assigned a drive letter, it appears as a separate entity in File Explorer. A hard disk can have one or more volumes.

- **Mounted drive.** A mounted drive is a volume that is mapped to an empty folder on an NTFS-formatted disk. A mounted drive does not get a drive letter and does not appear separately in File Explorer. Instead, it behaves as though it were a subfolder on another volume.

- **Format.** To format a disk is to prepare it for storage by using a particular file system (such as NTFS).

- **File system.** A file system is a method for organizing folders (directories) and files on a storage medium. Windows 10 supports the following file systems: FAT (File Allocation Table), NTFS, exFAT (Extended File Allocation Table; optimized for use with flash drives), CDFS (Compact Disc File System; also sometimes identified as ISO-9660), and UDF (Universal Disk Format). Windows 10 does not currently support the new Resilient File System (ReFS, for short) but this support is likely to arrive in a future update.

- **Basic disk and dynamic disk.** The two principal types of hard-disk organization in Windows are called basic and dynamic:

  - A basic disk can be subdivided into as many as four partitions. (Disks that have been initialized using a GUID Partition Table can have more than four.) All volumes on a basic disk must be simple volumes. When you use Disk Management to create new simple volumes, the first three partitions it creates are primary partitions. The fourth is created as an extended partition using all remaining unallocated space on the disk. An extended partition can be organized into as many as 2,000 logical disks. In use, a logical disk behaves exactly like a primary partition.

  - A dynamic disk offers organizational options not available on a basic disk. In addition to simple volumes, dynamic disks can contain spanned or striped volumes. These last two volume types combine space from multiple disks.

- **Simple volume.** A simple volume is a volume contained entirely within a single physical device. On a basic disk, a simple volume is also known as a partition.

- **Spanned volume.** A spanned volume is a volume that combines space from physically separate disks, making the combination appear and function as though it were a single storage medium.

- **Striped volume.** A striped volume is a volume in which data is stored in 64-KB strips across physically separate disks to improve performance.

- **MBR and GPT disks.** MBR (master boot record) and GPT (GUID Partition Table) are terms describing alternative methods for maintaining the information regarding a disk's subdivisions. GPT disks support larger volumes (up to 18 exabytes) and more partitions (as many as 128 on a basic disk). You can convert a disk from MBR to GPT (or vice versa) only before a disk has been partitioned for the first time (or after all partitions have been removed). GPT is required on drives that contain the Windows partition on UEFI-based systems,

- **Active partition, boot partition, and system partition.** The active partition is the one from which an x86-based computer starts after you power it up. The first physical hard disk attached to the system (Disk 0) must include an active partition. The boot partition is the partition where the Windows system files are located. The system partition is the partition that contains the bootstrap files that Windows uses to start your system and display the boot menu.

Setting up a new hard disk

Whether you're installing Windows on a brand new hard disk or simply adding a new disk to an existing system, it's a good idea to consider how you want to use the new storage space before you begin creating volumes. If your goal is to set up a large space for backup or media storage, for example, you might want to devote the entire disk to a single volume. On the other hand, if your plan is to establish two or more separate volumes—perhaps one for each family member on a shared home computer—decide how many gigabytes you want to assign to each partition. You can change your mind later (see "Managing existing disks and volumes" later in this chapter), but it's easiest to adjust the number of volumes on a disk and their relative sizes before you've put a lot of data on the platter.

Installing Windows on a new disk

When you run the Windows 10 setup program on a computer with a single, raw hard disk, you are presented with a screen identifying the disk and its size. If you want to create a single volume encompassing the entire disk, you can click Next to proceed. Otherwise, you can click New, and then in the same screen you can choose the size of the volume you want to create for your Windows installation.

If you decide not to use the entire disk for Windows, you can create additional volumes from within the Setup program. But there's no particular need to do this. After you install Windows, you can use Disk Management to create one or more additional volumes in the unallocated space remaining on the disk.

> **For more information about setting up Windows, see Chapter 2, "Installing, configuring, and deploying Windows 10."**

Adding a new disk to an existing Windows installation

In the graphical view pane of Disk Management, a brand new hard disk, whether internal or external, appears like this:

To make this disk available for storage, you need to create one or more volumes, assign drive letters, label the volumes (if you don't want them to be identified in File Explorer as simply "New Volume"), and format the new volumes. You can carry out all of these steps from the New Simple Volume Wizard.

Specifying volume capacity

To begin, right-click anywhere in the area marked Unallocated and then click New Simple Volume. The New Simple Volume Wizard appears. Click Next to get past the welcome page. On the Specify Volume Size page, you're shown the maximum and minimum amounts of space you can devote to the new volume:

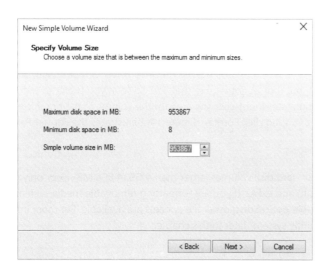

The wizard doesn't give you the option of designating volume space as a percentage of unallocated space, so if your goal is to create two or more volumes of equal size, you might want to do a bit of arithmetic before going on. In this example, if you wanted to split the disk into two equal partitions, you would enter 466933 in the Simple Volume Size In MB box.

Assigning a drive letter

After you have specified the volume size in megabytes and clicked Next, you are given the opportunity to assign a drive letter to the new volume. Note that the letters A and B, which used to be reserved for floppy disks, are no longer reserved:

Formatting the new volume

The Format Partition page, which follows the Assign Drive Letter Or Path page, gives you a chance to do just that, but it does not require that you do so. If you prefer to wait, you can always do the formatting later (right-click the area for the volume in the graphical view pane of Disk Management and then click Format). Figure 14-2 illustrates the Format Partition page.

Your choices are as follows:

- **File System.** For hard disk volumes larger than 4 GB (4,096 MB), your only options are NTFS (the default) and exFAT. If you are formatting removable media such as USB flash drives or a writable optical disc, other file systems are available. For more information, see "Choosing a file system" later in this chapter.

- **Allocation Unit Size.** The allocation unit size (also known as the cluster size) is the smallest space that can be allocated to a file. The Default option, in which Windows selects the appropriate cluster size based on volume size, is the best choice here.

- **Volume Label.** The volume label identifies the drive in File Explorer's Computer window. The default label is "New Volume." It's a good idea to give your new volume a name that describes its purpose.

Figure 14-2 The Format Partition page lets you specify your new volume's file system, allocation unit size, and volume label.

Select the Perform A Quick Format check box if you want Disk Management to skip the sometimes lengthy process of checking the disk media. Select Enable File And Folder Compression if you want all data on the new volume to use NTFS compression. (This option, which you can also apply later, is available only on NTFS volumes. For more information, see "Increase storage space with NTFS compression" later in this chapter.)

The wizard's final page gives you one more chance to review your specifications. You should actually take a moment to read this display before you click Finish.

After Disk Management has done its work and disk formatting is complete, a dark blue bar appears over the new volume in the console's graphical view pane:

If your disk still has unallocated space (as the disk in this example does), you can add another volume by right-clicking that part of the display and then clicking New Simple Volume again.

Choosing a file system

Whether you're setting up a new disk or reformatting an existing one, the process of formatting entails choosing a file system. The choices available to you depend on the type of media you are formatting. With hard disks, the only options made available by Disk Management are NTFS and exFAT. If you want to format a hard disk in FAT32, you need to use the Format command with the /FS switch at the command prompt. (Type **format /?** at the command prompt for details.) The only good reason to do this, however, is for the sake of compatibility with devices running non-Microsoft operating systems that don't natively support NTFS. (See "The Advantages of NTFS" later in this chapter.)

If you're formatting a USB flash drive, on the other hand, FAT32 or exFAT is a reasonable choice. Because NTFS is a journaling file system, reading and writing files on NTFS disks involves more disk input/output than similar operations on FAT32 and exFAT disks. Flash drives can perform a finite number of reads and writes before they need to be replaced—hence, they may have a longer life expectancy under FAT32 or exFAT than under NTFS. On UEFI systems, FAT32 is required for bootable installation media. (For more information about exFAT, see "exFAT vs. FAT32" later in this chapter.)

Choosing the right UDF version for optical media

If you're formatting a writable CD or DVD disc, your choices are various flavors of the Universal Disk Format (UDF). UDF, a successor to the Compact Disk File System (CDFS), is an evolving specification. Windows 10 can format discs using version 1.50, 2.00, 2.01, or 2.50. (Windows 10 can also use—but not format—discs using the latest version, which is 2.60.) Which to choose? It depends on whether you want the CDs or DVDs that you generate to be readable on systems running earlier versions of Windows or Windows Server 2003. The differences are as follows:

- **Version 1.50.** Can be read on systems running Windows 2000 and later.

- **Version 2.00 or 2.01.** Cannot be read on Windows 2000. Can be read on Windows XP Service Pack 3 and later. Note that version 2.01 is a minor revision of version 2.00. There is no reason to prefer version 2.00.

- **Version 2.50.** Can be read only on computers running Windows Vista or later.

All of these variants are afforded read/write support by Windows 10.

Choosing between UDF and mastered optical media

You do not have to format a CD or DVD (using one of the compatible UDF flavors) to store files on it. You can burn files to optical media by copying files to a temporary folder and transferring them en masse to the CD or DVD. Using UDF is somewhat more convenient because it allows you to read and write CD or DVD files as though they were stored on a USB flash drive or floppy disk. But the older method, sometimes called Mastered or ISO, offers greater compatibility with computers running other operating systems, and it's the only method that allows you to burn audio files and play them back on consumer audio devices.

The advantages of NTFS

NTFS offers a number of important advantages over the earlier FAT and FAT32 file systems:

- **Security.** On an NTFS volume, you can restrict access to files and folders by using permissions. (For information about using NTFS permissions, see "What are ACLs?" in Chapter 6, "Managing user accounts, passwords, and credentials.") You can add an extra layer of protection by encrypting files if your edition of Windows 10 supports it. On a FAT or FAT32 drive, anyone with physical access to your computer can access any files stored on that drive.

- **Reliability.** Because NTFS is a journaling file system, an NTFS volume can recover from disk errors more readily than a FAT32 volume. NTFS uses log files to keep track of all disk activity. In the event of a system crash, Windows 10 can use this journal to repair file-system errors automatically when the system is restarted. In addition, NTFS can dynamically remap clusters that contain bad sectors and mark those clusters as bad so that the operating system no longer uses them. FAT and FAT32 drives are more vulnerable to disk errors.

- **Expandability.** Using NTFS-formatted volumes, you can expand storage on existing volumes without having to back up, repartition, reformat, and restore.

- **Efficiency.** On partitions greater than 8 GB, NTFS volumes manage space more efficiently than FAT32. The maximum partition size for a FAT32 drive created by Windows 10 is 32 GB; by contrast, you can create a single NTFS volume of up to 16 terabytes (16,384 GB) using default settings, and by tweaking cluster sizes you can ratchet the maximum volume size up to 256 terabytes.

- **Optimized storage of small files.** Files on the order of a hundred bytes or less can be stored entirely within the Master File Table (MFT) record, rather than requiring a minimum allocation unit outside the MFT. This results in greater storage efficiency for small files.

exFAT vs. FAT32

Microsoft introduced the Extended FAT (exFAT) file system first with Windows Embedded CE 6.0, an operating system designed for industrial controllers and consumer electronics devices. Subsequently, exFAT was made available in Windows Vista Service Pack 1 (SP1). Its principal advantage over FAT32 is scalability. The exFAT file system removes the 32-GB volume and 4-GB file-size limitations of FAT32. It also handles more than 1,000 files per directory. Its principal disadvantage is limited backward compatibility. Some non-PC consumer electronics devices may be able to read earlier FAT systems but not exFAT.

If you're formatting a flash drive and you expect to store large video files on it, exFAT might be a good choice for the file system. And if you're planning to take that flash drive to a photo kiosk at your local convenience store, FAT32 is definitely the way to go.

Inside OUT

Formatting does not remove a volume's data

Whatever formatting options you choose, you are warned that the action of formatting a volume makes that volume's data inaccessible. That's true. Whatever data is there when you format will no longer be available to you by normal means after you format. Unless you use the /P switch, the data remains in some form, however. If you're really concerned about covering your tracks, either use the format /P:x (where x represents the number of passes) or wipe the disk after you format it by using the command-line program Cipher.exe, with the /W switch. (Type **cipher /?** at the command prompt for details.) For information about other ways to clean a disk, see "Permanently wiping all data from a disk" later in this chapter.

Managing existing disks and volumes

No matter how well you plan, your approach to deploying storage resources is likely to change over time. Disk Management can help you adjust to changing requirements. You can expand volumes (assuming space is available), shrink volumes, reformat, relabel, assign new drive letters, and more. We'll consider these options next.

Extending a volume

Disk Management will be happy to make an NTFS volume larger for you, provided unallocated space is available on the same or another hard disk. To accomplish the expansion, right-click the volume you want to expand and then click Extend Volume. Click Next to move past the Extend Volume Wizard's welcome page. The Select Disks page, shown in Figure 14-3, appears.

Figure 14-3 The Extend Volume Wizard lets you extend a volume into unallocated space on the same or another hard disk with free space.

The Selected list, on the right side of this dialog box, initially shows the disk whose volume you intend to extend. The Maximum Available Space In MB box shows you how much larger you can make the volume, assuming you want to confine your expansion to the current disk. The Select The Amount Of Space In MB box, initially set to equal the maximum available space, is where you declare the number of megabytes you want to add to the volume, and the Total Volume Size In Megabytes (MB) box shows you how big your volume is about to become. When you're ready to continue, click Next, review your orders on the ensuing page, and then click Finish. If your volume resided on a basic disk to begin with, it will remain basic after the expansion—provided that the space into which you expanded was contiguous with the original volume. Note that no separate formatting step is required; the new territory acquires the same formatting as the original.

Volume extension is subject to the following limitations:

- Only NTFS-formatted volumes can be extended.

- A logical drive can be extended only within the extended partition that contains it.

- The system and boot partitions can be extended only into contiguous unallocated space.

- You cannot extend a striped volume.

Inside OUT
Increase storage space with NTFS compression

If you're thinking of expanding a partition because you're short of space, consider compressing your files and folders instead. You can compress individual files, particular folders, or entire volumes. Items compressed in this manner are decompressed on the fly when you open them and compressed again when they are closed. You won't achieve huge savings in storage space this way—less than you would get by using compressed (zipped) folders—but the convenience of NTFS is high and the cost, in terms of performance, is virtually unnoticeable. To compress a volume, open This PC in File Explorer, right-click the volume, click Properties, and then, on the General tab of the properties dialog box, select Compress This Drive To Save Disk Space. To compress a particular folder or file, right-click it in File Explorer, click Properties, and then click Advanced on the General tab of the properties dialog box. In the Advanced Attributes dialog box, select Compress Contents To Save Disk Space. Note that this form of compression is available only on NTFS volumes and that NTFS compression is incompatible with encryption that uses the Encrypting File System. You can have one or the other, but not both.

Shrinking a volume

Provided that space is available, you can shrink an NTFS-formatted volume to make more space available for other volumes. To do this, right-click the volume in either the volume list or graphical view pane and then click Shrink Volume. Disk Management responds by analyzing the disk, and then it reports the amount of shrinkage possible, as shown next:

Enter the number of megabytes by which you want to reduce your volume, and then click Shrink. Disk Management defragments the disk, moving all its data to a contiguous block, and then performs the shrink.

Be aware that page files and volume shadow copy files cannot be moved during the defragmentation process. This means that you might not have as much room to shrink as you would like. Microsoft also advises that the amount by which you can shrink a volume is "transient" and depends on what is happening on the volume at the time. In other words, if you are trying to eliminate, say, 10 GB from the volume, and Disk Management can manage only 7, take the 7 and then try for more later.

Deleting a volume

Deleting a volume is easy—and irreversible. All data is lost in the process, so be sure you have backed up or no longer need whatever the volume currently contains. Then right-click the volume and click Delete Volume. The volume reverts to unallocated space, and if it happens to have been the last volume on a dynamic disk, the disk itself is converted to basic.

Converting a FAT32 disk to NTFS

To convert a FAT or FAT32 disk to NTFS, use the command-line Convert utility. The essential syntax is

```
convert d: /fs:ntfs
```

where d is the drive letter you want to convert. For information about optional parameters, type **convert /?** at the command prompt.

The Convert utility can do its work within Windows if the drive to be converted is not in use. However, if you want to convert the system volume or a volume that holds a page file, you might see an error message when you run Convert. In that case, you must schedule the conversion to occur the next time you start Windows. After you restart the computer, you'll see a prompt that warns you that the conversion is about to begin. You have 10 seconds to cancel the conversion. If you allow it to proceed, Windows will run the Chkdsk utility and perform the conversion automatically. During this process, your computer will restart twice.

Assigning or changing a volume label

In Windows 10, as in previous versions of Windows, you can assign a descriptive text label to any volume. Assigning a label is purely optional, but it's a good practice, especially if you have a multiboot system or if you've set up separate volumes to keep your data organized. You can use Data as the label for your data drive, Music for the drive that holds your collection of digital tunes, and so on.

You can enter a volume label when you format a new volume, or you can do it at any time afterward by right-clicking a volume (in Disk Management or in File Explorer), clicking Properties, and entering text in the edit field near the top of the General tab.

Assigning and changing drive letters

You can assign one and only one letter to a volume. For all but the following volumes, you can change or remove the drive letter at any time:

- The boot volume

- The system volume

- Any volume on which the page (swap) file is stored

To change a drive-letter assignment, right-click the volume in Disk Management and then click Change Drive Letter And Paths. (You can do this in either the upper or lower pane.) To replace an existing drive letter, select it and click Change. To assign a drive letter to a volume that currently has none, click Add. Select an available drive letter from the Assign The Following Drive Letter list, and then click OK twice.

> ### TROUBLESHOOTING
>
> *The drive letter for my card reader has disappeared*
>
> Windows 10 does not display empty drives by default. If your computer has a set of drives for memory cards, you may be accustomed to seeing those drives listed in File Explorer whether the drives are empty or not. If you want to make the empty drives visible, open File Explorer, click the View tab, and then select Hidden Items.

Mapping a volume to an NTFS folder

In addition to (or in place of) a drive letter, you can assign one or more paths to NTFS folders to a volume. Assigning a drive path creates a mounted volume (also known as a mounted
drive, mounted folder, or volume mount point). A mounted volume appears as a folder within
an NTFS-formatted volume that has a drive letter assigned to it. Besides allowing you to side-
step the limitation of 26 drive letters, mounted volumes offer these advantages:

- You can extend storage space on an existing volume that's running low on free space.
  For instance, if your digital music collection has outgrown your drive C, you can create a
  subfolder of your Music folder and call it, say, More Music. Then you can assign a drive
  path from a new volume to the More Music folder—in effect increasing the size of your
  original Music folder. The More Music folder in this example will appear to be part of the
  original Music folder but will actually reside on the new volume.

- You can make commonly used files available in multiple locations. Say you have an
  enormous collection of clip art that you store on drive X, and each user has a subfolder
  in his or her Documents folder where desktop publishing files are stored. In each of
  those personal folders, you can create a subfolder called Clip Art and assign that folder's
  path to volume X. That way, the entire clip art collection is always available from any
  user's desktop publishing folder, and no one has to worry about creating shortcuts to X
  or changing drive letters while they work.

To create a mounted volume, follow these steps:

1. In Disk Management, right-click the volume you want to change (you can do this in
    either the graphical view pane or the volume list pane), and then click Change Drive
    Letter And Paths.

2. Click Add to open the Add Drive Letter Or Path dialog box.

3. Select Mount In The Following Empty NTFS Folder. (This is the only option available if
    the volume already has a drive letter assigned.)

4. Click Browse. The Browse For Drive Path dialog box that appears shows only NTFS
    volumes, and the OK button is enabled only if you select an empty folder or click New
    Folder to create one.

5. Click OK to add the selected location in the Add Drive Letter Or Path dialog box, and
    then click OK to create the drive path.

You can manage files and subfolders in a mounted volume just as though it were a regular
folder. In File Explorer, the folder icon will be marked by a shortcut arrow. If you right-click the

folder icon and then click Properties, the General tab will reveal that the folder is actually a mounted volume, as shown next.

And, as Figure 14-4 shows, if you click the Properties button within that properties dialog box, you'll see more details about the drive to which the folder is mapped.

If you use the Dir command in a Command Prompt window to display a folder directory, a mounted volume is identified as <JUNCTION> (for junction point, yet another name for a mounted volume), whereas ordinary folders are identified as <DIR> (for directory, the MS-DOS term for a folder).

CAUTION

When creating mounted volumes, avoid establishing loops in the structure of a drive— for example, by creating a drive path from drive X that points to a folder on drive D and then creating a drive path on drive D that points to a folder on drive X. Windows allows you to do this, but it's invariably a bad idea, because an application that opens subfolders (such as a search) can go into an endless loop.

To see a list of all the mounted drives on your system, click View, Drive Paths in Disk Management. A dialog box like the one shown in Figure 14-5 appears. Note that you can remove a drive path from this dialog box; if you do so, the folder remains in the same spot it was previously located, but it reverts to being a regular, empty folder.

Figure 14-4 The properties dialog box for a mounted drive identifies the volume that actually holds its files.

Figure 14-5 This dialog box lists all the mounted drives on a system and shows the volume label, if any, of each mounted drive.

> ➤ For instructions on how to make a USB flash drive bootable so that you can use it to install Windows 10, see "Making bootable media" in Chapter 2. For details on how to mount an ISO file so you can run the setup program without requiring external media, see "Upgrade directly from an ISO file," also in Chapter 2.

Checking the properties and status of disks and volumes

You can check the properties of any drive—including the volume label, file system, and amount of free space available—by right-clicking the drive in File Explorer's This PC folder and then clicking Properties. You can see the same details and more in Disk Management. Most of the crucial information is visible in the volume list, the tabular pane that appears by default at the top of the Disk Management window. Slightly less information is available in the graphical view at the bottom of the window. Of particular interest is information about the status of a disk or volume. Figure 14-6 shows where to look for this information.

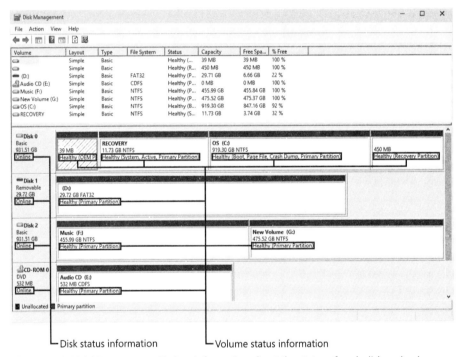

Figure 14-6 Disk Management displays information about the status of each disk and volume.

Under normal circumstances, the status information displayed here should report that each disk is online and each volume is healthy. Table 14-1 lists all possible disk status messages you might see on a system running Windows 10, along with suggested actions for resolving possible errors.

Table 14-1 Disk status messages

Status	Description	Action required
Online	The disk is configured correctly and has no known problems.	None.
Online (Errors)	The operating system encountered errors when reading or writing data from a region of the disk. (This status message appears on dynamic disks only.)	Right-click the disk, and then click Reactivate Disk to return its status to Online. If errors continue to occur, check for damage to the disk.
Offline	The disk was once available but is not currently accessible. The disk might be physically damaged, or it might be disconnected. (This status message appears on dynamic disks only.)	Check the physical connections between the disk and the power supply or disk controller. After repairing connections, right-click the disk and then click Reactivate Disk to return its status to Online. If the damage cannot be repaired, delete all volumes, right-click the disk, and then click Remove Disk.
Foreign	The disk was originally installed on another computer and has not yet been set up for use on your computer. (This status message appears on dynamic disks only.)	Right-click the disk, and then click Import Foreign Disks.
Unreadable	All or part of the disk might be physically damaged, or (in the case of a dynamic disk) the dynamic disk database might be corrupted.	Restart the computer. If the problem persists, right-click the disk and then click Rescan Disks. If the status is still Unreadable, some data on the disk might be recoverable with third-party utilities.
Missing	The disk is corrupted, disconnected, or not powered on. (This status message appears on dynamic disks only.)	After you reconnect or power on the missing disk, right-click the disk and click Reactivate Disk to return its status to Online.
Not Initialized	The disk does not contain a valid signature. It might have been prepared on a system running a non-Microsoft operating system, such as Unix or Linux, or the drive might be brand new.	If the disk is used by another operating system, do nothing. To prepare a new disk for use with Windows 10, right-click the disk and click Initialize Disk.
No Media	A disc is not inserted in the drive. (This status message appears only on removable media drives, such as CD and DVD drives.)	Insert a disc in the drive, and then click Action, Rescan Disks.

Table 14-2 describes volume status messages you're likely to see.

Table 14-2 Volume status messages

Status	Description	Action required
Healthy	The volume is properly formatted and has no known problems.	None.
Healthy (At Risk)	Windows encountered errors when reading from or writing to the underlying disk. Such errors are often caused by bad blocks on the disk. After encountering an error anywhere on the disk, Disk Management marks all volumes on that disk as Healthy (At Risk). (This status message appears on dynamic disks only.)	Right-click the disk, and then click Reactivate Disk. Persistent errors often indicate a failing disk. Back up all data, and run a thorough diagnostic check using the hardware manufacturer's software; if necessary, replace the disk.
Healthy (Unknown Partition)	Windows does not recognize the partition; this occurs with some partitions created by another operating system or by a computer manufacturer that uses a partition to store system files. You cannot format or access data on an unknown partition.	If you're certain the partition is unnecessary, use Disk Management to delete it and create a new partition in the free space created.
Initializing	Disk Management cannot determine the disk status because the disk is initializing. (This status message appears on dynamic disks only.)	Wait. The drive status should appear in a few seconds.
Failed	The dynamic disk is damaged or the file system is corrupted.	To repair a failed dynamic volume, check to see whether the disk is online. (If not, right-click the disk, and then click Reactivate Disk.) Right-click the volume, and then click Reactivate Volume. If the failed volume is on a basic disk, be sure that the disk is properly connected.
Unknown	The boot sector for the volume is corrupted, and you can no longer access data. This condition might be caused by a virus.	Use an up-to-date virus-scanning program to check for the presence of a boot-sector virus.

Permanently wiping all data from a disk

Formatting a volume results in a root folder that appears to be empty. However, as we mentioned earlier in this chapter, someone with data-recovery tools might be able to restore deleted files even after you format the volume. If you're discarding or recycling an old computer or hard disk, you don't want to risk the possibility of it landing in the hands of someone who might search it for recoverable data that can be used for identity theft or other nefarious purposes.

If your old disk is headed for the dumpster, you can ensure that the data can't be recovered by removing the disk drive from the computer and physically destroying the disk. Using tools as varied as a power saw, drill, torch, or sledge hammer, you can render the disk inoperable. Although this method is effective, it has several disadvantages: it takes time, considerable physical effort, and has all the usual risks associated with tools. (Be sure you're wearing safety goggles.) Perhaps most important, you're left with a disk that can't be sold or donated to someone who can use it.

As we mentioned earlier, the Format command (with the /P switch) and the Cipher command (with the /W switch) can be used to overwrite everything on a disk, but these tools are impractical for cleaning the system partition.

A better solution is to use a third-party disk-wiping tool. A free one that we like is Darik's Boot And Nuke (DBAN), which you can download from *www.dban.org*. DBAN is a bootable disk that securely wipes a computer's hard disks. If you're worried that DBAN or another purported disk-wiping utility might surreptitiously steal your data before destroying it, remove your concerns by disconnecting your computer from your network before using the program.

If your disk contains highly sensitive material and you want to be absolutely sure its data can't be recovered, search for a utility that conforms to the United States Department of Defense DoD 5220.22-M standard for clearing and sanitizing media. This standard requires each sector to be overwritten with different characters several times, thus defeating even the most sensitive data-recovery tools. Programs that meet the standard include Active@ KillDisk (*www.killdisk.com*) and BCWipe (*www.jetico.com*).

Working with virtual hard disks

Disk Management can create virtual hard disks in the VHD format used by the Windows 10 Hyper-V Manager program. A .vhd file encapsulates all the characteristics of a simple disk volume in a single file. Once created, initialized, and formatted, it appears as a disk drive in File Explorer and Disk Management, but you can copy it, back it up, and do anything else with it that you might do with an ordinary file.

> ➤ For more information about Hyper-V Manager, see Chapter 22, "Running virtual machines with Hyper-V."

To create a virtual hard disk, open Disk Management and click Action, Create VHD. Disk Management responds with the Create And Attach Virtual Hard Disk dialog box:

Specify a file name with a fully qualified path. It's easiest to do this with the help of the Browse button, but note that the file cannot be stored in your %SystemRoot% (usually C:\Windows) folder. If you want the disk to expand in size as you add files to it, select Dynamically Expanding. Otherwise, select Fixed Size (Recommended). Either way, you must also specify a size (that's an initial size if you select Dynamically Expanding). The minimum size is 3 MB; the maximum is the amount of free space available on your (real) disk.

New in Windows 10 is the option to create a virtual hard disk in either of two formats. The VHD format supports disks up to 2 TB, which can be used on systems running Windows 7, Windows 8 or 8.1, or Windows 10. The VHDX format supports much larger disks, up to 64 TB, but is not supported by earlier versions of Windows. The VHDX format was introduced with Windows Server 2012, and the option to create gigantic virtual disks is perhaps primarily of interest to server administrators. VHD is still the default format in Windows 10. However, because metadata in VHDX disks continuously tracks changes (a service not provided in VHD), they are, as the dialog box indicates, more resilient to power failures. For that reason, you might prefer the newer format even if your size requirements are well under 2 TB. Provided that you don't require interoperability with Windows 7 or Windows 8 or 8.1, we don't know of a good reason not to prefer VHDX.

After you have finished with the Create And Attach Virtual Hard Disk dialog box, Disk Management adds the new virtual disk to its graphical view pane as an unknown, uninitialized disk with unallocated space:

Right-click the area at the left side of this display (with the disk number), and then click Initialize Disk. The Initialize Disk dialog box that appears gives you the option of setting up a disk with a master boot record or a GUID Partition Table:

Select MBR (Master Boot Record) unless you're working with a very large disk. After completing these steps, you can follow the procedures described earlier in this chapter to create one or more volumes on the new disk. After you have created a volume, formatted it, and assigned it a drive letter, the disk appears like any other in Disk Management and File Explorer.

To remove a virtual hard disk, right-click the disk-number box at the left side of Disk Management's graphical view pane, and then click Detach VHD. Disk Management informs you that deleting the disk will make it unavailable until you reattach it. The dialog box also reminds you of the location of the file that encapsulated your virtual hard disk.

To reattach a deleted virtual disk, click Action, Attach VHD in Disk Management. Then type or browse to the location of the VHD or VHDX file. (It will be identified in File Explorer as Hard Disk Image File.)

Checking disks for errors

Errors in disk media and in the file system can cause a wide range of problems, from an inability to open or save files to blue-screen errors and widespread data corruption. Windows is capable of recovering automatically from many disk errors, especially on drives formatted with NTFS.

To perform a thorough inspection for errors, you can run the Windows Check Disk utility (Chkdsk.exe). Two versions of this utility are available—a graphical version that performs basic disk-checking functions, and a command-line version that provides a much more extensive set of customization options.

To check for errors on a local disk, follow these steps:

1. In File Explorer, open This PC, right-click the icon belonging to the drive you want to check, and then click Properties.

2. On the Tools tab, click Check. (If you're using a standard account, you'll need to supply credentials for an account in the Administrators group to execute this utility.) Unless Windows is already aware of problems with the selected disk, you are likely to see a message similar to the following:

3. If you want to go ahead and check the disk, click Scan Drive. Windows will perform an exhaustive check of the entire disk. If there are bad sectors, Windows will locate them and recover readable information where it can.

The command-line version of Check Disk gives you considerably more options. It also allows you to set up regular disk-checking operations using Task Scheduler (as described in "Using Task Scheduler" in Chapter 19, "Automating tasks and activities"). To run this command in its simplest form, open a Command Prompt window using the Run As Administrator option, and then type **chkdsk** at the prompt. This command runs Chkdsk in read-only mode, displaying the status of the current drive but not making any changes. If you add a drive letter after the command (*chkdsk d:*, for instance), the report applies to that drive.

To see descriptions of the command-line switches available with the chkdsk command, type **chkdsk /?**. Here is a partial list of the available switches:

- **/F** Instructs Chkdsk to fix any errors it detects. This is the most commonly used switch. The disk must be locked. If Chkdsk cannot lock the drive, it offers to check the drive the next time you restart the computer or to dismount the volume you want to check before proceeding. Dismounting is a drastic step; it invalidates all current file handles on the affected volume and can result in loss of data. You should decline the offer. When you do, Chkdsk will make you a second offer—to check the disk the next time you restart your system. You should accept this option. (If you're trying to check the system drive, the only option you're given is to schedule a check at the next startup.)

- **/V** On FAT32 volumes, /V displays verbose output, listing the name of every file in every directory as the disk check proceeds. On NTFS volumes, this switch displays cleanup messages (if any).

- **/R** Identifies bad sectors and recovers information from those sectors if possible. The disk must be locked. Be aware that this is a time-consuming and uninterruptible process.

The following switches are valid only on NTFS volumes:

- **/I** Performs a simpler check of index entries (stage 2 in the Chkdsk process), reducing the amount of time required.

- **/C** Skips the checking of cycles within the folder structure, reducing the amount of time required.

- **/X** Forces the volume to dismount, if necessary, and invalidates all open file handles. This option is intended for server administrators. Because of the potential for data loss, it should be avoided.

- **/L[:size]** Changes the size of the file that logs NTFS transactions. If you omit the size parameter, this switch displays the current size. This option is intended for server administrators. Because of the potential for data loss, it also should be avoided in normal use.

- **/B** Reevaluates bad clusters.

Optimizing disks for better performance

On a relatively new system with a speedy processor and plenty of physical memory, hard disk performance is the single biggest bottleneck in everyday operation. Even with a zippy hard disk, it takes time to load large data files into memory so that you can work with them. The problem is especially noticeable with movies, video clips, DVD-burning projects, databases, ISO image files, and virtual hard disks, which can easily take up multiple gigabytes, sometimes in a single file.

On a freshly formatted disk, files load fairly quickly, but performance can degrade over time because of disk fragmentation. To understand how fragmentation works, it helps to under-stand the basic structure of a hard disk. The process of formatting a disk divides it into sectors, each of which contains space for 512 bytes of data. The file system combines groups of sectors into clusters, which are the smallest units of space available for holding a single file or part of a file.

On any NTFS volume greater than 2 GB in size, the cluster size is 4 KB. Thus, when you save a 200-MB video clip, Windows divides the file into roughly 50,000 pieces. When you save this file for the first time on a freshly formatted, completely empty hard disk, Windows writes it in contiguous clusters. Because all the clusters that hold individual pieces of the file are physi-cally adjacent to one another, the mechanical components of the hard disk can work very effi-ciently, scooping up data in one smooth operation. As a bonus, the hard disk's onboard cache and the Windows disk cache are able to anticipate the need for data and fetch nearby clusters that are likely to contain other parts of the file, which can then be retrieved from fast cached memory rather than from the relatively slow disk.

Unfortunately, hard disks don't stay neatly organized for long. When you add data to an exist-ing file, the file system has to allocate more clusters for storage, typically in a different physical location on the disk. As you delete files, you create gaps in the once-tidy arrangement of con-tiguously stored files. As you save new files, especially large ones, the file system uses all these bits of free space, scattering the new files over the hard disk in many noncontiguous pieces. The resulting inefficiency in storage is called fragmentation; each time you open or save a file on a badly fragmented disk, disk performance suffers, sometimes dramatically, because the disk heads have to spend extra time moving from cluster to cluster before they can begin reading or writing data.

The Optimize Drives service in Windows 10 runs as a low-priority background task that defragments your disks at regularly scheduled intervals. By default, the program kicks off once a week in the middle of the night, without requiring any attention from you. If you would like a different schedule, or if you want to optimize certain disks and not others, type **dfrgui** at a command prompt. The Optimize Drives dialog box appears:

Here you can analyze the fragmentation level of particular disks, optimize a disk ad hoc, or reconfigure the system's background defragmentation schedule. To reconfigure, click Change Settings. The frequency options are Daily, Weekly, and Monthly:

By clicking the Choose button, you can turn optimization on or off for particular drives.

Working with solid state drives

Many newer computers are equipped with a solid state drive (SSD), which is a chunk of flash memory instead of a spinning magnetic disk coupled with an onboard disk controller and the requisite power and data connectors. Such drives can provide improved performance, increased battery life, better durability, reduced likelihood of damage caused by drops and shocks, faster startup times, and reductions in noise, heat, and vibration. These benefits come at a price: SSDs typically cost more and have less storage capacity than current hard disk drive (HDD) models, although the gap is closing.

Conventional hard disk drives are typically the biggest performance bottleneck in any computing environment. If you can speed up disk activity, especially reads, the effects on system startup and application launch times can be breathtaking. On our test platform, which has a conventional hard disk and a solid state drive configured for dual booting, the total boot time when using the SSD is less than half the time (about 30 seconds) than when booting from the HDD. Close examination of log files created by the Windows System Assessment Tool (WinSAT), which are stored in %SystemRoot%\Performance\WinSAT\DataStore, shows radically higher throughput and faster times in the DiskMetrics section of the SSD-based system.

Although the underlying technology in SSDs and HDDs is completely different, for the most part the devices are treated identically by Windows, and you don't need to concern yourself with the differences. Behind the scenes, Windows does several things differently on SSDs, including the following:

- SuperFetch, ReadyBoost, ReadyBoot, and ReadyDrive, features designed to overcome hard disk bottlenecks, are unnecessary and are disabled by default on most SSDs. (Windows analyzes disk performance and disables these features only on SSDs that are fast enough to make these features superfluous.)

- When creating a partition on an SSD, Windows properly aligns the partition for best performance.

- Windows 10 supports the TRIM command. SSDs have to erase blocks of data before those blocks can be reused; they can't write directly over deleted data as rotating disks can. The TRIM command makes this process more efficient by reclaiming deleted space in the background. You can find more details in this Wikipedia article: *wikipedia.org/wiki/Trim_(computing)*.

Optimizing solid state drives

If your system includes one or more SSDs and you have read that defragmentation is inappropriate with such drives, you might be startled to see something akin to the following in the Optimize Drives dialog box:

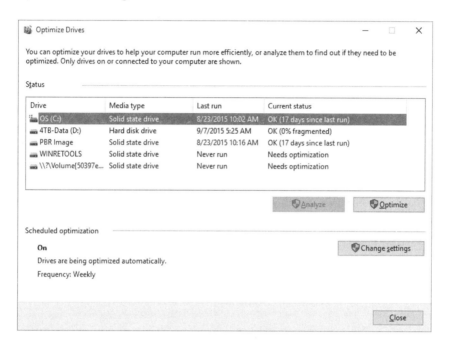

Rest assured that the optimization that Windows performs automatically at (by default) weekly intervals is retrimming, not defragmenting. (See the comments about the TRIM command in the preceding section.) For an interesting discussion of the application of TRIM to SSDs and the issues in general surrounding optimization with such drives, see Scott Hanselman's blog post at *bit.ly/defrag-ssd*.

That blog post includes a quotation from an unnamed Microsoft spokesperson indicating that Windows *does* defragment SSDs once a month provided that System Restore is enabled. This is done to improve performance of the System Restore process on drives that have become fragmented. In our view, there is no good reason to interfere with this optimization.

Monitoring disk usage

The Windows 10 Storage page lets you see at a glance how your various storage assets are being consumed. Go to Settings, System, click on Storage in the list of subsections at the left, and you will be presented with a display comparable to the following:

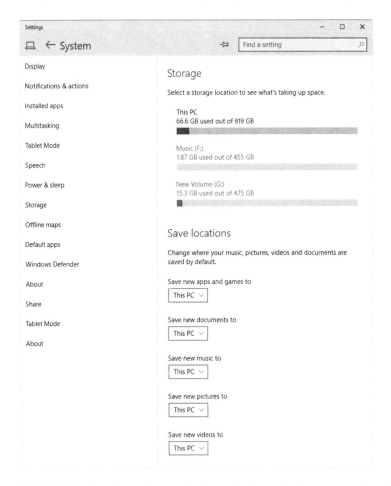

This initial display shows a bar graph for each volume, letting you see at a glance how much storage is in use and how much remains. The controls below the bar graphs provide an easy way to change the default storage locations for various categories of files—documents, music, pictures, and so on.

➤ For a detailed discussion of how this feature works, see "Managing disk space" in Chapter 15, "System maintenance and performance."

Changing default save locations

In the Save Locations section of the initial Storage Sense display, you'll find a set of drop-down lists for various categories of files—apps and games, documents, music, pictures, and videos. These controls let you change the locations where new items are saved by default. All of these categories, except for apps and games, represent libraries, and changing the default storage location simply adds a new location to the library. Opening the Save New Music To list and switching from This PC to Music (F:), for example, expands the Music Library to include drive F, as Figure 14-7 shows.

Figure 14-7 Changing the default save location for a file type expands the library, if any, associated with that file type.

Note that if the volume to which you redirect new saves does not already include an appropriate folder for the selected document type, Windows creates the folder. In Figure 14-7, for example, the folder F:\Craig\Music did not exist before we changed the default save location for music. Also note that the previous save folder (in this case, C:\Users\Craig\Music) becomes a public save location. If you subsequently change the default save location again, the previous save location remains in the library (and, of course, the folder and its contents also remain). You can change the library locations by using the Manage command in File Explorer.

➤ For information about libraries, see "Working with libraries" in Chapter 12.

Using Storage Spaces

Storage Spaces is a technology introduced with the server editions of Windows in 2012 and with Windows 8 and Windows 8.1. The technology allows you to aggregate collections of disks into "storage pools" and then create virtualized disks ("storage spaces") within those pools. For example, you could take two 3-TB disks (Serial-Attached SCSI, Serial ATA, or USB) and use Storage Spaces to create from them a single 6-TB virtualized disk.

You can also use Storage Spaces to establish resiliency for critical data. For example, using your two 3-TB disks, you could create a mirrored storage space in which each file saved on one of the physical disks is mirrored on the other; if one of the physical disks fails, your data is preserved.

Three types of resiliency are available:

- **Two-way mirror.** The system writes two copies of your data. You can lose one physical disk without data loss. A minimum of two physical disks is required. The amount of storage available is half of the total storage pool.

- **Three-way mirror.** The system writes three copies of your data. You can lose two physical disks without data loss. A minimum of three physical disks is required, and the amount of storage available is one-third of the storage pool.

- **Parity.** The system stripes data across physical disks while also maintaining parity information that allows it to protect and recover your data more efficiently in the event of drive failure. A minimum of three drives is required.

Simple (nonresilient) storage spaces are recommended if you require a large virtual disk in preference to separate physical disks. You might make this choice, for example, if you have a very large media collection and several older (hence smaller) disks that are not currently in service. Simple storage spaces are also a good choice for space-intensive operations (video editing, for example) that do not require resiliency. Files in a simple storage space are striped across physical disks, resulting in better performance.

Use parity for maximum resiliency, but note that write performance is degraded by the requirement for the system to calculate and store parity information. This choice might be ideal for archival storage.

Note the following:

- You can create a storage space only on freshly formatted blank disks. Storage Spaces will erase all data on the physical components of a pool (with due warning to you, of course) before setting up the storage space, and such erased data cannot be recovered via the Recycle Bin or other data-recovery tools.

- Storage spaces should not be used as a substitute for backups. They do not protect you against theft, fire, or other comparable adversities.

To set up a storage space, type **storage spaces** in the search box. (Or you can go to Control Panel and search for it there.) Click Create A New Pool And Storage Space and respond to the UAC prompt. A display comparable to the one shown next appears.

After noting the warning about the erasure of existing data on the available drives, select the drives you want to use, and then click Create Pool. The Create A Storage Space window appears, as shown next.

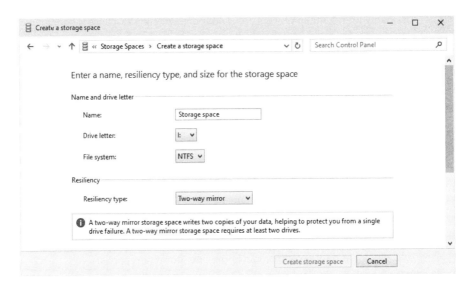

Choose a drive letter, file system, and resiliency type, and then click Create Storage Space.

For much more information about Storage Spaces, see *bit.ly/storage-spaces* and *bit.ly/ storage-spaces-faq*.

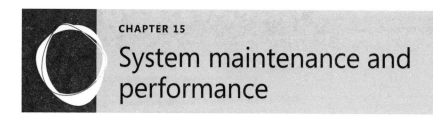

System maintenance and performance

Expectations for how a Windows 10 device should perform are defined by a host of factors. Among them is your threshold of patience, but for big jobs, such as converting and editing video files, time is literally money. For those tasks it's worth spending a little effort tweaking and tuning to shave a few minutes off the time needed to complete them.

For the most part, Windows 10 works acceptably out of the box. Yes, it's possible to improve performance for some tasks, but we don't believe there is a secret formula, magic bullet, or special MakeRocketShipGoFast registry value that will suddenly send your system zooming into warp speed. Our formula for getting great performance out of a Windows PC is much more prosaic: start with quality parts, make sure everything has the right drivers and is up to date, and then look at ways to speed you through your workday and make games go faster.

We also know that performance problems can crop up unexpectedly. This chapter covers a number of tools that you can use to establish a performance baseline and identify the cause of performance issues. Our goal in this chapter is to help you measure performance accurately and to understand the routine maintenance tasks that can keep a system running smoothly and prevent performance problems from occurring in the first place.

We begin with the single most important maintenance tool of them all: Windows Update.

Keeping Windows up to date

In Windows 10, the Windows Update service delivers security fixes, performance and reliability improvements, and updated device drivers, just as its predecessors have done for two decades. But this release also assigns a crucial new role to this core Windows feature. In the "Windows as a Service" model, Windows Update delivers regular upgrades to Windows 10, with new and improved features alongside the bug fixes.

Windows Update and its associated services, such as the Background Intelligent Transfer Service (BITS), should run automatically, with little or no attention required from you. We strongly suggest checking in at regular intervals to confirm that updates are being delivered as expected and that the various Windows Update services are working properly.

Inside OUT

Don't fear automatic updates

Over the past decade, Microsoft and other software companies, large and small, have occasionally delivered updates that caused new problems. Among conservative IT pros and Windows experts, it became practically dogma to stand out of the line of fire when updates were first released. Historically, problematic updates are usually identified within the first week or two and either pulled or fixed, making it safe to deploy them after a suitable delay.

So why are things different this time around? Are monthly updates in Windows 10 more trustworthy than their predecessors? The crucial difference is the introduction of the Windows Insider program, which allows a large group of early adopters to test updates in the Fast and Slow Insider tracks before updates are released to the general population.

Yes, it's still possible for a seemingly innocuous update to cause problems for some users, but the risk is much lower now because those updates will have been tested more fully than ever before. For truly mission-critical systems, where any downtime could be disastrous and a conservative approach is imperative, consider upgrading to Windows Enterprise edition, where the Long Term Servicing Branch is available.

One major change in the servicing model for Windows is likely to dismay traditionalists who want the option to sort through updates at their leisure, accepting some, delaying others, and rejecting still others.

In recent years most newly discovered vulnerabilities in Windows have been patched quickly—usually before they became widespread problems. In fact, many of the worst outbreaks were based on vulnerabilities that had been patched months or years earlier. Windows users who installed the updates promptly were able to avoid infection, whereas those who failed to keep their systems updated fell victim. With Windows 10, Microsoft has taken additional steps to ensure that more systems are updated quickly—namely by installing updates automatically in many cases.

Windows 10 has no supported mechanism for consumers and small businesses to skip individual updates, although it's possible to choose the installation time for the next batch of updates, which has the practical effect of postponing updates for several days.

The level of control you have over how and when updates are installed depends on which edition of Windows you have and on settings controlled by your network administrator:

- With Windows 10 Home, new features, bug fixes, and security updates are pushed to your computer automatically. You don't need to take any additional action aside from observing the occasional reminders to restart your computer. (When Windows does require a restart, you can control when it occurs, as shown next.) As a result, Windows 10 Home systems are always up to date; users who want to skip or postpone certain updates do not have that option. In Microsoft parlance, this servicing "ring" is called the Current Branch.

- Users of Windows 10 Pro can use the default settings and receive Current Branch servicing. An additional option, not available in Windows 10 Home, allows you to select Defer Upgrades from the Windows Update Advanced Options page. This option shifts update delivery to the Current Branch for Business; security updates arrive through Windows Update when they are released, but feature upgrades are delayed several months, until they have been thoroughly tested by users in the Insider preview program and by the general public in the Current Branch. Administrators can use an update manager, Windows Update for Business, to deploy this policy throughout a network.

- Organizations that deploy Windows 10 Enterprise get the same servicing options as Windows 10 Pro: they can receive all features, fixes, and security updates immediately via Windows Update and Current Branch, or they can configure updates with Current Branch for Business to receive them under the direction of an administrator using Windows Update for Business. Enterprises also have the option to manage updates using Windows Server Update Services (WSUS). One additional option is available: the Long Term Servicing Branch. Like Current Branch for Business, this option allows system administrators to control when updates are installed using Windows Update for Business or WSUS. But they can also opt to install only security updates, without installing any new features.

- Windows 10 Education, which most closely resembles Windows 10 Enterprise in terms of features, has the same update servicing options as Windows 10 Pro.

➤ For a full discussion of how Microsoft delivers security updates, see "Staying on top of security updates" in Chapter 7, "Securing Windows 10 devices."

The tools for managing updates are no longer in the old-style Control Panel. Search for **Windows Update** and the following results, all included as part of the modern Settings app, should appear at the top of the results list:

Click or tap Check For Updates to open the Windows Update page in Settings. A list of available updates appears at the top of the page. If the updates have been installed and require a restart, you see a suggested restart time similar to the one shown in Figure 15-1.

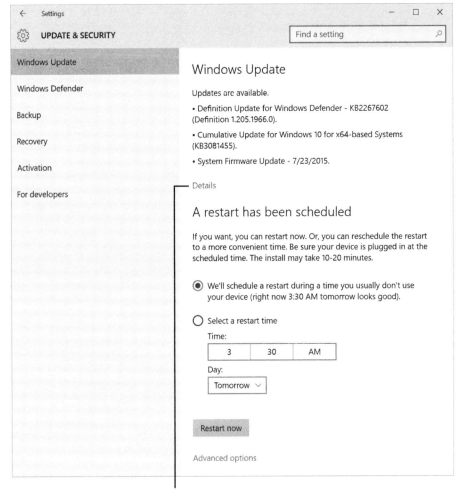

Click here to see more details about an update

Figure 15-1 In Windows 10, updates are installed automatically. If one or more updates requires a restart, you can adjust the suggested time to one that's more convenient.

If the suggested time is inconvenient, click Select A Restart Time and then choose an alternative time and day from the respective controls.

You also have the option of restarting manually. This option is ideal if you know you're going to be away from the PC for a meeting or lunch break that will last longer than the few minutes it takes to install a batch of updates. Save your existing work and close any open files, then click Restart Now. Be sure to wait for all open apps to close before you head out the door. It's highly annoying (and a big drag on productivity) to come back from a meeting and discover that the restart hasn't taken place because a dialog box was open, waiting for your okay.

In previous Windows versions, you had a wide range of configuration options for Windows Update. In Windows 10, the Advanced Options list contains the three items shown in Figure 15-2.

Figure 15-2 Windows 10 is designed for automatic delivery of updates, with only a few configuration options available.

As we noted earlier, the default Windows Update settings allow Windows 10 to install updates and restart automatically if necessary. You can exert slightly more control over the process by changing the Choose How Updates Are Installed option to Notify To Schedule Restart. You can't delay the restart indefinitely, however. If you haven't responded to the notification within six days, the system restarts automatically, typically overnight.

The first check box in the middle of the page allows you to expand the scope of Windows Update to include other Microsoft products, such as perpetual-license versions of Microsoft Office. A second check box allows you to defer large upgrades while still allowing important security updates to be installed. This option is especially useful if you're traveling and can't afford the bandwidth or the time required to install a major upgrade package.

Two other options are available via subtle links at the bottom of the Advanced Options page.

Click Choose How Updates Are Delivered to open the page shown in Figure 15-3. This peer-to-peer feature, which is new in Windows 10, allows you to share updates with devices on your local network rather than requiring a connection to Microsoft's update servers. In a small office or lab, this can significantly reduce the amount of data you download through your Internet connection. The last option allows you to share updates over the Internet at large, using Microsoft's peer-to-peer service.

Figure 15-3 Enabling this peer-to-peer option can speed up installation of large updates on a small network, reducing the demands on your Internet connection.

Clicking the View Your Update History link shown in Figure 15-2 reveals a list that includes the name of each installed Windows update, the date on which it was installed, and a link that includes the update's KB number.

Most of the options for Windows Update have been moved to the modern Windows 10 Settings app. Clicking the Uninstall Updates option on the View Your Update History page reveals a noteworthy exception, as shown in Figure 15-4. This list, which uses the old-style Control Panel interface, displays all updates that have been installed for Windows and other Microsoft products using Windows Update.

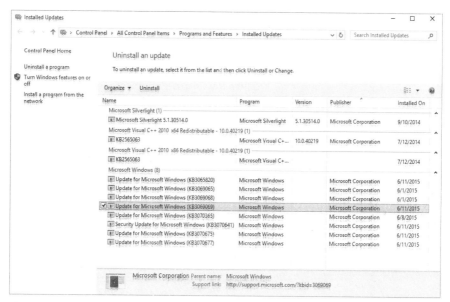

Figure 15-4 If an update is causing problems, you can select it from this list and use the Uninstall option to remove it for troubleshooting purposes.

From this page, you can confirm that a particular update has been installed by referring to its KB number in the list of installed items. A support link at the bottom of the page lets you see details about the selected update. The Uninstall option appears above the list and allows you to remove an update. This option should be a last resort for troubleshooting and used only when you suspect that a recently installed update is causing serious performance or reliability issues.

Inside OUT

Other software needs updates, too

On a typical Windows PC, it's not unusual to find many apps, services, plug-ins, and utilities that also update themselves automatically. Microsoft Edge and Internet Explorer include Adobe's Flash Player, for example, which is updated automatically through Windows Update. Third-party browsers that support Flash-based content require separate updates for the Flash Player plug-in. Likewise, it's crucial to ensure that Oracle's Java, which is regularly targeted by malware writers, has the most recent security updates.

Other programs and features you're likely to use on a PC running Windows 10 also require updates. This list includes Microsoft Office and Office 365 and offline content for the Maps app. Apps acquired from the Windows Store automatically update themselves as well. Many third-party programs and services, including web browsers and cloud-based file-storage services, include their own updaters, which typically run in the background or as scheduled tasks.

In general, it's a good idea to allow these updaters to run. Studies have shown repeatedly that most malware arrives through exploits that target vulnerabilities for which security patches have long been available. Keeping all installed software up to date is an excellent way to avoid being a victim.

TROUBLESHOOTING

Windows Update is stuck in a reboot loop

In some cases, Windows Update can get stuck in a loop, unable to complete the installation of one or more updates and continually repeating the unsuccessful update process each time you restart.

The solution? Reset Windows Update completely, removing content from the update cache and starting with fresh downloads. In most cases, that's enough to get things unstuck.

Microsoft has created a help resource for diagnosing and fixing Windows Update problems, which is available at *support.microsoft.com/kb/971058*. At the time we wrote this chapter, the automated Fix-It tool on that page was not yet compatible with Windows 10. As an alternative, you can follow the manual instructions on that page, which involve stopping several services, removing the folder containing updates in progress, and reregistering a list of system files.

Mastering Task Manager

The easiest way to open Task Manager is with its keyboard shortcut, Ctrl+Shift+Esc. (You can also press Ctrl+Alt+Delete and then click or tap Task Manager.) Task Manager's instant accessibility is its most endearing trait, especially when something appears to have gone awry. Its executable file, Taskmgr.exe, runs at a Base Priority of High, allowing it to kick into action even when another program running at Normal priority is refusing to surrender control. When you need to stop an application (or process) that doesn't respond to the usual measures, or if your system suddenly slows down and you want to know who's eating your processor cycles, Task Manager is your best friend.

If you're upgrading from Windows 7, you're in for a treat. The new Task Manager debuted in Windows 8, and in our humble opinion it is awesome. We'll repeat that keyboard shortcut, Ctrl+Shift+Esc, because we think every Windows user should memorize it. Pressing that combination opens Task Manager using the simple view shown in Figure 15-5.

Figure 15-5 In its Fewer Details view, Task Manager shows only apps that were started by the current user, with the option to end a task that is nonresponsive.

The short list shows only processes that were started by and can be directly controlled by the current user account. If a program has hung, you'll see "Not responding" after its entry in the list, and you can use the End Task button to kill the app and start fresh.

Click More Details to see Task Manager in all its multitabbed, information-rich glory. Figure 15-6 shows this dramatically expanded display, with the Processes tab selected.

Figure 15-6 In the More Details view, Task Manager includes a much longer list of running processes, with real-time performance information for each one.

Although the list of running apps in Figure 15-6 looks similar to the one in the simpler view, scrolling down reveals a much longer list, grouped into three categories: Apps, Background Processes, and Windows Processes. Processes that have multiple child windows have an arrow at their left, allowing you to expand the entry and see the titles of Microsoft Office document windows, Skype sessions, and the like.

You can end a task in the Apps group with minimal consequences (you'll lose any unsaved work); however, attempting to end a task in the Windows Processes group is equivalent to pulling the plug on Windows, as the following stern warning message makes clear:

In the More Details view the totals at the top of each of the four performance-related headings show total resource use for that category. You can click any column heading to sort by that value, making it possible to see at a glance which program is hogging the CPU or using more memory than its fair share. (We discuss performance monitoring strategies in more detail later in this chapter.)

Inside OUT

Why is the System process using so much memory?

Any experienced Windows user who has tracked per-process memory usage in previous versions of Windows might be startled to see the System process using far more RAM than it seemingly should (look back at Figure 15-6 for an example). Relax. That's not a bug; it's a feature, specifically a new memory-management subsystem that improves performance by compressing memory pages for processes you haven't used recently. If the system needs the memory, it will reclaim it quickly by flushing those compressed pages to disk.

Inside OUT

Restart Explorer.exe to fix shell-related problems

In the expanded view of Task Manager, you'll find an entry for Windows Explorer under the Name heading on the Processes tab. If you have multiple File Explorer windows open, each of them will be listed as a child task under that heading. Occasionally, for any of a variety of reasons, the main Windows shell process (Explorer.exe) can become unresponsive. When that happens, clicking the taskbar or Start button does nothing, and the search box is unusable as well. The cure? Open Task Manager, select Windows Explorer on the Processes tab (it might be in any of the three groups), and look in the lower right corner, where the button normally labeled End Task now reads Restart. Click this button to close all existing instances of Explorer.exe and restart the Windows shell.

When you right-click any item in the Processes list, you'll see several choices on a shortcut menu. Click Go To Details to jump to Task Manager's Details tab.

Windows veterans will feel right at home on the Details tab, which is a dense, data-rich list that was the default view in Task Manager in Windows 7 and earlier editions. It shows the executable file for the original process, along with technical details like those shown in Figure 15-7.

Figure 15-7 To show an executable file in its parent folder, select the item on the Details tab and then use the Open File Location option on the shortcut menu.

As with the Processes tab, right-clicking any entry on this list displays a shortcut menu with some technical options. The four at the bottom of the menu are most useful for troubleshooting:

- Click Open File Location to locate the file responsible for the running process. Often, just knowing which folder this file appears in is enough to help ease your mind about a process with a name and description that don't provide useful details.

- Click Search Online to open a browser window and pass the name and description of the selected executable file to the default search engine. This is a useful way to get additional information about a mysterious file, but beware of information from unknown and untrusted sources—the search results occasionally lead to scam sites bent on convincing you to buy bogus security software.

- The Properties menu choice leads directly to the properties dialog box for the associated executable file, where the Details tab includes copyright information and other relevant data drawn from the file itself. That information can help you decide whether a file is legitimate or needs further investigation.

● Finally, for processes that are running as Windows services, you can click the Go To Service(s) option, which takes you to the Services tab and highlights all the individual services associated with that process. For an instance of Svchost.exe, the list might number a dozen individual services.

Inside OUT

Get to know the Process ID column

The default arrangement of columns on the Processes tab does not include the Process Identifier (PID) column, although you can add it by right-clicking any visible column heading and clicking PID in the list of available columns. The PID column is shown by default on the Details and Services tabs, where it's extremely useful in enabling you to see which processes are running as part of the same Svchost.exe instance. To find out what's inside a particularly busy Svchost process, make a note of its PID and then switch to the Services tab and sort by the PID column. The associated services will appear in a block using that PID.

As was true with its predecessors, Task Manager's Details tab includes the option to display many more columns than the handful that are shown by default. To add or remove columns, right-click any visible column heading and then click Select Columns. That action opens the dialog box shown in Figure 15-8.

The list of available columns is overwhelming and highly technical. Some provide interesting information you can't find elsewhere, though. For example, on a device running 64-bit Windows 10, the Platform column lets you sort 32-bit and 64-bit processes quickly, while the Elevated column distinguishes processes that are running with full administrative privileges (usually in the context of the SYSTEM account). If you're experiencing issues with display corruption, show the GDI Objects column and then sort its values in descending order to locate processes that might be to blame.

Figure 15-8 If you're comfortable interpreting technical information about resources associated with a running process, you can add columns to the Details tab in Task Manager.

Managing startup programs and services

One of the most common performance problems occurs when Windows automatically loads an excessive number of programs at startup. The result, especially on systems with limited resources, can be unpleasant: startup takes an unnecessarily long time, applications that you never use steal memory from programs you use frequently, and the page file, which swaps programs and data from memory to disk when RAM fills up, gets more of a workout than it should. Some programs, such as antivirus utilities, need to start up automatically. But in many cases, you're better served by running programs when you need them and closing them when they're not needed.

Overcrowded startups are often a "feature" on computer systems sold in retail outlets, where Windows is preinstalled along with a heaping helping of applications. In some cases, the bundled programs are welcome, but a free software program is no bargain if it takes up memory and you never use it.

Task Manager's Startup tab, shown in Figure 15-9, lets you see at a glance which programs are starting automatically. Using the Disable button or the equivalent option on the shortcut menu, you can disable any option that you determine is slowing down your system.

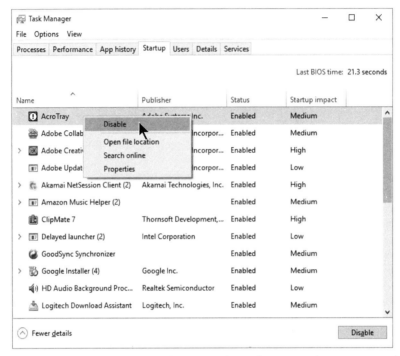

Figure 15-9 The Startup tab in Task Manager shows all programs that start automatically with Windows, with an easy option to disable those you prefer to start manually.

By default, the Startup tab shows only a gross measurement of the effect of a program on startup time. This value is displayed under the Startup Impact heading as High, Medium, or Low. To discover more details about the precise impact of an app that runs at startup, right-click the column headings on the Startup tab and add the two columns shown next—Disk I/O At Startup and CPU At Startup—which quantify just how much disk activity and CPU usage occur when the program starts.

Managing disk space

At the dawn of the Windows 10 era, several long-term trends have converged to make data storage more of a performance issue than it has been in years.

For many years, the trend with conventional hard disks was simple: more storage space at a lower cost per gigabyte. Each new Windows version required more space than its predecessor, but the accompanying new generation of hardware meant there was plenty of room for system files and data.

The advent of solid state drives (SSDs) and flash memory changed all that. SSDs are dramatically faster than conventional hard disks. They're also more reliable than hard disks because they have no moving parts. But SSDs are far more expensive per gigabyte than conventional hard disks, causing PC makers to choose smaller default disks for new PCs. Couple that trend with the arrival of small, cheap tablets that run Windows 10 with 32 GB of total storage or less and you have a recipe for chronic space shortage.

On a desktop PC, you have the option to expand storage by replacing the primary drive with one that's faster, larger, or both; on most full-size desktop PCs, you can also install additional drives to make room for extra data files. Many portable devices, on the other hand, provide built-in primary storage that is soldered to the system board and can't be replaced. For some portable devices, the option to expand storage using inexpensive removable media is available. Microsoft's Surface Pro 3, for example, includes a slot that accepts up to 128 GB of removable storage in the form of a MicroSD card, which can be treated as dedicated storage and used for File History.

> ➤ **For a full discussion of the ins and outs of managing hard drives and SSDs in Windows 10, see Chapter 14, "Managing disks and drives." For a discussion of how to use removable storage for backup, see "Using File History to protect files and folders" in Chapter 16, "Backup, restore, and recovery."**

Managing storage on a Windows 10 device involves two separate challenges:

● Setting default file locations to make best use of available storage, and

● Performing occasional maintenance to ensure that useful space (especially on the system drive) isn't being wasted with unnecessary files.

For an overview of how much total storage is available and what's in use on a Windows 10 device, open Settings, System, and then click or tap Storage to see a page like the one shown in Figure 15-10. This example shows a desktop PC with a 500-GB SSD used as the system drive (C) and a much larger (3-TB) hard drive configured as drive D.

Figure 15-10 The Storage page in Settings shows all available disks, with an indication of how much space is currently in use on each one.

Inside OUT

Why is actual storage capacity lower than advertised disk sizes?

When you use Microsoft's built-in disk utilities to view the storage capacity of a disk, the capacity is reported by using the binary system (base 2) of measurement: 1 KB is 1,024 bytes, 1 MB is 1,024 KB, 1 GB is 1,024 MB, and so on. Thus, measured in binary terms, 1 GB is calculated as 1,073,741,824 bytes. But the makers of storage devices and the PC makers who build SSDs and hard disks into their products typically advertise storage using the convenient metric that 1 GB is equal to 1 billion bytes. That difference is why a system advertised with 32 GB of storage displays only about 28 GB when detailed in Disk Management and other Windows tools. Fortunately, those same tools also report the number of bytes of storage, which allows more accurate comparisons with the advertised space.

With small portable devices, you can accomplish the same goal, on a smaller scale, by installing an expansion card. Figure 15-11, for example, shows a Surface Pro 3 with a 128-GB SSD as the system drive and a 128-GB Micro SDXC card used for data storage.

Figure 15-11 Adding a removable Micro SDXC card doubled the total storage capacity of this Windows 10 PC.

Regardless of how many drives are available, you can see which types of files are using that space. Open Storage in Settings and click any drive to show a breakdown of storage space in use, color coded by file type as in Figure 15-12.

Figure 15-12 This is just the start of a long list that displays a detailed breakdown of how much space is in use, grouped by type of file.

Click or tap any category to see more details about what's in it. Here are some examples of what you'll find in each category:

- **System And Reserved.** This category is typically large and includes files that are essential to the operation of the system. The actual amounts of storage in use depend on the type of device and how much memory it contains. Figure 15-13, for example, shows the breakdown for this category on a Windows 10 desktop PC with 16 GB of RAM (note in particular the large hibernation file).

Figure 15-13 The System And Reserved category shows how much space is in use by Windows, space reserved for virtual memory, and hibernation files.

- **Apps And Games.** This category includes default apps as well as those you have downloaded from the Windows Store.

  In theory, you can relocate apps to a secondary drive, such as a MicroSD card, preserving space on the system drive. This feature is not enabled in the initial release of Windows 10 for PCs and tablets, although it works as expected on Windows 10 Mobile.

- **Documents, Pictures, Music, Videos.** These separate categories show how much space is in use in the default save locations for the respective files types. Note that this value is not the total found in the libraries of the same names.

- **Mail.** This value measures the space used by local copies of messages saved using the default mail app. Clicking or tapping the Manage Mail button will take you to the default email app: Mail or Microsoft Outlook, for example.

- **OneDrive.** The total amount of space occupied by local copies of files synced from OneDrive.

- **Desktop.** This total should be small unless you use the desktop as a dumping ground for downloads and other potentially large files.

- **Maps.** If you have a large collection of offline maps, this category can get fairly large.

- **Other Users.** Displays the total amount of space in use for data files from other user accounts, not broken down by file types.

- **Temporary Files.** This category includes files that are managed by Windows but are not typically necessary for the operation of a Windows 10 device. On the system shown in Figure 15-14, it's possible to recover more than 20 GB of storage space with a few clicks.

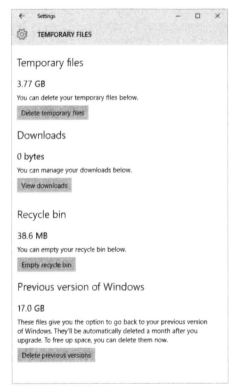

Figure 15-14 Several of the options in this category allow you to free up large amounts of disk space.

- **Other.** If you have large collections of files that don't slot into the standard categories, you might see a very large Other category. Figure 15-15 shows an example of the types of large files that might show up in this category, including Hyper-V virtual machines and associated VHD files, Windows image backups, and recorded TV programs.

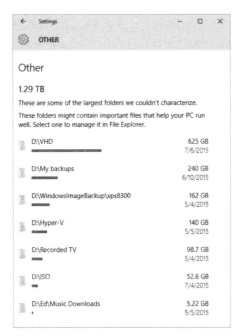

Figure 15-15 Developers and IT pros are likely to have large amounts of space in use for files that don't fit into standard categories and wind up under the Other heading.

As you click to navigate deeper into the categories in the Storage section of Settings, you'll find buttons and links that allow you to manage files contained in that category by using File Explorer.

On systems with multiple drives (including removable media), you can change the default location for specific file types. If you have a large music collection, for example, you might prefer to store MP3 files on an SD card rather than on your main system drive. To make that possible, open the Storage page in Settings and adjust the options under the Save Locations heading, as shown in Figure 15-16.

Figure 15-16 You can change the default location for new files you save in default categories. Existing files remain in their current locations.

When you set the default save location for these categories to a secondary drive, Windows 10 creates folders on the secondary drive, with subfolders that correspond to the category name for each file type within a folder named after your user account name.

You can also examine how much storage is currently available and in use by opening File Explorer, right-clicking a disk icon in This PC, and then clicking Properties. Figure 15-17 shows an example of what you might see.

Figure 15-17 Open the properties dialog box for a disk to see the total disk capacity and how much space is in use. Click Disk Cleanup to open the utility of the same name.

Click Disk Cleanup to run the utility of the same name (Cleanmgr.exe). Note that this utility initially opens in standard user mode, allowing you to manage files available to your user account but blocking access to system files. To enable the full range of Disk Cleanup options, click Clean Up System Files and enter the credentials for an administrator account if necessary. That restarts the utility and unlocks access to the full range of cleanup options, as shown in Figure 15-18.

Figure 15-18 When you start Disk Cleanup using administrative credentials, you have the option to remove Windows installation files and previous Windows versions.

CAUTION

It's tempting to obsess over disk space usage and use every trick to create as much free space as possible. That strategy might come back to haunt you, however. If you remove previous Windows installations, for example, you lose the ability to roll back to a previous version to recover from compatibility problems. As a general rule, it's good to keep at least 20 percent of total disk capacity free. That allows enough room to process temporary files properly without affecting performance dramatically. Beyond that baseline, think long and hard before deleting what might be important files.

Power management and battery life

Power management features in Windows 10 can be broadly divided into two groups. Features in the first group apply universally to all Windows devices, even those that are permanently tethered to AC power. Allowing a PC or tablet to sleep or hibernate cuts the amount of power it consumes, which translates into monetary savings for you and a benefit for society at large.

For portable devices, including Ultrabooks, hybrid devices, and tablets, paying attention to power management has additional productivity benefits. Anything you do to extend the battery life of a portable device means you don't have to quit working because your battery has given up the ghost.

On a portable device, a flyout control, visible with a tap of the battery icon in the notification area, shows how much charge your battery is currently holding. If the device is disconnected from AC power, this display offers an estimate of how many hours and minutes you can continue working. If you're plugged in, the display shows how much longer until the battery is fully charged, as in the example in Figure 15-19.

Tap to display power status   Tap to adjust screen brightness

Figure 15-19 Tap the battery icon on a portable device running Windows 10 to display this flyout control, which gives an up-to-date picture of your current battery status.

That battery indicator isn't just a status box, however. It's actually an entry point to multiple settings where you can fine-tune how a portable device uses power.

The screen brightness button, for example, cycles through brightness settings (25 percent, 50 percent, 75 percent, and 100 percent). Lowering the display brightness saves energy but makes the display dimmer and hence possibly more difficult to see well. For watching movies on a long-haul flight in a darkened jumbo jet, the power-saving setting has many advantages.

To adjust additional settings, click or tap Power & Sleep Settings. Figure 15-20 shows the corresponding options on a battery-equipped device—in this case, a Microsoft Surface Pro 3. (Although this option is also available in the Settings app on a desktop PC sans battery, only one option is available in each group, and the Wi-Fi option is missing completely. Other portable PCs may show a slightly different set of options, depending on which power-saving features are supported in hardware.)

POWER & SLEEP

Screen

On battery power, turn off after

| 4 minutes ⌄ |

When plugged in, turn off after

| 10 minutes ⌄ |

Sleep

On battery power, PC goes to sleep after

| 15 minutes ⌄ |

When plugged in, PC goes to sleep after

| 30 minutes ⌄ |

Wi-Fi

☐ On battery power, stay connected to Wi-Fi while asleep

☑ When plugged in, stay connected to Wi-Fi while asleep

Related settings

Additional power settings

Figure 15-20 On a battery-powered device, you can fine-tune these settings for better performance when the device is plugged in to AC power and better battery life when it's unplugged.

As with several other Windows features, the transition of power-management settings from the traditional Control Panel to the modern Settings app is not yet complete. Clicking the Additional Power Settings link at the bottom of the Power & Sleep page in Settings opens the Power Options page in Control Panel, where you'll find an extensive selection of power settings, some extremely esoteric.

The old-school Power Options in Control Panel, shown in Figure 15-21, is based on power plans, which represent a collection of saved settings. With older versions of Windows, it wasn't uncommon to find at least three power plans, with a hardware maker sometimes defining its own plan as well. In the Windows 10 era, you're likely to find a single Balanced plan that should work for most use cases.

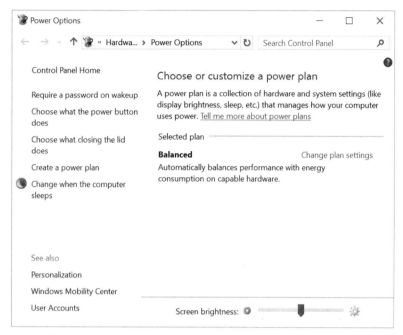

Figure 15-21 Default power options in Windows 10 include a single Balanced power plan. You can create additional plans for special purposes.

Your options here include the following (the list you see on a PC or mobile device will vary based on the capabilities of your hardware):

- **Require A Password On Wakeup.** This is an essential security option for a portable device or one that is in a place where it can be accessed by strangers or coworkers. For a home PC, you might choose the convenience of not requiring a password.

- **Choose What The Power Button Does.** These settings allow you to define whether pressing the power button shuts down the device, puts it to sleep, hibernates the device, turns off the display, or does nothing. If your device has multiple power, sleep, and/or standby buttons, you might see additional options here.

- **Choose What Closing The Lid Does.** This option, available on laptop devices, has the same choices as the previous option.

- **Create A Power Plan.** Click to copy the current settings to a new power plan, which then appears in the list of available plans and can be customized separately.

- **Choose When To Turn Off The Display.** This option, typically found on desktop systems, allows you to blank the screen to save energy.

- **Change When The Computer Sleeps.** Allows you to define the period of inactivity that must elapse before turning off the display or putting the computer to sleep. Battery-powered devices have separate options for when they're running on battery and when they are plugged in. (See Figure 15-22 for an example.)

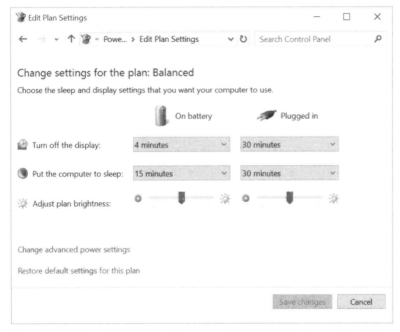

Figure 15-22 To maximize battery life on a portable PC, set the sleep option to the minimum acceptable amount. When the PC is plugged in, you might prefer to set the sleep option to a higher value for the convenience of instant access.

For each option, the choices in the drop-down list range from 1 minute (probably more annoying than most people will accept) to 5 hours (useful if you want the computer to sleep only when you're away for a long time). To disable either option, choose Never from the drop-down list.

If those options aren't sufficient, click the Change Advanced Power Settings option to open the advanced options dialog box shown in Figure 15-23.

Figure 15-23 These advanced options give you incredibly granular control over power management settings in Windows 10.

Inside OUT

Adjust Hibernate options for maximum battery life

To maximize battery life on a portable device, make use of the Hibernate option, which shifts from Sleep mode at an interval you define. Hibernation saves the current state of the system as well as the contents of memory to a hidden file (Hiberfil.sys), and then shuts down the computer. That effectively cuts power use to zero. Resuming from hibernation is much faster than a cold start, and when you resume you're back where you left off, with apps and files open exactly as they were. To adjust this option, open the Advanced Settings dialog box and change the values in the Hibernate After setting under On Battery. Switching from the default 240 minutes to, say, 30 minutes can significantly extend the battery life of a device that you use intermittently.

A new feature in Windows 10, Battery Saver mode, allows you to apply a group of power-saving settings with a single click or tap. Battery Saver mode, which stops many background processes and limits notifications, kicks in automatically when the battery level drops below a predefined threshold; you can also turn on Battery Saver mode manually, even on a device with a fully charged battery, as a preventive measure.

To change settings for this feature (available only on a battery-powered device), search for **Battery Saver** and open the Settings page shown in Figure 15-24. For aggressive management of battery life, set the threshold higher than the default 20 percent. You can also define exceptions for background operation for critical apps.

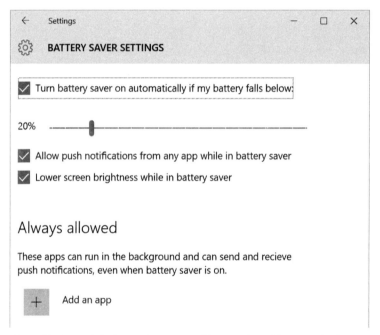

Figure 15-24 By default, your laptop or tablet goes into this aggressive battery-saving mode when your battery drops to 20 percent. You can adjust the settings to be more or less aggressive.

Monitoring and improving system performance

As we noted at the beginning of this chapter, the out-of-the-box performance of a Windows 10 PC should be acceptable, assuming that the device you're using is capable of the work you're asking it to perform. A small tablet with a low-power mobile processor will almost certainly struggle at a processor-intensive task like video processing, for example.

But even a workstation-class PC can perform poorly if you have a problem with a major subsystem or if Windows is configured incorrectly. In our experience, the most common causes of poor performance (in no particular order) are these:

- **Defective hardware.** Memory and disk errors are most obvious when they cause system crashes, but hardware-related problems can also cause performance to drag. Check with your hardware manufacturer to see what diagnostic tools are available.

- **Outdated or flawed device drivers.** PC and device makers are responsible for supplying drivers for the individual hardware components that go into their hardware. If you do a clean install, Windows might install a generic driver instead of one written specifically for that device. We have seen performance problems vanish immediately after a simple driver upgrade. Always be certain you're using the best possible drivers for all system devices. (Don't assume that a newer driver is automatically better than an older one, however; any driver update has the potential to cause new problems.)

- **Inadequate hardware resources.** Windows 10 should perform basic tasks well on even low-end hardware that was designed and built five or more years ago. But more demanding tasks, such as digital media encoding, can push some systems to the breaking point. The performance monitoring tools we identify later in this chapter should help you identify areas where hardware resources are being pushed to the limit.

- **Out-of-control processes or services.** Sometimes, a program or background task that normally runs just fine will spin out of control, consuming up to 100 percent of CPU time or grabbing increasing amounts of memory or other system resources. In the process, of course, performance of all other tasks slows down or grinds to a halt. Knowing how to identify and kill this sort of process or service and prevent it from recurring is a valuable troubleshooting skill.

  ➤ For instructions on how to identify programs that run automatically at startup or when you sign in, see "Managing startup programs and services" earlier in this chapter.

- **Malware.** Viruses, Trojan horse programs, spyware, and other forms of unwanted software can wreak havoc on system performance. Be sure to check for the possibility that malware is present on a system that exhibits otherwise unexplained performance problems.

Windows 10 offers two valuable tools for monitoring the performance of your system in real time. To gain access to these tools, type **resource** in the search box. The two items shown here should appear at the top of the list.

Task Manager has been a mainstay of Windows through many versions. It received a dramatic rewrite in Windows 8, adding detailed performance monitoring tools. For zeroing in on performance issues with even more detail, you can use an advanced tool called Resource Monitor. In combination, these tools allow you to keep an eye on CPU, memory, disk, and network usage, with the ability to isolate troublesome processes. We describe both of these utilities in detail in the following sections.

Monitoring performance with Task Manager

The Performance tab of Task Manager gives you a quick overview of your system's performance as measured in multiple dimensions, including CPU, memory, disk, and network usage. The small thumbnail graphs at the left report current data in real time; clicking any of these thumbnails displays a much larger version, with additional information below the chart. Figure 15-25 shows the performance data for a desktop PC, roughly 30 seconds after opening Task Manager.

The graphs to the right show 60 seconds' worth of data, with updates at one-second intervals. In Figure 15-25, for example, the CPU graph shows a large spike to 100 percent usage (which occurs, ironically, when you open Task Manager), followed by several additional spikes as other activities make demands on the CPU.

Keeping this pane open as you work allows you to see what the impact of a given activity is. For example, you might monitor CPU usage when encoding a video file to see whether the operation pins CPU usage at 100 percent; if so, that might be evidence that you need to upgrade your desktop PC to one with a more powerful CPU that's capable of doing the same work faster, generating less heat and allowing you to do other things while the task completes in the background.

Figure 15-25 The Performance tab of Task Manager gives you a big-picture view of resource usage.

Inside OUT

How long has your PC been running?

Many of the details below the performance graph on the CPU tab in Task Manager are obscure and only of use to developers. You probably don't need to know how many handles are in use by your current workload, for example. But one detail here is interesting as a benchmark of stability. The Up Time measure shows the amount of time that has elapsed, in days, hours, minutes, and seconds, since the machine was last restarted. Thanks to monthly updates that include mandatory restarts, it's unlikely you'll ever see this number go beyond 30 days.

The Memory option offers a snapshot of memory usage, as shown in Figure 15-26. Note that the total amount of memory is visible above the graph, with details about the physical memory itself (number of sticks and slots, for example) below, alongside the amount of RAM in use and the amount available.

Figure 15-26 Use the Memory option on the Performance tab to see how much of your system's RAM is in use. If the value is at 100 percent, it's time to close some apps to improve performance.

On this page, a detailed Memory Composition bar chart appears below the main graph. At first glance, it appears to be just an alternate view of the main Memory Usage chart, but hover the mouse pointer over any segment to see its real purpose. The ScreenTips that appear over each segment explain what each one represents.

The Disk options, likewise, graph the performance of all nonremovable disks on the current system. Each disk gets its own entry on the left side, with details about the selected disk's performance on the right, as shown in Figure 15-27. The top graph depicts the percentage of time the disk is busy processing read or write requests; the bottom graph shows the disk transfer rate.

Figure 15-27 The Disk options in Task Manager let you see the throughput of a fixed disk and determine whether a particular activity is causing a bottleneck.

> ➤ For a discussion of how to use the networking performance information from Task Manager (Ethernet, Wi-Fi, and Bluetooth), see Chapter 5, "Networking essentials."

Inside OUT
What happened to the Windows Experience Index?

Beginning with Windows Vista, Microsoft published a set of numbers purporting to quantify your system's performance in five distinct areas. These numbers were merged into an overall score. In Windows 10, these values are no longer reported on the System Properties page. However, they're still available if you're willing to run the Windows System Assessment Tool (Winsat.exe).

Using WinSAT, as it's known for short, you can run a full performance analysis (type **winsat formal** at an elevated command prompt) or test individual Windows subsystems (type **winsat –?** for the full syntax). You can also save the output as an XML file or redirect the verbal output of the tests to a text file for subsequent review. To see the most recent set of detailed results, type **winsat query** in a Command Prompt window. This report shows the raw test results instead of the Windows Experience Index scores and provides a more detailed look at your system's performance.

Windows keeps a history of WinSAT performance results that you can use for comparisons. You'll find them in %SystemRoot%\Performance\WinSAT\DataStore, each one stamped with the date and time it was run. Minor variations in results between WinSAT runs are normal, and usually occur because of other processes and services interfering with resource usage. Keeping even an informal record of detailed results over time can help you determine whether a significant change in test scores is normal or a sign of a problem to be found and fixed.

Using Resource Monitor to pinpoint performance problems

Like the Performance tab in Task Manager, Resource Monitor gives you both instantaneous and recent-history readouts of key performance metrics. Also like Task Manager, Resource Monitor can show you, in excruciating detail, what each process is doing.

To open Resource Monitor, you can search for it from the Start menu or use its command line, **perfmon /res**, from an elevated Command Prompt window. But the fastest way is to click the link at the bottom of the Task Manager Performance tab. This is, in our opinion, the preferred way to use this utility. Start with a quick overview from Task Manager, and if you need more information call on Resource Monitor. (Note that you must supply administrative credentials to run this tool.)

When you first open Resource Monitor, you see the Overview tab shown in Figure 15-28, which provides both detailed tables and charts that summarize performance in four areas.

Figure 15-28 Use the check boxes in the top section of Resource Monitor to limit the results to a specific process. ScreenTips show details for files that are truncated in the list below.

Tabs along the top of the Resource Monitor window allow you to switch to a different context and focus on a specific type of resource usage. The basic layout of each tab is similar and consists of a handful of common elements.

One or more tables contain details about the resource featured on that tab. The first table on each tab is called the key table; it contains a list of all processes currently using the selected resource, with a check box to the left of each process that allows you to filter the data displayed in additional tables on the tab. The key table at the top of the Overview tab lists all running processes in a display that is similar to the Processes tab of Task Manager.

Resource Monitor is overkill for most performance troubleshooting tasks. But it shines when you want to see exactly which process or file is responsible for an unexplained burst of activity.

CHAPTER 16

Backup, restore, and recovery

In the Unabridged Edition of Murphy's Law, you'll find an entire chapter of corollaries that apply to computers in general and your important data files in particular. Murphy says, "Anything that can go wrong will go wrong." That's certainly true of hard disks and solid state drives (SSDs), where it's not a matter of whether they'll fail but when. When a hard disk fails catastrophically or an SSD suddenly becomes unreadable, any data files on that device are gone, as are your Windows installation and all your apps and settings.

Even if your hardware never lets you down, human error can wreak havoc with data. You can press the wrong key and inadvertently delete a group of files you meant to move. If you're not paying attention, you might absent-mindedly click the wrong button in a dialog box, saving a new file using the same name as an old one, wiping out a week's worth of work in the process.

Some of the most important new features in Windows 10 let you recover quickly from either type of disaster.

In this chapter, we explain how to use the backup tools included with Windows 10, which allow you to prepare for the inevitable day when you need to restore a lost file (or an entire drive's worth of files). We also explain your options for resetting Windows when the operating system becomes damaged, for whatever reason. And finally, we offer a guide to the venerable but still useful System Restore feature.

An overview of Windows 10 backup and recovery options

Through the years, the backup and recovery tools in Windows have evolved, but their fundamental purpose has not changed. How well you execute your backup strategy will determine how easily you're able to get back to where you were after something goes wrong—or to start over with an absolutely clean slate. When you reach into the recovery toolkit, you're hoping to perform one of the following three operations:

- **Full reset.** If you're selling or giving away a PC or other device running Windows 10, you can reset it to a clean configuration, wiping personal files in preparation for the new owner. Some Windows users prefer this sort of clean install when they just want to get a fresh start, minus any cruft from previous installations.

- **Recovery.** The "stuff happens" category includes catastrophic hardware failure, malware infection, and system corruption, as well as performance or reliability problems that can't easily be identified with normal troubleshooting. The recovery process involves reinstalling Windows from a backup image or a recovery drive.

- **File restore.** When (not if) you accidentally delete or overwrite an important data file or (ouch) an entire folder, library, or drive, you can call on a built-in Windows 10 tool to bring back the missing file. This same feature also lets you find and restore earlier versions of a saved file—an original, uncompressed digital photo, for example, or a Word document that contains a section you deleted and now want to revisit.

For quick access to the full range of options available, use the search box. Figure 16-1 shows the results for the keywords **backup** (left) and **recovery** (right).

Figure 16-1 These two sets of search results provide an excellent overview of your backup and recovery options in Windows 10.

In Windows 10, the primary built-in tool for backing up files is called File History. Its job is to save copies of your local files—every hour, if possible—so that you can find and restore your personal documents, pictures, and other data files when you need them.

Inside OUT

Integrating the cloud into your backup strategy

It's tempting to think of OneDrive and other cloud-based storage services as a primary backup. But that strategy is potentially dangerous as well. Cloud services can fail, and online accounts can be compromised. In either case, if your only backup is in the cloud, you risk losing files. And even when you think you have a backup, it might not be what you expect. Your cloud backups of photos, for example, might be converted to a lower resolution than the original images, meaning that your only copy of a priceless photo is an inferior compressed version.

Having a complete archive of files backed up to the cloud does offer the reassurance that you can recover any or all of those saved files in the event of an accident or natural disaster, such as a fire or flood, that wipes out your primary device and its separate local backup. Given the ubiquity and relatively low cost of online storage services, in fact, it's probably prudent to keep copies of important files in two separate cloud-based services. Just remember that those distant archives are not a replacement for comprehensive local backups on an external storage device or a networked PC.

File History was introduced in Windows 8 and has evolved since. Still, it's designed to be simple and not full featured, which is why Windows 10 also includes the old-style Windows 7 Backup And Restore tool. You'll find both backup solutions on the Backup page in Settings, under the Update & Security heading, as shown in Figure 16-2.

Despite its advanced age, the Windows 7 backup tool can still do one impressive digital magic trick that its newer rivals can't: It can create an image of the system drive that can be restored to an exact copy of the original saved volume, complete with Windows, drivers and utilities, desktop programs, settings, and data files. System image backups were once the gold standard of backup and are still a perfect way to capture a known good state for quick recovery.

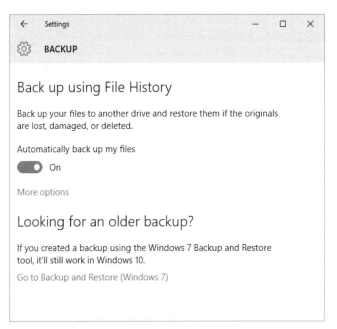

Figure 16-2 Once you've designated an external drive for File History, its controls are deceptively simple. For fine-tuning, click the More Options link.

The disadvantage of a full image backup is that it's fixed at a moment in time and doesn't capture files created, changed, or deleted since the image was created. If your primary data files are located in the cloud or on a separate volume from the system drive, that might not be a problem.

Over the decades, the clean install has taken on almost magical properties among some Windows users. This classic recovery option involves reinstalling Windows from installation media, installing custom drivers, rebuilding connections to network resources, restoring data files, reinstalling apps, and redoing individual preferences. You can still follow that old-school routine, if you're willing to spend the time and energy. But there are faster, easier ways in Windows 10.

In Windows 8, Microsoft formally introduced a "push button reset" feature with two options. Windows 10 simplifies this feature under a single Reset heading, which allows you to reinstall Windows with the option to keep or discard personal data files. This option allows you to reset a misbehaving system on the fly, rolling back with relative ease to a clean, fully updated Windows 10 installation minus any third-party programs or drivers that might be causing problems.

The Recovery page in Settings, which sits alongside Backup in the Update & Security group, gives the Reset option top billing, as shown in Figure 16-3. (The middle option, Go Back To An Earlier Build, is available because this machine is configured to receive preview releases of Windows 10 through the Windows Insider program. If you've upgraded to Windows 10 within the past month, you might see the option to go back to Windows 8.1 or Windows 7 in that middle position.)

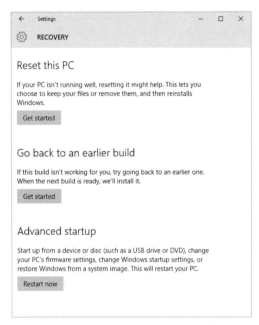

Figure 16-3 All of these recovery options allow you to reinstall Windows to work around performance problems or to get a fresh start.

Windows 10 also includes a built-in option to turn a USB flash drive into a bootable recovery drive. The recovery drive allows you to restore Windows, even after a complete system drive failure.

Inside OUT

Do you need the OEM recovery image?

The Windows 10 Reset feature, in a major change from Windows 8.1, is capable of reinstalling Windows without requiring a recovery partition or any external media. Instead, it uses the existing Windows system files to create a new, clean, side-by-side copy. The result, at least in theory, allows you to recover the sometimes significant disk space used by OEM recovery images.

The OEM image restores the device to its original, factory-installed configuration, complete with custom drivers and utilities as well as bundled (and potentially unwanted) software. Depending on when the machine left the factory, this option is likely to be significantly out of date. Unless you're running short of space for storing data, this partition is worth keeping on any device that's still under warranty.

You can safely remove the OEM recovery image if you are confident that you have a reliable way to restore your system to a clean image (to pass it along to a new owner, for example). Creating your own recovery drive or system image, as we explain in this chapter, fills either bill. Removing the OEM partition might require a trip to the Command Prompt window and some judicious use of the DiskPart utility, as we explain in "Managing disks from the command prompt" in Chapter 14, "Managing disks and drives."

In the remainder of this chapter, we discuss these backup and recovery options in more detail.

Using File History to protect files and folders

As we noted earlier, the File History feature was introduced in Windows 8 as a replacement for the Backup And Restore tool in Windows 7. Although you can delve into advanced settings if you dig deeply enough, File History is designed as a "set it and forget it" feature. After you enable this backup application, it first copies all files in the backup location and then scans the file system at regular intervals (hourly, by default), looking for newly created files and changes to existing files. Copies of each new or changed file are stored on a secondary drive, usually an external device.

You can browse the backed-up files by date and time—or search the entire history—and then restore any or all of those files to their original location or to a different folder.

But first, you have to go through a simple setup process.

Setting up File History

Although the File History feature is installed by default, it's not enabled until you designate a drive to serve as the backup destination. This can be a second internal hard disk or an external storage device, such as an external hard drive, or a network location.

CAUTION

Be sure you specify a File History volume that is on a separate physical drive from the one that contains the files you're backing up. Windows will warn you, sternly, if you try to designate a separate volume on the same physical drive as your system drive. The problem? One sadly common cause of data loss is failure of the drive itself. If the backups and original files are stored on the same drive, a failure wipes everything out. Having backups on a separate physical drive allows them to remain independent.

To turn on File History for the first time, open Settings, and then open the Backup page (under the Update & Security heading). Click Add A Drive to scan for available File History drives. Figure 16-4 shows a system that has a 32-GB external drive available for use as a File History location. Selecting that drive turns on the File History service and begins the hourly backup process.

Figure 16-4 Before you can enable File History, you must specify a drive (preferably external) to hold the backed-up files.

When you first enable File History, it creates a full copy of all files in the locations you've designated for backup. That list contains either the default locations or your customized list (we describe how to create a custom backup list in the next section).

The drive you designate as a File History drive must be either an internal or external hard drive (that category includes SSDs). Removable drives, such as USB flash drives, are not eligible. The File History setup wizard will show you only eligible drives when you set up File History for the first time.

In a home or small office that contains multiple computers, you have the option of specifying a shared network location as the File History location. This option is available only from the classic Control Panel; when prompted to select a File History drive, click the Add Network Location link below the list of available drives and browse to a network share where you have sufficient permissions. The newly added drive (in *servername**sharename* syntax) shows up in the list, as shown in Figure 16-5.

Click to select a shared network drive

Figure 16-5 After you successfully add a network location to File History, its full network path appears in this list of available destinations for saving backup history.

If the drive you select has previously been used as a File History destination, you see one additional choice, as shown in Figure 16-6. After selecting a drive from the list at the top, you can choose an existing backup location. That option is the correct choice if you're reconnecting to a File History drive after successfully restoring Windows 10 and you want your old backups to be available as well.

Figure 16-6 If the volume you select in the list above has already been used for File History, you need to select an existing backup from the list below.

There's nothing complicated or proprietary about File History volumes.

- When you use an external drive, Windows creates a FileHistory folder, with a separate subfolder for each user. Thus, on a device that includes multiple user accounts, each user's files can be backed up separately.

- Within each user's private folder are separate subfolders, one for each device backed up. This folder arrangement allows you to use a single external drive to record File History backups on different devices.

- Each individual backup set includes two folders. The Configuration folder contains XML files and, if necessary, index files to allow speedier searches. The Data folder contains backed-up files, which are stored in a hierarchy that matches their original location.

- Backed-up files are not compressed. File names are the same as the original, with a date and time stamp appended (in parentheses) to distinguish different versions. As a result, you can browse a File History drive in File Explorer and use search tools to locate a file or folder without using the File History app.

CAUTION

Files stored on a File History drive are not encrypted by default. Anyone who has physical possession of the drive can freely read any files stored there. If you're concerned about confidential information contained in an external File History drive, we recommend that you encrypt the drive (see "Encrypting with BitLocker and BitLocker To Go" in Chapter 7, "Securing Windows 10 devices," for detailed instructions). As an alternative, consider saving File History to a shared network folder for which you have appropriate permissions.

File History is yet another example of a feature caught in the transition from the classic Windows Control Panel to the new Settings app. The overlap between old interface and new is more pronounced here than elsewhere. From the old Control Panel or the new Settings app, you can select a File History drive or change the backup interval and time period for saving backups. The latter two options, identical in effect but different in appearance, are shown here.

By default, File History checks your designated drives and folders once an hour, saving copies of any new or changed files as part of the operation. You can adjust this setting in either direction, choosing from nine intervals that range from every 10 minutes (if you really hate the idea of ever losing a saved file) to once daily.

File History backups are saved by default forever (you receive a warning when your File History drive is full), although you can alter the Keep Saved Versions setting to 1, 3, 6, or 9 months or 1 or 2 years. The set-it-and-forget-it Until Space Is Needed setting allows File History to automatically jettison old backups to make way for new ones when the drive is full.

As you can see, the options in Settings and Control Panel overlap but aren't identical. As of the initial release of Windows 10, for example, the options to share a File History drive with others in a homegroup and to quickly view File History event logs are available only in the Advanced Settings section of the classic Control Panel.

TROUBLESHOOTING

Some files are missing from File History backups

Because of the unique way that File History organizes and names backed-up files, you might find that some files aren't backed up properly. The most common cause occurs when appending a version date and time to the name of a file. The addition of those 26 characters can cause the file name in the File History folder to exceed the maximum path limit of 260 characters. That situation is most likely to occur when a file is deeply nested inside multiple subfolders. You can spot these errors easily in the File History event logs and resolve them by moving the original files or subfolders to a location with a path name that's sufficiently shorter.

Choosing locations to back up

By default, File History backs up all folders in the current user profile (including those created by third-party apps) as well as the contents of local folders that have been added to custom libraries.

> ➤ For an overview of what's in a default user profile and instructions on how to work with libraries, see Chapter 12, "Organizing and searching for files."

To manage the list of folders backed up by File History, open the Backup page in Settings (under the Update & Security category) and then click More Options. Scroll down to view the folder list on the Backup Options page, as shown in Figure 16-7.

To remove any folder from this list, select its name and then click or tap Remove. To add a folder from any local drive, click or tap Add A Folder and then select the location using the Select Folder dialog box.

NOTE

Although the OneDrive folder is included by default in the list of folders to be backed up by File History, only files that are synced to the local drive are actually backed up.

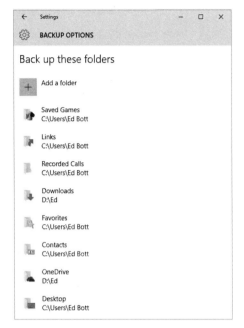

Figure 16-7 Individual profile folders relocated to a separate drive (as with the Downloads and OneDrive folders here) are automatically backed up by File History.

At the end of the list is an Exclude These Folders option, shown in Figure 16-8. It's useful when you want to avoid filling your File History drive with large files that don't require backing up. If you routinely put interesting but ephemeral video files into a subfolder in your Downloads folder, you might choose to exclude that Videos subfolder completely from File History, while leaving the rest of the Downloads folder to be backed up.

When a File History drive fills up, you can either change the settings to remove old backed-up files and make room for new ones or swap in a new drive. If you choose the latter option, click or tap the Stop Using Drive button on the Backup Options page, remove the old drive, and set up the new one.

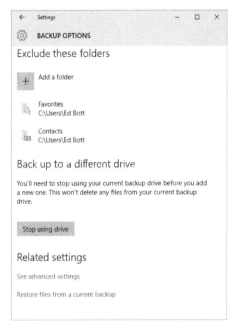

Figure 16-8 These File History options allow you to exclude folders that are part of a folder that would otherwise be backed up. The Stop Using Drive button lets you switch to a new File History drive.

Restoring files and folders

To find and restore a backed-up file, folder, or drive, you can use File Explorer or the File History app (C:\Windows\System32\FileHistory.exe).

The File Explorer option is the simplest way to locate a previous version of a file you've been working on, or to restore the contents of a folder as it existed at a specific date and time in the past.

Details of each previously saved copy are stored on the Previous Versions tab in the properties dialog box for a file, folder, or drive. To view this tab, open File Explorer, right-click the item whose history you want to inspect, and then click Restore Previous Versions. Figure 16-9 shows the history of an Excel spreadsheet with 10 saved versions from the previous week available.

Figure 16-9 The properties dialog box for any file, folder, or drive lists available File History back-ups here. Open the file to see a read-only copy, or use the Restore To option to save a copy of the selected version in a safe location, without disturbing the current version.

From the Previous Versions tab, you can take any of the following actions:

- **Open.** This command works only with files, opening a read-only copy of the document in the application associated with that file type. The file name in the title bar includes the File History date and time stamp. Note that this command has no effect on folders and drives.

- **Open In File History.** Click the arrow to the right of the Open command to choose this option, which displays the current selection (file, folder, or drive) in the File History app. (We describe this app's workings shortly.)

- **Restore.** Click this option to restore the selected version to its original location. If the original file still exists, you'll see the Replace Or Skip Files dialog box, which gives you an opportunity to change your mind or save the new file as a copy in the same location. (If you want to restore a copy without deleting the original, click Compare Info For Both Files and then select the check box for both the original file and the restored previous version. The restored copy will have a number appended to the name to distinguish it from the original.)

- **Restore To.** Click the arrow to the right of the Restore command to choose this option, which allows you to save a backed-up file in a location of your choice. This option is handy when you want to keep the current version of the file, perhaps to add material to it from the restored file.

The File History app offers a distinctly different take on browsing backup files. Although it resembles File Explorer in some respects, it adds a unique dimension—the ability to choose a set of saved files from a specific date and time to scan, scroll through, or search.

You can start the File History app in several ways:

- From the Settings app, look for Restore Files From A Current Backup, at the bottom of the Backup Options page.

- Using the classic Control Panel, open File History and click Restore Personal Files in the links at the left of the settings.

- From File Explorer, open the Previous Versions tab for a folder and then click Open With File History.

Figure 16-10 shows the File History app, which has an address bar, navigation controls, and a search box along the top, very much like File Explorer. What's different are the time stamp (above the file browsing window) and three controls (below the window) that allow time control without the need for flux capacitors or other imaginary time-machine components.

Address bar   Search box   Folders and libraries
                                         selected for backup

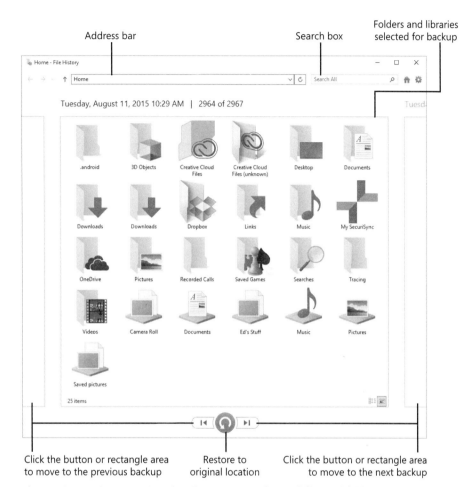

Click the button or rectangle area   Restore to   Click the button or rectangle area
to move to the previous backup   original location   to move to the next backup

Figure 16-10 In its Home view, the File History app shows all files and folders set for regular backup. Scroll left for older files, right for more recent backups.

As with File Explorer, you can use the search box in the upper right to narrow the results by file type, keyword, or file contents. Because file names rarely provide enough detail to determine whether a specific file is the one you're looking for, File History has a preview function. Click a file to show its contents in the File History window. Figure 16-11 shows one such preview of a PowerPoint presentation, with the full path and filename in the address bar and a scroll bar along the right for moving through the document in the preview window.

The option to restore entire folders is especially useful when you're switching to a new PC. After you complete one last backup on your old PC, plug the File History drive into your new

PC, and then use the big green Restore button to copy your backed-up files to corresponding locations on the new PC.

Figure 16-11 File History is capable of previewing most popular file types, including images, PDF files, and Office documents like this PowerPoint presentation.

As with File Explorer, you can change the view of files in the File History browsing window. Two shortcuts in the lower right corner allow you to quickly switch to Details or Large Icons view, although you have a total of eight predefined views, available from the well-hidden shortcut menu shown in Figure 16-12.

Inside OUT

Transfer your File Explorer smarts to File History

There's no need to open a menu or click a tiny icon to change the view in File History. Any of the eight predefined views, from Content through Extra Large Icons, can be invoked with its keyboard shortcut, Ctrl+Shift+*number*. Any number between 1 and 8 works, with Ctrl+Shift+2 switching to Large Icons view and Ctrl+Shift+6 to Details view. These same shortcuts work in File Explorer as well.

Figure 16-12 The gear icon in the upper right corner of the File History app leads to a menu with eight view settings. Details view (top) and Large Icons (bottom) work the same as in File Explorer.

Using the Reset option to recover from serious problems

One of the signature features of Windows 8 was a feature that turned out to be quietly revolutionary: a way for any user, even those without technical skills, to reset Windows to its original configuration using a Refresh or Reset command.

Windows 10 significantly refines that capability under a single Reset command. The most important change eliminates the need to have a disk-hogging OEM recovery image in a dedicated partition at the end of the hard drive. In Windows 10, that recovery image and its associated partition are no longer required. Instead, Windows 10 accomplishes recovery operations by rebuilding the operating system to a clean state using existing system files.

This push-button reset option has the same effect as a clean install, without the hassles of finding drivers and without wiping out potentially valuable data. The Reset This PC option is at the top of the list on the Recovery page in Settings, as shown earlier in Figure 16-3. It's also the featured choice on the Troubleshoot menu when you restart in the Windows Recovery Environment, as shown in Figure 16-13.

Figure 16-13 You can reset your Windows 10 PC by starting the Windows Recovery Environment and choosing the top option shown here.

When you reset a PC, Windows 10 and its drivers are restored to the most recent rollup state. The reset PC includes all updates except those installed in the last 28 days, a design that allows recovery to succeed when a freshly installed update is part of the problem.

For PCs sold with Windows 10 already installed, any customized settings and desktop programs installed by the manufacturer are restored with the Windows 10 reset. These customizations are saved in a separate container, which is created as part of the OEM setup process.

All Windows apps included with Windows 10 by default (Photos, Weather, Groove Music, and Mail and Calendar, for example) are restored, along with any Windows apps that were added to the system by the OEM or as part of an enterprise deployment. App updates are downloaded and reinstalled via the Store automatically after recovery.

Windows desktop programs are not restored and must be manually reinstalled. Likewise, any previously purchased Windows apps are discarded and must be reinstalled from the Store.

Resetting a PC isn't something you do accidentally. The process involves multiple confirmations, with many opportunities to bail out if you get cold feet or realize that you need to do just *one* more backup before you irrevocably wipe the disk. The first step offers you the option to keep your personal files or remove everything, as shown in Figure 16-14.

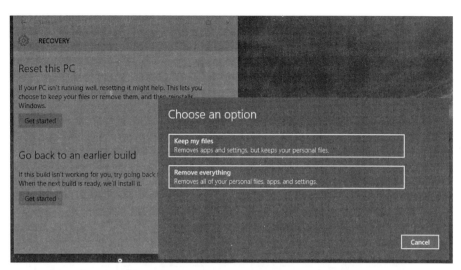

Figure 16-14 The Reset This PC option lets you choose whether to keep files for all user accounts or remove everything and start with a completely clean slate.

The Remove Everything option removes all user data, including user accounts, apps, and personalization settings. This option is useful when you plan to sell or give away an existing PC.

If the system contains multiple volumes that are visible in File Explorer, such as a dedicated data volume or an OEM-created utility partition, you're given the option to wipe all drives clean or just the system drive, as shown in Figure 16-15.

Figure 16-15 If you're resetting a PC because you plan to give it away or sell it, choose the All Drives option here; reset only the Windows system drive if you have a secondary drive that contains valuable data files.

The reset process also includes an option to scrub data from the drive so that it cannot easily be recovered using disk utilities. As the explanatory text in Figure 16-16 makes clear, the Remove Files And Clean The Drive option can add hours to the process. Note that this option, while thorough, is not certified to meet any government or industry standards for data removal.

Figure 16-16 Choose the first option if you're resetting a PC for a trusted friend or family member to use. The second option might be worth the time if your PC was used for work or contained sensitive information.

If you've made it this far through the process, you have only one more confirmation to get through. That dialog box shows the choices you've made, with one last Cancel option. To plunge irreversibly ahead, click Reset, shown in Figure 16-17.

The fresh recovery image is applied to the newly cleaned Windows partition, and a new Boot Configuration Data store is created on the system partition. After the PC restarts, each user must go through the standard procedures for setting up the PC and creating a new user account, a process formally known as the out-of-box experience (OOBE) phase.

Figure 16-17 This is your last chance to back out when resetting a PC.

The reset option is a tremendous time-saver, but it's not all-powerful. Your attempts to reset Windows can be thwarted by a handful of scenarios:

- If operating system files have been heavily corrupted or infected by malware, the reset process will probably not work.

- If the problem is caused by a cumulative update that is more than 28 days old, the reset might not be able to avoid that problem.

- If a user chooses the wrong language during the OOBE phase on a single-language Windows version (typically sold in developing countries and regions), a complete reinstallation might be required.

If the reset option doesn't work, it might be time for a more drastic solution: reinstalling with the assistance of a recovery drive.

Creating and using a recovery drive

If you upgraded to Windows 10 over an existing copy of Windows 8.1 or Windows 7, the one thing you didn't get out of the deal was a shiny disk. Relax—you don't need it. Windows 10 includes the capability to turn a USB flash drive into a recovery drive that you can use to perform repairs or completely reinstall Windows.

The Recovery Media Creator (C:\Windows\System32\RecoveryDrive.exe) creates a bootable drive that contains the Windows Recovery Environment. If you select the Back Up System Files To The Recovery Drive option, as shown in Figure 16-18, the utility creates a bootable drive that can be used to fully restore Windows, skipping most of the setup process.

Figure 16-18 You'll typically need a USB flash drive with a capacity of at least 8 GB to create a recovery drive that includes backed-up system files.

Inside OUT

Turn a recovery drive into installation media

The Recovery Media Creator creates a FAT32-formatted drive that's fully capable of booting and installing Windows 10. In fact, you can use that drive as a shortcut to turn an ISO file, such as those available to MSDN subscribers, into a full-fledged Windows installer. Skip the option to back up system files to the recovery drive. Open the newly created recovery drive in one File Explorer window. Double-click the ISO file to mount it as a virtual drive in a separate File Explorer window and then copy the entire contents of the mounted ISO drive by dragging them to the recovery drive, overwriting any existing files. The resulting drive can be used for clean installs on any PC.

To use the recovery drive, configure your PC so that you can boot from the USB flash drive. (That process, which is unique for many machines, might involve tapping a key or pressing a combination of buttons such as Power+Volume Up when restarting.)

If you see the Recover From A Drive option selected as shown here, congratulations—the system recognized your recovery drive and you are (fingers crossed) a few minutes away from being back in business.

Creating and restoring a system image backup

Windows 10 includes the Windows Backup program (Sdclt.exe) originally released as part of Windows 7. Its feature set is basically the same as its predecessor, and it's included primarily for compatibility with backups created using that older operating system.

If you have a working backup routine based on the Windows 7 Backup program, we don't want to stand in your way. The version included with Windows 10 does all the familiar tasks you depend on, and we suggest you carry on. After all, the best backup program is the one you use.

For Windows 10, there are better backup utilities, but we continue to recommend the Windows Backup program for the one task it does exceptionally well: Use it to make a system image backup that can re-create a complete PC configuration, using a single drive or multiple drives. Restoring that system image creates a perfect copy of the system configuration as it existed on the day that system image was captured.

You don't need to install, update, and activate Windows, reinstall all your applications, and then configure your applications to work the way you like; instead, you boot into the Windows Recovery Environment, choose an image file to restore, and then complete the process by restoring from your latest file backup, which is likely to be more recent than the image. The image files that Windows Backup creates are largely hardware independent, which means that—with some limitations—you can restore your backup image to a new computer of a different brand and type. (Just be prepared to jump through some activation hoops on the new PC.)

Inside OUT

Use a system image to save your custom configuration

The single greatest use for a system image backup is to clean up an OEM configuration, leaving Windows intact, removing unwanted software, and installing your favorite apps. Being able to return to a baseline configuration quickly is a trick that IT pros learned long ago, as a way of deploying Windows in large organizations. By mastering the system image backup feature, you can accomplish the same result even in an environment with a few PCs instead of a thousand.

Creating a system image backup

Type **backup** in the search box to find the Windows 7 Backup And Restore tool, shown in Figure 16-19.

Figure 16-19 The vintage Windows 7 backup tool isn't necessary for file backup tasks, but it's ideal for capturing a complete image of a Windows installation for disaster recovery.

NOTE

When you first open Windows Backup, a message alerts you that the program has not been set up. You can ignore the Set Up Backup link forever if you simply want to create a system image backup (an excellent idea if you just finished performing a clean installation with all your drivers and programs installed and ready to use). Click the Create A System Image link in the left pane.

Ignore the options in the center of that window and instead click the Create A System Image link at the left side of the window. That opens the efficient Create A System Image Wizard. The first step asks you to define a destination for your system image, as shown in Figure 16-20.

Figure 16-20 The best location for a system image backup is an external hard disk. Avoid the DVD option.

The ideal destination for a system image backup is a local hard disk, internal or external. If the Windows Backup program detects a drive that qualifies, it suggests that destination in the list of hard disks at the top of the dialog box.

The second option lets you choose a DVD writer as the target for the backup operation. You'll need to supply two, three, and maybe more blank discs to store the image backup. Although this option might have made sense in a bygone era, it's downright quaint today. Most new PCs don't even include a DVD drive, making backups stored on that media inconvenient at best and potentially useless. Even when a DVD drive is available, a single corrupted disc in the series can ruin the whole backup.

TROUBLESHOOTING

Windows Backup says your drive is not a valid location

If you try to choose a removable drive that is not a hard drive, such as a USB flash drive or SD card, Windows Backup will return this error message: "The drive is not a valid backup location." In its conventional backup role, Windows Backup can save data files on just about any storage medium. System image backups, however, must be saved on a hard disk, a DVD, or a network location.

When you create a system image backup, the resulting image file stores the complete contents of all selected drives during its first backup. If the backup target is a local (internal or external) hard drive, subsequent backup operations store only new and changed data. Therefore, the subsequent, incremental backup operation typically runs much faster, depending on how much data has been changed or added since the previous image backup operation.

If you choose a shared network folder as the backup destination, you can save only one image backup. Any subsequent image backup wipes out the previous image backup.

Inside OUT

Save multiple image backups on a network

If you specify a shared network folder as the destination for an image backup, beware of the consequences if you try to reuse that location for a subsequent backup of the same computer. If the backup operation fails for any reason, the older backup will be overwritten, but the newer backup will not be usable. In other words, you'll have no backup.

You can avoid this risk by creating a new subfolder in the shared network folder to hold each new image backup. The disadvantage, of course, is that each image file will occupy as much space as the original disk, unlike an incremental image backup on an external hard drive, which stores only the changed data.

If you have multiple hard drives, Windows displays a dialog box like the one shown in Figure 16-21, in which you choose the volumes you want to include in the backup. By default, any volume that contains Windows system files is selected. If other drives are available, you can optionally choose to include them in the image backup as well.

Figure 16-21 The Windows boot volume (indicated by the logo on the drive icon) and other system volumes must be included in a system image. Other volumes, such as a dedicated data drive, are optional.

The disk space requirements for an image-based backup can be substantial, especially on a well-used system that includes lots of user data files. Windows Backup estimates the amount of disk space the image will use (as shown in Figure 16-21) and will warn you if the destination you choose doesn't have sufficient free disk space.

After you confirm your settings, click Start Backup to begin the process of building and saving your image.

System images are stored in virtual hard disk (.vhd) format. Although the data is not compressed, it is compact because the image file does not include the hard drive's unused space and some other unnecessary files, such as hibernation files, page files, and restore points. Incremental system image backups on a local drive are not written to a separate folder. Instead, new and updated files (actually, the changed blocks in those files) are written to the same .vhd file. The older blocks are stored as shadow copies in the .vhd file, allowing you to restore any previous version.

The final step of the image backup process offers to help you create a system repair disc on a writable CD or DVD. This option might be useful for an older PC, but it's redundant if you've already created a recovery drive as described in the previous section.

Restoring a system image backup

The system image capabilities in Windows Backup are intended for creating an emergency recovery kit for a single PC. In that role, they function exceptionally well. If your hard drive fails catastrophically, or if you want to wipe your existing Windows installation and start with a clean custom image you created a few weeks or months ago, you've come to the right place.

Your options (and potential gotchas) become more complex if you want to use these basic image backup and restore tools to work with a complex set of physical disks and partitions, especially if the disk layout has changed from the time you created the original image.

In this chapter, we assume that you have created an image backup of your system disk and want to restore it to a system that is essentially the same (in terms of hardware and disk layout) as the one you started with. In that case, you can restart your computer using a recovery drive or a Windows 10 installation drive and then choose the Repair Your Computer option.

Choose Advanced Options and then select System Image Recovery, as shown in Figure 16-22.

Figure 16-22 Booting into the Windows Recovery Environment allows you to wipe the current device clean and replace its contents with a saved system image backup.

If the backup deities are smiling, you should see the dialog box shown here. Assuming that Windows recognized the drive containing your system image backup, your most recent system image backup should be available in the first (recommended) option.

If you're restoring the most recent image backup to the same system on which it was originally created and the backup is stored on an external hard drive attached to the computer, your job is easy. The latest system image should be available for your selection. Verify that the date and time and other details of the image match the one you want to restore, and then click Next to continue.

If the image file you're planning to restore from is on a network share or if you want to use a different image, choose Select A System Image and then click Next. You'll see a dialog box that lists additional image files available on local drives. Select the correct file, and click Next to select an image created on a specific date if more than one is available. If the image file you're looking for is in a shared network folder, click the Advanced button and then click Search For A System Image On The Network. Enter the network location that contains your saved image, along with a user name and password that have authorized access to that location.

Restoring an image backup completely replaces the current contents of each volume in the image file. The restore program offers to format the disk or disks to which it is restoring files before it begins the restore process; if you have multiple drives or volumes and you're nervous about wiping out valuable data files, it offers an option to exclude certain disks from formatting.

The important point to recognize about restoring a system image is that it replaces the current contents of system volumes with the exact contents that existed at the time of the image backup you select. That means your Windows system files and registry will be returned to health (provided the system was in good shape when you performed your most recent backup and that no hardware-related issues have cropped up since then). Whatever programs were installed when you backed up your system will be restored entirely. All other files on the restored disk, including your documents, will also be returned to their prior states, and any changes made after your most recent backup will be lost.

CAUTION

If you keep your documents on the same volume as your system files, restoring a system image is likely to entail the loss of recent work—unless, of course, you have an up-to-date file backup or you have the good fortune to have made an image backup almost immediately before your current troubles began. The same is true if you save documents on a volume separate from your system files but have included that data volume in your image backup. If you have documents that have not been backed up, you can avoid losing recent work by copying them to a disk that will not be affected by the restore process—a USB flash drive, for example, or some other form of removable media. You can use the Command Prompt option in the Windows Recovery Environment to copy these documents. (For details about using the Command Prompt option, see "Working at the Command Prompt" in Chapter 21, "Working with Command Prompt and Windows Powershell.") If you do have a recent file backup, you can restore files after you have restored the image backup and your system is running again.

NOTE

The main hardware limitation for restoring a system image backup is that the target computer must have at least as many hard drives as the source system, and each drive must be at least as big as its corresponding drive in the source system. This means, for example, that you can't restore a system image from a system that has a 500-GB hard drive to a system with a 256-GB SSD, even if the original system had far less than 256 GB of data on its drive. Keep in mind also that on a system with multiple hard drives, the BIOS determines which one is the bootable drive, and this is the one on which Windows will restore the image of your system volume. (You have no choice in the matter, aside from reconnecting the drives or, if your BIOS permits it, selecting a different bootable drive.)

If your new computer meets the space requirements, restoring a system image should work. This is true even when the source and target computers use different disk controllers. Similarly, other differences—such as different graphics cards, audio cards, processors, and so on—shouldn't prevent you from restoring a system image to a different computer, because hardware drivers are isolated from the rest of the image information and are rebuilt as part of the restore process.

TROUBLESHOOTING

Your backup folders are "empty"

If you use File Explorer to browse to the folder containing your system image backup, when you rest the mouse pointer over a folder name, the pop-up tip might identify it as an "Empty folder." Alarmed, you right-click the folder and choose Properties, only to find that the folder apparently contains 0 bytes, 0 files, and 0 folders. Don't worry. This is the normal condition when your backups are stored on an NTFS volume because, by default, only the System user account has permission to view the files. (That's a reasonable security and reliability precaution, which prevents you or another user from inadvertently deleting a key backup file.) If you're confident of your ability to work safely with backup files in their native format, the solution is simple: Double-click the folder name. Follow the prompts, including a User Account Control (UAC) consent dialog box, to permanently add your user account to the folder's permissions list, giving you Full Control access to the folder.

Configuring system protection options

The System Restore feature has been part of Windows since the turn of the twenty-first century. It's a relatively minor part of the recovery toolkit now, but it can be useful for quickly undoing recent changes that introduced instability. When System Restore is enabled, the Volume Shadow Copy service takes occasional snapshots of designated local storage volumes. These snapshots occur before Windows Update installs new updates and when supported software installers run. The snapshots can also be created manually—a sensible precaution before making any system-level changes.

System Restore snapshots make note of differences in the details of your system configuration—registry settings, driver files, third-party applications, and so on—allowing you to undo changes and roll back a system configuration to a time when it was known to work correctly.

NOTE

In Windows 7, the volume snapshots created by System Restore also included a record of changes to data files on designated drives, allowing you to restore previous versions of those data files. In Windows 10, this capability has been moved into the File History feature, which we describe in detail earlier in this chapter.

It's worth noting that System Restore monitors all files that it considers system-related, which includes executable files and installers. If you downloaded the latest version of a favorite utility and stored it in your Downloads folder, it would be removed if you rolled back to a System Restore checkpoint from before it was downloaded.

Inside OUT

What's in a restore point?

Restore points in Windows 10 include a full copy of the registry at the time of the snapshot as well as information about changes made to specific files on that volume since the previous snapshot was created. Historically, files are monitored if they include any of 250+ file name extensions specifically designated for monitoring. This list (which cannot be modified) contains many file types that are clearly programs and system files, with extensions such as .exe, .dll, and .vbs. But it also includes other files that you might not think of as system files, including .inf and .ini, and some that are truly head-scratchers, such as .d01 through .d05 and .d32. (Apparently .d06 through .d31 are unmonitored.) The entire list is available at *bit.ly/restore-points-windows*. It's most useful for programmers and system administrators, but you might want to take a look at it if you're curious why System Restore deleted a file.

To check the status of System Protection, open System in Control Panel and click the System Protection link in the left pane. (To go directly to the System Properties dialog box, click Start, type **systempropertiesprotection**, and press Enter.) The resulting dialog box, shown in Figure 16-23, lists all available NTFS-formatted drives (internal and external). The value under Protection Settings indicates whether restore points are being created automatically for each drive.

Using the System Properties dialog box, you can enable or disable automatic monitoring for any local drive. By design, system protection is fully enabled for the system drive and is disabled for all other local drives.

You can also manually create a restore point at any time for all drives that have system protection enabled. Click the Create button at the bottom of the System Protection tab to open the Create A Restore Point dialog box shown in Figure 16-24. Enter a meaningful description (you can't leave the box blank, although you can tap the Spacebar to leave that box effectively blank) and then click Create to enter the descriptive text.

Figure 16-23 By default, System Restore monitors changes to the system drive. Select another drive and click Configure to enable System Protection for that drive.

Figure 16-24 When you create a restore point manually, you're required to enter a description that will help you identify it later.

To turn system protection on or to adjust the amount of space it uses, select a drive from the Available Drives list and then click Configure. That opens the dialog box shown in Figure 16-25.

Figure 16-25 Use this slider to adjust the amount of disk space used by System Restore snapshots.

The information under the Disk Space Usage heading shows both the current usage and the maximum amount of space that will be used for snapshots before System Protection begins deleting old restore points to make room for new ones. Microsoft has not yet published its rules for how it reserves space for system protection in Windows 10. In our tests, we typically see this value set to 5 percent of the disk, up to a maximum of 10 GB, on volumes that are larger than 64 GB.

To adjust the maximum amount of disk space available for volume snapshots, click the System Protection tab in the System Properties dialog box, select a drive letter from the list of available drives, click Configure, and move the Max Usage slider to the value you prefer. For drives greater than 64 GB in size, you can choose any value between 1 percent and 100 percent.

If you're concerned about disk space usage and you're confident that you won't need to use any of your currently saved restore points, you can click the Delete button under the Disk Space Usage heading to remove all existing restore points without changing other System Protection settings.

NOTE

The default location for System Restore data is *d*:\System Volume Information, where *d* is the letter of each drive. Each restore point is stored in its own subfolder, under a name that includes a unique 32-character alphanumeric identifier called a GUID. This location cannot be changed. On an NTFS drive, these files are not accessible to users, even those in the Administrators group; the default NTFS permissions grant access only to the System account, and there is no easy way to view these files or to take ownership of them (nor should you even consider doing so, as these data structures are not intended for use by anything other than a program working through tightly controlled application programming interfaces).

Rolling back to a previous restore point

After you configure System Protection, it runs silently and automatically, making as-needed snapshots of your system configuration. In this section, we explain how to make use of those snapshots.

The System Restore utility provides controlled access to snapshots created by the System Protection feature. It can't perform miracles—it won't bring a dead hard drive back to life, unfortunately—but it can be a lifesaver in any of the following situations:

- You install a program that conflicts with other software or drivers on your system. If uninstalling the program doesn't cure the problem, you can restore your system configuration to a point before you installed the program. That should remove any problematic files or registry settings that were left behind by the uninstaller.

- You install one or more updated drivers that cause performance or stability problems. Rather than using the Roll Back Driver command in Device Manager, use System Restore to replace the new, troublesome driver (or drivers) with those that were in place the last time you saved a restore point.

- Your system develops performance or stability problems for no apparent reason. This scenario is especially likely if you share a computer with other family members or coworkers who have administrator accounts and are in the habit of casually installing untested, incompatible software and drivers. If you know the system was working properly on a certain date, you can use a restore point from that date, undoing potentially harmful changes made since then and, if all goes well, returning your system to proper operation.

CAUTION

Don't count on System Restore to protect you from viruses, worms, Trojan horses, and other malware. Use Windows Defender or a reliable and up-to-date third-party antivirus program.

The quickest way to get to System Restore is to type **rstrui** at a command prompt. You can also click System Restore on the System Protection tab of the System Properties dialog box to find this well-hidden feature.

If you're running under a standard user account, you'll need to enter an administrator's credentials in a UAC dialog box to continue.

When the System Restore wizard appears, it might recommend the most recent restore point. To see a complete list of available restore points, select Choose A Different Restore Point and click Next. That displays a list of recent restore points, as shown in Figure 16-26.

Figure 16-26 You must select the check box at the bottom of this dialog box to see more than the five most recent restore points.

If the restore point you're looking for is older than the oldest entry in the list, select Show More Restore Points to see the full list.

What impact will your choice of restore points have? To see a full list of programs and drivers that will be deleted or restored, select the restore point you're planning to use, and then click Scan For Affected Programs. That displays a dialog box like the one shown in Figure 16-27, highlighting every change you've made since that restore point was created. (Note that this list does not warn you about any executable files that might be deleted from your Desktop, Downloads, or other folders).

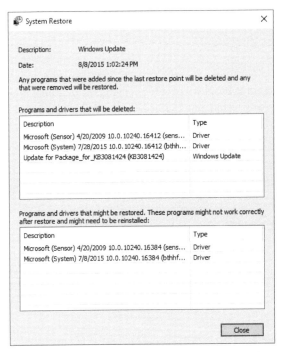

Figure 16-27 Look at this report before using System Restore to roll back to an earlier configuration so that you know what changes the operation will make.

After selecting a restore point, click Next to display a series of confirmation dialog boxes, including the one in Figure 16-28. After successfully convincing the system that, yes, you really want to do this, it creates a new restore point and then begins replacing system files and registry settings with those in the previous restore point you selected. As part of the restore process, your computer will restart and various messages will appear, all counseling you to be patient and not to interfere with the goings-on.

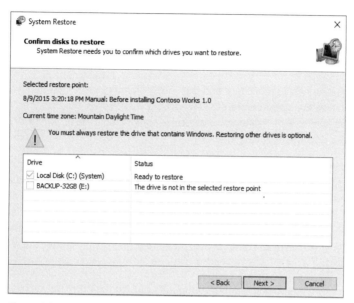

Figure 16-28 Review the descriptions carefully as you prepare to roll back to a previous restore point. After you begin the System Restore operation, it cannot be interrupted.

When System Restore reinstates a previously saved configuration using a restore point, your data files—documents, pictures, music files, and the like—are not tampered with in any way. (The only exception is if you or a program created or saved a file using file name extensions from the list of monitored extensions, as described in the previous section.) Before System Restore begins the process of returning your system to a previous restore point, it creates a new restore point—making it possible for you to return to the present if this time machine doesn't meet your expectations.

When the process is complete, do some testing to see whether the restoration fixed the problem you were encountering. If it has not and you want to return the system to the state it was in before you restored it, retrace your steps to System Restore. At or near the top of the list of available restore points, you will find one labeled Undo: Restore Operation. Choose that one and you're back where you started.

System Restore do's and don'ts

You don't have to be a science-fiction aficionado to appreciate the hazards of time travel. Here are some to be aware of:

- If you create a new user account and then use System Restore to roll back your system configuration to a point before the new account was created, the new user will no longer be able to sign in, and you will receive no warning. (The good news is that the new user's documents will be intact.)

- System Restore does not uninstall programs, although it does remove executable files, dynamic-link libraries (DLLs), and registry entries created by the installer. To avoid having orphaned program shortcuts and files, view the list of programs and drivers that will be affected when you return to the restore point you're about to roll back to. If you don't want the program anymore, uninstall it in the normal way before running the restore operation. If you want to continue using the program, reinstall it after the restore is complete.

- Any changes made to your system configuration using the Windows Recovery Environment are not monitored by System Protection. This can produce unintended consequences if you make major changes to system files and then roll back your system configuration with System Restore.

- Although you can restore your system to a previously saved restore point from the Windows Recovery Environment, you cannot create a new restore point from that location. As a result, you cannot undo a restore operation that you perform by starting from the Windows Recovery Environment. You should use System Restore in this mode only if you are unable to start Windows normally to perform a restore operation.

As they say, stuff happens. That might not be exactly how the famous quote goes, but it's certainly true whenever hardware and software are involved.

Although Windows has generally become more stable and reliable over time, it will never be perfect. Apps hang (stop responding) or crash (shut down unexpectedly). Once in a while, a feature of Windows walks off the job without warning. And on rare occasions, the grim BSOD ("blue screen of death," more formally known as a Stop error or bugcheck) arrives, bringing your whole system to a halt.

In a fully debugged, perfect world, such occurrences would never darken your computer screen. But you don't live there, and neither do we. So the prudent course is to prepare for the unexpected. That starts with making regular backups, of course, along with system restore points. But it also entails learning to use the many tools that Windows provides for diagnosing errors and recovering from problems. Those tools are the subject of this chapter.

> ➤ For information about creating regular backups and image backups as well as information about system restore points, see Chapter 16, "Backup, restore, and recovery."

Getting to know your troubleshooting toolkit

As any detective will tell you, solving a mystery requires evidence. If your mystery involves inexplicably slow performance or crashes, you have several places to look for clues.

Built-in troubleshooters

The most obvious first step on the road to resolving performance issues is the aptly named Troubleshooting section in the classic Control Panel. By default, it displays a list of the most commonly used troubleshooters included with Windows 10, as shown in Figure 17-1.

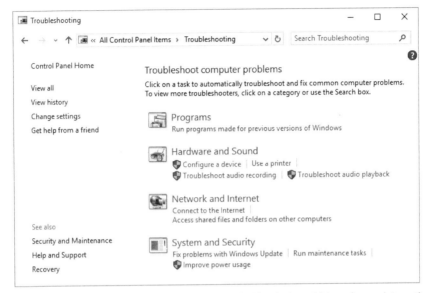

Figure 17-1 Each of the troubleshooters included with Windows 10 launches an interactive problem-solving tool that steps you through diagnosis and resolution of common problems.

Click the View All link on the left of the Troubleshooting page to see an expanded list that includes modules for fixing more esoteric problems, such as issues with search and indexing or with the Background Intelligent Transfer Service.

There's nothing magical about any of these troubleshooters. Their purpose is to ensure that you check the most common causes of problems, including some that might seem obvious (Is the network cable plugged in? Is the printer turned on?). Running a troubleshooter can result in easy fixes for some issues; more importantly, it establishes a baseline for further troubleshooting.

A troubleshooter might lead you through several steps and ask you to check settings or connections. At the end, it displays its results, which include a View Detailed Information link that displays a troubleshooting report similar to the one shown in Figure 17-2.

Figure 17-2 The troubleshooting report lists issues and indicates whether they were fixed. Click the Detection Details link to see more granular information about that item.

Inside OUT
Microsoft Fix It provides another self-repair option

Using technology similar to the troubleshooting packs, Microsoft Fix It provides online configuration settings and solutions to a variety of problems. Typically, a Fix It solution allows you to automatically apply a system setting that would otherwise require manual work, such as editing the registry. You can find a full listing of existing Fix It solutions at *support2.microsoft.com/fixit*, although many of the entries there apply only to earlier Windows versions. It's more common to find a new Fix It associated with a Knowledge Base article that identifies a workaround or mitigation for a security or reliability issue before an update is available.

Windows Error Reporting

Often an early indication that something is amiss is an error message informing you that an application is "not responding"—as if you hadn't figured that out already. If the application doesn't come back to life, you kill the process with Task Manager and move on, ideally without losing any data.

While all that's happening, the Windows Error Reporting (WER) service runs continuously in the background, keeping track of software and driver installations (successful and otherwise) as well as crashes, hangs, and other system events that indicate a possible problem with Windows. (In fact, although the service and programs that enable the feature are called Windows Error Reporting, the term you're more likely to see in Windows is *problem reporting*.) Microsoft provides this diagnostic information to the developers of the program that caused the error (including Microsoft developers when the issue occurs with a feature in Windows, Office, or another Microsoft program). The goal, of course, is to improve quality by identifying problems and delivering fixes through Windows Update.

In previous versions, Windows was downright chatty about reporting crashes, successful updates, and minor speed bumps. In Windows 10, most of these problem reports (including diagnostic reports sent after successful upgrades) are completely silent, but each report is logged. You can use the history of problem reports on a system to review events and to see whether any patterns demand additional troubleshooting.

To open the Problem Reports log, type **problem reports** in the search box and then click View All Problem Reports. Figure 17-3 shows a portion of the error history for a computer that was upgraded to Windows 10 in the first month after it was available.

Figure 17-3 The list of saved problem reports displays only the two most recent reports in each group; click More to see earlier reports.

If the words *Solution Available* appear in the Status column for an item, right-click that item and then click View Solution. Note also that the shortcut menu includes commands to group the entries in the list of problem reports by source (the default view, shown in Figure 17-3), summary, date, or status—or you can choose Ungroup to see the entire, uncategorized list. With the list grouped or not, you can sort by any field by clicking the field's column heading.

You can see a more detailed report about any event in this log by double-clicking the event. The Description field is usually written clearly enough to provide potentially useful information. The rest of the details might or might not be meaningful to you, but they could be helpful to a support technician. Some reports include additional details sent in a text file that you can inspect for yourself. In Figure 17-4, for example, a file called WERInternalMetadata.xml captures information about the Windows installation and its memory use. None of this information is personal or linked to your PC.

Figure 17-4 You can review the contents of a problem report, including any additional information sent as file attachments, before or after it's sent.

By default, Windows 10 configures your system so that it sends a generous amount of diagnostic and feedback information, including error reports that could inadvertently contain personal information. If you are concerned about data use or privacy, you can dial back the amount of diagnostic information by using the Feedback & Diagnostics page under the Privacy heading in Settings. Figure 17-5 shows the default settings.

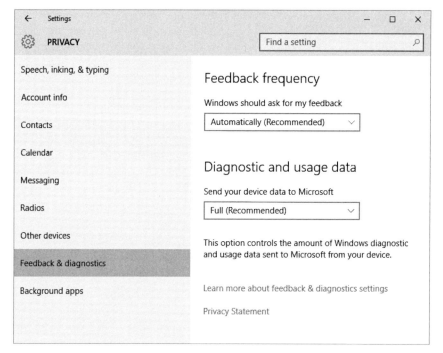

Figure 17-5 If you're concerned about sensitive data leaking out as part of diagnostic reports, consider changing the Diagnostic And Usage Data setting from its default of Full.

The Feedback Frequency setting at the top of this page controls how often Microsoft asks you about your use of features. If you prefer to be left alone, set this to Never.

The second heading, Diagnostic And Usage Data, allows you to specify how much diagnostic information your Windows 10 device sends to Microsoft servers as part of its normal operation. Much of that information is from problem reports, which rarely mean much by themselves but can be tremendously important as part of a larger data set to pinpoint the cause of problems. There are three available settings:

- **Basic.** This level includes data that is fundamental to the operation of Windows and Windows Update. It includes information about the capabilities of your device, what is installed, and whether Windows is operating correctly (which includes sending basic error reports to Microsoft). No personally identifiable information is included.

- **Enhanced.** Along with the data sent with the Basic setting, this setting adds data about how you use Windows (how often you use certain features or apps, for example) and collects enhanced diagnostic information, such as the memory state of your device when a system or app crash occurs. Information sent to Microsoft also includes reliability data for devices, the operating system, and apps.

- **Full (Recommended).** This setting, which is enabled by default, includes the full set of information from the Basic and Enhanced levels and turns on advanced diagnostic features that provide much more detailed error reports. These reports might include system files or memory snapshots that could include the contents of a file or message you were working on when the problem occurred. If a report inadvertently contains personal or sensitive information, Microsoft's privacy policy says the information will not be used to identify, contact, or target advertising to you.

The basic report that Windows Error Reporting transmits typically includes information such as the application name and version, module name and version, exception (error) code, and off-set. Hardware reports include Plug and Play IDs, driver versions, and other system details. The likelihood that any of these items will convey personally identifiable information is essentially nil. The process does transmit your IP address to a Microsoft server, but Microsoft's privacy statement asserts that the IP address is used only to generate aggregate statistics and will not be used to identify you.

In work environments, your network administrators will almost certainly disable the sending of advanced error reports that might inadvertently disclose confidential information.

If privacy is a major concern, you should, of course, read Microsoft's privacy statement for this feature, which is available at *bit.ly/win10-feedback-privacy*. Although most people are under-standably reluctant to send information to a faceless corporation, remember that this is a two-way street. You're sending information about a problem, and there's a good chance that, in return, you'll receive a solution to the problem, as explained in the next section. (Remember, too, that the engineers who analyze the problem information to develop solutions are not faceless!)

Reliability Monitor

Windows 10 keeps track of a wide range of system events. For a day-by-day inventory of these events, type **reliability** in the search box and then click the top result, View Reliability History. That opens Reliability Monitor, shown in Figure 17-6.

Figure 17-6 Reliability Monitor rates your system's stability on a scale of 1 (wear a crash helmet) through 10 (smooth sailing). This PC has had a rough week.

Each column in the graphical display represents events of a particular day (or week, if you click that option in the upper left corner). Each red X along the first three lines below the graph (the various "Failures" lines) indicates a day on which problems occurred. The "Warnings" line describes minor problems unrelated to system reliability, such as a program whose installation process didn't complete properly. The last line below the graph—the line marked Information—identifies days on which an app or an update was installed or removed. You can see the details about the events of any day by clicking on the graph for that day. Reliability Monitor retains its system stability records for one year, giving you plenty of history to review.

This history is most useful when you begin experiencing a new problem and are trying to track down its cause. Examine the critical events for the period when the problem began, and see whether they correspond with an informational item, such as a program installation. The alignment of these events could be mere coincidence, but it could also represent the first appearance of a long-term problem. Conjunctions of this sort are worth examining. If you think a new software application has destabilized your system, you can try uninstalling it.

Double-clicking any item exposes its contents, which are filled with technical details that are potentially useful, confusing, or both.

Although the various signatures and details for each such incident by themselves are probably just baffling, they're much more useful in the aggregate. Armed with a collection of similar reports, an engineer can pin down the cause of a problem and deliver a bug fix. If a previously common error suddenly stops appearing in the logs, chances are it was resolved with an update.

Note also that you can click the link in the Action column to take additional steps, such as searching for a solution or viewing the technical details of a particular event.

Event Viewer

Technically, we should probably have included Event Viewer (Eventvwr.msc) in the previous section. It is, after all, just another troubleshooting tool. But we think that this, the most powerful of all the diagnostic tools in Windows 10, deserves its own section in this chapter.

In Windows, an *event* is any occurrence that is potentially noteworthy—to you, to other users, to the operating system, or to an application. Events are recorded by the Windows Event Log service, and their history is preserved in one of several log files, including Application, Security,

Setup, System, and Forwarded Events. Event Viewer, a Microsoft Management Console (MMC) snap-in supplied with Windows, allows you to review and archive these event logs, as well as other logs created by the installation of certain applications and services.

You can examine the history of errors on your system by creating a filtered view of the Application log in Event Viewer. Why would you want to do this? The most likely reasons are to troubleshoot problems that have occurred, to keep an eye on your system to forestall problems, and to watch out for security breaches. If a device has failed, a disk has filled close to capacity, a program has crashed repeatedly, or some other critical difficulty has arisen, the information recorded in the event logs can help you—or a technical support specialist—figure out what's wrong and what corrective steps are required.

To start Event Viewer, find it by searching for **event** and then click Event Viewer or View Event Logs in the search results. Figure 17-7 offers an overview of Event Viewer.

Figure 17-7 Event Viewer's console tree (left) lists available logs and views; the details pane (center) displays information from the selected log or view; the Actions pane (right) provides a menu of tasks relevant to the current selection.

NOTE
Event Viewer requires administrator privileges for full functionality. If you start Event
Viewer while signed in as a standard user, it starts without requesting elevation. However, the Security log is unavailable, along with some other features. To get access to all
logs, right-click and choose Run As Administrator.

When you select the top-level folder in Event Viewer's console tree, the details pane displays
summary information, as shown in Figure 17-7. This view lets you see at a glance whether any
significant events that might require your attention have occurred in the past hour, day, or
week. You can expand each category to see the sources of events of that event type. Seeing
a count of events of various types in various time periods is interesting—but not particularly
useful in and of itself. If you see an unusually large number of recent errors from a particular
source, for example, you might want to see the full list to determine whether a particular error
needs closer examination. Right-click an event type or an event source under Summary Of
Administrative Events, and then click View All Instances Of This Event, as shown here.

The resulting filtered list of events is drawn from multiple log files, sparing you from having
to search in multiple places. Armed with this information, you can quickly scroll through and
examine the details of each one, perhaps identifying a pattern or a common factor that will
help you find the cause and, eventually, the cure for whatever is causing the event.

Types of events

As a glance at the console tree confirms, events are recorded in one of several logs. The following default logs are visible under the Windows Logs heading:

- **Application.** Application events are generated by applications, including programs you install, programs that are preinstalled with Windows, apps from the Windows Store, and operating system services. Program developers decide which events to record in the Application log and which to record in a program-specific log under Applications And Services Logs.

- **Security.** Security events include sign-in attempts (successful and failed) and attempts to use secured resources, such as an attempt to create, modify, or delete a file.

- **Setup.** Setup events are generated by application installations.

- **System.** System events are generated by Windows itself and by installed features, such as device drivers. If a driver fails to load when you start a Windows session, for example, that event is recorded in the System log.

- **Forwarded Events.** The Forwarded Events log contains events that have been gathered from other computers.

Under the Applications And Services Logs heading, you'll find logs for individual applications and services. The other logs generally record events that are system-wide in nature, but each log in Applications And Services Logs records the events related only to a particular program or feature. The Applications And Services Logs folder contains a Microsoft\Windows folder, which in turn contains a folder for each of hundreds of features that are part of Windows 10. Each of these folders contains one or more logs.

Viewing logs and events

When you select a log or a custom view from the console tree, the details pane shows a list of associated events, in reverse chronological order, with each event occupying a single line. A preview pane below the list displays the contents of the saved event record. Figure 17-8 shows one such listing from the System log.

Each event is classified by severity level (more on that shortly) and has a date and time stamp. The Source column reports the application or Windows feature that generated the event, and each entry has an Event ID—a numerical value that you can use as part of the criteria when filtering for similar events or searching for solutions online. The Task Category column is provided for some events but is blank for many others.

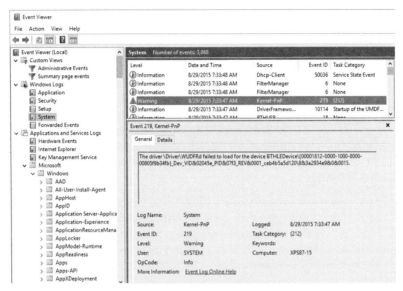

Figure 17-8 All the details you need for an individual event are visible in this preview pane. Double-click an event to see those same details in a separate window.

NOTE

The Windows Event Log service records the date and time each event occurred in Coordinated Universal Time (UTC), and Event Viewer translates those time values into dates and times appropriate for your own time zone.

Events in most log files are classified by severity, with one of three entries in the Level field: Error, Warning, or Information. Error events represent possible loss of data or functionality. Examples of errors include events related to a malfunctioning network adapter and loss of functionality caused by a device or service that doesn't load at startup. Warning events represent less significant or less immediate problems than error events. Examples of warning events include a nearly full disk, a timeout by the network redirector, and data errors on local storage. Other events that Windows logs are identified as information events.

The Security log file uses two different icons to classify events: a key icon identifies Audit Success events, and a lock icon identifies Audit Failure events. Both types of events are classified as Information-level events; "Audit Success" and "Audit Failure" are stored in the Keywords field of the Security log file.

Inside OUT

Export data from Event Viewer

You can save selected events, all events in the current view, or all events in a particular log to a file for archival purposes, for further analysis in a different program, or to share with a technical support specialist. (To select events for exporting, hold down the Ctrl key and click each event you want to include.) The command to export events is on the Action menu, but the command name varies depending on the current view and selection: Save Selected Events, Save Filtered Log File As, Save Events In Custom View As, or Save Events As.

Saving event data in Event Viewer's native (.evtx) format creates a file that you can view only in Event Viewer (or a third-party application capable of reading native event logs). However, Event Viewer can export log data to XML and to tab-delimited or comma-delimited text files, and you can easily import these into database, spreadsheet, or even word-processing programs.

The preview pane shows information about the currently selected event. (Drag the split bar between the list and preview pane up to make the preview pane larger so that you can see more details, or double-click the event to open it in a separate dialog box that includes Next and Previous buttons and an option to copy the event to the Clipboard.)

The information you find in Event Viewer is evidence of things that happened in the past. Like any good detective, you have the task of using those clues to help identify possible issues. One hidden helper, located near the bottom of the Event Properties dialog box, is a link to more information online. Clicking this link opens a webpage that might provide more specific and detailed information about this particular combination of event source and event ID, including further action you might want to take in response to the event.

Filtering the log display

As you can see from a cursory look at your System log, events can pile up quickly, obscuring those generated by a particular source or those that occurred at a particular date and time. Sorting and grouping can help you to find that needle in a haystack, but to get the hay out of the way altogether, use filtering. With filtering, you can select events based on multiple criteria; all other events are hidden from view, making it much easier to focus on the items you currently care about.

To filter the currently displayed log or custom view, click Filter Current Log or Filter Current Custom View in the Actions pane on the right. A dialog box like the one shown in Figure 17-9 appears. To fully appreciate the flexibility of filtering, click the arrow by each filter. You can, for example, filter events from the past hour, 12 hours, day, week, month, or any custom time period you specify. In the Event Sources, Task Category, and Keywords boxes, you can type text to filter on (separate multiple items with commas), but you'll probably find it easier to click the arrow and then click each of the items you want to include in your filtered view. In the Includes/Excludes Event IDs box, you can enter multiple ID numbers and number ranges, sepa-rated by commas; to exclude particular event IDs, precede their number with a minus sign.

Figure 17-9 If you don't select any Event Level check boxes, Event Viewer includes all levels in the filtered results. Similarly, any other field you leave blank includes all events without regard to the value of that property.

Click OK to see the filtered list. If you want to save your criteria for reuse later, click Save Filter To Custom View in the Actions pane on the right. To restore the unfiltered list, in the Event Viewer window, click Clear Filter.

NOTE

Event Viewer also includes an anemic search capability, which you access by clicking Action, Find. You can perform more precise searches by filtering.

Dealing with Stop errors

If Windows has ever suddenly shut down, you've probably experienced that sinking feeling in the pit of your stomach. When Windows 10 encounters a serious problem that makes it impossible for the operating system to continue running, it does the only thing it can do, just as every one of its predecessors has done in the same circumstances. It shuts down immediately and displays an ominous text message whose technical details begin with the word *STOP*. Because a Stop error typically appears in white letters on a blue background, this type of message is often referred to as a blue-screen error or the Blue Screen of Death (BSOD). When a Stop error appears, it means that there is a serious problem that demands your immediate attention.

Windows 10 collects and saves a variety of information in logs and dump files, which a support engineer or developer armed with debugging tools can use to identify the cause of Stop errors. You don't have to be a developer to use these tools, which are available to anyone via download from *bit.ly/windows-debugging-tools*. (Don't worry; you can't break anything by simply inspecting a .dmp file.) If you know where to look, however, you can learn a lot from these error messages alone, and in many cases you can recover completely by using standard troubleshooting techniques.

Customizing how Windows handles Stop errors

When Windows encounters a serious error that forces it to stop running, it displays a Stop message and then writes debugging information to the page file. When the computer restarts, this information is saved as a crash dump file, which can be used to debug the specific cause of the error.

You can customize two crucial aspects of this process by defining the size of the crash dump files and specifying whether you want Windows to restart automatically after a Stop message appears. By default, Windows automatically restarts after a Stop message and creates a crash dump file optimized for automatic analysis. That's the preferred strategy in response to random, isolated Stop errors. But if you're experiencing chronic Stop errors, you might have more troubleshooting success by changing these settings to collect a more detailed dump file and to stop after a crash.

To make this change, open Settings, type **advanced** in the search box, and then click View Advanced System Settings in the results list. (Or, in the Run or search box, type the undocumented command **systempropertiesadvanced** and press Enter.)

On the Advanced tab of the System Properties dialog box, under Startup And Recovery, click Settings. Adjust the settings under the System Failure heading, as shown in Figure 17-10.

Figure 17-10 By default, Windows keeps a kernel memory dump and restarts automatically after a Stop error. You can pick a larger or smaller dump file here.

If you want Windows to pause at the Stop error message page, clear the Automatically Restart check box and click OK.

From the same dialog box, you can also define the settings for crash dump files. By default, Windows sets this value to Automatic Memory Dump, which saves a kernel memory dump after a crash. This option includes memory allocated to kernel-mode drivers and programs, which are most likely to cause Stop errors. Because this file does not include unallocated memory or memory allocated to user-mode programs, it will usually be smaller in size than the amount of RAM on your system. The exact size varies, but in general you can expect the file to be no larger than one-third the size of installed physical RAM, and much less than that on a system with 16 GB of RAM or more. The crash files are stored in %SystemRoot% using the file name Memory.dmp. (If your system crashes multiple times, each new dump file replaces the previous file.)

If disk space is limited or you're planning to send the crash dump file to a support technician, you might want to consider setting the system to store a small memory dump (commonly called a mini dump). A small memory dump contains just a fraction of the information in a kernel memory dump, but it's often enough to determine the cause of a problem.

What's in a Stop error

The exact text of a Stop error varies according to what caused the error. But the format is predictable. Don't bother copying down the error code from the blue screen itself. Instead, look through Event Viewer for an event with the source BugCheck, as shown in the example in Figure 17-11.

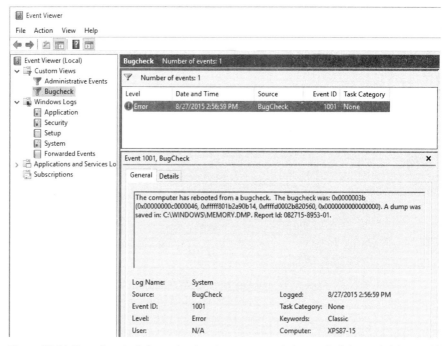

Figure 17-11 Decoding the information in a Stop error can help you find the underlying problem and fix it. Start with the error code—0x0000003b, in this example.

You can gather important details from the bugcheck information, which consists of error number (in hexadecimal notation, as indicated by the 0x at the beginning of the code) and up to four parameters that are specific to the error type.

Windows 10 also displays the information in Reliability Monitor, under the heading Critical Events. Select the day on which the error occurred and double-click the "Shut down unexpectedly" entry for an event with Windows as the source. That displays the bugcheck information in a slightly more readable format than in Event Viewer, as shown next, even using the term *BlueScreen* as the Problem Event Name. (For more information, see "Reliability Monitor," earlier in this chapter.)

For a comprehensive and official list of what each error code means, see the MSDN "Bug Check Code Reference" at *bit.ly/bugcheck-codes*. A code of 0x00000144, for example, points to problems with a USB 3 controller, whereas 0x0000009F is a driver power state failure. (Our favorite is 0xDEADDEAD, which indicates a manually initiated crash.) In general, you need a debugger or a dedicated analytic tool to get any additional useful information from a memory dump file.

Isolating the cause of a Stop error

If you experience a Stop error, don't panic. Instead, run through the following troubleshooting checklist to isolate the problem and find a solution:

- **Don't rule out hardware problems.** In many cases, software is the victim and not the cause of blue-screen errors. Common hardware failures such as a damaged hard disk or a corrupted SSD, defective physical RAM, an overheated CPU chip, or even a bad cable can result in Stop errors. If the errors seem to happen at random and the message details vary each time, there is a very good chance that you are experiencing hardware problems.

- **Check your memory.** Windows 10 includes a memory diagnostic tool that you can use if you suspect a faulty or failing memory chip. To run this diagnostic procedure, type **memory** in the search box and click Windows Memory Diagnostic in the search results. This tool, shown here, requires a restart to run its full suite of tests, which you can perform immediately or defer until your next restart.

- **Look for a driver name in the error details.** If the error message identifies a specific file name and you can trace that file to a driver for a specific hardware device, you might be able to solve the problem by disabling, removing, or rolling back that driver to an earlier version. The most likely offenders are network interface cards, video adapters, and disk controllers. For more details about managing driver files, see "Updating and uninstalling drivers" in Chapter 13, "Hardware."

- **Ask yourself, "What's new?"** Be suspicious of newly installed hardware and software. If you added a device recently, remove it temporarily and see whether the problem goes away. Take an especially close look at software in the categories that install services or file-system filter drivers—these hook into the core operating system files that manage the file system to perform tasks such as scanning for viruses. This category includes backup programs, multimedia applications, antivirus software, and DVD-burning utilities. You might need to permanently uninstall or update the program to resolve the problem.

- **Search Microsoft Support.** Make a note of the error code and all parameters. Search Microsoft Support using both the full and short formats. For instance, if you're experiencing a KMODE_EXCEPTION_NOT_HANDLED error, use 0x1E and 0x0000001E as your search keywords.

- **Check your system BIOS or firmware.** Is an update available from the manufacturer of the system or motherboard? Check the BIOS or firmware documentation carefully; resetting all BIOS options to their defaults can sometimes resolve an issue caused by overtweaking.

- **Are you low on system resources?** Stop errors are sometimes the result of a critical shortage of RAM or disk space. If you can start in Safe Mode, check the amount of physical RAM installed and look at the system and boot drives to see how much free disk space is available.

- **Is a crucial system file damaged?** To reinstall a driver, restart your computer, press F8, and start Windows in Safe Mode. In Safe Mode, only core drivers and services are activated. If your system starts in Safe Mode but not normally, you very likely have a problem driver. Try running Device Manager in Safe Mode and uninstalling the most likely suspect. Or run System Restore in Safe Mode. If restoring to a particular day cures the problem, use Reliability Monitor to determine what changes occurred on or shortly after that day.

Troubleshooting with alternative boot options

Before there was Reset, there was Safe Mode.

The recovery and reset options in Windows 10 make some traditional troubleshooting techniques less important than they used to be. Booting into Safe Mode, for example, used to be a mandatory step for recovering from problems. On modern hardware, with UEFI firmware and solid state drives, it's literally impossible to interrupt the boot process to switch into Safe Mode.

If you can start Windows and get to the sign-in screen, you can then hold down Shift and click the Power button in the lower right corner of that screen. Clicking Restart while holding down Shift makes an alternative boot menu available, with some interesting troubleshooting options.

To get to the Startup Settings menu, open Settings, Update & Security, Recovery, and then click Restart Now under Advanced Startup. After restarting, you can tap Troubleshoot, Advanced Options, and finally Startup Settings to reach the blue, full-screen menu shown in Figure 17-12. The nine choices shown there (one additional option is on the next screen) allow you to start Windows in modes that make some forms of troubleshooting easier.

The three choices in the middle enable Safe Mode, which starts Windows using a built-in administrator account, using only services and drivers that are absolutely required to start your system. The operating system runs with a generic video driver, with support for keyboard, mouse, monitor, local storage, and default system services. In Safe Mode, Windows does not install support for audio devices and nonessential peripherals. USB flash drives, hard disks, keyboard, and mouse are supported. All programs that normally run when you sign in (programs in your Startup folder, for example) are bypassed.

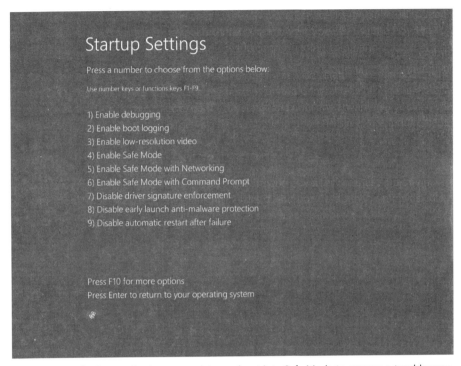

Figure 17-12 The Startup Settings menu lets you boot into Safe Mode to remove a troublesome program or driver that is preventing you from signing in normally.

In Safe Mode, you can access certain essential configuration tools, including Device Manager, System Restore, and Registry Editor. If Windows appears to work properly in Safe Mode, you can safely assume that there's no problem with the basic services. Use Device Manager, Driver Verifier Manager, and Event Viewer to try to figure out where the trouble lies. If you suspect that a newly installed device or program is the cause of the problem, you can remove the offending software while you're running in Safe Mode. Use Device Manager to uninstall or roll back a hardware driver; use Control Panel to remove a desktop program or utility. Then try restarting the system normally to see whether your changes have resolved the problem.

One important troubleshooting tool that is not available in Safe Mode is Backup And Restore. To restore a system image backup, for example, you need to use the Windows Recovery Environment, not Safe Mode.

If you need access to network connections, choose the Safe Mode With Networking option, which loads the base set of Safe Mode files and adds drivers and services required to start Windows networking.

The third Safe Mode option, Safe Mode With Command Prompt, loads the same stripped-down set of services as Safe Mode, but it uses the Windows command interpreter (Cmd.exe) as a shell instead of the graphical Windows Explorer (Explorer.exe, which also serves as the host for File Explorer). This option is unnecessary unless you're having a problem with the Windows graphical interface. The default Safe Mode also provides access to the command line. (Press Windows key+R, and then type **cmd.exe** in the Run dialog box.)

The six additional choices on the Startup Settings menu are of use in specialized circumstances:

- **Enable Debugging.** This choice starts Windows in kernel debug mode and requires a physical connection to another computer running a debugger.

- **Enable Boot Logging.** With this option enabled, Windows creates a log file that lists the names and status of all drivers loaded into memory. To view the contents of this file, look for Ntbtlog.txt in the %SystemRoot% folder. If your system is hanging because of a faulty driver, the last entry in this log file might identify the culprit.

- **Enable Low-Resolution Video.** This option starts the computer in 640 by 480 resolution using the current video driver. Use this option to recover from video problems that are caused not by a faulty driver but by incorrect settings, such as an improper resolution or refresh rate.

- **Disable Driver Signature Enforcement** Use this option if Windows is refusing to start because you installed an unsigned user-mode driver. Windows will start normally, not in Safe Mode. (Note that you cannot disable the requirement for signed kernel-mode drivers.)

- **Disable Early Launch Anti-Malware Protection.** This is one of the core security measures of Windows 10 on a UEFI-equipped machine. Unless you're a security researcher or a driver developer, we can't think of any reason to disable this important security check.

- **Disable Automatic Restart After Failure.** Use this option if you're getting Stop errors (blue-screen crashes) and you want the opportunity to see the crash details on the Stop error screen instead of simply pausing there before restarting.

The second page of the Advanced Boot Options menu includes a single menu choice that starts the Windows Recovery Environment. (We discuss this and other recovery tools in more detail in Chapter 16.)

PART 4

Windows 10 for experts and IT pros

Using advanced system management tools

In this chapter, we look at a handful of programs and management consoles that can help you attain greater mastery over Windows. We start with tools for unearthing details about your system—its hardware, software environment, running programs and services, and so on. In the remainder of the chapter, we discuss the Services console, Registry Editor, and a variety of specialized tools that use the Microsoft Management Console.

Viewing details about your system

For answers to basic questions about your operating system and computer, there's no better place to start than the System application, which displays the current Windows edition and whether it is a 32-bit or 64-bit version; basic system details, including processor type and installed memory; details about the computer name and network membership (domain or workgroup); and the current activation status.

Windows 10 offers two versions of this information. On a tablet or touchscreen-enabled system, you'll probably use the new Settings app, which is pinned to the Start menu by default. Open Settings, tap System, and then tap About to display details like those shown in Figure 18-1.

An alternative display that includes most of the same information is in the old-style Control Panel, shown in Figure 18-2. The simplest way to get to the System settings page in Control Panel is to right-click the Start button (or press Windows key+X) and then click System on the Quick Link menu. If File Explorer is open, right-click This PC and click Properties to reach the same destination.

Figure 18-1 This About page, found in the new Settings app, includes basic details about the local PC along with options to change its name and join a corporate network.

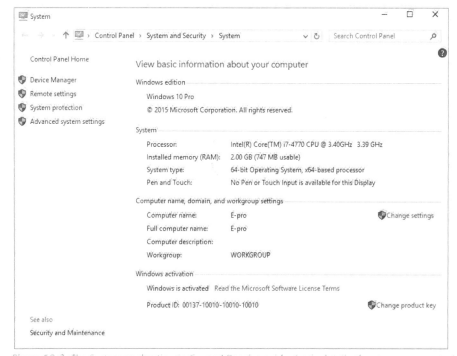

Figure 18-2 The System application in Control Panel provides basic details about your computer's configuration.

For the most exhaustive inventory of system configuration details in a no-frills text format, Windows offers three tools that provide varying levels of technical information, which we describe in the rest of this section.

Systeminfo

Systeminfo.exe is a command-line utility, installed in the Windows\System32 folder, that displays information about your Windows version, BIOS, processor, memory, network configuration, and a few more esoteric items. Figure 18-3 shows sample output.

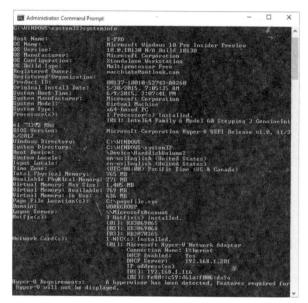

Figure 18-3 The command-line utility Systeminfo.exe provides an easy way to gather information about all your network computers in a single database.

To run Systeminfo, open a Command Prompt window, type **systeminfo**, and then press Enter. In addition to the list format shown in the figure, Systeminfo offers two formats that are useful if you want to work with the information in another program: Table (fixed-width columns) and CSV (comma-separated values). To use one of these formats, append the /FO switch to the command, along with the Table or Csv parameter. You'll also need to redirect the output to a file. For example, to store comma-delimited information in a file named Info.csv, enter the following command:

```
systeminfo /fo csv > info.csv
```

The /S switch allows you to get system information about another computer on your network. (If your user name and password don't match that of an account on the target computer, you'll also need to use the /U and /P switches to provide the user name and password of an authorized account.) When you've gathered information about all the computers on your network, you can import the file you created into a spreadsheet or database program for tracking and analysis. The following command appends information about a computer named Bates to the original file you created:

```
systeminfo /s Bates /fo csv >> info.csv
```

Windows Management Instrumentation command-line utility

This tool with the extra-long name is better known by the name of its executable, Wmic.exe, which is located in the Windows\System32\Wbem folder. Wmic provides an overwhelming amount of information about hardware, system configuration details, and user accounts. It can be used in either of two ways.

Enter **wmic** from a command prompt and the utility runs in console mode, allowing you to enter commands and view output interactively. Alternatively, you can add global switches or aliases, which constrain the type of output you're looking for, and see the output in a Command Prompt window or redirect it to a file. For example, use the following command to produce a neatly formatted HTML file:

```
wmic qfe list brief /format:htable > %temp%\hotfix.html
```

You can then open that file in a web browser to see a list of all installed updates on the current system. To see the full syntax for Wmic, open a Command Prompt window and type **wmic –?**.

System Information

System Information—often called by the name of its executable, Msinfo32.exe—is a techie's paradise. It displays a wealth of configuration information in a simple tree-and-details arrangement, as shown in Figure 18-4. You can search for specific information, save information, view information about other computers, and even view a list of changes to your system.

To start System Information, type **msinfo32** at a command prompt or in the search box.

Figure 18-4 System Information is for viewing configuration information only; you can't use it to actually configure settings.

You navigate through System Information much as you would through File Explorer or any of the other Windows management tools that use the Microsoft Management Console (MMC): click a category in the left pane to view its contents in the right pane. To search for specific information, use the Find What box at the bottom of the System Information window. (If the Find bar is not visible, press Ctrl+F, or click Edit and then clear the check box next to Hide Find.)

The Find feature is basic but effective. Here are a couple of things you should know:

- Whenever you type in the Find What box to start a new search, Find begins its search at the top of the search range (the entire namespace unless you select Search Selected Category Only)—not at the current highlight.

- Selecting Search Category Names Only causes the Find feature to look only in the left pane. When this check box is cleared, the text in both panes is searched.

Using the System Information tool, you can preserve your configuration information—which is always helpful when reconstructing a system—in several ways:

- Save the information as an .nfo file. You can subsequently open the file (on the same computer or on a different computer with System Information) to view your saved information. To save information in this format, click File, Save. Saving this way always saves the entire collection of information.

- Save all or part of the information as a plain-text file. To save information as a text file, select the category of interest and click File, Export. To save all the information as a text file, select System Summary before you export.

- You can print all or part of the information. Select the category of interest; click File, Print; and be sure that Selection is selected under Page Range. To print everything, select All under Page Range—and be sure to have lots of paper on hand. Depending on your system configuration and the number of installed applications, your report could top 100 pages. (Even better, consider "printing" to PDF and saving the results.)

Regardless of how you save your information, System Information refreshes (updates) the information immediately before processing the command.

Inside OUT

Save your system information periodically

Saving system configuration information when your computer is working properly can turn out to be very useful when you have problems. Comparing your computer's current configuration with a known good baseline configuration can help you spot possible problem areas. You can open multiple instances of System Information to display the current configuration in one window and a baseline configuration in another. Save the configuration in OneDrive, and you'll be able to retrieve the information even after a hard-disk replacement.

Managing services

A *service* is a specialized program that performs a function to support other programs. Many services operate at a very low level (by interacting directly with hardware, for example) and need to run even when no user is signed in. For this reason, they are often run by the System account (which has elevated privileges) rather than by ordinary user accounts. In this section, you'll learn how to view installed services; start, stop, and configure them; and install or remove them. We'll also take a closer look at some of the services used in Windows 10 and show you how to configure them to your advantage.

For the most complete view of services running on your computer, use the Services console. You can also view running services and perform limited management functions by using Task Manager. In this section, we discuss both tools.

Using the Services console

You manage services with the Services snap-in (Services.msc) for Microsoft Management Console, shown in Figure 18-5. To view this snap-in, type **services** in the search box and then click the Services desktop app at the top of the results list. (You must have administrator privileges to gain full functionality in the Services console. Running it as a standard user, you can view service settings, but you can't start or stop most services, change the startup type, or make any other configuration changes.)

Figure 18-5 Use the Services console to start, stop, and configure services.

The Extended and Standard views in the Services console (selectable by clicking a tab near the bottom of the window) have a single difference: the Extended view provides descriptive information of the selected service in the space at the left edge of the details pane. This space also sometimes includes links for starting, stopping, or pausing the selected service. Unless you need to constrain the console display to a small area of your screen, you'll probably find the Extended view preferable to the Standard view.

The Services console offers plenty of information in its clean display. You can sort the contents of any column by clicking the column title, as you can with similar lists. To sort in reverse order, click the column title again. In addition, you can do the following:

- Start, stop, pause, resume, or restart the selected service, as described in the following section.

- Display the properties dialog box for the selected service, in which you can configure the service and learn more about it.

Most of the essential services are set to start automatically when your computer starts, and the operating system stops them as part of its shutdown process. A handful of services that aren't typically used at startup are set with the Automatic (Delayed Start) option, which starts the associated service two minutes after the rest of startup completes, making the startup process smoother. The Trigger Start option allows Windows to run or stop a service as needed in response to specific events; the File History service, for example, doesn't run unless you enable the File History feature.

But sometimes you might need to manually start or stop a service. For example, you might want to start a seldom-used service on the rare occasion when you need it. (Because running services requires system resources such as memory, running them only when necessary can improve performance.) On the other hand, you might want to stop a service because you're no longer using it. A more common reason for stopping a service is because it isn't working properly. For example, if print jobs get stuck in the print queue, sometimes the best remedy is to stop and then restart the Print Spooler service.

Inside OUT

Pause instead of stopping

If a service allows pausing, try pausing and then continuing the service as your first step instead of stopping the service. Pausing can solve certain problems without canceling jobs in process or resetting connections.

Starting and stopping services

Not all services allow you to change their status. Some prevent stopping and starting altogether, whereas others permit stopping and starting but not pausing and resuming. Some services allow these permissions to only certain users or groups. For example, most services allow only members of the Administrators group to start or stop them. Which status changes are allowed and who has permission to make them are controlled by each service's discretionary access control list (DACL), which is established when the service is created on a computer.

NOTE

In Windows 10, software installers can stop and restart running applications and services by using a feature called Restart Manager (introduced in Windows Vista). A handful of system services are considered critical, however, and cannot be restarted manually or programmatically except as part of a system restart. These critical services include Smss.exe, Csrss.exe, Wininit.exe, Logonui.exe, Lsass.exe, Services.exe, Winlogon.exe, System, Svchost.exe with RPCSS, and Svchost.exe with DCOM/PnP.

To change a service's status, select it in the Services console. Then click the appropriate link in the area to the left of the service list (if you're using the Extended view and the link you need appears there). Alternatively, you can use the Play/Pause/Stop controls on the toolbar or right-click and use the corresponding command.

You can also change a service's status by opening its properties dialog box and then clicking one of the buttons on the General tab. Taking the extra step of opening the properties dialog box to set the status has only one advantage: you can specify start parameters when you start a service by using this method. This is a rare requirement.

Configuring services

To review or modify the way a service starts up or what happens when it doesn't start properly, view its properties dialog box. To do that, simply double-click the service in the Services console. Figure 18-6 shows an example.

Figure 18-6 Specify a service's startup type on the General tab, where you can also find the actual name of the service (in this case, BthHFSrv) above its display name.

Setting startup options

On the General tab of the properties dialog box (shown in Figure 18-6), you specify the startup type:

- **Automatic (Delayed Start).** The service starts shortly after the computer starts in order to improve startup performance and user experience.

- **Automatic.** The service starts when the computer starts.

- **Manual.** The service doesn't start automatically at startup, but it can be started by a user, program, or dependent service.

- **Disabled.** The service can't be started.

The Trigger Start option cannot be configured manually from the Services console. Instead, you have to use SC (Sc.exe), a command-line program that communicates with the Service Control Manager. If you'd rather not tinker with the arcane syntax of this command, try the free Service Trigger Editor, available from Core Technologies Consulting, at *bit.ly/servicetriggereditor.*

You'll find other startup options on the Log On tab of the properties dialog box, as shown in Figure 18-7.

Figure 18-7 On the Log On tab, you specify which user account runs the service.

> **NOTE**
>
> If you specify a sign-in account other than the Local System account, be sure that account has the requisite rights. Go to the Local Security Policy console (at a command prompt, type **secpol.msc**), and then go to Security Settings\Local Policies\User Rights Assignment and assign the Log On As A Service right to the account.

Specifying recovery actions

For a variety of reasons—hardware not operating properly or a network connection being down, for example—a service that's running smoothly might suddenly stop. Settings on the Recovery tab of the properties dialog box allow you to specify what should happen if a service fails. Figure 18-8, for example, shows the default settings for the Windows Firewall service.

Figure 18-8 Use the Recovery tab to specify what should happen if a service fails.

You might want to perform a different action the first time a service fails than on the second or subsequent failures. The Recovery tab enables you to assign a particular response to the first failure, the second failure, and all subsequent failures, from among these options:

- **Take No Action.** The service gives up trying. In most cases, the service places a message in the event log. (Use of the event log depends on how the service was programmed by its developers.)

- **Restart The Service.** The computer waits for the time specified in the Restart Service After box to elapse and then tries to start the service.

- **Run A Program.** The computer runs the program that you specify in the Run Program box. For example, you could specify a program that attempts to resolve the problem or one that alerts you to the situation.

- **Restart The Computer.** Drastic but effective, this option restarts the computer after the time specified in the Restart Computer Options dialog box elapses. In that dialog box, you can also specify a message to be broadcast to other users on your network, warning them of the impending shutdown.

Viewing dependencies

Many services rely on the functions of another service. If you attempt to start a service that depends on other services, Windows first starts the others. If you stop a service upon which others are dependent, Windows also stops those services. Before you either start or stop a service, therefore, it's helpful to know what other services your action might affect. To obtain that information, go to the Dependencies tab of a service's properties dialog box, as in the example shown in Figure 18-9.

Figure 18-9 The Dependencies tab shows which services depend on other services.

Managing services from Task Manager

Using the Services tab in Windows Task Manager, you can start and stop services and view several important aspects of the services, both running and available, on your computer. You can also use this as a shortcut to the Services console.

To open Task Manager, use any of the following techniques:

- Right-click Start (or press Windows key+X), and then click Task Manager on the Quick Link menu.

- Right-click the taskbar, and then click Task Manager.

- Press Ctr+Alt+Delete, and then click Task Manager.

- Press Ctrl+Shift+Esc.

The Services tab is shown in Figure 18-10.

Figure 18-10 By sorting on the Status column, you can see which services are running and which are stopped.

To start, stop, or restart a service, right-click its name on the Services tab and then click Start, Stop, or Restart.

Using the Services tab, you can also associate a running service with its process identifier (PID) and then further associate that PID with other programs and services being run under that PID. For example, Figure 18-10 shows several services running with PID 1220. Right-clicking one of the services with PID 1220 gives you two options, one to stop the service and one called Go To Details. Clicking the latter option opens the Details tab in Task Manager with the particular process (typically Svchost.exe) highlighted.

Determining the name of a service

As you view the properties dialog box for different services, you might notice that the service name (shown at the top of the General tab) is often different from the name that appears in the Services console (the display name) and that neither name matches the name of the service's executable file. (Many services run as part of a service group, under Services.exe or Svchost.exe.) The General tab (shown earlier in Figure 18-6) shows all three names.

So how does this affect you? When you work in the Services console, you don't need to know anything other than a service's display name to find it and work with it. But if you use the Net command to start and stop services from a Command Prompt window, you might find using the actual service name more convenient; it is often much shorter than the display name. You'll also need the service name if you're ever forced to work with a service's registry entries, which can be found in the HKLM\System\CurrentControlSet\Services*service* subkey (where *service* is the service name).

And what about the executable name? You might need it if you or a user you support have problems running a service; in such a case, you need to find the executable and check its permissions. Knowing the executable name can also be useful, for example, if you're using Windows Task Manager to determine why your computer seems to be running slowly. Although the Processes tab and the Services tab show the display name (under the Description heading), because of the window size it's sometimes easier to find the more succinct executable name.

Editing the Windows registry

The Windows registry is the central storage location that contains configuration details for hardware, system settings, services, user customizations, applications, and every detail, large and small, that makes Windows work.

> ### NOTE
> The registry is the work of many hands, over many years, and capitalization and word spacing are not consistent. With readability as our goal, we have made our own capitalization decisions for this book, and our treatment of names frequently differs from what you see in Registry Editor. No matter. Capitalization is irrelevant. Spelling and spacing must be correct, however.

Although it's convenient to think of the registry as a monolithic database, its contents are actually stored in multiple locations as separate *hive* files, alongside logs and other support files. Some of those hive files are read into memory when the operating system starts; hive files that contain user-specific settings are stored in the user profile and are loaded when a new user signs in.

The Boot Configuration Database (BCD) has its own file on the boot drive. The core hives for Windows—the Security Account Manager (SAM), Security, Software, and System—are securely stored in %SystemRoot%\System32\Config. Two hives that contain settings for local and network services are located in %SystemRoot%\ServiceProfiles\LocalService and %SystemRoot%\ServiceProfiles\NetworkService, respectively. User-specific hives are stored as part of the user profile folder.

The Hardware hive is unique in that it has no associated disk file. This hive, which contains details about your hardware configuration, is completely volatile; that is, Windows 10 creates it anew each time you turn your system on.

NOTE

You can see where the hives of your system physically live by examining the values associated with HKLM\System\CurrentControlSet\Control\HiveList. Windows assigns drive letters after assembling the registry, so these paths do not specify drive letters.

You can't work with hive files directly. Windows 10 is designed in such a way that direct registry edits by end users are generally unnecessary. When you change your configuration by using the Settings app or Control Panel, for example, Windows writes the necessary updates to the registry for you. Likewise, when you install a new piece of hardware or a new program, the setup program makes the required registry changes; you don't need to know the details.

On the other hand, because the designers of Windows couldn't provide a user interface for every conceivable customization you might want to make, sometimes working directly with the registry is the only way to make a change. Even when it's not the only way, it might be the fastest way. Removing or modifying registry entries is occasionally a crucial part of troubleshooting and repair as well. Windows includes a registry editor that you should know how to use—safely. This section tells you how.

CAUTION

Most Microsoft support articles contain a dire warning about the risks associated with editing the registry. We echo those warnings here. An incorrect registry modification can render your system unbootable and in some cases might require a complete reinstall of the operating system. Use Registry Editor at your own risk.

Understanding the Registry Editor hierarchy

Registry Editor (Regedit.exe) offers a unified view of the registry's contents as well as tools for modifying its contents. You won't find this important utility on the All Apps list, however, and it doesn't show up when you type its name in the search box. To start Registry Editor, you must use the name of its executable file, Regedit.exe, or type **regedit** at a command prompt.

Figure 18-11 shows a collapsed view of the Windows 10 registry, as seen through Registry Editor.

Figure 18-11 The registry consists of five root keys, each of which contains many subkeys.

The Computer node appears at the top of the Registry Editor tree listing. Beneath it, as shown here, are five root keys: HKEY_CLASSES_ROOT, HKEY_CURRENT_USER, HKEY_LOCAL_MACHINE, HKEY_USERS, and HKEY_CURRENT_CONFIG. For simplicity's sake and typographical convenience, this book, like many others, abbreviates the root key names as HKCR, HKCU, HKLM, HKU, and HKCC, respectively.

Root keys, sometimes called *predefined keys,* contain subkeys. Registry Editor displays this structure in a hierarchical tree in the left pane. In Figure 18-11, for example, HKLM is open, showing its top-level subkeys.

Subkeys, which we call keys for short, can contain subkeys of their own, which can be expanded as necessary to display additional subkeys. The status bar at the bottom of the Registry Editor window shows the full path of the currently selected key: HKLM\System\ DriverDatabase, in the previous figure.

The contents of HKEY_LOCAL_MACHINE define the workings of Windows itself, and its subkeys map neatly to several of the hives we mentioned at the start of this section. HKEY_USERS contains an entry for every existing user account (including system accounts), each of which uses the security identifier, or SID, for that account.

> ### NOTE
> For a detailed discussion of the relationship between user accounts and SIDs, see "What are security identifiers?" in Chapter 6, "Managing user accounts, passwords, and credentials."

The remaining three predefined keys don't exist, technically. Like the file system in Windows—which uses junctions, symlinks, and other trickery to display a virtual namespace—the registry uses a bit of misdirection (implemented with the REG_LINK data type) to create these convenient representations of keys that are actually stored within HKEY_LOCAL_MACHINE and HKEY_USERS:

- HKEY_CLASSES_ROOT is merged from keys within HKLM\Software\Classes and HKEY_ USERS*sid*_Classes (where *sid* is the security identifier of the currently signed-in user).

- HKEY_CURRENT_USER is a view into the settings for the currently signed-in user account, as stored in HKEY_USERS*sid* (where *sid* is the security identifier of the currently signed-in user).

- HKEY_CURRENT_CONFIG displays the contents of the Hardware Profiles\Current subkey in HKLM\SYSTEM\CurrentControlSet\Hardware Profiles.

Any changes you make to keys and values in these virtual keys have the same effect as though you had edited the actual locations. The HKCR and HKCU keys are generally more convenient to use.

Registry values and data types

Every key contains at least one value. In Registry Editor, that obligatory value is known as the default value. Many keys have additional values. The names, data types, and data associated with values appear in the right pane.

The default value for many keys is not defined. You can therefore think of an empty default value as a placeholder—a slot that could hold data but currently does not.

All values other than the default always include the following three components: name, data type, and data. Figure 18-12, for example, shows customized settings for the current user's lock screen (note the full path to this key in the bottom of the Registry Editor window).

Figure 18-12 Selecting a key on the left displays all of its values on the right.

The SlideshowEnabled value (last in the list) is of data type REG_DWORD. The data associated with this value (on the system used for this figure) is 0x00000000. The prefix 0x denotes a hexadecimal value. Registry Editor displays the decimal equivalent of hexadecimal values in parentheses after the value.

The registry uses the following data types:

- **REG_SZ** The SZ indicates a zero-terminated string. This is a variable-length string that can contain Unicode as well as ANSI characters. When you enter or edit a REG_SZ value, Registry Editor terminates the value with a 00 byte for you.

- **REG_BINARY** The REG_BINARY type contains binary data—0s and 1s.

- **REG_DWORD** This data type is a "double word"—that is, a 32-bit numeric value. Although it can hold any integer from 0 to 232, the registry often uses it for simple Boolean values (0 or 1) because the registry lacks a Boolean data type.

- **REG_QWORD** This data type is a "quadruple word"—a 64-bit numeric value.

- **REG_MULTI_SZ** This data type contains a group of zero-terminated strings assigned to a single value.

- **REG_EXPAND_SZ** This data type is a zero-terminated string containing an unexpanded reference to an environment variable, such as %SystemRoot%. (For information about environment variables, see "Interacting with PowerShell" in Chapter 21, "Working with Command Prompt and Windows PowerShell.") If you need to create a key containing a variable name, use this data type, not REG_SZ.

Internally, the registry also uses REG_LINK, REG_FULL_RESOURCE_DESCRIPTOR, REG_RESOURCE_LIST, REG_RESOURCE_REQUIREMENTS_LIST, and REG_NONE data types. Although you might occasionally see references in technical documentation to these data types, they're not visible or accessible in Registry Editor.

Registry virtualization

One of the longstanding fundamental principles of security in Windows is that it prevents applications running under a standard user's token from writing to system folders in the file system and to machine-wide keys in the registry, while at the same time enabling users with a standard account to run applications without running into "access denied" roadblocks.

Many applications that require administrator-level access are still in use in Windows 10, but standard users can run them without hassle. That's because User Account Control uses registry virtualization to redirect attempts to write to subkeys of HKLM\Software. (Settings in HKLM apply to all users of the computer, and therefore only administrators have write permission.) When an application attempts to write to this hive, Windows writes instead to a per-user location, HKCR\VirtualStore\Machine\Software. Like file virtualization, this is done transparently; the application (and all but the most curious users) never know this is going on behind the scenes.

NOTE
When an application requests information from HKLM\Software, Windows looks first in the virtualized key if it exists. Therefore, if a value exists in both the VirtualStore hive and in HKLM, the application sees only the one in VirtualStore.

Note that because the virtualized data is stored in a per-user section of the registry, settings made by one user do not affect other users. Running the same application in Windows XP, which doesn't use virtualization and therefore looks only at the actual HKLM hive, presents all users with the same settings. This can lead to confusion by users who are accustomed to sharing an application in Windows XP and find that it works differently in Windows 10.

Inside OUT

Copy virtualized registry entries to other user accounts

The hive that stores virtualized registry data, HKCR\VirtualStore\Machine\Software, can also be found in HKU*sid*_Classes\VirtualStore\Machine\Software, where *sid* is the security identifier of the user who is currently signed in. If you want to make sure that a certain application works identically for a different user, you can copy that application's subkey to the corresponding HKU subkey for the other user.

➤ For more information about UAC and virtualization, see "Preventing unsafe actions with User Account Control" in Chapter 7, "Securing Windows 10 devices."

NOTE

Registry virtualization is an interim solution to application compatibility problems. It was introduced with Windows Vista; at that time, nearly 10 years ago, Microsoft announced its intention to remove the feature from a future version of the operating system. It is still a feature in Windows 10. For more information about registry virtualization, see *w7io.com/22502*.

Backing up and restoring parts of the registry

The two most important things to know about Registry Editor are that it copies your changes immediately into the registry and that it has no Undo command. Registry Editor doesn't wait for you to issue a File, Save command (it has no such command) before making changes in the registry files. And after you have altered some bit of registry data, the original data is gone forever—unless you remember it and restore it yourself or unless you have some form of backup that you can restore. Registry Editor is therefore a tool to be used sparingly and cautiously; it should not be left open when not in use.

Before you make any changes to the registry, consider using System Restore to set a restore point, which includes a snapshot of the registry as it currently exists. This precaution allows you to roll back any ill-advised changes.

➤ For information about using System Restore, see "Rolling back to a previous restore point" in Chapter 16, "Backup, restore, and recovery."

In addition, you can use the Export command in Registry Editor to back up the branch of the registry where you plan to work.

Registry Editor can save all or portions of your registry in any of the four different formats described here:

- **Registration Files.** The Registration Files option creates a .reg file, a text file that can be read and edited in Notepad or a similar program. A .reg file can be merged into the registry of a system running any version of Windows. When you merge a .reg file, its keys and values replace the corresponding keys and values in the registry. Using .reg files allows you to edit your registry "offline" and add your changes to the registry without even opening Registry Editor. You can also use .reg files as an easy way to share registry settings and copy them to other computers.

- **Registry Hive Files.** The Registry Hive File format saves a binary image of a selected portion of the registry. You won't be able to read the resulting file (choose one of the text-file options if that's what you need to do), but if you need to restore the keys you've worked on, you can be confident that this format will do the job correctly.

  Registry hive file is the format of choice if you want to create a backup before working in Registry Editor. That's because when you import a registry hive file, it restores the entire hive to exactly the way it was when you saved it. (The .reg file types, when merged, restore all the saved keys and values to their original locations, which repairs all deletions and edits. But the process does not remove any keys or values that you added.) Note, however, that a registry hive file has the potential to do the greatest damage if you import it to the wrong key; see the caution in the following section.

- **Win9x/NT4 Registration Files.** The Win9x/NT4 Registration Files option also generates a .reg file, but one in an older format used by earlier versions of Windows. The principal difference between the two formats is that the current format uses Unicode and the older format does not. We can't think of a real-world scenario where you would actually want to use this legacy format.

- **Text Files.** The Text Files option, like the Registration Files option, creates a file that can be read in Notepad or another text editor. The principal advantage of this format is that it cannot accidentally (or intentionally) be merged into the registry. Thus, it's a good way to create a record of your registry's state at a particular time. Its disadvantage, relative to the .reg file format, is its size. Text files are considerably larger than corresponding .reg files, and they take longer to create.

To export a registry hive, select a key in the left pane, and then on the File menu, click Export. (Easier yet: right-click a key and click Export.) In the Save As Type list in the Export Registry File dialog box, select one of the four file types. Under Export Range, select Selected Branch. The resulting file includes the selected key and all its subkeys and values.

If you need to restore the exported hive from a registry hive file, select the same key in the left pane of the Registry Editor window, click Import on the File menu, and specify the file. You'll see a confirmation prompt letting you know that your action will overwrite (replace) the current key and all its subkeys. This is your last chance to make sure you're importing the hive into the right location, so take a moment to make sure you've selected the correct key before you click Yes.

CAUTION

Importing a registry hive file replaces the entire content of the selected key with the contents of the file—regardless of its original source. That is, it wipes out everything in the selected key and then adds the keys and values from the file. When you import, be absolutely certain that you've selected the correct key.

If you saved your backup as a .reg file, you use the same process to import it. (As an alternative, you can double-click the .reg file in File Explorer without opening Registry Editor.) Unlike with a registry hive file, however, the complete path to each key and value is stored as part of the file and it always restores to the same location. This approach for recovering from registry editing mishaps is fine if you did not add new values or subkeys to the section of the registry you're working with; it returns existing data to its former state but doesn't alter the data you've added.

TROUBLESHOOTING

You used a registry cleaner and your system is no longer working properly

The registry is often inscrutable and can appear messy. Misguided attempts at cleanup can cause unexpected problems that are nearly impossible to troubleshoot, which explains why Microsoft is so insistent with its warnings that improper changes to the registry can prevent your computer from operating properly or even booting. We've never found a so-called registry cleaner that justifies the risk it inevitably entails. If you find yourself with a misbehaving system after using a registry cleaner, use the Reset option to recover your system and start over. And this time, don't bother to install that unnecessary utility.

Browsing and editing with Registry Editor

Because of the registry's size, looking for a particular key, value, or data item can be daunting. In Registry Editor, the Find command (on the Edit menu; also available by pressing Ctrl+F) works in the forward direction only and does not wrap around when it gets to the end of the registry. If you're not sure where the item you need is located, select the highest level in the left pane before issuing the command. If you have an approximate idea where the item you want is located, you can save time by starting at a node closer to (but still above) the target.

After you have located an item of interest, you can put it on the Favorites list to simplify a return visit. Open the Favorites menu, click Add To Favorites, and supply a friendly name (or accept the default). If you're about to close Registry Editor and know you'll be returning to the same key the next time you open the editor, you can skip the Favorites step because Registry Editor always remembers your last position and returns to that position in the next session.

Registry Editor includes a number of time-saving keyboard shortcuts for navigating the registry. To move to the next subkey that starts with a particular letter, simply type that letter when the focus is in the left pane; in the right pane, use the same trick to jump to the next value that begins with that letter. To open a key (revealing its subkeys), press the Right Arrow key. To move up one level in the subkey hierarchy, press the Left Arrow key; a second press collapses the subkeys of the current key. To move to the top of the hierarchy, press Home. To quickly move between the left and right panes, use the Tab key. In the right pane, press F2 to rename a value, and press Enter to open that value and edit its data. Once you get the hang of using these keyboard shortcuts, you'll find it's usually easier to zip through the subkey hierarchy with a combination of arrow keys and letter keys than it is to open outline controls with the mouse.

Changing data

You can change the data associated with a value by selecting a value in the right pane and pressing Enter or by double-clicking the value. Registry Editor pops up an edit window appropriate for the value's data type.

Adding or deleting keys

To add a key, select the new key's parent in the left pane, open the Edit menu, point to New, and click Key. The new key arrives as a generically named outline entry, exactly the way a new folder does in File Explorer. Type a new name. To delete a key, select it and then press Delete.

Adding or deleting values

To add a value, select the parent key, open the Edit menu, and point to New. On the submenu that appears, click the type of value you want to add. A value of the type you select appears in the right pane with a generic name. Type over the generic name, press Enter twice, enter your data, and press Enter once more. To delete a value, select it and press Delete.

Using .reg files to automate registry changes

The .reg files created by the Export command in Registry Editor are plain text, suitable for reading and editing in Notepad or any similar editor. Therefore, they provide an alternative method for editing your registry. You can export a section of the registry, change it offline, and then merge it back into the registry. Or you can add new keys, values, and data to the registry by creating a .reg file from scratch and merging it. A .reg file is particularly useful if you need to make the same changes to the registry of several different computers. You can make and test your changes on one machine, save the relevant part of the registry as a .reg file, and then transport the file to the other machines that require it.

Figure 18-13 shows a .reg file. In this case, the file was exported from the HKCU\Software\Microsoft\Windows\CurrentVersion\Explorer\Advanced key, shown in Figure 18-14.

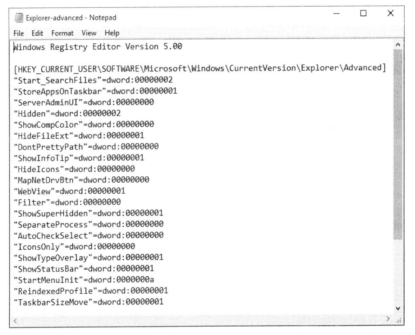

Figure 18-13 A .reg file is a plain-text file suitable for offline editing. This .reg file was exported from the key shown in Figure 18-14.

Figure 18-14 This key's name, values, and data are recorded in the .reg file shown in Figure 18-13.

Identifying the elements of a .reg file

As you review the examples shown in the two figures, note the following characteristics of .reg files:

- **Header line.** The file begins with the line "Windows Registry Editor Version 5.00." When you merge a .reg file into the registry, Registry Editor uses this line to verify that the file contains registry data. Version 5 (the version used with Windows 7 and later versions, including Windows 10) generates Unicode text files, which can be used with all supported versions of Windows as well as the now-unsupported Windows XP and Windows 2000.

- **Key names.** Key names are delimited by brackets and must include the full path from the root key to the current subkey. The root key name must not be abbreviated. (Don't use HKCU, for example.) Figure 18-13 shows only one key name, but you can have as many as you please.

- **The default value.** Undefined default values do not appear in .reg files. Defined default values are identified by the special character @. Thus, a key whose default REG_SZ value was defined as MyApp would appear in a .reg file this way:

```
"@"="MyApp"
```

- **Value names.** Value names must be enclosed in quotation marks, whether or not they include space characters. Follow the value name with an equal sign.

- **Data types.** REG_SZ values don't get a data type identifier or a colon. The data directly follows the equal sign. Other data types are identified as shown in Table 18-1:

Table 18-1 Data types identified in .reg files

Data type	Identifier
REG_BINARY	hex
REG_DWORD	dword
REG_QWORD	hex(b)
REG_MULTI_SZ	hex(7)
REG_EXPAND_SZ	hex(2)

A colon separates the identifier from the data. Thus, for example, a REG_DWORD value named "Keyname" with value data of 00000000 looks like this:

```
"Keyname"=dword:00000000
```

- **REG_SZ values.** Ordinary string values must be enclosed in quotation marks. A backslash character within a string must be written as two backslashes. Thus, for example, the path C:\Program Files\Microsoft Office\ is written like this:

```
"C:\\Program Files\\Microsoft Office\\"
```

- **REG_DWORD values.** DWORD values are written as eight hexadecimal digits, without spaces or commas. Do not use the 0x prefix.

- **All other data types.** All other data types—including REG_EXPAND_SZ, REG_MULTI_SZ, and REG_QWORD—appear as comma-delimited lists of hexadecimal bytes (two hex digits, a comma, two more hex digits, and so on). The following is an example of a REG_MULTI_SZ value:

```
"Addins"=hex(7):64,00,3a,00,5c,00,6c,00,6f,00,74,00,00,75,00,73,00,5c,00,\
31,00,32,00,33,00,5c,00,61,00,64,00,64,00,69,00,6e,00,73,00,5c,00,\
64,00,71,00,61,00,75,00,69,00,2e,00,31,00,32,00,61,00,00,00,00,00,00,00,00
```

- **Line-continuation characters.** You can use the backslash as a line-continuation character. The REG_MULTI_SZ value just shown, for example, is all one stream of bytes. We've added backslashes and broken the lines for readability, and you can do the same in your .reg files.

- **Line spacing.** You can add blank lines for readability. Registry Editor ignores them.

- **Comments.** To add a comment line to a .reg file, begin the line with a semicolon.

Using a .reg file to delete registry data

.Reg files are most commonly used to modify existing registry data or add new data. But you can also use them to delete existing values and keys.

To delete an existing value, specify a hyphen character (minus sign) as the value's data. For example, to use a .reg file to remove the value ShellState from the key HKCU\Software\Microsoft\Windows\CurrentVersion\Explorer, add the following lines to the .reg file:

```
[HKEY_CURRENT_USER\Software\Microsoft\Windows\CurrentVersion\Explorer]
"ShellState"=-
```

To delete an existing key with all its values and data, insert a hyphen in front of the key name (inside the left bracket). For example, to use a .reg file to remove the key HKCR\.xyz\shell and all its values, add the following to the .reg file:

```
[-HKEY_CLASSES_ROOT\.xyz\shell]
```

Merging a .reg file into the registry

To merge a .reg file into the registry from within Registry Editor, open the File menu and click Import. Registry Editor adds the imported data under the appropriate key names, overwriting existing values where necessary.

The default action for a .reg file is Merge—meaning merge with the registry. Therefore, you can merge a file into the registry by simply double-clicking it in File Explorer and answering the confirmation prompt.

Using Microsoft Management Console

Microsoft Management Console (MMC) is an application that hosts tools for administering computers, networks, and other system components. By itself, MMC performs no administrative services. Rather, it acts as the host for one or more modules, called *snap-ins*, which do the useful work. MMC provides user-interface consistency so that you or the users you support see more or less the same style of application each time you need to carry out some kind of computer management task. A combination of one or more snap-ins can be saved in a file called a Microsoft Common Console Document or, more commonly, an MMC console.

Creating snap-ins requires expertise in programming. You don't have to be a programmer, however, to make your own custom MMC consoles. All you need to do is run MMC, start with a blank console, and add one or more of the snap-ins available on your system. Alternatively, you can customize some of the MMC consoles supplied by Microsoft or other vendors simply by adding or removing snap-ins. You might, for example, want to combine the Services console with the Event Viewer console, the latter filtered to show only events generated by services. You might also want to include a link to a website that offers details about services and service-related errors. Or perhaps you would like to simplify some of the existing consoles by removing snap-ins that you seldom use.

MMC consoles use, by default, the file-name extension .msc, and .msc files are associated by default with MMC. Thus, you can run any MMC console by double-clicking its file name in a File Explorer window or by entering the file name at a command prompt. Windows 10 includes several predefined consoles; the most commonly used ones, described in Table 18-2, can be easily found by typing their name in the search box.

Inside OUT

Avoiding User Account Control problems with MMC consoles

Consoles can be used to manage all sorts of computer hardware and Windows features: with a console you can modify hard-drive partitions, start and stop services, and install device drivers, for example. In other words, MMC consoles perform the types of tasks that User Account Control (UAC) is designed to restrict. In the hands of someone malicious (or simply careless), consoles have the power to wreak havoc on your computer.

Therefore, when using an MMC console, you're likely to encounter a User Account Control request for permission to continue. If UAC is enabled on your computer, the type of request you get and the restrictions that are imposed depend on your account type and the console you're using. Some consoles, such as Device Manager (Devmgmt.msc), display a message box informing you that the console will run with limitations. (In effect, it works in a read-only mode that allows you to view device information but not make changes.) Others block all use by nonadministrative users. To ensure that you don't run into an "access denied" roadblock when performing administrative tasks while signed in with a standard account, always right-click and then click Run As Administrator.

Table 18-2 Useful predefined consoles

Console name (file name)	Description
Computer Management (Compmgmt.msc)	Includes the functionality of the Task Scheduler, Event Viewer, Shared Folders, Local Users And Groups, Performance Monitor, Device Manager, Disk Management, Services, and WMI Control snap-ins, providing control over a wide range of computer tasks.
Device Manager (Devmgmt.msc)	Uses the Device Manager snap-in to enable administration of all attached hardware devices and their drivers. See Chapter 13 for more information on configuring hardware.
Event Viewer (Eventvwr.msc)	Uses the Event Viewer snap-in to display all types of logged information. See "Event Viewer" in Chapter 17, "Troubleshooting," for details.
Performance Monitor (Perfmon.msc)	Uses the Performance Monitor snap-in to provide a set of monitoring tools far superior to Performance Monitor in earlier Windows versions. See Chapter 15, "System maintenance and performance," for details.
Services (Services.msc)	Uses the Services snap-in to manage services in Windows. For details, see "Managing startup programs and services" in Chapter 15.
Task Scheduler (Taskschd.msc)	Uses the Task Scheduler snap-in for managing tasks that run automatically. For details, see "Using Task Scheduler" in Chapter 19, "Automating tasks and activities."
Windows Firewall With Advanced Security (Wf.msc)	Uses the Windows Firewall With Advanced Security snap-in to configure rules and make other firewall settings. For details, see "Advanced tools for managing Windows Firewall" in Chapter 7.

If you use your computer very often—and if you're reading this book you probably do—you likely find yourself performing certain ordinary tasks repeatedly. Such tasks might include routine maintenance activities, such as backing up your data or cleaning deadwood from your hard disk, or they might be jobs that require many steps. Computers excel at repetitive actions, and Windows 10 provides several ways to automate such tasks:

- **Task Scheduler.** Probably the most important automation tool at your disposal is Task Scheduler, which lets you set up automated routines that are triggered by events or by a schedule and requires no programming expertise.

- **Batch programs.** A carryover from the earliest days of MS-DOS, batch programming still offers an easy, reliable way to run sequences of tasks. Most Windows programs can be started from a command prompt, which means they can be started from a batch program.

- **Windows Script Host.** This feature allows you to run scripts written in VBScript, JScript, and other languages. Although learning how to use Windows Script Host is more difficult than learning to create batch programs, scripts can interact with the operating system and with other programs in more powerful ways.

- **Windows PowerShell.** Windows PowerShell is a .NET-based command-line shell and scripting language tailored to work with Windows. If you're serious about scripting Windows 10, you'll want to take a look at Windows PowerShell. Chapter 21, "Working with Command Prompt and Windows PowerShell," provides an introduction to this important topic as well as references for further study.

Using Task Scheduler

Task Scheduler is a Microsoft Management Console (MMC) snap-in that supports an extensive set of triggering and scheduling options. You can run programs or scripts at specified times, launch actions when a computer has been idle for a specified period of time, run tasks when particular users sign in or out, and so on. Task Scheduler is also tightly integrated with the

Event Viewer snap-in, making it easy for you to use events (an application crash or a disk-full error, for example) as triggers for tasks.

To launch Task Scheduler, in the search box, type **sched**. In the results list, click Task Scheduler (Desktop App) or Schedule Tasks (Settings). Alternatively, press Windows key+R and type **taskschd.msc** in the Open box.

Figure 19-1 shows a sample of Task Scheduler in its default layout. As you can see, the window is divided into three regions—a console tree on the left, the Actions pane on the right, and, in between, various informative windows in the details pane. The console tree shows you which computer you're working with (the local machine or a network computer) and provides a folder tree of currently defined tasks. You can create your own folders here to organize the tasks that you create yourself, or you can add new tasks to existing folders.

Figure 19-1 Like many other MMC snap-ins, Task Scheduler presents a console tree, the Actions pane, and various informative windows.

The Actions pane provides a menu of things you can do. Some, but not all, of the items here are also available on the menus at the top of the window. If your screen is too crowded with the Actions pane displayed, you can hide—and redisplay—it using the button at the right end of the toolbar, directly below the menu bar.

In the center part of the window, initially you see an overview message (this is a bit of static text; once you've read it, you can hide it by clicking the collapse arrow at the right), a status report of all tasks that have run (or were scheduled to run) during some period of time (by default, the most recent 24 hours), and a summary of all the currently enabled tasks. Entries in the Task Status list have outline controls; click an item's plus sign to see more details.

The Task Status and Active Tasks areas are not updated automatically. To get the latest information, click Refresh at the bottom of the screen, in the Actions pane, or on the Action menu.

If this is your first visit to Task Scheduler, you might be surprised by the number of active tasks that Windows and your applications have already established. To see which tasks managed by Task Scheduler are currently running, click Display All Running Tasks in the Actions pane.

To satisfy your curiosity about what an active task does and how it has been set up, you need to locate it in the console tree. Expand the outline entries as needed, and browse to an item of interest. The entries in the console tree are virtual folders, each of which can contain subfolders or one or more tasks. When you select a folder, the upper part of the details pane lists all tasks stored in the folder. The lower area of the pane, meanwhile, shows a tabbed display of the properties of the selected task. Figure 19-2 shows the Customer Experience Improvement Program folder selected in the console tree, the task named KernelCeipTask selected in the upper area of the details pane, and the General tab of the KernelCeipTask properties displayed in the lower area. (The Actions pane has been hidden in this figure.)

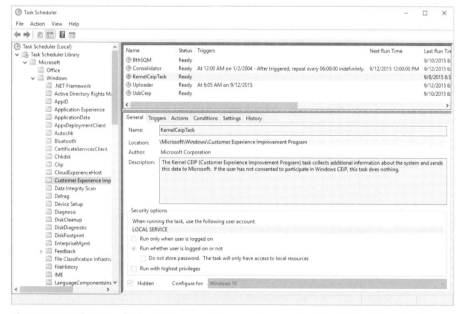

Figure 19-2 Selecting a folder in the console tree produces a list of that folder's tasks in the upper part of the details pane and a properties display in the lower part.

The properties display that appears is read-only. To edit the properties associated with a task, right-click the task name and then click Properties (or double-click the task's entry). That will open a read/write dialog box in a separate window.

With the exception of the History tab, the properties dialog box is identical to the Create Task dialog box, one of the tools you can use to create a new task; we'll explore that dialog box in some detail in the following section, "Creating a task." The History tab allows you to see exactly how, whether, and when a task has run. Figure 19-3 shows the History tab for the ProactiveScan task in the Microsoft\Windows\Chkdsk folder.

Figure 19-3 The History tab lets you confirm that a scheduled task is running as expected.

NOTE

If the History tab is disabled, click Enable All Tasks History in the Actions pane.

When you display the History tab, the relevant portion of the Event Viewer snap-in snaps in, showing you all the recent events related to the selected task. (Only the top of that pane is visible in Figure 19-3, directly below the properties pane.) This is exactly what you would see if you ran Eventvwr.msc, navigated in the console tree to Applications And Services Logs\ Microsoft\Windows\TaskScheduler\Operational, and filtered the resulting log to show events related to the selected task. (Obviously, if you want this information, it's quicker to find it in the

Task Scheduler console than in the Event Viewer console.) If a task you've set up is not being triggered when you expect it to or not running successfully when it should, you can double-click the appropriate event entry and read whatever details the event log has to offer.

Inside OUT
Use the History tab to troubleshoot tasks

The Windows 10 Task Scheduler maintains an ample history of the events generated by each task. If a task is failing regularly or intermittently, you can review all the causes by scrolling through the History tab on the task's properties display.

Task Scheduler terminology

As you go through the steps to create or edit a task, you'll encounter the following terms:

- **Trigger.** The time at which a task is scheduled to run or the event in response to which a task runs. A task can have multiple triggers.

- **Action.** What the task does. Possible actions include starting a program, sending an email message, and displaying a message on the screen. A task can have multiple actions, in which case the actions occur sequentially in the order in which you assign them.

- **Condition.** An additional requirement that, along with the trigger, must be met for the task to run. For example, a condition might stipulate that the task run only if the computer has been idle for 10 minutes or only if it's running on AC power.

- **Setting.** A property that affects the behavior of a task. With settings, you can do such things as enable a task to run on demand or set retry parameters to be followed if a task fails to run when it's triggered.

Creating a task

You can set up tasks on your own computer or any other computer to which you have access. If you're administering a remote computer, start by selecting the top item in the console tree—the one that says Task Scheduler (Local) if you haven't yet connected to a remote computer. Then click Connect To Another Computer in the Actions pane or on the Action menu.

To begin creating a new task, select the folder in the console tree where you want the task to reside. (If you need to create a new folder for this purpose, right-click the folder's parent in the console tree and click New Folder.)

You can create a new task in the Task Scheduler snap-in by using a wizard or by filling out the Create Task dialog box. The wizard, which you launch by clicking Create Basic Task (in the Actions pane or on the Action menu), is ideal for time-triggered tasks involving a single action. It's also fine for setting up a task to run when you sign in or when Windows starts. For a more complex task definition, you need to work through the Create Task dialog box. Select the folder where you want the task to appear (in the console tree), and then click Create Task in the Actions pane or on the Action menu. Figure 19-4 shows the General tab of the Create Task dialog box.

Figure 19-4 On the General tab, type a name for your new task and indicate the security context it should run in.

The one required entry on the General tab is a name for the task; everything else is optional. The task's author is you (you can't change that), and unless you specify otherwise, the task will run in your own security context. If you want it to run in the security context of a different user or group, click Change User Or Group and fill out the ensuing dialog box.

The circumstance under which you're most likely to need to change the security context is when you're setting up tasks to run on another computer. If you intend to run programs with which another user can interact, you should run those in the other user's security context. If you run them in your own, the tasks will run noninteractively (that is, the user will not see them).

Regardless of which user's security context the task is to run in, you have the option of allowing the task to run whether that user is signed in or not. If you select Run Whether User Is Logged On Or Not, you will be prompted for the user's password when you finish creating the task. If you don't happen to have that password, you can select Do Not Store Password. As the text beside this check box indicates, the task will have access to local resources only.

Creating a task to run with elevated privileges

If the task you're setting up is one that would generate a User Account Control (UAC) prompt if it is run interactively, you'll want to select Run With Highest Privileges. If you're setting up a task to run with elevated privileges in the context of a user who does not have administrative credentials, you are asked to supply credentials when you complete the task-setup process.

Creating a hidden task

Windows XP Service Pack 2 introduced the ability to create hidden tasks—tasks that did not ordinarily appear in the Windows XP Scheduled Tasks folder. Such tasks could be created only by means of an application programming interface (API). In Windows 10 and other recent versions of Windows, you can create such tasks without using the API by selecting the Hidden check box. Presumably the reason to do this is to make tasks that you set up for other users less visible (hence, less subject to alteration or deletion) on their target machines.

Note, however, that anyone with administrative credentials can make hidden tasks visible by clicking View, Show Hidden Tasks. And anyone running Task Scheduler can alter or delete tasks at will, regardless of who created them.

Configuring a task to run in a different operating system

If you're setting up a task on a remote computer that's running an operating system other than Windows 10, open the Configure For list and choose appropriately. Note that some applications that create scheduled tasks as part of their installation might configure those tasks for Windows 7, Windows Vista, or Windows XP. These tasks should run properly on Windows 10.

Setting up a task's trigger or triggers

Tasks can be triggered in the following ways:

- On a schedule

- At sign-in

- At startup

- On idle

- On an event

- At task creation or modification

- On connection to a user session

- On disconnection from a user session

- On workstation lock

- On workstation unlock

You can establish zero, one, or several triggers for a task. If you don't set any triggers, you can still run the task on demand (unless you clear the Allow Task To Be Run On Demand check box on the Settings tab of the Create Task dialog box). This gives you a way to test a new task before committing it to a schedule, for example. If you set multiple triggers, the task runs when any one of the triggers occurs.

To set up a trigger, click the Triggers tab in the Create Task dialog box, and then click New. In the New Trigger dialog box (shown in Figure 19-5), choose the type of trigger you want from the Begin The Task list.

Figure 19-5 A task can have zero, one, or several triggers. Advanced Settings options let you set delay, repeat, and expiration parameters.

Note the Advanced Settings options at the bottom of the dialog box shown in Figure 19-5. These choices—which let you establish delay, repeat, and expiration parameters (among other things)—are not so easy to find when you're reviewing a task that you or someone has already created. They don't appear in the read-only version of a task's properties, and in the read/write version of the properties dialog box, you need to select a trigger (on the Triggers tab) and click Edit to see or change the advanced settings.

Triggering a task on schedule   Time-triggered tasks can be set to run once or to recur at regular intervals. The choices are probably self-explanatory, with the possible exception of the Synchronize Across Time Zones check box. Time triggers are governed by the clock of the machine on which the task is to run, unless you select this check box—in which case, they are based on coordinated universal time (UTC). You might want to go with UTC if you're trying to coordinate time-triggered tasks on multiple machines in multiple time zones.

Triggering a task at sign-in   Sign-in tasks can be set for any user or a specific user or user group. If the user whose sign-in triggers the task is not the user in whose security context the task is running, the task will be noninteractive—in other words, essentially invisible. (The user can note the presence of the task—and terminate it—by running Windows Task Manager, going to the Users tab, and expanding the current user to see a list of running processes.)

Triggering a task at startup   If you set a task to be triggered at startup, the trigger takes effect when you start your own computer (assuming you have Task Scheduler set to configure the local machine) but before you sign in. Therefore, if you intend for the task to run on your own system, be sure to choose Run Whether User Is Logged On Or Not on the General tab of the Create Task dialog box. Otherwise, the task will never run.

If you use the Change User Or Group button on the General tab to specify another user on your domain and you select Run Only When User Is Logged On, the startup-triggered task will run on the remote system when you restart your own, provided the specified user actually is signed in.

Triggering a task on idle   If you set a task to be triggered when your computer is idle, you should also go to the Conditions tab of the Create Task dialog box to specify what you mean by idle. For information about how Task Scheduler defines idleness, see "Starting and running a task only if the computer is idle" later in this chapter.

Note that you need to set an idle trigger on the Triggers tab only if idleness is the only trigger you want to use. If you're setting one or more other triggers but want to ensure that the task starts only when the computer is idle, select Start The Task Only If The Computer Is Idle For on the Conditions tab.

Using an event to trigger a task   Anything that generates an item in an event log can serve as a task trigger. The simplest way to use this feature is to launch Event Viewer (Eventvwr.msc), find the event that you want to use as a trigger, right-click it in Event Viewer, and click Attach

Task To This Event. This action launches the Create Basic Task Wizard, with the trigger portion of the wizard already filled out. The new task appears in a folder called Event Viewer Tasks (newly created for you if it doesn't already exist), and you can modify the task if needed by selecting it there and opening its properties dialog box.

> ➤ For information about events and event logs, see "Event Viewer" in Chapter 17, "Troubleshooting."

It's possible, of course, to create an event-driven task directly in Task Scheduler—by selecting On An Event in the New Trigger dialog box. If you set up the task in this fashion, you need to supply the Log, Source, and Event ID information yourself. It's more trouble to do it this way, and there's no need.

Triggering at task creation or modification   The option to trigger a task at task creation or modification gives you an easy way to run a task the moment you finish setting it up or edit it subsequently. You can use this setting for testing purposes or, by combining it with other triggers, to make a task run immediately as well as subsequently.

Triggering a task at user connection or disconnection   The options On Connection To A User Session and On Disconnect From A User Session give you some flexible ways to run tasks in response to user activities. Option buttons associated with these choices let you specify whether the settings apply to any user or to a particular user or group. Additional options make the trigger apply to remote connections and disconnections or to local connections and disconnections. Setting a trigger to a particular user on the local computer, for example, enables you to run a task in response to that user's connection via Remote Desktop Connection or the Switch User command.

Triggering a task at workstation lock or unlock   Like several other triggering choices, the On Workstation Lock and On Workstation Unlock options can be configured to apply to a particular user or group or to anyone who locks or unlocks the computer.

Setting up a task's action or actions

Besides its name (which you supply on the General tab of the Create Task dialog box), the only other task parameter you must provide is the action or actions the task is supposed to perform. This you do by clicking New on the Actions tab and filling out the rest of the dialog box.

Opening the Start A Program drop-down menu, you will find three choices: Start A Program, Send An E-Mail, and Display A Message. The second and third of these, however, have been deprecated since Windows 8. So leave Action set at Start A Program, and then supply the program (or script) name, optional arguments, and an optional start location.

You can specify one or several actions. Multiple actions are carried out sequentially, with each new action beginning when the previous one is complete.

The Start A Program option can be applied to anything that Windows can execute—a Windows program, a batch program or script, a document associated with a program, or a shortcut. You can use the Browse button to simplify entry of long path specifications, add command-line parameters for your executable on the Add Arguments line, and specify a start-in folder for the executable. If your program needs elevated privileges to run success-fully, be sure that you select Run With Highest Privileges on the General tab of the Create Task dialog box.

Starting and running a task only if the computer is idle

On the Conditions tab of the Create Task dialog box (shown in Figure 19-6), you can require that the computer be idle for a specified period of time before a triggered task can begin. To do this, select Start The Task Only If The Computer Is Idle For, and specify the time period in the field to the right. Other check boxes in the Idle section of the Conditions tab let you spec-ify what should happen if the task starts to run during a required idle period but the computer subsequently becomes active again.

Figure 19-6 You can configure a task to run only when the computer is idle, only when it's running on AC power, or only when it's connected to a network.

Task Scheduler defines idleness as follows:

- If a screen saver is running, the computer is presumed to be idle.

- If a screen saver is not running, the system checks for idleness every 15 minutes, considering the machine to be idle if no keyboard or mouse input has occurred during that
interval and if the disk input/output (I/O) and CPU usage figures were 0 percent for 90
percent of that time.

In addition to specifying a required period of idleness, you can tell Windows to wait some
period of time after a task has been triggered before beginning to determine whether the
computer is idle. Clearly, adjusting the idle parameters is a bit of an art; if you have precise
requirements for some reason, you might need to experiment and test to get things just the
way you want them.

Requiring AC power

If you're setting up a task to run on a portable computer, consider whether you want the task
to begin running while the computer is running on battery power. If you do not, select Start
The Task Only If The Computer Is On AC Power in the Power section of the Conditions tab.
A second check box below this one lets you specify whether the task, once it begins, should
cease if the computer switches to battery power.

Waking the computer to run a task

If it's essential that your task run at some particular time, whether or not the computer is
asleep, be sure to select Wake The Computer To Run This Task on the Conditions tab. Once
roused, the computer will then perform whatever duties you've assigned, returning to sleep on
completion in accordance with whatever power plan is in effect.

If you do not want to disturb your computer's rest, you might want to stipulate that the task
run as soon as possible after the machine wakes. You can do that by selecting Run Task As
Soon As Possible After A Scheduled Start Is Missed on the Settings tab of the Create Task dialog box.

Requiring a network connection

If your task requires access to network resources, be sure to select Start Only If The Following
Network Connection Is Available on the Conditions tab. Then use the drop-down list directly
below this check box to specify which network connection is required. You might want to use
this option in conjunction with Run Task As Soon As Possible After A Scheduled Start Is Missed,
a check box on the Settings tab.

Running a task on demand

You can run a scheduled task on demand as well as in response to various time or event triggers. You can turn this feature off for a task by clearing the Allow Task To Be Run On Demand
check box on the Settings tab. But unless you're concerned that another user with access to
your system might run a task against your wishes, it's hard to imagine why you would want to
disallow on-demand execution.

To run a task on demand, assuming you have not disallowed it, locate the task's folder in the
console tree, right-click the task in Task Scheduler's upper pane, and then click Run.

Scheduling tasks with the Schtasks command

Task Scheduler provides a friendly and versatile method of creating and managing scheduled
tasks. In some instances, however, you might find it easier to manage scheduled tasks from a
command prompt. For these occasions. Windows provides the Schtasks command, a replacement for the venerable At command that was included with earlier versions of the Windows
NT platform. With Schtasks, you can create, modify, delete, end, view, and run scheduled
tasks—and, of course, you can incorporate the command in batch programs and scripts.

Tasks created via Schtasks appear in the top-level folder (Task Scheduler Library) in the Task
Scheduler console tree, and you can edit, run, or delete them from there as well as from the
command prompt.

Schtasks is a rather complex command with lots of command-line switches and other parameters, but it has only six main variants:

- **Schtasks /Create.** This variant, which you use to create a new scheduled task, is the
  most complex because of all the available triggering options, conditions, and settings.
  For details, type **schtasks /create /?** at the command prompt.

- **Schtasks /Change.** This variant allows you to modify an existing task. Among other
  things, you can change the program that the task runs, the user account under which
  the task runs, or the password associated with that user account. For details, type
  schtasks /change /? at the command prompt.

- **Schtasks /Delete.** This variant deletes an existing task or, optionally, all tasks on a
  computer.

- **Schtasks /End.** This variant stops a program that was started by a scheduled task.

- **Schtasks /Query.** This variant displays, with optional verbosity, all scheduled tasks
  on the local or a remote computer. You can use arguments to restrict the display to

particular tasks or tasks running in particular security contexts. For details, type **schtasks /query /?** at the command prompt.

● **Schtasks /Run.** This variant runs a specified task on demand.

A few examples should give you an idea of the power of the Schtasks command. Suppose, for example, that you want to run OneNote 2013 every four hours at 20 minutes past the hour. Assuming the OneNote executable exists at the specified location on your computer, the following command sets you up:

```
schtasks /create /tn "Run OneNote" /tr "%programfiles%\Microsoft Office 15\root\
office15\onenote.exe" /sc hourly /mo 4 /st 00:20:00
```

In this example, the /tn switch specifies the name of the task, /tr specifies the path to the executable program, /sc specifies the schedule type, /mo specifies the interval, and /st specifies the starting time.

The following example creates a task that runs a script on the last Friday of each calendar quarter. (The script isn't included with Windows; it's just an example.)

```
schtasks /create /tn "Quarterly wrap-up" /tr c:\apps\qtrwrap.vbs /sc monthly /mo last
/d fri /m mar,jun,sep,dec
```

By default, tasks scheduled via the Schtasks command run under the user account that's currently signed in. To make them run under a different account, use the /ru switch followed by the account name you want to use; you also need to know the sign-in password for that account. To use the built-in System account, append /ru "System" to the command. No password is required for the System account, but because only administrators can use Schtasks, this doesn't present a problem.

Automating command sequences with batch programs

A batch program (also commonly called a *batch file*) is a text file that contains a sequence of commands to be executed. You execute the commands by entering the file name at a command prompt. Any action you can take by typing a command at a command prompt can be encapsulated in a batch program.

When you type the name of your batch program at the command prompt (or when you specify it as a task to be executed by Task Scheduler and the appropriate trigger occurs), the command interpreter opens the file and starts reading the statements. It reads the first line, executes the command, and then goes on to the next line. On the surface, this seems to operate just as though you were typing each line yourself at the command prompt. In fact, however, the batch program can be more complicated because the language includes replaceable parameters, conditional and branching statements, the ability to call subroutines, and so on.

Batch programs can also respond to values returned by programs and to the values of environment variables.

Batch programming is a venerable art, having been with us since the earliest days of MS-DOS (long before Windows was so much as a twinkle in Microsoft's eye). These days there are more powerful scripting tools at your disposal. Nevertheless, if you have already invested some time and energy in learning the language of batch programming, that investment can continue to serve you in Windows 10. Your batch programs will run as well as they ever have, and you can execute them in response to events by means of Task Scheduler.

Automating tasks with Windows Script Host

Microsoft Windows Script Host (WSH) provides a way to perform more sophisticated tasks than the simple jobs that batch programs are able to handle. You can control virtually any component of Windows and of many Windows-based programs with WSH scripts.

To run a script, you can type a script name at a command prompt or double-click the script's icon in File Explorer. WSH has two nearly equivalent programs—Wscript.exe and Cscript.exe—that, with the help of a language interpreter dynamic-link library such as Vbscript.dll, execute scripts written in VBScript or another scripting language. (Cscript.exe is a command-line program; Wscript.exe is its graphical counterpart.)

With WSH, the files can be written in several different languages, including VBScript (a scripting language similar to Microsoft Visual Basic) and JScript (a form of JavaScript). All the objects are available to any language, and in most situations you can choose the language with which you are most comfortable. WSH doesn't care what language you use, provided the appropriate interpreter dynamic-link library is available. VBScript and JScript interpreters come with Windows 10; interpreters for Perl, KiXtart (Kix), Python, Rexx, and other languages are available elsewhere.

Advanced networking

For most users of Windows at home or in a small office, HomeGroup and the other network-ing methods and procedures described in Chapter 5, "Networking essentials," provide all the needed connectivity. In these environments, accessing shared files, media, and printers throughout a local area network is easily achieved.

But there's much more to networking, enough to fill another book the size of this one. In this chapter, we touch upon a few of these more complex features.

We begin with a look at other ways to share resources over a network. While HomeGroup has the advantage of being easy to set up and use, it doesn't allow you to apply resource permis-sions on a granular level. If you need to provide different types of access to individual users, you can use the procedures in this section. Another limitation of HomeGroup is that it works only with Windows 7 and later versions; if your network includes computers running other operating systems or older versions of Windows, this section is for you.

In this chapter we also look at situations in which accessing shared files and printers is not enough; you want access to an *entire computer*. With Remote Desktop, you can do exactly that, and a section of this chapter is devoted to showing you how.

Networked devices don't always communicate the way they should, so we conclude with a survey of network troubleshooting tools included with Windows and explain sound proce-dures for using them.

Viewing network status

If you're familiar with earlier Windows versions, you probably know Network And Sharing Center as the place to go for a quick overview of your network connections and the condition of your network. And, if you're experiencing problems with your network, it serves as a launch pad to various diagnostic tools.

➤ For more information, see "Network And Sharing Center" in Chapter 5.

As you've seen with other Control Panel applications, much of the functionality of Network And Sharing Center from previous Windows versions has made the transition to Settings in Windows 10. Take a look by opening Settings, Network & Internet, which is shown in Figure 20-1.

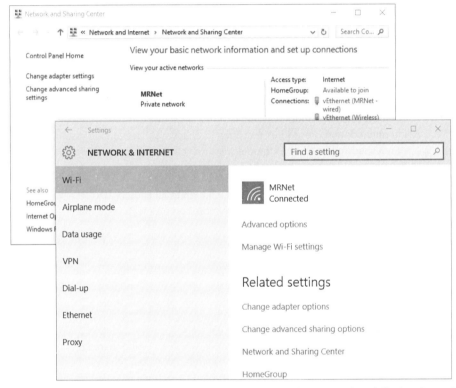

Figure 20-1 Network & Internet in Settings will someday supplant Network And Sharing Center. In the meantime, a link in the Settings app leads to the Control Panel app.

Inside OUT

Easily open Network & Internet or Network And Sharing Center

The quickest way to get to either network settings app is to click or tap the network icon in the notification area of the taskbar. To open Network & Internet in Settings, click the icon and then click **Network Settings**. To open the Network And Sharing Center in Control Panel, right-click or long tap the network icon in the taskbar and then choose **Open Network And Sharing Center.**

Sharing resources with other users

The simplest way to share files, digital media, printers, and other resources in a small network is with HomeGroup, a feature we cover in Chapter 5. Convenient as it is, however, HomeGroup isn't appropriate for all networks. First, it's designed for use in a home, where you fully trust everybody. Hence, it has limited abilities for applying different access requirements to various objects and for various users. Second, HomeGroup works only on computers running Windows 7 and later. Computers running earlier versions of Windows or other operating systems must use different methods for sharing and accessing network resources.

These other methods are fully supported in Windows 10 and can be used alongside Home-Group if you want to. The underlying system of share permissions and NTFS permissions for controlling access to objects remains in Windows 10, working much like it has in previous versions of Windows going all the way back to Windows NT in the early '90s.

> ➤ For more information about HomeGroup, see "Sharing files, digital media, and printers in a homegroup" in Chapter 5.

Understanding sharing and security models in Windows

Much like Windows 7, Windows 10 offers two ways (aside from HomeGroup) to share file resources, whether locally or over the network:

- **Public folder sharing.** When you place files and folders in your Public folder or its subfolders, those files are available to anyone who has a user account on your computer. Each person who signs in has access to his or her own profile folders (Documents, Music, and so on), and *everyone* who signs in has access to the Public folder. (You'll need to dig a bit to find the Public folder, which doesn't appear by default in the left pane of File Explorer. Navigate to C:\Users\Public. If you use the Public folder often, pin it to the Quick Access list in File Explorer.)

  By default, all users with an account on your computer can sign in and create, view, modify, and delete files in the Public folders. The person who creates a file in a Public folder (or copies an item to a Public folder) is the file's owner and has Full Control access. All others who sign in locally have Modify access.

  Settings in Advanced Sharing Settings (accessible from Settings, Network & Internet; see the next section for details), determine whether the contents of your Public folder are made available on your network and whether entering a user name and password is required for access. If you turn on password-protected sharing, only network users who have a user account on your computer (or those who know the user name and password for an account on your computer) can access files in the Public folder. Without password-protected sharing, everyone on your network has access to your Public folder files if you enable network sharing of the Public folder.

You can't select which network users get access, nor can you specify different access levels for different users. Sharing via the Public folder is quick and easy—but it's inflexible.

- **Advanced sharing.** By choosing to share folders or files outside the Public folder, you can specify precisely which user accounts are able to access your shared data, and you can specify the types of privileges those accounts enjoy. You can grant different access privileges to different users. For example, you might enable some users to modify shared files and create new ones, enable other users to read files without changing them, and lock out still other users altogether.

You don't need to decide between sharing the Public folder and sharing specific folders because you can use them both simultaneously. You might find that a mix of sharing styles works best for you; each has its benefits:

- Sharing specific folders is best for files that you want to share with some users but not others—or if you want to grant different levels of access to different users.

- Public folder sharing provides a convenient, logical way to segregate your personal documents, pictures, music, and so on from those that you want to share with everyone who uses your computer or your network.

Configuring your network for sharing

If you plan to share folders and files with other users on your network through options other than those available in the HomeGroup feature, you need to take a few preparatory steps. (If you plan to share only through HomeGroup and with others who use your computer by signing in locally, you can skip these steps. And if your computer is part of a domain, some of these steps—or their equivalent in the domain world—must be done by an administrator on the domain controller. We don't cover those details in this book.)

1. **Be sure that all computers use the same workgroup name.** With versions of Windows newer than Windows XP, this step isn't absolutely necessary, although it does improve network discovery performance. For details, see the sidebar, "Renaming your workgroup."

2. **Be sure that your network's location is set to Private.** This setting provides appropriate security for a network in a home or an office. For details, see "Setting network locations" in Chapter 5.

3. **Be sure that Network Discovery is turned on.** This should happen automatically when you set the network location to Private, but you can confirm the setting—and change it if necessary—in Advanced Sharing Settings, which is shown in Figure 20-2. To open Advanced Sharing Settings, go to Network & Internet or Network And Sharing Center. In either app, click Change Advanced Sharing Options.

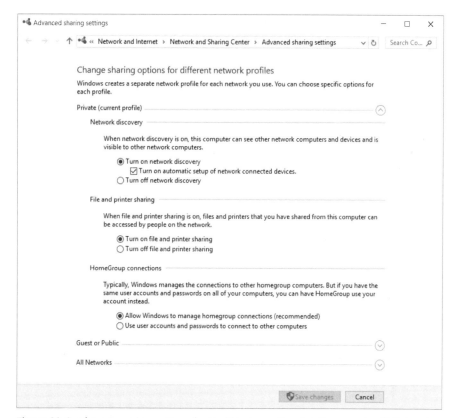

Figure 20-2 After you review settings for the Private profile, click the arrow by All Networks to see additional options.

4. **Select your sharing options.** In Advanced Sharing Settings, make a selection for each of the following network options. You'll find the first two under the Private profile; to view the remaining settings, expand All Networks.

    ▪ **File And Printer Sharing.** Turn on this option if you want to share specific files or folders, the Public folder, or printers; it must be turned on if you plan to share any files (other than media streaming) over your network.

    The mere act of turning on file and printer sharing does not expose any of your computer's files or printers to other network users; that occurs only after you make additional sharing settings.

    ▪ **HomeGroup Connections.** If you use a homegroup for sharing, it's generally best to use the default setting, Allow Windows To Manage Homegroup Connections (Recommended). With this setting, when a user at a computer that is also part of a homegroup attempts to use a shared resource on your computer, Windows connects using the HomeGroupUser$ account.

When a user connects from a computer that is not a member of the homegroup, Windows first tries to authenticate using that person's sign-in credentials; if that fails, Windows uses the built-in Guest account (if password-protected sharing is off) or prompts for credentials (if password-protected sharing is on). If you select Use User Accounts And Passwords To Connect To Other Computers, homegroup computers work like nonhomegroup computers instead of using the HomeGroupUser$ account.

- **Public Folder Sharing.** If you want to share items in your Public folder with all network users (or, if you enable password-protected sharing, all users who have a user account and password on your computer), turn on Public folder sharing. If you do so, network users will have read/write access to Public folders. With Public folder sharing turned off, anyone who signs in to your computer locally has access to Public folders, but network users do not.

- **Media Streaming.** Turning on media streaming provides access to pictures, music, and video through streaming protocols that can send media to computers or to other media playback devices.

- **File Sharing Connections.** Unless you have very old computers on your network, leave this option set to 128-bit encryption, which has been the standard for most of this century.

- **Password Protected Sharing.** When password-protected sharing is turned on, network users cannot access your shared folders (including Public folders, if shared) or printers unless they can provide the user name and password of a user account on your computer. With this setting enabled, when another user attempts to access a shared resource, Windows sends the user name and password that the person used to sign in to his or her own computer. If that matches the credentials for a local user account on your computer, the user gets immediate access to the shared resource (assuming permissions to use the particular resource have been granted to that user account). If either the user name or the password does not match, Windows asks the user to provide credentials.

  With password-protected sharing turned off, Windows does not require a user name and password from network visitors. Instead, network access is provided by using the Guest account. As we explain in Chapter 6, "Managing user accounts, passwords, and credentials," this account isn't available for interactive use but can handle these tasks in the background.

5. **Configure user accounts.** If you use password-protected sharing, each person who accesses a shared resource on your computer must have a user account on your computer. Use the same user name as that person uses on his or her own computer and the same password as well. If you do that, network users will be able to access shared resources without having to enter their credentials after they've signed in to their own computer.

Renaming your workgroup

A workgroup is identified by a name; all computers in a workgroup must be in the same local area network and subnet, and all must share the same workgroup name. In Windows 10, the workgroup name is largely invisible and irrelevant; when you open the Network folder or look at a network map, Windows displays all computers in the network, regardless of which workgroup they're in. (However, network discovery is faster when all computers are in the same workgroup.) The default name for a workgroup in recent Windows versions is WORKGROUP.

To set the workgroup name, follow these steps:

1. In the search box or in Control Panel, type **workgroup**, and then click Change Workgroup Name.

2. On the Computer Name tab of the System Properties dialog box, click Change, which displays the following dialog box:

3. In the Computer Name/Domain Changes dialog box, select Workgroup and type the name of the workgroup (15-character maximum; the name can't include any of these characters: ; : < > * + = \ | / ? ,). Then click OK in each dialog box.

4. Restart your computer.

Sharing files and folders from any folder

Whether you plan to share files and folders with other people who share your computer or those who connect to your computer over the network (or both), the process for setting up shared resources is the same as long as the Sharing Wizard is enabled. We recommend that you use the Sharing Wizard even if you normally disdain wizards. It's quick, easy, and certain to make all the correct settings for network shares and NTFS permissions—a sometimes daunting task if undertaken manually. Once you've configured shares with the wizard, you can always dive in and make changes manually if you need to.

To be sure the Sharing Wizard is enabled, open Folder Options. (Type **folder** in the search box and choose File Explorer Options. Or, in File Explorer, click View, Options.) In the dialog box that appears, shown next, click the View tab. Near the bottom of the Advanced Settings list, see that Use Sharing Wizard (Recommended) is selected.

With the Sharing Wizard at the ready, follow these steps to share a folder or files:

1.   In File Explorer, select the folders or files you want to share. (You can select multiple objects.)

2.   Right-click and choose Share With, Specific People. (Alternatively, click or tap the Share tab and then click Specific People in the Share With box. You might need to click the arrow in the Share With box to display Specific People.) The File Sharing dialog box appears, as shown in Figure 20-3.

Figure 20-3 For each name in the list, you can click the arrow to set the access level—or remove that account from the list.

3.   In the entry box, enter the name or Microsoft account for each user with whom you want to share. You can type a name in the box or click the arrow to display a list of available names; then click Add. Repeat this step for each person you want to add.

The list includes all users who have an account on your computer, plus Everyone. If you've joined a homegroup, the list also includes any Microsoft accounts that have been linked to user accounts on any PC that is part of the homegroup. Guest is included if password-protected sharing is turned off. If you want to grant access to someone who doesn't appear in the list, click Create A New User, which takes you to User Accounts in Control Panel. (This option appears only if your computer is not joined to a homegroup.)

NOTE

If you select Everyone and you have password-protected sharing enabled, the user must still have a valid account on your computer. However, if you have turned off password-protected sharing, network users can gain access *only* if you grant permission to Everyone or to Guest.

4. For each user, select a permission level. Your choices are:

- **Read.** Users with this permission level can view shared files and run shared programs, but they cannot change or delete files. Selecting Read in the Sharing Wizard is equivalent to setting NTFS permissions to Read & Execute.

- **Read/Write.** Users assigned the Read/Write permission have the same privileges you do as owner: they can view, change, add, and delete files in a shared folder. Selecting Read/Write sets NTFS permissions to Full Control for this user.

NOTE

You might see other permission levels if you return to the Sharing Wizard after you set up sharing. Contribute indicates Modify permission. Custom indicates NTFS permissions other than Read & Execute, Modify, or Full Control. Mixed appears if you select multiple items and they have different sharing settings. Owner, of course, identifies the owner of the item.

5. Click Share. After a few moments, the wizard displays a page like the one shown in Figure 20-4.

Figure 20-4 The Sharing Wizard displays the network path for each item you've shared.

6. In the final step of the wizard, you can do any of the following:

- Send an email message to the people with whom you're sharing. The message includes a link to the shared folder or file.

- Copy the network path to the Clipboard. This is handy if you want to send a link via another application, such as a messaging app. (To copy the link for a single item in a list, right-click the share name and choose Copy Link.)

- Double-click a share name to open the shared item.

- Open a search folder that shows all the folders and files you're sharing.

When you're finished with these tasks, click Done.

Creating a share requires privilege elevation, but after a folder has been shared, the share is available to network users no matter who is signed in to your computer—or even when nobody is signed in.

Inside OUT

Use advanced sharing to create shorter network paths

Confusingly, when you share one of your profile folders (or any other subfolder of %SystemDrive%\Users), Windows creates a network share for the Users folder—not for the folder you shared. This isn't a security problem; NTFS permissions prevent network users from seeing any folders or files except the ones you explicitly share. But it does lead to some long Universal Naming Convention (UNC) paths to network shares. For example, sharing the PDW subfolder of Documents (as shown in Figure 20-4) creates the network path \\CARL-SURFACE\Users\Carl\Documents\PDW. If this same folder had been anywhere on your computer outside the Users folder, no matter how deeply nested, the network path would instead be \\CARL-SURFACE\PDW. Other people to whom you granted access wouldn't need to click through a series of folders to find the files in the intended target folder.

Network users, of course, can map a network drive or save a shortcut to your target folder to avoid this problem. But you can work around it from the sharing side too: use advanced sharing to share the folder directly. (Do this after you've used the Sharing Wizard to set up permissions.) For more information, see "Setting advanced sharing properties" following the next section. (And while you're doing that, be sure the share name you create doesn't have spaces. Eliminating them makes it easier to type a share path that works as a link.)

Stopping or changing sharing of a file or folder

If you want to stop sharing a particular shared file or folder, select it in File Explorer and on the Share tab, click Stop Sharing. (Or right-click and choose Share With, Stop Sharing.) Doing so removes access control entries that are not inherited. In addition, the network share is removed; the folder will no longer be visible in another user's Network folder.

To change share permissions, right-click and choose Share With, Specific People. In the File Sharing dialog box (shown earlier in Figure 20-3), you can add users, change permissions, or remove users. (To stop sharing with a particular user, click the arrow by the user's name and choose Remove.)

Setting advanced sharing properties

With Advanced Sharing, you configure network shares independently of NTFS permissions. (For more information about this distinction, see the sidebar "How shared resource permissions and NTFS permissions work together" later in this chapter.) To open Advanced Sharing, right-click a folder, choose Properties, and click the Sharing tab. Or, if the Sharing Wizard is disabled, select a folder in File Explorer and on the ribbon's Share tab (or the right-click Share With menu) choose Advanced Sharing. Both methods display the Sharing tab, which is shown in Figure 20-5.

Figure 20-5 The Share button under Network File And Folder Sharing summons the Sharing Wizard, but it's available only when the wizard is enabled.

NOTE

The Sharing tab is part of the properties dialog box for a folder, but not for files. Also, when the Sharing Wizard is disabled, the Advanced Sharing button appears on the ribbon only when you select a single folder. Only the Sharing Wizard is capable of making share settings for files and for multiple objects simultaneously.

To create or modify a network share using advanced settings, follow these steps:

1. On the Sharing tab, click Advanced Sharing to display the Advanced Sharing dialog box.

2. Select Share This Folder, as shown next.

3. Accept or change the proposed share name.

NOTE

If the folder is already shared and you want to add another share name (perhaps with different permissions), click Add and then type the name for the new share.

The share name is the name that other users will see in their own Network folders. Windows initially proposes to use the folder's name as the share name. That's usually a good choice, but you're not obligated to accept it. If you already have a shared folder with that name, you'll need to pick a different name.

4. Type a description of the folder's contents in the Comments box.

   Other users will see this description when they inspect the folder's properties dialog box in their Network folder (or use Details view).

5. To limit the number of users who can connect to the shared folder concurrently, specify a number in the box. Windows 10 permits up to 20 concurrent network connections. (If you need to share a resource with more users, you must use Windows Server.)

6. Click Permissions.

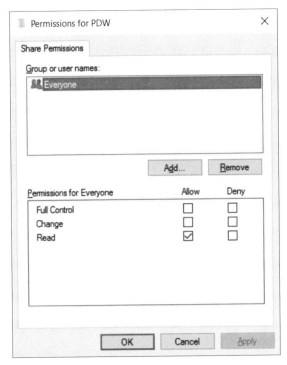

The default shared resource permission associated with a new share is Read access to Everyone.

CAUTION

When you share a folder, you also make that folder's subfolders available on the network. If the access permissions you set for the folder aren't appropriate for any of its subfolders, either reconsider your choice of access permissions or restructure your folders to avoid the problem.

7. In the Group Or User Names list, select the name of the user or group you want to manage.

    The shared resource permissions for the selected user or group appear below in the permissions list.

8. Select Allow, Deny, or neither for each access control entry:

    - **Full Control.** Allows users to create, read, write, rename, and delete files in the folder and its subfolders. In addition, users can change permissions and take ownership of files on NTFS volumes.

    - **Change.** Allows users to read, write, rename, and delete files in the folder and its subfolders but not create new files.

    - **Read.** Allows users to read files but not write to them or delete them.

    If you select neither Allow nor Deny, it is still possible that the user or group can inherit the permission through membership in another group that has the permission. If the user or group doesn't belong to another such group, the user or group is implicitly denied permission.

NOTE

To remove a name from the Group Or User Names list, select it and click Remove. To add a name to the list, click Add to open the Select Users Or Groups dialog box, where you can enter the names of the users and groups you want to add.

How shared resource permissions and NTFS permissions work together

The implementation of shared resource permissions and NTFS permissions is confusingly similar, but it's important to recognize that these are two separate levels of access control. Only connections that successfully pass through both gates are granted access.

Shared resource permissions control *network* access to a particular resource. Shared resource permissions do not affect users who sign in locally. You set shared resource permissions in the Advanced Sharing dialog box, which you access from the Sharing tab of a folder's properties dialog box.

NTFS permissions (also known as discretionary access control lists, DACLs) apply to folders and files on an NTFS-formatted drive. For each user to whom you want to grant access, you can specify exactly what that user is allowed to do: run programs, view folder contents, create new files, change existing files, and so on. You set NTFS permissions on the Security tab of the properties dialog box for a folder or file.

It's important to recognize that the two types of permissions are combined in the most restrictive way. If, for example, a user is granted Read permission on the network share, even if the account has Full Control NTFS permissions on the same folder, the user gets only read access when connecting over the network. In effect, the two sets of permissions act in tandem as "gatekeepers" that winnow out incoming network connections. An account that attempts to connect over the network is examined first by the shared resource permissions gatekeeper. The account is either rejected or allowed to enter with certain permissions. It's then confronted by the NTFS permissions gatekeeper, which might strip away (but not add to) some or all of the permissions granted at the first doorway. In many advanced sharing scenarios, it's common practice to simply configure the shared folder with Full Control permissions for Everyone and then configure NTFS permissions to control access as desired.

In determining the effective permission for a particular account, you must also consider the effect of group membership. Permissions are cumulative; an account that is a member of one or more groups is granted all the permissions granted explicitly to the account as well as all permissions granted to each group of which it's a member. The only exception to this rule is Deny permissions, which take precedence over any conflicting Allow permissions.

Inside OUT

Review and change your sharing and NTFS permissions settings

A tool in File Explorer opens a dialog box that shows NTFS permissions and share permissions in a format that's sometimes easier to decipher than the properties dialog box. Select a single folder or file in File Explorer and then, on the ribbon's Share tab, click Advanced Security. Here, in addition to viewing each type of permission, you can determine the *effective access*, which shows for a specific user or group the cumulative effect of various permissions and group memberships. (On a small network, the easiest way to specify a user on the Effective Access tab is to click Select A User, Advanced, Find Now.)

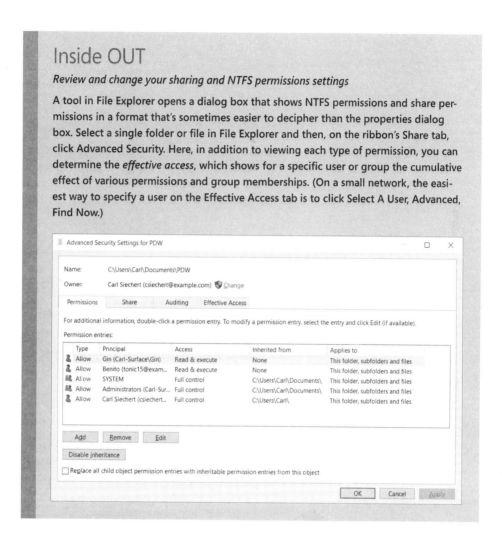

Sharing a printer

Although Windows doesn't have a wizard for sharing a printer over the network, the process is pretty simple. You configure all options for a printer—whether you plan to share it or not—by using the printer's properties dialog box, which you access from Devices And Printers in Control Panel.

To make a printer available to other network users, right-click a printer and click Printer Properties. On the Sharing tab, select Share This Printer and provide a share name, as shown in Figure 20-6.

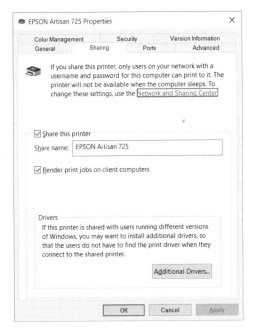

Figure 20-6 The share name can include spaces.

Unlike for shared folders, which maintain separate share permissions and NTFS permissions, a single set of permissions controls access to printers, whether by local users or by network users. (Of course, only printers that have been shared are accessible to network users.)

When you set up a printer, initially all users in the Everyone group have Print permission for documents they create, which provides users access to the printer and the ability to manage their own documents in the print queue. By default, members of the Administrators group also have Manage Printers permission—which allows them to share a printer, change its properties, remove a printer, and change its permissions—and Manage Documents permission, which lets them pause, restart, move, and remove all queued documents. As an administrator, you can view or modify permissions on the Security tab of the printer properties dialog box.

Setting server properties

In addition to setting properties for individual printers by using their properties dialog boxes, you can set other properties by visiting the Print Server Properties dialog box. To get there, select a printer in the Devices And Printers folder, and then click Print Server Properties. You'll find more details in "Fine-tuning hardware and printer settings" in Chapter 13, "Hardware."

The first three tabs control the list of items you see in the properties dialog box for a printer:

- The Forms tab controls the list of forms that you can assign to trays using the Device Settings tab in a printer's properties dialog box. You can create new form definitions and delete any that you create, but you can't delete any of the predefined forms.

- The Ports tab lets you configure the ports that appear on the Ports tab in a printer's properties dialog box.

- The Drivers tab offers a list of all the installed printer drivers and provides a centralized location where you can add, remove, or update drivers.

On the Advanced tab you can specify the location of spool files (you might want to change to a folder on a different drive if, for example, you frequently run out of space on the current drive when you attempt to print large documents) and set notification options.

Inside OUT

Use the Print Management console

Users of Windows 10 Pro and Enterprise editions have a tool that places all print management tasks in one convenient console. Print Management (Printmanagement.msc), shown here, provides a place for managing printers, drivers, queues, and shares. If your edition includes Print Management, you can start it by typing **print** in the search box and then clicking Print Management.

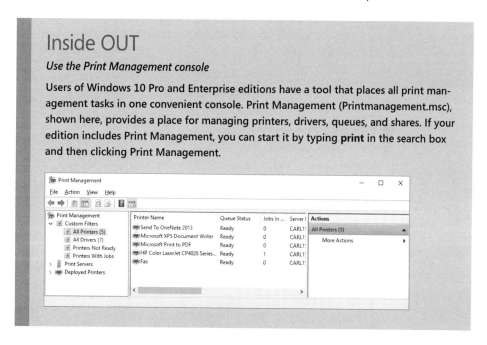

Finding and using shared resources on a Windows network

The Network folder is your gateway to all available network resources, just as This PC is the gateway to resources stored on your own system. The Network folder (shown in Figure 20-7) contains an icon for each computer that Windows discovers on your network; double-click a computer icon to see that computer's shared resources, if any.

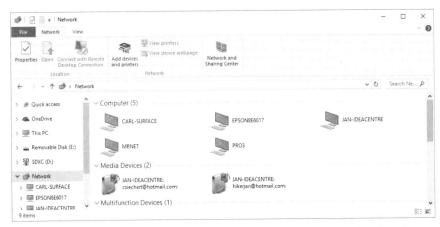

Figure 20-7 The Network folder shows all computers on your network, not just those in your workgroup.

To open a shared folder on another computer, double-click its icon in the Network folder. If you have the proper permissions, this action displays the folder's contents in File Explorer. It's not always that easy, however. If the user account with which you signed in doesn't have permission to view a network computer or resource you select, a dialog box asks you to provide the name of an account (and its password, of course) that has permission. Don't be fooled by the Domain reference below the User Name and Password boxes; in a workgroup, that value refers to the local computer.

Perhaps the trickiest part of using shared folders is fully understanding what permissions have been applied to a folder and which credentials are in use by each network user. It's important to recognize that *all network access is controlled by the computer with the shared resources*; regardless of what operating system runs on the computer attempting to connect to a network share, it must meet the security requirements of the computer where the shared resource is actually located.

Working with mapped network folders

Mapping a network folder makes it appear to applications as though the folder is part of your own computer. Windows assigns a drive letter to the mapped folder, making the folder appear like an additional hard drive. You can still access a mapped folder in the conventional manner by navigating to it through the Network folder. But mapping gives the folder an alias—the assigned drive letter—that provides an alternative means of access.

To map a network folder to a drive letter, follow these steps:

1. Open This PC in File Explorer, and on the ribbon's Computer tab, click Map Network Drive. (Alternatively, after you open a computer in the Network folder, right-click a network share and choose Map Network Drive.)

2. Select a drive letter in the Drive box. You can choose any letter that's not already in use.

3. In the Folder box, type the path to the folder you want or, more easily, click Browse and navigate to the folder.

4. Select Reconnect At Sign-In if you want Windows to connect to this shared folder automatically at the start of each session.

5. If your regular sign-in account doesn't have permission to connect to the resource, select Connect Using Different Credentials. (After you click Finish, Windows asks for the user name and password you want to use for this connection.)

6. Click Finish.

In File Explorer, the "drive" appears under This PC.

If you change your mind about mapping a network folder, simply right-click the folder's icon in your This PC folder. Choose Disconnect on the resulting shortcut menu, and the connection will be severed.

Connecting to a network printer

To use a printer that has been shared, open the Network folder in File Explorer and double-click the name of the server to which the printer is attached. If the shared printers on that server are not visible, return to the Network folder, click to select the server, and then, on the ribbon's Network tab, click View Printers. Right-click the printer and choose Connect. Alternatively, from the Devices And Printers folder, click Add A Printer and use the Add Printer Wizard to add a network printer.

Connecting to another computer with Remote Desktop

Sharing computer resources over a network, when properly configured, gives you access to all the files you might need, wherever they're stored. But sometimes even that is not enough. You might need to run a program that is installed only on another computer, or you might need to configure and manage another computer's files and settings in ways that can be done only by sitting down in front of that computer. As it turns out, there is an alternative to direct physical access: Remote Desktop. By using a Remote Desktop session, you can operate a computer by remote control over a local network or over the Internet.

With Remote Desktop, applications run on the remote computer; your computer is effectively used as a dumb terminal. You can use a low-powered computer—an inexpensive laptop or even an old desktop clunker—and enjoy the speed and power of the remote computer. Remote Desktop connections are encrypted, so your information is secure, even if you're making a connection over the Internet.

The basic requirements for using Remote Desktop are pretty simple: you need two computers that are connected via a local area network, the Internet, or a dial-up connection.

NOTE
The computer that you want to control—the one at the remote location—is called the *remote computer*. The computer you want to use to control the remote computer is called the *client computer*.

These are the requirements for the two computers:

- **Remote computer.** You need a computer running Windows 10 Pro, Enterprise, or Education. (Windows 10 Home does not include the software required for hosting Remote Desktop sessions.) The remote computer can also use Windows 8 or 8.1 (Pro or Enterprise editions), Windows 7 (Professional, Enterprise, or Ultimate editions), Windows Vista (Business, Enterprise, or Ultimate editions), Windows XP Professional (or Windows XP Media Center or Tablet PC editions), Windows Home Server, or Windows Server. This computer must have a connection to a local area network or to the Internet. If you're going to connect to this computer over the Internet, its Internet connection must have a known, public IP address. (For ways around this last requirement, see the next section, "Configuring your network for Remote Desktop connections.")

● **Client computer.** You can access Remote Desktop from a computer running any version of Windows or Windows Phone. Remote Desktop client software from Microsoft is also available for iOS, Mac OS X, and Android; third-party apps are available for Linux and other operating systems. To find one, search for "RDP apps." (RDP is short for *Remote Desktop Protocol*, the networking protocol that enables Remote Desktop.)

Configuring your network for Remote Desktop connections

When you enable Remote Desktop on Windows 10 Pro, Enterprise, or Education, the remote computer listens for incoming connections on port 3389. Enabling Remote Desktop also creates an exception in Windows Firewall that allows authenticated traffic on this port.

That makes Remote Desktop easy to use over a local network where no third-party security software is installed. But it doesn't solve the many problems you face when trying to connect to Remote Desktop over the Internet. To connect through the Internet, you must be able to reach the remote computer by using a known public IP address, and you have to get through a router and past any security software in between the two computers. If you're sitting in a hotel room or an airport, connecting to Remote Desktop poses several challenges imposed by firewalls, routers, and IP addresses. The solutions to these issues depend on your specific hardware configuration, but we can offer some general advice.

If the remote computer is connected to the Internet through a router, you need to accomplish two tasks. First, you have to ascertain the router's public IP address. (Depending on your ISP, this public address can change over time. See the following tip for a workaround.) Then you have to configure the router to forward Remote Desktop Protocol traffic it receives on port 3389 to the remote computer.

To find the router's IP address, open its browser-based administration interface and find the status screen. The public IP address is typically labeled as the WAN (wide area network) address; don't use the local area network (LAN) address, which is the private IP address used to forward traffic to computers on your local network.

To make sure RDP traffic reaches your remote PC, look for a "port forwarding" page in the same router administration interface (it's often buried within an advanced configuration section). You'll need to specify the local (private) IP address of the remote computer and tell the router that you want all traffic on port 3389 to be forwarded to that PC instead of being discarded. Figure 20-8 shows this configuration on a Linksys router, allowing incoming Remote Desktop requests to be forwarded to a computer with a local (private) IP address of 192.168.10.25.

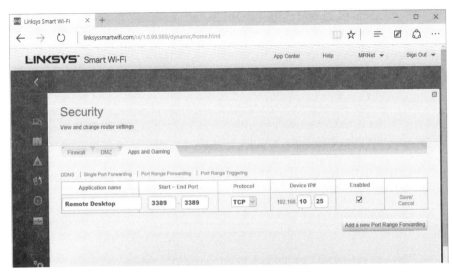

Figure 20-8 Every router has a different configuration interface, but the basic concepts of port forwarding are similar to the one shown here, which will forward traffic on port 3389 to a local PC with the specified private IP address.

Inside OUT

Use dynamic DNS to avoid IP address confusion

Using a bare IP address for Remote Desktop connections is easy but potentially risky. If you forget the public IP address assigned to your computer, you'll be unable to make a connection. Worse, if your ISP decides to change your IP address, you'll be stymied until you discover the new address, which is a challenge if you're away from home. The solution is to use a dynamic DNS service, such as those offered by Dyn (*dyndns.com*), No-IP (*noip.com*), and Duck DNS (*duckdns.org*). (A web search for "dynamic DNS service" will turn up many more options.) Such services map the public IP address on your router to a domain name that doesn't change. Dynamic DNS services typically rely on software installed on your remote computer, which notifies the service provider's domain name servers if your IP address changes. Because the domain name server correlates your domain name with its current IP address, you (or anyone you designate) can always find your computer by using your registered domain name instead of a numeric IP address.

Enabling inbound remote desktop connections

If you intend to connect to a remote computer—whether it's at home while you're away, at work when you're out of the office, or just down the hall—you must first enable Remote Desktop on that computer. To set up a computer running Windows 10 Pro, Enterprise, or Education to accept Remote Desktop connections, follow these steps:

1. Open System in Control Panel. Right-click the Start button and choose System; or, in Control Panel, open System And Security, System.) In the left pane, click Remote Settings. (Or use the undocumented command **systempropertiesremote**.)

2. Under Remote Desktop, select Allow Remote Connections To This Computer, as shown here:

Unless you anticipate that you will need to access your computer from a computer running an ancient version of Remote Desktop Connection, leave Allow Connections Only From Computers Running Remote Desktop With Network Level Authentication (Recommended) selected. This requires Remote Desktop version 6 or later, but all versions of Windows and Windows Server released since 2007 (that is, Windows Vista or later, or Windows Server 2008 or later) meet this requirement. In addition, versions of Remote

Desktop that support Network Level Authentication are available for earlier Windows versions and for other operating systems.

At this point, the current user account and any user account that is a member of the local Administrators group can be used to connect remotely to the computer, provided that the account has a sign-in password. (As a security precaution, accounts that use a blank password cannot be enabled for remote connections.)

3. If you want to change which users can connect remotely, click Select Users. The Remote Desktop Users dialog box appears.

- To add a user to the Remote Desktop Users group, click Add. Then type the user's name in the Select Users Or Groups dialog box that appears (or click Advanced, Find Now to select names from a list). You can type the name of any local user account or, if your computer is in a domain, any domain user account. You can add multiple users by separating each user name with a semicolon.

- To delete a user from the Remote Desktop Users group, select the user's name in the Remote Desktop Users dialog box and click Remove.

That's all you need to do to set up the remote computer. Windows configures rules for Remote Desktop in Windows Firewall when Remote Desktop is enabled, allowing connection requests on port 3389 to be received from any IP address.

If your connection has to pass through a router to get to your computer, be sure you take the additional steps outlined earlier in "Configuring your network for Remote Desktop connections." If you have replaced Windows Firewall with a third-party software firewall, you need to configure it to allow incoming access to TCP port 3389.

Using Remote Desktop Connection

If you've enabled incoming remote connections on your PC at home or in the office and verified that your network and firewall have the welcome mat out (for visitors with suitable credentials only, of course), you're ready to begin using Remote Desktop Connection. In the search box, type **remote** and then click Remote Desktop Connection. A dialog box like the one shown in Figure 20-9 appears. In the Computer box, type the name of the remote computer or its IP address.

Figure 20-9 You can specify the remote computer by name or IP address.

NOTE

After a successful connection to a remote desktop, the name of the remote computer is added to the drop-down list in the Computer box. Thereafter, you can simply select it from the list (if it isn't already selected) instead of typing the name each time.

In addition, if Remote Desktop Connection is pinned to your taskbar or Start menu (or if it's in the Start menu's recently used list), the name of each computer to which you've successfully connected appears on the Jump List. By using the Jump List and saved sign-in credentials, you can bypass this dialog box completely.

TROUBLESHOOTING

Your firewall blocks outbound access

If you use a third-party firewall that blocks unknown outbound traffic to the Internet, it prevents your initial attempt to connect to your remote desktop. Configure the firewall to enable Mstsc.exe (the file name of the Remote Desktop Connection program) to make outbound TCP connections on port 3389.

If you're willing to accept the default settings (about which we'll go into great detail shortly), you can click Connect at this point.

If you're signed in to the client computer using an account other than one that's authorized on the remote computer, Windows first displays a request for credentials, as shown here. After you enter your credentials and they're approved, Windows initiates the Remote Desktop Connection session.

The remote computer's sign-in screen then appears on your computer, either in a window or a full-screen display. Enter your password; other sign-in options (that is, PIN, picture password, or biometric sign-in) are not available for a remote connection.

If the account you use for the remote connection is already signed in to the remote computer—or if no one is signed in to the remote computer—the remote computer's desktop then appears on your computer.

If a different user account is signed in to the remote computer, Windows lets you know that you'll be forcing that person to sign out and gives you a chance to cancel the connection. On the other end, the signed-in user sees a similar notification that offers a short time to reject the remote connection before it takes over. It's important to note that only one user at a time can control the desktop of a computer running Windows. Whoever is currently signed in has the final say on whether someone else can sign in.

While you're connected to the remote computer, the local display on that computer (if it's turned on) does not show what you see on the client computer but instead shows the lock screen. A person who has physical access to the remote computer can't see what you're doing (other than the fact that you are signed in remotely).

An alternative client: Remote Desktop universal app

The Remote Desktop Connection program that's included with Windows is a desktop app, and it has changed very little in the past 15 years. A newer alternative, a modern app called Remote Desktop, is available via the Store. Remote Desktop, shown here in a preview release, supports connections to remote computers in much the same way as Remote Desktop Connection, albeit in a streamlined, modern-looking app.

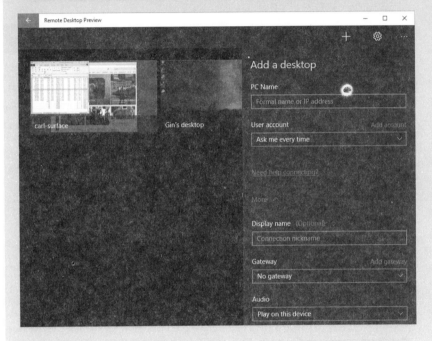

The Remote Desktop modern app also offers several additional features not found in Remote Desktop Connection. Its visual approach shows all your remote connections on the home screen, allowing you to open one with a single click or tap. Within a single window, it allows you to connect to multiple remote desktops simultaneously. (You can use multiple instances of the traditional Remote Desktop Connection app for concurrent connections, but the modern app makes it easier to see and manage multiple sessions.)

In addition, Remote Desktop includes several performance enhancements that optimize your connection quality. And, of course, as a modern app, it's touch friendly.

Don't be confused when looking for this app in the Store. An older version of the Remote Desktop app, designed for Windows 8.1, is still available as well, although it offers a completely different user experience. If you see a hamburger menu in the upper left corner, you have the older one and should seek out the newer, Universal version in the Store.

Changing screen resolutions and display settings

When you connect to a remote computer using Remote Desktop Connection, the remote computer takes over your entire screen. It uses the resolution of the client computer, regardless of the resolution set on the remote computer. Along the top of the screen, in the center, a small title bar appears, as shown next. This title bar, dubbed the *connection bar* in Remote Desktop Connection, lets you switch between your own desktop and the remote desktop. The Minimize, Maximize, and Restore buttons work as they do in other programs.

The pushpin button locks the connection bar in place. If you click the pushpin, the connection bar disappears completely, retracting into the top of the screen. To make the connection bar reappear, "bump" the mouse pointer to the top edge of the screen. To keep the connection bar visible at all times, click the pushpin again. The Close button disconnects the remote computer (but does not sign you out of the remote computer) and closes Remote Desktop Connection. You can pick up where you left off by reopening Remote Desktop Connection and reconnecting or by signing in locally at the remote computer.

Inside OUT

Move the connection bar

If the connection bar covers a part of the screen that you need to see, you can move it instead of hiding it altogether with the pushpin button. Simply slide it left or right.

You might prefer to use less than your full screen resolution for the remote desktop. (This option is especially useful if you have a large monitor and the work you want to do with Remote Desktop is just another task among several.) You must set the resolution—along with a number of other options—before you connect to the remote computer. After you start Remote Desktop Connection, click the Show Options button (shown in Figure 20-9) to expand the dialog box. Then click the Display tab, which is shown in Figure 20-10. You can set the screen resolution to any size that is supported on the client hardware, from 640 by 480 up to the current resolution of the client computer (not the remote computer). Set it to full screen by moving the slider all the way to the right.

Figure 20-10 Screen resolution is determined by the client computer.

Remote Desktop Connection allows the use of multiple monitors, although you should be aware that this feature requires that the remote computer is running Windows 7 or later. To configure the connection for use with more than one monitor, select Use All My Monitors For The Remote Session.

Accessing local resources

While you use Remote Desktop Connection, it's immediately apparent that you have control of the remote computer. You see its desktop, Start menu, and so on. That's terrific if the remote computer has everything you need. But you'll often want to use local resources and information from the client computer as well as from the remote computer. In addition, you might want to move information between the two computers. With Remote Desktop Connection, you can do so easily by clicking Show Options to expand the Remote Desktop Connection dialog box and then adjusting any of the options on the Local Resources tab, shown in Figure 20-11.

Figure 20-11 Configure these Remote Desktop Connection settings before you make the connection—you can't change settings while the connection is active.

The following options are available:

- **Remote Audio.** If your music collection is on the remote PC and you want some tunes at your current location, click Settings and select Play On This Computer. If you want both computers to be silent, choose Do Not Play. After clicking Settings, you can also tell Remote Desktop Connection whether to pay attention to the microphone (or other audio input) on the client computer.

- **Keyboard.** When you press a Windows keyboard shortcut such as Alt+Tab, do you want the shortcut to take effect on the remote machine or on your client computer?

- **Printers.** When this option is selected, your local printers appear in the remote computer's Printers folder. Their entries have "(from *clientcomputername*)" appended to each printer name. To print to a local printer, select its name in the Print dialog box from any application.

- **Clipboard.** When you copy or cut text or graphics on either the remote computer or the local computer, it's saved on the Clipboard in both locations. The Clipboard contents are then available for pasting in documents on either computer. Similarly, you can cut or copy files or folders from a File Explorer window on either computer and paste them into a folder on the other computer. Clear this option if you want to keep the contents of the two Clipboards separate.

The More button leads to additional devices in the Local Devices And Resources category. Smart cards are automatically enabled, and serial ports are disabled by default. Local drives and Plug and Play devices are also disabled by default. They can be enabled individually in this dialog box, as shown in Figure 20-12. These options are most useful if you're expecting to do most or all of your work with the Remote Desktop session in full-screen view and you don't want to continually flip back to your local desktop for file-management tasks.

Figure 20-12 You control which (if any) client computer resources are available in the Remote Desktop Connection window.

TROUBLESHOOTING

You receive a security warning when you try to sign in remotely

Remote Desktop Connection considers any connections to local hard drives to be a potential security risk. As a result, you'll see an extra security dialog box ("Do you trust this remote connection?") if you choose to make any local drives or Plug and Play devices available on the remote desktop. If you're comfortable with the configuration you've chosen, click Connect. If you want to adjust the connect settings, click the Details button to expand the dialog box. Then clear the check box for any category of resources.

Inside OUT

Use your pen in Remote Desktop Connection

In addition to keyboard, mouse, and touch input, if your client computer supports the use of a pen or stylus, you can use it in a Remote Desktop session. You won't see pens mentioned on the Local Resources tab because no configuration is required. You'll need to have Windows 10 or Windows Server 2016 on the remote computer and the client computer. This feature allows you to add handwriting and other drawings even if the remote computer has no built-in pen capability. You can use the full pen capabilities of the local computer; for example, pens that vary in line width based on the pressure you apply to the screen can use this feature on remote documents.

Using the keyboard with Remote Desktop Connection

When the Remote Desktop Connection window is active, almost every key you press is passed to the remote computer. Certain key combinations, however, can be processed by the client computer, depending on the setting you make in the Keyboard section of the Local Resources tab of the Remote Desktop Connection dialog box (shown in Figure 20-11). You can specify that the key combinations shown in the first column of Table 20-1 are sent to the remote computer all the time, only when the remote desktop is displayed in full-screen mode, or never.

If you select On This Computer, key combinations from the first column of Table 20-1 are always applied to the client computer. To get the equivalent function on the remote computer, press the key combination shown in the second column. The same is true if you select Only When Using The Full Screen and the remote session is displayed in a window.

If you select On The Remote Computer, key combinations from the first column are applied to the remote computer. Key combinations in the second column are ignored (unless they have some function in the active application on the remote desktop). The same is true if you select Only When Using The Full Screen and the remote session is displayed in full-screen mode. One exception is the Ctrl+Alt+Delete combination, which is always applied to the client computer. Regardless of your Local Resources tab setting, you must press Ctrl+Alt+End to obtain the same result on the remote computer.

Table 20-1 Special keys in Remote Desktop Connection

Key combination for local session	Equivalent key combination for Remote Desktop session	Description
Alt+Tab	Alt+Page Up	Switches between programs
Alt+Shift+Tab	Alt+Page Down	Switches between programs in reverse order
Alt+Esc	Alt+Insert	Cycles through programs in the order they were started
N/A	Ctrl+Alt+Break	Switches the remote desktop between a window and full screen
Ctrl+Alt+Delete	Ctrl+Alt+End	Displays the Windows Security screen
Ctrl+Esc	Alt+Home	Displays the Start menu
Alt+Spacebar	Alt+Del	Displays the Control menu of the active window (does not work when using Remote Desktop in full-screen mode)
Shift+Print Screen	Ctrl+Alt+Plus Sign (on numeric keypad)	Captures a bitmap image of the remote desktop and places it on the remote computer's Clipboard
Alt+Print Screen	Ctrl+Alt+Minus Sign (on numeric keypad)	Captures a bitmap image of the active window and places it on the remote computer's Clipboard

Configuring performance options

When you first use Remote Desktop Connection, you might notice that the remote desktop doesn't display a background. Disabling the background is one of several settings you can make that affect the perceived performance of your remote session. How you set these options depends in large measure on the speed of the connection between the two computers. If you're using a dial-up connection, you should disable as many features as possible to reduce the amount of information that must be transmitted across the wire and keep the mouse and windows movements responsive. On the other hand, if you're connecting to another desktop over a fast local area network, you might as well enable all features to enjoy the full experience of working at the remote computer.

The performance-related options are on the Experience tab of the Remote Desktop Connection dialog box, shown in Figure 20-13. To quickly select an appropriate set of prepackaged options, select the speed of your connection from the list box. Use those settings or select your own options.

Figure 20-13 Remote Desktop Connection has a default collection of settings for each connection speed.

Saving a Remote Desktop configuration

Changes you make in the expanded Remote Desktop Connection dialog box are automatically saved in a hidden file named Default.rdp (stored in your default save location for documents) and they're used the next time you open Remote Desktop Connection. But you might want to have several different Remote Desktop Connection configurations for connections to different computers. If you have a portable computer, you might want different settings for use with different connections to the same computer (for example, a slow Wi-Fi connection from a hotel versus a fast LAN at your branch office).

You can also save your credentials (user name and password) along with the other settings. To do so, enter your user name under Logon Settings on the General tab and select Allow Me To Save Credentials. You'll be prompted to save the password (in encrypted form, of course) when you sign in. Note that not all remote operating systems allow the use of saved credentials.

To save a configuration, make all your settings, click the General tab, and click Save As.

To reuse a stored configuration at a later time, start Remote Desktop Connection, click Show Options, click Open, and then double-click the stored file. More simply, select it from the Jump

List for Remote Desktop Connection (on the taskbar or Start menu), or double-click the stored file in File Explorer.

Ending a remote session

When you're through with a Remote Desktop Connection session, you can lock, sign out, or disconnect. If the remote computer is running Windows 10, you'll find these options in the usual places where comparable options appear on your local computer: Lock and Sign Out appear when you click the user name at the top of the remote session's Start menu, and Disconnect appears when you click Power on the remote Start menu. For remote machines running earlier Windows versions, these options appear in the lower right corner of the remote session's Start menu. (You must click the arrow to see all the options.)

Locking the computer keeps the remote session connected and all programs running, but it hides everything behind a sign-in screen that requests a password; this is comparable to pressing Windows key+L to lock your computer.

Signing out closes all your programs, exits your user session, and disconnects.

If you disconnect without signing out, your programs continue to run on the remote computer, but the remote connection is ended. The sign-in screen is visible on the remote computer, and it's available for another user. If you sign in later—either locally or through a remote connection—you can pick up right where you left off. As an alternative to the Start menu command, you can disconnect by simply clicking the Close button on the connection bar of the remote session.

Troubleshooting network problems

Network connectivity problems can be a source of great frustration. Fortunately, Windows 10 includes several tools and wizards that can help you identify and solve problems. Even better, Windows has built-in network diagnostic capabilities, so in many cases, if there is a problem with your network connection, Windows knows about it before you do, displays a message, and often solves the problem.

When a network-dependent activity (for example, browsing to a website) fails, Windows works to address the most common network-related issues, such as problems with file-sharing, website access, newly installed network hardware, connecting to a wireless network, and using a third-party firewall.

If you encounter network problems that don't trigger an automatic response from Windows, you should first try to detect and resolve the problem with one of the built-in troubleshooters.

In Network And Sharing Center, click Troubleshoot Problems to display the choices shown in Figure 20-14.

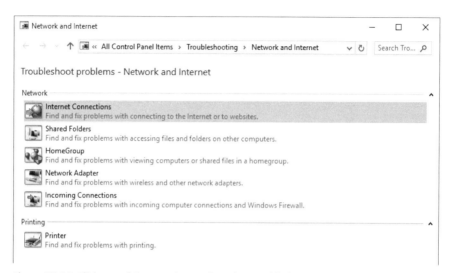

Figure 20-14 Click any of these options to launch a troubleshooter that performs numerous diagnostic and corrective steps.

Inside OUT

Skip the troubleshooting menu

You can bypass Network And Sharing Center and the troubleshooting menu shown in Figure 20-14. Simply right-click the network icon in the notification area and choose Troubleshoot Problems; doing so launches right into a network troubleshooter.

Each of the troubleshooting wizards performs several diagnostic tests, corrects some conditions, suggests actions you can take, and ultimately displays a report that explains the wizard's findings. Sometimes, the problem is as simple as a loose connection.

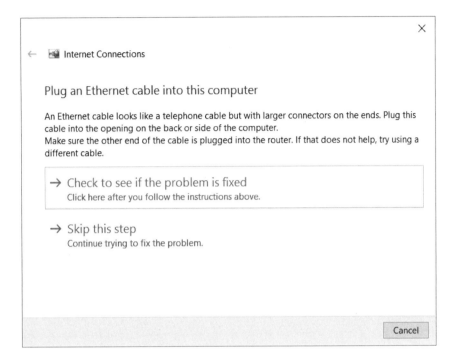

Other situations might point to problems outside your network.

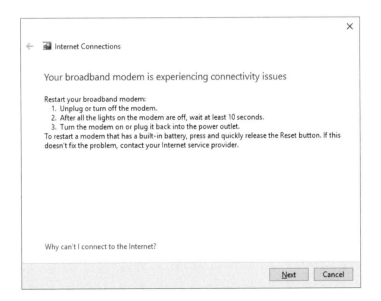

If the diagnostic capabilities leave you at a dead end, you'll find that restarting the affected network hardware often resolves the problem, because the hardware is forced to rediscover the network. The first step in troubleshooting is to isolate the problem. Here is a good general procedure:

1. Isolate the problem. Does it affect all computers on your network, a subset of your network, or only one computer?

2. If it affects all computers, try restarting the Internet device (that is, the cable or DSL modem). If it doesn't have a power switch, unplug it for a few moments and plug it back in.

3. If the problem affects a group of computers, try restarting the router to which those computers are connected.

4. If it affects only a single computer, try repairing the network connection for that computer. In Network And Sharing Center, click Change Adapter Settings. (Alternatively, in Settings, Network & Internet, click Change Adapter Options.) Then, in Network Connections, select the connection and click Diagnose This Connection. If the troubleshooter doesn't resolve the problem, select the connection and click Disable This Network Device; then click Enable This Network Device, which causes Windows to reinitialize it.

Troubleshooting HomeGroup problems

The HomeGroup troubleshooting wizard provides a good example of how these troubleshooters work. If you're having problems seeing shared resources in a homegroup and you didn't have the benefit of the troubleshooter's assistance, you'd need to check the following settings, among others:

- The network location profile must be set to Private.

- In Windows Firewall With Advanced Security, you need to ensure that the following groups of rules are enabled on private networks:
    - Core Networking
    - Network Discovery
    - HomeGroup
    - File/Printer Sharing
    - Windows Media Player
    - Windows Media Player Network Sharing

- The following services must be configured so that they can run:

    - HomeGroup Listener

    - HomeGroup Provider

    - Function Discovery Provider Host

    - Function Discovery Resource Publication

    - Peer Name Resolution Protocol

    - Peer Networking Grouping

    - Peer Networking Identity Manager

Running the HomeGroup troubleshooter—which you can launch from HomeGroup or by right-clicking HomeGroup in File Explorer as well as from the list of troubleshooters shown in Figure 20-14—checks each of these items and more. When you get to the wizard's last window, you can click View Detailed Information to see a troubleshooting report that lists the potential problems that the wizard attempted to identify and fix.

Network troubleshooting tools

When the troubleshooters don't solve the problem, it might be time to dig deeper into the Windows toolbox. Windows contains an assortment of utilities you can use to diagnose, monitor, and repair network connections. Table 20-2 lists some of the more useful networking-related command-line utilities and summarizes how you can use them. To learn more about each utility, including its proper syntax, open a Command Prompt window and type the executable name followed by /?.

Table 20-2 Windows network command-line utilities

Utility name	What it's used for
Get MAC Address (Getmac.exe)	Discovers the Media Access Control (MAC) address and lists associated network protocols for all network cards in a computer, either locally or across a network.
Hostname (Hostname.exe)	Displays the host name of the current computer.
IP Configuration Utility (Ipconfig.exe)	Displays all current Transmission Control Protocol/Internet Protocol (TCP/IP) network configuration values, and refreshes Dynamic Host Configuration Protocol (DHCP) and DNS settings.
Name Server Lookup (Nslookup.exe)	Displays information about Domain Name System records for specific IP addresses and/or host names so that you can troubleshoot DNS problems.
Net services commands (Net.exe)	Performs a broad range of network tasks. Type **net** with no parameters to see a full list of available command-line options.

Utility name	What it's used for
Netstat (Netstat.exe)	Displays active TCP connections, ports on which the computer is listening, Ethernet statistics, the IP routing table, and IPv4/IPv6 statistics.
Network Command Shell (Netsh.exe)	Displays or modifies the network configuration of a local or remote computer that is currently running. This command-line scripting utility has a huge number of options, which are fully detailed in Help.
PathPing (Pathping.exe)	Combines the functions of Traceroute and Ping to identify problems at a router or network link.
TCP/IP NetBIOS Information (Nbtstat.exe)	Displays statistics for the NetBIOS over TCP/IP (NetBT) protocol, NetBIOS name tables for both the local computer and remote computers, and the NetBIOS name cache.
TCP/IP Ping (Ping.exe)	Verifies IP-level connectivity to another Internet address by sending Internet Control Message Protocol (ICMP) packets and measuring response time in milliseconds.
TCP/IP Route (Route.exe)	Displays and modifies entries in the local IP routing table.
TCP/IP Traceroute (Tracert.exe)	Determines the path to an Internet address, and lists the time required to reach each hop. It's useful for troubleshooting connectivity problems on specific network segments.

As is the case with other command-line utilities, the Windows PowerShell environment includes cmdlets that offer much of the same functionality along with the scripting capability of PowerShell. (Indeed, one of the commands shown in Table 20-2—Netsh—displays a notice that it might be removed from future versions of Windows. The trend in Windows command-line utilities, certainly, is moving away from Command Prompt toward PowerShell. However, because of the one-off nature of troubleshooting tasks—the topic of this section—our emphasis here is on command-line utilities that run in a Command Prompt window.)

You can get a list that includes many of the more commonly used network-related cmdlets by entering at a PowerShell prompt

```
get-command -module nettcpip, netadapter
```

➤ For more information about PowerShell, see "An introduction to Windows PowerShell" in Chapter 21, "Working with Command Prompt and Windows PowerShell." For details about the Net TCP/IP cmdlets, go to *w7io.com/20401*. On that page, you'll also find (using the navigation pane on the left) details about other network-related cmdlets, including those for Network Adapter, Network Connection, and Network Connectivity Status.

Troubleshooting TCP/IP problems

Transmission Control Protocol/Internet Protocol (TCP/IP) is the default communications protocol of the Internet; in Windows 10, it's installed and configured automatically and cannot be removed. Most of the time, your TCP/IP connection should just work, without requiring any manual configuration. When you encounter problems with TCP/IP-based networks, such as an inability to connect with other computers on the same network or difficulty connecting to external websites, the problems might be TCP/IP related. You'll need at least a basic understanding of how this protocol works before you can figure out which tool to use to uncover the root of the problem.

Setting IP addresses

Networks that use the TCP/IP protocol rely on *IP addresses* to route packets of data from point to point. On a TCP/IP network, every computer has a unique IP address for each protocol (that is, TCP/IPv4 and TCP/IPv6) in use on each network adapter. An IPv4 address consists of four 8-bit numbers (each one represented in decimal format by a number from 0 through 255) separated by periods. An IPv6 address consists of eight 16-bit numbers (each one represented in hexadecimal format) separated by colons. In addition to the IP address, each computer's TCP/IP configuration has the following additional settings:

- A *subnet mask*, which tells the network how to distinguish between IP addresses that are part of the same network and those that belong to other networks

- A *default gateway*, which is a computer that routes packets intended for addresses outside the local network

- One or more *Domain Name System (DNS) servers*, which are computers that translate domain names (such as *www.microsoft.com*) into IP addresses

Windows provides several methods for assigning IP addresses to networked computers:

- **Dynamic Host Configuration Protocol (DHCP).** This is the default configuration for Windows 10. A DHCP server maintains a pool of IP addresses for use by network devices. When you connect to a network, the DHCP server assigns an IP address from this pool and sets subnet masks and other configuration details. Many corporate networks use DHCP to avoid the hassle of managing fixed addresses for constantly changing resources; all versions of Windows Server include this capability. Most routers and residential gateways also incorporate DHCP servers that automatically configure computers connected to those devices.

- **Automatic Private IP Addressing (APIPA).** When no DHCP server is available, Windows automatically assigns an IP address in a specific private IP range. (For an explanation of how private IP addresses work, see the sidebar "Public and private IP addresses.") If all computers on a subnet are using APIPA addresses, they can communicate with one another without requiring any additional configuration. APIPA was introduced with Windows 98 and works the same in all versions of Windows released since that time.

- **Static IP Addressing.** By entering an IP address, subnet mask, and other TCP/IP details in a dialog box, you can manually configure a Windows workstation so that its address is always the same. This method takes more time and can cause some configuration headaches, but it allows a high degree of control over network addresses.

  Static IP addresses are useful if you plan to set up a web server, a mail server, a virtual private network (VPN) gateway, or any other computer that needs to be accessible from across the Internet. Even inside a local network, behind a router or firewall, static IP addresses can be useful. For instance, you might want to configure the router so that packets entering your network on a specific port get forwarded to a specific computer. If you use DHCP to assign addresses within the local network, you can't predict what the address of that computer will be on any given day. But by assigning that computer a static IP address that is within the range of addresses assigned by the DHCP server, you can ensure that the computer always has the same address and is thus always reachable.

- **Alternate IP Configuration.** This feature allows you to specify multiple IPv4 addresses for a single network connection (although only one address can be used at a time). This feature is most useful with portable computers that regularly connect to different networks. You can configure the connection to automatically acquire an IP address from an available DHCP server, and you can then assign a static backup address for use if the first configuration isn't successful.

To set a static IP address, follow these steps:

1. In the Network Connections folder, select the connection whose settings you want to change. On the command bar, click Change Settings Of This Connection. (Alternatively, right-click the icon and choose Properties.)

2. In the list of installed network items, select Internet Protocol Version 4 (TCP/IPv4) or Internet Protocol Version 6 (TCP/IPv6), and then click Properties.

3. In the Internet Protocol (TCP/IP) Properties dialog box, select Use The Following IP Address and fill in the blanks. You must supply an IP address, a subnet mask (for IPv6, the length of the subnet prefix, which is usually 64 bits), and a default gateway.

4. Select Use The Following DNS Server Addresses, and then fill in the numeric IP addresses for one or more DNS servers as well. Figure 20-15 shows the dialog box with all fields filled in.

Figure 20-15 When assigning static IP addresses, you must fill in all fields correctly. To avoid making a mistake that could cause you to lose your network connectivity, select Validate Settings Upon Exit.

5. Click OK to save your changes.

Public and private IP addresses

Any computer that is directly connected to the Internet needs a public IP address—one that can be reached by other computers on the Internet—so that information you request (webpages and email, for instance) can be routed back to your computer properly. When you connect to an Internet service provider, you're assigned a public IP address from a block of addresses registered to that ISP. If you use a dial-up connection, your ISP probably assigns a different IP address to your computer (drawn from its pool of available addresses) each time you connect. If you have a persistent connection to your ISP via a DSL or cable modem, your IP address might be permanent—or semipermanent if you turn off your computer when you leave your home or office to travel and your assigned IP address is changed when you reconnect on your return.

On a home or small office network, it's not necessary to have a public IP address for each computer on the network. In fact, configuring a network with multiple public addresses can increase security risks and often requires an extra fee from your ISP. A safer, less costly solution is to assign a single public IP address to a router or residential gateway (or a computer that performs that function). All other computers on the network connect to the Internet through that single address. Each of the computers on the local network has a private IP address that is not directly reachable from the outside world. To communicate with the Internet, the router on the edge of the network uses a technology called Network Address Translation (NAT) to pass packets back and forth between the single public IP address and the multiple private IP addresses on the network.

The Internet Assigned Numbers Authority (IANA) has reserved the following three blocks of the IP address space for use on private networks that are not directly connected to the Internet:

- 10.0.0.0–10.255.255.255
- 172.16.0.0–172.31.255.255
- 192.168.0.0–192.168.255.255

In addition, the Automatic Private IP Addressing feature in all post-1998 Windows versions uses private IP addresses in the range 169.254.0.0 through 169.254.255.255.

Routers and residential gateways that use NAT almost always assign addresses from these private ranges. Linksys routers, for instance, typically assign addresses starting with 192.168.1.x. If you're setting up a small business or a home network that will not be connected to the Internet, or that will be connected through a single proxy server, you can freely use these addresses without concern for conflicts. Just make sure that all the addresses on the network are in the same subnet.

Checking for connection problems

Anytime your network refuses to send and receive data properly, your first troubleshooting step should be to check for problems with the physical connection between the local computer and the rest of the network. Assuming your network connection uses the TCP/IP protocol, the first tool to reach for is the Ping utility. When you use the Ping command with no parameters, Windows sends four echo datagrams—small Internet Control Message Protocol (ICMP) packets—to the address you specify. If the machine at the other end of the connection replies, you know that the network connection between the two points is alive.

To use the Ping command, open a Command Prompt window (Cmd.exe) and type the command **ping *target_name*** (where *target_name* is an IP address or the name of another host machine). The return output looks something like this:

```
C:\>ping www.example.com

Pinging www.example.com [93.184.216.34] with 32 bytes of data:
Reply from 93.184.216.34: bytes=32 time=54ms TTL=51
Reply from 93.184.216.34: bytes=32 time=40ms TTL=51
Reply from 93.184.216.34: bytes=32 time=41ms TTL=51
Reply from 93.184.216.34: bytes=32 time=54ms TTL=51

Ping statistics for 93.184.216.34:
    Packets: Sent = 4, Received = 4, Lost = 0 (0% loss),
Approximate round trip times in milli-seconds:
    Minimum = 40ms, Maximum = 54ms, Average = 47ms
```

If all the packets you send come back properly in roughly the same time, your TCP/IP connection is fine and you can focus your troubleshooting efforts elsewhere. If some packets time out, a "Request timed out" message appears, indicating that your network connection is working but one or more hops between your computer and the target machine are experiencing problems. In that case, repeat the Ping test using the –n switch to send a larger number of packets; **ping –n 30 192.168.1.1**, for example, sends 30 packets to the computer or router at 192.168.1.1.

NOTE
The –n switch is case-sensitive; don't capitalize it.

A high rate of timeouts, also known as *packet loss*, usually means the problems are elsewhere on the network and not on the local machine. (To see the full assortment of switches available for the Ping command, type **ping** with no target specified.)

If every one of your packets returns with the message "Request timed out," the problem might be the TCP/IP connection on your computer or a glitch with another computer on that network. To narrow down the problem, follow these steps, in order, stopping at any point where you encounter an error:

1. Ping your own machine by using any of the following commands:

   ```
   ping ::1
   ping 127.0.0.1
   ping localhost
   ```

   These are standard addresses. The first line is the IPv6 address for your own computer; the second line is the IPv4 address; the third line shows the standard host name. If your local network components are configured correctly, each of these three commands should allow the PC on which the command is run to talk to itself. If you receive an error, TCP/IP is not configured properly on your system. For fix-it details, see "Repairing your TCP/IP configuration" later in this chapter.

2. Ping your computer's IP address.

3. Ping the IP address of another computer on your network.

4. Ping the IP address of your router or the default gateway on your network.

5. Ping the address of each DNS server on your network. (If you don't know these addresses, see the next section for details on how to discover them.)

6. Ping a known host outside your network. Well-known, high-traffic websites are ideal for this step, assuming that they respond to ICMP packets.

7. Use the PathPing command to contact the same host you specified in step 6. This command combines the functionality of the Ping command with the Traceroute utility to identify intermediate destinations on the Internet between your computer and the specified host or server.

Inside OUT
Choose your test site carefully

In some cases, pinging an external website results in a string of "Request timed out" messages, even when you have no trouble reaching those sites. Don't be misled. Some popular sites block all ICMP traffic, including Ping packets, as a routine security measure. Some routers and residential gateways are also configured to block certain types of ICMP traffic. Try pinging several sites before concluding that your Internet connection is broken.

If either of the two final steps in this process fails, your problem might be caused by DNS problems, as described later in this chapter. (For details, see "Resolving DNS issues.") To eliminate this possibility, ping the numeric IP address of a computer outside your network instead. (Of course, if you're having DNS problems, you might have a hard time finding an IP address to ping!) If you can reach a website by using its IP address but not by using its name, DNS problems are indicated.

If you suspect that there's a problem on the Internet between your computer and a distant host or server, use the Traceroute utility (Tracert.exe) to pinpoint the problem. Like the Ping command, this utility works from a command line. You specify the target (a host name or IP address) by using the syntax **tracert *target_name***, and the utility sends out a series of packets, measuring the time it takes to reach each hop along the route. Timeouts or unusually slow performance indicate a connectivity problem. If the response time from your network to the first hop is much higher than the other hops, you might have a problem with the connection to your Internet service provider (ISP); in that case, a call to your ISP's support line is in order. Problems farther along in the traceroute might indicate congestion or hardware problems in distant parts of the Internet that are out of your ISP's hands. These symptoms might disappear when you check another URL that follows a different path through the Internet.

If your testing produces inconsistent results, rule out the possibility that a firewall program or Network Address Translation (NAT) device (such as a router or residential gateway) is to blame. If you're using Windows Firewall or a third-party firewall program, disable it temporarily. Try bypassing your router and connecting directly to a broadband connection such as a DSL or cable modem. (Use this configuration only for testing and only very briefly because it exposes your computer to various attacks.)

If the Ping test works with the firewall or NAT device out of the picture, you can rule out network problems and conclude that the firewall software or router is misconfigured. After you complete your testing, be sure to enable the firewall and router again!

Diagnosing IP address problems

On most networks, IP addresses are assigned automatically by Dynamic Host Configuration Protocol (DHCP) servers; in some cases, you may need (or prefer) to use static IP addresses, which are fixed numeric addresses. Problems with DHCP servers or clients can cause network connections to stop working, as can incorrectly assigned static IP addresses.

To see details of your current IP configuration, follow these steps:

1. In Settings, Network & Internet, click Change Adapter Options.

2. Double-click the icon for the connection about which you want more information. (Alternatively, you can select the icon and click View Status Of This Connection on the command bar.)

3. Click Details to see the currently assigned IP address, subnet mask, and default gateway for this connection. (If you have IPv4 and IPv6 connectivity, the Network Connection Details dialog box shows information for both.) In the following example, you can tell that the IP address was automatically assigned by the DHCP server in a router; details indicate that DHCP is enabled and the DHCP server address matches that of the router.

You can also get useful details of your IP configuration by using the IP Configuration utility, Ipconfig.exe, in a Command Prompt window. Used without any parameters, typing **ipconfig** at a command prompt displays the DNS suffix, IPv6 and/or IPv4 address, subnet mask, and default gateway for each network connection. To see exhaustive details about every available network connection, type **ipconfig /all**.

The actual IP address you see might help you solve connection problems:

- If the address is in the format 169.254.*x.y*, your computer is using Automatic Private IP Addressing (APIPA). This means your computer's DHCP client was unable to reach a DHCP server to be assigned an IP address. Check the connection to your network.

- If the address is in one of the blocks of IP addresses reserved for use on private networks (for details, see the sidebar "Public and private IP addresses" earlier in this chapter), make sure that a router or residential gateway is routing your Internet requests to a properly configured public IP address.

- If the address of your computer appears as 0.0.0.0, the network is either disconnected or the static IP address for the connection duplicates an address that already exists on the network.

- Make sure you're using the correct subnet mask for computers on your local network. Compare IP settings on the machine that's having problems with those on other computers on the network. The default gateway and subnet mask should be identical for all network computers. The first one, two, or three sets of numbers in the IP address for each machine should also be identical, depending on the subnet mask. A subnet mask of 255.255.255.0 means the first three IP address numbers of computers on your network must be identical—192.168.0.83 and 192.168.0.223, for instance, can communicate on a network using this subnet mask, but 192.168.1.101 will not be recognized as belonging to the network. The gateway machine must also be a member of the same subnet. (If you use a router, switch, or residential gateway for Internet access, the local address on that device must be part of the same subnet as the machines on your network.)

NOTE

Are you baffled by subnets and other related technical terms? For an excellent overview of these sometimes confusing topics, read Knowledge Base article 164015, "Understanding TCP/IP Addressing and Subnetting Basics" (*w7io.com/1908*), which offers information about IPv4. For comparable details about IPv6, see the "Introduction to IPv6" white paper at TechNet (*w7io.com/1909*).

Repairing your TCP/IP configuration

If you suspect a problem with your TCP/IP configuration, try either of the following repair options:

- **Use the automated repair option.** Right-click the connection icon in Network Connections and click Diagnose.

- **Release and renew your IP address.** Use the **ipconfig /release** command to let go of the DHCP-assigned IPv4 address. Then use **ipconfig /renew** to obtain a new IP address from the DHCP server. To renew an IPv6 address, use **ipconfig /release6** and **ipconfig /renew6**.

NOTE

If these methods don't work, you can use the Netsh utility to restore the TCP/IP stack to its original configuration when Windows was first installed. The utility restores all registry settings relating to the TCP/IP stack to their original settings, which is effectively the same as removing and reinstalling the protocol. The utility records a log of the changes it makes. For details about this drastic, but effective, solution, see Microsoft Knowledge Base article 299357 (*w7io.com/299357*). Another option is to uninstall and reinstall the network adapter, as described in "Enabling and disabling individual devices" in Chapter 13.

Resolving DNS issues

The Domain Name System (DNS) is a crucial part of the Internet. DNS servers translate host names (*www.microsoft.com*, for instance) into numeric IP addresses so that packets can be routed properly over the Internet. If you can use the Ping command to reach a numeric address outside your network but are unable to browse websites by name, the problem is almost certainly related to your DNS configuration.

Here are some questions to ask when you suspect DNS problems:

- **Do your TCP/IP settings point to the right DNS servers?** Inspect the details of your IP configuration, and compare the DNS servers listed there with those recommended by your Internet service provider. (You might need to call your ISP to get these details.)

- **Is your ISP experiencing DNS problems?** A misconfigured DNS server (or one that's offline) can wreak havoc with your attempts to use the Internet. Try pinging each DNS server to see whether it's available. If your ISP has multiple DNS servers and you encounter problems accessing one server, remove that server from your TCP/IP configuration temporarily and use another one instead.

- **Have you installed any "Internet accelerator" utilities?** Many such programs work by editing the Hosts file on your computer to match IP addresses and host (server) names. When Windows finds a host name in the Hosts file, it uses the IP address listed there and doesn't send the request to a DNS server. If the owner of the server changes its DNS records to point to a new IP address, your Hosts file will lead you to the wrong location.

Temporary DNS problems can also be caused by the DNS cache, which Windows maintains for performance reasons. If you suddenly have trouble reaching a specific site on the Internet and you're convinced there's nothing wrong with the site, type this command to clear the DNS cache: **ipconfig /flushdns**.

A more thorough solution is offered by **ipconfig /registerdns**, which renews all DHCP leases (as described in the previous section) *and* reregisters all DNS names.

Inside OUT
Translate names to IP addresses and vice versa

The Nslookup command is a buried treasure in Windows. Use this command-line utility to quickly convert a fully qualified domain name to its IP address. You can tack on a host name to the end of the command line to identify a single address; type **nslookup ftp.microsoft.com**, for instance, to look up the IP address of Microsoft's File Transfer Protocol (FTP) server. Or type **nslookup** to switch into interactive mode. From this prompt, you can enter any domain name to find its IP address. If you need more sophisticated lookup tools, you can find them with the help of any search engine. A good starting point is DNSstuff (*w7io.com/22201*), which offers an impressive collection of online tools for looking up domains, IP addresses, and host names. The site also offers form-based utilities that can translate obfuscated URLs and dotted IP addresses, both of which are widely used by spammers to cover their online tracks.

Working with Command Prompt and Windows PowerShell

Windows 10, like all previous versions of Windows, lets you enter commands, run batch programs, and run applications by typing commands in a Command Prompt window. If you're accustomed to performing administrative tasks at the command line, you can go on doing that in Windows 10. But this latest version of Windows, like its most recent predecessors, also includes a more powerful tool for performing administrative tasks at the command line. This newer, more versatile shell is called Windows PowerShell.

This chapter provides only a cursory introduction to the legacy Command Prompt and Windows PowerShell, with an emphasis on the latter. We presume that if you're perusing this chapter, you already have some familiarity with Command Prompt (if not, a quick scan of the bibliosphere will turn up several worthwhile references); we will confine ourselves therefore to a few tips and tricks. If your work calls on you to administer systems through scripts, you will find it worth your while to dive into Windows PowerShell. This chapter provides an overview of this newer, more versatile shell, and points you to additional resources.

Working at the command prompt

To get to the command prompt, run Cmd.exe. You can do this by double-clicking any shortcut for Cmd.exe, but since you like to type, you might find it easiest to press Windows key+R, and then type **cmd.** To open a second or subsequent Command Prompt window when one is already open, you can type **start** in the window that's already running.

Running with elevated privileges

Your activities in a Command Prompt session are subject to the same User Account Control (UAC) restrictions as anything else you do in Windows. If you use Command Prompt to launch a program (for example, Regedit) that requires an administrative token, you will be asked to confirm a UAC prompt before moving on. If you plan to run several such tasks from Command Prompt, you might prefer to run Cmd.exe itself with elevated privileges. To do this, right-click any shortcut for Command Prompt and then click Run As Administrator. Alternatively, type **cmd** in the search box, and then press Ctrl+Shift+Enter. Windows displays the word *Administrator* in the title bar of any Command Prompt window running with elevated privileges.

Starting Command Prompt at a particular folder

If you run Cmd.exe from a shortcut or from %SystemRoot%\System32, the session begins with that folder as the current directory. (*Directory* is the MS-DOS-era term for *folder*, and you will encounter it frequently in command names, help files, and so on.) If you run Cmd from the Start menu, it begins in your %UserProfile% folder. To run a Command Prompt session at a different folder, hold down the Shift key while you right-click the folder in File Explorer. On the shortcut menu, click Open Command Window Here.

Starting Command Prompt and running a command

The /C and /K command-line arguments allow you to start a Command Prompt session and immediately run a command or program. The difference between the two is that **Cmd /C** *commandstring* terminates the Command Prompt session as soon as *commandstring* has finished, whereas **Cmd /K** *commandstring* keeps the Command Prompt session open after *commandstring* has finished. Note the following:

- You must include either /C or /K if you want to specify a command string as an argument to Cmd. If you type **cmd** *commandstring*, the command processor simply ignores *commandstring*.

- While *commandstring* is executing, you can't interact with the command processor. To run a command or program and keep the Command Prompt window interface, use the Start command. For example, to run Mybatch.bat and continue issuing commands while the batch program is running, type

```
cmd /k start mybatch.bat
```

- If you include other command-line arguments along with /C or /K, /C or /K must be the last argument before *commandstring*.

Using AutoRun to execute commands when Command Prompt starts

By default, Command Prompt executes on startup whatever it finds in the following two registry values:

- The AutoRun value in HKLM\Software\Microsoft\Command Processor

- The AutoRun value in HKCU\Software\Microsoft\Command Processor

The AutoRun value in HKLM affects all user accounts on the current machine. The AutoRun value in HKCU affects only the current user account. If both values are present, both are executed—HKLM before HKCU. Both AutoRun values are of data type REG_SZ, which means they can contain a single string. To execute a sequence of separate Command Prompt statements, therefore, you must use command symbols or store the sequence as a batch program and then use AutoRun to call the batch program.

You can also use group policy objects to specify startup tasks for Command Prompt.

Editing the command line

When working at a command prompt, you often enter the same command multiple times or enter several similar commands. To assist you with repetitive or corrective tasks, Windows includes a feature that recalls previous commands and allows you to edit them on the current command line. Table 21-1 lists these editing keys and what they do.

Table 21-1 Command-line editing keys

Key	Function
Up Arrow	Recalls the previous command in the command history
Down Arrow	Recalls the next command in the command history
Page Up	Recalls the earliest command used in the session
Page Down	Recalls the most recently used command
Left Arrow	Moves left one character
Right Arrow	Moves right one character
Ctrl+Left Arrow	Moves left one word
Ctrl+Right Arrow	Moves right one word
Home	Moves to the beginning of the line
End	Moves to the end of the line
Esc	Clears the current command
F7	Displays the command history in a scrollable pop-up box
F8	Displays commands that start with the characters currently on the command line
Alt+F7	Clears the command history

Using command symbols

Old-fashioned programs that take all their input from a command line and then run unaided can be useful in a multitasking environment. You can turn them loose to perform complicated processing in the background while you continue to work with other programs in the foreground.

To work better with other programs, many command-line programs follow a set of conventions that control their interaction:

- By default, programs take all of their input as lines of text typed at the keyboard. But input in the same format also can be redirected from a file or any device capable of sending lines of text.

- By default, programs send all of their output to the screen as lines of text. But output in the same format also can be redirected to a file or another line-oriented device, such as a printer.

- Programs set a number (called a *return value*) when they terminate to indicate the results of the program.

When programs are written according to these rules, you can use the symbols listed in Table 21-2 to control a program's input and output or chain programs together.

Table 21-2 Command symbols

Symbol	Function
<	Redirects input
>	Redirects output
>>	Appends redirected output to existing data
|	Pipes output
&	Separates multiple commands in a command line
&&	Runs the command after && only if the command before && is successful
||	Runs the command after || only if the command before || fails
^	Treats the next symbol as a character
(and)	Groups commands

The redirection symbols

Command Prompt sessions in Windows allow you to override the default source for input (the keyboard) or the default destination for output (the screen).

Redirecting output   To redirect output to a file, type the command followed by a greater than sign (>) and the name of the file.

Using two greater than signs (>>) redirects output and appends it to an existing file.

Redirecting input   To redirect input from a file, type the command followed by a less than sign (<) and the name of the file.

Redirecting input and output   You can redirect both input and output in a command line. For example, to use Batch.lst as input to the Sort command and send its output to a file named Sorted.lst, type the following:

```
Sort < batch.lst > sorted.lst
```

Standard output and standard error   Programs can be written to send their output either to the standard output device or to the standard error device. Sometimes programs are written to send different types of output to each device. You can't always tell which is which because, by default, both devices are the screen.

The Type command illustrates the difference. When used with wildcards, the Type command sends the name of each matching file to the standard error device and sends the contents of the file to the standard output device. Because they both go to the screen, you see a nice display with each file name followed by its contents.

However, if you try to redirect output to a file by typing something like this:

```
type *.bat > std.out
```

the file names still appear on your screen because standard error is still directed to the screen. Only the file contents are redirected to Std.out.

Windows allows you to qualify the redirection symbol by preceding it with a number. Use 1> (or simply >) for standard output and 2> for standard error. For example:

```
type *.bat 2> err.out
```

This time the file contents go to the screen and the names are redirected to Err.out.

The pipe symbol

The pipe symbol (|) is used to send, or pipe, the output of one program to a second program as the second program's input. Piping is commonly used with the More utility, which displays multiple screenfuls of output one screenful at a time. For example:

```
help dir | more
```

This command line uses the output of Help as the input for More. The More command filters out the first screenful of Help output, sends it to the screen as its own output, and then waits for a keystroke before sending more filtered output.

Customizing Command Prompt windows

You can customize the appearance of a Command Prompt window in several ways. You can change its size, select a font, and even use eye-pleasing colors. And you can save these set-tings independently for each shortcut that launches a Command Prompt session so that you can make appropriate settings for different tasks.

To customize a Command Prompt window, you make settings in a properties dialog box that you can reach in any of three ways:

- Right-click a shortcut that opens a Command Prompt window, and then click Properties on the shortcut menu. Changes you make here affect all future Command Prompt ses-sions launched from this shortcut.

- Click the Control menu icon in a Command Prompt window, and then click Proper-ties on the Control menu. (If Command Prompt is running in full-screen mode, press Alt+Enter to switch to window display.) Changes you make here affect the current ses-sion. When you leave the properties dialog box, you'll be given the option of propagat-ing your changes to the shortcut from which this session was launched.

- Click the Control menu icon in a Command Prompt window, and then click Defaults on the Control menu. Changes here do not affect the current session. Instead, they affect all future sessions, except those launched from a shortcut whose properties you have modified.

Setting the window size and position

To change the screen position where a newly launched Command Prompt window appears, open the window's properties dialog box and click the Layout tab.

The dialog box maintains two different sizes—the screen buffer size and the window size. The width for both sizes is specified in columns (characters); the height is specified in rows (text lines).

The screen buffer settings control the size of the "virtual screen," which is the maximum extent of the screen. Standard screen sizes are 80 by 25, 80 by 43, or 80 by 50, but you can set your Command Prompt session to any size you want.

The window size settings control the size of the Command Prompt window on your screen. In most cases, you'll want it to be the same size as the screen buffer. But if your screen is crowded, you can reduce the window size. If you do, scroll bars are added. The window size settings cannot be larger than the screen buffer size settings.

Because you size a window by specifying how many rows and columns of characters it should have, the size of those characters also affects the amount of space the window occupies on your display. For information about changing the character size, see "Selecting a font" below.

Setting the window size and position visually

Rather than guess at the settings for window size and position, you can drag the borders of a Command Prompt window to adjust its size and drag its title bar to adjust its position. To retain the settings for future sessions, click the Control menu icon, click Properties, and click the Layout tab. You'll see the settings that reflect the window's current condition. Click OK to apply these settings.

Selecting a font

Applications in a Command Prompt window can display only one font at a time. Your choice is limited, as you'll see if you click the Font tab in the Command Prompt window's properties dialog box.

Make a selection in the Font list first because your choice here determines the contents of the Size list. If you select the Consolas or Lucida Console font, you'll find point sizes to choose from in the Size list. If you select Raster Fonts, you'll find character widths and height in pixels.

Setting colors

You can set the color of the text and the background of the Command Prompt window. You can also set the color of the text and the background of pop-up windows that originate from the command prompt, such as the command history window.

To set colors, click the Colors tab in the Command Prompt window's properties dialog box. Here you can set separate foreground and background colors for the Command Prompt window and pop-up windows, such as the command history window.

An introduction to Windows PowerShell

Microsoft describes Windows PowerShell as a "task-based command-line shell and scripting language designed especially for system administrators." That means that you can use PowerShell for the same kinds of tasks you're accustomed to performing with Cmd.exe, and you can use its scripting power to automate routine work. If you're a Windows user who occasionally likes to take advantage of the power of text-based command-line tools such as Ipconfig or Netsh, you'll find that PowerShell lets you interact with the operating system in all the old familiar ways—and a good many new ones as well. If you're accustomed to using batch programs, VBScript, or JScript to automate administrative tasks, you can retain your current scripting investment but take advantage of the additional capabilities afforded by PowerShell's object orientation and .NET Framework foundation as your scripting needs grow.

CAUTION

If you use Netsh to configure TCP/IP, you should familiarize yourself with equivalent procedures in PowerShell. In 2015, Microsoft began displaying the following message in response to the **netsh /interface** command: "Microsoft recommends that you transition to Windows PowerShell if you currently use netsh to configure and manage TCP/IP." Type **Get-Command –Module NetTCPIP** at the Windows PowerShell prompt to view a list of commands to manage TCP/IP. As of this writing, **netsh/interface** continues to work, but the message suggests that it might not always.

Among the advantages that PowerShell offers over previous shells and scripting platforms are the following:

- **Integration with the .NET Framework.** Like more traditional development languages, such as C#, PowerShell commands and scripts have access to the vast resources of the .NET Framework.

- **Object orientation and an object-based pipeline.** All PowerShell commands that generate output return .NET Framework objects rather than plain text, eliminating the need for text parsing when the output of one command provides input to a second (that is, when one command is "piped" to another).

- **A consistent, discoverable command model.** All of PowerShell's commands (or "cmdlets," as they are called) use a verb-noun syntax, with a hyphen separating the two components. All cmdlets that read information from the system begin with Get; all those that write information begin with Set. These and other similar consistencies make the language easy to learn and understand. Each cmdlet has a help topic that can be retrieved by typing **get-help *cmdletname*** (where *cmdletname* is the name of a cmdlet). A –Whatif parameter lets you test the effect of a cmdlet before you execute it.

- **Universal scripting capability.** A PowerShell script is a text file, with the extension .ps1, containing PowerShell commands. Any commands that can be used interactively can be incorporated into a script, and scripting structures, such as looping, branching, and variables, can also be used interactively—that is, outside the context of a script.

- **A focus on administrators.** PowerShell includes features of particular interest to system administrators, such as the ability to work with remote computers; access to system resources such as files, folders, registry keys, events, and logs; and the ability to start and stop services.

- **Extensibility.** Developers can extend the PowerShell language by importing modules—packages of PowerShell commands and other items.

The following pages introduce PowerShell. Our discussion focuses primarily on the use of PowerShell as an interactive command shell because PowerShell scripting is itself a book-length subject. For sources of additional information, see "Finding additional PowerShell resources" later in this chapter.

Starting PowerShell

To launch Windows PowerShell, type **power** into the search box; the Windows PowerShell application should appear at or near the top of the results list. Nearby you will also find the 64-bit and 32-bit versions of the Windows PowerShell Integrated Scripting Environment (ISE). The ISE is a multitabbed graphical environment of particular use for developing and debugging scripts.

As Figure 21-1 shows, PowerShell's default appearance differs minimally from that of Cmd.exe. The caption *Windows PowerShell* and the letters *PS* at the beginning of the command prompt may be the only details you notice.

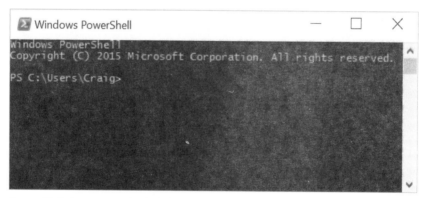

Figure 21-1 An uncustomized (default) PowerShell window looks a lot like Cmd.exe.

Interacting with PowerShell

If you're an old hand at the command prompt but new to PowerShell, the first thing you might want to try is using some of Cmd.exe's familiar internal commands. You'll discover that such items—for example, *dir*, *cd*, *md*, *rd*, *pushd*, and *popd*—still work in PowerShell. Redirection symbols, such as > to send output to a file and >> to append output to a file, work as well, and you can pipe lengthy output to More, just as you are accustomed to doing in Cmd.exe. PowerShell uses aliases to map Cmd.exe commands to its own cmdlets. Thus, for example, *dir* is an alias for the PowerShell cmdlet *Get-Childitem*; *cd* is an alias for PowerShell's *Set-Location*.

You can create your own aliases to simplify the typing of PowerShell commands that you use often; for details, see "Using and creating aliases" later in this chapter.

Like any other command prompt, PowerShell can be used to launch executables. Typing **regedit**, for example, launches Registry Editor; typing **taskschd** launches Task Scheduler. (Note that PowerShell also lets you work directly with the registry without the use of Registry Editor; for details, see "Working with the registry" later in this chapter.)

Using cmdlets

The core of PowerShell's native vocabulary is a set of cmdlets, each consisting of a verb, followed by a hyphen, followed by a noun—as, for example, *Start-Service*. A cmdlet may be followed by one or more parameters; each parameter is preceded by a space and consists of a hyphen connected to the parameter's name followed by a space and the parameter's value. So, for example,

```
Get-Process -Name iexplore
```

returns information about any currently running processes named iexplore.

With parameters that accept multiple values, you can use a comma to separate the values. For example,

```
Get-Process -Name iexplore, winword, excel
```

would generate information about Word and Excel as well as Internet Explorer.

Many cmdlets use positional parameters. For example, the –Name parameter for *Get-Process* is positional. PowerShell expects it to come first, so you may omit –Name and simply specify the names of the processes in which you're interested.

If you omit both the first positional parameter and its value, PowerShell typically assumes a value of *. So, for example,

```
Get-Process
```

returns information about all running processes, as shown in Figure 21-2.

In some cases, if you omit values for an initial positional parameter, PowerShell will prompt you to supply the parameter. For example, in response to

```
Get-Eventlog
```

PowerShell will do you the courtesy of prompting for the name of an event log. (Event logs are large; it wouldn't be reasonable to ask for all of them at once.)

For information about any particular cmdlet, type **get-help** followed by the cmdlet name.

Figure 21-2 Typing *Get-Process* without parameters produces information about all running processes.

Using the pipeline

The pipe operator (|) lets you supply the output of one cmdlet as input to another. You can connect as many cmdlets as you please in this manner, as long as each cmdlet to the right of a pipe operator understands the output of the cmdlet to its left. Because PowerShell cmdlets return full-fidelity .NET objects rather than text, a cmdlet to the right of a pipe operator can operate directly on properties or methods of the preceding cmdlet's output.

The following paragraphs provide examples of the use of piping to format, filter, and sort the output from various Get- cmdlets.

Formatting output as a list   The default output from many Get- cmdlets is a table that presents only some of the resultant object's properties (about as many as the width of your display is likely to accommodate). For example, the cmdlet

```
Get-Service
```

generates a three-column display that includes only the Status, Name, and DisplayName properties.

If you pipe the same output to *Format-List*,

```
Get-Service | Format-List
```

PowerShell, no longer constrained by display width, can display more of the object's properties (see Figure 21-3), including in this case such useful items as the dependencies of each service and whether the service can be paused or stopped.

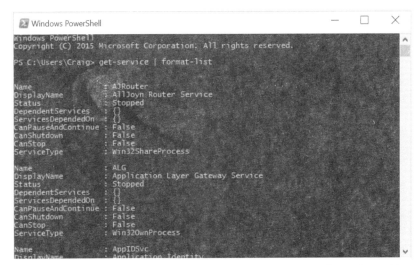

Figure 21-3 Piping a cmdlet to *Format-List* allows you to see more of a resultant object's properties.

In some cases, the *Format-List* cmdlet, with no parameters, is equivalent to *Format-List –Property **. But this is by no means always the case. For example,

```
Get-Process | Format-List
```

returns four properties for each process: ID, Handles, CPU, and Name. Asking for all properties produces a wealth of additional information.

To generate a list of particular properties, add the –Property parameter to *Format-List* and supply a comma-separated list of the properties you want to see. To see what properties are available for the object returned by a cmdlet, pipe that cmdlet to *Get-Member*:

```
Get-Process | Get-Member -Itemtype property
```

(Omitting the –Itemtype parameter returns methods as well as properties.)

Creating a multicolumn list with *Format-Wide*   By piping a cmdlet to *Format-Wide*, you can generate a multicolumn list displaying a single property, comparable to a List view in File Explorer. Use the –Column parameter to specify the number of columns you want. For example,

```
Get-Childitem hkcu:\appevents\eventlabels | Format-Wide -Column 2
```

generates a two-column list of the subkeys of HKCU:\Appevents\Eventlabels.

Formatting output as a table   Perhaps you want tabular output but with different properties from those that your cmdlet gives you by default. *Format-Table* does the trick. For example,

```
Get-Service | Format-Table -Property name, dependentservices, servicesdependedon
```

generates a table consisting of these three enumerated properties. Note that PowerShell's console output is constrained by your console width, no matter how many properties you ask to see. For results that are too wide to display, redirect output to a file (using the > operator) or try the *Out-Gridview* cmdlet, described next.

Generating an interactive graphical table with *Out-Gridview*   Piping output to *Out-Gridview* generates a graphical tabular display that you can filter, sort, and copy easily into other programs, such as Excel, that accommodate tabular data. For example,

```
Get-Process | Select-Object * | Out-Gridview
```

produces output comparable to that shown in Figure 21-4. Note that in this example, *Get-Process* is piped first to *Select-Object* * because *Out-Gridview*, unlike *Format-Table*, does not include a –Property parameter. *Select-Object* * passes all properties of the object returned by *Get-Process* along the pipeline to *Out-Gridview*.

_NounName	Name	Handles	VM	WS	PM	NPM	Path	Comp
Process	ApplicationFr...	293	2,199,249,801,216	27,189,248	14,331,904	20,528	C:\WINDO...	Micro
Process	audiodg	331	2,199,110,033,408	13,955,072	11,714,560	15,952		
Process	chrome	234	222,879,744	19,996,672	14,618,624	23,464	C:\Program...	Goog
Process	chrome	197	233,340,928	33,521,664	30,523,392	21,888	C:\Program...	Goog
Process	chrome	932	336,797,696	68,988,928	39,989,248	51,920	C:\Program...	Goog
Process	conhost	168	2,199,119,544,320	13,713,408	5,484,544	14,808	C:\WINDO...	Micro
Process	csisyncclient	628	339,951,616	30,035,968	35,225,600	35,112	C:\Program...	Micro
Process	csrss	427	2,199,081,062,400	3,031,040	1,544,192	14,208		
Process	csrss	434	2,199,109,603,328	7,245,824	2,113,536	29,704		
Process	dasHost	136	2,199,047,012,352	2,727,936	1,236,992	7,536		
Process	dwm	4,336	2,199,374,393,344	102,391,...	89,645,056	31,304		
Process	explorer	1,970	2,199,533,977,600	108,212,...	45,109,248	82,880	C:\WINDO...	Micro
Process	firefox	741	688,422,912	234,340,...	209,289,...	85,048	C:\Program...	Mozil
Process	fontdrvhost	49	2,199,085,252,608	3,170,304	831,488	5,976		
Process	Idle	0	65,536	4,096	0	0		
Process	InputPersona...	267	2,199,124,881,408	17,747,968	2,891,776	15,064	C:\Program...	Micro

Figure 21-4 The *Out-Gridview* cmdlet produces a graphical tabular display that you can sort, filter, and copy into a spreadsheet.

You can manipulate the *Out-Gridview* display with techniques comparable to those used by many other programs:

- To sort the display, click a column heading; click a second time to reverse the sort.

- To change the position of a column, drag its heading. You can also rearrange columns by right-clicking any column head, choosing Select Columns, and then using the Move Down and Move Up buttons in the Select Columns dialog box.

- To remove columns from the display, right-click any column heading, click Select Columns, and then use the << button in the Selected Columns dialog box.

- To perform a quick filter, enter text in the line labeled Filter. For example, to limit the display in Figure 21-4 to processes with properties containing the word Microsoft, type **Microsoft** on the Filter line.

- To filter on one or more specific columns, click the Add Criteria button. In the dropdown list that appears, select check boxes for the columns on which you want to filter and then click Add.

Filtering output with *Where-Object* To filter output from a cmdlet, pipe it to the *Where-Object* cmdlet. With *Where-Object* you encapsulate filtering criteria in a script block, between curly braces. The following example filters output from *Get-Service* so that only services whose status is Stopped are displayed:

```
Get-Service | Where-Object {$_.Status -eq "Stopped"}
```

Sorting output with *Sort-Object* The *Sort-Object* cmdlet lets you sort the output from a cmdlet on one or more of the resultant object's properties in a variety of useful ways. If you omit the –Property parameter, *Sort-Object* sorts on the default property. For example,

```
Get-Childitem | Sort-Object
```

sorts the contents of the current directory by Name, the default property in this case. To sort on multiple properties, follow –Property with a comma-separated list. *Sort-Object* sorts on the first named property first, sorting items with identical values for the first property by the second property, and so on. Sorts are ascending by default; to sort in descending order, add the parameter –Descending.

By piping *Sort-Object* to *Select-Object* you can do such things as returning the largest or smallest *n* items in a resultant object. For example,

```
Get-Process | Sort-Object –Property WS | Select-Object -Last 10
```

returns the processes with the 10 largest values of the working set (WS) property. Using –First 10 instead of –Last 10 would give you the items with the smallest values.

Piping output to the printer   To redirect output to the default printer, pipe it to *Out-Printer*. To use a nondefault printer, specify its name, in quotation marks, after *Out-Printer*. For example,

```
Get-Content C:\Users\Craig\Documents\Music\Sonata.sib | Out-Printer "Microsoft Print
To PDF"
```

sends the content of C:\Users\Craig\Documents\Music\Sonata.sib to the device named Microsoft Print To PDF.

Using PowerShell features to simplify keyboard entry

PowerShell is a wordy language and doesn't take kindly to misspellings. Fortunately, it includes many features to streamline and simplify the task of formulating acceptable commands.

Using and creating aliases   An alias is an alternative formulation for a cmdlet. As mentioned earlier, PowerShell uses aliases to translate Cmd.exe commands to its own native tongue—for example, *cd* to *Set-Location*. But it includes a great many more simply for your typing convenience; *gsv*, for example, is an alias for *Get-Service*. And you can create aliases of your own.

To see what aliases are currently available (including any that you have created yourself during the current session), type **get-alias**. To see whether an alias is available for a particular cmdlet, pipe *Get-Alias* to *Where-Object*, like this:

```
Get-Alias | Where-Object { $_.definition -eq "Set-Variable" }
```

This particular command string inquires whether an alias is available for the *Set-Variable* cmdlet. If you type this, you'll discover that PowerShell offers two—*sv* and *set*.

To create a new alias, type **set-alias *name value***, where *name* is the alias and *value* is a cmdlet, function, executable program, or script. If *name* already exists as an alias, *Set-Alias* redefines it. If *value* is not valid, PowerShell won't bother you with an error message—until you try to use the alias.

Aliases that you create are valid for the current session only. To make them available permanently, include them in your profile. See "Using your profile to customize PowerShell" later in this chapter.

Abbreviating parameter names   Aliases are dandy for cmdlets, but they're no help for parameter names. Fortunately, PowerShell allows you to abbreviate such names. The commands *Get-Process –name iexplore* and *Get-Process –n iexplore* are equivalent. As soon as you've typed enough of a parameter name to let PowerShell recognize it unambiguously, you can give your fingers a rest. And, of course, you can combine aliases with parameter abbreviations to further lighten your load.

Using Tab expansion   As a further convenience, PowerShell lets you complete the names of files, cmdlets, or parameters by pressing Tab. Type part of a name, press Tab, and PowerShell presents the first potential completion. Continue pressing Tab to cycle through all the possibilities. Note, however, that Tab expansion works only with the noun portion of a cmdlet; type the verb and the hyphen, and then you can use Tab expansion for the noun.

Using wildcards and regular expressions   Like all its Windows-shell predecessors, PowerShell supports the * and ? wildcards, the former standing in for any combination of zero or more characters, the latter for any single character. PowerShell also provides a vast panoply of "regular expressions" for matching character strings. For details about regular expressions in PowerShell, type **get-help about_regular_expressions**.

Recalling commands from the command history   PowerShell maintains a history of your recent commands, which makes it easy to reuse (or edit and reuse) a command that you've already entered. To see the history, type **get-history**. Each item in the history is identified by an ID number. Type **invoke-history *ID*** to bring an item to the command line. On the command line, you can edit an item before executing it. With the exception of Alt+F7, the editing keys available in Cmd.exe (see Table 21-1) work the same way in PowerShell.

The number of history items retained in a PowerShell session is defined by the automatic variable $MaximumHistoryCount. By default, that variable is set to 64. If you find you need more, you can assign a larger number to the variable. For example, to double the default for the current session, type **$MaximumHistoryCount = 128**. To change the history size for all sessions, add a variable assignment to your profile. For more information, see "Using your profile to customize PowerShell" later in this chapter.

Using PowerShell providers for access to file system and registry data

PowerShell includes a set of built-in providers that give you access to various kinds of data stores. Providers are .NET Framework–based programs, and their data is exposed in the form of drives, comparable to familiar file-system drives. Thus, for example, you can access a key in the HKLM registry hive with a path structure similar to that of a file-system folder; for example, the path HKLM:\Hardware\ACPI specifies the ACPI key of the Hardware key of the HKLM hive. Or, to use a quite different example, you can use the command *Get-Childitem env:* to get a list of current environment variables and their values.

Table 21-3 lists PowerShell's built-in providers. For more information about providers, type **get-help about_providers**.

Table 21-3 Built-in providers

Provider	Drive	Data store
Alias	Alias	Currently defined aliases
Certificate	Cert X509	Certificates for digital signatures
Environment	Env	Windows environment variables
FileSystem	(varies)	File-system drives, directories, and files
Function	Function	PowerShell functions
Registry	HKLM, HKCU	HKLM and HKCU registry hives
Variable	Variable	PowerShell variables
WSMan	WSMan	WS-Management configuration information

The following paragraphs provide some basic information about working with the file system and registry.

Working with the file system   For very simple file-system operations, you might find that familiar Cmd.exe commands are adequate and easier to use than PowerShell cmdlets. The built-in aliases listed in Table 21-4 let you stick with time-honored methods. PowerShell supports the familiar single period (.) and double period (..) symbols for the current and parent directories, and it includes a built-in variable, $Home, that represents your home directory (equivalent to the HomePath environment variable).

Table 21-4 File-system aliases

Alias	PowerShell cmdlet
cd	*Set-Location*
chdir	*Set-Location*
copy	*Copy-Item*
del	*Remove-Item*
dir	*Get-Childitem*
move	*Move-Item*
md, mkdir	*New-Item*
rd, rmdir	*Remove-Item*
type	*Get-Content*

The PowerShell cmdlets, however, include valuable optional parameters:

- **–Confirm and –Whatif.** The –Confirm parameter, used with *Copy-Item*, *Move-Item*, *Remove-Item*, or *Clear-Content*, causes PowerShell to display a confirmation prompt before executing the command. (*Clear-Content* can be used to erase the contents of a file.) If you use the –Whatif parameter, PowerShell shows you the result of a command without executing it.

- **–Credential.** Use the –Credential parameter to supply security credentials for a command that requires them. Follow –Credential with the name of a user, within double quotation marks. PowerShell will prompt for a password.

- **–Exclude.** The –Exclude parameter allows you to make exceptions. For example, *Copy-Item directory1*.* directory2 –Exclude *.log* copies everything, excluding all .log files, from Directory1 to Directory2.

- **–Recurse.** The –Recurse parameter causes a command to operate on subfolders of a specified path. For example, *Remove-Item x:\garbagefolder*.* –Recurse* deletes everything from X:\Garbagefolder, including files contained within that folder's subfolders.

- **–Include.** The –Include parameter, used in conjunction with –Recurse, allows you to restrict the scope of a command. For example, *Get-Childitem c:\users\craig\documents* –Recurse –Include *.xlsx* restricts a recursive listing of C:\Users\Craig\Documents to files with the extension .xlsx.

- **–Force.** The –Force parameter causes a command to operate on items that are not ordinarily accessible, such as hidden and system files.

For detailed information about using these parameters with *Set-Location*, *Get-Childitem*, *Move-Item*, *Copy-Item*, *Get-Content*, *New-Item*, *Remove-Item*, or *Get-Acl*, type **get-help cmdletname**.

Working with the registry   The built-in registry provider provides drives for two registry hives, HKLM and HKCU. To change the working location to either of these, type **set-location hklm:** or **set-location hkcu:**. Use standard path notation to navigate to particular subkeys, but enclose paths that include spaces in quotation marks; for example, *set-location "hkcu:\control panel\accessibility"*.

To display information about all subkeys of a key, use *Get-Childitem*. For example,

```
Get-Childitem -Path hkcu:\software\microsoft
```

returns information about all the subkeys of HKCU:\Software\Microsoft.

To add a key to the registry, use *New-Item*. For example,

```
New-Item -Path hkcu:\software\mynewkey
```

adds the key mynewkey to HKCU:\Software. To remove this key, type **remove-item –path hkcu:\software\mynewkey**.

To copy a key, use *Copy-Item* and specify the source and destination paths; like this, for example,

```
Copy-Item -Path hkcu:\software\mykey hkcu:\software\copyofmykey
```

To move a key, use *Move-Item*. The command

```
Move-Item -Path hkcu:\software\mykey -Destination hkcu:\software\myrelocatedkey
```

copies all properties and subkeys associated with HKCU:\Software\Mykey to HKCU:\Software\ Myrelocatedkey and deletes HKCU:\Software\Mykey.

To display the security descriptor associated with a key, use *Get-Acl*. To see all the properties of the security descriptor, pipe this to *Format-List –Property **. For example,

```
Get-Acl -Path hkcu:\software\microsoft | Format-List -Property *
```

generates a display comparable to this:

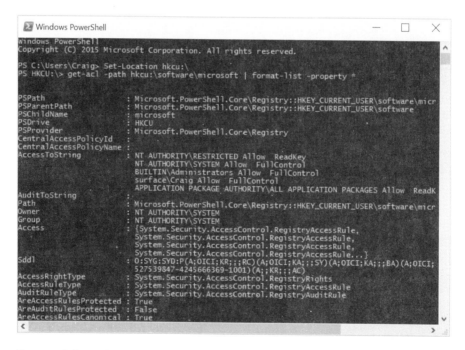

For more information about working with the registry, type **get-help registry**.

Discovering PowerShell

PowerShell provides plenty of resources to help you learn as you go. You can display help information about any cmdlet by typing **get-help *cmdletname***. For example, to read help about *Get-Help*, type **get-help get-help**. If you omit the first *get,* PowerShell helpfully pipes the help text to More. So, for example, if you type **help get-help**, PowerShell will pause the output after each screenful.

Among the useful parameters for *Get-Help* are the following:

- **–Examples.** To display only the name, synopsis, and examples associated with a particular help text, add the –Examples parameter.

- **–Parameter.** To get help for a particular parameter associated with a cmdlet, include –Parameter. Specify the parameter name in quotation marks.

- **–Detailed.** To get the description, syntax, and parameter details for a cmdlet, as well as a set of examples, use the –Detailed parameter. (Without this parameter, the examples are omitted; with –Examples, the syntax information is omitted.)

- **–Full.** For the works, including information about input and output object types and additional notes, specify –Full.

- **–Online.** For the latest information that Microsoft has, including additions or corrections to the native output of *Get-Help*, specify –Online. The relevant information, from the Microsoft TechNet Script Center, will appear in your browser.

PowerShell includes a compiled HTML (.chm) help file, which you can run from the Jump List that appears on the recent items or pinned items section of your Start menu (or on the taskbar if you pin PowerShell there). But the information made available via the –Online parameter is more current and more accurate than that provided in the .chm file. For the most recent updates visit the "Scripting with Windows PowerShell" page at Microsoft TechNet, *bit.ly/scripting-with-powershell*.

Getting help on conceptual topics

The PowerShell help resources include a number of entries on conceptual topics, such as operators, parameters, variables, and pipelines. These topics all begin with *about*. You can generate a list by typing **get-help about*** or **get-help –category "helpfile"**. To read information about aliases, for example, type **get-help about_aliases**. Note that the TechNet site described in the previous section also includes these conceptual topics.

Finding the right cmdlet to use

The *Get-Command* cmdlet can help you figure out which cmdlet is the right one to use for a given task. Type **get-command** with no arguments to get the names and definitions of all available cmdlets, functions, and aliases. *Get-Command* can also give you information about non-PowerShell executables. If you type **get-command ***, for example, you'll get a huge list including all files in all folders included in your current Path environment variable.

Either global list (with or without the non-PowerShell executables) is likely to be less than useful when you just want to know which cmdlets are available for use with a particular object. To get such a focused list, add the –Noun parameter. For example, type **get-command –noun eventlog** to get a list of the cmdlets that use that noun; you'll be rewarded with the names and definitions of *Clear-Eventlog*, *Get-Eventlog*, *Limit-Eventlog*, *New-Eventlog*, *Remove-Eventlog*, *Show-Eventlog*, and *Write-Eventlog*. You can get a list focused similarly on a particular verb by using the –Verb parameter.

Scripting with PowerShell

A PowerShell script is a text file with the extension .ps1. You can create a script in any plain text editor (Notepad will do fine), or you can use the Integrated Scripting Environment (ISE).

Anything that you do interactively with PowerShell you can also do in a script. The reverse is true as well; you can take lines from a script, including those that involve looping or branching structures, and execute them individually outside the context of a script. For example, if you type

```
For ($i=1; $i -le 5; $i++} { "Hello, World" }
```

at the PowerShell command prompt, PowerShell will perform the familiar greeting five times.

Using PowerShell's history feature, you can easily transfer commands that you have used interactively into a script. That way you can test to see what works and how it works before committing text to a .ps1 file.

For example, the command

```
Get-History | Foreach-Object { $_.commandline } >> c:\scripts\mynewscript.ps1
```

appends the Commandline property from each item in your current history to the file C:\Scripts\Mynewscript.ps1. (If the path doesn't exist, the command returns an error.) Once you have transferred your history to Mynewscript.ps1 in this manner, you can edit it in Notepad by typing **notepad c:\scripts\mynewscript.ps1**.

Running PowerShell scripts

Although files with the extension .ps1 are executable PowerShell scripts, running one is not quite as straightforward as double-clicking a .bat file. In the first place, if you double-click a .ps1 file in File Explorer, you'll get an Open File—Security Warning dialog box, from which the only forward step leads to Notepad. In effect, the default action for a PowerShell script in File Explorer is Edit.

Second, the first time you try to run a script by typing its name at the PowerShell command prompt, you might well see a distressing message displayed in red letters and with possibly unwelcome detail. This means that PowerShell has declined to run your script "because the execution of scripts is disabled on this system." You need to change PowerShell's execution policy.

Third, even after you've cleared the execution-policy hurdle, you might still be rebuffed if you try to run a script stored in the current directory. That's because PowerShell requires a full path specification—even when the item you're running is stored in the current directory. For example, to run Displayprocessor.ps1, which resides in the current directory, you must type **.\displayprocessor**.

Getting and setting the execution policy

PowerShell's power can be used for evil ends. The majority of Windows users will never run PowerShell, but many will have .ps1 files lying about on their system or will download them inadvertently. To protect you from malice, PowerShell disables script execution until you explicitly enable it. Enabling execution requires a change to the execution policy.

Note that your profile script (if you have one) is subject to the same execution policy as any other script. (See "Using your profile to customize PowerShell" later in this chapter.) Therefore, it's pointless to set an execution policy by means of a profile script; that script itself will not run until you've enabled script execution elsewhere.

The following execution policies, listed here from least permissive to most, are available:

- **Restricted.** The default policy. No scripts are allowed to run.

- **AllSigned.** Any script signed by a trusted publisher is allowed to run. PowerShell presents a confirmation prompt before running a script signed by a publisher that you have not designated as "trusted."

- **RemoteSigned.** Scripts from local sources can run. Scripts downloaded from the Internet (including scripts that originated as email or instant-messaging attachments) can run if signed by a trusted publisher.

- **Unrestricted.** All scripts can run, but PowerShell presents a confirmation prompt before running a script from a remote source.

- **Bypass.** All scripts are allowed to run.

Execution policies can be set separately for the following scopes:

- **Process.** Affects the current PowerShell session only. The execution policy is stored in memory and lost at the end of the session.

- **CurrentUser.** The execution policy is stored in a subkey of HKCU and applies to the current user only. The setting is retained between PowerShell sessions.

- **LocalMachine.** The execution policy is stored in a subkey of HKLM and applies to all users at this computer. The setting is retained between PowerShell sessions.

If policies are set at two or more of these scopes, the Process policy takes precedence over the CurrentUser policy, which takes precedence over the LocalMachine policy. Execution policy can also be set via Group Policy, however, and settings made in that manner trump any of the foregoing scopes. (Group Policy settings can be made in either the Computer Configuration or User Configuration node; a Computer Configuration setting trumps any other.)

To see the execution policies in effect at all scopes, type **get-executionpolicy –list**.

To set an execution policy, use *Set-ExecutionPolicy*. To set a policy at the LocalMachine scope, you need to be running PowerShell with administrative privileges.

The default scope for *Set-ExecutionPolicy* is LocalMachine, so if you're planning to apply a policy to all users at your computer, you can omit the –Scope parameter. For example, if you're comfortable disabling all of PowerShell's script-execution security measures, including warning prompts, you can type **set-executionpolicy bypass.** For a slightly more protective environment, type **set-executionpolicy unrestricted**.

To set a policy at the CurrentUser or Process scope, add –Scope followed by CurrentUser or Process. Note that you can also set an execution policy at the Process scope by adding an –executionpolicy argument to a command that launches PowerShell. For example, from a command prompt in Cmd.exe, in PowerShell, or on the Start menu, you could type **power-shell –executionpolicy unrestricted** to launch PowerShell with the Unrestricted execution policy at the Process scope.

To remove an execution policy from a particular scope, set that scope's policy to Undefined. For example, if you have set a Process policy to, say, Bypass, and you would like PowerShell to revert to the policy at the next level of precedence (CurrentUser, if a policy is set there, or LocalMachine, if not), type **set-executionpolicy undefined –scope process**.

Using your profile to customize PowerShell

Your profile is a script that PowerShell executes at the beginning of each session. You can use it to tailor your PowerShell environment to your preferences. Your profile must have the following path and file name:

$Home\Documents\WindowsPowerShell\Profile.ps1

where $Home is a system-generated *PowerShell* variable corresponding to the environment variable UserProfile. You can see where this is on your system by typing **$profile**, and you can edit an existing profile by typing **notepad $profile**. If you have not yet created a profile, you can type the following:

```
if (!(test-path $profile)){New-Item -Type file -Path $profile -Force}
```

PowerShell will create the file for you in the appropriate folder. Then you can type **notepad $profile** to edit the blank file.

You can use your profile to customize PowerShell in a variety of ways. Possibilities to consider include changing the default prompt and creating new aliases.

PowerShell's prompt is derived from a built-in function called Prompt. You can overwrite that function with your own. For example, the function

```
Function prompt {"PS [$env:computername] $(Get-Date) > "}
```

replaces the built-in PowerShell prompt with the letters PS, followed by your computer name, followed by the current date and time. For more information about PowerShell prompts, type **get-help about_prompts**.

To add new aliases to the ones that PowerShell already offers, simply include *Set-Alias* statements in your profile. (See "Using and creating aliases" earlier in this chapter.)

Using the PowerShell ISE

A feature introduced with PowerShell 2.0 allows you to issue commands and work with scripts in a graphical environment. This Integrated Scripting Environment (ISE) includes a command pane, a script pane, and an output pane. The output pane displays the results of any commands you issue in the command pane or any scripts that you run in the script pane.

The ISE supports multiple tabs, so you can open several scripts at once. Click File, New to open a new blank tab (for example, to write a new script) or File, Open to open an existing script in a new tab. To run the current script, click Run/Continue on the Debug menu, press F5, or click the green arrow in the middle of the toolbar. Other commands on the Debug menu allow you to set and remove breakpoints and step through execution.

The ISE offers all the usual amenities of a graphical environment. You can resize and rearrange the panes, for example. You can use the View menu's Zoom commands (or adjust the slider in the lower right corner of the window) to make the text display larger or smaller. And you can easily select and copy text from one pane to another or from the ISE to another application.

The ISE uses its own profile, separate from the one you use to customize PowerShell itself. The path and file name are as follows:

$Home\Documents\WindowsPowerShell\ProfileISE.ps1

and you create the file by typing:

```
if(!(Test-Path $profile)){New-Item –Type file -Path $profile -Force}
```

Finding additional PowerShell resources

This chapter's discussion of PowerShell has barely nicked the surface. For further exploration, we recommend the following:

- *Windows PowerShell 3.0 First Steps*, by Ed Wilson (Microsoft Press, 2013)

- *Windows PowerShell Cookbook*, third edition, by Lee Holmes (O'Reilly Media, 2013)

- "Windows PowerShell Scripting" (part of the Microsoft TechNet Script Center) at *bit.ly/ps-script-center*

- The "Hey, Scripting Guy!" blog at *bit.ly/scripting-guy*

- "Getting Started with Windows PowerShell" (part of the MSDN Script Center) at *bit.ly/get-started-powershell*

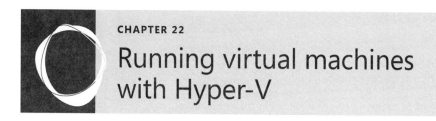

Hyper-V allows you to create and run *virtual machines*—effectively, computers within a computer. A console on your computer acts as a monitor for a virtual machine (sometimes called a *VM*), which generally has all the features and capabilities of a standalone computer. The only difference is that a virtual machine is running as a program on a host computer.

Hyper-V has long been a power feature in server editions of Windows, allowing IT managers to use a single server machine to host a variety of server roles, each in its own virtual machine. Beginning with Windows 8, Client Hyper-V is included in Pro and Enterprise editions of Windows, to the great delight of IT professionals, developers, security researchers, and tech enthusiasts. Client Hyper-V has most, but not all, of the features of Hyper-V Server. In Windows 10, Client Hyper-V gains some additional features, such as production checkpoints, better support of older operating systems, and the ability for users to change memory and other settings without first shutting down a virtual machine.

Virtual machines running under Hyper-V are useful in the following situations, among many others:

- People who have programs that work only in older versions of Windows can run them in a virtual machine.

- Developers who need to test their programs in different Windows versions or on different hardware configurations can set up a virtual machine for each target platform.

- Security researchers and curious users who want to test software of unknown provenance or explore potentially dangerous websites can do so safely within the confines of a virtual machine (assuming it's properly isolated from the host and the host network). If a virus or other malware is found, the host machine remains unscathed, and the virtual machine can be rolled back to a safe state.

- Tech enthusiasts who want to test a new beta (prerelease) version of Windows or other software can install it in a virtual machine. This way, they can try software without having to dedicate a physical machine (or worse, upgrading their main system to run an operating system that's not ready for prime time).

- Authors of books like this one can use virtual machines not only to test various setups, but also to capture images of screens that would be impossible to grab using ordinary screen-capture tools (for example, images showing sign-in screens or even Windows setup before Windows itself is fully functional).

To use Hyper-V, your system must meet certain minimum requirements and you might need to enable Hyper-V, as described in the next section. After that is done, you use Hyper-V Manager to create virtual machines. With enough system resources, you can then run one or more virtual machines, each in its own window. Because they function as independent computers, each virtual machine can run a different version of Windows—32-bit or 64-bit, old or new, server or desktop—or even other operating systems that work on PC-compatible hardware.

Setting up Hyper-V

Before you get started with Hyper-V, be sure your computer meets the system requirements. Because each virtual machine uses system resources on a par with a standalone computer, the requirements are somewhat steep:

- **64-bit version of Windows 10 Pro, Enterprise, or Education.** Hyper-V is unavailable on 32-bit versions and is also not part of Windows 10 Home.

- **At least 4 GB of RAM.** With 4 GB, you can probably run up to three virtual machines simultaneously. More machines require more RAM.

- **Copious disk space.** Each virtual machine is stored in files on your hard drive. The size can vary considerably depending on how you configure your virtual machines (for example, the size of the VM's virtual hard disks), how many checkpoints you save, and so on—but expect to use at least 20 GB of disk storage for each virtual machine.

- **CPU with Second Level Address Translation (SLAT) support.** Your computer must have a 64-bit processor that supports SLAT. Most 64-bit processors sold by Intel and AMD in the past few years have this capability.

With those prerequisites in place, you're ready to enable Hyper-V, which is not enabled by default. To do so, open Windows Features, shown in Figure 22-1. (In the search box, type **features** and then click Turn Windows Features On Or Off.)

Inside OUT

Determine whether your computer supports SLAT

A utility from Windows Sysinternals can tell you more than you need to know about your computer's CPU. Download Coreinfo from *bit.ly/sysinternals-coreinfo*. At an elevated command prompt, enter **coreinfo –v** to see results similar to this:

```
c:\>E:\Data\Downloads\Coreinfo\Coreinfo.exe -v

Coreinfo v3.31 - Dump information on system CPU and memory topology
Copyright (C) 2008-2014 Mark Russinovich
Sysinternals - www.sysinternals.com

Intel(R) Core(TM) i7-2600 CPU @ 3.40GHz
Intel64 Family 6 Model 42 Stepping 7, GenuineIntel
Microcode signature: 00000029
HYPERVISOR      -       Hypervisor is present
VMX             *       Supports Intel hardware-assisted virtualization
EPT             *       Supports Intel extended page tables (SLAT)
```

For an Intel processor (as shown here), an asterisk in the EPT line indicates SLAT support; a hyphen in that space indicates that the processor does *not* support SLAT. For an AMD processor, the line to look for is NP. Note that you'll get valid results only if Hyper-V is *not* already running. (But if it's already running, you didn't need to run this diagnostic test anyway, did you?)

Figure 22-1 To select all the Hyper-V-related entries, simply select the top-level Hyper-V check box.

Click the plus sign by the top-level Hyper-V entry to show all the subentries. If your computer does not fully support Hyper-V, the Hyper-V Platform entry is not available.

Inside OUT

Using Hyper-V on a computer that doesn't support SLAT

Hyper-V Management Tools, the first subentry under Hyper-V, can be installed on any computer running Windows 10. Therefore, even if the Hyper-V Platform entry is dimmed (which means your computer isn't capable of hosting virtual machines), you can use Hyper-V Management Tools to manage virtual machines that are hosted on a different physical computer (in most cases, a computer running Window Server). To create and run virtual machines on your own computer, you must enable Hyper-V Platform.

Select Hyper-V (which also selects all the available subentries) to enable it, and then click OK. After a few moments, Windows asks you to restart your computer.

Alternatively, you can enable Hyper-V by using Windows PowerShell. Use this cmdlet:

```
Enable-WindowsOptionalFeature –Online –FeatureName Microsoft-Hyper-V –All
```

Using Hyper-V Manager

Hyper-V Manager is the program you use to create, run, and manage your virtual machines. When you start Hyper-V Manager, the initial view, shown here, might leave you scratching your head. You're faced with a barren console window, one that has only one available action.

The trick is to select a "server" (in this case, your local computer) in the left pane, the console tree. (On computers that do not have Hyper-V Platform enabled, the only option is to choose the Connect To Server action, which lets you connect to a different computer running Hyper-V Platform.) Lots more information and options then appear, as shown in Figure 22-2.

Actions for Hyper-V host computer

Actions for selected virtual machine

Figure 22-2 When you select a local machine or remote server in the console tree (PRO3 in this example), Hyper-V Manager shows the virtual machines stored on that physical computer.

TROUBLESHOOTING

The name of your computer doesn't appear in the console tree

If your computer's name doesn't appear under Hyper-V Manager in the console tree, then it is not running Hyper-V Platform. Be sure you're running a 64-bit version of Windows 10, and be sure that your computer's processor supports Second Level Address Translation, as described in the previous section. If your computer meets the requirements, then check to be sure that Hyper-V Platform is selected in Windows Features.

When you select a server in the console tree, the center pane lists the virtual machines available on that server and shows a bit of information about the current state of each one. Below that, you'll see a list of checkpoints for the selected virtual machine. (A *checkpoint* captures the configuration and data of a virtual machine at a point in time. For more information, see "Working with checkpoints" later in this chapter.) At the bottom of the center pane, the

Summary, Memory, and Networking tabs show additional details about the selected virtual machine. Here you can see at a glance what IP address has been assigned to the virtual machine, how much memory is in use, and so on. The thumbnail image on the Summary tab also provides a convenient launching method for the virtual machine; double-click it to open a full-size screen in a new window.

As in other console applications, the right pane shows available actions for the items selected in the left and center panes. Figure 22-2, for example, shows the actions that apply to the PRO3 computer (the name of the local computer running Hyper-V) and to the virtual machine named Windows 8 Pro.

Creating a network switch

By default, a new virtual machine is set up as a standalone computer with no network connection. It can't connect to the Internet or to other computers on your network. In this connected world, you'll probably want to give your virtual machines a network connection.

To do that, you must first have a bit of networking infrastructure in place—namely, a virtual switch. A *virtual switch* connects the virtual network adapter in your virtual machine to the physical network adapter in your physical computer, thereby allowing the virtual machine to connect to the outside world.

> **NOTE**
> You can create and manage a virtual switch *after* you set up a virtual machine and then modify your virtual machine to use the virtual switch. Setting up the virtual switch before you set up your virtual machines simply saves a few steps.

To create a virtual switch or make changes to an existing one, in the Actions pane (or on the Action menu) click or tap Virtual Switch Manager. Then select the type of switch you want to create:

- **External.** This is the most common type because it binds the virtual switch to your computer's physical network adapter so you can access your physical network. Assuming your physical network adapter is connected to the Internet, your virtual machines also have Internet access.

- **Internal.** An internal virtual switch can be used only to make a connection among the virtual machines running on your physical computer, and between the virtual machines and your physical computer.

- **Private.** Use a private virtual switch to set up a network that comprises only the virtual machines running on your physical computer. This network is isolated from all physical computers, including the one on which it's installed.

When you click or tap Create Virtual Switch, you're asked for more details, as shown in Figure 22-3. Click OK to complete the switch creation.

Figure 22-3 If your computer has more than one physical network adapter, specify the one you want to use under External Network.

Creating a virtual machine

With your virtual network switch in place, you're ready to create a new virtual machine. To do that, in the Actions pane, click or tap New, Virtual Machine, which launches the New Virtual Machine Wizard. You navigate through the wizard, which leads you through the process of setting up a virtual machine, by using the Next and Previous buttons or the links along the left side. At any point in the wizard, you can click Finish to create a virtual machine that uses default values for any wizard pages you skip.

Specify name and location

After you step through the Before You Begin page, the wizard asks you to provide a name for your virtual machine. Enter a name or description that'll help you differentiate this virtual machine from others you might create. If you don't like the proposed storage location for the virtual machine files, select the check box and specify another, as shown in Figure 22-4.

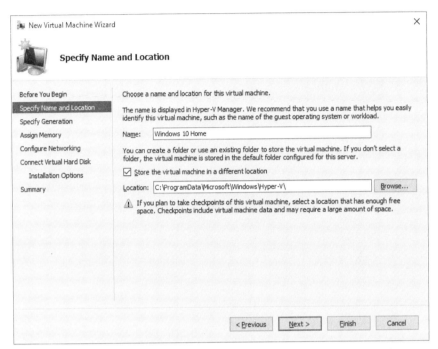

Figure 22-4 For our purposes, the operating system name provides a good name for a virtual machine, but you might have different needs.

The default location is %ProgramData%\Microsoft\Windows\Hyper-V\. (%ProgramData% is an environment variable that is set to C:\ProgramData on a standard Windows installation.) If your computer has a small system drive (common in systems that use a solid state drive for system files and a large hard disk for data files), you might want to store the files elsewhere. Keep in mind that a virtual machine can occupy 10–40 GB or more.

It is possible to move the virtual machine files after you create the machine, but it's not easy. Although some parts of a virtual machine (the virtual hard disk and the paging file, for example) can be moved by changing the settings of the virtual machine, this option isn't available for some of the core files. To completely move a machine at a later time, you can import a virtual machine, copy it, and store it in a different location. You're much better off choosing a suitable location *before* you create the virtual machine.

Specify generation

On the next wizard page, shown here, you select either Generation 1 or Generation 2 for the style of virtual machine you need.

This choice is new to Hyper-V in Windows 10 and offers some tradeoffs between compatibility and features.

Generation 1 supports a wide range of guest operating systems, including most versions of Windows (32-bit and 64-bit) and Linux. The virtual hardware in a generation 1 virtual machine is typical of that found in BIOS-based PCs for many years.

Generation 2 supports only a few guest operating systems: 64-bit versions of Windows 8, Windows 8.1, Windows 10, Windows Server 2012, and Windows Server 2012 R2. In addition, generation 2 removes support for attaching physical DVD drives and other older hardware to a virtual machine. But a generation 2 virtual machine has modern UEFI-based firmware, which enables Secure Boot and booting from a network adapter, SCSI hard drive, or DVD. In addition, generation 2 virtual machines enable new Hyper-V features, such as the ability to adjust memory or add a network adapter while the virtual machine is running.

If you're going to install one of the newer supported operating systems in your virtual machine, select Generation 2 to enable additional features. For an older operating system, you must stick with the default option, Generation 1.

NOTE
If you select Generation 2, you must install the operating system from an ISO file; you can't use a DVD.

Assign memory

On the Assign Memory page, shown in Figure 22-5, you specify the amount of RAM your virtual machine will have.

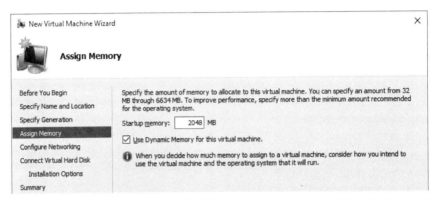

Figure 22-5 The Dynamic Memory option lets you use memory more efficiently when running multiple virtual machines.

If you enable Dynamic Memory, Hyper-V uses memory as a shared resource that can be reallocated as needed among running virtual machines. This way, each machine gets as much memory as it needs, but it doesn't reserve a fixed amount of memory (which would preclude other machines from using it).

Therefore, if you plan to run more than one virtual machine at once, we recommend that you select Dynamic Memory to get the best performance. Then set Startup Memory to at least the minimum amount required for the operating system you plan to install in this virtual machine.

If you plan to run only one virtual machine, or if you know how much memory your virtual machine will need to perform its given tasks, you can turn off Dynamic Memory and specify a fixed amount of memory. This setup works more like a physical computer, in that whatever memory you specify is the total amount of installed RAM in the virtual machine.

Configure networking

On the next wizard page, shown in Figure 22-6, you specify the virtual network switch where you want to connect your virtual machine's network adapter. The default option is Not Connected, which results in a virtual machine that's isolated from all other computers (physical and virtual) and from the Internet. Even to connect to the physical computer on which the virtual machine runs, you must create a virtual network switch and select it here.

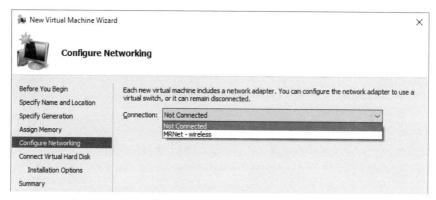

Figure 22-6 Select a virtual network switch to connect to the outside world.

The only available option is Not Connected

Before you can connect to a network, you must create a virtual network switch, as described earlier in "Creating a network switch." Each virtual network switch you create appears in the Connection list.

To determine which type of network switch you're using (External, Internal, or Private), you need to return to the Virtual Switch Manager.

Connect virtual hard disk

On the Connect Virtual Hard Disk page, shown in Figure 22-7, you set up the virtual machine's first virtual hard disk (VHD). (Just like a physical computer, a virtual machine can have multiple hard drives.) A virtual hard disk is actually a file in the VHD or VHDX format. By default, it's created in a subfolder of the virtual machine location you specified earlier. But you can override that default and store the virtual hard disk on any physical disk that's accessible to the host computer running Hyper-V.

Figure 22-7 With the first option, you create a virtual hard disk. The other options allow you to use an existing virtual hard disk.

In addition to specifying the name and location of your virtual hard disk file, you must specify the disk's capacity in gigabytes. Be sure you create a virtual hard disk that's big enough to store the operating system, programs, and data you plan to use on the virtual machine. Although you don't want to go overboard, don't worry too much about specifying a size that's too big. Because of the way data is stored in a virtual hard disk, the size of the VHDX file roughly corresponds with the amount of disk space in use rather than the size you specify, which is the maximum. However, its dynamically expanding nature also means that the VHDX file can grow to that maximum size; be sure that the physical hard drive where you store it has enough room to accommodate growth.

NOTE

You can change the location later, but it's a multistep process. And it is possible to resize a virtual hard disk after it has been created, but doing so brings some risk of data loss. (For more information, select the virtual hard disk in the Settings window for the virtual machine, and then click Edit.) Therefore, it's best to get it right from the beginning.

If you have an existing virtual hard disk you want to use instead of creating a new one, select the second or third option on this wizard page.

Installation options

Almost done! You use the wizard's next page, shown in Figure 22-8, to specify how and when you want to install an operating system in your new virtual machine.

Figure 22-8 If you choose Generation 2 on the Specify Generation page, the options for installing from a CD/DVD drive or floppy disk don't appear because generation 2 virtual machines don't support these types of physical devices.

Like a physical computer, a virtual machine is nothing without an operating system, so installing one should be your first order of business. Select the appropriate option, specify the location of your operating system installation media, and click Next.

This brings you to a Summary page, where you can review your settings before clicking Finish to complete the wizard.

At this point, even though you've specified installation options, you still don't have a working virtual machine. Now back in Hyper-V Manager, double-click the new virtual machine to open it in a Virtual Machine Connection window. Then click or tap the Start button on the toolbar or choose Start on the Action menu. This "powers on" your virtual machine and launches operating system setup from the location you specified in the wizard.

Running a virtual machine

As the final step in creating a virtual machine, described in the previous sections, you double-click the name of a virtual machine in Hyper-V Manager to open the machine in a Virtual Machine Connection window. You then click the Start button on the toolbar to power on the machine. This is one of two common ways to run a virtual machine. (The other is to use the Hyper-V Virtual Machine Connection program, which we describe in the following section.)

As shown in Figure 22-9, a virtual machine running in a Virtual Machine Connection window looks (and, for the most part, acts) just like a separate physical computer, except that it's contained in a window on your desktop.

Virtual Machine Connection menu and toolbar

Windows XP running in a window

Virtual Machine Connection status bar

Figure 22-9 For a nostalgic look back—or to run a legacy program that doesn't run properly on newer operating systems—you can run Windows XP in a Virtual Machine Connection window.

You use the toolbar at the top of the window (or the corresponding commands on the Action menu) to operate the virtual machine.

From left to right, the buttons have the following functions:

- **Ctrl+Alt+Del.** Because the Ctrl+Alt+Del key combination is reserved by Windows 10 on your physical computer, when you press it while you're using a virtual machine, the key combination goes to your host computer. There are two ways to mimic the effect of Ctrl+Alt+Del within a virtual machine: Press Ctrl+Alt+End or click or tap this toolbar button.

- **Start.** This button turns on a virtual machine that is off.

- **Turn Off.** This button turns the virtual machine off, but it does so by effectively unplugging the machine. This, of course, is not a graceful way to shut down a computer, and you'll lose any unsaved data.

- **Shut Down.** This is equivalent to using the Shut Down command on the Start menu, and the machine goes through the usual shut-down process. Note that some (usually older) operating systems do not support Shut Down, even with Integration Services enabled. For a virtual machine without this support, use commands within the virtual machine to shut down properly.

- **Save.** This button saves the virtual machine state and then turns it off, much like hibernation on a physical computer. When you next start the virtual machine, you return immediately to where you left off.

- **Pause/Resume.** Pausing a virtual machine stops it temporarily but does not fully release its resources, as the Turn Off, Shut Down, and Save options do.

- **Reset.** Resetting a virtual machine discards any changes and reboots using the last saved version.

- **Checkpoint.** This button creates a checkpoint, which is a snapshot of the virtual machine's state and its data. For more information, see "Working with checkpoints" later in this chapter.

- **Revert.** This button restores the virtual machine to its condition at the previous checkpoint and restarts the virtual machine.

- **Enhanced Session.** On guest operating systems that support it, this button toggles the virtual machine between basic session mode and enhanced session mode. For more information, see the next section, "Using enhanced session mode."

Within the Virtual Machine Connection window, you use the virtual machine just as you would a physical computer, with only a few exceptions:

- When you run an older guest operating system, using a mouse is not as fluid as it is when your guest operating system is Windows 8 or later. That's because once you click inside the virtual machine window, the mouse becomes trapped in that window. To release it, press Ctrl+Alt+Left Arrow.

- Not all of your physical computer's hardware is available in all virtual machines.

  For example, DVD drives are not available in generation 2 virtual machines. (You can, however, mount an ISO image as a DVD drive.) For generation 1 machines, only one virtual machine can use a physical DVD drive at any given time. (To release the DVD drive from one virtual machine so that you can use it in another, use commands on the DVD menu.)

  USB devices, audio devices, and some other local resources work only in enhanced session mode. (For more information, see "Using enhanced session mode.")

Inside OUT

Start a virtual machine automatically

By default, when you open a Virtual Machine Connection window, it opens with the machine turned off. If you want to save yourself the trouble of starting the virtual machine after you open it, you can change a setting for the virtual machine so that it starts automatically. In Hyper-V Manager, select the virtual machine; in the right pane, under the virtual machine name, click Settings; in the Settings dialog box, under Management, select Automatic Start Action and then select an option.

When you close the Virtual Machine Connection window, note that your virtual machine continues to run. By closing the window, all you're doing, in effect, is turning off the monitor. To shut down or turn off the virtual machine, you should use the appropriate buttons on the Virtual Machine Connection window. If that window is closed? You can reopen it by using Hyper-V Manager.

Using enhanced session mode

With previous versions of Hyper-V, access to your physical computer's hardware is quite limited. Your physical computer's screen, keyboard, and mouse could be redirected for use by the virtual machine, but connecting other devices is somewhere between difficult and impossible. Audio playback is not supported. In addition, capabilities for copying files between a virtual machine and its host computer are very limited in older Hyper-V versions. You could overcome some of these limitations (specifically, audio playback and file copying) by using Remote Desktop Connection to connect to a virtual machine, but that requires a working network connection to the virtual machine.

With Windows 10, Hyper-V adds *enhanced session mode*, which solves many of these shortcomings. With enhanced session mode, you can redirect the following resources from your physical computer to a virtual machine in a Virtual Machine Connection window:

- Audio devices

- Printers

- Plug and Play devices

- Clipboard (which allows you to copy and paste files and other information between the virtual machine and your physical computer)

Inside OUT

Determine at a glance whether you're in enhanced session mode

Need a quick way to tell whether your machine is running in enhanced session mode? Look at the speaker icon in the notification area of your virtual machine's taskbar. If it has a red X, that's because no audio device is available, which means you're in basic session mode.

Alas, enhanced session mode comes with its own limitations. First and foremost: enhanced session mode requires a guest operating system that supports it, and there are only a few that do (Windows 8.1, Windows 10, Windows Server 2012 R2). Of less importance, you'll also discover that in enhanced session mode you can't readily change the resolution of the virtual machine's monitor. (For a workaround, see the following tip.)

If your virtual machine is running an operating system that supports enhanced session mode, you can switch between basic and enhanced session mode by clicking or tapping the rightmost button on the Virtual Machine Connection toolbar.

Inside OUT

Change screen resolution for an enhanced mode session

Within an enhanced session mode window, using the normal Windows settings for changing screen resolution leads to this message: "The display settings can't be changed from a remote session." (Enhanced session mode, in effect, uses Remote Desktop Connection to connect to the virtual machine, hence the message about a "remote session.")

If you need to change the screen resolution, switch to basic session mode and then close the Virtual Machine Connection window. In Hyper-V Manager, click Connect to open a new Virtual Machine Connection window, and you'll be greeted by a dialog box in which you can specify the screen resolution, as shown here.

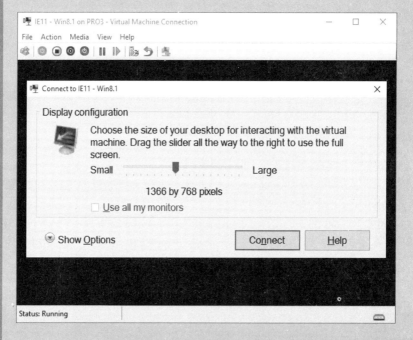

In this same dialog box, clicking Show Options adds a Local Resources tab to the dialog box. On that tab, you specify which local resources—that is, printers, drives, and other devices from the host computer—you want to use within the virtual machine. For more information about these settings, see "Using Remote Desktop Connection" in Chapter 20, "Advanced networking."

You can enable and disable enhanced session mode on a per-server or per-user basis. To view or change either setting, in Hyper-V Manager select the server and then, under the server name in the right pane, click or tap Hyper-V Settings. In the Hyper-V Settings dialog box that appears, you'll find enhanced session mode settings under Server and User.

Inside OUT

Get ready-to-run virtual machines

As part of its support for developers, Microsoft offers fully configured virtual machines that you can download and run. Each one has a different guest operating system with certain software installed. These virtual machines are for testing and evaluation and expire after a limited time, but instructions provided with the virtual machine files explain how to use the files after expiration. You can find these virtual machine files at *bit.ly/virtualmachines*.

Changing settings for a virtual machine

The settings you make when you create a new virtual machine are but a small subset of the settings you can apply to a virtual machine. You can change almost all the settings you make in the New Virtual Machine Wizard plus scores more. You can add virtual devices such as network adapters and hard drives, change the location of some of the files that make up the virtual machine, reconfigure devices at a granular level, and more.

To dive into these settings, in Hyper-V Manager select the name of the virtual machine and then, near the bottom of the Actions pane, click or tap Settings. A dialog box like the one shown in Figure 22-10 appears.

Many settings can be changed even while a machine is running (which is important for virtual machines running critical tasks), especially on generation 2 virtual machines.

Figure 22-10 The dizzying array of options on the Memory page—which is similar in complexity to many other pages in the Settings dialog box—will make you glad that the New Virtual Machine Wizard asks for only a single number.

Working with checkpoints

A *checkpoint* captures the data and configuration of a running virtual machine—a snapshot in time. Indeed, in earlier versions of Hyper-V, checkpoints were called snapshots. A checkpoint can be restored, allowing you to quickly and easily return your virtual machine to an earlier time—perhaps a time before that misguided software installation.

To capture a checkpoint, simply click or tap the Checkpoint button on the Virtual Machine Connection toolbar. You can provide a descriptive name for the checkpoint, but no other inter-action is required. The checkpoints you collect for a given virtual machine appear in the center of the Hyper-V window, as shown in Figure 22-11. To revert to an earlier checkpoint, select the checkpoint and, in the Actions pane, click or tap Apply.

Figure 22-11 When you select a checkpoint in the center pane, a list of applicable actions for that checkpoint appear in the bottom of the Actions pane.

Microsoft engineers have discovered that droves of Hyper-V users use checkpoints as a form of backup. (Although it doesn't provide the full capabilities of a more traditional backup program—such as the ability to restore individual folders and files—it's convenient and easy.) However, the checkpoint feature as implemented in earlier Hyper-V versions is far from ideal for backup. Because those checkpoints (now called standard checkpoints) include information on the virtual machine state, running applications, and network connections, restoring one often takes you to an unstable condition (for example, the same network connections might not be available).

In response, Client Hyper-V in Windows 10 adds a new type of checkpoint called a *production checkpoint*. A production checkpoint uses the Volume Snapshot Service (VSS) backup technology to save the data and configuration of a running virtual machine but not its state. This provides a much better backup solution, and it is now the default checkpoint in Hyper-V. You can still use standard checkpoints if you prefer; to make the switch, open Settings for a virtual machine and, under Management, click Checkpoints.

Windows 10 editions at a glance

Microsoft's lineup of Windows 10 editions is refreshingly simple.

Consumers and small businesses that acquire Windows on a new device or as an upgrade have their choice of two and only two editions: Windows 10 Home and Windows 10 Pro.

On corporate networks, you have the option to enable additional features by upgrading to the Enterprise edition. At universities and other institutions of learning, administrators can enable advanced features by upgrading to the Education edition, which is, except for a few small details, roughly equivalent to the Enterprise edition.

That makes a grand total of four editions, of which you are still only likely to encounter two.

Yes, the Windows 10 family also includes Windows 10 Mobile, which runs on smartphones and, at least in theory, on other small devices that have not yet appeared in the market. Sometime in the future, you might encounter embedded versions of Windows 10 for use in specialized machines (such as automated teller machines) and wearables. But our focus in this appendix is on the four versions of Windows 10 designed for use on traditional PCs and PC-like devices such as tablets.

That simple lineup is a stark and welcome improvement over the sometimes confusing assortment of previous Windows editions, and it makes our job in this appendix simple. We start with a recitation of the features you can find in all Windows 10 desktop editions and then, in separate sections, list the additional features available in individual editions.

You can use this information to decide whether to upgrade from Home to Pro when you're shopping for a new PC, for example. You can also use the data in these tables to help decide which PCs on a corporate network should be upgraded to the Enterprise edition using your organization's Volume License agreement.

We start with a brief discussion of hardware configurations. Table A-1 lists technical limits related to CPU and memory support that might affect your purchase or upgrade decision.

Table A-1 Supported hardware configurations in Windows 10

Hardware component	Supported configurations
Number of CPUs/cores	Windows 10 Home: One physical processor, unlimited cores Windows 10 Pro/Enterprise/Education: One or two physical processors, unlimited cores
Addressable memory (RAM)	32-bit (x86) editions: 4 GB maximum (because of 32-bit memory architecture, usable memory is typically 3.5 GB or less) 64-bit (x64) editions: 128 GB for Windows 10 Home, 512 GB for Windows 10 Pro/Enterprise/Education

Features available in all Windows 10 editions

With some minor exceptions, which are noted here, the features listed in Table A-2 are available in all retail editions of Windows 10 sold worldwide, including Windows 10 Home edition.

Table A-2 Features available in all Windows 10 editions

Feature	Description
Core Windows features	
Customizable Start menu and taskbar	Similar in concept to the Windows 7 Start menu, with the additional ability to pin apps as Windows 8–style live tiles.
Windows Update	Provides regular security updates, device drivers, and new features. Business editions have limited options to delay updates.
Fast User Switching	Allows a user to sign in to another user account without requiring the current user to sign out.
Hiberboot and InstantGo	These features, which are supported on most modern devices, allow faster startup as well as low-power, always-on updates even when a device is sleeping.
Settings app	Offers access to many system settings previously available only in Control Panel; uses an interface that scales to devices of different sizes and is especially usable on touch devices.
Virtual desktops	Allows collections of running apps to be arranged on separate virtual desktops, with keyboard shortcuts or gestures for switching between desktops.
Window snap	An upgrade to the classic Aero Snap behavior, with Snap Assist improving the usability of displaying two windows side by side. Allows snapping of up to four windows to any corner or side of a display; also supports multiple displays.
Task View	Quickly switch between running programs with a taskbar button, keyboard shortcuts, or touch gestures.

Feature	Description
Power management	In addition to support for classic Windows power schemes, includes new Battery Saver options for more aggressive control over battery life.
Ease Of Access features	High-contrast themes, Ease Of Access Center, Magnifier, Narrator, and On-Screen Keyboard.
Windows Mobility Center	Central location for managing power, display, network, and other settings on a notebook PC.
Windows PowerShell and Integrated Scripting Environment	Command-line shell and graphical host application for scripting administrative tasks.
Virtual hard drive (VHD) support	Create a new VHD; attach (mount) an existing VHD.
Display	
Touchscreen/pen support	With appropriate hardware and drivers, adds support for touch, multitouch, and pen input.
Tablet Mode and Continuum	Tablet Mode changes the layout of the Start menu, taskbar, and running programs for easier use on handheld touch devices. Continuum allows hybrid devices to switch modes when the keyboard is attached or removed.
Miracast	Allows streaming of audio and video from a Windows 10 device to a Miracast receiver, such as the Microsoft Wireless Display Adapter.
Multimonitor support	With properly configured hardware, extends the main display to include a second (or third, fourth, and so on) monitor.
Cortana and Search	
Windows Search	Indexed search of local files, programs, and settings, with ability to expand search to include cloud-based items and the web.
Cortana	Adds a "personality" and a natural language interface to Windows Search and allows access to an ever-expanding collection of web services.
Speech-based interaction	Allows hands-free activation with the "Hey Cortana" trigger phrase, as well as intelligent and trainable speech recognition.
Interest-based suggestions	Proactive display of news, sports scores, weather forecasts, traffic reports, and more, based on defined interests and linked calendars or other activities.
Intelligent actions	Create reminders, appointments, tasks, and spoken notes from speech or typed input.

Feature	Description
Security and reliability	
Trusted Platform Module (TPM) support	Supports the latest TPM specification for secure storage of system secrets such as encryption keys and configuration information.
Secure Boot and Early Launch Antimalware	On UEFI devices, ensures the integrity of boot files and prevents malicious software from acting before Windows has fully loaded.
Device encryption	Full disk encryption, even on Windows 10 Home devices, when signing in with a Microsoft account. BitLocker administration tools are available only with business editions.
Windows Hello	Biometric sign-in and authentication options enabled through support for compatible fingerprint readers, facial recognition devices, and iris scanners.
Microsoft Passport	Supports authentication to online resources using biometric credentials without transmitting passwords.
User Account Control	Allows the use of standard accounts for day-to-day use; includes Enhanced Protected Mode in Internet Explorer 11.
Security and maintenance notifications	Messages and updates about security and maintenance issues.
Windows Defender	Real-time antivirus and antispyware protection, with free updates.
Windows Firewall	Blocks unsolicited inbound network connections; includes advanced security interface to manage inbound and outbound connections.
System recovery drive/ Windows Recovery Environment	Provides the ability to access a troubleshooting/repair environment at startup without requiring original installation media.
Reset	Allows the user to recover from system corruption or compromise by reinstalling Windows, with options to keep or remove personal files and account information.
File History	Provides the ability to recover changed or deleted files from automatic or manual backups.
System image backup	Includes the capability to create a system image and restore Windows from a previously saved image.
Family safety	For accounts you designate as family members, provides the ability to set time limits on computer usage and block access to specific games, programs, and websites.
Windows Remote Assistance	Allows direct network connections between two Windows PCs for troubleshooting and repair.

Feature	Description
Sideloading of line of business apps	In managed environments, supports deployment of custom Windows apps directly, without requiring access to the Windows Store.
Mobile device management	Allows administrators to manage Windows 10 mobile devices from a management console. This feature is not available in Windows Home edition at launch but will be available later.
Installed apps	
Microsoft Edge	Default web browser for retail editions of Windows 10, updated through Windows Store; supports reading view, PDF viewing, ink comments, and Cortana integration.
Internet Explorer 11	Secondary web browser for Windows 10; provides compatibility with older websites and allows use of ActiveX controls and browser plug-ins.
Mail & Calendar	Allows sending, receiving, and managing email messages, appointments, and meeting invitations; supports industry-standard protocols as well as cloud services from Microsoft, Google, Apple, and Yahoo.
Maps	Online and offline support for maps covering the entire world; supports navigation functions on devices equipped with a GPS.
Photos	Allows viewing and basic editing of photos stored locally or in the cloud.
Alarms & Clock	Displays the current time, with the option to display multiple time zones; also includes stopwatch, alarm, and countdown features.
Calculator	Full-featured calculator that performs basic arithmetic as well as advanced statistical functions; also includes programmer and scientific modes and has the ability to convert units of measurement.
News, Weather, Sports, Money	A suite of information apps powered by MSN and connected via the current Microsoft account
Phone Companion	Manages synchronization with mobile devices, including those running non-Windows operating systems.
Xbox and other games	Allows access to casual games, including a preinstalled modern version of Solitaire; can also stream games from an Xbox One console.
Groove Music	Plays supported audio file formats, including MP3, WMA, AAC, and FLAC; also connects to Microsoft's Groove (previous Xbox Music) subscription service.
Camera	Controls built-in camera (front and back) for taking photos or communicating via programs such as Skype.

Feature	Description
Scan	Used to scan documents and send and receive faxes. Requires properly configured scanner, fax modem, or both.
XPS Document Writer and Viewer	Provides the capability to create and view documents using the XML Paper Specification.
Voice Recorder	Creates simple voice memos.
Networking	
Remote Desktop client	Connect via a network to a Remote Desktop host.
SMB network connections	Maximum of 20 simultaneous connections. Because each PC or device requires two Server Message Block (SMB) connections, 10 PCs or devices can be connected at once.
Ability to join a homegroup	Share local resources and access shared resources on other devices running Windows 7 or later versions that are part of the same homegroup.
Microsoft Wi-Fi	Automatically connects to Microsoft-managed Wi-Fi hotspots; requires subscription.

Windows 10 Pro

Windows 10 Pro includes the same core features as Windows 10 Home, with the addition of features that are primarily of interest to business users and corporate network administrators. All of the features listed in Table A-3 are also available in the Enterprise and Education editions.

Table A-3 Features available only in Windows 10 Pro, Enterprise, and Education editions

Feature	Description
Core Windows features	
Client Hyper-V	With proper hardware support, this hypervisor-based virtualization software allows users to create a virtual machine (VM), install Windows or another operating system on the VM, and use it as if it was a separate physical device.
Boot from virtual hard drive (VHD)	Configure a VHD as a boot device.
Language packs	Change the Windows 10 interface to display menus, dialog boxes, and other elements in a user-selected language.
Subsystem for Unix-based Applications	Compatibility subsystem for compiling and running custom Unix-based applications.
Encrypting File System	Enables strong encryption of files and folders on an NTFS-formatted volume.

Feature	Description
Management, security, and networking features	
BitLocker	Allows an entire drive to be encrypted, protecting its contents from unauthorized access if the computer is lost or stolen.
BitLocker To Go	Encrypts data on removable media such as USB flash drives.
Domain join/Group Policy management	Allows the device to join a Windows domain and be managed by using Active Directory and Group Policy.
Enterprise Data Protection	Provides advanced control over data files, including encryption and remote wipe. This feature is not available at launch.
Enterprise Mode Internet Explorer (EMIE)	Using network configuration files, administrators can define compatibility settings for sites accessed using Internet Explorer, including those on corporate intranets, enabling continued use of older web apps that aren't compatible with Microsoft Edge.
Assigned Access	A special configuration mode primarily for use on tablets and task-specific workstations that restricts the ability of a user to run any apps except those on an approved list.
Remote Desktop (server)	Allows remote access to the full Windows experience on the current PC; the connection is made using Remote Desktop Protocol from a client program running on any Windows PC, Mac, or supported mobile device.
Offline Files	Used to synchronize, cache, and index network files locally so that they are available when the computer is disconnected from the network.
Deployment features	
Azure Active Directory support	Allows a Windows 10 device to join Azure Active Directory, with single sign-in to cloud-hosted apps.
Business Store for Windows 10	Using this feature, an organization can provision apps and packaged Windows desktop programs in a restricted area of the Windows Store for installation by employees. This feature is not available at launch.
Windows Update for Business	Allows central management of security updates and new features delivered through Windows Update. The Current Branch for Business enhances stability by delaying delivery of new features until they have been thoroughly tested in the Current Branch.

Windows 10 Enterprise and Education

Windows 10 Enterprise edition is available as an upgrade to Volume License customers; it requires an underlying license for Windows 10 Pro. Windows 10 Education edition provides equivalent features for large networks in academic environments and allows upgrades from Windows 10 Home or Pro editions. Table A-4 lists features available only in these editions.

Table A-4 Features available only in Windows 10 Enterprise and Education editions

Feature	Description
Management and security features	
Granular control of user experience	Provides standard Start menu layouts defined by administrators, and prevents users from altering the standard user experience.
AppLocker	Enables administrators of enterprise networks to create an authorized list of programs that users can install and run.
Credential Guard	Supports multifactor authentication using smart cards and biometric information.
Device Guard	Allows organizations to lock down a Windows 10 device so that only approved apps and desktop programs can be installed or run, preventing the installation of most forms of malware and any unauthorized software.
Windows To Go Creator	Allows the installation of Windows 10 Enterprise or Education on certified, high-performance USB drives that can boot and run in secure, self-contained mode, isolated from access by the host PC.
Long Term Servicing Branch	Allows administrators to limit deployment of new features in Windows 10, installing reliability and security updates only; this feature is designed for use in mission-critical environments; available only in Enterprise edition.
Networking	
BranchCache	Increases network responsiveness of applications in environments running on Windows Server 2008 R2 and later.
DirectAccess	Provides secure connections (without a virtual private network, or VPN) between a client PC running Windows 10 and a remote server running Windows Server 2008 R2 or later.
Location-aware printing	Helps domain-joined computers find the correct printer when a user moves between office and home networks.

Help and support resources

We hope this book is helpful. We also know that even if we had unlimited pages and multiple volumes to fill, there's no way we could answer every question or cover every nook and cranny of a product as rich and diverse as Windows 10. And, of course, in the "Windows as a Service" model, Windows 10 continues to evolve with new and reworked features and apps that we weren't able to describe in this edition because they didn't exist when we wrote it.

So we've put together this appendix to serve as a compendium of places where you can go to find help, troubleshooting tips, how-to guides, drivers, utilities, and advice.

Our list starts with official resources, collated and curated by Microsoft, but we also include community-based resources where you are likely to find reliable answers.

Online help

Over the years, what longtime Windows users call "the Help file" has evolved, with the Internet serving as the greatest agent of change. As recently as Windows 7, a Help And Support link on the Start menu led to Compiled HTML Help (.chm) files, readable with a built-in Windows utility (Hh.exe) that acts like a special-purpose browser.

That utility is still included with Windows 10, and you can still find a few .chm files (mostly for third-party products) if you search hard enough, but for Windows 10 itself most help is available online, where it's easily updated without the hassle of having to deliver those updated files to a billion or so PCs.

So for most questions, your first stop should be Microsoft's search engine, Bing, which delivers results directly from Microsoft Help when you ask a question about Windows. Figure B-1 shows one such question, with the answer in a box above all other search results and the source clearly labeled as "Help from Microsoft."

If a specific search doesn't return the official answer you're looking for, you can try browsing through Windows Help online (*windows.com/help*), which contains instructions for common tasks, organized by category, with a search box to help deliver more refined results, as shown in Figure B-2.

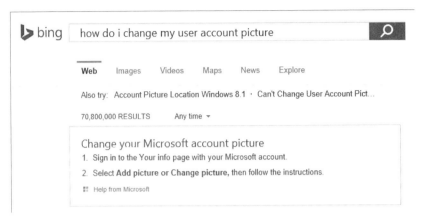

Figure B-1 Microsoft's Bing search engine delivers results directly from its collection of online Help from Microsoft if you ask the right questions.

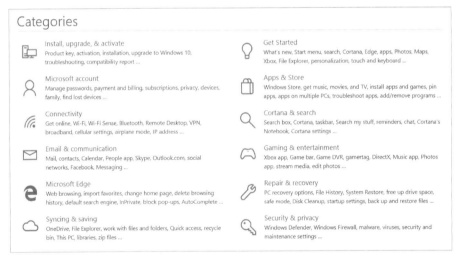

Figure B-2 Windows Help online is organized by category, with each entry shown here leading to a list of topics containing explanations and instructions.

Sometimes, of course, you're not looking for a detailed explanation or step-by-step instructions but simply trying to find a Windows setting without having to dig through menus or dialog boxes. For that type of chore, you have your choice of no fewer than three separate places to start a search.

- **The search box on the taskbar.** Entering a search term (in this case, the word **display**) in the search box on the taskbar returns a short but usually well-focused set of results.

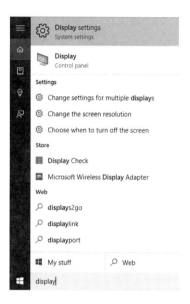

- **The Settings search box.** Click Settings on the Start menu (or use the keyboard short-cut Windows key+I) and enter a word or phrase in the search box in the upper right corner. Note that the top of the results list contains matching entries from the modern Settings app, followed by results from the desktop Control Panel, with the latter identifi-able by their unique icons, as shown here:

- **The Control Panel search box.** The classic desktop Control Panel has its own search box in the upper right corner. Entering a word or phrase here returns results exclusively from the All Control Panel Items list, as shown here. Its index does not include options from the modern Settings app.

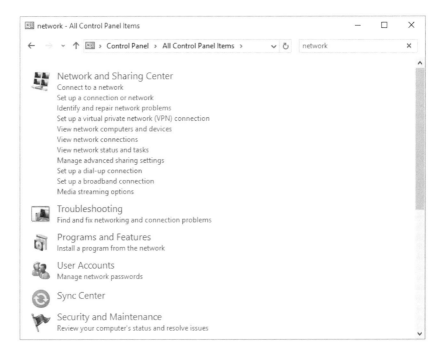

For traditionalists, one bit of help is available on a Windows 10 device, courtesy of a Windows Store app called Get Started. The app, shown in Figure B-3, is installed with Windows 10 and updated through the Windows Store.

The content in the Get Started app is basic, offers an overview of core features, and is aimed primarily at nontechnical users. Most of the readers of this book will probably find little new information there, but it's an excellent resource to suggest to friends, family members, and coworkers who could benefit from it.

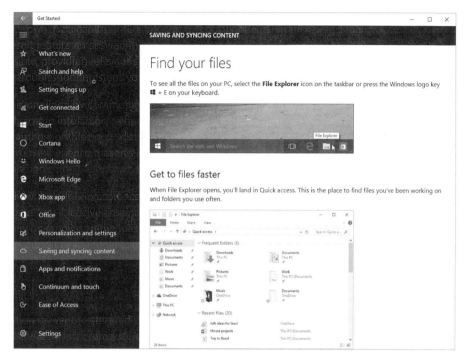

Figure B-3 The Get Started app is installed with Windows 10 and is intended primarily for beginners and nontechnical users.

You can open Get Started directly from the Start menu. An alternative entry point comes via pop-up tips that appear occasionally after you install Windows 10, suggesting that you try out new features. Those tips are designed to be unobtrusive and won't appear if you've already used the feature the tip is intended to introduce. But if you want to eliminate them completely, you'll find a Show Me Tips About Windows switch in Settings, under the System, Notifications & Actions category. Turn that setting off and you won't be bothered by those pop-ups.

> ➤ An additional source of detailed help in Windows 10 is available through the Troubleshooting section of Control Panel. We cover these guided tools as well as online Fix It resources in Chapter 17, "Troubleshooting."

Online reference material from Microsoft

Microsoft's commitment to ongoing support of Windows 10 includes an enormous library of training aids and reference material. This section lists the most important of these resources.

Microsoft Knowledge Base

Knowledge Base articles are official support documents that provide details about known issues, workarounds, security updates, new features, and anything else that the Microsoft Support organization deems worthy of formal publication.

Every Knowledge Base article has a unique ID number that you can use as a search term to locate a specific document. Security updates, for example, are documented with KB numbers so that IT pros can read details about what a specific update does.

To search for specific information in the Knowledge Base, start with this search term:

site:support.microsoft.com/en-us/kb "windows 10"

If your Windows 10 language is something other than US English, replace *en-us* with the prefix for your regional settings.

Save that search in your browser's Favorites bar or bookmarks and use it as the starting point for any future searches, appending your search terms in the search box. The results list will contain only documents that have been formally published in the Knowledge Base.

Microsoft TechNet

TechNet (*technet.microsoft.com*) is Microsoft's hub for technical information written primarily for IT pros. It includes news, technical articles, and downloads for all Microsoft products.

To focus exclusively on information about Windows 10, visit the Windows 10 TechCenter: *technet.microsoft.com/windows/dn798751*.

The TechNet library for Windows is continually expanding as new technical articles are added. It's worth bookmarking that page and visiting occasionally to see what's new.

Microsoft Virtual Academy

This online learning resource (*microsoftvirtualacademy.com*) is an excellent source of free training on a wide range of topics, including Windows 10. Available content includes prerecorded courses, live events (and archives of previous events), and books, with walk-throughs and demos bringing complex topics to life. New content is added regularly.

Getting technical support

If you can't find an answer in the Knowledge Base, or if a problem seems to be unique to your system configuration, you can turn to Microsoft's support forums for help.

Microsoft Community

For consumer versions of Windows and nontechnical users, start with the Microsoft Community forums at *answers.microsoft.com*. These threaded message boards are organized into categories—choose Windows, then Windows 10 to find the most relevant answers.

It's tempting to start by firing off a question, but a much better strategy is to use the search box in the upper right corner of the page to see whether anyone else has reported a similar issue. After entering the Windows 10 topic area, enter your search term and choose Current Scope from the drop-down list, as shown in Figure B-4. That step ensures that you see only answers that are relevant to Windows 10.

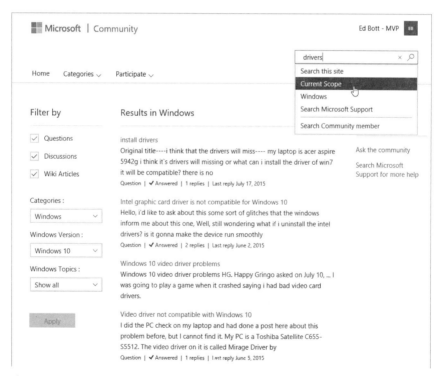

Figure B-4 Use the Current Scope option to limit search results to those matching the categories you selected from the lists on the left side of the Microsoft Community forums.

If your search doesn't turn up the answer you're looking for, click Ask The Community to begin composing a question of your own. (You can use this same form to start a discussion if you want to raise an issue that doesn't require an answer.) When posting to the Community forums, try to be as specific as possible, providing relevant details about your system configuration and hardware as well as any troubleshooting steps you've already tried and their results.

Note that support in these forums is provided by community members as well as Microsoft support personnel. You're also likely to run into an occasional Microsoft MVP (Most Valuable Professional), including one of the authors of this book. There's no guarantee you'll get a satisfactory answer, but we can testify from experience that this route has been successful for many people, including the authors of this book.

To keep track of a discussion, sign in with your Microsoft account and use the notification options at the bottom of any message. You'll receive an email at the address associated with your Microsoft account whenever anyone replies to the message; this is true regardless of whether you started the discussion yourself or found an existing discussion that you want to follow.

TechNet forums

If you're an IT pro and have a question or want to start a discussion with other like-minded and experienced individuals, go to the TechNet forums, *social.technet.microsoft.com/Forums*. Topics available here include a much broader range of Microsoft products and technologies than those covered in the Community forums, with a special emphasis on deploying and using Windows in the enterprise.

The basic rules of these more advanced message boards are similar to those we recommend for the Microsoft Community forums: search first, and ask a new question only if you can't find an existing discussion that addresses your issue.

Search options for the TechNet forums allow you to select multiple forums, shown on the left in Figure B-5, and then find specific topics within that selection by using a search box above the message list.

Use the filtering and sorting options (above the message list) to narrow your search further or make specific answers easier to locate.

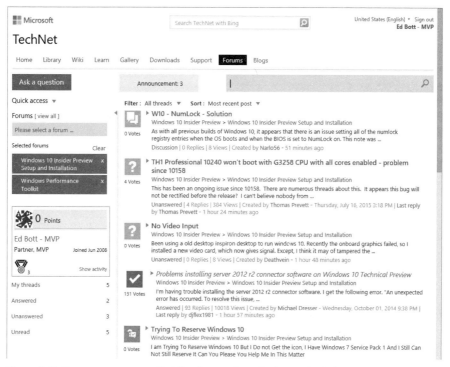

Figure B-5 Choose one or more TechNet forums from the list on the left, and then use the search box at the top of the message list to narrow your results.

Free and paid support from Microsoft

Getting answers from fellow Windows users has the advantage of being free and easily accessible, but sometimes you need formal support from Microsoft engineers.

Microsoft provides free support for security issues. If you suspect you've been infected with malware, for example, you can request and receive support at no charge. Other support options might be covered under a product warranty that's provided if you purchase Windows directly from Microsoft, or you can open a support ticket (called an "incident") for a fee.

To see your support options, you can visit the Microsoft Answer Desk online at *support.microsoft.com/contactus*. Listings on that page direct you to the appropriate technical support resources for different business categories.

As an alternative, use the Contact Support app, which is installed by default with Windows 10. Figure B-6 shows the options available for Windows support, which includes chat and telephone options.

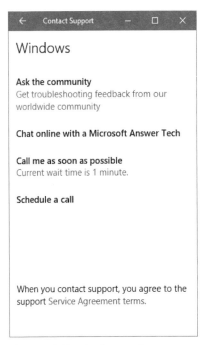

Figure B-6 Use the Contact Support app to chat online or talk with a support representative. Note that some options might require payment.

OneDrive and other cloud services

OneDrive, Microsoft's cloud-based file-storage service, is a crucial part of the Windows 10 experience. Every free Microsoft account starts with 15 GB of OneDrive storage. You can expand that storage with paid upgrades to OneDrive or get a massively increased cloud storage allotment with an Office 365 Home or Personal subscription.

That consumer version of OneDrive is separate from OneDrive for Business, which is associated with Office 365 Business and Enterprise subscriptions.

When we began planning this book, a year before Windows 10 was released to the public, we gave OneDrive its own chapter. In that chapter, we planned to explain how to store, sync, and share files between a Windows 10 device and Microsoft's two OneDrive services.

But shortly after releasing the first preview edition of Windows 10, Microsoft made the decision to completely rewrite its OneDrive synchronization client. As we write this appendix, more than a month after Windows 10 was officially released, we still haven't seen that new sync client. Instead, the OneDrive software that was included with the initial release of Windows 10 is essentially the same as what was in Windows 8 more than three years ago.

By the time you read this, that new software will probably be ready, or at least available in a preview release for Windows Insiders. As a result, our coverage here is deliberately general, designed to get you oriented with Microsoft's cloud services.

How OneDrive and OneDrive for Business work

Despite the brand name they share, Microsoft's two cloud-based file-storage services have different origins and different feature sets. Both are designed to allow access to files and folders in a web browser, but there are some big differences in how the two services work.

OneDrive, the consumer service, is designed for personal use, with special views that showcase photo libraries and albums, as well as the ability to store a music collection that can be streamed through Groove Music. OneDrive is the default storage option for Office 365 Home and Personal editions, although nothing prevents you from using it for work. (In fact, the authors, editors, and production professionals who collaborated on this book used OneDrive to exchange and share files.)

Files stored in OneDrive are organized into folders and subfolders just as they would be on a local drive. Figure C-1 shows the contents of a subfolder in the OneDrive Documents folder, as viewed in a web browser. Note the range of options available in the command bar for the selected file, as well as the additional menu choices available with a click.

Figure C-1 When using OneDrive in a web browser, you can perform most file-management tasks, with the ability to create, edit, and collaborate on Office documents.

OneDrive for Business offers a similar web-based view, as shown in Figure C-2. Note that subscription settings aren't accessible from the navigation pane on the left. That's because a OneDrive for Business subscription is managed by a company administrator, with additional security and collaboration options appropriate for use in an organization.

Figure C-2 OneDrive for Business offers a familiar web-based view of files and folders, with options that are more appropriate for collaboration in an organization.

When you sign in with a Microsoft account, OneDrive is just one of several services available. Clicking the menu button on the left (it looks like grid of nine squares and is sometimes referred to as the "waffle" button) displays the full range of options, shown here.

When you sign in to an Office 365 Business or Enterprise account, clicking the waffle-shaped menu button in the same location displays a larger group of options, and the OneDrive icon leads to OneDrive for Business.

Both services allow subscribers to share files and folders with other people. The consumer edition of OneDrive allows complete control of sharing, letting you make a file, a photo, or an entire folder public. You can also share access by using a link that doesn't require signing in to a Microsoft account.

Sharing options for OneDrive for Business are managed by a company administrator, who might apply restrictions on sharing files with other people, especially in folders that contain confidential company information.

Synchronizing files with Windows 10 devices

The whole point of OneDrive is to allow you to store your files in the cloud and then access those files from anywhere. One option, of course, is through a web browser. But Microsoft has also released platform-specific clients that allow you to browse, open, and synchronize those files on any device.

As we mentioned at the beginning of this chapter, the OneDrive sync client in the initial release of Windows 10 is a stopgap, to be replaced by a new utility that wasn't available at the time we finished this book. Figure C-3 shows the settings for that initial Windows 10 OneDrive client, with the option to choose which files and folders to sync between the cloud and the Windows 10 PC.

Figure C-3 The OneDrive sync client in the initial release of Windows 10 (July 2015) includes this interface for specifying which folders to sync between the cloud and a local device.

At the initial launch of Windows 10, synchronizing files with OneDrive for Business required a separate piece of client software, included with an Office 365 ProPlus installation. The new sync client will reportedly be able to handle both OneDrive and OneDrive for Business accounts, giving you the option to choose which folders in the cloud are synced to the local device and which are available only from the cloud. That's a crucial feature, especially if you have hundreds of gigabytes of photos, music and video files, and documents on OneDrive. Selective sync is an essential strategy for using OneDrive on devices that have limited local storage, such as laptop PCs, phones, and tablets.

Office 365 and Office Web Apps

Both OneDrive and OneDrive for Business allow you to create, edit, and collaborate on documents created in Office applications and saved in the broadly supported Office document formats.

To create a new Office document online, click New and then choose a file type from the menu, as shown here.

Both versions of OneDrive allow you to view and edit an Office document online, again using only a web browser. The feature set is limited compared with the full Office programs, as shown in the example in Figure C-4, but the Office Online apps maintain document fidelity, preserving features and formatting that might not be available in the web-based apps.

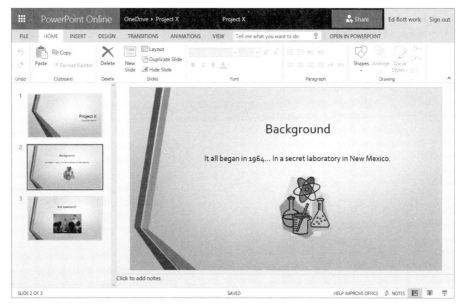

Figure C-4 You can open and edit any Office document in a web browser, with a ribbon-based user interface that's consistent with the full Office desktop apps.

Index to troubleshooting topics

Index

Symbols and Numbers

~ (tilde), 435, 439
* (wildcard character), 433, 439, 740
? (wildcard character), 435, 439, 740
7-Zip, 399
32-bit Windows 10
vs. 64-bit, 25
Hyper-V not available for, 752
product keys, 56
RAM limitations of, 774
64-bit Windows 10
vs. 32-bit, 25
Hyper-V available for, 752
product keys, 56

A

accent colors, 103–104
access control
effective access, viewing, 687
entries (ACEs), 191, 685
lists (ACLs), 190–192, 686
NTFS permissions with resource permissions, 686
NTFS vs. FAT file systems, 189
share permission options, 685
SIDs, 189–190
access point (Wi-Fi) security, 149
ACEs (access control entries), 191, 685
ACLs (access control lists), 190–192, 686
Action Center
accessing, 9
color options, 103–104
Connect pane, 334–335
enabling in Tablet Mode, 82
icon, hiding, 78
icon settings, 107–108
notifications settings, 76–78
opening, 63

quick actions, 107
activating Windows
32-bit vs. 64-bit keys, 56
activate now notices, 53–54
anonymous nature of, 57
changes in hardware requiring, 57
clean installs, 53, 56
command prompt for, 59
corporate volume licensing, 58
digital entitlement, 53
hardware fingerprints, 53, 57
installation IDs, 53, 57
Key Management servers, 58
license agreement enforcement function of, 52
malware interfering with, 54
OEM installations, 57–58
product keys, 52–56
retail copy activation, 57
silent activation, 52
Software Protection Platform, 52
by telephone manual activations, 57
upgrading from Windows 7 or 8, 54–56
validation of licenses, 53–54
Active Directory, 142. *See also* Azure Active Directory
Active@ KillDisk, 503
active partitions, 486
ActiveX controls
not supported by Microsoft Edge, 339–341
supported by Internet Explorer 11, 339
Trusted Sites zone blocking of, 381
UAC prompts from installing, 216
Add Printer Wizard, 469–470
add-ons, Internet Explorer 11, 372–373
Address Space Layout Randomization (ASLR), 202
Address toolbar, 75
administrator accounts
Administrator account, legacy, 195
Administrators group, 193

processors (CPUs)
assigning processes to specific cores, 252
Coreinfo utility, 753
Hyper-V requirements for, 752
number supported by various Windows editions, 774
percentage used, Task Manager, 251, 527, 550–551
requirements for Windows 10, 22
Resource Monitor statistics, 554–555
usage by apps, data on, 252–253
viewing type of, 625–627
product keys, 52–56
profiles. *See* **user profiles**
Program Compatibility Assistant, 248–249
programs. *See* **applications, desktop; apps**
properties, file
displaying in File Explorer, 407
editing, 409–411
properties dialog box, 408
varieties of, 407
properties of items, searches by, 436–437
Public folders, 673–674, 676
Public network location, 141–142, 150, 209
Public profile, 392–393
Python, 669

Q

queries. *See* **searches**
question marks (?) as wildcards, 435, 439, 740
Quick Actions, Mail app, 273–274

R

RAM. *See* **memory (RAM)**
ransomware, 198
ratings metadata, 407
Read & Execute permission, 192
Read permission, 192, 685
Reading List app, Windows, 303–305
reading lists, Microsoft Edge, 357–360
Reading View, Microsoft Edge, 13–14, 367–369
recovery
BitLocker recovery keys, 226–227
File History, with. *See* File History
file restore operation, 558
files and folders, methods for, 412–415
full reset operation, 558, 560

Go Back To An Earlier Build option, 561
new features of, 12
OEM recovery images, 562
recovery drives for, 579–581
Recovery Media Creator, 40
recovery operation, 558
Recovery page options, 561
Recycle Bin, 412–415
Remove Files And Clean The Drive option, 578
Reset command, 575–579
reset options, 560–562
of services, 635–636
system image backups, 582–590
System Restore, 590–598
USB bootable recovery, 561
Windows Recovery Environment, 45
Recycle Bin, 412–415
red eye removal, 323
Refresh command, 575
Regedit.exe. *See* **Registry Editor**
registry
AutoRun values, 726–727
BCD (Boot Configuration Database), 639
case insensitivity of, 638
changes made by Settings and Control Panel, 639
cleaners, danger of, 646
data types, 642–643, 650
deleting data in, 651
editing manually. *See* Registry Editor
header lines, 649
hive locations, 639
HKLM (HKEY_LOCAL_MACHINE), 641, 643
HKU (HKEY_USERS), 641
installations, changes made in during, 37
key names, 649
PowerShell manipulation of, 742–743
purpose of, 638
.reg files, 648–651
root keys, 640
Run key startup programs, 256
RunOnce startup programs, 257
service entries, 638
structure of, 638–639
subkeys, 640
values, 641–642, 647, 650
view of, collapsed, 640
virtualization of, 643–644

About the authors

Ed Bott is an award-winning author and technology journalist who has been researching and writing about Windows and PC technology, in print and on the Internet, for more than two decades. He has written more than 30 books, all on Windows and Microsoft Office, which in turn have been translated into dozens of languages and read worldwide. You can catch up with Ed's latest opinions and get hands-on advice at *The Ed Bott Report* on ZDNet (*zdnet.com/blog/bott*). You can also follow his lively and occasionally irreverent Twitter feed (@edbott). Ed and his wife, Judy, live in northern New Mexico with two English springer spaniels, Mackie and Lucy, who were adopted with the help of English Springer Rescue America (*springerrescue.org*). Both of those lucky dogs make cameo appearances in this book.

Carl Siechert began his writing career at age eight as editor of the *Mesita Road News*, a neighborhood newsletter that reached a peak worldwide circulation of 43 during its eight-year run. Following several years as an estimator and production manager in a commercial printing business, Carl returned to writing with the formation of Siechert & Wood Professional Documentation, a Pasadena, California, firm that specializes in writing and producing product documentation for the personal computer industry. Carl is a coauthor of more than 20 books, covering operating systems from MS-DOS 3.0 to Windows 10 and productivity applications from Microsoft Works 3 to Office 2013. In a convergence of new and old technology, Carl's company now operates a popular website for hobby machinists, *littlemachineshop.com*. Carl hiked the Pacific Crest Trail from Mexico to Canada in 1977 and would rather be hiking right now. He and his wife, Jan, live in Southern California.

Craig Stinson, an industry journalist since 1981, was editor of *Softalk for the IBM Personal Computer*, one of the earliest IBM-PC magazines. He is the author or coauthor of numerous books about Windows and Microsoft Excel. Craig is an amateur musician and reformed music critic, having reviewed classical music for various newspapers and trade publications, including *Billboard*, the *Boston Globe*, the *Christian Science Monitor*, and *Musical America*. He lives in Bloomington, Indiana.

Now that you've read the book...

Tell us what you think!

Was it useful?
Did it teach you what you wanted to learn?
Was there room for improvement?

Let us know at http://aka.ms/tellpress

Your feedback goes directly to the staff at Microsoft Press,
and we read every one of your responses. Thanks in advance!

 Microsoft